Developing Safer Online Environments for Children:

Tools and Policies for Combatting Cyber Aggression

Information Resources Management Association
USA

A volume in the Trending Topics
Book Series (TTBS) Book Series

Published in the United States of America by
    IGI Global
    Information Science Reference (an imprint of IGI Global)
    701 E. Chocolate Avenue
    Hershey PA, USA 17033
    Tel: 717-533-8845
    Fax: 717-533-8661
    E-mail: cust@igi-global.com
    Web site: http://www.igi-global.com

Library of Congress Cataloging-in-Publication Data

Names: Information Resources Management Association, editor.
Title: Developing safer online environments for children : tools and
  policies for combatting cyber aggression / Information Resources
  Management Association, editor.
Description: Hershey, PA : Information Science Reference, [2020] | Includes
  bibliographical references and index. | Summary: """This book explores
  the effects of cyberbullying and cyberstalking on children and examines
  solutions that can identify and prevent online harassment through both
  policy and legislation reform and technological tools"--Provided by
  publisher"-- Provided by publisher.
Identifiers: LCCN 2019032852 | ISBN 9781799816843 (hardcover) | ISBN
  9781799816850 (paperback) | ISBN 9781799816867 (ebook)
Subjects: LCSH: Cyberbullying--Prevention. | Cyberstalking--Prevention. |
  Internet and children.
Classification: LCC HV6773.15.C92 .D48 2020 | DDC 302.34/3--dc23
LC record available at https://lccn.loc.gov/2019032852

This book is published in the IGI Global book series Trending Topics (TTBS) (ISSN: pending; eISSN: pending)

British Cataloguing in Publication Data
A Cataloguing in Publication record for this book is available from the British Library.

The views expressed in this book are those of the authors, but not necessarily of the publisher.

For electronic access to this publication, please contact: eresources@igi-global.com.

Trending Topics Book Series (TTBS) Book Series

Mehdi Khosrow-Pour, D.B.A.

Information Resources Management
Association, USA

ISSN:pending
EISSN:pending

MISSION

Every day all over the world, researchers are making groundbreaking discoveries that address current challenges and solve complex problems across a variety of fields. Due to advancements in technology, changes in demographics, adjustments to societal norms, the development of political and economic structures, and more, new theories, methods, strategies, techniques, and applications are constantly being established in response to both existing and evolving issues.

Based on the success of IGI Global's latest Trending Topics Campaign, which provides news snippets and trending research breakthroughs relevant to IGI Global content, IGI Global has launched this new book series, titled the **Trending Topics Book Series**, which offers small anthologies of reprinted IGI Global book chapters and journal articles hand-selected by IGI Global's Executive Editorial Board on topics currently trending and stirring up discussion and/or controversy.

Spanning across topics such as the multigenerational workforce, legislation for sustainability, emotional branding, privacy on mobile devices, robotics in healthcare, and bio-based product development, this book series aims to provide researchers, academicians, professionals, and students with the most up-to-date studies in order to advance knowledge across all industries.

COVERAGE

- Bio-Based Product Development
- Women in STEM Fields
- Environmental Legislation and Sustainability
- Aging Workforce
- Plan S and Open Access Movements
- Inclusive Learning
- Emotional Branding
- Eco-Cities
- Business Sustainability
- Robotics in Healthcare

IGI Global is currently accepting manuscripts for publication within this series. To submit a proposal for a volume in this series, please contact our Acquisition Editors at Acquisitions@igi-global.com or visit: http://www.igi-global.com/publish/.

Titles in this Series

For a list of additional titles in this series, please visit:
https://www.igi-global.com/book-series/trending-topics-book-series/228608

Five Generations and Only One Workforce How Successful Businesses Are Managing a Multigenerational Workforce
Information Resources Management Association (USA)
Business Science Reference • © 2020 • 364pp • H/C (ISBN: 9781799804376) • US $215.00 (our price)

Developing Eco-Cities Through Policy, Planning, and Innovation Can It Really Work?
Information Resources Management Association (USA)
Engineering Science Reference • © 2020 • 350pp • H/C (ISBN: 9781799804413) • US $195.00 (our price)

701 East Chocolate Avenue, Hershey, PA 17033, USA
Tel: 717-533-8845 x100 • Fax: 717-533-8661
E-Mail: cust@igi-global.com • www.igi-global.com

Table of Contents

Section 2
Policy and Reform Solutions

Section 3
Technological Solutions

Preface

Within the past decade, there has been an alarming rise in the number of actions, trends, and online "challenges" designed to inflict emotional or physical harm on children. Cyberbullying, cyberstalking, cyber-harassment, and trolling are just some of the actions and behaviors showcased across the internet. Trends and challenges have included the Momo Challenge, which exposes children to a disturbing character who induces them to commit various dangerous acts, including running away from home and self-inflicting pain; and the Blue Whale Challenge, which purportedly assigned children tasks over a period of time that ultimately required them to self-harm and, possibly, commit suicide. Though such challenges are difficult to connect to actual suicides and are often sensationalized by the media, it is clear that children browsing the internet and posting on social media sites are at risk to become victims of cyber aggressive behavior.

More commonly, traditional bullying tactics, once inflicted on playgrounds and in schools, have moved online where they are more difficult to track and provide even more of a challenge for an adult to intercede on behalf of the victim. Emboldened by anonymity and the almost guaranteed chance of receiving no punishment for their actions, cyberbullies have the ability to harass their victims ceaselessly, offering no relief to those under attack. With children attached to the internet through multiple easily accessible devices, this harassment can lead to long-term mental suffering, social exclusion, depression, self-harm, and in extreme circumstances, suicide.

Internet safety is now at the top of the agenda as more individuals become aware of the need for developing online environments that are not only safe for children to use, but also instill and empower compassion, sensitivity, and confidence. Legislation, policies, and laws must be examined to ensure that chatrooms, social media profiles, videos, and more are continuously monitored for harmful content and malicious language. Additionally, new policies should be explored that hold cyberbullies accountable for their actions. Technological tools should also be implemented to help quickly detect and suppress malevolent and felonious activity.

In response to the need for advanced research that can offer innovative solutions to deal with these growing concerns and also as part of IGI Global's Trending Topics Book Series, which aligns with IGI Global's Trending Topics Campaign that showcases the latest research breakthroughs that are stirring up discussion and/ or controversy across a variety of fields, this publication, *Developing Safer Online Environments for Children: Tools and Policies for Combatting Cyber Aggression*, is comprised of reprinted IGI Global book chapters and journal articles that have been hand-selected by IGI Global's executive editorial board with the intent to adequately address the main issues facing the security and online safety of youth when utilizing the internet and social media sites.

Whether it be through protecting their privacy or combatting the use of the internet as a place to verbally attack and target a victim, the content found within this book centers on conceptual, methodological, and technical aspects and provides insights into emerging topics including but not limited to fake profile identification, trolling, victimization, digital privacy, and bystanders/witnesses.

Readers will come to understand the latest solutions for identifying and stopping culprits, as well as for preventing children from being exposed to such activity in the first place. Teachers, parents, IT specialists, psychologists, psychiatrists, sociologists, policy makers, law enforcement officers, criminal investigators, social media companies, internet safety organizations, government officials, as well as many others will find themselves equipped with strategies to identify, detect, and prevent cyber aggressive behavior and create a safer overall online environment for children of all ages. It will also empower academicians, researchers, and students with a better understanding of the challenges and prospective solutions for securing children's identity, privacy, and emotional wellbeing in a digitized era.

This publication is organized into three sections that provide comprehensive coverage of important topics. The sections are:

1.   Defining and Understanding Cyber Aggression
2.   Policy and Reform Solutions
3.   Technological Solutions

The following paragraphs provide a summary of what to expect from this invaluable reference source:

Section 1, "Defining and Understanding Cyber Aggression," opens this extensive reference source by providing the reader with a comprehensive understanding of the emotional and social impact that cyber aggression has on both children as victims and as bystanders/witnesses to the behavior. The first chapter in this section, "Offending, Victimization, Forensic Investigation, and Prevention of Cyberstalking," by Prof. Rejani Thudalikunnil Gopalan from Mahatma Gandhi Medical college and Hospital, India, focuses on the definition, typologies, characteristics of victims and offenders, forensic investigation, and prevention of cyber stalking. The second chapter in this section, "Developing an Understanding of Cyberbullying: The Emotional Impact and Struggle to Define," authored by Prof. Carol M. Walker of East Stroudsburg University, USA, serves to enhance the reader's understanding of the incidents of cyberbullying, to provide knowledge of the challenges researchers face in operationalizing cyberbullying that will enable all professionals to assist victims, and to offer techniques that may be implemented in the ethical practice of primary, secondary, or college educators as they work with Millennials and Neo-Millennials in the 21st century classroom. "Cyberbullying: Safety and Ethical Issues Facing K-12 Digital Citizens," the next chapter in this section, by Profs. Terry Diamanduros and Elizabeth Downs of Georgia Southern University, USA, explores the safety and ethical issues facing K-12 schools and the challenges associated with bullying and examines the phenomenon of the cyberbully-victim who moves from victim to perpetrator. The next chapter titled "Adolescent Victim Experiences of Cyberbullying: Current Status and Future Directions" is authored by Profs. Minghui Gao and Tonja Filipino of Arkansas State University, USA; Prof. Xu Zhao from The University of Calgary, Canada; and Prof. Mark McJunkin from Arkansas State University, USA and introduces a recent research study that disclosed adolescent victim experiences across seven major types of cyberbullying, significant gender and age differences, and reasons for not reporting incidents of cyberbullying to adults. In the final chapter of this section, "Cyberbullying Bystanders: Gender, Grade, and Actions Among Primary and Secondary School Students in Australia," Profs. Marilyn Anne Campbell, Chrystal Whiteford, and Krystle Duncanson from Queensland University of Technology (QUT), Brisbane, Australia; Prof. Barbara Spears from University of South Australia, Adelaide, Australia; Prof. Des Butler of the Faculty of Law, Queensland University of Technology (QUT), Brisbane, Australia; and Prof. Phillip Thomas Slee from Flinders University, Adelaide, Australia present a study that examines the gender and age of cyberbullying bystanders out of 2,109 upper primary and secondary school students in Australia. The actions the bystanders took when a peer was cyber-victimized are analyzed and implications for prevention and intervention in cyberbullying are discussed.

Section 2, "Policy and Reform Solutions," takes an in-depth look at current laws and legislation that are used to dissuade cyber aggression behavior across the globe and recommends further policies that can be implemented by schools, law enforcement, and governments. This section starts off with "Cyberbullying in Adolescence: Victimization and Adolescence," authored by Prof. Michael Pittaro from American Military University, USA & East Stroudsburg University, USA. The chapter discusses the criminalization of cyberbullying, especially in regard to cases in which cyberbullying led to an adolescent attempting suicide, and examines the extent to which law enforcement should be involved in cyberbullying incidents. The next chapter, "Cyber Bullying: Global and Local Practices on Awareness Raising," by Profs. Emıne Nılufer Pembecıoglu and Hatıce Irmaklı of Istanbul University, Turkey, explores global and local policies that can be implemented in middle schools, high schools, and colleges that provide cyberbullying prevention programs. The third chapter in this section, authored by Prof. Jiyoon Yoon from University of Texas Arlington, Arlington, USA and Prof. Katie Koo of Texas A & M University – Commerce, Commerce, USA, is titled "Implication of Cyberbullying on Under-Represented Students in Post-Secondary Education" and continues the discussion on rules and policies that can be implemented within schools and suggests specialized treatment and interventions for cyberbullies as a solution. In the chapter, "Legislative Response to Cyber Aggression: Federal and State-Local Policy Reform," by Prof. Ramona S. McNeal from University of Northern Iowa, USA and Profs. Susan M. Kunkle and Mary Schmeida of Kent State University, USA, a comprehensive look at federal and state-local legislative responses to cyber aggression is undertaken using several key cases as learning factors. Authored by Prof. Leslie J. Reynard from Washburn University, USA, the next chapter in this section, "Troll Farm: Anonymity as a Weapon for Online Character Assassination," investigates the nature of abusive communication online, the role anonymity plays in digital attacks, and psychological characteristics associated with trolls and cyber-bullies, and offers legal remedies as solutions. "Digital Privacy Across Borders: Canadian and American Perspectives," the last chapter in this section, contributed by Profs. Lorayne P. Robertson, Heather Leatham, James Robertson, and Bill Muirhead from the University of Ontario Institute of Technology, Canada, highlights some of the potential consequences of a lack of awareness of the risks associated with sharing information online and outlines the obligations of multiple parties (from the vendor to the end user) when students use online apps, including the teachers and parents who want to protect students' digital privacy. Employing policy analysis and a comparative approach, they examine federal, national, and local legislation, as well as curriculum responses to this issue in the USA and Canada.

Section 3, "Technological Solutions," presents coverage on technological tools that can be implemented to help with the detection and prevention of cyber aggressive behavior. The first chapter in this section, "Technological Help to Prevent and Reduce Cyberbullying," by Prof. Gilberto Marzano of Rezekne Academy of Technologies, Latvia, illustrates the progress that has been made to reduce cyber-bullying through technological means and discusses the notion of industry self-regulation. It also argues that the IT industry has a responsibility to respect societal obligations toward users, especially when users are children. The following chapter, "Empowering Technology Use to Promote Virtual Violence Prevention in Higher Education Context," authored by Profs. Miftachul Huda and Aminudin Hehsan from Universiti Teknologi Malaysia, Malaysia; Prof. Singgih Basuki from Sunan Kalijaga State Islamic University, Indonesia; Prof. Budi Rismayadi of Buana Per-juangan University, Indonesia; and Profs. Kamarul Azmi Jasmi, Bushrah Basiron, and Mohd Ismail Mustari from Universiti Teknologi Malaysia, Malaysia, proposes a model to empower technology use to promote virtual violence prevention in a higher education context and attempts to elucidate the stages employed amidst the users in empowering technology use through nurturing innovative approaches. Contributed by Profs. Michal E. Ptaszynski and Fumito Masui from Kitami Institute of Tech-nology, Japan, in the next chapter, "Brute Force Search Method for Cyberbullying Detection," a method for automatic detection of malicious internet contents based on a combinatorial approach resembling brute force search algorithms with applica-tion to language classification is presented as a solution to cyberbullying. The last chapter of this section, "Entropy-Based Identification of Fake Profiles in Social Network: An Application of Cyberbullying," by Profs. Geetika Sarna and M.P.S. Bhatia from Netaji Subhas Institute of Technology, Delhi, India, uses the concept of entropy and cross-entropy to identify fake profiles created for the intent of sending harassing/abusive information online as entropy works on the degree of uncertainty.

Although the primary organization of the contents in this work is based on its three sections, offering a progression of coverage of the important concepts, methodologies, technologies, applications, social issues, and emerging trends, the reader can also identify specific contents by utilizing the extensive indexing system listed at the end.

Section 1
Defining and Understanding Cyber Aggression

Chapter 1
Offending, Victimization, Forensic Investigation, and Prevention of Cyberstalking

Rejani Thudalikunnil Gopalan
Gujarat Forensic Sciences University, India

ABSTRACT

The term cyberstalking has been used to describe a variety of behaviors that involve repeated threats and/or harassment by the use of electronic mail or other computer-based communication that would make a reasonable person afraid or concerned for their safety. It is growing fast and creating problems, especially psychologically. This chapter mainly focused on its definition, typologies, characteristics of victims and offenders, forensic investigation, and its prevention. There is not much agreement on the definition of cyberstalking as it appeared recently due to technological advancement. Many of the researches were done on university students and the prevalence of cyberstalking among general population and special groups are not much known. But researches repeatedly confirm it as a growing issue. Technical advancements and thorough knowledge on technical details among researchers from different backgrounds poses a big problem to its complete understanding and prevention. Future research needs to focus on all these aspects.

DEFINITION AND TYPOLOGIES

Stalking can be defined as recurring unwelcome attention which causes people to fear for their own safety and for the safety of those closest to them (Baum, Catalano, Rand, & Rose, 2009). Stalking is an assembly of behaviors involving recurring and

DOI: 10.4018/978-1-7998-1684-3.ch001

persistent attempts to impose on another person unwanted communication and/or contact. These behaviors include repeated phone calls or letters as well as pursuit, approach, threats or assault by the perpetrator (Pathé, 2002). Being stalked includes being repetitively followed in a manner that causes a reasonable person to fear for his or her safety. The definition has two aspects that are behavioral and emotional. The behavioral represents the repeated pursuit of behaviors as experienced by the victims. Second is the emotional issues suffered by the victim in terms of fear, anxiety and distress. Stalking physically takes place in spatial proximity to the victim and increases the potential physical harm to the victim and, therefore, heightened fear of the realization of its probability (Reyns, 2010).

Cyberstalking is an electronic crime involving a perpetrator using the internet or other high tech communication devices to take advantage of systematic weaknesses, or to exploit a person's vulnerability, including stalking a person online (Stambaugh, Beaupre, Baker, Cassaday, & Williams, 2001). It is harassment on the Internet using various modes of transmission such as electronic mail (e-mail), chat rooms, newsgroups, mail exploders, and the World Wide Web (Deirmenjian, 1999). The term "cyberstalking" has been used to describe a variety of behaviors that involve: (a) repeated threats and/or harassment; (b) by the use of electronic mail or other computer-based communication; (c) that would make a reasonable person afraid or concerned for their safety (Fisher, Cullen, & Turner, 2000; U.S. Department of Justice, 2000). According to Petherick (2001), it is which is simply an extension of the physical form of stalking, is where the electronic mediums such as the Internet are used to pursue, harass or contact another in an unsolicited fashion. Cyber stalking doesn't involve any physical contact yet stalking through the internet has found favor among the offenders for certain advantages available like, ease of communication access to personal information and anonymity (Verma, 2016). As per Bocij and McFarlane (2002), cyber stalking is a group of behaviors in which an individual, group of individuals or organization uses information technology to harass one or more individuals. Such behavior may include, but are not limited to, the transmission of threats and false accusations, identity theft, data theft, damage to data or equipment, computer monitoring and the solicitation of minors for sexual purposes. Harassment is defined as:

a course of action that a reasonable person, in possession of the same information, would think causes another reasonable person to suffer emotional distress.

Any of the following categories may constitute the perpetration of cyberstalking: persistent unwanted contact, repeated unwanted harassment, persistent and unwanted sexual advances, or implied threats or acts of violence. The main difference between stalking and cyber stalking stems from the methods of perusal occupied. Cyber stalking adheres to the repeated pursuit of a victim by exploiting various electronic communicative avenues. These online behaviors are facilitated by technological innovations that liberate potential stalkers of the spatial restriction of their recurring perusal (Reyns, Henson, & Fisher, 2011; Reyns, 2010).

There are three primary ways of cyber stalking depending on the use of the internet:

1. **E-Mail Stalking:** This is direct communication through e-mail characterized by threatening, hateful, or obscene nature, or even send spam or viruses to harass others.
2. **Internet Stalking:** There is global communication through the Internet and the domain is more wide and public in comparison to e-mail stalking. Here stalkers can use a wide range of activities to harass their victims.
3. **Computer Stalking:** This is unauthorized control of another person's computer. In this type of stalking, the stalker exploits the working of the Internet and the Windows operating system in order to to assume control over the computer of the targeted victim (Ogilvie, 2000).

A number of typologies concerning stalking have been proposed by researchers. Zona et al., (1993) reported about three kinds of stalkers — erotomanics, love obsessionals and simple obsessionals. *Erotomanics* have the delusional belief that the target of interest, usually of higher status, is in love with the stalker. Cases involving *love obsessionals* are characterized by the absence of an existing relationship between the stalker and the victim (usually celebrities), yet the stalker has a fanatical love towards the subject. These stalkers tend to suffer from schizophrenia, or bipolar disorder, or some other psychiatric illness. The final group is the *simple obsessional,* where the stalker is usually an ex-partner of the victim and may wish to rekindle the relationship or may harass the victim for revenge. Harmon et al. (1995) classified stalkers in to two based on the nature of the attachment between victim and stalker (classified as affectionate/amorous or persecutory/angry), and the nature of the prior relationship between stalker and victim (i.e. personal, professional, employment, media, acquaintance, none and unknown). It was noted that *amorous/affectionate* harassers usually suffered from erotomanic features, and that the majority of stalkers of ex-intimates had narcissistic and paranoid personality traits. *Persecutory/angry* harassers not only stalked individuals but also large institutions who had wronged them (real or imagined) (Mullen, Pathé, & Purcell, 2000).

Wright et al. (1996) classified stalkers in to *domestic* or *nondomestic (*nature of the relationship between the victim and stalker), *nondelusional* or *delusional* (the content of the communications), *low, medium, high* (the level of risk to the victim in terms of aggression), *infatuation, possession, anger/retaliation, other* (the motive of the stalker) and *legal, suicide, psychiatric, other(*the outcome of the case for the stalker). Their system was developed from crime scene and common forensic findings, stalking cases, anecdotal reviews, newspaper accounts of stalking, as well as interviews with victims of stalkers.

Attempt was made to categorize stalkers based on psychiatric evaluation and Kienlen et al. (1997) divided stalkers into *psychotic* (with symptoms that ranged from schizophrenia, delusional disorder with erotomanic features, bipolar disorder) and *non-psychotic* (with disorders that ranged from mood disorder, alcohol and drug abuse, and personality disorder). Based on the stalkers' predominant motivation and the context in which stalking occurred, information about the nature of the prior relationship with the victim, and finally, a psychiatric diagnosis, Mullen et al. (1999) classified five types of stalkers:

1. **The Rejected Stalker:** Has had an intimate relationship with the victim (although occasionally the victim may be a family member or close friend), and views the termination of the relationship as unacceptable. Their behavior is characterized by a mixture of revenge and desire for reconciliation.
2. **Intimacy Seekers:** Attempt to bring to fruition a relationship with a person who has engaged their desires, and who they may also mistakenly perceive reciprocates that affection.
3. **Incompetent Suitors:** Tend to seek to develop relationships but they fail to abide by social rules governing courtship. They are usually intellectually limited and/or socially incompetent.
4. **Resentful Stalkers:** Harass their victims with the specific intention of causing fear and apprehension out of a desire for retribution for some actual or supposed injury or humiliation.
5. **Predatory Stalkers:** Are those who stalk for information gathering purposes or fantasy rehearsal in preparation for a sexual attack.

Ellison (1999) has classified cyber stalking as either "direct" or "indirect" based on the type of electronic communication used to stalk the victim and the extent to which the communication is private or public. Direct cyber stalking includes the use of pagers, cell phones and e-mail to send messages of hate, obscenities, and threats to intimidate a victim and it is the most common form of cyber stalking and most common way in which stalking begins (Wallace, 2000).

McFarlane and Bocij (2003) identified four categories of offenders:

1. **Vindictive Cyberstalkers:** Are characterized by relentless harassment of their victim without a specific reason. They are frequently suffering from psychological disorders.

2. **Composed Cyberstalkers:** Aim to cause constant annoyance and irritation to the targeted victim. They have no desire to establish a relationship with their victim, and are motivated to cause them distress.
3. **Intimate Cyberstalkers:** Are characterized by the desire to attract the attention or affection of their victim. They usually have detailed knowledge of the person being targeted.
4. **Collective Cyberstalkers:** Consist of a group of individuals harassing their victims through the use of communication technology.

Spitzberg and Cupach, (2007) classified eight categories of stalking and obsessive relational intrusion (ORI) behaviors such as:

1. **Hyper-Intimacy:** Typical courtship activities, but taken to an excessive level.
2. **Mediated Contacts:** All forms of communication efforts performed through technologies, including email, instant message (IM), the Internet, cell phones, etc. ·
3. **Interactional Contacts:** Activities oriented toward face-to-face or proximal conversation. This includes behaviors oriented toward direct contact such as physical approaches, appearing at various places, pursuing common activities and locations, etc.
4. **Pursuit and Surveillance:** The systematic attempt to secure knowledge or information about the victim without the victim's awareness. Following, watching, and/or monitoring the person or the person's behaviors. ·
5. **Invasion:** Activities that involve the violation of normatively prescribed personal and legal boundaries, such as the theft of information, breaking and entering into a person's premises, and trespassing, etc.
6. **Harassment and Intimidation:** Variety of aggressive verbal or nonverbal activities designed to bother, annoy, or otherwise stress the victim such as insults, seeking to harm the person's reputation, spreading rumors, calling non-stop, etc.
7. **Coercion and Threat:** Implicit or explicit suggestion of potential harm that may befall the victim. Threats may be against loved ones, pets, property, colleagues, the victim, or even to the pursuer (e.g., threatening to commit suicide), etc.
8. **Physical Aggression and Violence:** Involves vandalism, use of a weapon, assault, injury, attempted suicide and suicide, attempted rape and rape, and attempted homicide and homicide.

Though many typologies are available, each has its own merits and demerits and it is important how well these typologies help in detection and prevention of cyberstalking.

PREVALENCE

The prevalence of cyber stalking varies according to types. Mitchell, Becker-Blease, and Finkelhor (2005) found that individuals reported being victimized while using online sites in two forms, sexual and nonsexual. One method is harassment, which can be accomplished by:

... posting defamatory or embarrassing personal information about others, impersonating others online, stalking people online, threatening violence, and physical and emotional abuse.

Kennedy and Taylor (2010) conducted an anonymous, self-report surveys were completed polling experiences with harassment, stalking, and sexual assault and it was found that the majority of victimization types were reported infrequently, while rates of sexual assault overall were quite high compared to prior research. Types of victimization varied by where they were occurring: online or offline. Acts such as verbal harassment, pestering, unwanted behaviors, and sexual harassment were all fairly prevalent online, while other victimizations, such as being threatened or stalked, occurred more offline.

Mitchell, Finkelhor, and Wolak (2001) surveyed 1,501 frequent internet users between the ages of 10-17 (63% were 14 or older) and found that nearly one-fifth of the sample had been sexually solicited, which meant that an individual had made requests for sex, discussed sex when it was unwanted, or consensually discussed sex. It was also found that females and those who were between the ages of 14 and 17 were solicited at higher rates than those aged 10 to 13, while those between the ages of 10 and 13 reported being distressed by the solicitations more frequently than older teens. Mitchell, Finkelhor and Wolak (2007) reported that risk factors for solicitations were being female, using chat rooms frequently, talking about sex frequently online, revealing personal information, and being abused offline.

In a study among university students, Spitzberg and Hoobler (2002) reported that 59 percent of respondents felt that they had been cyberstalked, of which 19.6 percent felt threatened or were in fear for their personal safety. In another study of offline and online stalking, 11 percent of participants had been harassed. The majority of complainants were female (61 percent) and ages ranged from 17 to 42, with 55 percent aged 20 or younger (Burgess & Baker, 2002). It was reported that CyberAngels (a well-known Internet safety organization) receives some 500 complaints of cyberstalking each day, of which up to 100 represent legitimate cases and another Internet safety organization (Working to Halt Online Abuse) reports receiving an average of 100 cases per week (Dean, 2000; WHOA, 2001) which indicated it as a significant problem.

In an online survey of 6,379 participants involving users of the German social network StudiVZ, the prevalence of cyberstalking was estimated to be 6.3%. In various aspects, cyberstalking was comparable to offline stalking such as cyberstalking occurred most often in the context of ex-partner relationships; most of the victims were female and the majority of the perpetrators were male. The prevalence of cyberstalking is considerable. However, if stringent definition criteria comparable to those of offline stalking are applied, it is not a mass phenomenon (Dreßing, Bailer, Anders, Wagner, & Gallas, 2014). Previous studies also reported high prevalence rate of stalking. The lifetime prevalence of stalking was estimated at 4.5 percent of adults surveyed, translating into roughly 10 million people having been stalked at some point in their life (Basile, Swahn, Chen, & Saltzman, 2006). In an another study on a sample of 16,507 adults aged 18 and over, the lifetime stalking victimization rate for women was 16 percent and 5 percent for men (Black, Basile, Breiding, Smith, Walters, Merrick, Chen, & Stevens, 2011). In a meta-analysis of 103 research studies of stalking related incidents involving 70,000 individuals, authors found approximately three fourths of the perpetrators had some type of relationship with the victims and nearly half of all occurrences occurred between past romantic partners (Spitzberg, 2002). Overall, it is predicted nearly one in every five people will become a victim of stalking in their lifetimes, and women are almost two and a half times more likely than men to be victims (Spitzberg, 2002). In another meta-analysis of 175 research studies on stalking, representing over 120,000 cases, Spitzberg and Cupach (2007) reported 25% of the sample experienced stalking. Alexy, Burgess, Baker, and Smoyak (2005) have surveyed 756 students across 2 universities and reported 4 percent of their sample had been cyberstalked (32% of the total stalking cases). Sheridan and Grant, (2007) found 7 percent self-reported cyberstalking victimization was 7 percent and purely online was 4 percent and Paullet et al., (2009) reported 13 percent among 302 students at a mid-Atlantic university.

Cyber stalking often happens to celebrities and politicians because of the nature of work and in one study in New Zealand reported that politicians felt they (and their families) had become more exposed as a result of the Internet. Half of MPs had been personally approached by their harassers, 48% had been directly threatened and 15% had been attacked. Some of these incidents were serious, involving weapons such as guns, Molotov cocktails and blunt instruments (Every-Palmer, Barry-Walsh, & Pathé, 2015). In a recent study, the prevalence of cyberstalking among Italian nurses was 23.3% and 42.7% had to change their lifestyle and work. The cyberstalker was predominantly male (52%) and, in 49% of cases, was a patient. The victims reported moderate anxiety levels and depression and increased levels of depression in nurses experienced in computer use, website managers or blogs, and a negative correlation between anxiety level and experienced nurses. The cyberstalking is a phenomenon that occurs frequently among nurses. The nurse-patient relationship plays a central role in the development of the phenomenon and the victims reported stress-related disorders that affect working life. These preliminary results could sensitize hospital managers, politics and anti-violence centers in order to develop resolutive strategies (Comparcini, Simonetti, Lupo, Galli, Bocij, & Cicolini, 2016).

RISK FACTORS

Bocij and McFarlane (2003) pointed out how technology can encourage individuals to harass others. The central argument made is that technology both enables and invites participation in criminal or antisocial behavior from individuals who would not normally take part in such activities. One way in which this can be explained is by suggesting that some of the social and technological characteristics of the Internet act together in order to lower inhibitions and establish new norms. For instance, the anonymity offered by the Internet enables people to participate in activities such as encouraging violence against others with little fear of retaliation. In addition, by allowing a cyber stalker to harm another person at a distance, the victim is effectively depersonalized. In this way it can be argued that some of those who sympathize with the goals of far-right organizations may be reluctant to act in the offline world but more willing to act in the online world.

Social networking web site is a virtual environment where people can connect with each other and it is often used as a channel for harassment and intimidation. More victims reported to having been tracked down through social networks than on dating sites. Victims also can be tracked through search engines, online forums, message boards, chat rooms or electronic mail. In the case of cyber stalking, perpetrators were likely to be strangers, resulting in unclear motives for the harassment. It cannot be said that social networking is the cause of cyberstalking but it do facilitate (Hill, 2010; Smith, 2011).

Risk of Being Victim

Studies have found many factors related with being a victim of cyber stalking such as gender, age, social actors, and relationship status with offender. Studies have noticed that mostly cyberstalking victims are females (Bjorklund, Häkkänen-Nyholm, Sheridan, & Roberts, 2010; Reyns, Henson, & Fisher, 2011; Baum, Catalano, Rand, & Rose, 2009; Henson, Reyns, & Fisher, 2011; Spitzberg, 2002). Hitchcock (2000) reported that 90% of off-line stalking victims are female. Majority of the victims are females of average socioeconomic status with most victims between the ages of 18 and 29 (Goode, 1995; Brownstein, 2000; McCann, 2000; Sinwelski & Vinton, 2001). Stalking has become a problem to women and children on a larger part in comparison to men. Women are threatened, vandalized, assaulted when it comes to real world but the same things happen when cyber stalking takes place. Obscenity also adds up with the, threatens and harassment. No doubt men also become the prey of the same but its lower when it comes to females. Children also undergo the same trauma by adult predators and pedophiles. The victim is normally a person who is less thorough regarding internet services and its applications. The stalker is generally a person who is a paranoid with no self-esteem. But the traits differ from one stalker to another. Some harass to seek revenge or some do so for their own pleasure. While some just to do it for playing a mischief (Amita, 2016).

Relationship status with offender is a crucial factor in determining the risk for being a victim. Zona, et al. (1993) reported, 65% of off-line victims had a previous relationship with their stalker and up to 51% by Working to Halt Online Abuse (2003). Baum et al (2009) noted that 75% of victims were stalked by a known person, most commonly a neighbor, co-inhabitant, or past romantic partner/companion. Ending the relation, ill will, rage, and revenge were the most frequent reasons for cyberstalking (Baum, Catalano, Rand, & Rose, 2009; Spitzberg, 2002). But some argue that cyber stalking begins during a relationship and continues, even after it's termination, the stalker using his/her intimate knowledge of the victim's personal life as an aid in commission of the crime (Logan & Walker, 2009). McEwan, Mullen, and MacKenzie (2009) found that the type of prior relationship between stalker and victim is strongly associated with persistence, with prior acquaintances the most persistent, and strangers least. Being aged over 30, sending the victim unsolicited materials, and having an intimacy seeking or resentful motivation was also associated with greater persistence, as was the presence of psychosis. Lyndon, Bonds-Raacke and Cratty (2011) reported abundant anecdotes and warnings of inappropriate behaviors on social networking sites, particularly about Facebook. They studied whether individuals obsessively monitor or harass their ex-partners on Facebook (related to general "Facebook stalking") and, if so, whether those individuals would also engage in cyber obsessional pursuit (COP) and obsessive relational pursuit (ORI), which are categories of cyberstalking and stalking (Covert Provocation, Public Harassment, and Venting). They found that each category of Facebook harassment was related to perpetration of COP and ORI. Additionally, participants who engaged in COP were almost six times more likely to also perpetrate ORI. If participants admitted to engaging in some types of stalking behaviors, they did so online, offline, and on Facebook. Though studies reported that victims are known to the perpetrator, some studies also found that offenders are strangers to victims, never ever romantically involved or had any biological relationship (Sissing, 2013).

Victim's victim's past deviant internet behavior such as downloading pirated media, contacting someonein a threatening manner, and sending sexual images predicted high risk for victimization. Individuals who engaged in deviant onlinebehavior were found to be 14 times more likely to be victims of cyberstalking (Reyns, Henson, & Fisher, 2011). Marcum, Ricketts, and Higgins (2010) have conducted a survey to 100-level courses at a mid-sized university in the northeast, which questioned respondent on their Internet behaviors and experiences during the high school senior and college freshman time period. The findings of the study indicated that participating in behaviors that increased exposure to motivated offenders and target suitability in turn increased the likelihood of victimization for both genders.

Cyber stalking may cause victims to alter their lifestyles in terms of interpersonal, professional and general social functioning. For instance, victims may change their personal contact information such as telephone numbers, e-mail addresses or even their names. Moreover, they may remove their contact details from public portals, change their daily routines, suspend previously enjoyed activities, find new jobs and schools for their children, relocate and or end communication with family, friends or 66 colleagues. Naturally, victims squander a lot of energy, time and money in achieving the above-mentioned changes (Drahokoupilová, 2007).

Studies have indicated that females are more prone to cyberstalking especially youngsters and it do affect their life significantly.

Risk of Being Offender

Though many cyberstalkers maintain their anonymity by using internet technologies to conceal their actions (Wykes, 2007; Harrison, 2006), many factors related with offenders such as gender, social and mental characteristics, and pathology. Studies have reported that most of the cyberstalkers on both online and offline are males (Bjorklund, Häkkänen-Nyholm, Sheridan, & Roberts, 2010; Meloy & Gothard, 1995; Mullen, Pathé, & Purcell, 1999; Working to Halt Online Abuse, 2003). It ranges from 68% to 91.8%. When a victim was male, the offender was also male 41.3% of the time, female 42.5% of the time, and unknown 16.1% of the time; when a victim was a female; the offender was male 66.9% of the time, female 23.5% of the time, and unknown 9.3% of the time (Baum, Catalano, Rand, & Rose, 2009). Cyberstalkers are between the ages of 19 and 30 (Bjorklund, Häkkänen-Nyholm, Sheridan, & Roberts, 2010) and belongs to diverse socioeconomic backgrounds with either underemployment or unemployment (Meloy, 1996). It is also noted that most offenders stalked victims of the same ethnicity (Baum, Catalano, Rand, & Rose, 2009). Though studies have reported male as perpetrator, women admitted greater frequencies of cyberstalking perpetration than males in one study signaling that further research on frequency and motivation for cyberstalking among the sexes is necessary (Strawhun & Huss, 2013).

Studies have reported that many psychological factors are related with cyberstalkers. Off-line stalkers were above intelligence and older in comparison to other criminal offenders (McCann, 2000). Cyber stalkers have similar characteristics to the off-line stalkers and most of them are motivated to control the victim (Jenson, 1996; Ogilvie, 2000; Report on Cyberstalking, 1999). Factors such as social isolation, maladjustment and emotional immaturity, along with an inability to cope with failed relationships are common with off-line stalking groups (Kamphuis & Emmelkamp, 2000). Childhood sexual maltreatment predicted cyber and overt stalking for men and women and for men, narcissistic vulnerability and its interaction with sexual abuse predicted stalking behavior while for women, insecure attachment (for cyber and overt stalking) and alcohol expectancies (for cyber stalking) predicted stalking behavior (Ménard & Pincus, 2012).

Morrison (2001) examined the factors associated with violent/aggressive behavior in stalkers using a sample of 100 Canadian cases of persons charged with criminal harassment (more commonly known as stalking). Results revealed that the typical profile of a "simple obsessional" type of stalker was a middle-aged male, single or separated/estranged, with a history of emotional and/or anger management problems. The most common initial strategies used by the victims to cope with the stalkers were oriented towards legal resources. Initial legal remedies, including court orders or police warnings, seemed to be ineffective as a strategy to stop stalking given that most stalkers chose to ignore them. The study also provided partial support for a preliminary model of predictors of violent/aggressive behavior in stalkers. Stalkers with previous violent behaviors, strong negative emotions, and obsessional tendencies toward the victim may be most at risk of future violent and aggressive acts.

Mullen, et al. (1999) claims the majority of simple obsessional stalkers have some form of personality disorder and as a group have the greatest potential to become violent. Testimonies from stalking victims consistently revealed how personable, caring, and charismatic offenders seemed at first, but how those initially appealing features quickly transformed. Once an offender had won over his/her victim, the need to control emerged and behavior including outward acts of jealousy, aggression and threats, and mental abuse was displayed (Cox & Speziale, 2009). Prior attachment, jealousy, and violence issues within relationships are significant predictors of cyberstalking-related behaviors (Strawhun & Huss, 2013). Zona et al. (1993) reported that the love obsessional stalkers are those who have never met their victim. The erotomanic group is the smallest among stalkers and is motivated by the belief that the victim is in love with them, as a result of active delusions. Sheridan and Grant (2007) observed that cyberstalking was less likely to be perpetrated by ex-partners and was more often engaged by acquaintance or strangers.

It is also noted that cyberstalking has been connected to pedophilia. Of adults to stalk children on the internet, 74% were 20-49 years old and 95% were males (Alexy, Burgess, & Baker, 2005). Many studies have observed that offenders showed a tendency to display low to medium mental impairment when entering the criminal justice system, as well as nonconforming psychological states of being and antisocial behaviors (Prins, 2005; Kamphuis & Emmelkamp, 2005).

Rosenfeld (2003) was the first to conduct an empirical study on the relationship between stalkers and recidivism and it was found that half of the offenders repeated the offence. Personality disorder, particularly those that involve antisocial, borderline, or narcissistic behaviors, which are collectively referred to as "Cluster B" personality disorders, combination of a personality disorder and a history of substance abuse raised the risk of re-offending even higher. This is consistent with the findings associated with other criminal offender groups. Based on experience, those offenders with a history of mental illness and substance abuse have a higher than normal probability of re-offending (Pittaro, 2007).

Mainly offenders are found to be males, who may or may not have psychological disorders. Though many researches were conducted, clarity on many aspects related to offending is not clear.

THEORIES

Many theories were put forward to explain cyberstalking such as evolutionary theory, relational goal theory, and psychodynamic approaches. According to evolutionary approach, stalking evolved as one strategy among an armament of strategies for solving historically recurrent problems of mating and within gender competition (Duntley & Buss, 2012). As per Relational Goal Theory obsessive relational pursuers link the goal of having a particular relationship to higher-order goals such as happiness and self-worth (Spitzberg & Cupach, 2007). In the case of stalking, perpetrator goal is to make relation with victim as their happiness and self-worth depends on it. If this goal (i.e., relationship) becomes blocked, the individual experiences strain, frustration, and anger. They respond to this frustration by excessively ruminating about their failed objective. They will not stop until they feel they have achieved their goal and they believe the more persistent and intense methods of pursuit will eventually lead them to success. Attachment theory and object relations theory are used to explain stalking under paradigm of psychodynamic approach. Attachment theories suggest that those who stalk tend to have attachment issues stemming from childhood disruptions such as the loss of a caregiver, an emotionally or physically absent caregiver, or childhood emotional, physical, and/or sexual abuse In the cases of stalking, individuals with insecure-anxious attachment issues have the propensity to resort to stalking and other threatening behaviors in order to preserve or mend the bond and reduce the anxiety they experience from the rejection or abandonment. Likewise, the more unavailable or emotionally distant the object of pursuit gets the more intense and desperate the attempts become to try to reform the attachment (Kienlen, 1998; Meloy, 1998; Patton, Nobles, & Fox, 2010).

Another theory used to explain cyberstalking is the lifestyle exposure theory which suggests that the likelihood of victimization is dependent on lifestyle. This proposes that any change in the habitual activities of an individual or group, be it potential victims or wrongdoers, is enough to increase or decrease exposure to risk as well as present opportunities for victimization. The lifestyle exposure theory permits the predictability of victimization or potential victimization when lifestyle is taken into account. In other words, patterns, routines and daily schedules are exploited to the benefit of the perpetrator. In this way, not only can high risk individuals of cyber stalking be identified and targeted by cyber stalkers but also by protective agents concerned by the matter at hand (Davis, 2005).

The routine activity theory is based on the observations by Cohen and Felson pertaining crime to a product of the recurrent, routine activities and structuring of everyday life (SAGE dictionary of Criminology, 2006). In its original conception, the theory was designed to explain the volume and distribution of violent crimes or that of theft – cases in which both the victim and offender are physically present at the scene of the crime (Davis, 2005). The Routine activity theory was used to explore whether there is an increased risk while using online sites and whether the use of social networking sites should be deemed a risky act that may lead to various types of victimization. It looks for a convergence in time and location of motivated offenders, targets that are deemed suitable by the offender and a lack of guardianship over desired persons or things (De Coster, Estes, & Mueller, 1999).

Rational choice theory suggests that individuals, which in this case would be cyber stalkers, freely choose to commit a crime after weighing the prospective rewards against the potential risks. Since rational choice theory assumes that cyber stalkers will calculate the risks before committing a crime, it also assumes that such behaviors could be deterred if the risks were certain and the punishment was severe (Barkan, 2006).

Not a single theory is fully explaining the complexity of cyberstalking, more theories are yet to come in future.

FORENSIC INVESTIGATION

Cybercrime offending can be technically complex and legally intricate. Rapid advancements in the functionality of information communication technologies (ICTs) and innate disparities between systems of law globally are stark challenges for first responders, investigating authorities, forensic interrogators, prosecuting agencies, and administrators of criminal justice (Brown, 2015). Many cybercrimes are sophisticated and well-conceived, requiring police to apply technological expertise and deductive reasoning to unravel complex 'modus operandi' and substantiate elements of an offence and many cybercrime offenders have evaded prosecution due to weaknesses in substantive criminal laws that do not address technological means of offending (Bromby, 2006; Downing, 2005).

Criminal profiles are widely used in investigations to link together different crimes, to narrow down lists of suspects and to aid the process of investigation (Rogers, 2003). Offender profiling is a forensic technique used in criminal investigations for analyzing, assessing, and interpreting the physical evidence, the crime scene, the nature of the offence and the way it was committed. This aims to create a profile of the demographic and behavioral characteristics (e.g., gender, age, background, psychological disorders, guilt, anger) of an offender against the characteristics of those who have previously committed similar crimes. Profiles help build a bigger picture and reconstruct the crime, when there are too many unknowns (Kocsis, 2006; Turvey, 2011). Criminal profiling in simple terms is defined as:

A technique for identifying the major personality and behavioural characteristics of an individual based upon an analysis of the crimes he or she has committed (Douglas, Ressler, Burgess, & Hartman,1986).

Criminal Profiling in Prosecution Profiles have been proved useful in court in helping keep evidence in a case and proving a connection between one or several crimes and an offender (Ingram, 1998).

Criminal profiling models have two main approaches – inductive, where statistical information about committed crimes is used to generalize the behavior exhibited by these crimes, and deductive, where offender characteristics are derived from the specific case. It relies on data from criminal databases to identify a generalized behavioral pattern and personality traits of a typical offender in specific kind of cases (e.g., rape, serial homicides). After identifying a behavioral pattern or specific characteristics of a typical offender, the investigator can use criminal databases or records related to the defined characteristics to develop a group of potential suspects (Rogers, 2003). This method is less methodological and possibility of having errors caused by variable levels of honesty and perception bias of questionnaire respondents, or by case studies being taken from a wide range of time and increased possibility of unpredictable external influences on the case (Turvey, 2012). A deductive method takes a more personal approach, as it examines every case contextually and it relates to case-based investigation. It analyses evidence from the case in question focusing on specific behavioral and personality traits, and uses it to develop a profile of the specific characteristics of the probable offender (Turvey, 2012; 2011). It looks the case more in detail but it lacks access to a real case with the appropriate amount of case detail.

Profiling of cyber stalkers is difficult as it involves complex and sometimes unpredictable behaviours (Burmerster, Henry, & Kermes, 2005). Sheridan and Grant (2007) reported that cyberstalking is not fundamentally different from offline stalking and Bocij (2003) noticed many similarities and differences among offline stalkers. Though attempts are made to build profile like Barnes (2013) builds a cyberstalking victim profile in terms of their daily activities, relationship with technology, behaviour online, age group, lack of many studies and clarity is preventing to form a formal profile of cyberstalker and victim.

Digital forensics is a branch of forensic science, which encompasses the discovery, acquisition and investigation of information associated with digital devices. Originally used as a synonym for computer forensics, the term digital forensics has expanded to involve the investigation of any device capable of storing information in digital form. Digital forensics investigations have a variety of applications and the use of forensic techniques in the digital domain is increasingly an essential element of high-tech investigations, but also to support or refute the theory of a case in traditional civil and criminal investigations (Brown, 2015). The utility of Behavioural Evidence Analysis (BEA) has gained attention in the field of Digital Forensics in recent years. BEA is a deductive, case-based investigative strategy that analyses evidence from a specific case focusing on certain behavioral and personality traits to derive characteristics of the probable offender which is consisted of four steps: equivocal forensic analysis, victimology, crime scene characteristics, and offender characteristics. Victimology focuses on the reasons for being targeted, offender motivations and their relation with victim, and the traits of victims (e.g., physical characteristics, marital status, personal lifestyle). Crime scene characteristics explore motives and behavioral decisions of the offender and giving more evidence. Offender characteristics focus on the behavioral and personality characteristics of the offender to make a profile and equivocal forensic analysis reviews the case evidence scientifically, thoroughly and objectively to develop theories that are justified by actual facts (Turvey, 2011; Casey, 2011; Karmen, 2012). Recently, Rogers (2015) proposed a model which incorporates BEA into the process of digital forensics investigation which included six phases such as Case classification, context analysis, data collection, statistical analysis, timeline analysis/visualization, and decision/opinion.

Mutawa, Bryce, Franqueira, and Marrington (2015) explored the use of BEA for the investigation of cases of the possession and dissemination of Sexually Exploitative Imagery of Children (SEIC) and found that integrating BEA in digital investigations can greatly assist the investigator in assessing the reliability of digital evidence and the strength of associated conclusions. This can produce a more detailed reconstruction of evidence that can inform sentencing and prosecution in court. It can also assist in mapping and understanding offending behavior and the dynamics of offences. In another study on the utility of BEA for analyzing cyberstalking cases in terms of understanding the behavioral and motivational dimensions of offending, and the way in which digital evidence can be interpreted, the authors found that BEA helps to focus an investigation, enables better understanding and interpretation of victim and offender behavior, and assists in inferring traits of the offender from available digital evidence. These benefits can help investigators to build a stronger case, reduce time wasted to mistakes, and to exclude suspects wrongly accused in cyberstalking cases (Mutawa, Bryce, Franqueira, & Marrington, 2016). More studies are required to understand the use of BEA in digital investigation.

Criminal profiling and use of BEA are different methods aid in the criminal investigation and many methods are required for the effective investigation on cyber stalking as not much scientific information is available on cyberstalking. Profiling can help deal with extensive suspect pools and abundance of digital traces to investigate, leading to a successful case conclusion in less time or where otherwise none would be possible. However, the extent to which it can be applied to cybercrime altogether is not clear. There have been thorough attempts to profile hackers and other cybercriminals, suggesting that this should also be possible for cyber stalkers. There are studies that investigate application of existing profiling techniques and criminal typologies to cyberstalking. Most of these attempts have little to offer to real-life forensic investigations, and only have an academic significance. They cover cyber stalker profiling very broadly, only offering approximate typologies or templates and little detail. There is also little to no consideration to technical aspects of the crime. A possible reason for that is problematic access to detailed cases and hence the use of inductive methods by researchers, which, as a statistics-based method, offers little detail to the profile. Another problem is the lack of consideration for digital forensic investigation models and what profiling can offer to a real investigation, carried out according to such a methodology (Silde, 2013).

PREVENTION

The prevention of cyberstalking needs to be done with public education, and law and enforcement. Educating the public about cyberstalking and promoting multi—agency awareness campaigns would reduce the risk of being victim (Stambaugh, Beaupre, Icove, Baker, Cassaday, & Williams, 2000; Baum, Catalano, Rand, & Rose, 2009). Educating about the risk of adding strangers as friends, engaging in deviant activities (e.g., surfing sites depicting pornographic images), and associating online with deviant peers, educating on internet security measures and use these techniques to help control access to personal information on sites such as Facebook and Myspace are helpful in reducing the chance of victimization. Adults monitoring children and youth's internet use and making guidelines for them are also useful

(Reyns, Henson, & Fisher, 2011; Henson, Reyns, & Fisher, 2011; Marcum, Ricketts, & Higgins, 2010). Several studies of Internet use by adolescents have found that increasing numbers of young people are experiencing the following types of victimization while using computer-mediated communication (CMC) methods: unwanted exposure to sexual material, sexual solicitation, and unwanted nonsexual harassment (Mitchell, Finkelhor, & Wolak, 2003; 2007; O'Connell, Barrow, & Sange, 2002). Many students recommended appropriate prevention, education, and intervention strategies, mainly offline programs at the college level to battle cyberstalking (White & Carmody, 2014). Tokunaga and Aune (2015) reported that victims used seven general management tactics of which ignore/avoidance, active technological disassociation, and help seeking were the most common and using technology to move away from pursuers was reported as the most effective tactic for managing the unwanted relational pursuit. It is also suggested that victims' management responses were associated with the type of behaviors experienced.

It can be seen that addressing cyberstalking involves a variety of different approaches, including personal prevention strategies, legislative interventions, and technological solutions to current technological flaws. However, the first step in effectively responding to cyberstalking in particular and Internet-based crime in general, is to ensure that the understanding of the Internet is derived from a realistic appreciation of the nature of the new technologies themselves, rather than being rooted in a pre-Internet conception of information exchange mechanisms. Whilst it can be argued that some cybercrimes are not different from real world crimes in as much as they reflect the same range of offensive and dangerous behaviors, it also needs to be acknowledged that the Internet can magnify, distort, and ignore the attributes of the real world in ways we urgently need to address. Cyberstalking provides an illuminating example of cybercrime. The extent to which cyberstalking can be regulated and responded to by the criminal justice system depends in many respects upon the extent to which it emulates traditional stalking behaviors in the physical world. The new technologies are so different from the old that the old ways may no longer hold good, and we may need to reassess our thinking about the nature of the possible intervention strategies. In sum, while some of the traditional strategies will remain applicable in addressing cyberstalking, new and innovative legislative, technical, and investigative counter measures will almost certainly be necessary (Thapa & Kumar, 2011).

Bocij (2004) suggested few recommendations to prevent cyberstalking such as controlling information and communicative technology. Controlling information means controlling their personal information to ensure that it does not become accessible to others. The more active an individual is in the online realm, the more information is likely to be available to others and by controlling access to personal information, the danger posed by cyber stalkers is reduced. Communicative technology indicates that individuals should be thoroughly familiarized themselves with the particular site and its security measures before joining it which help them to understand the potential dangers implement security measures to protect their online security. He also gave three rules to online behavior such as one should behave appropriately when interacting in communicative technology, avoid any arguments and personal attacks within cyber space and personal information should not be disclosed to online platforms.

It is also important to educate the victims about cyberstalking, and encourage seeking legal help and also mental health services to reduce the distress associated with stalking. The involvement and law and enforcement and ensuring punishment for cybercrimes including cyber stalking would be beneficial. The laws should be updated with new developments in technology and crimes related to it. It is also important to protect oneself from cyber harassment and stalking and many suggestions available for the same. Hitchcock (2000) listed suggestions regarding staying safe online which are as follows:

1. Use your primary e-mail account only for messages to and from people you know and trust.
2. Get a free e-mail account from someplace like Hotmail, Juno, or Excite, and so forth, and use that for all of your other online activities.
3. When you select an e-mail username or chat nickname, create something gender-neutral and like nothing you have elsewhere or have had before. Try not to use your name.
4. Do not fill out profiles for your e-mail account, chat rooms, IM (instant messaging), and so forth.
5. Do set your options in chat or IM to block all users except for those on your buddy list.
6. Do learn how to use filtering to keep unwanted e-mail messages from coming to your e-mailbox.
7. If you are being harassed online, try not to fight back. This is what the harasser wants—a reaction from you. If you do and the harassment escalates, do the following:
    a. Contact the harasser and politely ask them to leave you alone.
    b. Contact their ISP and forward the harassing messages.
    c. If harassment escalates, contact your local police.
    d. If they cannot help, try the State Police, District Attorney's office and/ or State Attorney General.
    e. Contact a victims group, such as WHOA, SafetyED or CyberAngels.

GENERAL GUIDELINES FOR ONLINE INTERACTION SAFETY

Prevention

- Online identity. The information available on the net that allows someone to build a picture of them so consider using a gender neutral nickname may be safer than using a real name and makes it harder for potential cyber stalkers to access potential victims. Using pseudonyms in adult chat rooms and using gender-neutral names in other forms may be helpful.

- Being wary about what information you provide online, whether it is on a FaceBook or MySpace profile, in a blog, on a bulletin board, in the course of chat or in response to an online marketer's offer of an amazing deal. Once posted, forever online. Be attentive when making online posts by assuming that everything posted will be permanently recorded in cyber space. Even if an account is deleted, anyone on the Internet can easily print and save the posts, such as photos, contact information or status updates made.

- Personal information should remain personal. The more information posted online, the more at risk an individual may become to cyber stalking. It is important to be cautious about including personal mobile phone numbers in email footers.

- Know and manage online friends. Often communicative platforms are used to gain large numbers of friends – known and unknown to the user and there are tools on these communicative platforms which allow for the management of profiles. For instance, an Internet user can share certain information with certain friends or have multiple online pages that vary in content and magnitude. Adding strangers to social media risk for stalking.

- Use strong passwords. Passwords which are long, complex and alphanumeric are advisable as they are more difficult to figure out. It is always better to have different password for each online account occupied. Passwords should also be changed regularly, also make sure of not using a pet's name as a password and not sharing passwords with friends or colleagues.

- Use discretion when selecting profile pictures. Assume that people will use the information and pictures gained from profiles destructively. For instance, an already provocative picture could be further altered to humiliate and degrade the victim.

- Apply caution when clicking on links. It is suggested that Internet users be very careful when clicking on links as they may contain viruses or malware.

- Protection of laptops, personal computers - including use of passwords, caution in downloading potential spyware and attention to keeping virus protection up to date.

- Consider creating an additional e-mail account. The creation of an additional email account may be beneficial, in that all the online activity and interaction in the communicative technology can be linked to this delegated account as opposed to a personal one.

- Do not allow any site to scan an e-mail address book. Often, on joining a social network, a request is sent out to enter the individual's e-mail address and password in order to find out if there are any contacts that are also active on the same social network. This process allows for the social network to send an email to everyone ever e-mailed, informing them of the individual's participation in that specific social network.

- While making e-mail id, don't use full name and living place instead use a first name or surname as the user name identity.

- Be cautious of using of e-mail signature as it may expose full name, position and contact details so it is to be included when necessary and to known recipients and remove the contact details of the e-mail signature when sending e-mails to unknown recipients.

- Use blind carbon copy (BCC) when sending an e-mail to multiple recipients so that each recipient only sees his or her e-mail address.

- Regularly delete personal messages or encrypt old as it may prevent stalker to gain more information regarding the victim.

- As youngsters spend more time on online and often feel a sense of belonging to online communities which may put them on high risk for stalking, hence education and awareness about cyber stalking are must for them.

- Younger Internet users are encouraged to work securely from wireless networks and cautioned to choose networks that have a network security key and to connect to a standard or wired network that offers the best protection.

- Warn young users against becoming victim to cyber stalkers with intimate and romantic motives and are cautioned to avoid flirtation with unknown online friends. The participation in 'harmless' flirtation may give a potential cyber stalker the wrong indication of interest.

- Victims who are under the age of eighteen should tell their parents or another adult they trust about any harassments or threats.

- Experts suggest that in cases where the offender is known, victims should send the stalker a clear written warning. Specifically, victims should communicate that the contact is unwanted, and ask the perpetrator to cease sending communications of any kind. Victims should do this only once. Then, no matter the response, victims under no circumstances ever communicate with the stalker again.

- Victims should save copies of this communication in both electronic and hard copy for if the harassment continues; the victim may wish to file a complaint with the stalker's Internet service provider, as well as with their own service provider.
- Many Internet service provides offer tools that filter or block communications from specific individuals.
- As soon as individuals suspect they are victims on online harassment or cyber stalking, they should start collecting all evidence and document all contact made by the stalker. Save all email, postings or other communications in both electronic and hard-copy form. If possible, save all of the header information from e-mail and newsgroup postings. Record the dates and times of any contact with the stalker.
- Victims may also want to start a log of each communication explaining the situation in more detail. Victims may want to document how the harassment is affecting their lives and what steps they have taken to stop the harassment.
- Victims may want to file a report with local law enforcement or contact their local prosecutor's office to see what charges, if any, can be pursued. Victims should save copies of police reports and record all contact with low enforcement officials and the prosecutor's office.
- Victims who are being continually harassed may want to consider changing their e-mail address, Internet service provider, a home phone number, and should examine the possibility of using encryption software or privacy protection programs.
- Under no circumstances should victims agree to meet with the perpetrator face to face to work it out, or talk. No contact should ever be made with the stalker. Meeting a stalker in person can be very dangerous.
- Prevention of cyber stalking for business users should focus on two key roles: protecting the public from becoming victims of cyber stalking by employees through business resources and protecting the business and its staff from becoming victims of cyber stalking.
- Business owners can control their resources by means of an Acceptable Use Policy (AUP). An AUP clearly sets out how a company's Information Communication Technology (ICT) resources can be used as well as any prohibited behaviours and practices. The AUP should also list any penalties for the misuse of business facilities.
- Business owners can implement regular software audits. This involves the regular checks of computer systems to make sure that no pornography or private software is stored.

- Business owners can place controls on the use of company facilities for e-mails and web browsing in order to monitor the use of the Internet.
- It is necessary to take proper precautions when marketing a business online and to be done in secure and safe ways such as using a specialized e-mail address to advertise the business, avoid giving out any personal contact details, avoid publicizing personal and private information and avoid unhealthy rivalry and competition, including bad mouthing and slandering other business competitors.

(Bocij, 2004; Communication Technologies, nd; Miller & Morris, 2012; Online Privacy…nd; Small & Vorgan, 2008; Social Networking…,nd; Sissing, 2013; Thape & Kumar, 2011).

Intervention

Bocij (2004) warns that an offensive e-mail or online argument does not constitute a valid case of cyber stalking. So the first step in dealing with cyber stalking is establishing whether or not cyber stalking is actually taking place Understanding the concept of cyberstalking and legal definition of cyber stalking in concerned countries would be useful to decide upon the interventions. The decision whether or not to contact the cyber stalker is a difficult one and needs to be carefully considered. The decision to ignore the cyber stalker may cause him to lose interest or the cyber stalker may decide to retaliate and increase the cyber stalking behaviour. Similarly, the same results can be produced if the cyber stalker is contacted, confronted and asked to stop the behaviour. This plea to stop the cyber stalking may come across as weakness which further fuels the cyber stalker's destructive behaviour. In some situations it may be necessary for the victim to contact the cyber stalker to ask him to stop the cyber stalking behaviour. If an individual decides to do this, research suggests that this request should only be made once and subsequently all contact with the cyber stalker should seize. If the victim continues to entertain the cyber stalker, this behaviour is not only counterproductive but also dangerous in terms of escalation of the cyber stalking behavior (Bocij, 2004; Sissing, 2013).

Once it is understood that cyberstalking is happening, it is important to gather as much evidence as possible. It is suggested that all the evidence be saved on an external device such as an external hard drive or data disk and all the cyber-stalking-related communication should be saved as the cyber stalker's ISP or even identity may be traced. The victims may also make use of "screen grabber" applications to record and save cyber stalking messages. Make use of the security options available within social networks, e-mail facilities or cell phones to block the cyber stalkers. Also, increase cyber security measures on any online forums. After increasing online security measures, efforts should be made to search for the victim's name on the

Internet via major search engines such as Google or Yahoo with full name in order to check how much personal information is available to the public and consider deleting this information. It is important for the victim to find a supportive personal safety network of friends, family, and resources and always let this trusted network know of their whereabouts. Security measures at home, in a vehicle and at work, cyber safety measures, memorizing emergency numbers and keep them on speed dial, keep their cell phone charged, not accepting private calls and blocking the cyber stalker's number are a must. Victims should consider notifying his or her Internet service and they may take action depending on their internal policies. In addition to this, victims should make sure that the cyber stalker has no opportunity to download any programs that aid in monitoring their online activity. Victims can also purchase software to block, squelch, or ignore unwanted electronic communication and it would be advisable to contact one's Internet Service Provider since most ISPs have established policies in the online agreement prohibiting such abuse of services The ISP can immediately terminate the offender's service for violating this policy without fear of legal recourse by the offender However, the reality of the situation is that most ISPs have concentrated more on helping its customers avoid spam, unwanted pop-ups, and virus protection rather than protecting against online harassment Legal actions against perpetrator can be considered. IT specialists should seek to develop new and innovative ways to increase the traceability of online predators and make the necessary efforts to launch awareness programmes aimed at the various criminal justice role players as well as local communities to better equip them with knowledge and knowhow regarding IT vigilance (Bocij, 2004; Donovan & Bernier, 2009; Sissing, 2013; Hutton & Haantz, 2003).

Al-Khateeb, Epiphaniou, Zhraa, Barnes, and Short (2017) suggested that most offences were communicated through private channels such as emails and/or mobile texts/calls. A significant number of victims did not report this to their service provider because they did not know they could. While Police were recognized as the first-point-of-contact in such cases, 41.6% of our sample did not contact the Police due to reasons such as fear of escalation, guilt/sympathy and self-blaming. Experiences from those who have reported offences to service providers demonstrate that no or very little support was offered. Overall, the majority of participants shared the view that third-party intervention is required on their behalf in order to mitigate risks associated with cyberstalking. An independent specialist anti-stalking organization was a popular choice to act on their behalf followed by the Police and network providers. Incidents are taking place on channels owned and controlled by large, cross-border international companies providing mobile services, webmail and social networking. The lack of support offered to victims in many cases of cyberstalking can be identified as Corporate Social Irresponsibility (CSI). Awareness should be raised as regarding service providers' liability and social responsibility towards adopting better strategies.

Law enforcement officials have suggested that to prevent being a victim, people choose screen names that are gender and age ambiguous and if possible, avoid posting personal information in web profiles. Most importantly, be extremely cautious when meeting with an individual that was met online. It suggests that if a meeting is to take place that it is done in a public location and it is strongly advisable to bring a friend along. To aid in the investigation, cyber stalking victims should be advised to inform the perpetrator that the communication is unwanted and should cease immediately. It is also advisable to save all unaltered and unedited communication from the perpetrator that could be used as prosecutorial evidence (Petrocelli, 2005 in Pittaro, 2007).

Online support groups such as Working to Halt Online Abuse (WHOA) (http://www.haltabuse.org), CyberAngels (http://www.cyberangels.com), WiredPatrol (http://www.wiredpatrol.org), Web Police (http://www.intergov.org), and Network for Surviving Stalking (http://www.nss.org.uk), are informative and give a platform to express their anger, sadness and personal experiences to cyberstalking. Victims would be benefited from joining such groups. Unfortunately, there are several obstacles to treating this disorder. First, finding a qualified mental health professional that acknowledges this condition and specializes in this type of treatment may be a cumbersome task to accomplish (King, 1996). The literature on cyber stalking is scarce at best and the studies that have been done have been based on comparatively small sample populations. From what has been researched, it is doubtful that mental health professionals even have a general understanding of cyber stalking behaviors and are less likely to know how to approach and treat this particular offender. The Internet is one of the most resourceful advancements in technology to have ever been created by humankind, but it also has a malevolent side to it that cannot be discounted. Clinicians have only recently begun to understand the dangers associated with the Internet (Pittaro, 2007).

CONCLUSION

There is not much agreement on the definition of cyberstalking as it appeared recently due to technological advancement. Many of the researches were conducted among university students and the prevalence of cyberstalking among general population and special groups are not much known but researches repeatedly confirm it as growing issue but less information on nature and extent of cyber stalking happening. There is not much agreement or lack of universally accepted definitions leads to varied prevalence rates of cyberstalking. The information on vulnerable groups and individuals to cyberstalking is still not enough as same as our understanding of offenders. There is concern regarding the use of profiling and typologies in actual criminal investigation. Technical advancements and thorough knowledge on technical details among researchers from different backgrounds poses a big problem to its complete understanding and prevention. All these are preventing to make a much authentic preventive and intervention guidelines. Future researchers need to focus on all these aspects.

Though many prevention techniques are advised, it suffers from limitations too. For example, the idea that changing one's username "prevents" cyberstalking seems misleading—it does not get at the root of the problem, and may in fact buy into cyberstalker mentality (Baer, 2010). According to Cavelty (2014), current approaches to cyber-security are not working and the reason for this is a multi-dimensional and multi-faceted security dilemma. The threat arising from cyberspace to (national) security is a possible disruption to a specific way of life, one building on information technologies and critical functions of infrastructures, with relatively little consideration for humans directly. This non-focus on people makes it easier for state actors to militarize cyber-security and (re-)assert their power in cyberspace, thereby overriding the different security needs of human beings in that space. Paradoxically, the use of cyberspace as a tool for national security, both in the dimension of war fighting and the dimension of mass-surveillance, has detrimental effects on the level of cyber-security globally. A solution out of this dilemma is a cyber-security policy that is decidedly anti-vulnerability and at the same time based on strong considerations for privacy and data protection. Such a security would have to be informed by an ethics of the info sphere that is based on the dignity of information related to human beings.

The concept of cyber resilience has emerged in recent years in response to the recognition that cyber security is more than just risk management. Cyber resilience is the goal of organizations, institutions and governments across the world and yet the emerging literature is somewhat fragmented due to the lack of a common approach to the subject. This limits the possibility of effective collaboration across public, private and governmental actors in their efforts to build and maintain cyber resilience. In response to this limitation, and to calls for a more strategically focused approach, this paper offers a knowledge-based view of cyber security management that explains how an organization can build, assess, and maintain cyber resilience (Ferdinand, 2015).

As mentioned by Maple, Short, and Brown (2011), one clear message from the data collected is that many of the victims of cyber harassment are frustrated with the lack of help and support they feel is available. The key sources they want to be able to act are the Police and Service Providers, both in terms of providing actions that can stop on going harassment and also in providing support to those affected in dealing with its effects. This adds to the growing debate of whether legislative change is required to allow the police and encourage service providers to provide the help people need in cases of cyber harassment and if so, exactly what changes those should be.

Current understanding on cyber staking indicates that we still need to go a long way to understand its prevalence, causes, risks, prevention and intervention effectiveness.

REFERENCES

Al-Khateeb, H. M., Epiphaniou, G., Alhaboby, Z. A., Barnes, J., & Short, E. (2017). Cyberstalking: Investigating formal intervention and the role of Corporate Social Responsibility. *Telematics and Informatics*, *34*(4), 339–349. doi:10.1016/j. tele.2016.08.016

Al Mutawa, N., Bryce, J., & Marrington, A.(2015). Behavioural evidence analysis applied to digital forensics: an empirical analysis of child pornography cases using P2P networks. Academic Press. doi:10.1109/ARES.2015.49

Al Mutawa, N., Bryce, J., Franqueira, V. N. L., & Marrington, A. (2016). Forensic investigation of cyberstalking cases using Behavioural Evidence Analysis. *Digital Investigation*, *16*, S96–S103. doi:10.1016/j.diin.2016.01.012

Alexy, E. M., Burgess, A. W., Baker, T., & Smoyak, S. A. (2005). Perceptions of cyberstalking among college students. *Brief Treatment and Crisis Intervention*, *5*(3), 279–289. doi:10.1093/brief-treatment/mhi020

Amita, V. (2016). Cyber Crimes & Law. Central Law Publication. Retrieved from http://www.legalindia.com/cyber-stalking-the-impact-of-its-legislative-provisions-in-india/

Baer, M. (2010). Cyberstalking and the Internet Landscape We Have Created. *Virginia Journal of Law & Technology.*, *15*(154), 153–174.

Barkan, S. (2006). *Criminology: A sociological understanding* (3rd ed.). Upper Saddle River, NJ: Prentice Hall.

Basile, K. C., Swahn, M., Chen, J., & Saltzman, L. (2006). Stalking in the United States: Recent national prevalence estimates. [PubMed]. *American Journal of Preventive Medicine*, *31*(2), 172–175. doi:10.1016/j.amepre.2006.03.028

Baum, K., Catalano, S., Rand, M., & Rose, K. (2009). *Stalking victimization in the United States*. Washington, DC: U.S. Department of Justice.

Baum, K., Catalano, S., Rand, M., & Rose, K. (2009). *Stalking victimization in the United States*. Washington, DC: U.S. Department of Justice.

Björklund, K., Häkkänen-Nyholm, H., Sheridan, L., & Roberts, K. (2010). The Prevalence of Stalking Among Finnish University Students. [PubMed]. *Journal of Interpersonal Violence*, 25(4), 684–698. doi:10.1177/0886260509334405

Black, M. C., Basile, K. C., Breiding, M. J., Smith, S. G., Walters, M. L., Merrick, M. T., & Stevens, M. R. (2011). *National Intimate Partner and Sexual Violence Survey, 2010 summary report*. Atlanta, GA: National Center for Injury Prevention and Control of the Centers for Disease Control and Prevention.

Bocij, P. (2003). Victims of cyberstalking: An exploratory study of harassment perpetrated via the Internet. *First Monday*, 8(10). doi:10.5210/fm.v8i10.1086

Bocij, P. (2004). *Cyberstalking: Harassment in the Internet age and how to protect your family*. Westport, CT: Praeger Publishers.

Bocij, P., & McFarlane, L. (2002). Online harassment: Towards a definition of cyberstalking. *Prison Service Journal*, *139*, 31–38.

Bocij, P., & McFarlane, L. (2003). The Internet: A Discussion of Some New and Emerging Threats to Young People. *The Police Journal*, 76(1), 3–13. doi:10.1177/0032258X0307600102

Bocij, P., & McFarlane, L. (2003). Cyberstalking: The Technology of Hate.The Police Journal: Theory. *Practice and Principles*, 76(3), 204–221. doi:10.1350/pojo.76.3.204.19442

Bromby, M. (2006). Security against Crime: Technologies for Detecting and Preventing Crime. *International Review of Law Computers & Technology*, 20(1-2), 1–5. doi:10.1080/13600860600818235

Brown, C. S. D. (2015). Cyber-Attacks, Retaliation and Risk: Legal and Technical Implications for Nation-States and Private Entities. In J. L. Richet (Ed.), *Cybersecurity Policies and Strategies for Cyberwarfare Prevention* (pp. 166–203). Hershey, PA: IGI Global; doi:10.4018/978-1-4666-8456-0.ch008

Brownstein, A. (2000). In the campus shadows, women are stalkers as well as the stalked. *The Chronicle of Higher Education*, 47(15), 4042.

Burgess, A. W., & Baker, T. (2002). Cyberstalking. In J. Boon & L. Sheridan (Eds.), *Stalking and psychosexual obsession: Psychological perspectives for prevention, policing and treatment*. Chichester, UK: Wiley; doi:10.1002/9780470713037.ch12

Burmester, M., Henry, P., & Kermes, L. S. (2005). Tracking Cyberstalkers: A Cryptographic Approach. ACM SIGCAS Computers and Society, 35(3).

Cameron, S., & Brown, D. (2015). Investigating and Prosecuting Cyber Crime: Forensic Dependencies and Barriers to Justice. *International Journal of Cyber Criminology*, *9*(1), 55–119.

Casey, E. (2011). Investigative reconstruction with digital evidence. In E. Casey & B. E. Turvey (Eds.), *Digital evidence and computer crime: forensic science, computers and the internet* (pp. 255–273). Academic Press.

Cavelty, D. M. (2014). Breaking the cyber-security dilemma: Aligning security needs and removing vulnerabilities. [PubMed]. *Science and Engineering Ethics*, *20*(3), 701–715. doi:10.100711948-014-9551-y

Comparcini, D., Simonetti, V., Lupo, R., Galli, F., Bocij, P., & Cicolini, G. (2016). Cyberstalking among Italian nurses: a large multicentric study. Prof Inferm, 69(3), 150-158. doi: 10.7429 / pi.2016.693150

Cox, L., & Speziale, B. (2009). Survivors of stalking. *Affilia*, *24*(1), 5–18. doi:10.1177/0886109908326815

Curtis, L. F. (2012). Virtual vs. reality: an examination of the nature of stalking and cyberstalking (Master Thesis). Retrieved from http://citeseerx.ist.psu.edu/viewdoc/download?doi=10.1.1.467.5711&rep=rep1&type=pdf

Davis, L. (2005). *Victimology in South Africa*. Pretoria: Van Schaik.

De Coster, S., Estes, S., & Mueller, C. (1999). Routine activities and sexual harassment in the workplace. *Work and Occupations*, *26*(1), 21–49. doi:10.1177/0730888499026001003

Dean, K. (2000). The Epidemic of Cyberstalking. Wired News. Retrieved from http://www.wired.com/news/politics/0,1283,35728,00.html

Deirmenjian, J. (1999). Stalking in Cyberspace. [PubMed]. *The Journal of the American Academy of Psychiatry and the Law*, *27*(3), 407–413.

Donovan, F., & Bernier, K. (2009). *Cyber crime fighters: Tales from the trenches*. Indianapolis, IN: Que Publishing.

Douglas, J. E., Ressler, R. K., Burgess, A. W., & Hartman, C. R. (1986). Criminal Profiling from Crime Scene Analysis. *Behavioral Sciences & the Law*, *4*(4), 401–421. doi:10.1002/bsl.2370040405

Downing, R. W. (2005). Shoring Up the Weakest Link: What Lawmakers Around the World Need to Consider in Developing Comprehensive Laws to Combat Cybercrime. *Columbia Journal of Transnational Law*, *43*, 741–762.

DrahokoupilováJ. (2007). Cyberstalking. Available at: http://heinonline.org/HOL/Page?handle=hein.journals/mujlt1&div=36&g_sent=1&collection=journals

Dreßing, H., Bailer, J., Anders, A., Wagner, H., & Gallas, C. (2014). Cyberstalking in a large sample of social network users: Prevalence, characteristics, and impact upon victims. [PubMed]. *Cyberpsychology, Behavior, and Social Networking*, *17*(2), 61–67. doi:10.1089/cyber.2012.0231

Duntley, J. D., & Buss, D. M. (2012). The evolution of stalking. *Sex Roles*, *66*(5-6), 311–327. doi:10.100711199-010-9832-0

Ellison, L. (1999). Cyberspace 1999: Criminal, criminal justice and the internet. Fourteenth BI LETA Conference, York, UK. Retrieved from http://www.bileta.ac.uk/99papers/ellison.htm

Ellison, L., & Akdeniz, Y. (1998). Cyber-Stalking: the Regulation of Harassment on the Internet. In Criminal Law Review (pp. 29–48). Crime, Criminal Justice and the Internet.

Epiphaniou, G., Alhaboby, Z. A., Barnes, J., & Short, E. (2017). Cyberstalking: Investigating formal intervention and the role of Corporate Social Responsibility. *Telematics and Informatics*, *34*(4), 339–349. doi:10.1016/j.tele.2016.08.016

Every-Palmer, S., Barry-Walsh, J., & Pathé, M. (2015). Harassment, stalking, threats and attacks targeting New Zealand politicians: A mental health issue. [PubMed]. *The Australian and New Zealand Journal of Psychiatry*, *49*(7), 634–641. doi:10.1177/0004867415583700

Ferdinand, J. (2015). Building organisational cyber resilience: A strategic knowledge-based view of cyber security management. [PubMed]. *Journal of Business Continuity & Emergency Planning*, *9*(2), 185–195.

Fisher, B. S., Cullen, F. T., & Turner, M. G. (2000). *The sexual victimization of college women*. Washington, DC: National Institute of Justice, Bureau of Justice Statistics; doi:10.1037/e377652004-001

Goode, M. (1995). Stalking: Crime of the nineties? *Criminal Law Journal*, *19*, 21–31.

Harmon, R. B., Rosner, R., & Owens, H. (1995). Obsessional harassment and erotomania in a criminal court population. [PubMed]. *Journal of Forensic Sciences*, *40*(2), 188–196. doi:10.1520/JFS15339J

Harrison, C. (2006). Cyberspace and child abuse images. *Affilia, 21*(4), 365–379.

Henson, B., Reyns, B. W., & Fisher, B. S. (2011). Security in the 21st century. *Criminal Justice Review, 36*(3), 253–268.

Henson, B., Reyns, B. W., & Fisher, B. S. (2011). Security in the 21st century. *Criminal Justice Review, 36*(3), 253–268. doi:10.1177/0734016811399421

Hill, A.L., Rand, D.G., Nowak, M.A., & Christakis, N.A. (2010). Emotions as infectious diseases in a large social network: the SISa model. Proceeding of Biological Science, 277(1701), 3827–3835. doi:10.1098/rspb.2010.1217

Hitchcock, J. A. (2000). Cyberstalking. Link-Up, 17(4). Retrieved from http://www.infotoday.com/lu/ju100/hitchcock.htm

Hutton, S., & Haantz, S. (2003). Cyber stalking. Retrieved from http://www.nw3c.org

Ingram, S. (1998). If the Profile Fits: Admitting Criminal Psychological Profiles into Evidence in Criminal Trials. *Journal of Urban and Contemporary Law, 54*, 239–266.

Jenson, B. (1996). Cyberstalking: Crime, enforcement and personal responsibility of the on-line world. S.G.R. MacMillan. Retrieved from http://www.sgrm.com/art-8.htm

Kamphuis, J. H., & Emmelkamp, P. M. G. (2000). Stalking—A contemporary challenge for forensic and clinical psychiatry. [PubMed]. *The British Journal of Psychiatry, 176*(03), 206–209. doi:10.1192/bjp.176.3.206

Karmen, A. (2012). *Crime victims: an introduction to victimology.* Cengage Learning.

Kennedy, M. A., & Taylor, M. A. (2010). Online Harassment and Victimization of College Students. *Justice Policy Journal, 7*, 1–21.

Kienlen, K. K. (1998). Developmental and social antecedents of stalking. In J. R. Meloy (Ed.), *The psychology of stalking: Clinical and forensic perspectives* (pp. 52–65). San Diego, CA: Elsevier Science; doi:10.1016/B978-012490560-3/50022-0

Kienlen, K. K., Birmingham, D. L., Solberg, K. B., & O'Regan, J. T. (1997). A comparative study of psychotic and nonpsychotic stalking. [PubMed]. *The Journal of the American Academy of Psychiatry and the Law, 25*(3), 317–334.

King, S. A. (1996). Is the Internet Addictive, or Are Addicts Using the Internet? Retrieved February 18, 2006, from Web site: http://webpages.charter.net/stormking/iad.html

Kocsis, R. N. (2006). *What Is Criminal Profiling?* Springer; doi:10.1007/978-1-59745-109-3_1

Logan, T., & Walker, R. (2009). Partner stalking. [PubMed]. *Trauma, Violence & Abuse, 10*(3), 247–270. doi:10.1177/1524838009334461

Lyndon, A., Bonds-Raacke, J., & Cratty, A. D. (2011). College students' Facebook stalking of ex-partners. [PubMed]. *Cyberpsychology, Behavior, and Social Networking, 14*(12), 711–716. doi:10.1089/cyber.2010.0588

Maple, C., Short, E., & Brown, A. (2011). Cyberstalking in the United Kingdom An Analysis of the ECHO Pilot Survey. Retrieved from http://paladinservice. co.uk/wp-content/uploads/2013/12/ECHO_Pilot_Final-Cyberstalking-in-the-UK-University-of-Bedfordshire.pdf

Marcum, C. D., Ricketts, M. L., & Higgins, G. E. (2010). Assessing sex experiences of online victimization: An examination of adolescent online behaviors utilizing Routine Activity Theory. *Criminal Justice Review, 35*(4), 412–437. doi:10.1177/0734016809360331

McCann, J. T. (2000). A descriptive study of child and adolescent obsessional followers. [PubMed]. *Journal of Forensic Sciences, 45*(1), 195–199. doi:10.1520/JFS14660J

McEwan, T. E., Mullen, P. E., & MacKenzie, R. (2009). A study of the predictors of persistence in stalking situations. [PubMed]. *Law and Human Behavior, 33*(2), 149–158. doi:10.100710979-008-9141-0

McFarlane, L., & Bocij, P. (2003). An exploration of predatory behavior in cyberspace: Towards a typology of cyberstalkers. *First Monday, 8*(9), 1–12. doi:10.5210/fm.v8i9.1076

Meloy, J. R. (1996). Stalking (obsessional following): A review of some preliminary studies. *Aggression and Violent Behavior, 1*(2), 147–162. doi:10.1016/1359-1789(95)00013-5

Meloy, J. R. (1998). The Psychology of stalking. In J. R. Meloy (Ed.), *The psychology of stalking: Clinical and forensic perspectives* (pp. 2–21). San Diego, CA: Elsevier Science; doi:10.1016/B978-012490560-3/50020-7

Meloy, J. R., & Gothard, S. (1995). Demographic and clinical comparison of obsessional followers and offenders with mental disorders. [PubMed]. *The American Journal of Psychiatry, 152*(2), 25826.

Ménard, K. S., & Pincus, A. L. (2012). Predicting overt and cyber stalking perpetration by male and female college students. [PubMed]. *Journal of Interpersonal Violence, 27*(11), 2183–2207. doi:10.1177/0886260511432144

Ménard, K. S., & Pincus, A. L. (2012). Predicting overt and cyber stalking perpetration by male and female college students. [PubMed]. *Journal of Interpersonal Violence, 27*(11), 2183–2207. doi:10.1177/0886260511432144

Miller, B. N., & Morris, R. G. (2012). Cyber-related violence. In *Violent offenders: Theory, research, policy and practice*. London: Jones & Bartlett Learning.

Miller, G. (1999). Gore to release cyberstalking report, call for tougher laws. Latimes. com. Retrieved from http://www. latimes.com/news/ploitics/elect2000/pres/gore

Mitchell, K., Becker-Blease, K., & Finkelhor, D. (2005). Inventory of problematic Internet experiences encountered in clinical practice. *Professional Psychology, 36*(5), 498–509. doi:10.1037/0735-7028.36.5.498

Mitchell, K., Finkelhor, D., & Wolak, J. (2001). Risk factors for and impact of online sexual solicitation of youth. [PubMed]. *Journal of the American Medical Association, 285*(23), 3011–3014. doi:10.1001/jama.285.23.3011

Mitchell, K., Finkelhor, D., & Wolak, J. (2003). The exposure of youth to unwanted sexual material on the Internet: A national survey of risk, impact and prevention. *Youth & Society, 34*(3), 300–358. doi:10.1177/0044118X02250123

Mitchell, K., Finkelhor, D., & Wolak, J. (2007). Youth Internet users at risk for the more serious online sexual solicitations. [PubMed]. *American Journal of Preventive Medicine, 32*(6), 532–537. doi:10.1016/j.amepre.2007.02.001

Morrison, K. (2001). Predicting Violent Behavior in Stalkers: A Preliminary Investigation of Canadian Cases in Criminal Harassment. *Journal of Forensic Sciences, 46*(6), 1403–1410. doi:10.1520/JFS15163J

Mullen, P. E., Pathé, M., & Purcell, R. (2000). *Stalkers and their victims*. Cambridge, UK: Cambridge University Press; doi:10.1017/CBO9781139106863

Mullen, P. E., Pathé, M., Purcell, R., & Stuart, G. W. (1999). A study of stalkers. [PubMed]. *The American Journal of Psychiatry, 156*, 1244–1249.

O'Connell, R., Barrow, C., & Sange, S. (2002). Young peoples use of chat rooms: Implications for policy strategies and programs of education. Retrieved November 1, 2005, from http://www.uclan.ac.uk/host/cru/ publications.htm

Ogilvie, E. (2000). Cyberstalking, trends and issues in crime and criminal justice. Retrieved from http://www.aic. gov.au

Pathé, M. (2002). *Surviving stalking*. London: Cambridge University Press; doi:10.1017/CBO9780511544200

Pathé, M., & Mullen, P. E. (2002). The victim of stalking. In J. Boon & L. Sheridan (Eds.), *Stalking and Psychosexual Obsession: Psychological Perspectives for Prevention, Policing and Treatment* (pp. 1–22). West Sussex, UK: Wiley; doi:10.1002/9780470713037.ch1

Patton, C. L., Nobles, M. R., & Fox, K. A. (2010). Look who's stalking: Obsessive pursuit and attachment theory. *Journal of Criminal Justice, 38*(3), 282–290. doi:10.1016/j.jcrimjus.2010.02.013

Paullet, K. L., Rota, D. R., & Swan, T. T. (2009). Cyberstalking: An exploratory study of students at a mid-Atlantic university. *Issues in Information Systems, 2,* 640–649.

Petherick, W. (2001). Cyberstalking: Obsessional pursuit and the digital criminal. Retrieved from http://www.crimelibrary.com/criminology/cyberstalking/index.html

Petrocelli, J. (2005). Cyber stalking. *Law and Order, 53*(12), 56–58.

Prins, H. (2005). Mental disorder and violent crime: A problematic relationship. *Probation Journal, 52*(4), 333–357. doi:10.1177/0264550505058033

Report on Cyberstalking. (1999, August). Cyberstalking: A new challenge for law enforcement and industry. A Report from the Attorney General to The Vice President. Retrieved from http://www.usdoj.gov/criminal/ cybercrime/cyberstalking.htm

Reyns, B. W. (2010). A situational crime prevention approach to cyberstalking victimization: Preventive tactics for Internet users and online place managers. *Crime Prevention and Community Safety, 12*(2), 99–118. doi:10.1057/cpcs.2009.22

Reyns, B. W., Henson, B., & Fisher, B. S. (2011). Being pursued online: Applying cyberlifestyle- routine activities theory to cyberstalking victimization. *Criminal Justice and Behavior, 38*(11), 1149–1169. doi:10.1177/0093854811421448

Rogers, M.K. (2015). Psychological profiling as an investigative tool for digital forensics. Digital Forensics Threatscaes and Best Practices, 45-58. Doi:10.1016/B978-0-12-804526-8.00003-4

Rogers, M. (2003). The role of criminal profiling in the computer forensics process. *Computers & Security, 22,* 292–298. doi:10.10160167-4048(03)00405-x

Sheridan, L., & Grant, T. (2007). Is cyberstalking different? *Psychology, Crime & Law, 13*(6), 627–670. doi:10.1080/10683160701340528

Silde, A. (2013). Profiling the Cyberstalker (Master Thesis). Retrieved from file:///C:/Users/HP/Downloads/67-1-209-1-10-20140623%20(5).pdf

Sinwelski, S., & Vinton, L. (2001). Stalking: The constant threat of violence. *Affilia*, *16*(1), 46–65. doi:10.1177/08861090122094136

Sissing, S. K. (2013). A criminological exploration of cyber stalking in South Africa (Master Thesis). Retrieved from http://uir.unisa.ac.za/bitstream/handle/10500/13067/dissertation_sissing_sk.pdf?sequence=1

Smith, H. J., Dinev, T., & Xu, H. (2011). Information privacy research: An interdisciplinary review. *Management Information Systems Quarterly*, *35*(4), 989–1015. doi:10.2307/41409970

Spitzberg, B. H. (2002). The tactical topography of stalking victimization and management. *Trauma, Violence & Abuse*, *3*(4), 261–288. doi:10.1177/1524838002237330

Spitzberg, B. H., & Cupach, W. R. (2007). The state of the art of stalking: Taking stock of the emerging literature. *Aggression and Violent Behavior*, *12*(1), 64–86. doi:10.1016/j.avb.2006.05.001

Spitzberg, B. H., & Hoobler, G. (2002). Cyberstalking and the technologies of interpersonal terrorism. *New Media & Society*, *4*(1), 71–92. doi:10.1177/14614440222226271

Spitzner, L. (2002). *Honeypots: Tracking hackers*. Addison Wesley.

Stambaugh, H., Beaupre, D., Icove, D., Baker, R., Cassaday, W., & Williams, W. (2000). State and local law enforcement needs to combat electronic crime. U.S. Department of Justice, Office of Justice Programs, National Institute of Justice. Retrieved from U.S. Government website: https://www.ncjrs.gov/pdffiles1/nij/183451.pdf

Stambaugh, H., Beaupre, D., Icove, D., Baker, R., Cassaday, W., & Williams, W. (2001). Electronic crime needs assessment for state and local law enforcement. Retrieved September 1, 2005 from http://www.ojp.usdoj.gov/nij/pubs-sum/186276.htm

Stephenson, P. R., & Walter, R. D. (2011). Toward cyber crime assessment. Cyberstalking 6th Annual symposium on information assurance (ASIA'11)

Strawhun, J., Adams, N., & Huss, M. T. (2013). The assessment of cyberstalking: An expanded examination including social networking, attachment, jealousy, and anger in relation to violence and abuse. [PubMed]. *Violence and Victims*, *28*(4), 715–730. doi:10.1891/0886-6708.11-00145

Thapa, A., & Kumar, R. (2011). Cyber staking: Crime and challenge at the cyberspace. *International Journal of Computing and Business Research*, *2*(1).

Tokunaga, R. S., & Aune, K. S. (2015). Cyber-Defense: A Taxonomy of Tactics for Managing Cyberstalking. *Journal of Interpersonal Violence*, *32*(10), 1451–1475. doi:10.1177/0886260515589564

Turvey, B. E. (2011). A history of criminal profiling. In B. E. Turvey (Ed.), *Criminal profiling: An introduction to behavioural evidence analysis* (pp. 3–40). Oxford, UK: Elsevier.

U.S. Department of Justice. (2000). The electronic frontier: The challenge of unlawful conduct involving the use of the Internet. Report of the President's Working Group on Unlawful Conduct on the Internet. Washington, DC: Author. Retrieved March 20, 2003, from http://www. usdoj.gov/criminal/cybercrime/unlawful.htm

Verma, S. K., & Raman Mittal, R. (2004). *Legal Dimension of Cyberspace*. New Delhi: Indian Law Institute.

Wallace, B. (2000). Stalkers find a new tool—The Internet e-mail is increasingly used to threaten and harass, authorities say. SFGate News. Retrieved from http://sfgate.com/cgi-bin/article_cgi?file=/chronicle/ archive/2000/07/10/MN39633.DTL

White, W. E., & Carmody, D. (2014). Preventing Online Victimization College Students' Views on Intervention and Prevention. *Journal of Interpersonal Violence*. doi:10.1177/0886260515625501

Working to Halt Online Abuse. (2011). Online Harassment/Cyberstalking Statistics. Retrieved from http://www.haltabuse.org/resources/stats/index.shtml

Working to Halt Online Abuse (WHO). (2003). Online harassment statistics. Retrieved May 25, 2007 from http://www.haltabuse.org/resources/stats/index. shtml

Wright, J. A., Burgess, A. G., Burgess, A. W., Laszlo, A. T., McCrary, G. O., & Douglas, J. E. (1996). A typology of interpersonal stalking. *Journal of Interpersonal Violence*, *11*(4), 487–502. doi:10.1177/088626096011004003

Wykes, M. (2007). Constructing crime: Culture, stalking, celebrity and cyber. *Crime, Media, Culture*, *3*(2), 158–174. doi:10.1177/1741659007078541

Zona, M. A., Sharma, K. K., & Lane, A. J. (1993). Comparative study of erotomanic and obsessional subjects in a forensic sample. [PubMed]. *Journal of Forensic Sciences*, *38*(4), 894–903.

This research was previously published in Intimacy and Developing Personal Relationships in the Virtual World edited by Rejani Thudalikunnil Gopalan, pages 126-152, copyright year 2019 by Information Science Reference (an imprint of IGI Global).

Chapter 2
Developing an Understanding of Cyberbullying:
The Emotional Impact and Struggle to Define

Carol M. Walker
East Stroudsburg University, USA

ABSTRACT

When considering ethical practice for educators in the 21st Century it is imperative that teacher educators, school counselors, and administration are knowledgeable in all aspects of bullying via technology that youth and young adults are experiencing on school campuses throughout the country. The exponential proliferation of technology and social media has brought traditional bullying into cyberspace. The purpose of this chapter is to enhance the reader's understanding of the incidents of cyberbullying, to provide knowledge of the challenges researchers face in operationalizing cyberbullying that will enable all professionals to assist victims, and to proffer techniques that may be implemented in the ethical practice of primary, secondary, or college educators as they work with Millennials and Neo-millennials in the 21st Century classroom.

DOI: 10.4018/978-1-7998-1684-3.ch002

INTRODUCTION

Educators in the 21st Century face a new ethical dilemma when considering the use of technology for learning. The plethora of affordable technologies, used by Millennials and Neo-millennials, enhances the need for exploration into how they are used to bully others and the emotional toll that cyberbullying may take. The Internet and World Wide Web (WWW) enable scholars and educators to enhance their research and communication; however, when people are accessible on a 24/7 basis, via cell phones and the WWW, negative circumstances may also develop. All one has to do is read the newspaper or peruse the Web; cyberbullying events and the impact on today's youth and young adults is evident. Without prejudice between small towns or large city campuses, students are often susceptible to the unrelenting attacks, whether by strangers or those known to them.

In order to provide a comprehensive assessment of the events of cyberbullying that impact 21st Century youth and young adults in the United States, this chapter will evaluate literature associated with six main areas:

1. Bullying,
2. The influence of technology,
3. Cyberbullying and the student,
4. The struggle to define cyberbullying,
5. Proposals for cyberbullying education, and
6. Legal implications.

BACKGROUND

Traditional Face-to-Face Bullying

Historically considered an inherent part of childhood the idiom "Sticks and stones can break my bones, but words may never hurt me" was often the method provided for youth to deal with schoolyard harassment. It was not until the late 1960s and early 1970s that research into the aggressive behavior of bullying began, in Scandinavia. Bullying behavior was termed *"mobbing"* (Norway, Denmark) or *"mobbning"* (Sweden, Finland), and Dan Olweus was the first to apply empirical research to better understand the phenomenon (Olweus, 1993, p. 8).

Bullying Defined

Employing the model of mobbing, bullying was defined by Olweus, as "A student is being bullied or victimized when he or she is exposed, repeatedly and over time, to negative actions on the part of one or more students." To further define the expression, "negative actions" are delineated as the aggressive behavior of intentionally inflicting or trying to inflict "injury or discomfort upon another" such as "teasing, name calling, threatening, and taunting" or physical actions such as hitting, pushing, or restraining others. Finally, non-physical actions without the use of words are also considered. Actions such as "making faces or dirty gestures, intentional exclusion from a group, or refusing to comply with another's wishes" were also found to be bullying behavior. An imbalance of power, where one student does not have the same "physical or psychological" strength as another must also be present, whereas, the weaker student has trouble defending themselves (Olweus, 1986, 1991, as stated in Olweus, 1993, p. 9).

In 1982, the suicide of three Norwegian boys, due to bullying, initiated a national research project by the ministry of education, in Norway. From there bullying research reached the United States and other countries in the 1980s and 90s. Throughout this research, there have been disputes on how bullying should be defined and various definitions have come forth. A general acceptance of two main forms of bullying was established. Relational or indirect bullying consists of the non-physical and often indirect actions of teasing, social isolation, and intentional exclusion. Direct bullying is the physical or verbal attack of one individual against another (Olweus, 1993). Three features have become standard components of bullying definitions used in research and include events that inflict harm or fear on the victim, repeated unprovoked aggression against an individual due to a real or perceived difference in power, and events that typically occur within familiar social circles (Burgess, Garbarino, & Carlson, 2006).

The bullying actions of youth that have resulted in serious injury, suicidal ideation, and the suicide death of many individuals has moved bullying from the normative behavior of youth into the spotlight of media headlines, both nationally and internationally, as adults work to understand the events and assist the victims (Bauman & DelRio, 2006; Burgess, et al., 2006). Research evaluating gender, homicide and suicide, sexual orientation, and the emotional impact of bullying will be discussed.

Bullying and Gender

Social Dominance theory indicated differences in the levels of social dominance orientation (SDO) in correlation to gender in which males have a higher level of SDO than females (Pratto, Sidanius, Stallworth, & Malle, 1994). Throughout research, several studies have considered the differences in bullying behaviors between males and females.

SanAntonio and Salzfass (2007) surveyed 7th and 8th grade youth to analyze bullying variances between big city, rural, and small city schools to find that 72% of respondents had experienced relational bullying. Gender impact was specified in the type of bullying, with boys often bullying girls with debasing comments regarding their appearance and demands for sexual interactions, often involving oral sex. Other researchers have found that high school boys were more likely to bully via overt, direct bullying, while girls were significantly higher in relational bullying. (Fitzpatrick, Dulin, & Piko, 2007; Griffin-Smith & Gross, 2006).

To better understand the impact of bullying on the college level, Chapell et al. (2004) surveyed 1,025 undergraduate students. Results indicated that almost 25% of students had experienced bullying at least once or twice with 1.1% having occurred very frequently. In addition, males reported being a bully more frequently than females. Chapell et al. (2006) found a positive correlation between being a bully in elementary school, high school, and college. Interestingly, the role of those being bullied continued into college, almost three-quarters of those bullied in college also reported being the victim of bullying in elementary school and high school.

Bullying and Homicide or Suicide

The increased frequency of school shootings and reports of self-harm by those being bullied lends one to evaluate the connection between bullying and these extreme reactions. The history of school shootings dates back to 1974, when a student, who was setting fires in the school, resorted to violence and shot the school custodian who discovered his actions. In 1982, a 17-year-old student shot and killed his English teacher based on the concern that she was trying to commit him to a mental institution. In 1997, a fourteen-year-old boy, Michael Carneal, brought a shotgun to school to regain his reputation with force, and several students were killed (Burgess et al., 2006).

Noted to be primarily a middle class event, the lethal violence of school shootings and suicide brings great concern to adults as they try to formulate an understanding of what precipitated the events (Twemlow, 2008). Numerous studies indicate that most school shooters had been bullied (Burgess et al., 2006; Chapell et al., 2006).

Often times, school violence followed instances of ostracism and romantic rejection. Leary, Kowalski, Smith, and Phillips (2003) found that bullying events of this nature instigated 14 of 15 school shootings.

Serious suicide attempts are frequently precipitated with interpersonal or relationship disputes (Beautrais, 2000). The drastic rise of suicide rates for young people have placed them as the group with the highest risk in one-third of all countries. Klomek, Sourander, and Gould (2010) provided a literature review of 31 empirical studies, which evaluated both cross-sectional and longitudinal research articles and found that bully-victims are repeatedly reported to exhibit high levels of suicidal ideation.

Bullying and Sexual Orientation

As humanity becomes more aware of individual differences in sexual orientation, the intolerable aspect of harassment due to lack of understanding is bound to occur. Sexual minority students, described by Bishop and Casida (2011) as "most often gay, lesbian or bisexual, but including anyone who does not or is perceived to not fit the common heterosexual stereotype," (p. 134) are frequently bullied in United States schools with humiliating words such "fag, queer, dyke, homo, and gay" being heard by 51% of on a daily basis (p. 135). Craig, McInroy, McCready, DiCesare, and Pettaway (2015) found that sexual minority youth and young adults were more concerned regarding offline bullying than incidents with information and communication technologies (ICTs).

Homophobia was the primary factor of such harassment. San Antonio and Salzfass (2007) found that in the incidences of relational bullying reported in their research, the second most common reason stated was from students perceived as being gay. When surveyed, 74% of individuals (N = 713) perceived their college campus as homophobic (Rankin, 2005).

Bullying and the Emotional Impact of Victims

The choice of three young men to take their lives due to bullying was the impetus for the seminal research of Olweus (1993). Suicidal ideation has brought young adults into the highest risk categories in one-third of countries. But what of the others who are bullied and do not reach that level of despair? One must also consider the other impacts of bullying on adolescents and young adults.

Kim, Catalano, Haggerty, and Abbott (2011) conducted a longitudinal study of 957 young people in the Pacific Northwest who had participated in the Raising Healthy Children project. Participants were recruited, in 1993 – 1994, from first and second grades in 10 suburban public elementary schools. Data were collected annually each spring and were used to determine if bullying in the fifth grade would predict problem behaviors at age 21. Seventy-eight percent of participants had reported being involved in bullying acts, "at least once in the last year," during their 5th grade experience. When surveyed again at age 21, 33% of those involved in bullying in 5th grade reported being involved with violence, over 67% reported drinking heavily at least once, and 42% reported using pot at least once. Other cross sectional research indicated that students who have been bullied experienced poor grades, increased high school dropout rates, poor psychological adjustments, physical problems associated with stress, and low self-esteem (Bauman & Del Rio, 2006; Bishop & Casida, 2011; Bonanno & Hymel, 2013; Olweus, 1993).

MAIN FOCUS OF THE CHAPTER

The Impact of Technology

The exponential increase of technology and social networking services (SNS) has changed the way teachers must work with students as they strive to create ethical learning environments. Sampasa-Kanyinga and Hamilton (2015) found the percentage of students cyberbullied increased significantly with increased time on SNS. Research regarding the trends in cyberbullying from 2006 – 2012 indicated a 6% increase of cyberbullying victimization from 15% to 21%; results were significantly higher for students of both genders (Schneider, O'Donnell, & Smith, 2015). Individuals use social media to communicate with people they know or with those unknown to them. This has led to challenges with bullying that have grown and transformed in the last decade to allow cyberbullies to intensify attacks in this "always on" generation (Abbott, 2011; Davison & Strein, 2014; Gross, 2009; Kowalski, Limber & Agatston, 2008). These challenges increase the need for educators to understand not only the occurrence of cyberbullying but also methods to address the issue in the ethical K-12 classroom.

Cyberbullying and the Teenager

While technology enhances the ability to connect socially with others, it also has provided bullies with an outlet to harass victims remotely and has eliminated the safe-haven that was historically found in their homes. The advent of student participation in 24/7 communications may increase the emotional impact it has on the individual with potential violence as the chosen recourse. This is accentuated when the victim is unable to determine who is perpetrating the harassment. In addition, the school-age cyberbully who does not see the emotional pain of the victim, due to the distance technology provides, may not fully realize the harm they have caused. Zych, Ortega-Ruiz, and Rey (2015) provided an in-depth review of 309 articles and found that research reported similar effects on teenagers worldwide.

When individuals can be frequently harassed via technology the outcome may be more emotional upset and violence in the nation's schools. Unlike traditional bullying, the cyberbully has access to the victim at any time, thus eliminating the person's ability to seek solace at home away from the bully (Burnham et al., 2011; Davison & Stein, 2014; Gross, 2009; Kowalski & Limber, 2007; Raskauskas & Stoltz, 2007). Ybarra, Diener-West, and Leaf (2007) found that cyberbullying that occurred twelve or more times a year may result in increased behavior problems for students, with one in five participants stating they brought a weapon to school within the month prior to the survey. In a survey of 1,454 twelve to seventeen-year-old individuals, Juvonen & Gross' (2008) research indicated that 19 percent of the respondents had been cyberbullied seven or more times in the past year.

When youth or young adults can surreptitiously attack others with bullying behavior the consequences may be more intense for the victim. The WWW allows individuals to bully others without revealing their identity (Kowalski & Limber, 2007; Patchin & Hinduja, 2006). When a person does not know who is perpetrating the harassment, this may lead to a greater disparity of power between the bully and the victim. The ability for people to bully others anonymously prohibits the target from knowing if there are one or several bullies. This brings additional concern to the victim with many people being their potential tormentor (Klomek et al., 2010; Kowalski & Limber, 2007; Raskauskas & Stoltz, 2007).

Slonje and Smith (2008) surveyed 360 students, in Sweden. One student considered cyberbullying to be "extremely immature and a sign of lacking respect for people's equal worth and freedom" (p. 150). However, another felt that the ability "to get to someone anonymously" increased the concern that it would become "more and more common" (p. 151). It is this ability to remain anonymous that empowered some bullies who may not have harassed others in a face-to-face environment (Vandesbosch & Cleemput, 2008). The opportunity to bully without experiencing the emotional impact that the harassment brings to the victim prevents the bully from knowing if they have gone too far. When using technology, the cyberbully may feel that their bullying behavior is in jest. Inability to observe the victim's emotional anxiety may allow them to continue this misperception of their actions (Kowalski & Limber, 2007; Raskauskas & Stoltz, 2007).

The use of camera phone technology has led to additional apprehensions for victims when pictures that are taken in more personal settings, such as school locker rooms, are disseminated quickly via social media or picture messaging (Kowalski

& Limber, 2007). Slonje and Smith (2008) found that an image disseminated on the Internet had the highest emotional impact on its victims. As youth become savvier with the use of technology, the webcam must also be considered a source of concern.

As with the suicides of bully victims in 1982, cyberbullying has also brought increased attention and concern from the media, as young adults take their lives after being harassed or victimized via technology. Media stories resonate with brokenhearted family members struggling to understand why their loved ones took their own lives. Parents are all too often frustrated due to the lack of action taken by school and local officials as they tried to end the harassment their children experienced (McNeil, Herbst, Hamashige, Mascia, & Jessen, 2010). Knowledge of these events may strengthen teachers' ability to address issues of digital citizenship and assist students.

Hay, Meldrum, & Mann (2010) examined the impact of bullying and cyberbullying behaviors from the underpinnings of Agnew's general strain theory. The researchers noted higher levels of the internalizing deviance (self-harm) and suicidal ideation for all respondents. The emotional strain of surreptitious attacks combined with the daily struggles and feelings of hopelessness that young adults experience as they try to understand life may lead to poor mental health and youth suicide (Bonanno & Hymel, 2013; Duong & Bradshaw, 2014; Hinduja & Patchin, 2010).

Implications of Gender and Culture

As technology enhances the ability to become a global society, a better understanding of the affect that gender and culture have on teenage cyberbullying is essential. Study results vary regarding the amount of impact that cyberbullying has on the school environment, but it is clear that bullying via technology is a multi-cultural concern (Zych et al., 2015). Cyberbullying has become a global concern, and additional research is essential to provide an understanding of the impact cyberbullying has on K – 12 students (Zych, et al., 2015). Juvonen and Gross (2008) found that 72 percent of youth queried reported being cyberbullied at least once in the past year and that youth who are bullied in school face a much higher probability of being cyberbullied. Ybarra, Diener-West, and Leaf (2007) disputed this finding with survey results that indicated 64 percent of those bullied on-line were not being harassed in school (N = 1,500 between ages of 10 – 17 years). In a cross-cultural comparison, Li (2008) found that 25 percent of the Canadian subjects surveyed (157, 12 – 15-year-old middle school students) and 60 percent of Chinese students (202, 11 – 14 years-old) reported being cyberbullied. Additionally, Caucasian and Hispanic youth, in America, were most prone to frequently use the Internet to harass others (Ybarra & Mitchell, 2007).

As children enter middle and high school, there are differences in the level of concern and acknowledgement of technology-based bullying behaviors between boys and girls. When evaluating age and gender, research indicated that cyberbullying and victimization are higher in the middle school than in high school (Raskauskas, 2007; Williams & Guerra, 2007). Although the veiled style of female bullying was often less evident, a majority of girls viewed cyberbullying as a concern and were more likely than boys to report occurrences (Agatston, Kowalski, & Limber, 2007; Dilmac, 2009; Li, 2005; Li, 2006; Rice et al., 2015; Sampasa-Kanyinga & Hamilton, 2015; Wolak, Mitchell, & Finkelhor, 2007). Male youth were more likely to be involved in overt cyberbullying behaviors and less likely to view the behavior as problematic (Agatston, Kowalski, & Limber, 2007; Dilmac, 2009; Li, 2005; Raskauskas & Stoltz, 2007; Ybarra & Mitchell, 2007). In focus group discussions, Smith et al. (2008) found that girls were more likely to be cyberbullied, due to the difference in how males and females address conflict, one participant stated: "girls hold grudges for longer, boys deal with it there and then and get it over with" (p. 380).

Sengupta and Chaudhuri (2011) explored the impact of social networking sites (SNS). The researchers analyzed data from the Pew Internet American Life Online Teen Survey (data gathered in 2006) with informative results. Twenty-five percent of respondents had been cyberbullied. When queried on their use of SNS, results indicated that teenage girls were 63% more likely to set up a site. This led to girls being 250% more likely to be harassed online than boys, with that percentage rising to 300 for girls who used SNS as a forum for flirting. Children who needed affiliation or inclusion, that was not found at home or in school, turned to the Internet for friendship and the feeling of being included (Solberg, Olweus, & Endresen, 2007).

Emotions play a large part in considering the events of cyberbullying. An individual's need to feel included or powerful distinctly impacted their experience on the Internet. When evaluating the personality aspects of the bully, it was evident that children who were raised in abusive or neglectful homes were more likely to bully others (Baldry, Farrington, & Sorrentino, 2015; Crothers & Kolbert, 2008; Dilmac, 2009). Additionally, the cyberbully presented higher levels of aggression. Their need to feel dominant may have led to bullying behavior via the Internet (Beran & Li, 2005; Dilmac, 2009; Patchin & Hinduja, 2006; Raskauskas & Stoltz, 2007).

Konig, Gollwitzer, and Steffgen (2010) used an online survey and evaluated the use of cyberbullying as an act of revenge. Of the 473 teenaged respondents, over 79% were classified as cyberbullies. Of those, 31% reported being victims of traditional bullying within the past six months. Revenge was frequently the reason for cyberbullying (Hinduja & Patchin, 2009; Ybarra & Mitchell, 2007).

Cyberbullying on the College Campus

When young adults leave their homes and enter college, they do so with mixed emotions of trepidation and excitement. Venturing onto the college campus with great expectations of good things to come may leave them vulnerable to the unexpected negativity that Internet and cell phone harassment can generate. Although many may consider the sophomoric actions of cyberbullying left behind with high school days, Chapell et al. (2006) found that over half of respondents who admitted to being bullies in high school also bullied others at college.

Although there is a strong body of empirical literature addressing bullying and a growing amount of research to understand the impact of cyberbullying on teenagers, research on the college level remains limited (Coleyshaw, 2010). In addition, this author can substantiate the concerns of Coleyshaw (2010) who stated that "any attempt to apply theory to student-to-student bullying in the university context has, as yet, not been afforded a significant level of attention" (p. 378). Of the articles reviewed, only two provided a theoretical foundation for analysis of data (Akbulut & Eristi, 2011; Walker, Sockman, & Koehn, 2011).

Often researchers will select a specific sample within a population to investigate. A desire to understand the cyberbullying experienced by ethnic minorities led Abbott (2011) to query 137 individuals. Participants who self-identified as Caucasian or European American were considered mortalities and 117 surveys were included in the final analysis.

The survey instrument utilized was developed by the researcher based on the constructs of Kowalski, Limber, and Agatston (2008) and Willard (2007) and queried participants on "flaming, harassment, griefing, cyberstalking, denigration, impersonation, outing/trickery, and exclusion" (p. 71). The survey did not limit the experience to adulthood or college, it asked if participants "ever had been or ever had experienced" the events provided. Many respondents included an incident remembered from high school. Cyberbullying was defined as:

Bullying that occurs via the internet [sic] or other electronic methods of communication. This may include: email, instant messages, chat rooms, on message boards, on a website, in an online game, or through text messages, pictures or images sent to a cellular phone (p. 168).

The results were interesting with 27% who knew someone who had been a victim of cyberbullying, 18% knew someone who had cyberbullied others, 19% were victims of cyberbullying, and 7% were cyberbullies. However, when individual questions were asked regarding the general concepts, such as flaming, griefing, etc., that fit the *definition of cyberbullying* in the literature review the results ranged from 65% (flaming) to 13% (outing/trickery).

Akbulut and Eristi (2011) examined the victimization among college students, in Turkey. In an effort to access students who were likely to replicate those of teaching professionals only third year students were included, ranging in age from 18 to 23 years. Thirty-three percent (N=254) of the junior class voluntarily completed the 56-question survey that included items addressing both cyberbullying and victimization.

Similar to Abbott (2011), Akbulut and Eristi's survey also worked to establish instances of "flaming, harassment, cyberstalking, denigration, masquerade, exclusion, outing and trickery" (p. 1160). The authors avoided the term 'cyberbullying' to prevent a self-selection bias. They supported this choice with research from Juvonen and Gross (2008).

The results for cyberbullying indicated being blocked in instant messaging at the highest percentage (42.8%), with the use of social applications for gossiping or inappropriate chats at 34.7%. Exclusion from online groups (25%) and hiding identities (21.6%) were the least reported. Interestingly, a significant relationship was noted between being a bully and being a victim in cyberspace with 25 of the 28 instances queried.

Prior to the research in 2011, Akbulut worked with Sahin and Eristi (2010b) to develop a scale to investigate cybervictimization experienced by "online social utility members" (p. 167). Individuals were recruited via a Turkish online social utility; of the 896 respondents, 45.2% were college students. The researchers used the same qualifiers as in the 2011 study to determine instances of cyberbullying (flaming etc.) and the term 'cyberbullying' was excluded to prevent self-selection bias. A two-step study procedure was utilized to confirm the inclusion of instances of cyberbullying in the survey instrument. This resulted in a high internal consistency coefficient ($\alpha = .97$).

Akbulut, Sahin, and Eristi (2010a) began their inquiry into the instances of online victimization via an analysis of data, gathered in February 2009, from 1,470 individuals (Mean age = 23). A survey was linked to a "popular social network application in Turkey" (p. 195) for one week and participants were given credits to be used in the application. The researchers did not use the term 'cyberbullying' to reduce selection bias and found that 56% of respondents reported experiencing at least one case of victimization.

The highest incidents reported were cursing in instant messaging programs (56%), masquerading (53%), receiving harassing e-mails/instant messaging (52%). It is here that the cultural differences may be indicated as it is hard to conceive of Americans of the same age group considering swearing via the Internet as victimization. There were significant relationships noted in socioeconomic status, frequency of use of the Internet, and for time of use (night use reported more problems than afternoon or evenings).

Turkish research was conducted by Aricak (2009) to evaluate the psychiatric symptomatology of university students whom experienced harassing behavior via the Internet. Aricak gathered data from 695 undergraduate students (M_{age} = 19.34, SD = 1.19) in the Education department at Selcuk University, from October to December 2007. Two instruments were utilized, a cyberbullying questionnaire (queried "have you ever," not specified to college experience) and the Symptom Check List-90-Revised (SCL90), used to evaluate psychological symptom patterns such as obsessive-compulsive, depression, anxiety, hostility, etc.

Findings indicated 19.7% of respondents having been cyberbullied at least one time and 54.4% were a victim of cyberbullying "at least once in their lifetime" (p. 171). A significant positive correlation was indicated in hostility and psychoticism in relation to being a cyberbully. The analysis between interpersonal sensitivity and psychoticism related to being exposed to cyberbullying resulted in a significant negative correlation. Those who reported more interpersonal sensitivity were less likely to be cyberbullied.

Concern "prompted by shock at the Clementi suicide and the increasing reports of incidents on college campuses" motivated the research of Baldasare, et al. (p. 130, 2012) which provided qualitative data regarding students understanding of the phenomenon of cyberbullying. The authors utilized a grounded theory approach to analyze information provided by 30 undergraduate college students (M_{age} = 20.47, SD = 2.3) to uncover major themes of student understanding of the events of cyberbullying.

Findings indicated that participants were divided in the concept of intent with cyberbullying. "Many participants" (p. 136, please note, no *n* provided) indicated that harm may occur unintentionally when a receiver is hurt via messages sent with technology and therefore, intent and repetition should be present to indicate cyberbullying. However, "more participants" (Baldasare et al., 2012, p. 137) replied that the receiver's interpretation of the event was the defining factor with one student stating, "I think maybe the definition needs to capture, like, really emphasize the way the recipient feels, not necessarily the way the person intended it" (Baldasare et al., 2012, p. 137). In addition, participants considered the ability to post anonymously as a factor in cyberbullying, noting that the lack of face-to-face interaction removed the personal factor, "It's almost like bullying a machine, so it doesn't matter" (Baldasare et al., 2012, p. 138). Finally, the respondents consistently identified women as being more involved in cyberbullying than men.

Dilmac (2009) also gathered data from the Selcuk University from 666 participants from the Education department (M_{age} = 19.29, SD = 1.14) to evaluate the events of cyberbullying correlated with the Adjective Check List to identify personal traits of an individual via an analysis of their social needs. The researcher utilized an operational definition of cyberbullying from Belsey (2008) as "involving the use of information in communication technologies to support deliberate, repeated, and hostile behaviour by an individual or group that is intended to harm others" (http://cyberbullying/.ca). It should be noted that Bill Belsey is often credited with originating the term cyberbullying (Spears, Slee, Owens, & Johnson, 2009). Similar to Aricak, Dilmac utilized the terminology 'cyberbully' and did not limit respondents to college cyberbullying experienced. Findings indicated an impact of personality on cyberbullying: aggression and succorance ("soliciting sympathy, affection, and emotional support from others") positively predicted cyberbullying, whereas endurance and affiliation ("seeking and sustaining numerous personal friendships") were negatively correlated with cyberbullying (p. 1313).

Concern regarding the *cyberimmersion* of individuals born after 1980 in the First World motivated Englander, Mills and McCoy (2009) to evaluate the impact of exposure to user-generated content that college students experienced. Data were gathered from 283 undergraduate students. Individuals participated for course credit or as a course requirement. The survey queried respondents regarding their experiences with cyberbullying in high school and college. Eight percent of participants reported being cyberbullied while at college via e-mail and 3% admitted being a cyberbully at college.

Johnson (2011) presented a convenience sample of 577 undergraduate students enrolled in communication classes at two Midwestern universities. Participants' age ranged from 17 to 55 (M_{age}=22), and the majority were in their first year of college. A $15 gift card or extra credit points were given to the participants. Respondents completed a "Cyber-bullying Target Scale" in which they replied to questions such as *"In the past, I have been cyber-bullied a lot"* (p.82). All questions were generalized with "in the past" and did not specify during the college years. A Likert Scale was constructed to query emotional responses to the messages, feelings regarding the content of the messages, and for specific instances of being or having been a cyberbully.

Results indicated that victims of cyberbullying were more likely to be absent from school. However, there was a negative correlation between grades and being victimized via technology. The researcher found a positive relationship between being a target of cyberbullying and loneliness and peer rejection. In addition, results indicated the effects of cyberbullying message exposure remain salient for the victim and are easily recalled. Participant data were operationalized to describe cyberbullying as:

A *message perceived to be: mean/hostile, hurtful, abusive, coercive, making fun, casting one negatively (such as calling one names), or as lies or rumors. This study reveals that cyberbullying is clearly demonstrated when these negative actions occurs via some form of media, such as cell phone, email, text or IM, chat rooms or social networking (p. 136).*

Kenworthy, Brand, and Bartrum (2012) provided a service-learning platform to educate undergraduate college student regarding the incidents and impact of cyberbullying. The researchers taught undergraduate students how to educate secondary students to avoid, recognize, and address cyberbullying. With the goal to benefit the undergraduate as well as the younger student. From September 2010 to January 2011, undergraduate students created informative presentations for over 10,000 students in secondary schools. Utilizing the definition of cyberbullying as "a method of bullying using technology ... to bully verbally, socially, or psychologically" (p. 86) the authors guided 77 undergraduate students as they researched, designed and performed presentations for secondary students.

Pre and post-program data from 331 secondary students indicated a significant difference in their knowledge accuracy regarding cyberbullying and in behavior changes they would adopt to reduce bullying in their areas. In addition, the university students indicated a strong value gained from the program. One participant noted that the project had "changed my life" (Kenworthy et al., 2012, p. 95). Responses to a post-presentation questionnaire indicated that while 44% had never thought about cyberbullying issues before, 86% noted that the experience would change their online behavior.

Research conducted at a large western Canadian university formed the data set for Leenaars and Rinalid (2010) as they queried students' experiences with indirect aggression. This mixed method study gathered survey data via four scales to measure direct and indirect aggression, expressions of aggression, gender role identification (BSRI), and behavior assessment for children. In addition, a random subset of participants ($n=18$) completed three days of daily journaling with paper and pen. Forty-two participants ($M_{age}=20.43$) completed the measures.

The Direct and Indirect Aggression scale (DIAS) questions focused participants on events "in the past year" such as "gossiped about someone with whom you were angry" and "have you been shut out of a group" (p. 136). Results indicated that 7% of respondents were indirect aggressors, 10% were direct, and 5% were both. There was a significant relationship with indirect victimization and hyperactivity, sensation seeking, and mania (p. 137). Older participants were less likely to experience aggression, hyperactivity, sensation seeking, or mania. There were no significant sex differences noted.

The qualitative portion of Leenaars and Rinaldi's (2010) research was reviewed with an inductive thematic analysis and found that participants were likely to express emotionally how the incident affected them with a subtheme of revenge, thus explaining why some victims become the aggressor. Aggression was viewed as a method of attaining or maintaining control and indirect aggression was related to psychosocial maladjustment (alcohol abuse, anxiety, sense of inadequacy, hyperactivity). Gossiping was noted to be harmless entertainment with one participant stating, "it's always going to happen, no matter what, it's just like natural that people do that" (p. 145).

Schenk (2011) provided an experiment analysis to determine the psychological impact of cyberbullying victimization for college students. A sample of 799 participants, who ranged in age from 18 – 24 (M_{age}=20.01, SD=2.41), completed the survey. This sample was further divided into group of "victims" (8.6%: replied yes to having experienced cyberbullying at least four times or more and to a question specifically about being a victim of cyberbullying) and a control group (CG) (n=69). No significant differences were found in the demographics between experimental and control groups.

This researcher focused specifically on "during your time at WVU" to determine the prevalence, psychological impact, and coping strategies of college students when faced with cyberbullying. Several measures were distributed: a researcher developed Internet Experience Questionnaire (IEQ), a questionnaire focused on the symptoms of psychopathology (Symptom Checklist-90-Revised), a Likert-type scale to determine suicidal ideation, and a five point Likert Scale to determine five personality traits (neuroticism, extraversion, openness to new experiences, agreeableness, and conscientiousness).

Results indicated that victims of cyberbullying were significantly higher in depression, anxiety, phobic anxiety, and paranoid subscales. In addition, 5.7% of victims (n=4) reported attempting suicide (CG=0%) and 10.1% had frequent suicidal ideations (CG = 0%). Interestingly, phone calls were the most prevalent media of victimization (80%) of the five measured (also text messaging, Internet, picture/video messaging, and masquerading). The most common attack for both genders was an attack on their self-worth (e.g. "your worthless"). An interesting statistic since decades have been spent helping adolescents and children develop self-esteem and self-worth. The second most common for females was regarding sexual activity (e.g. "slut") and for males was sexual orientation (e.g. "gay"). The third most prevalent was the same for both genders, attacks on appearance (e.g. "ugly"). The victims of cyberbullying were likely to victimize others; 60.8% reported cyberbullying others at least two to three times (33.3%) and possibly four or more times (27.5%).

An investigation of the use of technology communication devices to cyberbully was conducted by Walker, et al. (2011) to determine the covert events that surround the undergraduate college students' experience of cyberbullying. A total of 131 students were surveyed in a northeastern US college. The researchers presented the following definition of cyberbullying:

The use of information and communication technologies such as e-mail, cell phone and pager text messages, instant messaging, personal Web sites or blogs and online personal polling Web sites. The technology is used to promote deliberate, repeated, and hurtful behavior by an individual or group with the intent to harass or embarrass (p. 32).

While the demographic data specified where the student was living (on campus, at home, off campus but not at home) during the current college semester, the questions did not specifically address "while at college." Results indicated that up to 54% of respondents knew someone who had been cyberbullied (with cell phones: text, pictures, video or messages). One hundred percent of male participants knew someone who had been cyberbullied. Eleven percent (n=14) had been cyberbullied, with 14% of those (n=2) having been bullied over ten times. When queried about specific instances of communications that were repeated and undesired, results ranged from 3% (receiving threatening pictures or images) to 34% (someone pretending to be someone else). Receiving unwanted tokens of affection, excessively 'needy' or demanding messages, and 'friending' others to get information about you were also reported at higher than 30 percent.

Smith, Grimm, Lombard, and Wolfe (2012) surveyed 340 undergraduate students at the Ohio University (210 females, 130 male) with 22 closed and one open-ended question. Results indicated that 37% of respondents knew someone who had been cyberbullied, 3% (n=10) admitted to being a cyberbully and 16.7% were the target of cyberbullying. Statistical significance was noted in four areas. Students who self-identified as being a member of a Greek society were significantly more likely to observe someone they knew being targeted by cyberbullying. Though reverse of the hypothesis, a significant relationship was also noted with college living arrangements; students living off-campus were more likely to know someone who had been cyberbullied than on-campus individuals. Though not hypothesized, the authors noted statistically significance in the response of female and non-heterosexual students in being more likely to know someone who had been cyberbullied in college.

Williams (2011) surveyed 67 students from a nursing program in a private Christian university and evaluated relational aggression in the adult population. The participants ranged in age from 19 to 55 (M_{age}=27.03, SD=10.75). Questions were directed for "now or within the last year" and utilized a measure to self-report aggression and social behavior. No definition or reference to cyberbullying was presented. Findings indicated a negative correlation between age and intentional negative actions within a relationship when one did not get what they wanted. Age was also negatively correlated with reactive relational aggression (intentionally hurting, spreading rumors about, or excluding someone due to anger).

An examination of these research articles indicated the necessity for more college-based research. Of the articles available, seven were based in the United States and six were international research (Turkey and Canada). From the studies in the U.S., three did not query incidents specific to the college experience (Abbott, 2011; Johnson, 2011; and Walker et al., 2011). The remaining four articles provided a glimpse of the events that are occurring on college campuses (Englander et al., 2009; Schenk, 2011; Williams, 2011). Williams (2011) queried adult aggression not specific to cyber-events. Participants' range of ages in Williams (2011) and Johnson (2011) prohibit any generalizations to the undergraduate college student. The following section will delineate the emotional impact of cyberbullying for young adults, as well as the relationship of cyberbullying with gender and sexual orientation.

The Emotional Toll of Cyberbullying

The same undesirable emotions experienced with cyberbullying by teenagers were also reported for young adults. Individuals often turned to electronic media to air disputes and to seek retribution following arguments and relationship break-ups (Hoff & Mitchell, 2009). Those who felt alone and lonely often turned to social media for that feeling of inclusion. Social media, such as Facebook, was designed to allow individuals to create human connections and expand their social networks. Social connections are essential for individuals to maintain a physiological and emotional balance. (Cacioppo, 2008; Madge, Meek, Wellens, & Hooley, 2009).

Reports of cyberbullying victimization for college-aged individuals ranged widely from eight to fifty-six percent. The range of those who were cyberbullies was from three to 20 percent. Lee (2004) provided a literature review and delineated six key concepts that are utilized in cyberbullying definitions: intent, hurt, repetition, duration, power, conflict, and provocation. Other authors questioned the validity of a definition that was primarily adapted from the original concept of Olweus in the 1980s. The range of percentages reported for cyberbullying may be due to lack of consistency in data gathered due to a non-standardized definition.

People who were bullied via technology often experienced a heightened emotional impact due to the anonymity that the bully was allowed. In addition, victims reported feeling psychosocial maladjustments such as alcohol abuse, anxiety, and sense of inadequacy (Aricak, 2009; Akbulut et al., 2010a; Hoff & Mitchell, 2009; Leenaars & Rinaldi, 2010; Paullet & Pinchot, 2014; Rivituso, 2014; Spitzberg & Hoobler, 2002).

Rivituso (2014), through interpretive phenomenological analysis, indicated six emotional impact themes that included feeling of fear and vulnerability, distrust of technology and mistrust of people, an impact on victim self-esteem, reactions of stress, depression, and embarrassment, and frustration that lead to self-blame (p. 73). While most respondents reported varying levels of emotional upset, Schenk (2011) had "approximately 12" participants deny being bothered by cyberbullying events experienced. Abbott (2011) noted that the majority of school shootings in the United States were by individuals who have been bullied.

The tragic suicide death of Tyler Clementi, on September 22, 2010, catapulted the discussion of college-level victimization via social media and the WWW into the mainstream media (Cloud, 2010). Schenk (2011) was the only research article to report on suicide attempts or thoughts. The depth of depression that some victims feel when cyberbullied indicates the necessity for more research to better understand the impact of the proliferation of social media accessibility for college aged individuals.

Cyberbullying and Sexual Orientation

Another seldom-studied area of technologically based harassment involved those in the minority of sexual orientation (LGBT). Research that has analyzed events of cyberbullying correlated with sexual orientation have found that self-identified LGBT individuals reported receiving communications that harassed, threatened and insulted them, from people known and unknown to them, based on their sexuality (Abbott, 2011; Walker, 2012, 2015). Schenk (2011) found the second highest incidents of cyberbullying for college-aged males based in sexual orientation harassment.

Duong and Bradshaw (2014) evaluated the results of 951 youth in grades 9 through 12 who self-identified as LGB (lesbian, gay, bisexual) from a survey of 11,877 students. There were statistically significant differences in the prevalence of engaging in physical fights and attempting suicide for those who experienced cyberbullying.

Thus a new understanding and definition for the events of relational bullying, now perpetrated via the anonymous environment of the WWW, must be considered. As Olweus defined bullying in the last several decades of the 20th century, so must researchers today work to define the new form of aggression, cyberbullying, to protect this generation of youth from further harm.

The Current Understanding of Cyberbullying

A comprehensive literature review of cyberbullying research, focused on adolescents and young adults, revealed that there is little agreement regarding the wording and incidents that qualify as a bullying event propagated via technology. Most researchers have merely expanded Olweus' definition to include technology (Leenaars & Renaldi, 2010; Burnham, Wright, & Houser, 2011; Wright, Burnham, Inham, & Ogorchock, 2009). Li (2006) considered cyberbullying to be a "bullying problem occurring in new territory" (p. 166). Slonje and Smith (2008) expanded Olweus' concept of bullying to define cyberbullying as aggression that utilized modern technology specifically the WWW and cell phones.

Spears, et al. (2009) expressed concern regarding the definition of cyberbullying via their qualitative research. The authors acknowledged the repetitive nature of Olweus' definition of bullying as having "common agreement" (p. 153) amongst researchers, yet questioned what the actual concept of repetition, a requirement in Olweus' definition, involved in the new atmosphere of cyberspace. Students interviewed considered cyberbullying to be something via technology that was used to intimidate or put down another. They described cyberbullying based on its emotional impact with it "sounding cruel, vicious, obscene, torturous, powerful and even silent" (p. 192). Those cyberbullied stated it "felt unnerving, demeaning, inescapable, unsafe, vulnerable, and trapped within a huge power imbalance" (192 – 193). Repetition was implied via plural responses but not specifically indicated as a necessity to inflict pain.

Ybarra et al. (2012) conducted online research among children ages 6 – 17 to measure three commonly exclusive aspects of bullying: type, mode of communication, and environment (p. 54). Utilizing two separate "mini-surveys" data were gathered based on the prevalence rate of bullying. Participants were randomly provided one of four different versions of the survey: one that included a definition and the word "bully", a definition-only form, a "bully" only form, and a form that included a variety of behavioral events that included items such as being hit, kicked, or pushed around; threatening or aggressive comments made to you; called mean names; teased in a nasty way; and rumors being spread about them. The respondents then indicated the mode of transmission (in person, by phone call, text message, or online) with the largest majority (25%) being bullied in person and 10% being bullied online. The authors indicated that the "gold standard" of three criteria (differential power, repetition, and over time) was met by all measures. The researchers stated that although their research indicated twice as many youth reported in-person bullying, the findings allowed a separate count rate for online experiences and thus could be extrapolated to cyberbullying.

Other researchers moved away from Olweus and conducted research based on various definitions that included the concepts of harmful or cruel events to provide different conceptualizations and create a common language (Abbott, 2011; Vandebosch & Van Cleemput, 2008). Willard (2007) considered it to be the transmission of "cruel" text or pictures via technology (p.1). Terms such as aggressive, intentional, repetitive, willful and repeated, defamatory, and hostile are frequently utilized by those researchers working to understand the impact of negative communications via technology (Englander, et al., 2009; Hoff & Mitchell, 2009; Johnson, 2011; Smith et al., 2008).

The Internet and proliferation of technological contact that Millennials and Neo-millennials have access to has changed the face of communication in the 21st Century. The ability for any individual to create and publish information via user-generated content providers such as YouTube, Instagram, Facebook, Google+, True Blab, Chatroulette, and the myriad of other Web 2.0 programs that are exponentially growing has led to an environment of "information exposure" in which individuals disseminate vast amounts of personal and confidential information, that often is damaging and incriminating, to the world via the web (Englander et al., 2009, p. 216).

The increased negative emotional impact that victims have reported due to the anonymity that the Internet provides, lends Hoff and Mitchell (2009) to consider cyberbullying to be more than a modern form of an old event but more akin to victimization with an intent to "terrorize and assert dominance" (p. 659). The reported extent of cyberbullying victims varies greatly in percentages, despite similarities in other demographics such as age, location, and gender. These varying results have increased the necessity for an operational definition for cyberbullying that will be universally accepted and provide more standardized reporting from victims and bullies alike (Abbott, 2011; Patchin & Hinduja, 2015; Vandebosch & Van Cleemput, 2008; Ybarra et al., 2012).

Much research has indicated a relationship between the extent of use of technology and youth and young adults being cyberbullied. Therefore, one may consider the logical aspect of eliminating the threat of cyberbullying by having the victim disconnect from social media and Smart phones. However, today's youth and young adults have been weaned on technology. To ask them to "unplug" from the WWW or cellular phones may be as unrealistic as asking a baby-boomer to live without electricity.

Based in the theoretical framework of the Social Dominance Theory, Walker (2012, 2014) evaluated the current definition of cyberbullying. This definition, taken from the Olweus research of the twentieth century, was reviewed to determine if it remains relevant to determine the extent and emotional impact of relational bullying that twenty-first century students may experience when using social media and cellular technology.

The research queried the extent of emotional impact that one incident of cyberbullying had on the victims, in light of the tragedies that are befalling schools and college campuses in the twenty-first century. It was clear that the criteria of repetition in the definition of cyberbullying must be eliminated. Youth and young adults need the support of administration, educators and counselors when cyberbullied – even if the incident only happens once. In addition, data results did not support the concept of social dominance as an instigator for being a cyberbully. When young adults advocate for themselves and stand up to the cyberbully, it is imperative that perpetrators be held accountable whether they "intended" to inflict pain or not (also supported by Patchin & Hinduja, 2015).

The author acknowledges that cyberbullying may be an intentional act, deliberately conducted to hurt or scare the recipient. However, findings of current research indicate that the use of the traditional bullying definition (Olweus, 1993) to evaluate the impact of bullying behaviors in cyberspace is not comprehensive. The necessity to re-define cyberbullying is at the forefront of concern to assure that all acts of cyberbullying; whether intentional and repeated or a single, random event are recognized. This will allow victims to advocate for themselves and receive the help necessary from teachers, counselors, and school administrators.

This concern is supported by qualitative research conducted by Baldasare et al. (2012) with most participants stating that the receiver's interpretation of the event should provide the defining factor. One participant stated, "I think maybe the definition needs to capture, like, really emphasize the way the recipient feels, not necessarily the way the person intended it" (Baldasare et al., 2012, p. 137).

Spears et al. (2009) utilized triangulation of qualitative data to evaluate the human dimensions of cyberbullying. Participants reported cyberbullying as looking like "ostracism, exclusion, and intimidation" (p. 192) and sounding "cruel, vicious, obscene, torturous, and powerful" (p. 192). In addition, cyberbullying felt "unnerving, demeaning, inescapable, and unsafe" (p. 193).

Vandesbosch and Van Cleemput (2008) also utilized qualitative research with 53 focus groups. When asked to define cyberbullying, the participants noted events such as spreading personal conversations, gossip, manipulating and sending personal pictures, sending messages with sexual comments, or humiliating someone online (p. 500).

Current research garnered expressions of emotions that included embarrassment, creepy, scary, stalkerish, derogatory, racist, anger, hurt, and frustrating (Walker, 2012). Therefore, the following definition is proffered:

Cyberbullying is the use of web-based communication media or hand-held technologies by an individual or group to deliver slanderous, harassing, demeaning, obscene, racist or other offensive messages, images, or video either directly or indirectly that result in emotional harm to the target of the communication (p. 131).

SOLUTIONS AND RECOMMENDATIONS

Programs to Enhance Ethical Digital Citizenship

As society moves forward, it is through the education of our youth regarding these new communication challenges and how to deal with them that the future will be improved. Cyberbullying is not old wine in a new bottle. It is a new challenge that teachers face. The following are research-based suggestions for educators of Millennials and Neo-millennials to enhance their ability to provide a positive and healthy classroom atmosphere.

Schultze-Krumbholz, Schultze, Zagorscak, Wölfer, and Scheithauer (2016) evaluated the effect of empathy training on cyberbullying (N=897; M_{age} = 13.36, SD=1.00) via the "Media Heroes" preventive intervention for schools. Based in the theory of planned behavior, "Media Heroes" intervention intended to change student actions and beliefs through education that included edification of legal implications and training to promote cognitive and affective empathy. Online and social skills were also addressed and social learning (ex. model learning, role-playing) was utilized to enhance student understanding (p. 148). Students who did not receive the training (CG) had a significant decrease in their ability to show affective empathy. Those who received the intervention did not experience the decrease in affective empathy, had a significant increase in cognitive empathy, and a significant decrease in cyberbullying events.

The ConRed Program evaluated by Del Rey, Casas, and Ortega (2016) also provided methods to cope with cyberbullying. The program worked in a whole-school model with students to evaluate Internet dependence, bullying, and empathy and was based in the theory of normative social behavior that posits the behavior of youth to be influenced by perceived social conventions. The study (N = 375; M_{age} = 13.80, SD=1.47) included three primary interventions: training to develop social competencies, safe use of the Internet, and bullying prevention (p. 125). Results indicated significant differences in student cybervictimization, along with increased interpersonal independence for those students who received the training, while those who were not trained experienced increased cyberbullying.

Legal Implications of Cyberbullying for Classroom Policy and Practice

It is important to provide a general understanding of the legal implications educators and administrators face when addressing issues of cyberbullying. As of April 2015, all states have enacted bullying prevention laws (see www.laws.cyberbullying.us and www.stopbullying.gov for the most current information).

To enhance a principled classroom environment and protect students and themselves, teachers must understand the importance of documentation. U.S. courts have repeatedly emphasized the First Amendment rights of free expression of students. The exception to free speech are events that "substantially or materially disrupts learning, interfere with the educational process or school discipline, utilize school-owned technology to harass, or threaten other students or infringe on their civil rights" (Hinduja & Patchin, 2015, p. 3). Thus, when a teacher suspects cyberbullying the burden falls on school personnel to investigate and be able to demonstrate with ample documentation and evidence that the events resulted in a substantial interference of student learning. Hinduja and Patchin (2011, 2012, 2015) provided numerous court cases that involve student versus school district legislation in cyberbullying cases too lengthy to review in this chapter but recommended for future review.

CONCLUSION

The hectic day-to-day environment in the average classroom may inhibit in-depth research and individual use of major programs. However, all educators who desire to enhance the moral actions of students can achieve this goal through the use of curriculum that addresses communicating with technology and doing so with decency. The simple inclusion of teachable moments within the classroom would enable the educator to emphasize media and information literacy (MIL). Teachers who emphasize digital citizenship, interpersonal, intercultural, and social media communication decency can provide a basis for the orientation and integration of social media ethics and etiquette in and out of the K-12 classroom (UNESCO, 2014).

Similar to research conducted by Kenworthy et al. (2102) the K-12 educator could create a service-learning platform to educate secondary students through creating lessons on cyberbullying knowledge and prevention for elementary students. This project could advance students' knowledge of how to recognize, avoid, and address cyberbullying and may become a vital part of enhancing digital citizenship for all students involved.

In closing, this author sincerely hopes that all who read this chapter benefit. No more powerful words can be reiterated than those of Ravi when he was interviewed regarding his involvement in the tragic suicide death of Clementi, "I just wish I had talked to him more . . .." (Sloan, 2012).

REFERENCES

Abbott, M. (2011). *Cyberbullying experiences of ethnic minorities*. (Doctoral dissertation). Retrieved from ProQuest dissertations & theses. (Order No. 3480015).

Agatston, P. W., Kowalski, R., & Limber, S. (2007). Students' perspectives on cyber bullying. *The Journal of Adolescent Health*, *41*(6), 59–60. doi:10.1016/j.jadohealth.2007.09.003 PMID:18047946

Akbulut, Y., & Eristi, B. (2011). Cyberbullying and victimisation among Turkish university students. *Australasian Journal of Educational Technology*, *27*(7), 1155–1170. doi:10.14742/ajet.910

Akbulut, Y., Sahin, Y. L., & Eristi, B. (2010a). Cyberbullying victimization among Turkish online social utility members. *Journal of Educational Technology & Society*, *13*(4), 192–201.

Akbulut, Y., Sahin, Y. L., & Eristi, B. (2010b). Development of a scale to investigate cybervictimization among online social utility members. *Contemporary Educational Technology*, *1*(1), 46–59.

Aricak, O. T. (2009). Psychiatric symptomatology as a predictor of cyberbullying among university students. *Eurasian Journal of Educational Research*, *34*, 167–184.

Baldry, A. C., Farrington, D. P., & Sorrentino, A. (2015). "Am I at risk of cyberbullying?" A narrative review and conceptual framework for research on risk of cyberbullying and cybervictimization: The risk and needs assessment approach. *Aggression and Violent Behavior*, *23*, 1359–1789. doi:10.1016/j.avb.2015.05.014

Bauman, S., & Del Rio, A. (2006). Preservice teachers' responses to bullying scenarios: Comparing physical, verbal, and relational bullying. *Journal of Educational Psychology*, *98*(1), 219–231. doi:10.1037/0022-0663.98.1.219

Beautrais, A. L. (2000). Risk factors for suicide and attempted suicide among young people. *The Australian and New Zealand Journal of Psychiatry*, *34*(3), 420–436. doi:10.1080/j.1440-1614.2000.00691.x PMID:10881966

Beran, T., & Li, Q. (2005). Cyber-harassment: A study of a new method for an old behavior. *Journal of Educational Computing Research*, *32*(3), 265–277. doi:10.2190/8YQM-B04H-PG4D-BLLH

Bishop, H. N., & Casida, H. (2011). Preventing bullying and harassment of sexual minority students in schools. *The Clearing House: A Journal of Educational Strategies, Issues and Ideas*, *84*(4), 134–138. doi:10.1080/00098655.2011.564975

Bonanno, R. A., & Hymel, S. (2013). Beyond hurt feelings: Investigating why some victims of bullying are at greater risk for suicidal ideation. *Merrill-Palmer Quarterly: Journal of Developmental Psychology, 56*(3), 420–440. doi:10.1353/mpq.0.0051

Burgess, A., Garbarino, C., & Carlson, M. I. (2006). Pathological teasing and bullying turned deadly: Shooters and suicide. *Victims & Offenders, 1*(1), 1–14. doi:10.1080/15564880500498705

Cacioppo, J. T., & William, P. (2008). *Loneliness: Human nature and the need for social connection*. New York, NY: W. W. Norton.

Chapell, M., Casey, D., De la Cruz, C., Ferrell, J., Forman, J., Lipkin, R., ... Whitaker, S. (2004). Bullying in university by students and teachers. *Adolescence, 39*, 53–64. PMID:15230065

Chapell, M. S., Hasselman, S. L., Kitchin, T., Lomon, S. N., MacIver, K. W., & Sarullo, P. L. (2006). Bullying in elementary school, high school, and college. *Adolescence, 41*(164), 633–648. PMID:17240771

Cloud, J. (2010). Bullied to death? *Time, 176*(16), 60–63. PMID:21032985

Coleyshaw, L. (2010). The power of paradigms: A discussion of the absence of bullying research in the context of the university student experience. *Research in Post-Compulsory Education, 15*(4), 377–386. doi:10.1080/13596748.2010.526799

Craig, S. L., McInroy, L. B., McCready, L. T., DiCesare, D. M., & Pettaway, L. D. (2015). Connecting without fear: Clinical implications of the consumption of information communication technologies by sexual minority youth and young adults. *Clinical Social Work, 43*(2), 159–168. doi:10.100710615-014-0505-2

Crothers, L. M., & Kolbert, J. B. (2008). Tackling a problematic behavior management issue: Teachers' intervention in childhood bullying problems. *Intervention in School and Clinic, 43*(3), 132–139. doi:10.1177/1053451207311606

Davison, C. B., & Stein, C. H. (2014). The dangers of cyberbullying. *North American Journal of Psychology, 16*(3), 595–606.

DelRay, R., Casas, J. A., & Ortega, R. (2016). Impact of the ConRed program on different cyberbullying roles. *Aggressive Behavior, 42*(2), 123–135. doi:10.1002/ab.21608 PMID:26351131

Dilmac, B. (2009). Psychological needs as a predictor of cyber bullying: A preliminary report on college students. *Educational Sciences: Theory and Practice, 9*(3), 1307–1325.

Duong, J., & Bradshaw, C. (2014). Associations between bullying and engaging in aggressive and suicidal behaviors among sexual minority youth: The moderation role of connectedness. *The Journal of School Health, 84*(10), 636–645. doi:10.1111/josh.12196 PMID:25154527

Englander, E., Mills, E., & McCoy, M. (2009). Cyberbullying and information exposure: User-generated content in post-secondary education. *International Journal of Contemporary Sociology, 46*(2), 215–230.

Fitzpatrick, K. M., Dulin, A. J., & Piko, B. F. (2007). Not just pushing and shoving: School bullying among African American adolescents. *The Journal of School Health, 77*(1), 16–22. doi:10.1111/j.1746-1561.2007.00157.x PMID:17212755

Griffin Smith, R., & Gross, A. M. (2006). Bullying: Prevalence and the effect of age and gender. *Child & Family Behavior Therapy, 28*(4), 13–37. doi:10.1300/J019v28n04_02

Gross, E. F. (2009). Logging on, bouncing back: An experimental investigation of online communication following social exclusion. *Developmental Psychology, 45*(6), 1787–1793. doi:10.1037/a0016541 PMID:19899932

Hay, C., Meldrum, R., & Mann, K. (2010). Traditional bullying, cyber bullying, and deviance: A general strain theory approach. *Journal of Contemporary Criminal Justice, 26*(2), 130–147. doi:10.1177/1043986209359557

Hinduja, S., & Patchin, J. W. (2010). *Bullying beyond the schoolyard: Preventing and responding to cyberbullying*. Thousand Oaks, CA: Sage Publications.

Hinduja, S., & Patchin, J. W. (2011). Cyberbullying: A review of the legal issues facing educators. *Preventing School Failure, 55*(2), 71–78. doi:10.1080/104598 8X.2011.539433

Hinduja, S., & Patchin, J. W. (2012). *School Climate 2.0: Preventing Cyberbullying and Sexting One Classroom at a Time*. Thousand Oaks, CA: Corwin. doi:10.4135/9781506335438

Hinduja, S., & Patchin, J. W. (2013). Social influences on cyberbullying behaviors among middle and high school students. *Journal of Youth and Adolescence, 42*(5), 711–722. doi:10.100710964-012-9902-4 PMID:23296318

Hinduja, S., & Patchin, J. W. (2015). Cyberbullying legislation and case law: Implications for school policy and practice. *Cyberbullying Research Center*. Retrieved from www.cyberbullying.us

Hoff, D. L., & Mitchell, S. N. (2009). Cyberbullying: Causes, effects, and remedies. *Journal of Educational Administration, 47*(5), 652–665. doi:10.1108/09578230910981107

Johnson, C. L. (2011). *An examination of the primary and secondary effects of cyber-bullying: Development and testing of a cyber-bullying moderator/mediator model.* (Doctoral dissertation). Retrieved from ProQuest dissertations & theses. (Order no. 3454251).

Juvonen, J., & Gross, E. F. (2008). Extending the school grounds? Bullying experiences in cyberspace. *The Journal of School Health, 78*(9), 496–505. doi:10.1111/j.1746-1561.2008.00335.x PMID:18786042

Kim, J. M., Catalano, R. F., Haggerty, K. P., & Abbott, R. D. (2011). Bullying at elementary school and problem behaviour in young adulthood: A study of bullying, violence, and substance abuse from age 11 to age 21. *Criminal Behaviour and Mental Health, 21*(2), 136–144. doi:10.1002/cbm.804 PMID:21370299

Klomek, A., Sourander, A., & Gould, M. (2010). The association of suicide and bullying in childhood to young adulthood: A review of cross-sectional and longitudinal research findings. *Canadian Journal of Psychiatry, 55*(5), 282–288. PMID:20482954

Kowalski, R. M., & Limber, S. P. (2007). Electronic bullying among middle school students. *The Journal of Adolescent Health, 41*(6), 22–30. doi:10.1016/j.jadohealth.2007.08.017 PMID:18047942

Kowalski, R. M., Limber, S. P., & Agatston, P. W. (2008). *Cyber bullying: Bullying in the digital age.* Malden, MA: Blackwell. doi:10.1002/9780470694176

Leary, M. R., Kowalski, R. M., Smith, L., & Phillips, S. (2003). Teasing, rejection, and violence: Case studies of the school shootings. *Aggressive Behavior, 29*(3), 202–214. doi:10.1002/ab.10061

Leenaars, L., & Rinaldi, C. M. (2010). Male and female university students' experiences of indirect aggression. *Canadian Journal of School Psychology, 25*(1), 131–148. doi:10.1177/0829573509350062

Li, Q. (2006). Cyberbullying in schools: A research of gender differences. *School Psychology International, 27*(2), 157–170. doi:10.1177/0143034306064547

Madge, C., Meek, J., Wellens, J., & Hooley, T. (2009). Facebook, social integration, and informal learning at university: It is more for socializing and talking to friends about work than for actually doing work. *Learning, Media and Technology, 34*(2), 141–155. doi:10.1080/17439880902923606

McNeil, L., Herbst, D., Hamashige, H., Mascia, K., & Jessen, M. (2010). Bullied to death? *People*, *73*(7), 62–65.

Olweus, D. (1993). *Bullying at school: What we know and what we can do*. Malden, MA: Blackwell.

Patchin, J. W., & Hinduja, S. (2006). Bullies move beyond the schoolyard. *Youth Violence and Juvenile Justice*, *4*(2), 148–169. doi:10.1177/1541204006286288

Patchin, J. W., & Hinduja, S. (2015). Measuring cyberbullying: Implications for research. *Aggression and Violent Behavior*, *23*, 69–74. doi:10.1016/j.avb.2015.05.013

Paullet, K., & Pinchot, J. (2014). Behind the screen where today's bully plays: Perceptions of college students on cyberbullying. *Journal of Information Systems Education*, *25*(1), 63–69.

Pratto, F., Sidanius, J., Stallworth, L. M., & Malle, B. F. (1994). Social dominance orientation: A personality variable predicting social and political attitudes. *Journal of Personality and Social Psychology*, *67*(4), 741–763. doi:10.1037/0022-3514.67.4.741

Raskauskas, J., & Stoltz, A. D. (2007). Involvement in traditional and electronic bullying among adolescents. *Developmental Psychology*, *43*(3), 564–575. doi:10.1037/0012-1649.43.3.564 PMID:17484571

Rice, E., Petering, R., Rhoades, H., Winetrobe, H., Goldbach, J., Plant, A., ... Kordic, T. (2015). Cyberbullying perpetration and victimization among middle-school students. *American Journal of Public Health*, *105*(3), e66–e72. doi:10.2105/AJPH.2014.302393 PMID:25602905

Rivituso, J. (2014). Cyberbullying victimization among college students: An interpretive phenomenological analysis. *Journal of Information Systems Education*, *25*(1), 71–75.

Sabella, R. A., Patchin, J. W., & Hinduja, S. (2013). Cyberbullying myths and realities. *Computers in Human Behavior*, *29*(6), 2703–2711. doi:10.1016/j.chb.2013.06.040

Sampasa-Kanyinga, H., & Hamilton, H. A. (2015). Use of social networking sites and risk of cyberbullying victimization: A population-level study of adolescents. *Cyberpsychology, Behavior, and Social Networking*, *18*(12), 704–710. doi:10.1089/cyber.2015.0145 PMID:26539738

SanAntonio, D. M., & Salzfass, E. A. (2007). How we treat one another in school. *Educational Leadership*, *64*(8), 32–38.

Schenk, A. (2011). *Psychological impact of cyberbully victimization among college students.* (master's thesis). Retrieved from ProQuest dissertations & theses: (Order No. 1501716)

Schneider, S. K., O'Donnell, L., & Smith, E. (2015). Trends in cyberbullying and school bullying victimization in a regional census of high school students, 2006-2012. *The Journal of School Health, 85*(9), 611–620. doi:10.1111/josh.12290 PMID:26201758

Schultz-Krumbholz, A., Schultze, M., Zagorscak, P., & Wölfer, R. (2016). Feeling cybervictims' pain – The effect of empathy training on cyberbullying. *Aggressive Behavior, 42*(2), 147–156. doi:10.1002/ab.21613 PMID:26349848

Sengupta, A., & Chaudhuri, A. (2011). Are social networking sites a source of online harassment for teens? Evidence from survey data. *Children and Youth Services Review, 33*(2), 284–290. doi:10.1016/j.childyouth.2010.09.011

Sloan, D. (Producer). (2012, March 23). *20/20 Tonight: Rutgers Ravi exclusive.* [Television broadcast]. New York, NY: ABC News. Available at http://abcnews.go.com/2020/video/2020-tonight-rutgers-ravi-exclusive-15988475

Slonje, R., & Smith, P. K. (2008). Cyberbullying: Another main type of bullying? *Scandinavian Journal of Psychology, 49*(2), 147–154. doi:10.1111/j.1467-9450.2007.00611.x PMID:18352984

Smith, K. J., Grimm, J., Lombard, A. E., & Wolfe, B. (2012). Cyberbullying: It doesn't stop after high school graduation. In L. A. Wankel & C. Wankel (Eds.), *Misbehavior online in higher education* (pp. 127–155). Bingley, UK: Emerald Group. doi:10.1108/S2044-9968(2012)0000005013

Smith, P. K., Mahdavi, J., Carvalho, M., Fisher, S., Russell, S., & Tippett, N. (2008). Cyberbullying: Its nature and impact in secondary school pupils. *Journal of Child Psychology and Psychiatry, and Allied Disciplines, 49*(4), 376–385. doi:10.1111/j.1469-7610.2007.01846.x PMID:18363945

Solberg, M. E., Olweus, D., & Endresen, I. M. (2007). Bullies and victims at school: Are they the same pupils? *The British Journal of Educational Psychology, 77*(2), 441–464. doi:10.1348/000709906X105689 PMID:17504556

Spears, B., Slee, P., Owens, L., & Johnson, B. (2009). Behind the scenes and screens: Insights into the human dimension of covert and cyberbullying. *The Journal of Psychology, 217*(4), 189–196. doi:10.1027/0044-3409.217.4.189

Spitzberg, B. H., & Hoobler, G. (2002). Cyberstalking and the technologies of interpersonal terrorism. *New Media & Society, 4*(1), 71–92. doi:10.1177/14614440222226271

Twemlow, S. W. (2008). Assessing adolescents who threaten homicide in schools: A recent update. *Clinical Social Work Journal, 36*(2), 127–129. doi:10.100710615-007-0100-x

United Nations Educational, Scientific, and Cultural Organization. (2014). *Paris declaration on media and information literacy in the digital era.* Retrieved from http://www.unesco.org/new/en/communication-and-information/resources/news-and-in-focus-articles/in-focus-articles/2014/paris-declaration-on-media-and-information-literacy-adopted/

Vandebosch, H., & Van Cleemput, K. (2008). Defining cyberbullying: A qualitative research into the perceptions of youngsters. *Cyberpsychology & Behavior, 11*(4), 499–503. doi:10.1089/cpb.2007.0042 PMID:18721100

Walker, C. (2015). An analysis of cyberbullying among sexual minority university students. *Journal of Higher Education Theory and Practice, 15*(7), 44–50.

Walker, C. M. (2012). *Twenty first century cyberbullying defined: An analysis of intent, repetition, and emotional response.* (Doctoral dissertation). Retrieved from http://hdl.handle.net/2069/1894

Walker, C. M. (2014). Cyberbullying redefined: An analysis of intent and repetition. *International Journal of Education and Social Science, 1*(5), 59–69.

Walker, C. M., Rajan Sockman, B., & Koehn, S. (2011). An exploratory study of cyberbullying with undergraduate university students. *TechTrends: Linking Research and Practice to Improve Learning, 55*(2), 31–38. doi:10.100711528-011-0481-0

Willard, N. E. (2007). *Cyberbullying and cyberthreats: Responding to the challenge of online social aggression, threats, and distress.* Champaign, IL: Research Press.

Williams, K. C. (2011). *A study of the presence of relational aggression in the adult population.* (master's thesis). Retrieved from ProQuest dissertations & theses. (Order no. 1494246)

Williams, K. R., & Guerra, N. G. (2007). Prevalence and predictors of Internet bullying. *The Journal of Adolescent Health, 41*(6), 14–21. doi:10.1016/j.jadohealth.2007.08.018 PMID:18047941

Wolak, J., Mitchell, K. J., & Finkelhor, D. (2007). Does online harassment constitute bullying? An exploration of online harassment by known peers and online-only contacts. *The Journal of Adolescent Health, 41*(6), 51–58. doi:10.1016/j.jadohealth.2007.08.019 PMID:18047945

Wright, V. H., Burnham, J. J., Inman, C. T., & Ogorchock, H. N. (2009). Cyberbullying: Using virtual scenarios to educate and raise awareness. *Journal of Computing in Teacher Education, 26*(1), 35–42.

Ybarra, M., & Mitchell, K. (2007). Prevalence and frequency of Internet harassment instigation: Implications for adolescent health. *The Journal of Adolescent Health, 41*(2), 189–195. doi:10.1016/j.jadohealth.2007.03.005 PMID:17659224

Ybarra, M. L., Boyd, D., Korchmaros, J. D., & Oppenheim, J. K. (2012). Defining and measuring cyberbullying within the larger context of bullying victimization. *The Journal of Adolescent Health, 51*(1), 53–58. doi:10.1016/j.jadohealth.2011.12.031 PMID:22727077

Ybarra, M. L., Diener-West, M., & Leaf, P. J. (2007). Examining the overlap in Internet harassment and school bullying: Implications for school intervention. *The Journal of Adolescent Health, 41*(6), 42–50. doi:10.1016/j.jadohealth.2007.09.004 PMID:18047944

Zych, I., Ortega-Ruiz, R., & Del Rey, R. (2015). Scientific research on bullying and cyberbullying: Where have we been and where are we going. *Aggression and Violent Behavior, 24*, 188–198. doi:10.1016/j.avb.2015.05.015

KEY TERMS AND DEFINITIONS

Bullying: The act of one individual repeatedly and intentionally asserting physical or relational dominance over another individual who is in a position of less power.

Cyberbullying: The use of web-based communication media or hand-held technologies by an individual or group to deliver slanderous, harassing, demeaning, obscene, racist, or other offensive messages, images, or video either directly or indirectly that result in emotional harm to the target of the communication.

Cyberimmersion: The extensive, 24/7, use of the World Wide Web to interact with others, garner information, or entertain oneself.

Cyberspace: All aspects of the World Wide Web.

Homophobia: A prejudiced and illogical fear or dislike of individuals who are not heterosexual.

Hyperconnectivity: The use of digital technology to connect with individuals anytime and anywhere.

Internet: The worldwide computer network utilized for the storage and dissemination of information.

Millennials: The generation of individuals born between the early 1980s through the early 2000s.

Neo-Millennials: The generation of individuals born after the early 2000s.

Social Dominance Orientation (SDO): an individual's preference for social inequality among groups.

Social Media: User-generated platforms that allow individuals to share ideas, information, images, and video via the World Wide Web.

Suicidal Ideation: The contemplation of ending ones life based on emotional distress.

Web 2.0: Sites located on the World Wide Web that allow user-generated content that is interactive and operational.

Web-Based Aggression: The use of the World Wide Web to present hostile or violent dialogue via text, audio, or video content.

World Wide Web (WWW): An open source information space hosted via the Internet that permits the interconnection of web-based documents and other resources via a uniform resource locator (URL).

This research was previously published in Teacher Education for Ethical Professional Practice in the 21st Century edited by Oliver Dreon and Drew Polly , pages 236-259, copyright year 2017 by Information Science Reference (an imprint of IGI Global).

Chapter 3
Cyberbullying:
Safety and Ethical Issues Facing K-12 Digital Citizens

Terry Diamanduros
Georgia Southern University, USA

Elizabeth Downs
Georgia Southern University, USA

ABSTRACT

This chapter describes cyberbullying with a focus on K-12 students. Cyberbullying has evolved with the increased use of information and communication technology. As electronic information becomes more a part of everyday life, there has been a negative aspect to the use of computers and mobile technology. Cyberbullying presents a complex set of issues that can negatively impact students' safety and wellbeing. Cyberbullying includes many of the same issues as traditional bullying but extends the aggression beyond the physical schoolyard. In addition to the cyberbully perpetrator, these aggressive acts include cybervictims and often find the cyberbully-victims who move from victim to perpetrator. This chapter explores the safety and ethical issues facing K-12 schools and the challenges associated with this electronic form of aggression.

INTRODUCTION

The effects of bullying on children have been well-documented (Graham, 2016; Salmivalli, 2010; Zych, Ortega-Ruiz, & Del Rey, 2015). Bullying has been a part of the human experience since our earliest ancestors and is an element of group culture not confined to the human experience as bullying behaviors are demonstrated

DOI: 10.4018/978-1-7998-1684-3.ch003

by many different species (Sherrow, 2011). In modern society, bullying has been documented in print as early as the 18th century (Koo, 2007) and continues to be a global concern (Gorzig & Frumkin, 2013; Zych, et al., 2015). As the internet and electronic media have become a pervasive part of global cultures, information and communication technology has been used as a format for bullying. The face-to-face, traditional schoolyard bullying still exists. However, an additional form of willful and repeated aggression now uses electronic transmission to deliver threats. Cyberbullying is currently a threat to the physical and emotional safety of K-12 students, and schools have an ethical obligation to create environments that reduce the instances of all forms of willful and repeated aggression.

BACKGROUND

The contemporary research on bullying has its origins with groundbreaking studies conducted by Olweus (1994), in the 1970's. Beginning with Olweus' early research, there has been a proliferation of studies on the topic (Zych et al., 2015). According to Olweus (1994), "A student is being bullied or victimized when he or she is exposed, repeatedly and over time, to negative actions on the part of one or more other students" (p. 1173). Another essential element of bullying includes an imbalance of power (Olweus & Limber, 2017). Bullies are thought to be motivated by status within the peer group (Salmivalli, 2010). The bully personality has been described as aggressive, impulsive, lacking empathy, having a desire to dominate others, and a positive attitude toward violence (Olweus, 1994). Victims have been characterized as anxious, insecure, or are victimized just because they are different (Graham, 2016). Bullying is a dynamic concept that involves more than the bully and victim. As research in the field expanded, a third category of bully-victim has emerged that describes those children who have been victims and who, in turn, bully others (Buelga, Martinez-Ferrer, Cava, 2017; Kochel, Ladd, Bagwell, & Yabko, 2015; Salmivalli, 2010). The traditional concept of bullying usually describes a schoolyard experience in which the bully and victim are in close physical proximity (Kowalski, Morgan, & Limber, 2012). However, as the 20th century came to an end, the internet added a new dimension to the schoolyard bullying problem.

The internet has changed many facets of our lives. With the ubiquitous influx of personal media in the 1990's a new delivery formats for bullying began to evolve. Email, texting, instant messaging, social media, social networks, digital video hosting, digital imaging, and other media sharing networks provided limitless platforms and formats for inappropriate aggressive behavior. The term that evolved to describe bullying through information and communication technology is cyberbullying. William Belsey is credited with coining the term at the turn of this century (Gregoire, 2013).

Olweus and Limber (2017) suggests that cyberbullying should be considered a form of bullying. A majority of students who have experienced cyberbullying have also been bullied in a traditional form. Bullying and cyberbullying include the common elements of intentional harm, repetition, and an imbalance of power (Menesini, 2012). Different definitions have been developed as the concept of cyberbullying has been studied. One common definition for cyberbullying is intentional and repetitive harmful and aggressive behavior through the use of electronic media (Hinduja & Patchin, 2009; Smith et al., 2008).

Although the definitions for cyberbullying contain the essential elements of bullying, some researchers suggest that there are features of electronic media that result in additional issues. Electronic media offers a tool that disassociates the bully from the victim, there is no longer the face-to-face confrontation associated with schoolyard method of bullying. The use of electronic media also provides the opportunity for total anonymity in which the victim does not know who the perpetrator is. The unique possibility for anonymity in an act of cyberbullying, where the victim does not know the identity of the bully, may increase feelings of vulnerability in the situation (Dooley, Pyzalski, & Cross, 2009).

Patchin and Hinduja (2015a, b) have conducted an extensive review of published research on cyberbullying. They report ranges of 0.4% to 92% for reports of cyberbullying victims and 1.0% to 60.4% for offenders. They conclude that probably 25% of teens have been victims of cyberbullying. Juvonen and Gross (2008) found 72% of the students they surveyed had experienced at least one incident of cyberbullying in the previous year.

There are various reasons for the discrepancy of reported cyberbullying incidents. One issue in the research is the discrepancy of factors included in the definition and the types of technology studied (Juvonen & Gross, 2008; Kowalski, Giumetti, Schroeder, & Lattanner, 2014; Zych, et al., 2015). Another possible issue is the use of self-report measures and non-experimental methodology (Kowalski, Giumetti, Schroeder, & Lattanner, 2014). The high incidence of reported cyberbullying experiences is troubling as it impacts academic achievement, mental health, and depression (Hinduja & Patchin, 2014). It also has an effect physical health, pain, appetite, and sleep (Zych et al, 2015). Due to the extensive reported incidents of cyberbullying and the broad spectrum of emotional and physical impacts, schools need to address the safety and ethical issues surrounding cyberbullying.

Student Safety and Emotional Harm Related to Cyberbullying

For the past decade, cyberbullying has become a challenge for schools and poses a significant concern for the safety of youth. Although this form of bullying can occur off school grounds, it can generate a school environment in which students may not feel safe if they know that the online bully attends their school or if they fear their peers will see the negative, hurtful posts or images of them and begin to bully them at school. While cyberbullying from someone whose identity is unknown may be perceived as more threatening and inducing more fear and anxiety, cyberbullying by someone whose identity is known to the victim can be quite harmful (Dooley et al., 2009; Nocentini, Calmaestra, Schultze-Krumboltz, Scheithauer, Ortega, & Menesini, 2010). Online harassment and aggression create significant stressors for the victim, which impact his/her emotional well-being. Victims of cyberbullying experience psychological distress that can lead to serious mental health problems (Feinberg & Robey, 2008). Some victims of cyberbullying are so emotionally distraught that they become suicidal threatening their own personal safety. Negative psychological outcomes of cyberbullying are not limited to the victims. Cyberbullying offenders are more likely to engage in risky behaviors that pose a threat to their safety (Ybarra & Mitchell, 2004). Additionally, young persons involved in cyberbullying both as a victim and as perpetrator are also vulnerable to the emotional harm associated with online aggression and are thought to be more emotionally troubled than cybervictims and cyberbullies (Sourander, Brunstein Klomek, Ikonen, Lindroos, Luntamo, Koskelainen, Ristkari, & Helenius, 2010). Recently, digital self-harm in which a young person posts negative messages about him/herself has gained the attention of professionals in the field.

Perceived Safety at School and the Role of School Climate

The anonymity and elusiveness of cyberbullying can undermine the school environment and lead to the cyberbullying victim wondering if the person perpetrating the online bullying is a peer at school. Without knowing the identity of the cyberbully, the victim may become wary about his/her surroundings and begin to scan his/her environment in an effort to avoid possible cruel encounters (Feinberg & Robey, 2008). The cyberbullying victim may not know who to trust and may worry that others have seen the negative messages posted online which can lead to their feeling fearful at school. If the cyberbully's identity is known, the victim may fear that the bullying will become physical which creates a sense of feeling unsafe at school.

Victims of both traditional bullying and cyberbullying have reported feeling unsafe at school. In a study examining fifth-grade students' feelings of safety at school, approximately 24% of the students in the sample indicated that they always or sometimes felt unsafe at school (Jacobson, Riesch, Temkin, Kedrowski, & Kluba, 2011). A majority of the students feeling unsafe reported that they had bullied or teased others. Approximately 33% of the students participating in the survey reported feeling stressed while about 50% reported believing they were at slight or great risk as a result of feeling unsafe. The authors noted that the possibility that students who feel unsafe at school may be likely to engage in risky behaviors, such as carrying a knife or gun for protection, needs careful consideration since it could possibly jeopardize their safety.

Older students who had experienced cyberbullying have also reported being scared for one's safety. In a sample of 13-16 year old Finnish adolescents, approximately 23% of students who identified as a victim of cyberbullying reported being fearful for their safety (Sourander et al., 2010). The authors of the study noted that, while victims of traditional bullying can seek refuge in their own homes, cyberbullying victims are vulnerable to online bullying 24 hours a day. The study revealed that adolescents who were targets of cyberbullying were more likely than cyberbullies or cyberbully-victims to feel unsafe at school and uncared about by their teachers. The degree to which cybervictims feel unsafe at school is illustrated in the findings of one study in which cybervictims were 8 times more likely to carry a weapon to school than other youth (Ybarra, Dierner-West, & Leaf, 2007).

While the above studies focus on a sense of safety at school following cybervictimization, some studies have examined the role of school climate and its perception among students who have experienced cyberbullying. Hinduja and Patchin (2012a) examined the perception of school climate among students who had been either a victim of cyberbullying or who have bullied others electronically. Students participating in the study were asked whether they felt safe at school, enjoyed going to school, believed that their teachers cared about them, and believed that teachers at their school really attempt to help them be successful. The results of their study indicated that students who identified as having cyberbullied others or being a victim of cyberbullying were less likely to agree with these items and have a poorer perception of the school's climate than students who did not acknowledge having cyberbullying experiences.

School climate and school safety were the focus of a recent meta-analysis of research on cyberbullying in which these factors were examined as protective factors against cyberbullying (Kowalski, Giumetti, Schroeder, & Lattanner, 2014). The results of the analysis indicated school climates in which school staff displayed respect, fairness, and kindness and school safety were inversely related to engagement in cyberbullying. Hence, positive, supportive school climates in which students felt safe limited involvement in cyberbullying. Therefore, students were less likely to engage in cyberbullying if they attended schools in which they felt supportive and safe but more likely to experience online victimization if they attended a school in which they did not feel supported or safe.

Emotional Harm

As noted above, many youth who experience cyberbullying feel unsafe and stressed. The cruel act of bullying someone online behind a wall of anonymity can lead to emotional harm for the victim of online aggression. But the negative emotional outcomes of cyberbullying also are associated with the cyberbully and the cyberbullying bully-victim who has been the target of hurtful messages and the perpetrator engaged in posting cruel messages about others online. In a rare, yet serious form of cyberbullying, some youth's struggles with emotional problems result in their posting hurtful messages and images online about themselves. Emotional harm associated with cyberbullying can lead to such a deep sense of hopelessness that the young person's escape from his/her torment results in suicide.

Cyberbullying Victim

One of the earliest national studies investigating online victimization and youth safety surveyed a sample of 1501 individuals between the ages of 10-17 who use the internet on a regular basis (Finklehor, Mitchell, & Wolak, 2000). Of the youth surveyed, six percent reported being the victim of online harassment. Results of the study indicated that, of the youth who acknowledged being the target of online harassment, 31% reported feeling very or extremely upset, 19% were very or extremely afraid, 18% were very or extremely embarrassed, 32% reported at least one symptom of stress, almost 50% who had experienced distressing episodes had at least one symptom of stress, and 18% exhibited five or more symptoms of depression after the incident. A five year follow up study found an increase in the percentage of youth reporting incidences of online harassment; nine percent of the youth surveyed indicated being the recipient of online harassment and three percent reported an incident of online harassment that was distressing enough to leave them feeling very or extremely upset and afraid (Wolack, Mitchell, & Finkelhor, 2006). Youth reported 34% of the incidences as very or extremely upsetting, 24% as very or extremely frightening, and 22% as very or extremely embarrassing. Additionally, approximately one-third of the youth experiencing online harassment reported having at least one symptom of stress. The findings of these surveys indicate that incidences of online harassment can negatively impact the child or adolescent, rendering them upset, afraid, and stressed.

More recently, negative reactions and outcomes related to cyberbullying incidences experienced by victims have been consistently reported across multiple studies. In a study that examined the effects of online aggression on adolescents' emotional regulation and psychosocial adjustment, the results indicated that the most frequent emotional reactions reported among victims of cyberbullying were anger, humiliation, sadness, embarrassment, and fear (Gianesini & Brighi, 2015). Psychological outcomes linked to cybervictimization include depressive symptoms, emotional distress, low self-esteem and self-worth, loneliness, social withdrawn and isolation, peer problems, hopelessness, and poor school performance (Gianesini & Brighi 2015; Hinduja & Patchin, 2010; Kowalski, Limber, & Agatston, 2012; Perren, Dooley, Shaw, & Cross, 2010; Sourander, et al., 2010). In a comprehensive literature review of studies investigating negative outcomes associated with cybervictimization, Nixon (2014) found reports of depression, anxiety, anger, embarrassment, and decreased self-esteem across multiple studies. Additionally, it has been reported that higher levels of cybervictimization were found to be associated with higher levels of depressive symptoms such as sadness, hopelessness, and powerlessness (Raskauskas & Stoltz, 2007). To determine the association between cybervictimization and depression as well as the association between cybervictimization and anxiety over time, Rose and Tynes (2015) surveyed students in grades 6 through 12 over a three year period. The results of their study revealed that the percentage of students reporting high cybervictimization increased at years 2 and 3 as did the percentage of students reporting depression and those reporting anxiety. Perren et al. (2010) conducted a study investigating the relationship between cybervictimization and depression in a sample of Swiss and Australian adolescents found that, when controlling for traditional bullying, cybervictimization accounted for a significant amount of the variance in adolescent symptomatology. Although some of these negative outcomes may also be experienced by victims of traditional bullying, the emotional harm resulting from cyberbullying may be greater given that it can occur at any time of the day or night, the wider audience it reaches, the degree of anonymity involved, and the power that the digital messages and images can have (Campbell, Spears, Slee, Butler, & Kift, 2012; Feinberg & Robey, 2008).

Victims who have poor coping skills and a limited support system may be more likely to engage in risk-taking behaviors as a means of dealing with the emotional distress that they experience following the cyberbullying incident. For example, Mitchell, Ybarra, and Finkelhor (2007) examined the relationship of online victimization to substance use, delinquent behavior, and depression in a sample of youth whose ages ranged from 10 to 17 years and found that cyberbullying victims were 2.5 times more likely to acknowledge depressive behaviors, 2.2 times more likely to acknowledge that they had engaged in delinquent behaviors, and 2.0 times more likely to acknowledge that they had engaged in substance use. Similar results were found in a study examining the impact of cyberbullying among multiethnic sample of adolescents which revealed an increased likelihood of substance use, depression, and suicide attempts among cyberbullying victims (Goebert, Else, Matsu, Chung-Do, & Chang, 2011).

As noted earlier, victims of online aggression may experience depression, loneliness, social isolation, low self-worth, and a sense of hopelessness which renders a child or adolescent emotionally vulnerable and susceptible to thoughts of self- harm. There have been numerous reports in the news about suicide among youth who have been victims of cyberbullying. Ryan Halligan and Megan Meier are two well-known cases involving cyberbullying which resulted in both teens' hanging themselves. Other cases of suicide involving cyberbullying have been reported in the media. Researchers have also studied the relationship between online victimization and suicide.

Hinduja and Patchin (2010) conducted a study examining the relationship between cyberbullying victimization and suicidal ideation in a sample of 1963 adolescents attending middle school. The results of their study revealed that both traditional and cyberbullying experiences were linked to suicidal ideation in comparison to youth who reported no experiences of peer aggression. Of the youth responding to the survey, 20% reported that they had seriously considered attempting suicide. The results also indicated that traditional and cyberbullying victimization was a stronger predictor of suicidal ideation and behaviors than traditional and cyberbullying offending. Furthermore, the results of their study indicated that victims of traditional bullying and cyberbullying were more likely to have attempted a suicide attempt than their peers who had not experienced traditional or cyberbullying experiences. Specifically, traditional bullying victims were 1.7 times more likely to have attempted suicide than those who had not experienced traditional bullying while cyberbullying victims were 1.9 times more likely to have attempted suicide in comparison to peers who had not experienced cyberbullying. These results indicate the significant impact of cyberbullying victimization on the emotional well-being of youth and the risk that it poses to their safety. It should be noted that, while some victims of cyberbullying do commit suicide, their experience of cyberbullying may not have been the sole contributor to their suicide as there may have been other factors that may have influenced their mental health status and contributed to the decision that led to the suicide (Kowalski, Limber, & Agatston, 2012; Hinduja & Patchin, 2012b).

Cyberbullying Offender

The negative outcomes associated with cyberbullying experiences are not limited to the victim. While many studies have examined the emotional outcomes among cyberbullying victims, fewer studies have focused on the emotional reactions and mental health problems of cyberbullies. Emotional reactions reported by cyberbullies about their involvement in cyberbullying include the following: no reactions, feelings of guilt, feeling good, being ashamed, and feeling confident (Gianesini & Brighi, 2015). Studies have demonstrated an association of mental health problems among youth who cyberbullying others. As early as 2004, Ybarra and Mitchell (2004) found that, in the sample of youth they surveyed, 16% of youth who identified as an online aggressor reported symptoms of severe depression. Depressive symptomatology also was reported in a study by Didden et. al (2009) who explored cyberbullying in a sample of youth with intellectual and developmental disabilities. The results of their study found a positive correlation between cyberbullying others and feeling depressed; the more one cyberbullies others the more depressive feelings they report.

Similar mental health outcomes associated with cyberbullies have been reported in other studies. In a sample of Australian 6th to 12th grade students who acknowledged cyberbullying others, Campbell, Slee, Spears, Butler, and Kift (2013) examined cyberbullies' perceptions of the emotional harm and impact that they inflict on their victims through cyberbullying as well as perceptions of their own mental health. The results indicated that most participants in the study who identified as a cyberbully did not believe that their actions were cruel or caused any harm to their victim. In comparison to students who did not have any cyberbullying experiences, cyberbullies participating in the study reported higher scores of anxiety, depression, and stress.

Behavioral problems have also been identified in bullies of online aggression. In a sample of Finnish youth between the ages of 13-16, Sourander and colleagues (2010) found that cyberbullies report conduct problems, low prosocial behaviors, hyperactivity, and frequent drinking and smoking. Other studies have also reported behavioral problems among cyberbullies that include delinquent behavior, dropping out of school, and substance use (Ybarra & Mitchell, 2004). A strong association between cyberbullying others and exhibiting aggressive behaviors at school was found in a sample of 12-13 year old youth in the UK (Fletcher, Fitzgerald-Yau, Jones, Allen, Viner, & Bonell, 2014).

Cyberbullying Bully-Victim

For some youth, their involvement in cyberbullying will have a dual role in that they are the target of cyberbullying at the hands of someone else but are also actively harassing others online. This dual role may be an attempt at gaining a sense of power in response to possible feelings of helplessness experienced as a victim of online aggression. Being in the role of both the bully and victim may render a young person psychologically vulnerable. Several studies report that this category of participants in cyberbullying experience more emotional problems than individuals having a status of victim only or bully only. Kowalski and Limber (2013) conducted a study in which 931 students in grades 6 through 12 completed a survey about their experiences with cyberbullying. The authors categorized participants in the study into four groups: cybervictims, cyberbullies, cyberbully-victim, and no involvement in cyberbullying. Measures of anxiety, depression, self-esteem, and suicidal ideation were administered.

The findings of the study revealed that the cyberbully-victim participants had more negative scores on measures of anxiety, depression, and self-esteem in comparison to participants in the other three groups. This finding was particularly evident in male participants. As Kowalski and Limber (2013) note, these results are consistent with previous studies indicating that cyberbullying bully-victims experience many of the emotional problems associated with cybervictims while they also experience behavioral problems often associated with cyberbullies (Kowalski, Limber & Agatston, 2012).

The emotional vulnerability of the bully-victim engaged in cyberbullying is also evident in other studies. Sourander et. al (2010) found that individuals in their study who were cyberbully-victims experience several psychological risk factors and were considered to be the most troubled in comparison to cyberbullies or cybervictims. Similarly, Ybarra and Mitchell (2004) found that aggressor/targets of online harassment were likely to report serious psychosocial challenges such as problematic behaviors and substance use.

Digital Self-Harm

A form of cyberbullying that has recently gained the attention of professionals is digital aggression toward one self. Digital self-harm is defined as "anonymous online posting, sending, or otherwise sharing of hurtful content about oneself" (Patchin & Hinduja, 2017). It is a more severe form of cyberbullying which poses serious safety issues for youth and has resulted in suicide for some youth and occurs when an individual posts or sends negative, hurtful messages online about oneself through electronic means such as email, social media, or other online platforms (Patchin & Hinduja, 2017). One of the first studies conducted on digital self-harm found that, in a sample of college students, nine percent had engaged in digital self-harm while in high school (Englander, 2012). The results also indicated that more boys acknowledged posting negative messages or images about themselves than girls. Among the participants who acknowledged involvement in posting negative information about themselves, the primary motivation for engaging in digital self-harm was to get attention. A more recent study on this rare form of cyberbullying found that, in a sample of 5593 adolescents between the ages of 12-17 who were surveyed, six percent reported engaging in digital self-harm (Patchin & Hinduja, 2017). The findings of this study also indicated that boys were more likely than girls to engage in digital self-harm. Another finding of the study was that youth who were depressed or had engaged in off-line self-harm were more likely to participate in digital self-harm. This is a concerning finding given that, as the authors point out, depression is often a precursor to suicide and digital self-harm might potentially be a precursor to suicide. Additionally, the study demonstrated a link between digital self-harm and traditional and online bullying.

Effects of Cyberbullying on Motivation and Academic Achievement

The implication of being victimized by bullies or cyberbullies extends beyond the emotional effect of these events. Traditional bullying often takes place in the school environment and although cyberbullying takes place through an electronic medium, it also often involves classmates. One outcome of these types of aggressive behaviors is the impact on academic achievement.

Glew, Fan, Katon, Rivara and Kernic (2005) found that both victims and bully-victims had lower academic achievement. Van der Werf (2014) found that increasing the frequency of bullying has a lasting negative impact on academic achievement. Also, bullying seems to have a more pronounced effect on younger student victims (van der Werf, 2014) although it can continue into the college years (Young-Jones, Fursa, Byrket, & Sly, 2015). Beyond the academic implications, a low level of academic performance can cause students to become targets of bullying (Young-Jones et al., 2015). Therefore, teachers, administrators, and parents should be aware of the needs of underperforming students and the possibilities of additional negative impact beyond academics.

Academic achievement is a complicated outcome that results from a combination of variables including access to resources, teacher input, time on task, and environment. The majority of literature discusses student victim status as it relates to academic achievement as a result of participation or psychosocial maladjustment (Fan & Dempsey, 2017). One important component of academic achievement that has not been included in these discussions is the amount of effort put forth by the student as a result of their motivation (Gamboa, Rodriguez, & Garcia, 2013). Academic motivation influences how students think, behave, perform, and work in the school environment. It is important to recognize the complexity of academic motivation and not attempt to oversimplify a multifaceted construct that includes such diverse components as age, ethnicity, socio-economic status, and cultural background (Linnenbrink & Pintrich, 2002). However, research indicates that the impact of aggressive behavior from peers can have an influence on motivation (Fan & Dempsey, 2017; Young-Jones et al., 2015). Young-Jones et al. (2015) found that victims of these incidents have significantly lower academic motivation than non-victims.

The effect of interfering with school success and academic achievement can have long-term implications on life success; both the victim and the bully might suffer the effects through various aspects of their lives. School success has an impact on one's ability to flourish beyond K-12 and therefore, influences the overall socio-economic outcome of students' lives (van der Werf, 2014).

Ethical Issues Related to Cyberbullying

The very nature of cyberbullying makes it a playing field for acting unethically. Behind a digital screen of anonymity, cyberbullies can become disinhibited and engage in cruel acts that they might not pursue in a face to face situation in which their identity would be known. Bystanders who are aware of the cyberbullying that is occurring are faced with an ethical dilemma of how to respond to the cyberbullying: ignore the cyberbullying and take no action to help the cybervictim, encourage the continuation of the cyberbullying by joining the cyberbullying in tormenting the cybervictim, or attempt to intervene so that the online aggression ceases and the cybervictim is no longer subjected to the emotional harm inflicted by the cyberbullying.

Bystanders

The role of the bystander has gained much attention in recent years. Bystanders are individuals who are aware of cyberbullying that is occurring by seeing cruel messages or rumors about someone posted online or having heard about someone being cyberbullied. Some bystanders may even be encouraged by the cyberbullies to participate in posting hurtful information about a peer online. This can place them in an ethical dilemma in that they have to decide how to respond by ignoring the cyberbullying that is occurring, participating in the cyberbullying, or intervening in some way to prevent the online harassment that is occurring.

Some bystanders decide to ignore the cyberbullying and not intervene. Research studies have found that, when presented with a simulated case of cyberbullying, most participants in the study selected not to intervene or felt helpless to help (Shultz, Heilman, & Hart, 2014). There are a number of potential explanations for taking no actions (Bastiaensens et al., 2016). Some individuals who are aware that cyberbullying is occurring may believe that it is none of their business so they take a passive stance in the situation and do not want to get involved. Their decision to ignore the online bullying may be a reflection of their fear that they might become a target of the cyberbully if they take a firm stand to report the situation or to intervene in some way. Another reason for ignoring the cyberbullying and not taking action may be related to their belief that any action that they take would be ineffective in stopping the online bullying. If an individual had attempted to intervene in similar situations in the past by telling an authority figure and no actions were taken to stop the bullying, he/she may believe that any attempts to report the situation or intervene would not bring about change to protect the victim. If the decision is to ignore the cyberbullying, one must consider the consequences of that decision.

The decision to passively accept the online harassment allows the victim continued exposure to cruel, hurtful, and embarrassing messages. Bystanders who take this course of action may be apathetic to the suffering of the cybervictim and does not care about the emotional harm inflicted onto the cybervictim. By having a passive role, the bystander allows the torment experienced by the cybervictim to continue, leaving that victim in a very emotionally vulnerable position of feeling helpless and powerless. Additionally, ignoring the online bullying gives the cyberbully more power and control over the situation and, by taking no action, the bystander is encouraging the cyberbully to continue harming the cybervictim which can be viewed as reinforcing the cyberbullying (Bastiaensens et al., 2016).

Some bystanders may be aware of cyberbullying that is occurring at the hands of their peers and may be encouraged to participate in the online aggression by those doing the online bullying. Some reasons for joining in the online aggression may be to avoid becoming the target of the online aggression if they refuse to participate in posting cruel messages about the cybervictim. Other individuals may begin to participate in the online aggression because they succumb to social influences by their peers. Bastiaensens et al. (2016) examined the social influence of others on the bystander's decision to join in cyberbullying among a sample of adolescents. The outcome of their study revealed that bystanders' perception of peers' approval of cyberbullying was related to more social pressure to participate in the cyberbullying.

The third decision of a bystander regarding how to respond to known cases of cyberbullying calls for the individual to respond and take some form of action to help the victim. Some individuals identify with the victim and have empathy for them. Shultz, Heilman, and Hart (2014) found that participants in their study who identified with the cybervictim had higher empathy scores than those who identified with the cyberbully. They also found that the most frequently given reason for intervening is to defend the victim and mediate the situation. Some bystanders may experience a struggle in their desire to help the cybervictim and their caution in making sure their actions cause no harm to the victim. This can be dilemma for some youth in that they want to do the "right" thing to help the cybervictim and end the torment for that victim while being mindful that they respond in a way that does not cause harm to the cybervictim. Some studies have found that the decision to defend the cyberbullying victim was related to the expectation that the cybervictim would feel better as a consequence of defending and the value associated with helping to make the cybervictim feel better (Pöyhönen, Juvonen, & Salmivalli, 2012).

SOLUTIONS AND RECOMMENDATIONS

Cyberbullying is a phenomenon that has posed a challenge to schools for over a decade. It can have a significant impact on the safety and emotional well-being of children and adolescents. Schools need to be proactive in establishing safe, supportive environments in which students believe that others care about them and are concerned for their well-being.

Role of Schools in Addressing Cyberbullying

There are several ways in which schools can be proactive in addressing cyberbullying. School professionals such as school psychologists and school media specialists can work with school administrators to educate students, teachers, and parents about cyberbullying and its impact on youth (Diamanduros, Downs, & Jenkins, 2008; Diamanduros & Downs, 2015). Strategies that can help address cyberbullying among students include the following: promoting awareness of cyberbullying in the school, establishing a cyberbullying prevention program, creating a positive school environment, and developing a school policy that addresses cyberbullying.

Promoting Awareness of Cyberbullying

One of the first steps that schools can take is promoting awareness of cyberbullying among school personnel, students, and parents. In-service workshops led by school psychologists, school counselors, and school media specialists can be provided for teachers, administrators, and school staff (Diamanduros, Downs, & Jenkins, 2008). The focus of the workshops can include the definition of cyberbullying, its prevalence among youth, the psychological impact on students, the need for a prevention program to address cyberbullying in the school, and the importance of establishing a school policy. A resource that may be useful for teachers and administrators is Willard's (2007a) *Educator's Guide to Cyberbullying: Addressing the Harm Caused by Online Social Cruelty*. This resource provides information about cyberbullying and ways in which schools can address cyberbullying among students.

School psychologists, school counselors, and school media specialists can collaborate with teachers to plan classroom presentations and activities on cyberbullying. The focus of these presentations should be to teach students about cyberbullying and address what it is, how it can psychologically affect others, potential dangers associated with cyberbullying, consequences of engaging in cyberbullying, and responsible internet use (Diamanduros, Downs, & Jenkins, 2008). Classroom activities can include the use of cyberbullying crossword puzzles (Patchin & Hinduja, 2014a), word-finding activities (Patchin & Hinduja, 2014b), researching cyberbullying to learn more about it (Patchin & Hinduja, 2014c), and digital citizenship activities (Hinduja & Patchin, 2015a) such as those that are available at the Cyberbullying Research Center website (https://cyberbullying.org/).

Informational sessions about cyberbullying can be provided to parents so that they become more aware of the impact that cyberbullying can have on youth. These sessions can focus on a general overview of the research on technology use among youth and the potential harm that can occur when technology is used to harass others. Parents can be provided with information about how to recognize signs of cyberbullying and how to respond if they discover that their child has been involved in a cyberbullying experience (Diamanduros, Downs, & Jenkins, 2008). Providing parents with resources about how to communicate with their child regarding internet safety and misuse of technology to harm others would be helpful. Hinduja and Patchin's (2013a) resource *Cyberbullying Prevention: Questions Parents Should Ask Their Children about Technology* is a useful tool that helps initiating a conversation with their child about cyberbullying. Some parents may find prepared scripts, such as *Cyberbullying Scripts for Parents to Promote Dialogue and Discussion* (Hinduja & Patchin, 2013b) useful when discussing cyberbullying with their child. Another available resource that may be helpful to parents is Willard's (2007b) *Parent Guide to Cyberbullying and Cyberthreats* which provides information on ways to help prevent their child from becoming a victim or a perpetrator of online bullying.

Cyberbullying Prevention

Schools have a responsibility to provide a safe learning environment for all students. Developing a plan to address cyberbullying is critical in order to address cyberbullying among students. A team of school professionals such as school psychologists, school counselors, school media specialists, and teachers can work together to develop a plan to address cyberbullying and to organize cyberbullying prevention activities (Diamanduros, Downs, & Jenkins, 2008). The plan could extend to other schools in the district. As Feinberg (2003) points out, it is helpful if the school district has a clear prevention plan that is implemented consistently in all the schools so that students receive consistent training in prevention as move to other schools when they advance in grades.

It is important that schools are aware of their state legislation regarding bullying and cyberbulling. Many states in the U.S. require that schools have an established policy on bullying prevention that includes cyberbullying (Hinduja & Patchin, 2015b). Schools can be proactive in addressing cyberbullying by incorporating cyberbullying prevention into an existing bullying prevention program or implementing a cyberbullying prevention program that helps students to understand what it is, how it impacts others, and how to respond if it occurs. For schools seeking to develop their own cyberbullying prevention program, the inclusion of certain components is essential. According to Diamanduros, Downs, and Jenkins (2008), a cyberbullying prevention program should address the following components: a) the need for students to feel safe at school, b) a clear definition of cyberbullying and how it occurs, c) the prevalence of cyberbullying, d) the impact that it has on individuals, e) an understanding of possible legal consequences associated with cyberbullying, f) the need to take a firm stand against cyberbullying, g) the need to report known incidences of cyberbullying, and h) the need for bystanders to intervene and report incidences of cyberbullying. Additionally, it is important that a prevention program also addresses the need to understand that a) electronic messages can be traced, b) personal information needs to remain private, c) internet safety guidelines and online etiquette rules need to be used, d) use of the internet requires respect for others, and e) one must be a responsible user of technology (Diamanduros, Downs, and Jenkins, 2008).

For schools seeking commercial cyberbullying prevention programs, there are several tools available. One program, *Cyber Bullying: A Prevention Curriculum*, consists of two separate curriculums for grades 3-5 and 6-12 and is available through the Violence Prevention Works website from Hazelden Publishing. The curriculum includes an explanation of cyberbullying, how it is harmful to others, how to interact with others online in a respectful way, and how to respond if cyberbullying occurs. Another resource that is designed to address cyberbullying among 11-15 year old youth is the program *Let's Fight It Together: What We Can Do to Prevent Cyberbullying* produced by Childnet International (2014). This useful resource consists of a video, lesson plans, and a teacher's guide which provides information about cyberbullying such as how it impacts others, strategies to help prevent it, and ways in which to respond if it occurs such as blocking the bully, save the evidence, and tell an adult. To address any cyberbullying targeted toward LGBTQ students, the resource *Gone Too Far* published by Childnet International (2016) can be used in the classroom. This resource is designed for adolescents and consists of a video that focuses on cyberbullying of LGBTQ students and accompanying lesson plans and teacher's guide. Both of these resources, *Let's Fight It Together: What We Can Do to Prevent Cyberbullying* and *Gone Too Far* are sponsored by the U.K. Safer Internet Center and are available on the Childnet International website. In addition to being used in the U.K., *Let's Fight It Together: What We Can Do to Prevent Cyberbullying* has been adapted to be used with Australian students.

Prevention efforts can also involve teachers utilizing lesson plans on internet safety and students becoming ethical digital citizens. A useful tool that can be used for these sessions include the *Scope and Sequence: Common Sense K-12 Digital Citizenship Curriculum* (Common Sense Education, 2015). This resource consists of grade-differentiated units consisting of lesson plans, interactive activities, tip sheets, and video clips for K-12 students. It is aligned with the Common Core standards as well as standards established by the American Association of School Librarians (AASL) and International Society of Technology Education (ISTE). Another available program is i-Safe's DC[4] Digital Programming package that includes K-12 lesson plans and videos on various topics such as cyberbullying, internet safety, appropriate online behavior, and cell phone safety. It also is aligned with the Common Core and AASL standards and is available on the i-Safe Ventures website (http://isafe.org/?q=content/i-safe-dc4-digital-programming).

Creating a Positive School Environment

In addition to implementing a cyberbullying prevention program, it is important that schools help to create a positive learning environment in which students feel safe. As mentioned earlier, evidence indicates that schools with a positive environment in which students feel safe have fewer incidents of cyberbullying (Hinduja & Patchin, 2012a; Kowalski, Giumetti, Schroeder, & Lattanner, 2014). There are several activities that school can engage in to create a positive learning environment. Hinduja and Patchin (2015c) recommend the following activities to promote a positive, safe school environment:

- Promote awareness of cyberbullying and the harm that it can cause to others.
- Encourage open communication between school staff and students so that students have at least one trusted adult whom they can seek help from if needed.
- Learn the names of students in order to form a connection with them and develop a relationship with them.
- Establish relationships with parents, professional, and local organizations to address cyberbullying.
- Launch an anonymous reporting system that is safe and private so that students can report incidents of cyberbullying without worries of retaliation and follow through on investigating each report.
- Cultivate a sense of hope, compassion, and positivity within the school by providing support and empathy when needed.
- Build positive social norms in which youth are recognized for using technology appropriately and acknowledge student successes and the positive things that they do.
- Engage the help of students in promoting positivity in the school and empower them to become involved in prevention efforts.

- Conduct an assessment to determine the extent of cyberbullying among students, factors that may contribute to the cyberbullying, and negative consequences that occur in response to cyberbullying.
- Be diligent in learning new technologies and how they can be misused to hurt others.

All of these activities help to foster an environment in which students feel safe, supported, and cared for by school personnel which also fosters positive interactions with their peers.

School Policy on Cyberbullying

As mentioned earlier, it is imperative that schools are aware of their state's legislation regarding school policies on bullying and cyberbullying. School policies should address specific components of the state legislation on bullying and cyberbullying. It should be clear that the purpose of the school policy is to protect students, staff, and the school environment as well as to document that cyberbullying is prohibited (Diamanduros, Downs, & Jenkins, 2008). The policy should also state clearly that the school has the authority to intervene in cases involving a student engaging in dangerous behavior that affects another student, the school staff, or the school environment (Aftab, 2007). Schools may tend to be reluctant to become involved in cyberbullying incidents that occur off school grounds because of legal issues related to violation of students' freedom of speech. However, it should be noted that schools have the right to intervene in cases involving cyberbullying that occurs off school grounds if the cyberbullying has resulted in a considerable disruption of the school environment (Aftab, 2007).

Key components of an effective school policy on cyberbullying have been proposed by Hinduja and Patchin (2015b). These components include the following:

- Detailed definitions of harassment, intimidation, and bullying including electronic versions
- Graduated penalties and remedial responses
- Reporting procedures
- Investigating procedures
- Using language that indicates that a student can be disciplined if his/her on or off-campus behavior and/or speech results in a considerable disruption in the school environment or violates the rights of other students.

A more detailed discussion of these key components can be found elsewhere (Hinduja & Patchin, 2015d).

FUTURE RESEARCH DIRECTIONS

Future research should expand the investigation of cyberbullying from the K-12 school setting to the college setting. At the college level, prevalence rates of cyberbullying among students could be examined along with psychological correlates such as psychological well-being, life satisfaction, social connectedness, and empathy. Academic correlates such as school engagement, academic identity, academic self-efficacy, and achievement also could be investigated.

REFERENCES

Aftab, P. (2007). *Parry Aftab's guide for schools*. Retrieved from http://www.stopcyberbullying.org/educators/guide for schools.html

Bastiaensens, S., Pabian, S., Vandebosch, H., Poels, K., Van Cleemput, K., DeSmet, A., & De Bourdeaudhuij, I. (2016). From normative influence to social pressure: How relevant others affect whether bystanders join in cyberbullying. *Social Development, 25*(1), 193–211. doi:10.1111ode.12134

Buelga, S., Martínez–Ferrer, B., & Cava, M. (2017). Full length article: Differences in family climate and family communication among cyberbullies, cybervictims, and cyber bully–victims in adolescents. *Computers in Human Behavior, 76*, 164–173. doi:10.1016/j.chb.2017.07.017

Campbell, M., Spears, B., Slee, P. T., Butler, D., & Kift, S. (2012). Victims' perceptions of bullying: Traditional and cyber and the psychosocial correlates of their victimisation. *Emotional & Behavioural Difficulties, 17*, 389–401. doi:10.1080/13632752.2012.704316

Campbell, M. A., Slee, P. T., Spears, B., Butler, D., & Kift, S. (2013). Do cyberbullies suffer too? Cyberbullies' perceptions of the harm they cause to others and to their own mental health. *School Psychology International, 34*(6), 613–629. doi:10.1177/0143034313479698

Childnet International. (2014). *Let's Fight It Together: What We Can Do to Prevent Cyberbullying*. Retrieved from http://www.childnet.com/resources/lets-fight-it-together

Childnet International. (2016). *Gone Too Far*. Retrieved from http://www.childnet.com/resources/pshetoolkit/cyberbullying/gone-too-far

Common Sense Education. (2015). *Scope and Sequence: Common Sense K-12 Digital Citizenship Curriculum.* Retrieved from https://www.commonsense.org/education/scope-and-sequence

Diamanduros, T., & Downs, E. (2015). Creating a safe school environment: How to prevent cyberbullying at your School. In School Library Management (7th ed.). Academic Press.

Diamanduros, T., Downs, E., & Jenkins, S. J. (2008). The role of school psychologists in the assessment, prevention, and intervention of cyberbullying. *Psychology in the Schools, 45*(8), 693–704. doi:10.1002/pits.20335

Didden, R., Scholte, R. H., Korzilius, H., de Moor, J. M., Vermeulen, A., O'Reilly, M., & Lancioni, G. E. (2009). Cyberbullying among students with intellectual and developmental disability in special education settings. *Developmental Neurorehabilitation, 12*(3), 146–151. doi:10.1080/17518420902971356 PMID:19466622

Dooley, J. J., Pyzalski, J., & Cross, D. (2009). Cyberbullying versus face-to-face bullying: A theoretical and conceptual review. *The Journal of Psychology, 217,* 182–188. doi:10.1027/ 0044-3409.217.4.182

Englander, E. (2012). *Digital self-harm: Frequency, type, motivations, and outcomes.* Retrieved from http://webhost.bridgew.edu/marc/ DIGITAL%20SELF%20 HARM%20report.pdf

Fan, W., & Dempsey, A. G. (2017). The mediating role of school motivation in linking student victimization and academic achievement. *Canadian Journal of School Psychology, 32*(2), 162–175. doi:10.1177/0829573516655228

Feinberg, T. (2003). Bullying prevention and intervention. *Principal Leadership Magazine, 4*(1), 10–14.

Feinberg, T., & Robey. (2008). Cyberbullying. *Principal Leadership, 9*(1), 10–14.

Finkelhor, D., Mitchell, K. J., & Wolak, J. (2000). *Online victimization: A report on the nation's youth.* National Center for Missing & Exploited Children. Retrieved from http://files.eric.ed.gov/fulltext/ED442039.pdf

Fletcher, A., Fitzgerald-Yau, N., Jones, R., Allen, E., Viner, R. M., & Bonell, C. (2014). Brief report: Cyberbullying perpetration and its associations with socio-demographics, aggressive behaviour at school, and mental health outcomes. *Journal of Adolescence, 37*(8), 1393–1398. doi:10.1016/j.adolescence.2014.10.005 PMID:25448835

Gamboa, L., Rodriguez, M., & Garcia, A. (2013).Differences in motivations and academic achievement. *Lecturas De Economia,* (78), 9-44.

Gianesini, G., & Brighi, A. (2015). Cyberbullying in the era of digital relationships: The unique role of resilience and emotion regulation on adolescents' adjustment. *Sociological Studies of Children and Youth, 19,* 1–46. doi:10.1108/S1537-466120150000019001

Glew, G. M., Fan, M., Katon, W., Rivara, F. P., & Kernic, M. A. (2005). Bullying, psychosocial adjustment, and academic performance in elementary school. *Journal of the American Medical Association, 159,* 1026–1031. PMID:16275791

Goebert, D., Else, I., Matsu, C., Chung-Do, J., & Chang, J. Y. (2011). The impact of cyberbullying on substance use and mental health in a multiethnic sample. *Maternal and Child Health Journal, 15*(8), 1282–1286. doi:10.100710995-010-0672-x PMID:20824318

Gorzig, A., & Frumkin, L. (2013). Cyberbullying experiences on-the-go: When social media can become distressing. *Journal of Psychosocial Research on Cyberspace, 7*(1), 1.

Graham, S. (2016). Victims of bullying in schools. *Theory into Practice, 55*(2), 136–144. doi:10.1080/00405841.2016.1148988

Gregoire, L. (2013, September). Cyberbullying. *The Walrus.* Retrieved from: https://thewalrus.ca/cyberbullying/

Hinduja, S., & Patchin, J. (2009). *Bullying Beyond the Schoolyard: Preventing and Responding to Cyberbullying.* Thousand Oaks, CA: Corwin.

Hinduja, S., & Patchin, J. W. (2010). Bullying, cyberbullying, and suicide. *Archives of Suicide Research, 14*(3), 206–221. doi:10.1080/13811118.2010.4941 33 PMID:20658375

Hinduja, S., & Patchin, J. W. (2012a). School climate 2.0: Preventing cyberbullying and sexting one classroom at a time. Thousand Oaks, CA: Sage (Corwin Press).

Hinduja, S., & Patchin, J. W. (2012b). Cyberbullying: Neither an epidemic nor a rarity. *European Journal of Developmental Psychology, 9,* 539–543. doi:.(2012).706448 doi:10.1080/17405629

Hinduja, S., & Patchin, J. W. (2013a). *Cyberbullying prevention: Questions parents should ask their children about technology.* Cyberbullying Research Center. Retrieved from https://cyberbullying.org/Questions-Parents-Should-Ask.pdf

Hinduja, S., & Patchin, J. W. (2013b). *Cyberbullying scripts for parents to promote dialogue and discussion*. Cyberbullying Research Center. Retrieved from https://cyberbullying.org/cyberbullying-scripts-for-parents-to-promote-dialog-and-discussion

Hinduja, S., & Patchin, J. W. (2014). *Cyberbullying identification, prevention, and response*. Cyberbullying Research Center. Retrieved from: https://cyberbullying.org/Cyberbullying-Identification-Prevention-Response.pdf

Hinduja, S., & Patchin, J. W. (2015a). *Digital citizenship activities: Ten ideas to encourage appropriate technology use among students*. Cyberbullying Research Center. Retrieved from http://cyberbullying.org/Digital-Citizenship-Activities-Educators.pdf

Hinduja, S., & Patchin, J. W. (2015b). *Cyberbullying and case law: Implications for school policy and practice*. Cyberbullying Research Center. Retrieved from https://cyberbullying.org/cyberbullying-legal-issue.pdf

Hinduja, S., & Patchin, J. W. (2015c). *Developing a positive school climate: Top ten tips to prevent bullying and cyberbullying*. Retrieved from https://cyberbullying.org/School-Climate-Top-Ten-Tips-To-Prevent-Cyberbullying.pdf

Hinduja, S., & Patchin, J. W. (2015d). *Bullying Beyond the Schoolyard: Preventing and Responding to Cyberbullying* (2nd ed.). Thousand Oaks, CA: Sage Publications.

Jacobson, G., Riesch, S. K., Temkin, B. M., Kedrowski, K. M., & Kluba, N. (2011). Students feeling unsafe in school: Fifth graders' experiences. *The Journal of School Nursing : The Official Publication of the National Association of School Nurses, 27*(2), 149–159. doi:10.1177/1059840510386612 PMID:20956581

Juvonen, J., & Gross, E. F. (2008). Extending the school grounds? Bullying experiences in cyberspace. *The Journal of School Health, 78*(9), 496–505. doi:10.1111/j.1746-1561.2008.00335.x PMID:18786042

Kochel, K. P., Ladd, G. W., Bagwell, C. L., & Yabko, B. A. (2015). Bully/victim profiles' differential risk for worsening peer acceptance: The role of friendship. *Journal of Applied Developmental Psychology, 41*, 38–45. doi:10.1016/j.appdev.2015.05.002 PMID:26309346

Koo, H. (2007). A timeline of the evolution of school bullying in differing social contexts. *Asia Pacific Education Review, 8*(1), 107–116. doi:10.1007/BF03025837

Kowalski, R. M., Giumetti, G. W., Schroeder, A. N., & Lattanner, M. R. (2014). Bullying in the digital age: A critical review and meta-analysis of cyberbullying research among youth. *Psychological Bulletin, 140*(4), 1073–1137. doi:10.1037/a0035618 PMID:24512111

Kowalski, R. M., & Limber, S. P. (2013). Psychological, physical, and academic correlates of cyberbullying and traditional bullying. *The Journal of Adolescent Health, 53*(1), S13–S20. doi:10.1016/j.jadohealth.2012.09.018 PMID:23790195

Kowalski, R. M., Limber, S. P., & Agatston, P. W. (2012). *Cyberbullying: Bullying in the digital age* (2nd ed.). Malden, MA: Wiley-Blackwell.

Kowalski, R. M., Morgan, C. A., & Limber, S. P. (2012). Traditional bullying as a potential warning sign of cyberbullying. *School Psychology International, 33*(5), 505–519. doi:10.1177/0143034312445244

Linnenbrink, E. A., & Pintrich, P. R. (2002). Motivation as an enabler for academic success. *School Psychology Review, 31*(3), 313.

Menesini, E. (2012). Cyberbullying: The right value of the phenomenon. *European Journal of Developmental Psychology, 9*(5), 544–552. doi:10.1080/17405629.2012.706449

Mitchell, K. J., Ybarra, M., & Finkelhor, D. (2007). The relative importance of online victimization in understanding depression, delinquency, and substance use. *Child Maltreatment, 12*(4), 314–324. doi:10.1177/1077559507305996 PMID:17954938

Nixon, C. L. (2014). Current perspectives: The impact of cyberbullying on adolescent health. *Adolescent Health, Medicine and Therapeutics, 5*, 143. doi:10.2147/AHMT.S36456 PMID:25177157

Nocentini, A., Calmaestra, J., Schultze-Krumboltz, A., Scheithauer, H., Ortega, R., & Menesini, E. (2010). Cyberbullying: Labels, behaviours and definition in three European countries. *Australian Journal of Guidance & Counselling, 20*(02), 129–142. doi:10.1375/ajgc.20.2.129

Olweus, D. (1977). Aggression and peer acceptance in adolescent boys: Two short-term longitudinal studies of ratings. *Child Development, 48*(4), 1301–1313. doi:10.2307/1128488 PMID:608360

Olweus, D. (1994). Bullying at school: Basic facts and effects of a school based intervention program. *Journal of Child Psychology and Psychiatry, and Allied Disciplines, 35*(7), 1171–1190. doi:10.1111/j.1469-7610.1994.tb01229.x PMID:7806605

Olweus, D., & Limber, S. P. (2017). Some problems with cyberbullying research. *Current Opinion in Psychology*, *19*, 139–143. doi:10.1016/j.copsyc.2017.04.012 PMID:29279213

Patchin, J. W., & Hinduja, S. (2014a). *Cyberbullying activity: Crossword puzzle.* Cyberbullying Research Center. Retrieved from https://cyberbullying.org/Words-Wound-Crossword-Puzzle.pdf

Patchin, J. W., & Hinduja, S. (2014b). *Cyberbullying activity: Word find.* Cyberbullying Research Center. Retrieved from https://cyberbullying.org/Words-Wound-Word-Find.pdf

Patchin, J. W., & Hinduja, S. (2014c). *Cyberbullying activity: Research.* Cyberbullying Research Center. Retrieved from https://cyberbullying.org/Words-Wound-Research-Activity.pdf

Patchin, J. W., & Hinduja, S. (2015a). *Cyberbullying victimization rates across peer reviewed journal articles (2003-2015).* Cyberbullying Research Center. Retrieved from https://cyberbullying.org/facts

Patchin, J. W., & Hinduja, S. (2015b). *Cyberbullying offending rates across peer reviewed journal articles (2003-2015).* Cyberbullying Research Center. Retrieved from https://cyberbullying.org/facts

Patchin, J. W., & Hinduja, S. (2017). Digital self-harm among adolescents. *The Journal of Adolescent Health*, *61*(6), 761–766. doi:10.1016/j.jadohealth.2017.06.012 PMID:28935385

Perren, S., Dooley, J., Shaw, T., & Cross, D. (2010). Bullying in school and cyberspace: Associations with depressive symptoms in Swiss and Australian adolescents. *Child and Adolescent Psychiatry and Mental Health*, *4*(1), 28. doi:10.1186/1753-2000-4-28 PMID:21092266

Pöyhönen, V., Juvonen, J., & Salmivalli, C. (2012). Standing up for the victim, siding with the bully or standing by? Bystander responses in bullying situations. *Social Development*, *21*(4), 722–741. doi:10.1111/j.1467-9507.2012.00662.x

Raskauskas, J., & Stoltz, A. D. (2007). Involvement in traditional and electronic bullying among adolescents. *Developmental Psychology*, *43*(3), 564–575. doi:10.1037/0012-1649.43.3.564 PMID:17484571

Rose, C. A., & Tynes, B. M. (2015). Longitudinal associations between cybervictimization and mental health among US adolescents. *The Journal of Adolescent Health, 57*(3), 305–312. doi:10.1016/j.jadohealth.2015.05.002 PMID:26115909

Salmivalli, C. (2010). Bullying and the peer group: A review. *Aggression and Violent Behavior, 15*(2), 112–120. doi:10.1016/j.avb.2009.08.007

Sherrow, H. (2011). The origin of bullying. *Scientific American.* Retrieved from: https://blogs.scientificamerican.com/guest-blog/the-origins-of-bullying/

Shultz, E., Heilman, R., & Hart, K. J. (2014). Cyber-bullying: An exploration of bystander behavior and motivation. *Cyberpsychology (Brno), 8*(4), 3. doi:10.5817/CP2014-4-3

Smith, P. K., Mahdavi, J., Carvalho, M., Fisher, S., Russell, S., & Tippett, N. (2008). Cyberbullying: Its nature and impact in secondary school pupils. *Journal of Child Psychology and Psychiatry, and Allied Disciplines, 49*(4), 376–385. doi:10.1111/j.1469-7610.2007.01846.x PMID:18363945

Sourander, A., Brunstein Klomek, A., Ikonen, M., Lindroos, J., Luntamo, T., Koskelainen, M., ... Helenius, H. (2010). Psychosocial Risk Factors Associated With Cyberbullying Among Adolescents: A Population-Based Study. *Archives of General Psychiatry, 67*(7), 720–728. doi:10.1001/archgenpsychiatry.2010.79 PMID:20603453

Van der Werf, C. (2014). The effects of bullying on academic achievement. *Desarrollo y Sociedad,* (74): 275–308. doi:10.13043/DYS.74.6

Willard, N. E. (2007a). *Educator's guide to cyberbullying: Addressing the harm caused by online social cruelty.* Retrieved from https://www.chino.k12.ca.us/site/handlers/filedownload.ashx?moduleinstanceid=3695&dataid=23989&FileName=EducatorsGuidetoCyberbullying.pdf

WillardN. E. (2007b). *Parent guide to cyberbullying and cyberthreats.* Retrieved from http://www.embracecivility.org/wp-content/uploadsnew/2012/10/appK.pdf

Wolak, J., Mitchell, K. J., & Finkelhor, D. (2006). *Online Victimization of Youth: Five Years Later.* Durham, NH: National Center for Missing and Exploited Children, University of New Hampshire. Retrieved from http://scholars.unh.edu/cgi/viewcontent.cgi?article=1053&context=ccrc

Ybarra, M., & Mitchell, K. (2004). Online aggressor/targets, aggressors, and targets: A comparison of associated youth characteristics. *Journal of Child Psychology and Psychiatry, and Allied Disciplines, 45*(7), 1308–1316. doi:10.1111/j.1469-7610.2004.00328.x PMID:15335350

Ybarra, M. L., Diener-West, M., & Leaf, P. J. (2007). Examining the overlap in Internet harassment and school bullying: Implications for school intervention. *The Journal of Adolescent Health, 41*(6), S42–S50. doi:10.1016/j.jadohealth.2007.09.004 PMID:18047944

Young-Jones, A., Fursa, S., Byrket, J. S., & Sly, J. S. (2015). Bullying affects more than feelings: The long-term implications of victimization on academic motivation in higher education. *Social Psychology of Education, 18*(1), 185–200. doi:10.100711218-014-9287-1

Zych, I., Ortega-Ruiz, R., & Del Rey, R. (2015). Scientific research on bullying and cyberbullying: Where have we been and where are we going. *Aggression and Violent Behavior, 24*, 188–198. doi:10.1016/j.avb.2015.05.015

This research was previously published in Emerging Trends in Cyber Ethics and Education edited by Ashley Blackburn, Irene Linlin Chen, and Rebecca Pfeffer, pages 65-90, copyright year 2019 by Information Science Reference (an imprint of IGI Global).

Chapter 4
Adolescent Victim Experiences of Cyberbullying:
Current Status and Future Directions

Minghui Gao
Arkansas State University, USA

Tonja Filipino
Arkansas State University, USA

Xu Zhao
The University of Calgary, Canada

Mark McJunkin
Arkansas State University, USA

ABSTRACT

This chapter started by introducing a recent research study that disclosed adolescent victim experiences across seven major types of cyberbullying, significant gender and age differences, and reasons for not reporting incidents of cyberbullying to adults. The chapter then related the research findings to major areas in the literature on the nature and forms of cyberbullying in contrast to traditional forms of bullying, its prevalence among school-aged youths, the effects of gender and age on adolescent victim experiences of cyberbullying, and the factors that contribute to adolescent attitude toward reporting cyberbullying incidents to adults. The chapter suggested that future research should further explore issues such as how various types of cyberbullying affect adolescent mental wellbeing, how age and gender affect school-aged youth victim experiences of various forms of cyberbullying, and how professionals and other adults may help adolescents counter cyberbullying.

DOI: 10.4018/978-1-7998-1684-3.ch004

INTRODUCTION

Cyberbullying is "a unique form of bullying" (Patchin & Hinduja, 2010, p. 614) that involves "sending or posting harmful or cruel text or images using the Internet or other digital communication devices" (Willard, 2004, p.1). The rapidly evolving information technology provides numerous easy avenues for spreading negative messages, and thus enables various forms of cyberbullying behaviors. Willard (2004) has identified the following forms of cyberbullying:

1. **Flaming:** Sending angry, rude, vulgar messages directed at a person or persons privately or to an online group;
2. **Denigration (put-downs):** Sending or posting harmful, untrue, or cruel statements about a person to the person or other people;
3. **Online harassment:** Repeatedly sending a person offensive messages;
4. **Cyberstalking:** Harassment that include threats of harm or is highly intimidating;
5. **Outing:** Sending or posting material about a person that contains sensitive, private, or embarrassing information, including forwarding private messages or images. Engag[ing] in tricks to solicit embarrassing information that is then made public;
6. **Masquerade:** Pretending to be someone else and sending or posting material that makes that person look bad or places that person in potential danger;
7. **Exclusion:** Actions that specifically and intentionally exclude a person from an online group.

In the following sections, we will first introduce a recent research study that we conducted to explore adolescent experience as victims of various forms of cyberbullying as well as their explanations of why they decide to report or not to report their victim experience of cyberbullying. We will then relate our main findings to major research areas in the literature on the nature and forms of cyberbullying and its prevalence among school-aged youths, the effects of gender and age on adolescent victim experiences of cyberbullying, and the factors that contribute to adolescent attitude toward reporting cyberbullying incidents to adults. Finally, we will end this chapter by pinpointing future directions pertaining to the understanding and intervention of school-aged youth's victim experiences of cyberbullying.

INTRODUCING A RECENT STUDY

Recently, we conducted a survey research to explore adolescent victim experiences of cyberbullying (Gao, Zhao, & McJunkin, 2016). The study aimed to answer the following research questions: 1) to what extent are adolescents exposed to different types of cyberbullying? 2) Is there any gender difference in adolescent victim experiences of cyberbullying? 3) Is there any age- or grade-related difference in adolescent victim experiences of cyberbullying? 4) To what extents are adolescent victims of cyberbullying willing to report their incidents to adults, and what factors contribute to their decision-makings about whether to report their experiences?

To collect both quantitative and qualitative information about respondents' experiences of cyberbullying, the first author devised the Adolescent Victims of Cyberbullying Questionnaire (AVCQ; see Appendix A). The AVCQ contains 15 questions that fall into three sections. The first section includes six questions that aim to solicit respondents' demographic information. The second section contains seven questions that address respondents' victim experiences with seven forms of cyberbullying behaviors identified by Willard (2004), including cyberstalking, denigration, exclusion, flaming, harassment, masquerade, and outing. The third section entails two questions that tap into respondents' decision-making and justifications regarding whether to report incidents of cyberbullying. The questionnaire was piloted, and Cronbach's alpha was calculated. The reliability coefficient for each item was high ($\alpha \geq .75$), which suggests that the AVCG was reliable. Students participating in the pilot study commented that the definitions of the various cyberbullying forms overall helped them understand the meanings of these terms while also giving suggestions for rewording. The questionnaire was revised by accommodating the students' feedbacks and then was employed as data collection tool for this study.

The researchers sent invitation to more than 300 students in Northeastern Arkansas schools and received 74 signed consent forms to participate in the study. The participants were directed to understand meanings of the seven cyberbullying types before responding to the questionnaire. Of the 74 completed questionnaires, 61 were valid and thus included in data analysis. The study sample (n= 61) included 21 tenth graders (12 girls and 9 boys), 20 eleventh graders (10 girls and 10 boys), and 20 twelfth graders (10 girls and 10 boys). Difference in the sample's gender-grade composition is not significant, $\chi^2 (2, N = 61) = 0.28, p = .87$. Quantitative data were analyzed using descriptive statistics, Chi-square analysis, Fisher's exact test (when the cell count is less than 5), and residual analysis (by calculating standardized residuals, or Std. Res). An alpha level of .05 was used for all statistical tests. Qualitative data were analyzed using thematic coding, and case and cross-case analysis. The results include four aspects as follows.

First of all, adolescent victim experiences varied across the seven types of cyberbullying. Table 1 presents the results. Sitting atop the list is flaming, with nearly half of the respondents indicating having been flamed (46%). Around one third of the respondents reported having been denigrated (34%), harassed online (33%), cyberstalked (31%), or outed (28%). At the bottom of the list are masquerade (20%) and exclusion (13%).

Secondly, a Pearson's Chi-square test for a 2 (gender) × 2 (cyberbullying) contingency table revealed that gender had significant impact on adolescent victim experiences of cyberstalking and online harassment. Table 2 shows the results. As can be seen, significant gender differences existed in the participants' experiences of cyberstalking ($\chi^2 = 4.99$, $p = .03$); more girls (44%) than boys (17%) reported having been victims of cyberstalking. In addition, marginally significant gender difference was also identified in adolescent victim experience of online harassment ($\chi^2 = 3.67, p = .06$); more girls (44%) than boys (21%) reported having been victims of online harassment. The analyses did not show significant gender differences in flaming ($\chi^2 = 2.90$, $p = .09$), denigration ($\chi^2 = 0.29$, $p = .60$), masquerade ($\chi^2 = 0.21, p = .65$), outing ($\chi^2 = 0.38, p = .54$), and exclusion (Fisher's exact test statistic value = 0.14, $p > .05$).

Thirdly, a Pearson's Chi-square test for a 2 (cyberbullying) × 3 (grade level) contingency table disclosed that 10th, 11th, and 12th graders differed significantly in their victim experiences of cyberbullying. When a significant Chi-square statistic value was identified, residual analysis was conducted by calculating *standardized residuals* (Std. Res) to find out the specific cell (i.e., grade level) that makes the greatest contribution to the Chi-square test result (Sharpe, 2015). Table 3 reveals the results.

Table 1. Frequency (%) of adolescents being cyberbullied (n = 61)

Type of Cyberbullying	Frequency (%)
1. Flaming	28 (46%)
2. Denigration	21 (34%)
3. Online Harassment	20 (33%)
4. Cyberstalking	19 (31%)
5. Outing	17 (28%)
6. Masquerade	12 (20%)
7. Exclusion	8 (13%)

Table 2. Frequency and chi-square statistics of cyberbullying by gender (n = 61)

Type of Cyberbullying	Gender		$\chi^2 p$ Value (df = 1)
	Female (n = 32)	Male (n = 29)	
1. Flaming	18 (56%)	10 (34%)	2.90 .09
2. Denigration	12 (37%)	9 (31%)	0.29 .60
3. Online harassment	14 (44%)	6 (21%)	3.67 .06
4. Cyberstalking	14 (44%)	5 (17%)	4.98 .03
5. Outing	10 (32%)	7 (24%)	0.38 .54
6. Masquerade	7 (23%)	5 (17%)	0.21 .65
7. Exclusion	2 (6%)	6 (21%)	0.14 >.05*

Note. * Fisher's exact test statistic value for cell(s) with expected frequency < 5.

Table 3. Frequency and chi-square statistics of cyberbullying by grade level (n = 61)

Type of Cyberbullying	Grade Level			$\chi^2 p$ Value (df = 2)
	10th (n = 21)	11th (n = 20)	12th (n = 20)	
1. Flaming	9 (43%)	9 (45%)	10 (50%)	0.22 .90
2. Denigration	6 (29%)	8 (40%)	7 (35%)	0.60 .74
3. Online harassment	4 (19%)	8 (40%)	9 (45%)	3.47 .18
4. Cyberstalking	4 (19%)	3 (15%)	12 (60%)	11.63 .003*
5. Masquerade	3 (14%)	2 (10%)	7 (35%)	4.53 .10
6. Outing	4 (19%)	4 (20%)	9 (45%)	4.35 .11
7. Exclusion	0 (0%)	2 (10%)	6 (30%)	8.34 .02*

Note. * Standardized residuals were calculated when chi-square results were significant.

As found out, significant grade differences existed in the participants' victim experiences of cyberstalking (χ^2 = 11.63, p = .003). Residual analysis indicated that 12th graders (Std. Res = 2.31) were significantly more likely to be victims of cyberstalking than 10th graders (Std. Res = -.99) and 11th graders (Std. Res = -1.29). In addition, significant grade differences were also found in the participants' victim experiences of online exclusion (χ^2 = 8.34, p = .02). Residual analysis suggested that 12th graders (Std. Res = 2.09) were more likely to be victims of online exclusion than their counterparts in 10th grade (Std. Res = -1.66) and 11th grade (Std. Res = -0.38). The same analysis, however, suggested that students from the different grades do not differ significantly in their victim experiences of flaming (χ^2 = 0.22, p = .90), denigration (χ^2 = 0.60, p = .74), online harassment (χ^2 = 3.47, p = .18), masquerade (χ^2 = 4.53, p = .10), and outing (χ^2 = 4.35, p = .11).

The fourth aspect of the results was about whether young people, as victims (and/ or witnesses) of cyberbullying, would report the incidents to adults (e.g., school personnel, health professionals, parents, etc.), and how they justify their decision. As Table 4 shows, regardless of gender, grade level, and types of cyberbullying, an overwhelming majority (70-90%) of the respondents mentioned that they would tackle the issue on their own rather than reporting incidents of cyberbullying to adults. Three common themes were identified from their justifications, including: (1) unawareness or underestimate of the negative effect of cyberbullying (e.g., "I don't care"; "It's no big deal" or "it is funny"); (2) fear of adult overreactions including restrictions on their Internet access (e.g., "the school staff will overreact"); and (3) determination to deal with cyberbullying on one's own (e.g., "I will deal with it"; "I can handle it myself.").

Specifically, among the 10th graders (n = 21), nine out of 12 girls (75%) and seven out of nine boys (78%) said they would not report. In regard to their justifications for not reporting their experiences, the girls either said they do not care, or mentioned that victims of cyberbullying should toughen up and not care about it. In contrast, the boys wrote that "the school counselor makes too big of a deal out of it", "the school counselor is not getting into the drama," or "I don't care enough," with one boy writing that his normal response to cyberbullying is "sometimes I laugh – it is funny."

Among the 11th graders (n = 20), seven girls (70%) and eight boys (80%) said they would not report, or if they witness any incident of cyberbullying, they would watch what is going on but would not participate in it. The girls did not want to report incidents of cyberbullying due to considerations of the potential negative consequences of doing so. The most common considerations they mentioned were either their parents might restrict their Internet access if they were aware of the issue, or they might get themselves into trouble by reporting the incidents, even though they had done nothing wrong themselves. The boys' justifications often emphasized the need/desire to deal with the issue by themselves. For example, some boys mentioned, "I'll deal with it," "[I] would fight them," and "the school staff would overreact." Others mentioned, "I do things on my own," and "I can handle myself."

Among the 12th graders (n = 20), eight girls (80%) and nine boys (90%) said that, when being the target of cyberbullying or witnessing it, they would not report the incidents to adults. Some girls said that as witnesses they would join in and cheer on the bullies. Others said they would just watch but not participate in it. Still others said they would try to help or befriend the victims. Very few boys responded to this question in the survey, but one boy mentioned that when being the target or witness of cyberbullying, his typical response would be to "go on with my life." With respect to their justification, a variety of responses were given. One girl said, "I don't care," and "grow up, it's no big deal!" Five boys answered that cyberbullying is "no big deal," and that people should "just ignore it."

Table 4. Frequency (%) of not reporting and justifications for behavioral decision

Grade	Gender	Not Reporting	Example of Justification
10th	F (n = 12)	9 (75%)	"Don't care"; "Toughen up"
	M (n = 9)	7 (78%)	"The school counselor makes too big of a deal out of it"; "not getting into the drama"; "I don't care enough"; "sometimes I laugh – it is funny"
11th	F (n = 10)	7 (70%)	"Parents would restrict Internet access"; "get oneself into trouble"
	M (n = 10)	8 (80%)	"I'll deal with it"; "would fight them"; "the school staff would overreact"; "I do things on my own"; "I can handle it myself"
12th	F (n = 10)	8 (80%)	"I don't care"; "grow up"; "it's no big deal"
	M (n = 10)	9 (90%)	"No big deal"; "just ignore it"
Total	N = 61	48 (79%)	—

Note. F = Girls, M = Boys

To sum up, limited by its small sample size (n = 61) and geographical homogeneity of the group of participants (one high school in a small town), findings of this study may not reflect national or even regional patterns in adolescents' experience of cyberbullying and thus should be interpreted with great caution. Therefore, its findings should be related to those of the large literature in this field so as to shed light on the way various forms of cyberbullying occur to adolescents in and perhaps beyond the participating school, the small town, or the state of Arkansas, for the reason that adolescents' access to the cyber world is not limited by their geographical location, and often not by their racial and social economic backgrounds.

MAJOR THEMES IN THE LITERATURE

With the recent study findings in mind, we reviewed the relevant literature in purpose of assessing the current status of knowledge about adolescent victim experiences of cyberbullying. It was found that although researchers have extensively explored cyberbullying and its impact on adolescent victims, few have investigated adolescent victim experiences of particular types of cyberbullying and, importantly, when and why the victims report their experience to adults. Therefore, starting with clarifying the nature of cyberbullying in contrast to traditional forms of bullying, our review focused on disclosing harms cyberbullying inflicts to youth wellbeing and major factors that affect school-aged youth experience of cyberbullying.

Cyberbullying vs. Traditional Bullying

Cyberbullying became a noticed phenomenon in the late 20th century following advances in information and electronic technologies such as the Internet and cell phones (Olweus, 1993). It has become prevalent among adolescents due to the distancing effect of technological devices that makes it easier for youth to say and do cruel things to others compared to what is typical in traditional face-to-face bullying situations (Donegan, 2012; National Center for Education Statistics, 2013; Center for Disease Control and Prevention, 2014). Cyberbullying involves individuals' spreading harsh, hostile, or simply negative messages via electronic devices and communication tools. Cyberbullying can take place on the Internet, through instant messaging (IM), chat rooms, on social networking sites, blogs, or gaming sites. According to Grigonis (2017), cyberbullying happens more often on Instagram at 42% than any other platforms, with Facebook following close behind at 37%, Snapchat at 31%, and YouTube at 10%. It can also crop up on mobile phones, through short message service (SMS), multimedia messaging service (MMS), or other technologies (Smith et al., 2008). By posting words and images online or sending messages via cell phones, harsh comments travel much quicker than they once did and can stick around much longer if not forever.

Comparing to traditional forms of bullying, what used to be verbal or physical is now viral. Rather than name-calling on the playground in front of a few people, harsh messages can now be posted online or sent to one person or a group of 100 or more in a matter of seconds. Unlike traditional bullies who are usually physically strong and fast, and who involve in face-to-face confrontations with their victims, cyberbullies can be anyone who has a desire to inflict "willful and repeated" harms by using computers, cell phones, and other electronic devices (Hinduja & Patchin, 2010, p. 208). Different from traditional bullying that usually occurs in school settings, cyberbullying can continue outside school and go beyond school hours (Smith et al., 2008). In fact, it can happen among youth wherever and whenever a respected adult is not present (Haber & Daley, 2011). That is, while past generations of youth would be safe from peer judgment and abuse once they arrive home from school, students today have only their wits to protect them from teasing, harassment, and threats that reach them online, anytime and anywhere (Mustacchi, 2009).

In the course of a few decades, there has been a sharp spike in the number of cyberbullying incidents among school-aged youth, with electronic bullying peaking in middle and high schools (Dehue, Bolman, & Völlink, 2008; Mendez-Baldwin, Cirillo, Ferrigno, & Argento, 2015; Patchin & Hinduja, 2010). A 2009 AP-MPV survey of 1,274 people aged 14-24 found that 50% of those surveyed experienced cyberbullying to some extent, and according to the 2011 AP-MPV survey, this figure has grown to 56% (Associated Press, 2011). According to statistics by the

2010-2011 School Crime Supplement, a total of 9% of students in grades 6–12 experienced cyberbullying (National Center for Education Statistics, 2013). The 2013 Youth Risk Behavior Surveillance Survey showed that 15% of high school students (grades 9-12) were electronically bullied in the year 2012 (Center for Disease Control and Prevention, 2014). According to Reportlinker (2017), 71% of young generations say they are concerned about cyberbullying. Among Internet users of Canadian between ages 15-29, one in five said they had been victims of cyberstalking or cyberbullying in the past five years (Hango, 2016). According to a 2016 report from the Cyberbullying Research Center, 33.8% of students between 12 and 17 were victims of cyberbullying in their lifetime (Enough.org, 2017). As Algar (2017) has revealed, cyberbullying has soared 351% in New York City schools in just two years.

Cyberbullying happens for many of the same reasons as traditional face-to-face bullying (Notar, Padget, & Roden, 2013). Bullies' behavior usually stems from psychosocial problems such as having too much or too little self-esteem, having inadequate parental care and supervision, lack of interest in school, depression or anxiety, having difficulty in controlling their emotions and impulses, and difficulty in following rules (Dombeck, 2007). According to a document published by the US federal government, two types of children are more likely to bully. The children who are popular may bully because they see it as a way to stay popular, and hurting others makes them feel powerful. The children who are less socially successful may bully because it may help them cope with their own low self-esteem or fit in with their peers, or because they have difficulty empathizing with those they hurt (Stopbullying.gov, n.d.). Research also shows that victims of traditional forms of bullying also tend to be victims of cyberbullying (Raskauskas & Stoltz, 2007).

However, compared to traditional forms of bullying, it is easier for young people to engage in cyberbullying due to several reasons. First, the distancing effect of technological devices allows cyberbullies to avoid facing their victims and also provides the illusion that cyberbullies will not get caught (Donegan, 2012). According to a survey of adolescents aged 13 to 17, most teens think people cyberbully others because cyberbullying is no big deal or has any tangible consequences, or because it is anonymous (National Crime Prevention Council, 2007). Second, cyberbullying provides the psychological experience that other forms of bullying do not. According to the same federal government document on Stopcyberbullying. org (n.d.), cyberbullies do harms as a form of entertainment when they are bored, have too much time on their hands, and have too many tech toys available to them. Many do it for laughs or to get a reaction. Furthermore, cyberbullying is also found to be significantly associated with factors such as the use of proactive aggression, justification of violence, exposure to violence, and less perceived social support of friends (Calvete, Orue, Estévez, Villardón, & Padilla, 2010). Other factors that contribute to cyberbullying include envy, prejudice, intolerance for disability, religion, gender, and negative emotions such as shame, guilt, and anger (Hoff & Mitchell, 2009; Jones, Manstead, & Livingstone, 2011). All this increases the harmful impact of cyberbullying on its victims; in extreme cases, it has also led to tragic suicide incidents (CBSNews, 2010; Friedman, 2010; Kennedy, 2010; Maag, 2007).

Harmful Impact of Cyberbullying on Youth Well-Being

Cyberbullying has harmful impact on its adolescent victims. On one hand, it is easier for the offender to strike blows against a victim without having to see the victim's physical response, and on the other hand, it is harder for responsible adults to detect and contain the situation. Cyberbullying can result in the lasting negative impact on its victims, including harming their mental health, social well-being, experience of schooling, and the quality of their future life and career as adults (Hoff & Mitchell, 2009; Mesch, 2009; Sahin, 2012).

School-aged youth are at a developmental stage where they develop social relationships outside family, and the quality of their peer relationships is significantly related to their behavioral outcomes (Mesch, 2009). Young people's social interactions with peers, including their experience of online socialization, provide opportunities for learning to develop their socio-emotional skills. Through interactions with peers, young people learn to negotiate relationships, take perspectives, and to meet their growing need for intimacy in peer relationship. Youth who report having high-quality peer relationships are found to be more confident, less aggressive, and more academically engaged; those who report having low-quality peer relationships are subject to loneliness, fear, and depression (Bukowski, Newcomb, & Hartup, 1996).

Cyberbullying has become an "emerging public health problem" (King, 2010, p. 849). As a manifestation of peer relationship problems such as break-ups, envy, intolerance, and ganging up (Mesch, 2009), cyberbullying has a pervasive influence on youth mental health, often leading the victims to feel depressed, sad, angry, frustrated, have low self-esteem and even suicidal thoughts. Victims of cyberbullying are found to be twice as likely to need help from a mental health professional and three times more likely to drop out of school than peers who do not report being cyberbullied (Connolly & Giouroukakis, 2012). Contrary to some naïve belief that the impact of cyberbullying is limited to initial responses and tends to fade soon, research indicates that the harm caused by cyberbullying has enduring negative impact on its victims, especially on their social well-being (Hoff & Mitchell, 2009; Mesch, 2009). Significant correlations have been found between adolescents' experience of cyberbullying and their feeling of loneliness (Sahin, 2012). In a research involving approximately 2,000 randomly selected middle school students from one of the largest school districts in the United States, Patchin and Hinduja (2010) found that cyberbullying victims and offenders both had significantly lower self-esteem than those who have not been subject to cyberbullying. This relationship persisted even controlling for gender, race, and age.

Cases of cyberbullying occur every day, but most real-life cyberbullying incidents contain more than one form of cyberbullying and few exemplify exactly a certain type of cyberbullying as defined previously. To shed light on the nature of real-life cyberbullying, however, let's take a look at a few high profile incidents. The story of Megan Meier is a noteworthy case that broke on national news about cyberbullying (Maag, 2007). Megan was a thirteen-year-old girl from Missouri who ended her own life after a MySpace romance ended online with a boy named Josh. Megan developed a crush on Josh until things suddenly went bad and he began insulting her. His final message to her was, "The world would be a better place without you." It was on that same day that Megan hanged herself in her room with a belt.

Another young female who chose to end her own life after becoming victim to cyberbullying, following a move to the United States from Ireland, was fifteen-year-old Phoebe Prince. According to Helen Kennedy of the New York Daily News (Kennedy, 2010), Phoebe Prince was cyberbullied by a number of students at her new school in Massachusetts. The students set out to humiliate Phoebe and make her feel unwelcomed. It was reported that Phoebe was called 'Irish slut' and 'whore' on Twitter, Craigslist, Facebook, and Formspring. Phoebe hanged herself after walking home from school and being hit by a Red Bull drink can thrown from a passing bus by the "Mean Girls."

Still another case that also gained major news attention is the tragedy of Tyler Clementi, an eighteen-year-old, Rutgers University college student. According to CBSNews (2012), Tyler was a freshman that jumped to his death from the George Washington Bridge after his roommate, Dhraun Ravi, recorded his intimate encounter with a man in the dorm room they shared. Ravi used a webcam to record Tyler and his partner from another room in the dormitory. Tyler jumped from the bridge a few days after the video was posted online (Friedman, 2010).

Gender and Age Differences in Cyberbullying

Researchers have not reached a consensus regarding gender and age differences in adolescents' experiences of cyberbullying. It has been argued that boys are more likely to bully in person, in the forms of physical, verbal, and relational bullying, whereas girls are more likely to bully online, and that cyberbullying is a higher risk for girls (Notar et al., 2013). This argument is supported by multiple studies. One study found that adolescent girls are more likely to be victims of cyberbullying than boys (25.8% girls versus 16% boys) (Adams, 2010 as cited in Notar et al., 2013). According to the website Enough.org (2017) which has amassed cyberbullying statistics from various sources, girls (40.6%) are more likely to be victims of cyberbullying than boys (28.8%), and girls dominate social media while boys tend to play video games (Cyberbullying Research Center, 2015); 54% of teens surveyed have witnessed online bullying; and 60% of teens who admit to being bullied online have told an adult, compared to 40% in 2013 (Cox, 2014). Another study found that girls reported feeling less safe at school and suffer more relational bullying (Humphrey & Symes, 2010).

Still another study showed that compared to girls, boys are more likely to be both offenders and victims of cyberbullying (Erdur-Baker, 2010). However, a study by Didden et al. (2009) found no evidence showing significant associations between cyberbullying and gender. In addition, existing literature suggests that overall students are bullied at all grade levels, in and away from school, but compared with younger kids, older students reported feeling safer at school and experiencing less relational victimizations (Humphrey & Symes, 2010). However, Didden et al. (2009) have also argued that there is no association between cyberbullying and age. These mixed findings raise the question of whether gender and age differences may be found when particular types of cyberbullying are examined. Certainly, according to our study (Gao, Zhao, & McJunkin, 2016) as introduced previously, gender and age differences do exist in several types of cyberbullying.

FUTURE RESEARCH DIRECTIONS

First of all, future research should further explore adolescent victim experiences of cyberbullying for better understanding and intervention of positive youth development. As mentioned earlier, the rapidly evolving information technology provides numerous easy avenues for spreading negative messages (Li, 2008; Notar, Padgett, & Roden, 2013). Being anonymous, cyberbullies can do tremendous harms to a large number of victims without taking a high risk of being punished (Snakenborg, Van Acker, & Gable, 2011). As a consequence, cyberbullies have invented multiple ways to harm their victims, including cyberstalking, denigration, exclusion, flaming, harassment, masquerade, and outing.

While there are cases of cyberbullying occurring multiple times a day, how young people may experience these different forms of cyberbullying largely remains unknown in the existing literature, despite the fact that research on cyberbullying in general has rapidly increased in recent years. Moreover, the current literature on cyberbullying victims, as previously discussed, has not reached a consensus regarding significant gender and age differences in the way young people experience of cyberbullying, pointing to the necessity of investigating whether gender and age differences exist in young people's experiences of particular forms of cyberbullying.

Most importantly, a key characteristic of cyberbullying, as noted earlier, is that it can happen anytime and anywhere, making it very hard for adults to detect and contain the situation itself and its impact on the victim. Furthermore, while cyberbullying victims often need help from health professionals, they may not want to report their experiences to adults and seek help. To increase our understanding of how to stop cyberbullying and reduce its negative impact on youth, social scientists need to investigate not only young people's experiences of various forms of cyberbullying but also the reasons behind their decisions on whether to report their experiences. Knowledge in this regard will help school officials, health professionals, and other responsible adults better understand the nature of cyberbullying and inform them of ways to support the victims and stop the bullies.

Second, future research should further explore how various types of cyberbullying affect adolescent mental wellbeing so as to find out coping strategies that might help prevent adolescents from conducting, and becoming victims of, cyberbullying. Recent research has pointed to both the prevalence of cyberbullying among school-aged youth (Dehue et al., 2008; Donegan, 2012; Mendez-Baldwin et al., 2015; Patchin & Hinduja, 2010) and its multiple and lasting negative effects on its victims (Connolly & Giouroukakis, 2012; King, 2010; Hoff & Mitchell, 2009; Mesch, 2009; Patchin & Hinduja, 2010; Sahin, 2012). Our recent study (Gao, Zhao, & McJunkin, 2016) contributes to the literature by looking into the extents to which adolescents either have witnessed or have been the targets of various forms of cyberbullying. It also explored their choices on whether to report incidents of cyberbullying to adults and their justifications for making the decision.

Consistent with the existing literature, results of our recent study suggest that the majority of the participants have experienced cyberbullying, either as witnesses or victims, further supporting the argument that cyberbullying in general is prevalent among school-aged youth (Dehue et al., 2008; Donegan, 2012; Mendez-Baldwin et al., 2015; Patchin & Hinduja, 2010). In addition, the present study contributes specific knowledge about the various extents to which adolescents are exposed to different forms of cyberbullying, including flaming (46%), denigration (34%), online harassment (33%), cyberstalking (31%), Outing (28%), masquerade (20%), and exclusion (13%). This finding provides a possible explanation to why the existing literature has documented a puzzling wide range of proportions (ranging from 9 through 15% to nearly 50%) of middle and high school students who reported having experienced cyberbullying (Center for Disease Control and Prevention, 2014; Associated Press, 2011; National Center for Education Statistics, 2013). With this being said, research up to date has provided very limited evidence regarding how different cyberbullying types may affect youth mental wellbeing and needs to explore further in this regard.

Third, future research should investigate further into how age and gender affect school-aged youth victim experiences of various forms of cyberbullying. Our recent study reveals that while school-aged youth are subject to all forms of cyberbullying, the factors of gender and age may make some adolescents more vulnerable than others to particular forms of cyberbullying. Girls were significantly more likely than boys to be victims of cyberstalking (44% versus 17%). Girls are also more likely to be subject to threats of harm or intimidation from the Internet. This finding is consistent with findings in the existing literature that females reported feeling less safe and more relational victimization (Humphrey & Symes, 2010). However, our recent study also challenges Humphrey and Symes's finding that in general older students reported feeling safer and less relational victimization than younger students. Results of our recent study suggest that grade-related differences in adolescents' experiences of cyberbullying vary by forms of cyberbullying. Specifically, compared to 10th and 11th graders, 12th graders are significantly more likely to experience two particular forms of cyberbullying: cyberstalking and exclusion. These findings all point to the necessity of investigating the mechanisms underlying the gender and grade-level difference in adolescents' experiences of particular forms of cyberbullying.

Last but not the least, future research should explore effective means to help adolescent counter cyberbullying. Our recent study provides strong evidence showing that adolescents' unwillingness to report incidents of cyberbullying is a key factor contributing to the prevalence of cyberbullying among school-aged youth and an important barrier against early detection and intervention to stop cyberbullying and mitigate its negative impact on youth. Cross gender and grade levels, an overwhelming majority of students would not report incidents of cyberbullying to adults. The present study identified several reasons that explain this phenomenon, including: adolescents' unawareness or underestimate of the negative effect of cyberbullying on themselves or on others, their concerns about school staff's overreaction and parents' restrictions on their Internet access, and above all, the belief that they should deal with situations of cyberbullying by themselves.

The finding that young people are either unaware of or underestimate the negative impact of cyberbullying is not surprising. The existing literature has documented that most teens think that cyberbullying is no big deal nor has any tangible consequences, or even that it is fun (National Crime Prevention Council, 2007). However, this seemingly simple finding, together with the finding of adolescents' fear of adults' overreaction and their determination to deal with cyberbullying themselves all deserve close attention and further investigation. Questions such as what makes adolescents perceive cyberbullying as harmless and even fun, where do they draw the line between friendly teasing and malicious attack and manipulation, what information help them make judgments about the nature of online behavior, how should adults deal with situations of cyberbullying in order to gain trust from adolescents are complicated psychological, legal, and ethical questions. Adding to the complexity is the fact that in the world of online socialization, individuals may be both bullies and victims. Some adolescents have been bullies themselves and are now receiving the cruelty of being bullied (Notar et al., 2013). Reporting one's cybervictim experiences means potentially disclosing one's online behaviors and, as a result, getting oneself into trouble.

The present study contributes to our knowledge of how school-aged youth experience different forms of cyberbullying and how factors such as gender, age, and perceptions of the nature of cyberbullying are related to their experiences. This knowledge has two important implications for educational and counseling practice. First, it informs educators, parents, and helping professionals of the multifarious nature of cyberbullying but also the groups of youth who are particularly vulnerable to the various forms of cyberbullying. Second, it points to the importance of preventive intervention in the efforts to stopping cyberbullying. Adults need to communicate effectively with young people, starting from early adolescence, about the nature of cyberbullying, its various forms, potential harms on the victims, and ethical ways of responding to situations of cyberbullying. This requires adults' knowledge of cyberbullying, good judgment of its nature, and strategies to have open conversations with adolescents to gain their trust.

Educators, parents, and helping professionals should not feel powerless facing the powerfully penetrating influences of the cyber world. After all, how young people behave in the cyber world themselves and how they respond to others' online behavior is ultimately shaped by the real world in which they are socialized by parents, teachers, and other important adults to think and act in ethical and responsible ways.

REFERENCES

Adams, C. (2010). Cyberbullying: How to make it stop. *Instructor, 120*(2), 44–49.

Algar, S. (2017, February 1). *Cyberbullying in city schools soars 351% in just two years*. Retrieved from www.nypost.com

Associated Press. (2011). *Executive summary: 2011 AP-MTV digital abuse study*. Retrieved from http://www.athinline.org/pdfs/MTV-AP_2011_Research_Study-Exec_Summary.pdf

Bukowski, W. M., Newcomb, A. F., & Hartup, W. (Eds.). (1996). *The company they keep*. Cambridge, UK: Cambridge University Press.

Calvete, E., Orue, I., Estévez, A., Villardón, L., & Padilla, P. (2010). Cyberbullying in adolescents: Modalities and aggressors' profile. *Computers in Human Behavior, 26*(5), 1128–1135. doi:10.1016/j.chb.2010.03.017

CBSNews. (2012, September 30). Tyler Clementi suicide sparks outrage, remorse. *CBSNews.* Retrieved from http://www.cbsnews.com/news/tyler-clementi-suicide-sparks-outrage-remorse/

Center for Disease Control and Prevention. (2014). *Youth risk behavior surveillance — United States 2013.* Washington, DC: U.S. Department of Health and Human Services. Retrieved from http://www.cdc.gov/mmwr/pdf/ss/ss6304.pdf

Connolly, M., & Giouroukakis, V. (2012). Cyberbullying: Taking control through research-based letter writing. *English Journal, 101*(6), 70–74.

Cox. (2014). *Cox 2014 Internet Safety Survey (conducted by The Futures Company).* Retrieved from http://docplayer.net/16377341-2014-teen-internet-safety-survey-conducted-by-the-futures-company.html

Cyberbullying Research Center. (2015). *2015 Cyberbullying Data.* Retrieved from https://cyberbullying.org/2015-cyberbullying-data

Cyberbullying Research Center. (2016). *2016 Cyberbullying Data.* Retrieved from https://cyberbullying.org/2016-cyberbullying-data

Dehue, F., Bolman, C., & Völlink, T. (2008). Cyberbullying: Youngsters' experiences and parental perception. *CyberPscyhology & Behavior, 11*(2), 217–223. doi:10.1089/cpb.2007.0008 PMID:18422417

Didden, R., Scholte, R. H. J., Korzilius, H., de Moor, J. M. H., Vermeulen, A., O'Reilly, M., ... Lancioni, G. E. (2009). Cyberbullying among students with intellectual and developmental disability in special education settings. *Developmental Neurorehabilitation, 12*(3), 146–151. doi:10.1080/17518420902971356 PMID:19466622

Dombeck, M. (2007, July 24). *The long-term effects of bullying.* Retrieved from https://www.mentalhelp.net/articles/the-long-term-effects-of-bullying/

Donegan, R. (2012). Bullying and cyberbullying: History, statistics, law, prevention and analysis. *The Elon Journal of Undergraduate Research in Communications, 3*(1), 33–42.

Enough.org. (2017, November 10). *Cyberbullying Statistics.* Retried from http://enough.org/stats_cyberbullying

Erdur-Baker, Ö. (2010). Cyberbullying and its correlation to traditional bullying, gender, and frequent and risky usage of internet-mediated communication tools. *New Media & Society, 12*(1), 109–125. doi:10.1177/1461444809341260

Friedman, E. (2010, September 29). Victim of secret dorm sex tape posts Facebook goodbye, jumps to his death. *ABC News*. Retrieved from http://abcnews.go.com/US/victim-secret-dorm-sex-tape-commits-suicide/story?id=11758716

Gao, M., Zhao, X., & McJunkin, M. (2016). Adolescents' experiences of cyberbullying: Gender, age, and reasons for not reporting to adults. *International Journal of Cyber Behavior, Psychology and Learning, 6*(4), 13–27. doi:10.4018/IJCBPL.2016100102

Grigonis, H. (2017, July 20). *Cyberbullying happens more often on Instagram*. Retrieved from https://www.digitaltrends.com/social-media/cyberbullying-statistics-2017-ditch-the-label/

Haber, J. D., & Daley, L. A. (2011). A cyberbullying protection plan. *Camping Magazine, 84*(2), 32–37.

Hango, D. (2016). *Insights on Canadian Society: Cyberbullying and cyberstalking among Internet users aged 15 to 29 in Canada*. Retrieved from https://www.statcan.gc.ca/pub/75-006-x/2016001/article/14693-eng.htm

Hinduja, S., & Patchin, J. (2010). Bullying, cyberbullying, and suicide. *Archives of Suicide Research, 14*(3), 206–221. doi:10.1080/13811118.2010.494133 PMID:20658375

Hoff, D. L., & Mitchell, S. N. (2009). Cyberbullying: Causes, effects, and remedies. *Journal of Educational Administration, 47*(2), 652–665. doi:10.1108/09578230910981107

Humphrey, N., & Symes, W. (2010). Responses to bullying and use of social support among pupils with autism spectrum disorders (ASDs) in mainstream schools: A qualitative study. *Journal of Research in Special Educational Needs, 10*(2), 82–90. doi:10.1111/j.1471-3802.2010.01146.x

Jones, S. E., Manstead, A. S. R., & Livingstone, A. G. (2011). Ganging up or sticking together? Group processes and children's responses to text-message bullying. *British Journal of Psychology, 102*(1), 71–96. PMID:21241286

Kennedy, H. (2010, March 29). Phoebe Prince, South Hadley High School's 'new girl,' driven to suicide by teenage cyber bullies. *New York Daily News*. Retrieved from http://www.nydailynews.com/news/national/phoebe-prince-south-hadley-high-school-new-girl-driven-suicide-teenage-cyber-bullies-article-1.165911

King, A. V. (2010). Constituency of cyberbullying laws: Keeping the online playground safe for both teens and free speech. *Vanderbilt Law Review, 63*(3), 845–884.

Li, Q. (2008). Cyberbullying in schools: An examination of preservice teacher's perception. *Canadian Journal of Learning and Technology, 34*(2). Retrieved from http://www.cjlt.ca/index.php/cjlt/article/view/494/225

Maag, C. (2007, November 28). A hoax turned fatal draws anger but no charges. *The New York Times*. Retrieved from http://www.nytimes.com/2007/11/28/us/28hoax.html?_r=0

Mendez-Baldwin, M., Cirillo, K., Ferrigno, M., & Argento, V. (2015). Cyberbullying among teens. *Journal of Bullying and Social Aggression, 1*(1). Retrieved from http://sites.tamuc.edu/bullyingjournal/cyber-bullying-among-teens/

Mesch, G. S. (2009). Parental mediation, online activities, and cyberbullying. *Cyberpsychology & Behavior, 12*(4), 387–393. doi:10.1089/cpb.2009.0068 PMID:19630583

Mustacchi, J. (2009). R U Safe? *Educational Leadership, 66*(6), 78–82.

National Center for Education Statistics. (2013). *Student reports of bullying and cyberbullying: Results from the 2011 school crime supplement to the National Crime Victimization Survey*. Washington, DC: U.S. Department of Education. Retrieved from https://nces.ed.gov/pubs2013/2013329.pdf

National Crime Prevention Council. (2007). *Teens and cyberbullying: Executive summary of a report on research*. Retrieved from http://www.ncpc.org/resources/files/pdf/bullying/Teens%20and%20Cyberbullying%20Research%20Study.pdf

Notar, C. E., Padgett, S., & Roden, J. (2013). Cyberbullying: A review of the literature. *Universal Journal of Educational Research, 1*(1), 1–9. doi:10.12189/ujer.2013.010101

Olweus, D. (1993). *Bullying at school: What we know and what we can do*. Cambridge, MA: Blackwell.

Patchin, J. W., & Hinduja, S. (2010). Cyberbullying and self-esteem. *The Journal of School Health, 80*(12), 614–621. doi:10.1111/j.1746-1561.2010.00548.x PMID:21087257

Raskauskas, J., & Stoltz, A. D. (2007). Involvement in traditional and electronic bullying among adolescents. *Developmental Psychology, 43*(3), 564–575. doi:10.1037/0012-1649.43.3.564 PMID:17484571

Reportlinker. (2017, June). *For America's youth, standing up to the cyberbully is now a life skill*. Retrieved from https://www.reportlinker.com/insight/americas-youth-cyberbully-life-skill.html

Şahin, M. (2012). The relationship between the cyberbullying/cybervictmization and loneliness among adolescents. *Children and Youth Services Review, 34*(4), 834–837. doi:10.1016/j.childyouth.2012.01.010

Sharpe, D. (2015). Your chi-square test is statistically significant: Now what? *Practical Assessment, Research & Evaluation, 20*(8). Retrieved from http://pareonline.net/getvn.asp?v=20&n=8

Smith, P. K., Mahdavi, J., Carvalho, M., Fisher, S., Russell, S., & Tippett, N. (2008). Cyberbullying: Its nature and impact in secondary school pupils. *Journal of Child Psychology and Psychiatry, and Allied Disciplines, 49*(4), 376–385. doi:10.1111/j.1469-7610.2007.01846.x PMID:18363945

Snakenborg, J., Van Acker, R., & Gable, R. A. (n.d.). Cyberbullying: Prevention and intervention to protect our children and youth. *Preventing School Failure, 55*(2), 88-95. doi: . doi:10.1080/1045988X.2011.539454

Stopbullying.gov. (n.d.). *Effects of bullying*. Retrieved from http://www.stopbullying.gov/at-risk/effects/index.html

StopCyberBullying.org. (n.d.). *What is cyberbullying, exactly?* Retrieved from http://www.stopcyberbullying.org/what_is_cyberbullying_exactly.html

Willard, N. (2004). *Educator's guide to cyberbullying: Addressing the harm caused by online social cruelty*. Retrieved from http://cyberbully.org

This research was previously published in Analyzing Human Behavior in Cyberspace edited by Zheng Yan, pages 236-254, copyright year 2019 by Information Science Reference (an imprint of IGI Global).

Chapter 5
Cyberbullying Bystanders:
Gender, Grade, and Actions among Primary and Secondary School Students in Australia

Marilyn Anne Campbell
Queensland University of Technology (QUT), Australia

Chrystal Whiteford
Queensland University of Technology (QUT), Australia

Krystle Duncanson
Queensland University of Technology (QUT), Australia

Barbara Spears
University of South Australia, Australia

Des Butler
Queensland University of Technology (QUT), Australia

Phillip Thomas Slee
Flinders University, Australia

ABSTRACT

Cyberbullying is a relatively new and serious form of bullying with negative social and emotional effects on both victims and perpetrators. Like traditional bullying, cyberbullying is a social phenomenon and often unfolds in the context of a large network of bystanders. This study examined gender and age of cyberbullying bystanders out of 2109 upper primary and secondary school students in Australia. The actions the bystanders took when a peer was cybervictimised were analysed. The results of the study suggested bystanders to cyberbullying were most likely not to do anything or help the person cyberbullied at the time. Girls were more prosocial in helping students who were cyberbullied than boys. In addition, those students who knew someone who was bullied in both ways were more likely to tell their parents and friends about it than those who knew someone who was cyberbullied only. Implications for prevention and intervention in cyberbullying are discussed.

DOI: 10.4018/978-1-7998-1684-3.ch005

INTRODUCTION

With the emergence of cyberbullying at the beginning of this century, there has been vigorous debate whether this kind of bullying through technology is a separate phenomenon or another form of bullying (Dooley, Pyzalski, & Cross, 2009). The definition of bullying is generally agreed to be a systematic abuse of power with physical, verbal and social forms often called traditional bullying (Smith et al., 2008). The debate centres on the theoretical and conceptual similarities and differences of cyberbullying and face-to-face or traditional bullying. While there are differences between traditional and cyberbullying, there are also differences between physical, verbal and social bullying. Despite these differences these forms of bullying are classified as bullying. The question becomes does cyberbullying have all the characteristics of a form of bullying with the intention to hurt, an imbalance of power and is usually repetitive or should the word bullying be removed from cyberbullying? Repetition in cyberbullying can be manifested in a different way, in that a single act may become viral and thus repeated but not necessarily by the same person. The intent to harm might be more difficult to detect with less emotional clues but as Langos (2012) argues following legal tradition that "intention is best determined based on how a reasonable person would perceive the perpetrator's conduct." (p. 288). It is often argued that the concept of imbalance of power is more difficult to distinguish in cyberbullying when the perpetrator is anonymous. However, returning to Olweus's (1993) original concept that the imbalance of power means that the person victimised cannot get the bullying to stop, then cyberbullying could be considered to meet this criteria. In 2014 both the United States Center for Disease Control and the Australian Research Alliance for Children and Youth issued statements that cyberbullying could be considered to be another form of bullying (Gladden, Vivolvo-Kantor, Hamburger, & Lumpkin, 2014; Hemphill, Heerde, & Gomo, 2014) although not all researchers agree.

One of the concepts first studied in traditional bullying is the role of the bystander. The prevalence and actions of bystanders are now the subject of examination in cyberbullying. The conception of bullying has progressed from a predominant focus on the bully-target dyad to a focus involving the social context in which bullying occurs and the many roles students play (Kochenderfer-Ladd & Troop-Gordon, 2010). Recognising the importance of the wider social context in bullying is consistent with viewing bullying from an ecological perspective (Rodkin & Hodges, 2003). The early work of Salmivalli, Lagerspetz, Björkqvist, Österman, and Kaukiainen (1996) has been influential in identifying and naming the diverse roles of students in traditional bullying; as well as the bully, the victim and the bully-victim, there are four bystander roles of reinforcers of the bully, assistants of the bully, defenders of the victim and outsiders.

Bystanders are usually considered to be individuals who are not in the role of bully or victim but who witness the bullying (Oh & Hazler, 2009). However, the definition of bystanders can also be expanded to include those peers who are told about the bullying incident (Stueve et al., 2006). These students are also able to perform actions in response to the bullying, similar to witnesses. This could be especially important in the case of cyberbullying. While there are public real-time transactions between the student who is bullying and the victim such as a in chatroom or on Facebook, there are times when the bullying is conducted by personal means to an individual such as by email or text messages where there are no direct witnesses (Menesini et al., 2012) and a friend may need to be shown the text or be forwarded the text to become aware of the bullying. These differences create a different landscape for a virtual network of peers and may alter how bystanders respond. For the purposes of this study, bystanders to cyberbullying refer to those peers who either have directly witnessed someone cyberbullied or know someone who has been cyberbullied, but without witnessing the episode personally. These "secondary" bystanders have as much potential as direct witnesses to influence bullying (Jones, Mitchell, & Turner, 2015).

Classic bystander effects are thought to account for lack of intervention by bystanders in some bullying episodes (Salmivalli, 2010); that is, the physical presence of other people in a potentially harmful situation inhibits individual helping behaviour through effects such as diffusion of responsibility and audience inhibition (Latane & Nida, 1981). However, Olweus (1993) outlined a number of group processes that can help explain how usually non-aggressive children may become involved as unhelpful bystanders in traditional bullying episodes. These processes include social contagion, weakening of the control of aggressive tendencies and cognitive changes concerning perception of the victim in those viewing the bullying.

Behaviours displayed by students categorised into bystander roles to traditional bullying range from supportive and consoling side-taking with the victim, to assisting the bullying by physically catching the victim. Bystanders to traditional bullying have been recognised as important players in the bullying process, as their actions can influence the persistence and escalation of bullying episodes, or alternatively, assisting in stopping them (O'Connell, Pepler, & Craig, 1999). For this reason, they have become an important target group for bullying intervention programs. Schools where students report that peers take action against bullying have been associated with decreased reports of victimisation (Denny et al., 2015).

Like traditional bullying, cyberbullying, is a social phenomenon and often involves a large network of students (Huang & Chou, 2010; Li, 2006, 2007). Research into bystander prevalence in cyberbullying has revealed that similar to traditional bullying, bystanders to cyberbullying form the largest group of participants (Gradinger, Strohmeier, & Spiel, 2009). The nature of technology also means there is a potential for a very large audience if the bullying is conducted by social media (Kowalski, Giumetti, Schroeder, & Lattanner, 2014). In addition, it has been shown in some studies that bystanders to cyberbullying play a similar role to bystanders to traditional bullying, sometimes escalating the cyberbullying by joining in or sometimes helping to support the victim and stand up to the bully (Machackova, Dedkova, Svcikova, & Cerna, 2016; Authors, 2015).

Participants in cyberbullying are usually physically separated by technology. This means the opportunity to view the emotional reactions of the victim or to observe the reactions of other bystanders to the cyberbullying may be limited. Also, the student who bullies and the bystander can choose to be anonymous. Technology also creates variation in the way that bystanders can be involved, including how they come to witness or know about the bullying and how they can directly respond in the cyberbullying episodes.

Preliminary studies on bystanders in cyberbullying incidents (grades spanning 7-9, 12 to 15-years old) have found that the majority of those who knew someone being cyberbullied chose to stay quiet and do nothing, rather than report the incident to an adult (Li, 2006, 2007). One study examined cyberbullying problems among Taiwanese junior high school students, including how bystanders respond to cyberbullying (Huang & Chou, 2010). Similar to the other studies, while they were the largest group involved in cyberbullying, they were found to be the least likely to report or talk to someone about a bullying incident in comparison to peers with past experience with cyberbullying in the role of victim or bully (Huang & Chou, 2010). Machackova et al. (2016) found in a sample of over 2, 000 Czech students aged from 12-18 years-old that most cyber bystanders offered some support to the person being victimised if they considered the cyberbullying incident to be severe.

Gender and age have been found to be important in understanding bystanders' behaviour in traditional bullying (Oh & Hazler, 2009; Trach et al., 2010). Girls and primary school aged students have been found to express more readiness to intervene to support a victim (Authors, 2014; Rigby & Johnson, 2006). Reasons suggested for higher levels of intervening and positive attitudes towards the victim with females has included less pressure to conform to dominant macho values together with advanced social maturity and higher empathy (Cowie, 2000). With increasing age, both male and female bystanders of traditional bullying have been reported to become increasingly passive in their behaviour when faced with bullying and less likely to directly intervene (O'Connell et al., 1999; Pozzoli & Gini, 2010; Trach et al., 2010).

In a recent study Machackova et al. (2016) found the female bystanders to cyberbullying helped the victim more than boys but there was no difference in age. However, two other studies have shown no differences in age or gender for bystanders' actions in helping a cybervictim (Machackova, Dedkova, Sevcikova, & Cerna, 2013) nor do they increase negative cyber bystander behaviour of forwarding hurtful messages (Barlinska, Szuster, & Winiewski, 2103). It is also unclear whether the contextual differences introduced by cyberbullying create differences in the way that bystanders to cyberbullying respond compared to traditional bullying. For example, the diffusion of responsibility could lead to not helping a victim or the anonymity afforded by technology could lead to more assistance to the victim.

Bullying through technology could still affect bystander actions. There is also considerable overlap of traditional and cyberbullying, where students are victimised by both forms (Authors, 2011; Jose, Kljakovic, Scheib, & Notter, 2011) which could influence bystander actions to cybervictimisation. In a large Canadian study over 50% of students who were victimised reported they were victimised by all four forms, physical, verbal, social and cyber (Waasdorp & Bradshaw, 2015). Students who were victimised, aged 10-20 years have reported that during victimisation by both traditional and cyber means that were higher rates of both negative and positive activity by the bystanders with some joining in with the cyberbullying, such as forwarding embarrassing images and others more likely to help (Jones et al., 2015). Therefore, it was decided to see if the actions of bystanders differed in relation to knowing if a person was cyberbullied only or was bullied in both ways.

This study therefore, investigated the prevalence of bystanders to cyberbullying and compared the actions of peers who knew about the cyberbullying to examine if there were gender or age differences. In addition, the actions of the bystanders to cyberbullying were compared when the victim was cyberbullied only and when the victim was traditionally as well as cyberbullied.

METHOD

Participants

Data for this study were drawn from a larger research project examining the incidences and consequences of traditional and cyberbullying bullying in Australian school students (Authors, 2012). Participants for this paper were drawn from a sample of 3,112 students (49% male ($n = 1,535$); 51% female ($n = 1,572$). Participants were aged between 9 and 16 years, M = 13.96, SD = 1.874. Schools that participated were located in three different states in Australia.

Measures

An anonymous, self-report paper-based survey was conducted (Authors, 2012). Participants were provided with the following written definition of cyberbullying:

Cyberbullying is when one person or a group of people repeatedly try to hurt or embarrass another person, using their computer or mobile phone, to use power over them. With cyber bullying, the person bullying usually has some advantage over the person targeted, and it is done on purpose to hurt them, not like an accident or when friends tease each other.

A reminder of this definition was included in other relevant sections of the survey. The following definition of traditional bullying was provided:

There are lots of different ways to bully someone. A bully wants to hurt the other person (it's not an accident), and does it repeatedly and unfairly (the bully has some advantage over the victim). Sometimes a group of students will bully another student.

The first part of the survey consisted of demographic information followed by two separate parallel sections on participants' experiences with cyberbullying and traditional bullying.

In the section on cyberbullying, students were asked "Has someone you know been cyberbullied this year?" Using a multiple response format participants were asked what actions they took in response to knowing about the cyberbullying: e.g., thinking about your most recent time that someone you know was cyberbullied, what did you do when they were cyberbullied? Responses which could be selected were: not doing anything; ignoring it; helping the person at the time or later; standing up to the person bullying; reporting to parents or friends; getting back at the bully later; making a joke of it; joining in; getting someone to stop it; telling an adult; standing by and watching. The same questions and bystander responses were then asked in the parallel section for traditional bullying.

Three categories of bystanders were created from the responses to: has someone you know been cyberbullied/face-to-face bullied this year. (1) bystanders to cyberbullying only; (2) bystanders to both traditional and cyber bullying; and (3) students who did know anyone bullied that year. In this paper bystanders to cyberbullying only and bystanders to both cyberbullying and traditional bullying are examined.

Procedure

The project was granted approval by an institutional ethics committee. Active consent was sought from parents and assent from students. Surveys were administered by research assistants in the students' classrooms. The survey took between 20-30 minutes to complete.

Analysis

As the study utilises nominal and ordinal level data, the analysis approach is largely based on cross-tabulations and simple descriptive percentages. Significant differences in proportions were examined via Pearson's Chi Square. The reader should note that the variable 'bystander actions' was a multiple response variable, which meant students could select more than one response. The PASW Statistics 23 package was used for statistical analyses.

RESULTS

Prevalence by Gender and Grade of Bystanders to Bullying

Most students (45.9%, $n =1, 417$) did not know anyone who was bullied at all in that year. There were 21% ($n = 669$) of students knew someone who was only traditionally bullied, 10.7% of students (n= 333) who knew someone who was cyberbullied but not traditionally bullied, and 16.4% ($n = 510$) students who knew of someone traditionally bullied and also cyberbullied (see Table 1).

No significant differences were found between gender and bystander groups. However, age was significantly associated with bystander groups ($x^2 = 9.431$, $df = 2$, $p<.05$, Cramer's $V = .106$). Results suggest a higher proportion of children aged 13 to 15 years knew someone who was bullied by both means (64.3%) compared to children aged 9 to 12 (58.8%) or 16 to 19. Participants who were 16 to 19 years of age (50.9%) knew less of these victims than other groups. Those aged 16 to 19 were more likely to know people who were cyberbullied only (49.1%) than other age groups.

Actions of Bystanders to Cyberbullying Related to Gender

Males were significant more likely to report ignoring the cyberbullying (8.8%) than females (2.6%) ($x^2=15.975$, $df = 1$, $p<.001$, Cramer's $V = .138$). Females were significantly more likely to do a range of positive helping behaviours. Results, presented in Table 2, suggest females were significantly more likely than males to tell their parents about it ($x^2=11.337$, $df =1$, $p<.001$, Cramer's $V = .116$), tell an adult at school about it ($x^2=5.628$, $df =1$, $p<.05$, Cramer's $V = .082$), tell their friends about it ($x^2=11.148$, $df=1$, $p=.001$, Cramer's $V= .115$), get someone to stop it ($x^2=3.886$, $df =1$, $p<.05$, Cramer's $V = .068$), help the person at the time being cyberbullied ($x^2=29.210$, $df =1$, $p<.001$, Cramer's $V = .186$) and stand up to the person that was doing it ($x^2=12.106$, $df=1$, $p=.001$, Cramer's $V = .120$). Bystander actions by gender in percentages are presented in Table 2.

Table 1. Prevalence of bystander groups by gender and grade

Bystander group (Total *n* = 2.939)	Gender		Grade		
	Female (*n* = 1,493) *n* (%)	Male (*n* = 1,445) *n* (%)	Primary (*n* = 759) *n* (%)	Middle (*n* = 1,559) *n* (%)	Senior (*n* = 619) *n* (%)
Bystander to cyberbullying only (*n* = 333)	209 (14.0)	124 (8.6)	80 (10.5)	183 (11.7)	70 (11.3)
Bystander to Traditional bullying only (*n* = 669)	338 (22.6)	330 (22.8)	201 (26.5)	364 (23.3)	104 (16.8)
Both (*n* = 510)	326 (21.8)	184 (12.7)	120 (15.8)	315 (20.2)	73 (11.8)
Neither (*n* = 1,427)	620 (41.5)	807 (55.8)	358 (47.2)	697 (44.7)	372 (60.1)

Table 2. Actions of bystanders to cyberbullying by gender

Actions	Males *n* = 308	Females *n* = 535
	% of cases	
I didn't do anything	21.1	21.3
I ignored it	8.8**	2.6**
I stood by and watched	1.3	1.5
I stood up to the person that was doing it	9.4*	18.3*
I got someone to stop it	2.3*	5*
At the time, I helped the person being cyber bullied	13**	29.3**
Later on, I helped the person being cyber bullied	3.6	6.5
I told an adult at school about it	1*	3.7*
I told my parents about it	4.5*	11.4*
I told my friends about it	5.5*	12.7*
I got back at the bully later	4.9	3.6
I made a joke of it	3.9	2.1
I joined in with the cyber bullying	1.9	0.6

Note. Multiple responses were allowed.

* $p < .05$

** $p < .001$

Actions of Bystanders to Cyberbullying and Age

There were no significant differences between age group and actions of bystanders to cyberbullying. The percentages of bystander actions by age groups are presented in Table 3.

Actions of Bystanders to Cyberbullying Only and Bystanders to Both Forms of Bullying

Table 4 presents percentages of those who knew about cyberbullying only and those who knew about both cyberbullying and traditional bullying in regards to their actions. The most common action for those students who witnessed cyberbullying only was to not do anything (24.6%), followed by helping the person being bullied at the time (20.1%). The most common action for students who witnessed both was to help the person at the time being cyberbullied (25.5%), followed by not doing anything (19%).

Table 3. Actions of bystanders to cyberbullying by year level

Actions	Age ranges	
	10-14years $n = 534$	15-19years $n = 309$
	% of cases	
I didn't do anything	22.1	19.7
I ignored it	4.9	4.9
I stood by and watched	1.1	1.9
I stood up to the person that was doing it	14.4	16.2
I got someone to stop it	4.7	2.9
At the time, I helped the person being cyber bullied	22.5	24.9
Later on, I helped the person being cyber bullied	5.1	6.1
I told an adult at school about it	2.8	2.6
I told my parents about it	10.3	6.5
I told my friends about it	10.1	10
I got back at the bully later	3.7	4.5
I made a joke of it	2.1	3.9
I joined in with the cyber bullying	0.7	1.6

Note. Multiple responses were allowed.

* $p<.05$

** $p<.001$

There was a statistically significant association between the groups and whether they told their parents about it (x^2=8.278, df=1, p<.05, Cramer's V = .099). Results suggest those who knew about both forms of bullying were more likely (11.2%) to tell their parents in comparison to those who only knew of cyberbullying (5.4%). In addition, those who knew of both forms of bullying were significantly more likely to tell their friends about it (x^2=11.633, df=1, p=.001, Cramer's V = .117).

DISCUSSION

The study found that while the majority of students did not know anyone who was bullied by any form, 21% of students knew someone who was traditionally bullied, 10.7% knew someone who had been cyberbullied that year and 16.4% knew someone who had been victimised by both cyber and traditional means. It was found that there were differences in the actions taken by bystanders to the cyberbullying depending on whether the cyberbullying was the only way in which the student was bullied or

Table 4. Actions of bystanders to cyberbullying by bystander group

Actions	Bystanders to cyber only n = 333	Bystanders to both forms n = 510
	% of cases	% of cases
I didn't do anything	24.6	19
I ignored it	5.1	4.7
I stood by and watched	0.9	1.8
I stood up to the person that was doing it	13.8	15.9
I got someone to stop it	2.7	4.9
At the time, I helped the person being cyber bullied	20.1	25.5
Later on, I helped the person being cyber bullied	4.8	5.9
I told an adult at school about it	2.1	3.1
I told my parents about it	5.4*	11.2*
I told my friends about it	5.7*	12.9*
I got back at the bully later	5.4	3.1
I made a joke of it	2.4	2.9
I joined in with the cyber bullying	1.2	1

Note. Multiple responses were allowed.

if the student was bullied both cyber and traditional means. Bystanders to both forms of bullying reported helping the person being bullied at the time and telling parents and friend about it more than those who knew students who were cyberbullied only.

These prevalence rates are in similar proportions to other studies of bystanders to cyberbullying (Bastiaensens et al., 2016; Quirk & Campbell,2014), although slightly lower than some (Beran & Wade, 2011; Steffgen & Konig, 2009).

The most frequent response among students involved as bystanders to cyberbullying victimisation as the only form of bullying experienced was to ignore it or do nothing. This is consistent with the findings of Li (2006, 2007) and Huang and Chou (2010). One explanation is that students who ignore bullying may not perceive the 'seriousness' of the bullying or deny that it is their duty to respond (Huang & Chou, 2010). An almost equal number of students told a friend and told a parent about the cyberbullying. This is not consistent with the findings of Huang and Chou (2010), whose research indicated bystanders to cyberbullying were far more likely to tell a classmate than a parent and also expressed a sense of hopelessness in terms of turning to an adult regarding cyberbullying issues. This indicates the need for schools to provide guidance to parents as well as students on how best to respond when they are approached for support with cyberbullying concerns. Adults at a school were told by the least number of students. This may reflect the view by students that cyberbullying belongs to the home domain and is out of the teacher's jurisdiction or power to manage (Smith et al., 2008) or potentially they fear reprisal within the schooling context.

Girls were significantly more prosocial in helping victims by not only helping the person being bullied at the time as well as later but they also stood up to the person doing the bullying more than boys. Girls got someone to stop the bullying and told friends, parents and teachers more than boys. These findings are similar to past studies where girls were shown to be more likely to support victims of traditional bullying than boys (O'Connell et al., 1999; Salmivalli et al., 1996). This is also consistent with other findings of bystanders to cyberbullying where girls were more prosocial than boys (authors, 2014), leading to an argument for gendered considerations by way of presentation and interventions.

There were no significant differences by age groups of young students (10-14 years-old) and older students (15-19 years-old) in the actions they reported they took when they knew someone had been cyberbullied. Both age groups were most likely to either do nothing or help the person at the time. This is similar to two other studies which found no age differences in the actions of bystanders to cyberbullying with students from 12-18 years of age (Machackova et al., 2016; Machackova et al., 2013).

Participants who were bystanders to both forms of bullying reported similar reactions to those who knew students who were cyberbullied only in that most did nothing or they helped the cybervictim at the time. However, there were significantly more students who knew peers victimised by both forms of bullying who told their friends and their parents about the bullying than those who knew someone who had been cyberbullied only.

Limitations

It is important to note the limitations of this study. First, this study relied solely on student self-report. Self-report is prone to social desirability effects, which result in higher rates of stated intervening in support of the victim (Rigby & Johnson, 2006). In light of the very high levels of reported helping behaviour among the participants, this needs to be taken into account. However, the impact of this may have been minimised by the assurance to participants of the anonymity of individual survey results. Second, this study was cross-sectional and the results produced mainly from descriptive statistics. This means that only preliminary associations can be drawn from the data.

CONCLUSION

Despite these limitations, this study adds to the emerging research on the nature of bystander behaviour in cyberbullying. There is minimal information about this often large network of peer bystanders and how they behave in the new cyber context in comparison to the traditional in-person context. Similar to bystanders in traditional bullying, bystanders to cyberbullying hold great potential for intervention and prevention work, as they form an important relational context for its occurrence. Most victims of cyberbullying do not go to anyone for support and when they do it is most likely to be a friend (Slonje & Smith, 2008). Bystanders to cyberbullying have the power to choose not to pass on a hurtful email, express disapproval on an online chat site or notify appropriate school authorities of its occurrence (Spears, Slee, Owens, & Johnson, 2008). They therefore have a powerful role in intervening and preventing hurtful bullying material from spreading (Huang, & Chou, 2010). Additionally, the earlier bystanders intervene the lower the chances of major negative impacts on the cyberbully victim. It is interesting to note that bystanders were more proactive when the student was who was cyberbullied was also bullied in traditional ways. With more information on how bystanders in cyberbullying are behaving and the similarities and differences to traditional bullying, educational preventive programs can be tailored to the bystanders, being mindful that students can engage in different roles in bullying at different times.

Future research may focus on examining influences on bystander actions using stronger inferential statistics to reveal the nature and causes of bystander behaviour in cyberbullying and may also examine the influence of different cyberbullying mediums (e.g., text, chat room and website) on how bystanders respond to the bullying. Finally, future research should focus on the development of theoretical frameworks to help explain bystander behaviour in the technological context.

REFERENCES

Authors (2015). On standby? A comparison of online and offline witnesses to bullying and their bystander behaviour. *Educational Psychology, 35,* 430-448. doi :10.1080/01443410.2014.893556

Authors. Victims' perceptions of traditional and cyberbullying, and the psychosocial correlates of their victimisation. *Emotional and Behavioural Difficulties, 17,* 389-401. doi:10.1080/13632752.2012.704316

Barlinska, J., Szuster, A., & Winiewski, M. (2013). Cyberbullying among adolescent bystanders: Role of the communication medium, form of violence, and empathy. *Journal of Community & Applied Social Psychology, 23*(1), 37–51. doi:10.1002/casp.2137

Bastiaensens, S., Pabian, S., Vandebosch, H., Poels, K., Van Cleemput, K., DeSmet, A., & De Bourdeaudhuij, I. (2015). From normative influence to social pressure: How relevant others affect whether bystanders join in cyberbullying. *Social Development, 25*(1), 193–211. doi:10.1111ode.12134

Beran, T., & Wade, A. (2011). Cyberbullying: The new era of bullying. *Canadian Journal of School Psychology, 26*(1), 44–61. doi:10.1177/0829573510396318

Brody, N., & Vangelisti, A. (2015). Bystander intervention in cyberbullying. *Communication Monographs.* doi:10.1080/03637751.2015.1044256

Campbell, M.A., Whiteford, C. Duncanson, K., Spears, B., Butler, D. & Slee, P.T. (2011, April). The prevalence of cyberbullying in Australia. *Proceedings of the 5th World conference and IV Iberoamerican congress on violence in school. Investigations, interventions, evaluations and public policies,* Mendoza, Argentina.

Campbell, M.A., Whiteford, C. Duncanson, K., Spears, B., Butler, D. & Slee, P.T. (2016). The modern day bystander: Online and face-to-face bystander actions in traditional bullying and cyberbullying. *Psychology and Education: An interdisciplinary journal, 53*(1/2), 13-23.

Denny, S., Peterson, E., Stuart, J., Utter, J., Bullen, P., Fleming, T., ... Milfont, T. (2015). Bystander intervention, bullying, and victimization: A multi-level analysis of New Zealand high schools. *Journal of School Violence, 14*(3), 245–272. doi:10 .1080/15388220.2014.910470

Dooley, J. J., Pyżalski, J., & Cross, D. (2009). Cyberbullying versus face-to-face bullying: A theoretical and conceptual review. *Zeitschrift für Psychologie. The Journal of Psychology, 217*, 182–188. doi:10.1027/0044-3409.217.4.182

Gladden, R. M., Vivolo-Kantor, A. M., Hamburger, M. E., & Lumpkin, C. D. (2014). Bullying surveillance among youths: Uniform definitions for public health and recommended data elements (Version 1.0). National Center for Injury Prevention and Control, Centers for Disease Control and Prevention and U.S. Department of Education.

Gradinger, P., Strohmeier, D., & Spiel, C. (2009). Traditional bullying and cyberbullying: Identification of risk groups for adjustment problems. *Zeitschrift für Psychologie. The Journal of Psychology, 217*, 205–213. doi:10.1027/0044-3409.217.4.205

Hemphill, S. A., Heerde, J. A., & Gomo, R. (2014). *A conceptual definition of school-based bullying for the Australian research and academic community.* Canberra: Australian Research Alliance for Children and Youth.

Huang, Y. Y., & Chou, C. (2010). An analysis of multiple factors of cyberbullying among junior high school students in Taiwan. *Computers in Human Behavior, 26*(6), 1581–1590. doi:10.1016/j.chb.2010.06.005

Jones, L., Mitchell, K., & Turner, H. (2015). Victim reports of bystander reactions to in-person and online peer harassment: A national survey of adolescents. *Journal of Youth and Adolescence, 44*(12), 2308–2320. doi:10.100710964-015-0342-9 PMID:26316304

Kochenderfer-Ladd, B., & Troop-Gordon, W. (2010). Introduction to the special issue contexts, causes, and consequences: New directions in peer victimization research. *Merrill-Palmer Quarterly, 56*(3), 221–230. doi:10.1353/mpq.0.0048

Kowalski, R., Giumetti, G., Schroeder, A., & Lattanner, M. (2014). Bullying in the digital age: A critical review and meta-analysis of cyberbullying research among youth. *Psychological Bulletin, 140*(4), 1073–1137. doi:10.1037/a0035618 PMID:24512111

Langos, C. (2012). Cyberbullying: The challenge to define. *Cyberpsychology, Behavior, and Social Networking, 15*(6), 285–289. doi:10.1089/cyber.2011.0588 PMID:22703033

Latane, B., & Nida, S. (1981). Ten years of research on group size and helping. *Psychological Bulletin, 89*, 308–324. doi:10.1037/0033-2909.89.2.308

Li, Q. (2006). Cyberbullying in schools: A research of gender differences. *School Psychology International, 27*(2), 157–170. doi:10.1177/0143034306064547

Li, Q. (2007). New bottle but old wine: A research of cyberbullying in schools. *Computers in Human Behavior, 23*(4), 1777–1791. doi:10.1016/j.chb.2005.10.005

Machackova, H., Dedkova, L., Sevcikova, A., & Cerna, A. (2013). Bystanders support of cyberbullied schoolmates. *Journal of Community & Applied Social Psychology, 23*(1), 25–36. doi:10.1002/casp.2135

Machackova, H., Dedkova, L., Sevcikova, A., & Cerna, A. (2016). Bystanders supportive and passive responses to cyberaggression. *Journal of School Violence*, 1–12; Advance online publication. doi:10.1080/15388220.2016.1222499

Machmutow, K., Perren, S., Sticca, F., & Alsaker, F. D. (2012). Peer victimisation and depressive symptoms: Can specific coping strategies buffer the negative impact of cybervictimisation. *Emotional & Behavioural Difficulties, 17*(3-4), 403–420. doi:10.1080/13632752.2012.704310

Menesini, E., Nocentini, A., Palladino, B. E., Frisén, A., Berne, S., Ortega-Ruiz, R., & Smith, P. K. (2012). Cyberbullying definition among adolescents: A comparison across six European countries. *Cyberpsychology, Behavior, and Social Networking, 15*(9), 455–463. doi:10.1089/cyber.2012.0040 PMID:22817693

OConnell, P., Pepler, D., & Craig, W. (1999). Peer involvement in bullying: Insights and challenges for intervention. *Journal of Adolescence, 22*(4), 437–452. doi:10.1006/jado.1999.0238 PMID:10469508

Oh, I., & Hazler, R. (2009). Contributions of personal and situational factors to bystanders reactions to school bullying. *School Psychology International, 30*(3), 291–310. doi:10.1177/0143034309106499

Olweus, D. (1993). *Bullying at school: What we know and what we can do*. Oxford, UK: Blackwell.

Olweus, D. (1993). *Bullying at school: What we know and what we can do*. New York: Blackwell.

Pozzoli, T., & Gini, G. (2010). Active defending and passive bystanding behavior in bullying: The role of personal characteristics and perceived peer pressure. *Journal of Abnormal Child Psychology, 38*(6), 815–827. doi:10.100710802-010-9399-9 PMID:20228996

Quirk, R., & Campbell, M. A. (2015). On standby? A comparison of online and offline witnesses to bullying and their bystander behaviour. *Educational Psychology: An International Journal of Experimental Educational Psychology, 35*(4), 430–448. doi:10.1080/01443410.2014.893556

Rigby, K., & Johnson, B. (2006). Expressed readiness of Australian school children to act as bystanders in support of children who are being bullied. *Educational Psychology, 26*(3), 425–440. doi:10.1080/01443410500342047

Rodkin, P. C., & Hodges, E. V. E. (2003). Bullies and victims in the peer ecology: Four questions for psychological and school professionals. *School Psychology Review, 32*, 384–400.

Salmivalli, C. (2010). Bullying and the peer group: A review. *Aggression and Violent Behavior, 15*(2), 112–120. doi:10.1016/j.avb.2009.08.007

Salmivalli, C., Lagerspetz, K., Björkqvist, K., Österman, K., & Kaukiainen, A. (1996). Bullying as a group process: Participant roles and their relations to social status within the group. *Aggressive Behavior, 22*(1), 1–15. doi:10.1002/(SICI)1098-2337(1996)22:1<1::AID-AB1>3.0.CO;2-T

Slonje, R., & Smith, P. K. (2008). Cyberbullying: Another main type of bullying? *Scandinavian Journal of Psychology, 49*(2), 147–154. doi:10.1111/j.1467-9450.2007.00611.x PMID:18352984

Smith, P. K., Mahdavi, J., Carvalho, M., Fisher, S., Russell, S., & Tippett, N. (2008). Cyberbullying: Its nature and impact in secondary school pupils. *Journal of Child Psychology and Psychiatry, and Allied Disciplines, 49*(4), 376–385. doi:10.1111/j.1469-7610.2007.01846.x PMID:18363945

Spears, B. A., Slee, P. T., Owens, L., & Johnson, B. (2008). *Behind the scenes: Insights into the human dimension of covert bullying*. Canberra: DEEWR.

Steffgen, G., & Konig, A. (2009). Cyberbullying: The role of traditional bullying and empathy. In B. Sapeo, L. Haddon, E. Mante-Meijer, L. Fortunati, T. Turk & E. Loos (Eds.), *The good, the bad and the challenging: The user and the future of information and communication technologies: Conference Proceedings* (Vol. 2, pp. 1041-1047). Brussels: COST office.

Stueve, A., Dash, K., ODonnell, L., Tehranifar, P., Wilson-Simmons, R., Slaby, R., & Link, B. G. (2006). Rethinking the bystander role in school violence prevention. *Health Promotion Practice, 7*(1), 117–124. doi:10.1177/1524839905278454 PMID:16410428

Trach, J., Hymel, S., Waterhouse, T., & Neale, K. (2010). Bystander responses to school bullying: A cross-sectional investigation of grade and sex differences. *Canadian Journal of School Psychology, 25*(1), 114–130. doi:10.1177/0829573509357553

Waasdorp, T., & Bradshaw, C. (2015). The overlap between cyberbullying and traditional bullying. *The Journal of Adolescent Health, 56*(5), 483–488. doi:10.1016/j. jadohealth.2014.12.002 PMID:25631040

This research was previously published in International Journal of Technoethics (IJT), 8(1); edited by Rocci Luppicini, pages 44-55, copyright year 2017 by IGI Publishing (an imprint of IGI Global).

Section 2
Policy and Reform Solutions

Chapter 6
Cyberbullying in Adolescence:
Victimization and Adolescence

Michael Pittaro
American Military University, USA & East Stroudsburg University, USA

ABSTRACT

The advent of the internet has revolutionized the way individuals conduct business, socialize, and search for information on any topic imaginable at any time. Nevertheless, with all its benefits, the internet also has a darker side for which new criminal opportunities have emerged and some traditional crimes have evolved and multiplied. One area of concern that has emerged since the advent of the internet is that of cyberbullying, a distinct type of deviant behavior that has attained worldwide attention from practitioners and scholars. This chapter examines cyberbullying as associated with the age, gender, race, and urbanicity of the victims versus the extent to which traditional face-to-face bullying took place within these same groups. Cyberbullying remains an elusive social problem for all because cyberbullying has been associated with school shootings, suicides, and other violence among adolescents. Discussion of the implications for practitioners and scholars will be included in that cyberbullying extends beyond the school grounds and well within the realm of public safety.

INTRODUCTION

Bullying is a widely used and internationally familiar form of victimization that had traditionally been perceived to be a common, customary rite of passage, which typically occurs during a child's early middle school to high school years. That is until the past few decades when researchers and practitioners started to look more

DOI: 10.4018/978-1-7998-1684-3.ch006

closely at the emotional and behavioral ramifications associated with bullying victimization, especially in relation to adolescence (Lusk, 2014). It is widely accepted that most adolescents have encountered, or will encounter, bullying at one or more times during adolescence (Lusk, 2014). Researchers have emphasized that with traditional, face-to-face bullying, adolescents typically assume one of three principal roles that include the bully, the victim, and what researchers and practitioners have deemed to be, the bystander (Lusk, 2014). As noted, up until recent decades, most adults have dismissed bullying as seemingly harmless normal childhood conduct that dissipates in time with both age and maturity. The adage, *kids will be kids*, was a commonly held and widely accepted belief embraced by parents, early childhood educators, school administrators, and criminal justice professionals. However, the apparent lack of knowledge and understanding of bullying accepted by adults over the past years has compelled bullying victims to develop ways to fend for themselves (Lusk, 2014).

In recent decades, there has been a change in basic assumptions in our collective understanding of bullying in that, the behavior is now recognized as a "pervasive social problem that may have a profound influence on the psychological and physiological well-being of the targeted victims" (Dempsey, 2010, p. 224). In fact, incidents of face-to-face bullying have come to be a distinct form of harmful and hurtful emotional and physical abuse that directly and adversely affects over one-third of today's youth, thereby, warranting international concern (National Crime Prevention Council, 2014). Ever since the mass shooting at Columbine High School on April 20, 1999, which at the time was the largest school massacre to date, bullying has become a major concern for law enforcement and other public safety organizations (Pittaro, 2008). In response to Columbine and the other mass school shootings that have taken place in recent years, schools and other youth organizations have been tasked with reducing incidents of bullying through preventative and intervention-type programs (Pittaro, 2008). The comprehensive criminal investigation that took place following the bloodbath at Columbine, strongly confirmed the fact that the majority of school shooters were bullied and responded to their victimization through retaliatory actions that were intended to harm the bullies and those who did nothing to prevent such incidents (Casebeer, 2012; Pittaro, 2008; Vossekuil, Fein, Reddy, Borum, & Modzeleski, 2002).

To compound matters further, the advent of the Internet and its obvious, vast capabilities to limitlessly transcend well beyond the physical world, has directly contributed to an increasingly growing phenomenon, whereby bullies have moved from the school's physical grounds into cyberspace (Campbell, 2005). Cyberbullying victims, as they are known within the research and practitioner literature, have described this contemporary form of bullying as relentless, inescapable, ruthless, and even more disturbing than traditional forms of bullying because, its potential reach is inexplicably vast, infinite, and immediate (Campbell, 2005; Pittaro, 2008). According to researchers, incidents, trends, and patterns relative to cyberbullying have contributed significantly to increases in juvenile deviancy where youth are using various forms of technology, including cellphones, tablets, computers, and other electronic devices to harass and-emotionally abuse targeted victims" (Lam, Cheng, & Liu, 2013). Bullying via the Internet, hereafter referred to as *cyberbullying* for clarity and consistency, can be initiated through every form of electronic media with Internet access, including email, instant messaging, chat rooms, social media, gaming systems, and similar technology (Patchin & Hinduja, 2014). Without a doubt, modern-day youth rely heavily, if not exclusively, on the Internet to socialize and in this context, to torment and harass peers. For that reason, indications suggest that the prevalence of cyberbullying will continue to strengthen and significantly increase in both incidents and the number of victims affected (Dooley, Pyzalski & Cross, 2009).

Researchers have indicated that the increase in incidents of cyberbullying will stem, albeit speculatively, from the absence of evidence-based intervention and prevention-based programs (Dooley et al., 2009). The lack of prevention programs in particular has manifested into a completely new and unique social problem like that of cyberstalking and other evolving crimes of the Internet, which if not addressed, will worsen and multiply (Dooley et al., 2009). Without comprehensive prevention and intervention strategies in place, cyberbullying will continue to elude and intensify as today's youth have virtually unlimited access to the Internet, most of which is unsupervised, not scrutinized, nor carefully monitored by adults (Slonje, Smith, & Frisen, 2012). While the traditional concerns of bullying still exist in relation to cyberbullying, additional trepidations have since surfaced now that bullying has evolved and expanded into cyberspace. The anonymity of the bully and his or her increased access to peers outside of the typical school day and beyond the school grounds has only enhanced and empowered the destructive, persistent, and limitless reach of the modern-day bully (Slonje et al., 2012). The detrimental influences of cyberbullying need to be further examined within the same constructs as traditional bullying due to the recent increases in highly publicized cases, involving cyberbullying, as well as society's heightened awareness as to how technology directly perpetuates such incidents.

Simply stated, cyberbullying remains a serious social problem for school officials, criminal justice practitioners because the phenomenon has been associated with school shootings, suicides, and poor academic performance leading to school failure, as well as acts of delinquency (Casebeer, 2012). More importantly, cyberbullying cannot be addressed using the commonly employed 'one-size-fits-all' approach used in criminal justice policy and practice because cyberbullying is a complex, systemic societal problem requiring a deeper understanding of the variables for which it is associated (Casebeer, 2012). Effective responses to combatting cyberbullying need to be introduced, adopted, and implemented so that the burden of preventing and addressing such aversive deviant behaviors does not rest solely with school officials, but rather in collaboration with criminal justice practitioners.

LITERATURE REVIEW

An estimated 657 million people worldwide have daily access to the Internet and that figure will undoubtedly rise considerably in response to constantly evolving advancements in technology (Marcum, Higgins, Freiberger, & Ricketts, 2014). As usage of the Internet has admittedly grown exponentially, so has the prevalence of online cruelty and criminality in the form of cybercrimes (Marcum et al., 2014). While cybercrimes are still considered relatively 'new' in comparison to traditional 'street' crimes that occur in the physical realm, one of the most widely recognized of all the cybercrimes continues to be that of cyberbullying, particularly during adolescence (Marcum et al., 2014). This increase is mostly attributed to the fact that today's youth have unlimited access to the Internet through portable electronic devices, including cellphones, tablets, computers, and even gaming consoles such as Xbox and PlayStation (Lam, Cheng, & Liu, 2013). Tokunaga (2010) estimated that the majority of youths in the United States, more than 97% of American children and adolescents, access the Internet daily through one or more of the electronic mediums and finds that the age of Internet exposure and usage is decreasing. These findings suggest that younger, elementary school-aged children are now vulnerable to being cyberbullied (Tokunaga, 2010).

Although bullying among youth, has had longstanding concerns, the obscurity of cyberbullying compounds the difficulty in identifying and intervening in order to stop such incidents, or at a minimum, significantly reduce the prevalence of such behaviors (Feinberg & Robey, 2009). Extensive research has been conducted concerning the nature of bullying as well as the theoretical explanations behind the significant growth and widespread diversity of bullying behaviors (Addington, 2013; Dixon, 2008). However, minimal research has been performed in the United States as to how incidents of cyberbullying correlate to various types of criminal victimization. Despite the increasing level of concern associated with the occurrence of cyberbullying incidents, there is a noticeable paucity of scientific research on the topic of cyberbullying and its association to criminal victimization.

Current research relating to incidents of bullying in children and adolescents have focused on how the environment in which the child lives and interacts with peers, caregivers, and adults, influences bullying behaviors, while cyberbullying focuses on new harmful implications of technology-initiated bullying (Patchin & Hinduja, 2014).

The research literature clearly acknowledged that cyberbullying victimization can result in significant emotional harm because it is essentially inescapable, relentless, and has far-reaching and limitless capabilities (Brockenbrough, 2001; Davis, Reich, & James, 2014; Donegan, 2012; Farrington, Loeber, Stallings, & Ttofi, 2011; Gini & Espelage, 2014; Gradinger, Strohmeier, & Spiel, 2009). Victims of "traditional" bullying often experience depression, anxiety, low self-esteem, physiological complaints, problems concentrating, school failure, and school avoidance whereas targets of cyberbullying suffer equal, if not greater harm in relation to the aforementioned difficulties, including psychological impairment (Li, 2007a; Li, 2007b; National Crime Prevention Council, 2014; Patchin & Hinduja, 2014; Schneider, O'Donnell, Stueve, & Coulter, 2012). The hurtful rumors, insinuations, and other malicious information being disseminated about the targeted victims can be transmitted broadly, instantaneously, and can be difficult, if not impossible, to remove anything related to the cyberbullying incidents once it has entered cyberspace (Feinberg & Robey, 2009).

Cyberbullying perpetrators can also remain anonymous whereas the heightened state of anxiety in not knowing the identity of the perpetrator or perpetrators can result in victims becoming hyper-vigilant in terms of constantly surveying their social environment, both cyber and physical, to avoid such malicious encounters (Pittaro, 2008). Incidents of cyberbullying can therefore lead to severe psychological distress, externalized criminal violence, and suicide in some victims who might feel as if they cannot escape the relentless barrage of hurtful information being disseminated by the perpetrators or bystanders (Feinberg & Robey, 2009). When combined with the anonymity of the perpetrator and the unknown location of where the cyberbullying originated online, jurisdictional matters become convoluted for law enforcement in not just identifying the perpetrator, but also in charging the perpetrator with crimes for which they can be legally prosecuted to the fullest extent of the law (Pittaro, 2008).

The investigation into the specific tactics used in bullying must be evaluated further in order to formulate a consistent way of dealing with the issue across multiple platforms, with the principal struggle coming from the fast-paced, continuous growth, and development of technology (Donegan, 2012). The research that does exist has mostly evaluated traditional bullying behaviors without regard to evaluating the unique characteristics associated with cyberbullying. For example, Morrison (2002) examined bullying and victimization from a restorative justice approach but did not address any elements of cyberbullying. Brockenbrough (2001), along with Farrington and colleagues (2011) also examined peer victimization and bullying, but without regard to cyberbullying. These studies suggest that research has not yet 'caught up' with the many widespread advances in technology used to terrorize victims, particularly younger individuals who may not have the cognitive coping skills and access to resources intended to obstruct, or at the very least minimize, deflect incidents of cyberbullying. The research concerning victimization and bullying must be reorganized to include a specific focus on the unique characteristics of, and influences in relation to, cyberbullying. Hence, the literature review that follows provides a sound, scientific baseline and highlights the identified gap of scholarly information available relative to cyberbullying.

CONTEMPORARY RESEARCH

Cyberbullying research that leads to a more comprehensive understanding of its profound influences on today's youth is important for many reasons. To begin, adolescence is one of the most critical stages in the development of emotional and cognitive schemes in an individual's life that will ultimately shape and influence the adult personality (Erdur-Baker, 2010). Secondly, cyberbullying is a phenomenon experienced by more than half of all high school students and even more middle school students (Kowalksi & Limber, 2007). Cyberbullying victimization can result in unyielding mental health ramifications that are self-destructive, including but not limited to, abusing drugs and alcohol as well as debilitating suicidal thoughts and ideations, and in some cases, retaliatory criminal behaviors and actions (Erdur-Baker, 2010). The importance of the relatively recent research pertaining to cyberbullying is that society is only now beginning to accept, but also expect, that electronic communication can be emotionally and physically harmful to the recipients of such targeted loathing and hostility.

Gini and Espelage (2014) concluded that cyberbullying victimization is related to an increased risk of suicidal ideations, thoughts, and attempts among targeted youth. For generations, traditional bullying was perceived to be an inevitable, and in most cases, a customary rite of passage for youth (Gini & Espelage, 2014). On the contrary, such behaviors can lead to a wide range of physiological and psychological concerns. Regardless as to whether bullying behaviors are carried out in person or online, bullying has been well documented within the pediatric and psychiatric research literature, concurrently and longitudinally, but not to the same depth and degree within the criminal justice literature (Gini & Espelage, 2014). As noted, the adverse consequences of such victimization are diverse and varied; nevertheless, cyberbullying is a risk factor for extremely destructive behaviors, including impelling the victim to commit suicide, whether performed overtly or covertly by the cyberbullying perpetrator (Gini & Espelage, 2014). The American Academy of Pediatrics has advised pediatricians to ask probing questions concerning bullying incidents during wellness examinations and patient visits and to screen for possible suicidal ideations and behaviors during these visits (Gini & Espelage, 2014). Victimization, including bullying-related incidents of suicide, have been clearly identified within the bullying literature and should therefore, be emphasized and addressed uniformly and consistently within school and community-based programs (Gini & Espelage, 2014).

Fanti, Demetriou, and Hawa (2012) recommend that future studies should explore the possible relationship among cyberbullying involvement, reporting, and the existence of effective coping strategies in greater depth. Moreover, research that concerns the association between cyberbullying and at-risk behaviors, including criminal victimization is urgently needed. Researchers support inclusion of cyberbullying prevention strategies in existing anti-bullying programs, but such programs must be shared throughout the entire adolescent school population and rather than being directed at the identified individual bullies or those who are perceived to be most at-risk for victimization/perpetration (Campbell, 2005; Kowalski, Limber, & Agatston, 2008; Williams & Guerra, 2007).

The transmutation of traditional bullying from the physical to the virtual world (i.e., cyberbullying) is a direct response to the advent of the Internet and the continued expansion of technology in which harmful communication can flourish (Davis, Reich, & James, 2014). Physical separation of the bully and the victim is no longer a limitation in the frequency, scope, and depth of harm being experienced by victims and doled out by perpetrators. As instances of bullying are no longer restricted to real world, physical settings, cyberbullying victimization has essentially worsened beyond traditional bullying, and as a direct result, cyberbullying is perceived to be inescapable, unavoidable, and incessant by targeted victims (Hinduja & Patchin, 2011; Patchin & Hinduja, 2006). The lack of a defined physical location in regard to potential criminal victimization creates a host of challenging issues for effective criminal justice responses and intervention due to perceived legal and jurisdictional limitations (Pittaro, 2008).

Rocque and Paternoster (2011) emphasized that one of the strongest findings within-juvenile delinquency literature is the relationship between school disengagement and involvement in the criminal justice system. The information within this chapter will contribute to the scientific literature by providing additional information regarding the demographic characteristics of adolescents most likely to be impacted by cyberbullying. Knowing these demographic characteristics can assist law enforcement officers in understanding the role of social-ecological theory in the application of bullying prevention programs that are designed to minimize juvenile disengagement, which in turn could reduce the all-to-familiar, school to prison pipeline (Meiners, 2011).

Cyberbullies use varieties of deceitful, manipulative tactics, including impersonating, outing and trickery, photo shopping, exclusion/ostracism, and denigration, all of which are highly visible to an indefinite audience (Hinduja & Patchin, 2008; Kowalksi, Limber & Agatson, 2008). Cyberbullies engage in mostly

137

passive-aggressive tactics that are intended to incessantly harass and provoke fear in their intended victims (Kowalksi et al., 2008). Instances of cyberbullying may include, but are not limited to emails, chatrooms, voting/rating websites, blogging sites, online gaming sites, virtual worlds, instant messaging, and text messaging, all of which are readily available at the-disposal of the cyberbully/perpetrator (Hinduja & Patchin, 2008; Kowalksi et al., 2008).

The disinhibition associated with cyberbullying incidents contributes to the extremity of hateful and harmful comments being spewed because it increases the perpetrator's level of confidence in saying something that would not likely be said in a face-to-face encounter (Bryce & Fraser, 2013). That is, deindividuation research suggests that individuals will behave differently online in comparison to face-to-face encounters (Kowalski et al., 2014). When online, individuals tend to say and do things that they normally would not do or say in a face-to-face encounter (Kowalksi et al., 2014). As a generalization, cyberbullies lack empathy for their hurtful behaviors; thereby, suggesting that lower feelings of empathy result in higher frequencies of cyberbullying (Lazuras, Barkoukis, Ourda, & Tsorbatzoudis, 2013). For instance, Ang and Goh (2010) concluded that male and female adolescent participants with low empathy levels were correlated with higher cyberbullying incidents, including incidents leading to victimization.

CYBERBULLYING VICTIMIZATION

Age

When evaluating cyberbullying, one must consider age since it is an important attribute to reflect upon from a research perspective. The age onset of cyberbullying appears to be decreasing as younger users' access the Internet with far more frequency than in past years (Willard, 2007). In addition, cyberbullying can continue into young adulthood, but higher prevalence rates have been recorded during the middle school years (Cunningham & Delaney, 2008; Slonje & Smith, 2008; Smith et al., 2008). Some research has found that cyberbullying increases with age (Vandenbosch & Van Cleemput, 2008b), whereas other studies uncovered no significant relationship concerning age (Hinduja & Patchin, 2008; Patchin & Hinduja, 2006). Therefore, the prevalence of cyberbullying as far as age is concerned, varies from study to study with no agreed upon percentages, yet at least anecdotally, most would agree that the prevalence of cyberbullying among adolescents is pronounced (den Hamer, Konijn, & Keijer, 2014). That being said, adolescents are the prime target group for cyberbullying research since evidence suggests that cyberbullying is immersed heavily within adolescent culture.

Gender

To date, research findings regarding the relationship between cyberbullying and gender remain unclear and mostly speculative (Slonje & Smith, 2008; Smith et al., 2008). However, with the perpetration and victimization of traditional bullying, males and females engage in and are the recipients of distinct types of bullying; thereby, establishing clear gender distinctions (Olweus, 1992). Hinduja and Patchin (2008) emphasized that gender differences in cyberbullying research outcomes may be related to sample size, assessment measures, socioeconomic status, and geographic location to name a few. However, anecdotal evidence indicated that girls engage in indirect forms of cyberbullying intended to disrupt social relationships more than males (Hinduja & Patchin, 2008). In contrast, several studies have concluded that adolescent boys are more likely than girls to be perpetrators of cyberbullying (Calvete, Orue, & Este vez, 2010; Dehue, Bolman, & Vo llink, 2008; Erdur-Baker, 2010; Fanti, Demetriou, & Hawa, 2012; Li, 2006; Li, 2007a). Other studies have determined that adolescent girls are more likely to engage in cyberbullying (Holfeld & Grabe, 2012; Kowalski & Limber, 2007; Pornari & Wood, 2010). Lastly, some studies have found no significant differences between the genders (Hinduja & Patchin, 2008; Smith et al., 2008). Admittedly, more research is necessary due to the conflicting findings that have been reported to date.

Reporting Victimization

Most studies do not focus on whether cyberbullying victims report being victimized, but if reporting is included, it is combined with reporting to a peer, teacher, parent, or another adult (Addington, 2013). Unlike studies that have focused on traditional bullying, cyberbullying research has rarely examined whether victims report their experiences to law enforcement (Addington, 2013). Addington (2013) determined that cyberbullying victims are more likely to inform a parent or friends as opposed to law enforcement authorities. One obvious reason why victims report such incidents to parents and friends is that the harassment is likely occurring outside of school hours since most schools do not allow cellphones to be accessed during the school day (Addington, 2013; Watkins & Maume, 2011). However, Tokunaga (2010) concluded that reporting the victimization to a parent occurs with less frequency than one would hope. The most common response from parents is to utilize avoidance strategies, namely deleting the messages, which is a short-term, typically ineffective response to a long-term problem (Parris, Varjas, Meyers, & Cutts, 2012; Tokunaga, 2010).

The primary reason cited as to why cyberbullying victims do not report their victimization to an adult, particularly a parent, is because the victim believes that the parent will either closely monitor and limit his or her access to electronic devices, or take the devices away altogether (Addington, 2013; Kowalski, Limber, & Agatson, 2012; Tokunaga, 2010). In fact, McQuade, Colt, and Meyer (2009) noted a marked decrease in instances of reporting from the preteen to teen years because the victims felt that the parents would respond by limiting their Internet access. Conversely, McQuade and colleagues (2009) reported a marked increase in the number of cyberbullying victims who informed friends from the preteen to teen years, which reaffirmed the victim's distrust of the parents' reaction or response, as well as that of other adults, to being cyberbullied.

Criminalization of Cyberbullying

Even more disturbing are those cases of cyberbullying in which victims are persistently harassed to the point where they take their own life. While it is not necessarily a new concept, the term *cyberbullicide*, has been used to describe how cyberbullying can contribute to the victim's decision to attempt suicide. In a 2010 survey administered to 2,000 middle school students, Hinduja and Patchin (2010) reported that cyberbullying victims were nearly twice as likely to attempt suicide in comparison to those who were not cyberbullied. Interestingly, the same study revealed that cyberbullying perpetrators were 1.5 times as likely to report having attempted suicide in comparison to those who were not cyberbullying perpetrators (Hinduja & Patchin, 2010).

While cyberbullying cannot definitively be the sole cause of adolescents who have attempted suicide, cyberbullying has been shown to increase the risk of suicide due to amplified feelings of depression, desperation, isolation, and hopelessness (Hinduja & Patchin, 2010). For example, in 2006, Megan Meier, who was 13 years old at the time, committed suicide following an incident where a neighbor created a fictitious profile on the social media site, Myspace, pretending to be a boy who expressed a romantic interest in Megan (Burton, Florell, & Wygant, 2013). The messages were initially thoughtful and innocently flirtatious but turned cruel and hurtful soon thereafter (Burton et al., 2013).-The neighbor who concocted this plan was criminally charged in one of the nation's first attempts to criminalize cyberbullying because they had encouraged Megan to commit suicide through their conversations with one another (Burton et al., 2013). Two years after Megan's death, the first cyberbullying trial was held within the United States in which the neighbor was successfully prosecuted (Burton et al., 2013). The trial drew international attention and condemnation, but more importantly, it brought cyberbullying to the forefront, prompting further research into this relatively new phenomenon (Benzmiller, 2013; Burton et al., 2013).

The Megan Meier case was only one in a series of highly publicized cases that followed in which teens committed suicide in response to being cyberbullied (Benzmiller, 2013). In reaction to widespread public outcry, politicians at all levels of government became involved by drafting and subsequently passing several legislative acts intended to create civil and criminal sanctions against cyberbullying perpetrators (Benzmiller, 2013). However, successfully criminalizing cyberbullying acts on a large-scale has proven to be difficult. In 2009, the *Megan Meier Cyberbullying Prevention Act* was drafted and introduced on the federal level in recognition of 13-year-old Megan Meier (Benzmiller, 2013). The bill, which called for imprisonment and/or a fine for any individual using "electronic communication to harass another person or cause him or her emotional distress" (Benzmiller, 2013, p.932), was introduced to the House Committee on Crime, Terrorism, and Homeland Security; however, the committee did not take action because the bill, as it was originally drafted, unconstitutionally threatened free speech as safeguarded under the First Amendment (Benzmiller, 2013).

At the state level, legislators have created similar statutes aimed to criminalize cyberbullying behaviors by charging those who bully others with a misdemeanor resulting in a fine and/or short term of imprisonment, depending on the severity of the cyberbullying incidents (Benzmiller, 2013). However, as in the *Megan Meier Cyberbullying Prevention* bill that was proposed, cyberbullying statutes at the state level have been criticized and challenged for failing to safeguard constitutionally protected free speech under the First Amendment (Benzmiller, 2013). While the legalities of cyberbullying legislation are still being debated, anecdotal evidence has suggested that parents are supportive of such legislation, including criminally charging perpetrators by the police agencies.

POLICE INVOLVEMENT WITH CYBERBULLYING

Very little research has been conducted in which police involvement in incidents of cyberbullying are considered; thereby, suggesting that police involvement is infrequent. As a result, little is known as to how the police have responded to incidents of cyberbullying victimization (Addington, 2013). Even when an adult is informed of cyberbullying behaviors, the police are typically not contacted; however, McQuade and colleagues (2009) claim that it is because the parents are mostly uncertain about involving the police in such matters. School officials are even less likely to involve the police in matters of cyberbullying but will instead report the victimization to the parents and leave the decision with them about whether they want to pursue the issue and file criminal charges (Kowalski et al., 2008). Further, research indicates that school officials might be hesitant or reluctant to report cyberbullying incidents to the police, especially when incidents occurred off school grounds, outside school hours, and may involve adolescents from another school (McQuade et al., 2009; Kowalski et al., 2008).

Nevertheless, serious allegations should be reported to the police, especially if the wrongdoing involves extortion, stalking, or threats to physically harm the victim (Kowalski, Limber, & Agatson, 2012). Therefore, the police should take the lead in the investigation of criminal wrongdoing while school administrators pursue internal violations of school or district-wide policies (Kowalski et al., 2012). To increase police involvement, McQuade and colleagues (2009) recommend-that the police utilize existing criminal laws including harassment, stalking, and terroristic threats to name a few; particularly if the state does not have a specific cyberbullying law in effect.

However, while schools serve a vital role in addressing cyberbullying, directing school officials to essentially police cyberbullying violations, even when those alleged violations do not occur during school hours or on school property, is not the most sound, logical approach (Fenn, 2013). Indeed, there are additional challenges to consider. For one, what if the victim is a member of that school district but the perpetrator is not? Secondly, it is important to know whether a student's constitutional rights are being violated regarding the First Amendment's freedom of speech clause. Determining when the speech becomes threatening, hurtful, or hateful can be quite subjective and therefore, open to legal interpretation.

POLICY IMPLICATIONS

As previously noted, there is no single, universally agreed upon definition of cyberbullying other than the acknowledgment that this behavior is inherently negative, it entails unwanted harassing behavior, and it is perpetrated through electronic means, namely the Internet (Stewart & Fritsch, 2011). While it has already been established that adolescents can be criminally charged for violating state and federal statutes that prohibit such behaviors, cyberbullying is not always indistinguishable to criminal actions that are legally proscribed within the state and federal penal codes. If specific statutes do not exist, cyberbullying perpetrators can be prosecuted using other cybercrime statutes, including cyberstalking and online harassment, or civilly through torts of defamation, libel, or intentional infliction of emotional stress; therefore, specific cyberbullying statutes are needed (Kowalski et al., 2012).

Stewart and Fritsch (2011) proposed that cyberbullying be categorized as cyber-deviance or cyber-violence since some acts of cyberbullying (i.e. – being ignored by others) are not necessarily violations of the penal code and within the legally proscribed definition of a crime. Although federal law enforcements agencies are the leading authorities in combatting cybercrime and enforcing cyber-laws, they have traditionally stood aside in matters involving cyberbullying unless the crime is particularly heinous or when local and state laws were deemed inadequate (Stewart &

Fritsch, 2011). However, Nathan and Sisaye (2015), have noted that law enforcement officers are more likely today to address cyberbullying cases. In fact, Nathan and Sisaye (2015) cited a 2014 survey by the Cyberbullying Research Center, which concluded that 94% of School Resource Officers (SROs) and 82% of traditional police officers agreed that cyberbullying incidents are serious and therefore, merit a police response.

Responses from law enforcement regarding incidents of cyberbullying have been predominately reactive rather than proactive because police agencies do not continuously or randomly surveil users' posts to web pages so as not to infringe upon constitutionally-safeguarded free speech and privacy (Stewart & Fritsch, 2011). However, school officials can and should alert law enforcement to these incidents if the school can clearly demonstrate a substantial disruption stemming from cyberbullying (Stewart & Fritsch, 2011). For example, in *J.S. v. Bethlehem Area School District* (2000), a student was expelled for creating a website that depicted graphic images of severed heads that included encouragement for the hiring of a "hitman" and other threatening comments about a specific teacher (Stewart & Fritsch, 2011). The Commonwealth Court of Pennsylvania upheld the expulsion of the student because the school had clearly demonstrated substantial disruption in that the website could be accessed from school computers and because the intended audience consisted of administrators, teachers, and students (Stewart & Fritsch, 2011). The behaviors and actions exhibited by the student were already prohibited and prosecutable under existing penal codes, including terroristic threats, harassment, menacing, stalking, and hate crimes, all of which can be applied to the prosecution of cyberbullying in jurisdictions that lack specific cyberbullying statutes (Stewart & Fritsch, 2011).

Although the reporting of cyberbullying incidents has increased, particularly regarding the reporting of incidents to adults, most adolescents do not feel comfortable reporting cyberbullying to law enforcement for fear that it could make the situation worse by enraging the perpetrator. When coupled with the vagueness of some cyberbullying criminal statutes, the lack of reporting makes investigating and prosecuting such crimes undeniably difficult (Stewart & Fritsch, 2011). This must change; however, the problem is compounded by the lack of resources needed to adequately aid law enforcement, particularly financially limited law enforcement agencies, which comprise the bulk of those within the United States (Stewart & Fritsch, 2011). For instance, nearly half of all local law enforcement departments within the United States employ 10 or fewer sworn officers. Further, smaller police departments have limited resources and training in cybercrimes, especially behaviors that comprise cyberbullying (Stewart & Fritsch, 2011). That being said, it is likely that smaller-sized police departments have had exposure to any type of formal training exclusively dedicated to investigating cybercrime in general but cyberbullying in particular. In turn, cybercrime investigations are likely to be limited to incidents that involve more recognizable and familiar cybercrimes such as online child pornography and exploitation, online fraud, and hacking. Moreover, these incidents are only investigated with aid and resources that are provided by state and federal law enforcement agencies (Stewart & Fritsch, 2011).

Therefore, it is strongly suggested that consistent, uniform training be extended to local law enforcement agencies, particularly smaller-sized departments that make up the bulk of America's law enforcement agencies with limited officers and resources, and that this training be provided by qualified state and federal law enforcement agencies that specialize in the investigation of cybercrimes, specifically cyberbullying (International Association of Chiefs of Police, 2010). Additionally, the procurement of resources is necessary to aid in the investigations, once again within smaller, local departments that have a limited staffing of sworn police officers. One suggestion would be to provide such smaller-sized law enforcement agencies with access to state and federal databases to aid in cyberbullying investigations. In addition, the nation's criminal laws must be amended to keep pace with-ever-evolving cybercrimes. Cyberbullying cannot be ignored nor discounted as being less serious or less worthy of investigation and prosecution in comparison to other criminal acts, cyber or otherwise, that result in victimization. If police officers and prosecutors are educated, trained, and knowledgeable about cyberbullying, such criminal justice practitioners will hopefully understand and appreciate the negative short and long-term ramifications that cyberbullying can have on targeted victims, and not dismiss or discount such acts as being trivial or less worthy of arrest and subsequent prosecution.

Stewart and Fritsch's (2011) study concluded that law enforcement expressed the need for uniform training, particularly for first responding officers who are initially tasked with interviewing victims and witnesses, collecting, and preserving electronic evidence, and subsequently providing courtroom testimony. Stewart and Fritsch's study also emphasized the need for a national certification program to accommodate and compliment cyberbullying training; thereby, ensuring the acquisition of reliable, standardized information that pertains to cyberbullying (2011). This well-defined need for cyberbullying training must not be exclusively intended for law enforcement, but should extend to prosecutors, defense attorneys, judges, and corrections officials so that they too, may appreciate and acknowledge the harmful effects of cyberbullying and its association with criminal victimization.

Resource needs must include, but not be limited to, equipment, support from leadership, and access to crime data, but more importantly, the formation of collaborative relationships such as joint task forces who are responsible for responding to the multi-jurisdictional nature of cyberbullying (Stewart & Fritsch, 2011). The formation of joint task forces that consist of federal, state, and local law enforcement agencies has many advantages, one of which includes access to information and intelligence that would otherwise be unavailable or limited, particularly within smaller police departments (Stewart & Fritsch, 2011). Since cybercrimes in general are evolving and expanding rapidly, the creation of a cybercrime divisions or units with the inclusion of a state police forensic labs to examine electronic evidence are also highly recommended (Stewart & Fritsch, 2011). In summary, prior research validates and affirms the need for more accurate statistical data that tracks cyberbullying incidents, trends, and patterns to better understand this behavior, as it pertains to both victims and perpetrators of such incidents.

Creation or Amendment of Cyberbullying Criminal Statutes

As of September 2014, 49 states and the District of Columbia had enacted bullying statutes apart from Montana (Hinduja & Patchin, 2014). Twenty of the 49 states that adopted such statutes included a subsection to address cyberbullying however, only 12 of those states included a criminal sanction specifically for cyberbullying (Hinduja & Patchin, 2014). McQuade, Colt, and Meyer (2009) emphasized that cyberbullying violations and subsequent criminal sanctions are not clearly outlined within the nation's existing laws which have led to vague legal interpretation of the language contained within the statutes. Therefore, to fulfill their role as law enforcers, police officers must be educated about the proper legal guidelines and processes required to investigate, criminally-charge, and prosecute cyberbullying crimes (Stewart & Fritsch, 2011).

RECOMMENDATIONS FOR FUTURE RESEARCH

Federal law enforcement agencies have assumed the lead in combating cybercrimes; however, cyberbullying, due to its localized nature, is more likely to be investigated by state or local law enforcement, yet such investigations to date have been severely strained (Stewart & Fritsch, 2011). A national study, would yield pertinent information necessary to determine and address apparent deficiencies within the nation's criminal justice system in response to combating cyberbullying on a larger scale, with all levels of law enforcement being educated, trained, and adequately equipped with training and resources.

LGBTQ Youth and Cyberbullying

The necessity for further investigation of demographic variables pertaining to the cyberbullies in relation to the demographic variables of the victims is important. Although there are inherent risks to studying participants who were perpetrators and victims of cyberbullying, qualitative research is indispensable in providing multiple levels of details that are often unavailable through quantitative research, particularly those which concern the lived experiences of cyberbullying perpetrators and victims (Carduff, Murray, & Kendall, 2015). This would be particularly informative if the research focused on Lesbian, Gay, Bisexual, Transgender, and Queer (LGBTQ) and those who are physically and/or mentally challenged, since they are typically excluded from wide-scale, national surveys, yet have an incredibly high probability of cyberbullying victimization (Wiederhold, 2014). Indeed, this population of students are vulnerable. For example, in October 2012, 15-year-old Amanda Todd hanged herself approximately one month after posting a video to YouTube in which she used a series of flash cards to tell her experience of being blackmailed into exposing her breasts via webcam, and of being bullied and physically assaulted (No Bullying, 2017). The video went viral after her death, resulting in international media attention. As of February 2017, the video has had more than 12 million views (No Bullying, 2017).

Criminal justice researchers and practitioners must remain vigilant by staying abreast of emerging or evolving forms of victimization as adolescents continue to become more technologically-savvy (Raskauskas & Huynh, 2015). Future research can play a significant role in combatting cyberbullying among children and adolescents by identifying and evaluating intervention and prevention programs and strategies to ensure the programs' effectiveness and generalizability, as well as research methodology including reliability and validity, in helping adolescents to cope with victimization from cyberbullies and other similar bullying behaviors.

The importance of future research stems from the fact that early identification, evaluation, and treatment for cyberbullying victimization during adolescence can prevent the development of behaviors that place adolescents at high-risk of delinquency, self-harm, and criminal aggression. Indeed, research demonstrates that adolescents who experience victimization are at a higher-risk for developing these maladaptive behaviors in response to being victimized (Pittaro, 2008). Therefore, future research should concentrate on present and emerging forms of victimization that are related to cyberbullying and the causes, associations, and outcomes, which take place predominantly among adolescents.

CONCLUSION

With the likely upsurge in cyberbullying incidents and the probable advancement of state and federal legislation that criminalize cyberbullying behaviors, criminal justice professionals will be called upon to investigate and perhaps prosecute such crimes if criminal charges are warranted. This literature review investigated demographic variables of the victims of cyberbullying and provided implications for the criminal justice sector by offering suggestions for further research. One of the strongest predictors of becoming a cyberbully perpetrator was being in a prior role as a cyber-victim (Vendenbosch & Van Cleemput, 2008b). In response, criminal justice professionals need to be able to minimize the incidents of cyberbullying by responding quickly and appropriately to reported incidents of cyberbullying and work closely with schools, parents, and victims in a positive, supportive role. More research is needed into this global epidemic to better understand and deter victimization of youth.

REFERENCES

Addington, L. A. (2013). Reporting and clearance of cyberbullying incidents: Applying "offline" theories to online victims. *Journal of Contemporary Criminal Justice, 29*(4), 454–474. doi:10.1177/1043986213507399

Ang, R. P., & Goh, D. H. (2010). Cyberbullying among adolescents: The role of affective and cognitive empathy, and gender. *Child Psychiatry and Human Development, 41*(4), 387–397. doi:10.100710578-010-0176-3 PMID:20238160

Benzmiller, H. (2013). The cyber-Samaritans: Exploring criminal liability for the "innocent" bystanders of cyberbullying. *Northwestern University Law Review, 107*(2), 927–962.

Brockenbrough, K. K. (2001). *Peer victimization and bullying prevention among middle school students* (Doctoral dissertation). Retrieved form ProQuest Dissertations and Theses, database. (UMI No. 3000186)

Bryce, J., & Fraser, J. (2013). 'It's common sense that it's wrong': Young people's perceptions and experiences of cyberbullying. *Cyberpsychology, Behavior, and Social Networking, 16*(11), 783–787. doi:10.1089/cyber.2012.0275 PMID:23745618

Bullying, N. (2017). *The top six unforgettable cases of cyberbullying*. Retrieved April 10, 2018, from https://nobullying.com/six-unforgettable-cyber-bullying-cases/

Burton, K., Florell, D., & Wygant, D. B. (2013). The role of peer attachment and normative beliefs about aggression on traditional bullying and cyberbullying. *Psychology in the Schools, 50*(2), 103–115. doi:10.1002/pits.21663

Calvete, E., Orue, I., Este'vez, A., Villardón, L., & Padilla, P. (2010). Cyberbullying in adolescents: Modalities and aggressors' profiles. *Computers in Human Behavior, 26*(5), 1128–1135. doi:10.1016/j.chb.2010.03.017

Campbell, M. A. (2005). Cyberbullying: An old problem in a new guise? *Australian Journal of Guidance & Counselling, 15*(2), 68–76. doi:10.1375/ajgc.15.1.68

Carduff, E., Murray, S. A., & Kendall, M. (2015). Methodological developments in qualitative longitudinal research: The advantages and challenges of regular telephone contact with participants in a qualitative longitudinal interview study. *BMC Research, 8*(1), 142–152. doi:10.118613104-015-1107-y PMID:25886625

Casebeer, C. (2012). School bullying: Why quick fixes do not prevent school failure. *Preventing School Failure, 56*(3), 165–171. doi:10.1080/1045988X.2011.633283

Cunningham, N. J., & Delaney, N. (2008, August). *Relationship between traditional bullying and cyberbullying in middle school girls.* Paper presented at a meeting of the American Psychological Association, Boston, MA.

Davis, K., Reich, J., & James, C. (2014). The changing landscape of peer aggression: A Literature review on cyberbullying and interventions. *Journal of Youth Development, 9*(1), 129–142. doi:10.5195/JYD.2014.77

Dehue, F., Bolman, C., & Völlink, T. (2008). Cyberbullying: Youngsters' experiences and parental perception. *Cyberpsychology & Behavior, 11*(8), 217–223. doi:10.1089/cpb.2007.0008 PMID:18422417

Dempsey, J. (2010). *Introduction to private security.* Belmont, CA: Cengage.

den Hamer, A., Konijn, E. A., & Keijer, M. G. (2014). Cyberbullying behavior and adolescents' use of media with antisocial content: A cyclic process model. *Cyberpsychology, Behavior, and Social Networking, 17*(2), 74–81. doi:10.1089/cyber.2012.0307 PMID:24015985

Dixon, R. (2008). Developing and integrating theory on school bullying. *Journal of School Violence, 7*(1), 83–114. doi:06 doi:10.1300/J202v07nOI

Donegan, R. (2012). Bullying and cyberbullying: History, statistics, law, prevention and analysis. *The Elon Journal of Undergraduate Research in Communications, 3*(1), 33–42.

Dooley, J. J., Pyżalski, J., & Cross, D. (2009). Cyberbullying versus face-to-face bullying: A theoretical and conceptual review. *Zeitschrift Für Psychologie. The Journal of Psychology, 217*(4), 182–188. doi:10.1027/0044-3409.217.4.182

Erdur-Baker, O. (2010). Cyberbullying and its correlation to traditional bullying, gender and frequent and risky usage of Internet-mediated communication tools. *New Media & Society, 12*(1), 109–125. doi:10.1177/1461444809341260

Fanti, K. A., Demetriou, A. G., & Hawa, V. V. (2012). A longitudinal study of cyberbullying: Examining risk and protective factors. *European Journal of Developmental Psychology*, *9*(2), 168–181. doi:10.1080/17405629.2011.643169

Farrington, D. P., Loeber, R., Stallings, R., & Ttofi, M. M. (2011). Bullying perpetration and victimization as predictors of delinquency and depression in the Pittsburgh youth study. *Journal of Aggression, Conflict and Peace Research*, *3*(2), 74–81. doi:10.1108/17596591111132882

Feinberg, T., & Robey, N. (2009). Cyberbullying. *Education Digest*, *74*(7), 26–31.

Fenn, M. (2013, April). A web of liability: Does new cyberbullying legislation put public schools in a sticky situation? *Fordham Law Review*, *81*, 2729–2768. Retrieved from http://fordhamlawreview.org/assets/pdfs/Vol_81/Fenn_April.pdf

Gini, G., & Espelage, D. (2014). Peer victimization, cyberbullying, and suicide risk in children and adolescents. *Journal of the American Medical Association*, *312*(5), 545–546. doi:10.1001/jama.2014.3212 PMID:25096695

Gradinger, P., Strohmeier, D., & Spiel, C. (2009). Traditional bullying and cyberbullying: Identification of risk groups for adjustment problems. *Zeitschrift FürPsychologie. The Journal of Psychology*, *217*(4), 205–213. doi:10.1027/0044-3409.217.4.205

Harrell, E. (2007). *Adolescent victimization and delinquent behavior*. El Paso, TX: LFB Publishing.

Hinduja, S., & Patchin, J. W. (2008). Cyberbullying: An exploratory analysis of factors related to offending and victimization. *Deviant Behavior*, *29*(2), 129–156. doi:10.1080/01639620701457816

Hinduja, S., & Patchin, J. W. (2010a). Bullying, cyberbullying, and suicide. *Archives of Suicide Research*, *14*(3), 206–221. doi:10.1080/13811118.2010.4941 33 PMID:20658375

Hinduja, S., & Patchin, J. W. (2010b). *Teen's use of technology*. Cyberbullying Research Center. Retrieved from Cyberbullying Research Center Website: http://www.cyberbullying.us/2010_charts/teen_tech_ use_2010.jpg

Hinduja, S., & Patchin, J. W. (2011). Cyberbullying and sexual orientation. *Cyberbullying Research Center*. Retrieved from http://cyberbullying.us/cyberbullying_sexual_orientation_fact_sheet.pdf

Hinduja, S., & Patchin, J. W. (2014). State cyberbullying laws: A brief review of state cyberbullying laws and policies. *Cyberbullying Research Center*. Retrieved from http://www.cyberbullying.us/Bullying_and_Cyberbullying_Laws.pdf

Holfeld, B., & Grabe, M. (2012). Middle school students' perspectives of and responses to cyber bullying. *Journal of Educational Computing Research*, *46*(4), 395–413. doi:10.2190/EC.46.4.e

International Association of Chiefs of Police. (2010). *Preparing and responding to cyberbullying: Tips for law enforcement*. Retrieved April 10, 2018, from http://www.theiacp.org/Portals/0/documents/pdfs/IACP_NCMEC_OJJDP_CyberbullyingTipCardforLawEnforcement.pdf

Kowalski, R. M., & Limber, S. P. (2007). Electronic bullying among middle school students. *The Journal of Adolescent Health*, *41*(6), S22–S30. doi:10.1016/j.jadohealth.2007.08.017 PMID:18047942

Kowalski, R. M., Limber, S. P., & Agatson, P. W. (2008). *Cyberbullying*. Malden, MA: Blackwell.

Kowalski, R. M., Limber, S. P., & Agatson, P. W. (2012). *Cyberbullying: Bullying in the digital age* (2nd ed.). Malden, MA: Wiley-Blackwell.

Lam, L. T., Cheng, Z., & Liu, X. (2013). Violent online games exposure and cyberbullying / victimization among adolescents. *Cyberpsychology, Behavior, and Social Networking*, *16*(3), 159–165. doi:10.1089/cyber.2012.0087 PMID:23253205

Lazuras, L., Barkoukis, V., Ourda, D., & Tsorbatzoudis, H. (2013). A process model of cyberbullying in adolescence. *Computers in Human Behavior*, *29*(3), 881–887. doi:10.1016/j.chb.2012.12.015

Li, Q. (2007a). Bullying in the new playground: Research into cyberbullying and cyber victimization. *Australasian Journal of Educational Technology*, *23*(4), 435–454. doi:10.14742/ajet.1245

Li, Q. (2007b). New bottle but old wine: A research of cyberbullying in schools. *Computers in Human Behavior*, *23*(8), 1777–1791. doi:10.1016/j.chb.2005.10.005

Lusk, B. (Producer) 2012, August 14). The relational aggression among youth: An interview with Michael Greene [Audio podcast manuscript]. *The Prevention Researcher Podcast*. Retrieved from www.tpronline.org/podcasts/transcript8.pdf

Marcum, C., Higgins, G., Freiberger, T., & Ricketts, M. (2014). Exploration of the cyberbullying victim/offender overlap by sex. *American Journal of Criminal Justice*, *39*(1), 538–548. doi:10.100712103-013-9217-3

McQuade, S. C., Colt, J. P., & Meyer, N. B. B. (2009). *Cyberbullying: Protecting kids and adults from online bullies.* Westport, CT: Praeger.

Meiners, E. R. (2011). Ending the school-to-prison pipeline: Building abolition futures. *The Urban Review, 43*(4), 547–565. doi:10.100711256-011-0187-9

Morrison, B. (2002). *Bullying and victimization in schools: A restorative justice approach.* Woden. Canberra, Australia: Australian Institute of Criminology. Retrieved from http://www.aic.gov.au/media_library/publications/tandi_pdf/tandi219.pdf

Nathan, L., & Sisaye, S. (2015, April 15). How should law enforcement respond to cyberbullying incidents? [Web log post]. Retrieved April 08, 2018, from https://www.stopbullying.gov/blog/2015/04/15/how-should-law-enforcement-respond-cyberbullying-incidents.html

National Crime Prevention Council. (2014). *Bullying: Information and resources to help prevent the serious problem of bullying.* Retrieved from http://www.ncpc.org/topics/bullying

Parris, L., Varjas, K., Meyers, J., & Cutts, H. (2012). High school students' perceptions of coping with cyberbullying. *Youth & Society, 44*(3), 284–306. doi:10.1177/0044118X11398881

Patchin, J. W., & Hinduja, S. (2006). Bullies move beyond the schoolyard: A preliminary look at cyberbullying. *Youth Violence and Juvenile Justice, 4*(2), 148–169. doi:10.1177/1541204006286288

Patchin, J. W., & Hinduja, S. (2014). *Bullying Beyond the School Yard* (2nd ed.). Newbury Park, CA: Corwin.

Pittaro, M. (2008). School violence and social control theory: An evaluation of the Columbine massacre. *International Journal of Criminal Justice Sciences, 2*(1), 1–12.

Pornari, C. D., & Wood, J. (2010). Peer and cyber aggression in secondary school students: The role of moral disengagement, hostile attribution bias, and outcome expectancies. *Aggressive Behavior, 36*(2), 81–94. doi:10.1002/ab.20336 PMID:20035548

Rauskauskas, J., & Huynh, A. (2015). The process of coping with cyberbullying: A systematic review. *Aggression and Violent Behavior, 23*(1), 118–125. doi:10.1016/j.avb.2015.05.019

Rocque, M., & Paternoster, R. (2011). Understanding the antecedents to the "school-to-jail" link. *The Journal of Criminal Law & Criminology, 101*(2), 633–665.

Schneider, S. K., O'Donnell, L., Stueve, A., & Coulter, R. W. S. (2012). Cyberbullying, school bullying, and psychological distress: A regional census of high school students. *American Journal of Public Health, 102*(1), 171–177. doi:10.2105/AJPH.2011.300308 PMID:22095343

Slonje, R., & Smith, P. K. (2008). Cyberbullying: Another main type of bullying? *Scandinavian Journal of Psychology, 49*(2), 147–154. doi:10.1111/j.1467-9450.2007.00611.x PMID:18352984

Slonje, R., Smith, P. K., & Frisen, A. (2012). The nature of cyberbullying, and strategies for prevention. *Computers in Human Behavior, 29*(1), 26–32. doi:10.1016/j.chb.2012.05.024

Stewart, D. M., & Fritsch, E. J. (2011). School and law enforcement efforts to combat cyberbullying. *Preventing School Failure, 55*(2), 79–87. doi:10.1080/1045988X.2011.539440

Tokunaga, R. (2010). Following you home from school: A critical review and synthesis of research on cyberbullying victimization. *Computers in Human Behavior, 26*(1), 277–287. doi:10.1016/j.chb.2009.11.014

Vandenbosch, H., & Van Cleemput, K. (2008). Defining cyberbullying: A qualitative research into the perceptions of youngsters. *Cyberpsychology & Behavior, 11*(4), 499–503. doi:10.1089/cpb.2007.0042 PMID:18721100

Vossekuil, B., Fein, R. A., Reddy, M., Borum, R., & Modzeleski, W. (2002). *The final report and findings of the "safe school initiative": Implications for the prevention of school attacks in the United States*. Washington, DC: U.S. Department of Education, U.S. Secret Service.

Watkins, A. M., & Maume, M. O. (2011). School victims and crime reporting. *Youth Violence and Juvenile Justice, 9*(4), 333–351. doi:10.1177/1541204011409069

Wiederhold, B. K. (2014). Cyberbullying and LGBTQ youth: A deadly combination. *Cyberpsychology, Behavior, and Social Networking, 17*(9), 569–570. doi:10.1089/cyber.2014.1521 PMID:25211134

Willard, N. (2007). *Educator's guide to cyberbullying and cyber threats*. Retrieved from http://csriu.org/cyberbully/docs/cbcteducator.pdf

Williams, R. W., & Guerra, N. G. (2007). Prevalence and predictors of Internet bullying. *The Journal of Adolescent Health, 41*(1), 14–21. doi:10.1016/j.jadohealth.2007.08.018 PMID:18047941

ADDITIONAL READING

Bauman, S., Toomey, R. B., & Walker, J. L. (2013). Associations among bullying, cyberbullying, and suicide in high school students. *Journal of Adolescence, 36*(2), 341–350. doi:10.1016/j.adolescence.2012.12.001 PMID:23332116

Cheng, K. (2012). Cyberbullying. *Neuropsychiatrie de l'Enfance et de l'Adolescence, 60*(5), S118–S119. doi:10.1016/j.neurenf.2012.05.505

Hinduja, S., & Patchin, J. W. (2010). Bullying, cyberbullying, and suicide. *Archives of Suicide Research, 14*(3), 206–221. doi:10.1080/13811118.2010.4941 33 PMID:20658375

Lee, E. B. (2017). Cyberbullying. *Journal of Black Studies, 48*(1), 57–73. doi:10.1177/0021934716678393 PMID:27805478

Litwiller, B. J., & Brausch, A. M. (2013). Cyber bullying and physical bullying in adolescent suicide: The role of violent behavior and substance use. *Journal of Youth and Adolescence, 42*(5), 675–684. doi:10.100710964-013-9925-5 PMID:23381779

Messias, E., Kindrick, K., & Castro, J. (2014). School bullying, cyberbullying, or both: Correlates of teen suicidality in the 2011 CDC youth risk behavior survey. *Comprehensive Psychiatry, 55*(5), 1063–1068. doi:10.1016/j.comppsych.2014.02.005 PMID:24768228

Moreno, M. A. (2014). Cyberbullying. *JAMA Pediatrics, 168*(5), 500–500. doi:10.1001/jamapediatrics.2013.3343 PMID:24791741

Reed, K. P., Nugent, W., & Cooper, R. L. (2015). Testing a path model of relationships between gender, age, and bullying victimization and violent behavior, substance abuse, depression, suicidal ideation, and suicide attempts in adolescents. *Children and Youth Services Review, 55*, 128–137. doi:10.1016/j.childyouth.2015.05.016

Sampasa-Kanyinga, H., Roumeliotis, P., & Xu, H. (2014). Associations between cyberbullying and school bullying victimization and suicidal ideation, plans and attempts among Canadian schoolchildren. *PLoS One, 9*(7), e102145. doi:10.1371/journal.pone.0102145 PMID:25076490

van Geel, M., Vedder, P., & Tanilon, J. (2014). Relationship between peer victimization, cyberbullying, and suicide in children and adolescents: A meta-analysis. *JAMA Pediatrics, 168*(5), 435–442. doi:10.1001/jamapediatrics.2013.4143 PMID:24615300

KEY TERMS AND DEFINITIONS

Adolescent: An individual in the developmental and physical stage of life between childhood and young adulthood.

Bullying: Abuse or mistreatment of an individual by someone who is perceived to be stronger, more powerful, and more influential.

Criminalization: A legal action that makes an activity illegal and therefore, a criminal offense.

Cyberbullying: Using electronic communication to intimidate, harass, or threaten another.

Cyberspace: The virtual environment in which communication occurs over computer networks.

Cybersuicide: A slang term used to suggest a suicide or attempted suicide influenced by one or more individuals using electronic communication.

Legislation: The act of creating and enacting laws.

School: An institution for educating children and adolescents.

Suicide: The act or intention of voluntarily taking one's own life.

Victimization: To treat someone cruelly, unfairly, or cause them physical, emotional, or sexual harm.

This research was previously published in Handbook of Research on School Violence in American K-12 Education edited by Gordon A. Crews, pages 267-285, copyright year 2019 by Information Science Reference (an imprint of IGI Global).

Chapter 7
Cyber Bullying:
Global and Local Practices on Awareness Raising

Emıne Nılufer Pembecıoglu

(iD) https://orcid.org/0000-0001-7510-6529
Istanbul University, Turkey

Hatıce Irmaklı
Istanbul University, Turkey

ABSTRACT

Cyber bullying is a serious and newly arising problem of today's world due to the negative intentions in using the recent technological improvements. However, despite its being a relatively new area, a significant number of studies conducted on this issue can be found. This chapter provides a general overview of the current literature with exemplary research to present some insight into the global and local practices in relation to any possible solution of prevention/intervention program for the cyber bullying problem. The global scale involves many studies of various scholars from several countries with different focuses while the local scale concentrates on the case of Turkey and the same of Turkish students or teachers.

INTRODUCTION[1]

Technological improvements, and new communication tools rising to the surface alongside them have introduced new ways of connection and interaction among individuals. Communication has been mostly moved to a digital, electronic and computer based platform. The recent generations who were born into a period of

DOI: 10.4018/978-1-7998-1684-3.ch007

rapid technological advancement and the ubiquitous use of electronic devices and the Internet, adapt to these tools quickly and include them in their daily routines and lives. And as expected, this situation also had positive effects on individuals and societies and life styles. Additionally, as Mishna, Cook, Gadalla, Daciuk and Solomon (2010) suggests, the exponential growth of electronic and computer-based communication and information sharing during the last decade has radically changed individuals' social interactions, learning strategies, and choice of entertainment. (p. 362)

However, the Internet and computer-based communication and interaction also created an online environment that can be used for negative purposes -and even malcontent- by everyone and more specifically, within the context of this study, mostly adolescents and teenagers. When entering the Web, a teenager moves in a space where usual barriers in physical life seem to disappear, and the connection with peers becomes easier (Mura, Topcu, Erdur-Baker & Diamantini, 2011, p. 3805). This enables the traditional form of bullying being performed at schools by the youth to be moved onto a digital platform and therefore it takes a new shape that is called "cyber bullying". This new form of bullying may have a stronger impact on children, teenagers and adolescents, moreso than the traditional one. The reason why is explained clearly by Kowalski, Limber and Agatston (2008):

Because of the nature of cyber space, a child who might wield little power over a victim face-to face may wield a great deal of power (and fear) in cyber space. More specifically, there is power in being anonymous, in assuming a false identity, in having the ability to spread rumors and lies to a wide audience, and in being able to harass a victim anywhere and anytime. (p.62)

Literacy is known to be a term mainly related to the ability to read and write, an ability that has been acquired by training. That's why most of the educational institutions prioritize media literacy as the main component of their curriculum. However, media literacy also means some kind of accomplishment, a mastership area of acquirement, attainment, a set of skills and specific forms of acquisition. Due to the fact that each society has a different form of literacy understanding, each country seems to be standing on the different point of the same ladder. Whereas some of the countries give more importance to the print data, some others value the visual sources more than the others. There seems to be more contradiction upon the traditional media and new media or social media credibility discussions. Relatively when the concept of bullying is regarded, the fallowing diagram could be useful.

Even if there were bullies around the society mainly known as a cruel and brutal fellow, a hired thug or an aggressive and violent young criminal, the actions of being bossy towards somebody else. These bullies usually discourage or frighten with threats or a domineering manner; intimidate the others. The action of bullying

Figure 1. The root of the word "bully" (http://wordvis.com/)

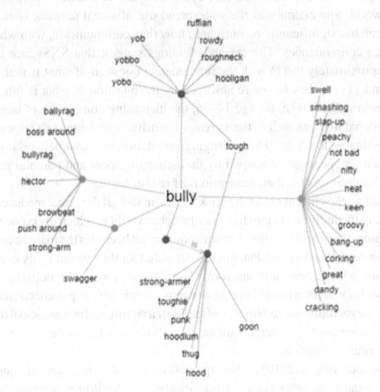

changed its character through the impact of technological substructure. Thus, the concept of cyber bullying appeared as a way to make it through more common way. As stated by Aboujaoude et all (2015) probably it's the review of an old problem gone viral. The old bullying actions were replaced by the other more technical and cruel ones in time. That's why the number of the scholarly articles on cyber bullying are more than 50.600. Whereas the link between cyber bullying seem to be a bit weak, Bhat, et all. (2010) address cyberbullying as a form of bullying using information and communications technology. So, from this perspective, it has got nothing to do with the media literacy or else.

Jackson, C. (2011) mentions a recent Pew Research Center report stating that 73% of teens between the ages of 12 and 17 use social networking, up from 55% just four years ago. Thus, sometimes it's hard for parents and educators to understand what healthy online behavior is. Jackson, states that social media can provide an opportunity for teens and adults to gain media literacy. Moreover, some researchers are finding that social media in the classroom can have positive psychological effects. Regarding this all, cyberbullying seems to be just a side effect of unhealthy media literacy style and it turns to be a behavior not to be cured or improved.

Livingstone (2014) mentions that cyber bullying is a term belonging to the adults' world. She claims that the widespread use of social network sites (SNSs) by children has significantly reconfigured how they communicate, with whom and with what consequences. The research findings suggest that SNSs face children (aged approximately 9–11) with the fundamental question of what is real or fake. By around 11–13, they are more absorbed by the question of what is fun, even if it is transgressive or fake. By age 14–16, the increasing complexity of their social and emotional lives, as well as their greater maturity, contributes to a refocusing on what is valuable for them. Their changing orientation to social networking online (and offline) appears to be shaped by their changing peer and parental relations, and has implications for their perceptions of risk of harm.

Regarding the current era as the "risk world" in fact all the posts, media channels are inviting the individuals into the risk of a cyber world in which everyone more or less becomes the bully or victim. Victimization or not becomes the main issue among the youngsters. Hinduja and Patchin (2010) state that the current study examining the extent to which a nontraditional form of peer aggression—cyberbullying—is also related to suicidal ideation among adolescents. Youth who experienced traditional bullying or cyberbullying, as either an offender or a victim, had more suicidal thoughts and were more likely to attempt suicide than those who had not experienced such forms of peer aggression.

Cowie and Colliety (2010) put the argument here in a different way. Although there is a case for sanctions, schools also have a critical role to play in preventing and reducing cyberbullying through a process of awareness-raising, (media literacy) the education of the emotions and active participation of children and young people themselves.

Livingstone and Brake (2010) noted that social networking sites provide opportunities and risks for young people. Opportunities include self presentation, learning, widening their circle of relationships, and managing privacy and intimacy. Risks are linked to opportunities and include loss of privacy, bullying, and harmful contacts. Livingstone and Brake highlighted the need for digital or media literacy initiatives related to social networking.

Defining Cyber Bullying

Due to the technological development rates, each country stands on the different step of the media literacy ladder. That means, even if the different societies use the social media or traditional media, the level of the media literacy could be different even in the same society, depending upon the geographical, educational, socio economical factors. That's why media literacy rates could be changing from one society to the other and thus, the immediate or delayed impact of the media could occur in different ways at different times.

Figure 2. Literacy rates could be different in different countries (https://ourworldindata.org/literacy)

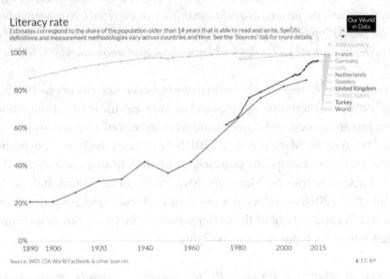

That means the types and occurrences of cyber bullying would be changing in different societies. This could easily be seen in the works of Nocentini, et all (2010) questioning cyber bullying in three European countries (Italy, Spain and Germany) or Menesini, et all (2012) trying to find out the definition of cyberbullying definition among Italian, Spanish, German, Sweden, Estonian, and French adolescents. Li, et all (2012) had a research on cyberbullying regarding a larger circle including, Australia, Austria, Canada, England, Finland, Italy, Japan, Portugal, South Korea, Spain and United States. As they put forward this seems to be "Cyberbullying in the global playground".

There are various scholars in contemporary literature who have defined cyber bullying. Since "cyber bullying" seems to be a *relatively new area* in some countries such as Turkey and it requires intensive and extensive research, there are still certain differences and variations in the conceptual framework among the researchers. According to Magsi, Agha and Magsi I. (2017), cyber or online bullying is a kind of abuse and stalking through electronic communication in which a person is threatened and intimidated (p.103). Similarly, Patchin and Hinduja (2006) defines cyber bullying as "willful and repeated harm inflicted through the medium of electronic text" (p. 152). Another definition is made by Vandebosch and Cleembut (2008) who concentrated on the perceptions of the youngsters, stating that "the term cyberbullying is often familiar to youngsters via the media and is usually equated with 'bullying via the Internet'" (p. 502). In addition, Vandebosch and Cleembut found out certain criteria in relation to the attributions of "cyber bullying" suggested by the students who were in their focus groups:

To be classified as cyberbullying, these Internet or mobile phone practices should be intended by the sender to hurt; part of a repetitive pattern of negative offline or online actions; and performed in a relationship characterized by a power imbalanced (based on real-life power criteria such as physical strength or age and/or on ICT related criteria such as technological know-how and anonymity). (p.502)

This shows that youngsters choose to name an online activity or practice as "cyber bullying" only under certain conditions and include real-life implications while doing so. Some researchers chose to investigate what cyber bullying means in particular regions. The study by Menesini et. al (2012) "addresses the issue of cyberbullying definition across six European countries, using data from a cross-national study" (p. 455). These countries are Germany, Sweden, Estonia, France, Italy and Spain. Nocentini et. al (2010) conducted a research in 3 European countries (Germany, Spain and Italy) and in light of the definitions and classifications in literature, they suggested four main types of cyber bullying:

Written-verbal behaviors: Phone calls, text messages, e-mails, instant messaging, chats, blogs, social networking communities, websites,

Visual behaviors: Posting, sending or sharing compromising pictures and videos through mobile phone or internet,

Exclusion: Purposefully excluding someone from an online group,

Impersonation: stealing and revealing personal information, using another person's name and account. (p. 130)

Overall, it can be said that cyber bullying is a form of bullying performed on a digital and online platform with the intentions of discomforting, harming and hurting other individuals or groups. As the other scholars presented in their research, it also might require particular attributes and types of behaviors to be called "cyber bullying" or to be classified as one of the subtypes of cyber bullying.

This study provides an overview of local and global practices in the present literature; with the subcategories of target audience/sample groups and country on the global level, and the case of Turkey on the local level. Particular exemplary studies are provided to show the diversity of the literature and to display certain illuminating aspects and observations. Additionally, it briefly presents their results to provide an insight for possible suggestions or solutions for the cyber-bullying problem.

LITERATURE REVIEW

Global Practices

Based on the Target Audience/Sample Groups

Middle Schools

Seeing as there are cross cultural, country based, and community-based studies in literature which have their focus on middle school students, it can be said that studies in this area are quite abundant and diverse in literature. For instance, in the study by Li (2008), a cross-cultural comparison was made. The target audience of the study was Canadian and Chinese adolescents in the middle school and their experiences and possible cultural differences were investigated with an anonymous questionnaire. Out of 157 Canadian and 202 Chinese students, "more Canadian students than Chinese students reported that they had cyberbullied others" (Li, 2008, p. 229) and "more Chinese students reported that adults in school tried to stop cyberbullying when notified" (Li, 2008, p. 230). The different patterns identified between Canadian and Chinese students' perceptions about adult intervention highlight the importance of culture in designing prevention/intervention programs (Li, 2008, p.223). Another study by Kowalski & Limber (2007) conducted research among 3767 middle school students in the US with a questionnaire. Of the students, 11% stated that they had been electronically bullied at least once in the last couple of months (victims only); 7% indicated that they were bully/victims; and 4% had electronically bullied someone else at least once in the previous couple of months (bullies only) (Kowalski & Limber, 2007, p. 22). An alternative research with a sample of middle school students was by You and Lim (2015). The sample included 3449 Korean middle school students and the long-term effects of individual and psychological factors on cyberbullying perpetration were examined (You & Lim, 2015). The findings indicated that longer use of the Internet, more previous bullying and victim experiences, a higher aggression level and lack of self-control are associated with more cyberbullying perpetration. (p. 172) Coelho, Sousa, Marchante, Bras and Romao (2016) did their research in Portugal and reported that out of 1039 middle school students, only 6.1% were aggressors and 10.1% were victims. In general, victimization prevalence was homogeneous between genders, but boys reported aggressive behaviors more frequently. (Coelho et al., 2016, p. 224) Lastly as an example for a community-based sample, research by Cooper and Blumenfeld (2012) can be given since it focused on middle school and high school students who were "identified as lesbian, gay, bisexual or with a same-sex attraction or as a LGBT-allied youth".

High Schools

Research and studies in the context of high school samples can also be found in the present literature. Similarly, to the samples of middle schools, there are several examples of studies being conducted in various countries or from different perspectives. For instance, the study by Kiriakidis and Lakes (2013) investigated on "exploring teachers' experiences in student-to-student cyber bullying" rather than the students. Apart from several significant results, it's important to point one particular outcome of the research since it emphasizes a possible solution and prevention for cyber bullying:

Findings included that the school district administrators and teachers should implement a cyber-bullying intervention program for student-to-student online safety. (Kiriakidis & Lakes, 2013, p.101)

Furthermore, Kyobe, Oosterwyk and Kabiawu (2016) concentrated on the mobile bullying and victimization in seven high schools in the case of South Africa. Their study suggests a conceptual framework that can be used "in developing solutions to the problem" (2). After an analysis of the responses by 3621 high school students, "mobile bullying was found to be more prevalent in public schools located in high safety risk areas and without anti-bullying policies (p.64)", "the aggressors are said to be largely friends of the victims (Kyobe et. al, 2016, p. 50)" and "the use of mobile phones could have greater cyber-bullying effect than the use of other electronic devices." (Kyobe et. al, 2016, p. 45) These outcomes highlight on the idea that anti-bullying policies are of importance to prevent cyber-bullying, the cyber-bullies do not necessarily have to be opponents or rivals and that the devices which can be accessed easily are used more often and commonly for cyberbullying. Moving from South Africa to Asia, the study by Chang et. al (2013) examined the relationship between mental health, cyber bullying and school bullying and their target audience consisted of Taiwanese high school students. Since this study provides an insight into the mental health aspect of cyber bullying, the research and its results carry quite the significance. The target audience consisted of 2992 students and the findings indicate that "students who had cyberbullying or victimization experiences tended to be involved in school bullying/victimization" and "cyber/school victims and bully-victims were more likely to have lower self-esteem, and cyber/school victims, bullies and bully-victims were at a greater risk for serious depression." (Chang et. al, 2013, p. 454)

Some studies focused on the relation between gender and cyber bullying. For instance, according to the study by Li (2006), when gender is considered, significant differences were identified in terms of bullying and cyberbullying. (p. 165) The target audience was 264 junior high school students in Canada. The results show that "males were more likely to be bullies and cyberbullies than their female counterparts" and "female cyberbully victims were more likely to inform adults than their male counterparts" (Li, 2006, p. 157). Other important outcomes of the study suggest that "the gender difference identified in this study underscores the importance of differentiated approaches for the research and possible intervention programs related to cyberbully issues" and "underscores the importance of awareness" (Li, 2006, p.167). Similar studies concentrating on different aspects can be found in the context of Israel and Lithuania. Tarablus, Heiman and Olenik-Shemesh (2015) examined the cyber bullying and socioemotional functioning with the case of Israel. 458 Israeli junior high school students were the sample group of the study. In Tarablus et. al (2015)'s study, results indicated that there is an overlap between involvement in cyber bullying and involvement in traditional bullying. The findings indicate that girls were more likely to be cyber victims than boys and that boys were more likely to be cyber bullies than girls" (p. 707).

An alternative example for a research conducted on high school students can be the study by Erentaite, Bergman and Zukauskiene (2012). Their sample consisted of 1667 high school students in Lithuania. The results indicated that very high levels of cyberbullying victimization are linked particularly to previous experiences of relational bullying (Erentaite et. al, 2012, p. 187). Erentaite et. al (2012) used the method of person-oriented analysis and it focuses on the patterns of victimization, which naturally appear in the sample and shows which combinations or co-occurrences are likely or unlikely to appear among the study participants (p.183). And it can be a useful method for future research and studies because in the context of this study, it allowed them to identify those patterns of traditional school victimization that were connected to further victimization in cyberspace. (Erentaite et al., 2012, p. 188)

Colleges / Universities

One of the most common sample groups in the literature of cyber bullying is college/ university students. It is obvious that the focus of the studies changes as the age range of the sample groups increase. For example, the article by Myers and Cowie (2017) makes a general overview of "the social and cultural contexts that either promotes or discourages cyberbullying among university students" in UK (Myers & Cowie, 2017, p.1172). It also highlights the legal aspect of the problem and examines the relation between cyberbullying and the law. Myers and Cowie (2017) also emphasize the importance of the age of the students as "those in higher and further education are young adults, rather than children in need of parental support" (p.1172).

Another study concentrating on university students is the one by Sobba, Paez and Bensel (2017). These researchers administered a survey to assess the perceived severity of cyberbullying among college students (Sobba et. al, 2017). The findings of their study revealed that college students perceive cyberbullying as a serious problem, yet they are unwilling to report the abuse (Sobba et. al, 2017, p. 576). Other outcomes were that there were predictors of perceived severity of cyber bullying such as age, gender and type of high school attended before college (Sobba et. al, 2017). Females were more likely to view cyberbullying as a serious issue compared to males (Sobba et. al, 2017, p. 576) and those who attended public schools were more likely to view cyberbullying as a serious issue than those who attended private schools (Sobba et. al, 2017, p. 576). Previous experience of cyberbullying influenced the perception of the problem's severity among college students (Sobba et. al, 2017). The study also suggests "firmer school policies" and "harsher legal strategies" to prevent cyberbullying in the university context.

As an example for an effective prevention program for cyber bullying, the study by Doane, Kelley and Pearson (2016) conducted a research using "Theory of Reasoned Action" based video prevention program with randomly chosen 167 college students in the United States. Findings of the study revealed that "a brief cyberbullying video is capable of improving, at one-month follow-up, cyberbullying knowledge, and cyberbullying perpetration behavior" (Doane et. al, 2016, p. 136).

In addition to its demonstrated efficiency and impact, according to Doane et. al (2016), a brief, Internet format for a cyberbullying prevention program is a low-cost option that would enable greater accessibility across a wide variety of settings and target populations than would traditional prevention programs and it could serve as a model for future cyberbullying prevention programs that may change attitudes toward cyberbullying and reduce cyberbullying behavior (p.144).

Taking the research to a more international level, Luker and Curchack (2017) investigated the international perceptions of cyberbullying within higher education with the sample of 1587 professionals from Australia, Canada, UK and USA. They focused on the professionals, reporting their perspectives, rather than the students'. The results of their study revealed that "cyberbullying is an international problem affecting higher education professionals similarly" and "the majority of participants, regardless of institutional role or country of origin, agreed that cyberbullying has long-lasting negative effects". (Lukar & Curchack, 2017, p. 152). On the other hand, approximately 10% of the participants reported that they considered cyber-bullying to be positive, which is why the study "calls for evidence-based, systematic policy development and implementation, including how to train those who see cyberbullying as a positive phenomenon" (Lukar & Curchack, 2017, p. 144).

Based on the Country

Another small subcategory of the literature review within the scope of this article can be based on the countries the research and studies are conducted in. In order to draw a clearer picture of the literature review, this subcategory can be divided into 2 main continents: North America and Europe. The reason being that the studies on cyber bullying presented in the literature review are most dominantly from the countries in these areas of the world or that they are made with cross-cultural perspectives.

North America

This subcategory presents exemplary studies conducted in the United States and Canada to display the diversity of the literature review. Starting with the United States, the study by Hicks, Clair and Berry (2016) provides a possible intervention program called "Solution-Focused Dramatic Empathy Training". It can be a functional example for future prevention or intervention programs. The target audience of the program consisted of 25 female middle school students. The program procedure follows firstly "a teaching session of solution-focused complimenting", secondly "asking students to write about a cyber-bullying incident they witnessed", enabling students "to enact the said incidents" and it ends with "a discussion on the feelings of the participants" and lastly "the counselor helping students to determine appropriate responses to counter any aggressive behaviors displayed" (Hicks et. Al, 2016, p.387) The main aim of the program is "to build empathy and self-concept as well as improve problem-solving and empathic responses to victims" (Hicks et. Al, 2016, p.386). As for the findings of the study, "student comments implied that they were able to experience the perspectives of others and understood the importance of being kind to one another after program implementation" and "these students also indicated they were trying to protect younger children or peer students of lower status who were victimized" (Hicks et. al, 2016, p. 385).

Grinshtyen and Yang (2016)'s research concentrates on the relationship between exposure to electronic bullying and absenteeism as a result of being afraid. This is another aspect of the consequences of the cyberbullying experiences of adolescents. The findings indicated that "electronic bullying was significantly associated with absences" (Grinshteyn & Yang, 2016, p.142). An additional important outcome from this study could be that "electronic bullying's association with absenteeism places it among already recognized negative influences such as depression and binge drinking, necessitating schools to implement policies to mediate the resulting harmful effects" (Grinshteyn et. al, 2016, p. 142). An alternative study targeting the students in the US is by Wang, Iannotti and Nansel (2009) and it examines four types of bullying, including cyber bullying and "their association with sociodemographic characteristics, parental support and friends" (Wang et. al, 2009, p. 368). The data obtained on 7182 middle school students from *Health Behavior in School-Aged Children 2005 Survey* and the questionnaire they used enabled them to investigate physical, verbal and relational forms of bullying. The results of their study indicated that "higher parental support was associated with less involvement across all forms and classifications of bullying" and "having more friends was associated with more bullying and less victimization for physical, verbal, and relational forms but was not associated with cyber bullying" (Wang, Iannotti & Nansel, 2009, p. 368).

An interesting aspect of the cyber violence and bullying has been focused on and studied by Yahner, Dank, Zweig and Lachman (2015) pertaining to physical and cyber dating violence and bullying between teens. The sample consisted of 5647 students and the results showed that "youth who perpetrated and/or experienced physical, psychological, and cyber bullying were likely to have also perpetrated/experienced physical and sexual dating violence, and psychological and cyber dating abuse" (Yahner, Dank, Zweig and Lachman, 2015, p. 1079). Additionally, the study by Litwiller and Brausch (2013) examined the relationship between victimization from both physical and cyber bullying and adolescent suicidal behavior (p. 675). The factors considered in the study were violent behavior, substance use and unsafe sexual behavior. A sample 4693 high school students were participants in a risk-behavior screening study. The findings of the study showed that "both types of bullying, cyber and physical, positively predicted suicidal behavior, substance use, violent behavior, and unsafe sexual behavior" (Litwiller et. al, 2013, p.681). This can be perceived as a critical sign of how instances of cyber bullying –and bullying in general- can negatively affect students.

In the case of Canada, there has been a national study on cyber bullying and children's experiences with it by Beran, Mishna, McInroy and Shariff (2015). The data was obtained from a sample of 1001 children from all Canadian cities. Overall the results indicated that "all children in Canada are at risk for bullying given that differential rates were not found among any demographic groups" (Beran, Mishna, McInroy & Shariff, 2015, p. 213). They also "identified a significant relationship between being cyberbullied and all forms of victimization and perpetration" (Beran et. al, 2015, p. 212). The fact that the findings of a national study displays how there aren't any differentials and that all children can be at risk of being cyber bullied strongly presents the critical and urgent need to find solutions or intervention/prevention programs for children and the youth. Concreating a different perspective, Coburn, Connolly and Roesch (2015) studied whether cyberbullying problem can be solved with a federal criminal legislation. Their outcome was that "Alternative approaches to dealing with the conflict, such as increasing the use of empirically based programs that teach youth to resolve interpersonal conflict and encourage them to disclose incidents of cyberbullying, would be more effective than federal criminal legislation at protecting young people from online victimization" (Coburn, Connolly & Roesch, 2015, p.567).

The study by Mishna, Khoury-Kassabri, Gadalla and Daciuk (2011) examined "the risk factors for involvement in cyber bullying" and additionally, bully-victims or in other words, the students who both cyber bullied others and have been bullied themselves. The sample of the study consisted of 2186 middle and high school students in Canada. One of the objectives of the study was also "to compare these to a fourth category of students who are not involved in the three categories of cyber bullying" and therefore "to explore the factors that contribute to involvement in cyber bullying" (Mishna et. al, 2011, p. 63). The results were striking, as the findings of the study revealed that "in traditional bullying the category of bully–victims represent the smallest and most vulnerable group of children, whereas in the current study the bully–victims' category emerged as common" (Mishna et. al, 2011, p 63). Another outcome which can be highlighted is that students are highly involved in cyber bullying, especially as victims and bully–victims (Mishna et. al, 2011, p.66). In light of this outcome, it can be said that other scholars or academics who wish to create or make intervention/prevention programs, should also consider the bully-victim category since it might provide valuable insight into different aspects and reasons regarding cyberbullying. In addition, females were more likely than males to be bully–victims, in contrast to research on traditional bullying, in which more males than females are typically involved as bully–victims (Mishna et. al, 2011, p. 63). This suggests that there are certain inconsistencies in the present literature and the findings may vary. An alternative study by Mishna, Saini and Solomon (2009) conducted in Canada focused on the perceptions of the adolescents. Their study gives a critical point of view about the need to understand the perceptions of the youth on online relationships and interactions; because it might be an important factor for figuring out solutions for the cyber-bullying problem. And it can be seen as follows:

Findings of the present study highlight the need to concurrently: 1) understand and attend to the importance and meaning of online relationships for children and youth (both those that are only online and those that are also known in "real life"); and 2) address the inherent risks in online communication and interactions. For example, a child or youth may give a trusted friend a password, without anticipating the risks should the relationship change, such as the friend becoming angry and using this password to perpetrate cyber bullying. What occurs within the context of what a child or youth considers a trusted friendship (for example giving a password or sending a picture) may quickly move into the realm of cyber space/Internet with its potential for immediate, anonymous, widespread and lasting distribution and access. (Mishna, Saini & Solomon, 2009, p.1226)

Overall, considering those exemplary and particular studies and research in such multicultural countries that host many origins and heritages and cultural backgrounds, it can be said that this problem is widespread and common leaving most of the youth of today's world at risk of being cyberbullied and provoking them to be a cyber-bully themselves.

Europe

There are other studies provided in this article conducted in the European region under different sections. However, it can be useful and eye-opening to present more exemplary studies to contribute. Another reason for presenting more research can be that it's common to conduct cross-nations studies in Europe and that provides more observations for other academics.

A study by Lievens (2014) "evaluates the applicability of the current legal framework to cyber bullying and sexting, two types of (potentially harmful) behavior that are increasingly occurring between peers in the social networking environment" (p. 251). While talking about the exemplary legal frameworks on bullying or "sexting" in other countries such as the US and Australia, Lievens (2011) explains that "in Europe, the debate on the legal consequences of sexting is much less active, perhaps because no high-profile cases have yet been brought before a court" (p. 255). That is why the current legal framework both on the Continental level and national level (Belgium) is questioned in this study. The result of the discussion by Lievens (2011) is that "with regard to cyberbullying the existing legislative provisions are sufficient to address the issue" and "new legislation to address this specific risk would not create an added value" (p. 267). In the article, sexting is discussed in the context of child pornography legislation and whether it could be associated with it or not. The final conclusion of Lievens (2011) is that "in the case of sexting, there currently is a mismatch with the current legislative framework" and "sexting should not be criminalized on the basis of child pornography legislation" (p. 267). If policymakers decide that new legislation needs to be drafted, such legislation will need to be carefully considered (Lievens, 2011). Similar research can be conducted within the framework of legal consequences and regulations in terms of the cyber bullying problem in other countries too, since it might highlight the solutions in the legal context.

The study by Tsitsika et. al (2015) was conducted in six European countries: Spain, Poland, the Netherlands, Romania, Iceland and Greece. The sample included 1030 students. The aim of the study was "to investigate the prevalence of cyber victimization and associated internalizing, externalizing and academic problems among adolescents in six European countries" (Tsitsika et. al, 2015, p. b2). The findings of the study revealed that "Romania was characterized by a high prevalence of cyber victimization" (p. 5). That is followed by Greece and "the lowest prevalence was in Spain and Iceland" (p.1). Additional outcomes are that "reports were more frequent among girls than boys" and that "cyber victimization was more frequent among adolescents using the internet and social networking sites for two or more hours daily" (Tsitsika et. al, 2015, p. 1). This can suggest that the usage of the internet can be another factor to be considered.

Brandtzæg, Staksrud, Hagen and Wold (2009) investigated the experiences of Norwegian children, presenting another research with the example of Norway. The study aimed "to examine whether children's experience of cyberbullying differs according to technological platforms and socio-demographic variables" (Brandtzæg et. al, 2009, p.349). The findings of this study revealed that "IM and email were the most likely platforms to be targeted for bullying" (p. 361) and that "most cyberbullying encountered in social networking sites was sexual and took place in communities in which the users are anonymous" (Brandtzæg et. al, 2009, p. 349). Females were more likely to experience cyber bullying, which is consistent with some other studies presented in this article.

A multi-nation study by Nasi, Rasanen, Kaakinen, Keipi and Oksanen (2016) examined whether routine activities could help predicting online harassment of youngsters in the USA, Finland, Germany and the UK, by using the "routine activity theory". The results of the study showed some differences based on the countries. Females were more likely to be victims than males in Finland, but not in other countries; those with an immigrant background had a higher likelihood of being victims in Germany, but not in other countries and lastly, the protective role of guardianship was supported in the USA and Germany (Nasi et. al, 2016, p. 419). According to Nasi et al. (2016)'s study, in terms of the cross-national comparison, the results suggest that the online context does not have a straightforward homogenizing effect when looking at the role of online harassment victimization in a multi-nation context (p. 427).

Lastly, the study by Haidar, Chamoun and Yamout (2016) can be given to show more diversity in the literature, since it focuses on the cyberbullying detection with the case of Arabic language. Along with a small background of all the technologies used in the field of cyber-bullying such as machine learning and NLP (natural language processing), an extensive survey was also conducted on "the techniques and advancements in multilingual cyberbullying detection" (Haidar etc. al, 2016, p. 165). It also proposes a solution plan for the problem of Arabic cyberbullying. This perspective of using such technologies for the cyber bullying detection online contributes to the literature by providing insight into more various and technical solutions which can be developed.

Local Practices: Turkey

There are also some research and studies being conducted in Turkey that can be found in the present literature and the amount of studies are growing gradually as the cyber bullying problem is being recognized more and more. Starting with Dilmaç (2009)'s study, it can be seen that this research focuses on the relationship between psychological needs and cyber bullying (p.1307). The sample included 666 undergraduate students studying in Konya, Turkey and data was collected using convenience sampling (Dilmaç, 2009). According to the findings of the study by Dilmaç (2009), aggression and succorance positively predict cyber bullying whereas interceptions negatively predicted it, and endurance and affiliation negatively predicted cyber victimization (Dilmaç, 2009, p. 1321). The study by Sezer, Yilmaz, Karaoglan Yilmaz (2014) concentrated on the teachers rather than students. They examined the "awareness levels of teachers with regard to cyber bullying" and "the extent of awareness levels of teachers in general, regarding the issue of personal cyber security in their daily lives and the precautions that can be taken in this context have been measured" (Sezer et. al, 2009, p. 674). A survey was made with a target audience of 184 teachers who worked in different cities in Turkey during one academic year. Though various studies will direct both the literature and the policy implementers (in Turkey); the findings of the study reveal that the teachers in the sample group of the study have an average level of awareness on cyber bullying, in general. (Sezer et. al, 2009, p. 674). Based on this outcome, it can be said that there is a need for an awareness raising programme targeting the teachers. This is also quite a critical factor since the teachers are the ones who guide the students that are the most at risk from cyber bullying activities. According to Sezer et. al (2009), determination of teachers' awareness on this subject through various studies direct both the literature and the policy implementers (p. 679)

Akbulut, Sahin and Eristi (2010) studied "cyberbullying victimization among Turkish members of an online social utility" (p. 192). The sample included 1470 participants. The findings revealed that "at least 56% of the participants experienced at least one instance of cyber bullying victimization" and this suggests that "the problem may be more serious in online social utilities" (Akbulut et. al, 2010, p. 198). Age, education level and Internet proficiency were not related to cyber victimization in this study. And another finding was that "regardless of age, education level and Internet proficiency, all participants had similar problems regarding victimization" (Akbulut et. al, 2010, p. 198) which emphasizes on the prevalence of cyber bullying in Turkish context as well. Ekşi (2012) conducted a research to find out to what extent do narcissistic personality traits predict internet addiction and cyber bullying in vocational high school students (p. 1694). The sample involved 508 students. The results of the study present many important points. However, in terms of the problem addressed in this article, in Ekşi (2012)'s study, it has been determined that the only variable predicting significantly "cyber bullying" behaviors in the sub-dimensions of internet addiction is "social isolation" (p. 1703). Such social isolation can be another critical point to be evaluated while trying to find solutions or create prevention/intervention programs.

And lastly, the study by d'Haenens and Ogan (2013) had a different perspective in their study. They focused on Turkish ethnic children in several European countries. Then they made a comparison of the data obtained with the data from Turkish children living in Turkey. The findings of the study revealed that "European majority children are more familiar than the two other groups with receiving sex-related images and messages and with face-to-face meetings with online contacts. By contrast, children in the Turkish diaspora are relatively more familiar with cyberbullying" (d'Haenens et. al, 2013, p. 41). Such cross-national studies focusing on a particular ethnic group and making a comparison with the ones living in the origin country can provide valuable insight into variables or factors such as cultural differences or environments that can affect the cyber bullying problem.

PRESS REVIEW

Whereas the cyber bullying seems to be a problem mainly associated with the new media and social networks, the traditional media gets also its share. That's why this research also dwells on the press review regarding how this new media had a negative impact on the society. Even if the main part of the society seem to be more modern, using smart phones, tablets, e-books, computers, etc. when it comes to getting information the traditional media seem to be more effective for all. That's why how cyber bullying is reflected and represented through the traditional media is very important. Interestingly, learning more about the cyber bullying is sometimes only possible through the traditional media. Thus, it could also be considered a kind of positive or negative contribution to the level of media literacy.

As a contribution to this research, a small sample group of the news about cyber bullying acts or related forms in Turkish press were analyzed. The main aim of presenting this press review is to support the arguments, assertions and findings of the academic research given above with real life cases and show how cyber-bullying problem is taking place and in what forms it is happening in Turkish society. A total of 15 news examples are provided along with their short analyses.

"Teens Facing Threats of Their Privacy Being Exposed Through WhatsApp Group Chat"[2]

The news was published online on the news section of a social content platform, called Onedio, on July 20, 2016; and reports of a Tumblr user creating a WhatsApp group chat and inviting other Tumblr users to the group by claiming that it will be "a new family" and "a new circle of real friends" for everyone included. The user demanded everyone who wanted to join the group chat to fill a form full of questions and rules about certain things such as sexual orientation, breast sizes, whether they would accept sending images of their private body parts or not. One of the Tumblr users joined the group and when s/he realized how young the other participants are and the topics discussed made her/him feel uncomfortable, s/he wanted to leave the chat group by messaging the group admin. However, the group admin claimed that s/he couldn't leave the group chat, because "s/he did not send 500 messages yet", which was one of the rules included in the form. After leaving the group chat, the user's phone number was shared in the whole group chat by the admin, encouraging everyone else to call and text this number, to harass her/him as a punishment. The news later covers the precautions parents can take to protect their children from such dangerous platforms or individuals online.

"Online Sexual Harassment of a Customer by an Instagram Boutique"[3]

Dated as October 25, 2016, this news was again published on Onedio, reporting that one of the employees in charge for the Instagram account of a boutique harassed a female customer through WhatsApp, after they had a discussion over a problem regarding the shipment. He started to send disturbing and disrespectful messages, including questions and claims about her private and sexual life. Even though she warned him and strongly wanted him to stop sending such infuriating messages, the employee did not stop. After contacting the authorities of the boutique through Instagram, she was sent explicit images of sexual parts of the employee in charge of the account at the moment. Later on, she has filed a criminal file, complained against, and sued the boutique and the said employee.

"Security Guard Fired After His Comment to a Nurse on Facebook" [4]

Published on the website of Hürriyet -a major newspaper-, dated as November 3, 2016; this piece of news reports that a security guard was fired from the company he was working for after he made a comment as "You're so beautiful and innocent" on a photo shared by a female nurse on Facebook. The verdict made by the court was for the company to employ him back, on the ground that "it was not a cyber-harassment, but a compliment at most". However, the supreme court reversed this judgement on the grounds that "it included harassment and caused the workflow to be disrupted" and prevented him being employed again.

"16-Year-Old Teen Kidnapped After Facebook Meet-Up" [5]

Another example is again published online on "Hürriyet" dated November 7, 2016; reports that a 43-year-old male created a Facebook profile with the pictures of his younger self from 25 years ago and added a 16-year old teen girl as a friend and they started to talk online. Thinking he was a 25-year-old male, the high schooler accepted to meet him after a certain period of time. Having found out that he was not the person he presented himself as, she tried to leave. However, he forced the girl to go with him kidnapping her and taking her to a completely different city. After missing reports by her parents, the police finally found the girl and arrested the perpetrator.

"16-Year-Old Teen Abused by Religion Teacher" [6]

This news was covered on the news section of the social content platform mentioned above, Onedio on November 19, 2018. It reports that the principal who is also a religion teacher of a school in Antalya, Turkey got arrested for harassing the 16-year-old sister of one of his students on Facebook. Based on the testimonies given, he invited the high schooler who dropped her sister off at the school to his room "for a cup of tea" and "offered to help with her studies" and kissed her. Afterwards, he contacted her through Facebook and kept trying to talk to her with the same excuse by asking questions about her private life and asking her to be his "girlfriend". Despite being married, he claimed that he "wanted to divorce his wife and marry her instead" in those messages sent online. The parents of the high schooler filed a criminal complaint regarding this issue after finding out about the online and real-life harassment.

"Disgusting Harassment Through Facebook" [7]

This news was published online on the website of Hürriyet, on December 12, 2016. It reports that a man in Tokat, Turkey created two Facebook profiles by using the information of two different teachers living in two different cities. He added their female students aged between 11-13 years old as friends on Facebook and they accepted the friend requests thinking he was actually their teacher. He insisted on having sexual conversations and asking students to send pictures of themselves wearing revealing clothes and making a video calls. When these conversations were found, the man got arrested and was sentenced with 2 years in prison.

"Young Girl Commits Suicide Because of Social Media Bullying"[8]

This headline belongs to a news published on Onedio dated as December 14, 2016. It reports that an 18-year-old girl from Texas, USA committed suicide after being bullied online for a year about her appearance and being "fat". Her peers created fake profiles on social media platforms, used Photoshop to change her pictures into degrading versions and shared her phone number on dating websites with the title of "Free Sex". After her suicide, it was found out that her peers still kept making such comments online about her. Her parents stated that they demanded justice for their daughter.

"Suicide Note Shared by Famous Twitter User Leaves Everyone Shocked"[9]

This news was published on the news section of Onedio on December 30, 2016. It reports that the owner of the famous Twitter account called "Kaç Saat Oldu?" ("How Long Has it Been?") shared a suicide note on Twitter stating the reason was mainly due to the online insults, harassment, and hate speech that he received from people online. It was also found out that in the recent past, he was beaten up and physically exposed to violence by a group of people in real life. In his suicide note, he stated that even though he recovered physically, he could not handle the psychological effects of the incident and the cyber harassment and hate speech he still received. The news also covers that after he shared the suicide note, his followers on Twitter and other famous account owners contacted him and convinced him to not commit suicide.

"Assassination Plan Through WhatsApp"[10]

Published online on Hürriyet's website, on January 13, 2016, the news reports that 8 students at Akdeniz University had conversations in a group chat on WhatsApp about one of their professors, strongly criticizing him about his grading them. The students went too far by talking about possible physical abuse, assassination and murder plans for their professor. One of the parents of these students saw these messages by chance and immediately went to the university to talk to the professor. After finding out about this conversation, the authorities took criminal action against, and inflicted disciplinary punishment to the students.

"Digital Civility Index and Turkey: What Are the Threats that Turkish Internet Users Face?" [11]

This news was published on the website, "Onedio" on February 13, 2017. It focuses on the percentage of the cyber harassment and threats that Turkish Internet users face online, based on the "Digital Civility Index" released by Microsoft every year. According to the Index, %71 of Turkish users online are being exposed to cyber threats. Even though there are other categories and rates of them covered in the Index, the most notable result is that the biggest threat for Turkish Internet users online is "damage to reputation".

As the exemplary news presented above show, cyber harassment and bullying can be in such various forms, on different platforms and received by several audiences. Not only the children and teens, but also the adults are at risk of being psychologically and physically abused online (which might also take place in real life later or before). It can have such harsh effects on individuals that it can lead them to devastating consequences, which is something that may be easily seen in the news of people attempting to or actually committing suicide or being kidnapped. Similar to the Digital Civility Index report, there can be many other reports or research clearly presenting the fact that cyber harassment and cyber bullying is a huge problem that poses a threat to everyone's physical and mental health who use the online platforms.

CONCLUSION

According to Narin and Ünal (2016) regarding the news reviewed as samples, moral panic frame is rarely used; and the technical frame which includes details about the problem is preferred by the news media in its stead. Besides, the supportive or critical frames targeting the existing policies about cyberbullying are also rarely brought up in the agenda. According to the news contents, families and educators are kept responsible and are usually blamed for the cyberbullying incidents rather than the police forces.

In a field study conducted in Turkey among children across the country it's been figured out that even if the kids have an access to television ranging from 200 up to 2000 channels they tend to determine between 2 to 6 channels of their own choice as their favorite ones (Pembecioğlu, 2013). Despite the regional differences in Internet access, it has been determined that almost every child has an access to a tablet or laptop computer during the day, while television is not the main medium to be wary of anymore. Mainly the schools support the info-technologies if not all the edutainment materials. Due to school assignments and careful follow-up of the family, limitations are brought to television for the kids yet, the same limitations are not followed for the other screens, such as laptops or mobile phones. Kids, feeling that have been observed continuously tend to make use of their computers for 'homework preparation' and 'spare time activities' use. However, mobile phone ownership could be as early as 6-7 years old specifically for the "better-off" families. It has been observed that many parents allow their children to communicate with their mobile phone even if it is for 'gaming' purposes. That means most of the kids are to an extent under the threat of cyberbullying, and their parents and teachers do not know much about the types, cases, causes or results, and mainly the impact of cyberbullying on children.

Regarding academics, cyber bullying is handled with psychological and sociological dimensions in the news and the methods of protection presented were supported by expert opinions and field studies. When the studies conducted in Turkey are considered, Baker and Kavşut (2007) stated that 28% of students aged 14-19 who use technology frequently use cyber bullying and 30% of them are exposed to bullying action. The study conducted by Arıcak et al. (2008), points out that the rate of bullying by Turkish students was 36%. Cited in Peker (2012), whereas Artillery found that 48% of students were cyber bullied in 2008, Ayas stated that 16% of secondary school students were bullied and 17% had bullied others by 2011. Dilmaç in another study found that by 2009, 23% of university students were bullied at least once, and 55% were exposed to bulimia at least once in their lives. In another study, the same year Arıcak found that 20% of students had at least one cyber bullying in their life and 54% had at least one case of being cyber victim.

According to Arıcak, cyberbullying in Turkey might arise in the following forms: to name, mock, threaten, to reveal a friend's condemnation or socially inappropriate / condemnatory behavior, to spread untrue rumors about a topic, to share/broadcast visuals or video recordings of one's personal life, putting people in difficult positions in social network sites such opening up a false account on Facebook, Twitter, Instagram and so on. These actions could also involve sharing inappropriate content in one's own social media account openly or using some other person's account for such purposes so that behaving in a manner that might damage that person's reputation, honour or face, and bring an end as to exclude that person from social media environments. Carrying out a large survey in Istanbul with 633 participants enrolled in the 9th, 10th 11th and 12nd grades, Küçük et al. (2017) checked the validity and reliability studies of Cyberbullying Scale As a result, "Cyberbullying Scale" was analyzed and found to be a valid and reliable scale. Family, school and students should be working in cooperation on the subject of Cyberbullying.

It's obvious that cyber bullying is a global problem thanks to the role of Internet in the globalization of today's world, which is explained clearly with the exemplary studies and news from the present literature and press review provided above. It has many aspects and dimensions which require professionals, researchers and scholars to work on, all together to be able to find a concrete solution to it. This study attempts to cast some light on possible solutions or intervention/prevention programs by going through the global and local practices in the literature. The main selection criterion of the studies was based on mainly showing the diversity of the literature on a small scale. Scholars, academics or professionals can benefit from this study to gain a general insight into cyber bullying problem.

Information age, brought society a difficult problem having its roots from the earliest times, caused by jealousy, brutal feelings, revenge and having a kind of malevolent instinct, all causing a huge impact on "the others" in society due to the harsh bullying action. Having the media and technology components, its impact gets larger and larger in nowadays. In public space and presentation of the news; using specific frameworks, templates, and stereotypes for the news is manifested as the sided news on the broadcast material. The media tries to be manipulating things by shaping the titles, only putting forward the causes, not much establishing the responsibility of the parts, neither maintaining the reality of the connection nor explaining the way the news is constructed or provided to the audience. This type of news mainly appears all in a form of dilemma without providing the audience a lesson to be learned. In fact, all these news formats could be formed in different ways in positive approaches. Apart from the public space the media never mentions the individual space. Not much awareness is raised through the media on the side of the individuals. People are not familiar with the bullying types and unprepared for any risk or occasion. Neither the word cyber nor bullying is common in Turkey and not much is published in newspapers. So, digging into the archives, the news is not labelled as they are in the other countries under the title of cyber bullying. Only in the recent few years has the concept became familiar to the public and classified as a general social problem.

REFERENCES

Aboujaoude, E., Savage, M. W., Starcevic, V., & Salame, W. O. (2015). Cyberbullying: Review of an old problem gone viral. *The Journal of Adolescent Health*, *57*(1), 10–18. doi:10.1016/j.jadohealth.2015.04.011 PMID:26095405

Akbulut, Y., Sahin, Y. L., & Eristi, B. (2010). Cyberbullying Victimization Among Turkish Online Social Utility Members. *Journal of Educational Technology & Society*, *13*(4), 192–201. Retrieved from http://www.ifets.info/journals/13_4/17.pdf

Aricak, T., Siyahhan, S., Uzunhasanoglu, A., Saribeyoglu, S., Ciplak, S., Yilmaz, N., & Memmedov, C. (2008). Cyberbullying among Turkish adolescents. *Cyberpsychology & Behavior*, *11*(3), 253–261.

Beran, T., Mishna, F., McInroy, B. L., & Shariff, S. (2015). Children's Experiences of Cyber bullying: A Canadian National Study. *Children & Schools*, *37*(4), 207–214. doi:10.1093/cs/cdv024

Bhat, C. S., Chang, S. H., & Linscott, J. A. (2010). Addressing cyberbullying as a media literacy issue. *New Horizons in Education*, *58*(3), 34–43.

Brandtzæg, B. P., Staksrud, E., Hagen, I., & Wold, T. (2009). Norwegian Children's Experiences of Cyberbullying When Using Different Technological Platforms. *Journal of Children and Media*, *3*(4), 349–365. doi:10.1080/17482790903233366

Chang, F.-C., Lee, C.-M., Hsi, W.-Y., Huang, T.-F., & Pan, Y.-C. (2013). Relationships among cyberbullying, school bullying, and mental health in Taiwanese adolescents. *The Journal of School Health*, *83*(6), 454–462. doi:10.1111/josh.12050 PMID:23586891

Coburn, I. P., Connolly, A. D., & Roesch, R. (2015). Cyberbullying: Is Federal Criminal Legislation the Solution? *Canadian Journal of Criminology and Criminal Justice*, *57*(4), 566–579. doi:10.3138/cjccj.2014.E43

Coelho, A. V., Sousa, V., Marchante, M., Bras, P., & Romao, M. A. (2016). Bullying and cyberbullying in Portugal: Validation of a questionnaire and analysis of prevalence. *School Psychology International*, *37*(3), 223–239. doi:10.1177/0143034315626609

Cooper, R. M., & Blumenfeld, W. J. (2012). Responses to Cyberbullying: A Descriptive Analysis of the Frequency of and Impact on LGBT and Allied Youth. *Journal of LGBT Youth*, *9*(2), 153–177. doi:10.1080/19361653.2011.649616

Cowie, H., & Colliety, P. (2010). Cyberbullying: Sanctions or sensitivity? *Pastoral Care in Education*, *28*(4), 261–268. doi:10.1080/02643944.2010.528017

D'Haenens, L., & Ogan, C. (2013). Internet-using children and digital inequality: A comparison between majority and minority Europeans. *Communications*, *38*(1), 41–60. doi:10.1515/commun-2013-0003

Dilmaç, B. (2009). Cyber bullying: A Preliminary Report on College Students. *Educational Sciences: Theory and Practice*, *9*(3), 1307–1325. Retrieved from https://eric.ed.gov/?id=EJ858926

Doane, N. A., Kelley, L. M., & Pearson, R. M. (2016). Reducing cyberbullying: A Theory of Reasoned Action-Based Video Prevention Program for College Students. *Aggressive Behavior*, *42*(2), 136–146. doi:10.1002/ab.21610 PMID:26349445

Ekşi, F. (2012). Examination of Narcissistic Personality Traits' Predicting Level of Internet Addiction and Cyber Bullying through Path Analysis. *Educational Sciences: Theory and Practice*, *12*(3), 1694–1706. Retrieved from https://files.eric.ed.gov/fulltext/EJ1000892.pdf

Erdur-Baker, Ö., & Kavşut, F. (2007). A new face of peer bullying: Cyber bullying. *Journal of Euroasian Educational Research*, 27(7), 31–42.

Grinshteyn, E., & Yang, Y. T. (2017). The association between electronic bullying and school absenteeism among high school students in the United States. *The Journal of School Health*, 87(2), 142–149. doi:10.1111/josh.12476 PMID:28076925

Haidar, B., Chamoun, M., & Yamout, F. (2016). *Cyberbullying Detection A Survey on Multilingual Techniques*. 2016 European Modelling Symposium, EMS 2016, Pisa, Italy. Retrieved from http://ieeexplore.ieee.org/document/7920246/

Hicks, F. J., Le Clair, B., & Berry, S. (2016). Using Solution-Focused Dramatic Empathy Training to Eliminate Cyber-Bullying. *Journal of Creativity in Mental Health*, 11(5). doi:10.1080/15401383.2016.1172533

Hinduja, S., & Patchin, J. W. (2010). Bullying, cyberbullying, and suicide. *Archives of Suicide Research*, 14(3), 206–221.

Jackson, C. (2011). Your students love social media... and so can you. *Teaching Tolerance*, 39, 38–41.

Kiriakidis, P. P., & Lakes, D. (2013). A Case Study of Student-to-student Cyber Bullying in one High School. *Romanian Journal of Multidimensional Education.*, 5(2), 101-118. Retrieved from http://revistaromaneasca.ro/category/2013/volume-5-issue-2-year-2013/

Kowalski, M. R., & Limber, P. S. (2007). Electronic Bullying Among Middle School Students. *The Journal of Adolescent Health*, 41(6), 22–30. doi:10.1016/j.jadohealth.2007.08.017 PMID:18047942

Kowalski, M. R., & Limber, P. S. (2007). Electronic Bullying Among Middle School Students. *The Journal of Adolescent Health*, 41(6), 22–30. doi:10.1016/j.jadohealth.2007.08.017 PMID:18047942

Kowalski, M. R., Limber, P. S., & Agatston, W. P. (2008). What is Cyber Bullying? In Cyber Bullying: Bullying in the Digital Age. Blackwell Publishing. doi:10.1002/9780470694176

Küçük, S., İnanıcı, M. A., & Ziyalar, N. (2017). Siber Zorbalık Ölçeği Türkçe Uyarlaması. *The Bulletin of Legal Medicine*, 22(3), 172–176.

Kyobe, E. M., Oosterwyk, W. G., & Kabiawu, O. (2016). The Nature Of Mobile Bullying & Victimization in the Western Cape High Schools of South Africa. *The African Journal of Information Systems*, 8(2), 45–69. Retrieved from http://digitalcommons.kennesaw.edu/ajis/vol8/iss2/3/

Li, Q. (2006). Cyberbullying in Schools: A Research of Gender Differences. *School Psychology International*, *27*(2), 157–170. doi:10.1177/0143034306064547

Li, Q. (2008). A cross-cultural comparison of adolescents' experience related to cyberbullying. *Educational Research*, *50*(3), 223–234. doi:10.1080/00131880802309333

Li, Q., Smith, P. K., & Cross, D. (2012). Research into cyberbullying. *Cyberbullying in the global playground: Research from international perspectives*, 1.

Lievens, E. (2014). Bullying and sexting in social networks: Protecting minors from criminal acts or empowering minors to cope with risky behaviour? *International Journal of Law, Crime and Justice*, *42*(3), 251–270. doi:10.1016/j.ijlcj.2014.02.001

Litwiller, J. B., & Brausch, M. A. (2013). Cyber Bullying and Physical Bullying in Adolescent Suicide: The role of Violent Behaviour and Substance Use. *Journal of Youth and Adolescence*, *42*(5), 675–684. doi:10.100710964-013-9925-5 PMID:23381779

Livingstone, S. (2014). Developing social media literacy: How children learn to interpret risky opportunities on social network sites. *Communications*, *39*(3), 283–303. doi:10.1515/commun-2014-0113

Livingstone, S., & Brake, D. R. (2010). On the Rapid Rise of Social Networking Sites: New Findings and Policy Implications. *Children & Society*, *24*(1), 75–83. doi:10.1111/j.1099-0860.2009.00243.x

Luker, M. J., & Curchack, C. B. (2017). International Perceptions of Cyberbullying Within Higher Education. *Adult Learning*, *28*(4), 144–156. doi:10.1177/1045159517719337

Magsi, H., Agha, N., & Magsi, I. (2017). Understanding Cyber Bullying in Pakistani Context: Causes and Effects on Young Female University Students in Sindh Province. *New Horizons*, *11*(1), 103-110. Retrieved from https://ourworldindata.org/literacy https://www.researchgate.net/profile/Habibullah_Magsi/publication/315474989_Understanding_cyber_bullying_in_Pakistani_context_Causes_and_effects_on_young_female_university_students_in_Sindh_province/links/58d13fb7a6fdcc8a864c9934/Understanding-cyber-bullying-in-Pakistani-context-Causes-and-effects-on-young-female-university-students-in-Sindh-province.pdf http://wordvis.com/

Menesini, E., Nocentini, A., Palladino, B. E., Frisén, A., Berne, S., Ortega-Ruiz, R., & Naruskov, K. (2012). Cyberbullying definition among adolescents: A comparison across six European countries. *Cyberpsychology, Behavior, and Social Networking*, *15*(9), 455–463. doi:10.1089/cyber.2012.0040 PMID:22817693

Mishna, F., Cook, C., Gadalla, T., Daciuk, J., & Solomon, S. (2010). Cyber Bullying behaviours among middle and high school students. *The American Journal of Orthopsychiatry*, *80*(3), 362–374. doi:10.1111/j.1939-0025.2010.01040.x PMID:20636942

Mishna, F., Khoury-Kassabri, M., Gadalla, T., & Daciuk, J. (2011). Risk factors for involvement in cyber bullying: Victims, bullies and bully-victims. *Children and Youth Services Review*, *34*(1), 63–70. doi:10.1016/j.childyouth.2011.08.032

Mishna, F., Saini, M., & Solomon, S. (2009). Ongoing and online: Children and youth's perceptions of cyber bullying. *Children and Youth Services Review*, *31*(12), 1222–1228. doi:10.1016/j.childyouth.2009.05.004

Mura, G., Topcu, C., Erdur-Baker, O., & Diamantini, D. (2011). An international study of cyber bullying perception and diffusion among adolescents. *Procedia: Social and Behavioral Sciences*, *15*, 3805–3809. doi:10.1016/j.sbspro.2011.04.377

Myers, A. C., & Cowie, H. (2017). Bullying at University: Social and Legal Contexts of Cyberbullying Among University Students. *Journal of Cross-Cultural Psychology*, *48*(8), 1172–1182. doi:10.1177/0022022116684208

Narin, B., & Ünal, S. (2016). Siber Zorbalık İle İlgili Haberlerin Türkiye Yazılı Basınında Çerçevelenişi. Akdeniz Iletisim, (26).

Nasi, M., Rasanen, P., Keipi, T., & Oksanen, A. (2016). Do routine activities help predict young adults' online harassment: A multi-nation study. *Criminology & Criminal Justice*, *17*(4), 418–432. doi:10.1177/1748895816679866

Nocentini, A., Calmaestra, J., Schultze-Krumbholz, A., Scheithauer, H., Ortega, R., & Menesini, E. (2010). Cyberbullying: Labels, behaviours and definition in three European countries. *Journal of Psychologists and Counsellors in Schools*, *20*(2), 129–142.

Patchin, W. J., & Hinduja, S. (2006). Bullies Move Beyond The School Yard A Preliminary Look at Cyber Bullying. *Youth Violence and Juvenile Justice*, *4*(2), 148–169. doi:10.1177/1541204006286288

Peker, A., Eroğlu, Y., & Çitemel, N. (2012). Boyun eğici davranışlar ile siber zorbalık ve siber mağduriyet arasındaki ilişkide cinsiyetin aracılığının incelenmesi. *Uluslararası İnsan Bilimleri Dergisi, 9*(1), 206–221.

Pembecioğlu, N. (2013). TRT Çocuk/çocuklar için eğitim hedeflerinin eğlenceli içeriğe dönüşmesi sürecinin araştırılması. *I. Türkiye Çocuk ve Medya Kongresi Bildiriler Kitabı, 1*, 473–511.

Sezer, Y., Yilmaz, K., & Karaoglan Yilmaz, F. G. (2015). Cyber bullying and teachers' awareness. *Internet Research, 25*(4), 674–687. doi:10.1108/IntR-01-2014-0023

Sobba, K. N., Paez, R. A., & Bensel, T. (2017). Perception of Cyberbullying: An Assessment of Perceived Severity among College Students. *TechTrends: For Leaders in Education & Training., 61*(6), 570–579. doi:10.100711528-017-0186-0

Tarablus, T., Heiman, T., & Olenik-Shemesh, D. (2015). Cyber Bullying Among Teenagers in Israel: An Examination of Cyber Bullying, Traditional Bullying and Socioemotional Functioning. *Journal of Aggression, Maltreatment & Trauma, 24*(6), 707–720. doi:10.1080/10926771.2015.1049763

Tsitsika, A., Janikian, M., Wojcik, S., Makaruk, K., Tzavela, E., Tzavara, C., ... Richardson, C. (2015). Cyberbullying victimization prevalence and associations with internalizing and externalizing problems among adolescents in six European countries. *Computers in Human Behavior, 51*, 1–7. doi:10.1016/j.chb.2015.04.048

Vandebosch, H., & Cleemput, V. K. (2008). Defining Cyberbullying: A Qualitative Research into the Perceptions of Youngsters. *Cyberpsychology & Behavior, 11*(4), 499–503. doi:10.1089/cpb.2007.0042 PMID:18721100

Wang, J., Iannotti, J. R., & Nansel, R. T. (2009). School Bullying Among Adolescents in the United States: Physical, Verbal, Relational and Cyber. *The Journal of Adolescent Health, 45*(4), 368–375. doi:10.1016/j.jadohealth.2009.03.021 PMID:19766941

Yahner, J., Dank, M., Zweig, M. J., & Lachman, P. (2015). The Co-Occurrence of Physical and Cyber Dating Violence and Bullying Among Teens. *Journal of Interpersonal Violence, 30*(7), 1079–1089. doi:10.1177/0886260514540324 PMID:25038223

You, S., & Lim, A. S. (2015). Longitudinal predictors of cyberbullying perpetration: Evidence from Korean middle school students. *Personality and Individual Differences, 89*, 172–176. doi:10.1016/j.paid.2015.10.019

ENDNOTES

[1]   This research was supported by the Scientific Research Projects Coordination Unit of Istanbul University. Project Number 23236 – Cyber Bullying: Local and Global Practices on Awareness Raising - Siber Zorbalık - Farkındalık Yaratmada Yerel ve Küresel Uygulamalar.

[2]   Retrieved from: https://onedio.com/haber/cocuklar-korktuklari-icin-tuzaga-surukleniyor-whatsapp-grubunda-ozel-paylasim-tehdidi-722089 (Last accessed: 17.02.2018).

[3]   Retrieved from: https://onedio.com/haber/instagram-uzerinden-satis-yapan-butikten-kadin-musterisine-igrenc-taciz-736443 (Last accessed: 17.02.2018).

[4]   Retrieved from: http://www.hurriyet.com.tr/hemsireye-cok-sade-ve-guzelsin-dedi-isinden-oldu-40267488 (Last accessed: 17.02.2018).

[5]   Retrieved from: http://www.hurriyet.com.tr/facebooktan-kandirilip-kacirilan-liseli-kiz-bulundu-40271297 (Last accessed: 17.02.2018).

[6]   Retrieved from: https://onedio.com/haber/ogrencisinin-16-yasindaki-ablasini-taciz-eden-din-ogretmeni-tutuklandi-739877 (Last accessed: 17.02. 2018).

[7]   Retrieved from: http://www.hurriyet.com.tr/facebookta-igrenc-taciz-40311008 (Last acccessed: 17.02.2018).

[8]   Retrieved from: https://onedio.com/haber/sosyal-medya-zorbaligi-bitmiyor-intihar-ettikten-sonra-bile-kotu-yorumlar-alan-kiz-744817 (Last accessed: 17.02.2018).

[9]   Retrieved from: https://onedio.com/haber/unlu-twitter-fenomeninin-takipcileriyle-paylastigi-intihar-notu-sosyal-medyayi-sarsti-748632 (Last accessed: 17.02.2018).

[10] Retrieved from: http://www.hurriyet.com.tr/whatsappta-suikast-plani-40039802 (Last accessed: 17.02.2018).

[11] Retrieved from: https://onedio.com/haber/turkiye-de-internet-kullanicilari-hangi-tehditlere-maruz-kaliyor-755950 (Last accessed:17.02.2018).

This research was previously published in Handbook of Research on Media Literacy Research and Applications Across Disciplines edited by Melda N. Yildiz, Minaz Fazal, Meesuk Ahn, Robert Feirsen, and Sebnem Ozdemir, pages 379-401, copyright year 2019 by Information Science Reference (an imprint of IGI Global).

Chapter 8
Implication of Cyberbullying on Under-Represented Students in Post-Secondary Education

Jiyoon Yoon
University of Texas Arlington, USA

Katie Koo
Texas A & M University - Commerce, USA

ABSTRACT

Cyberbullying is an emerging issue in the context of higher education as information and communication technologies increasingly become part of daily life at universities. This article offers a review of the major literature regarding cyberbullying, its victims and perpetrators, and its implications that impact disadvantaged students in higher education, specifically those who are in lower socio-economic situations. Post-secondary education has been an important pathway to guide students out of poverty by helping them lead successful lives. However, as in higher education, cyberbullying incidents have increased in educational situations, the bullied victims are more likely to report feelings of depression that cause an obstacle to their academic achievements in post-secondary education. The anonymous environments associated in cyberbullying can cause immorality of the cyberbullying perpetrators. To prevent cyberbullying on campus, this article provides cyberbullying rules and policies and suggests specialized treatment and interventions for cyber-bullies as a solution.

DOI: 10.4018/978-1-7998-1684-3.ch008

INTRODUCTION

The investigation of cyberbullying in post-secondary education has been substantive in recent years. Past studies focused primarily on bullying in the K–12 grades. It is assumed that maturity level has been reached by the time a student enters post-secondary education. However, cyberbullying is not limited to elementary, middle, or high school. It also occurs in post-secondary schooling. Research studies have continuously shown that cyberbullying is taking place at the post-secondary education level (Englander, 2007; Smith & Yoon, 2012). Statistics increased when students were asked about a time when they have witnessed cyber bullying occurring on social media sites such as Facebook and Twitter.

Recognizing and finding ways to eradicate cyberbullying is important as it can be an obstacle to students, especially underrepresented students, like women, minorities, and students in economically low status, who want to succeed in higher education. Post-secondary education has played an important role to move under-represented students out of poor socio-economic circumstances and help them to lead successful lives (NCVER, 2000). After training in post-secondary institutions students are hired more than those without college degrees. However, cyberbullying incidents in higher education have increased creating new obstacles for students with socio-economic and other disadvantages to complete their degrees in post-secondary education.

According to a survey conducted by researchers at the National Institutes of Health (Wang, Iannotti, & Nasel, 2009), the highest depression scores were reported in victims that had been bullied. Bully-victims are more likely to report feelings of depression than are other groups, which interfere with scholastic achievement, social skills, and feelings of well-being. This can, in turn, create an obstacle to students in post-secondary education, perhaps, especially minority and/or socio-economically disadvantaged students.

Common themes of cyberbullying incidents include targeting student's appearance, disability or health-status, grades, and economic situation (Anderson & Sturm, 2007). Cyberbullies are more likely to bully peers who appear vulnerable and poor, as well as having characteristics related to gender, race/ethnicity, color, religion, ancestry, sexual orientation or mental/physical/sensory ability levels. Therefore, bullying victims tend to be minority and/or socio-economically disadvantaged students who exhibit the following characteristics: anxiety, insecurity, low self-esteem, poor social skills, and fewer or withdrawal from friends (Banks, 1997). Willard (2007) also concurred that cyberbullying victims may be selected based on the characteristics of different sexual orientation, weight, hyperactivity, slow maturation rate when compared to peers, and identification as a loner or nonconformist, as well as being economically poor.

Protecting post-secondary students from cyberbullying is increasingly a matter of concern. Post-secondary education has produced successful students of various backgrounds and/or socio-economically disadvantaged students, to be effective in their future by ensuring their academic quality and college completion. As bullying has increased on college campuses, bullying victims tend to have lower grades and achievement test scores than their non–victimized peers, and feel generally less safe at, and connected to colleges (Nakamoto & Schwartz, 2009). Greater efforts must be directed toward reducing bullying and its devastating effects, and toward creating more positive college campus climates for all students. However, the concepts for policies of cyberbullying in post-secondary education can be nebulous and not well understood. Therefore, this paper offers a review of current knowledge of cyberbullying in higher education, what are the forms, extent, and characteristics, as well as, the cyberbullying landscape to help formulate plans of action and policies addressing cyber bullying issues.

CYBERBULLYING: DEFINITION

Cyberbullying is the newest form of bullying in school. It has emerged as students have become more adept at using computers, cell phones, other mobile devices, as well as Internet applications for communication, education, and socialization. Topics of abuse can be the same in cyberspace as in face-to-face communication. However, because of the rapidity and non-physical presence between victim and perpetrator, cyberbullying become more dangerous (Levy, 2011). The cyberbullying definition used in this article is by Holladay (2011), "cyberbullying is the repeated use of technology to harass, humiliate, or threaten" (p. 4). Cyberbullying is any harassment that occurs via Internet through computers and/or through mobile technologies and their applications. Cruel forum posts, posting fake profiles on websites, and cruel email messages are examples cyberbullying.

CYBERBULLYING: THE CAUSE FOR CONCERN

Cyberbullying has unique concerns. Cyberbullying can persistently and permanently harm the online reputation of everyone involved – not just the person being bullied, but those doing the bullying or participating in it. Digital devices offer an ability to immediately and continuously communicate 24 hours a day, so it can be difficult for children experiencing cyberbullying to find relief. With the new Web, from Web 1.0 to Web 2.0, static pages have changed to interactive and user-generated content for communication, entertainment, as well as education (Solomon & Schrum, 2010). But Web 2.0 social networking technologies have been criminal to cyberbullying evidenced in post-secondary educational institutions (Sellers et al., 2009; Walker, Sockman & Koehn, 2011). With the growing technological access and ease in higher education, academic cyberbullying has risen. Because of the rapid investment of educational technology infrastructures for student education, as well as students' own adoption of mobile devices, digital communication technologies have infiltrated colleges and universities. Samarawickrema and Stacey (2007) relayed that a majority of educational institutions are increasingly providing online, educational content to their students for program success, such as through learning management systems.

Increasing use of e-learning tools in higher education and a transition from Web 1.0 to Web 2.0 has changed the learning landscape as well as the roles of teachers and students on campus. With these changes in learning and communicating has come new forms of harassment. Cyberbullying can permeate educational classrooms via email, chatrooms, blogs, cell phones, video recorders, cameras, websites, and network printers to offensively communicate (Belsey, 2006; Campbell, 2005; Shariff, 2005). This paper was initially motivated by a cyberbullying incident that occurred spring semester 2010 on a Midwestern university's campus (Smith and Yoon, 2012). The incident involved university supplied wireless technology in university-owned facilities. Two Caucasian female students had harassed an African American female student via online social networking in the university dormitory lounge. The communication postings were horrific for the victim, which abhorred other students, faculty, staff, and administrators. It inspired students to organize and hold a silent march in opposition to the violent remarks, and the chancellor has been addressing the campus climate through various means since. Even though this university has adopted new language in the student conduct code to address cyberbullying, there was no policy directly dealing with this type of harassment at the time.

Cyberbullying can be as serious as physical threats and suicides. The negative effects of cyberbullying have been evidenced in a variety of ways and the cyberbullying victims are more likely to experience anxiety, depression, loneliness, unhappiness, and poor sleep (Ang & Goh, 2010; Bauchner, 2011; Beale & Hall, 2007; Englander, Mills & McCoy, 2009). According to Price and Dalgleish (2010), cyberbullying negatively impacts students in many ways: self-esteem and confidence plus relationships and scholarly activity can deteriorate with the increase in anger and depression as well as self-harming and suicidal thoughts. Making the issue worse is the fact that such negative effects of bullying often go unnoticed, as many victims feel the need to conceal the fact that they are being bullied because they are embarrassed or afraid of further bullying. More often than not victims respond passively to bullying. They tend to act anxious and appear less confident. They may become quieter in class and, as a result, the bullying can become a hindrance on their academic success. Therefore, bullying is a problem that, if left unattended, can become a significant hurdle in students' development.

Post-secondary Cyberbullying can go beyond harassment and hate-language to physical endangerment (Englander, Mills & McCoy, 2009; Shanahan & Kelly, 2012). Cyberbullying-related suicides in post-secondary education occurred in September 2010, on the campus of Rutgers University. A freshman committed suicide in apparent response to cyberbullying by students, one being his roommate. The roommate and the other student were charged with criminal actions arising out of the cyberbullying behavior (Schwartz, 2011). Even though cyberbullying is so harmful, it is harder to recognize because teachers and parents may not overhear or see cyberbullying taking place (Ybarra, Diener-West & Leaf, 2007). These severe cyberbullying cases have given rise to research about cyberbullying on post-secondary education as well as new anti-cyberbullying laws and policy development in schools and states (Noonan, 2011).

CHARACTERISTICS OF CYBERBULLYING VICTIMS

To resolve the issues of cyberbullying in post-secondary education, it is essential to investigate cyberbullying in the university system through the eyes of those who are the victims, perpetrators, and witnesses of cyberbullying. The research by Smith and Yoon (2012) investigated cyberbullying with 276 college students. The university is a comprehensive four-year university with the ethnicity that 70% of the student population is white, 10% international, 10% Asian, 3.8% Black, 2% Hispanic, and 3.6% others. In this case study, all participants were students enrolled at a mid-western university.

The results came through surveys and interviews. For those students stating they had been cyberbullied by another student, the targeted topics of offensive communication were relayed as follows:

1. 12.2% religion or creed
2. 12.2% sexual orientation
3. 10.2% gender
4. 8.2% race or ethnicity
5. 6.1% disability
6. 6.1% age
7. 4.1% marital status
8. 4.1% national origin
9. 2.0% color

10. 2.0% public assistance status
11. 2.0% veteran status
12. 6.1% unknown
13. 24.7% other

Over 30% relayed other or unknown reasons for the cyberbully attacks are, such as online learning problems, abusive relationships, sexual harassment, attack on clothes seen in profile picture/materialistic target/physical appearance, ethical decisions made which the victims did not approve, misinterpretation of not being able to provide assistance to the victims, more studious than victims, did not partake in (as many) parties, not (online) social enough, more (or less) knowledgeable than the victims, lack of online gaming skills, and misunderstanding of a joke or having fun.

Of the 10% stating they had been cyberbullied by another student, over 46% reported the extent being moderate with some short-term effect on life and learning. 14.3% selected that the cyberbullying had a great extent affecting life and learning and 3.6% as seriously impacting emotional health and/or physical trauma. These statistics show that over half of those reporting being victimized by another student during their university studies are at least having short-term negative effects on life and learning.

Also reported was witnessing cyberbullying behavior by a student towards an instructor. A little over 5% of the students relayed they had witnessed a student cyberbully an instructor during their university experience, but the majority had not (93.5%). Of those responding yes, 36 characteristics of the cyberbullying were selected. Over 80% related to the university's equal opportunity statement.

There was also witnessing of cyberbullying behavior by an instructor towards a student. Almost 3% (2.9%) of the students relayed they had witnessed an instructor cyberbully a student during their university experience, but the majority had not (94.9%). Of those responding yes, 19 characteristics of the cyberbullying were selected. Almost three-quarters (73.7%) related to the university's equal opportunity statement. Since a large percentage of these respondents named university aspects addressed as being important in their mission, this could be a problem that needs to be investigated.

The results of the case study by Smith and Yoon (2012) confirmed that cyberbullying incidents exist beyond student-to-student level and has grown to student-to-instructor rank in the post-secondary education. In another study (Baldasare. et al., 2012), the students in economically low stature may be more vulnerable to be victimized by cyberbullying and their learning on campus are negatively affected. These studies stimulate more studies about cyberbullying in higher education and associated policy-making to ensure all students are protected and provided a safe learning environment.

CYBERBULLYING VICTIMS WITH POVERTY

One of the common themes in cyberbullying victims is that they are from a poor socio-economic background (Anderson & Sturm, 2007). Cyberbullying is more likely to occur at home when students are alone (Garinger, 2006; Smith et al., 2008). Students home alone after school may be more likely to be in poverty as parent(s) may be working. As previously explained, cyberbullying victims are usually targeted because of their difference in comparison to other students (Willard, 2007). Students who do not fit in may become the prime targets of cyberbullying. In many contexts, female students, minority status and/or lower economic privilege may be more susceptible to the abuse. Li (2007) studied 177 urban school seventh grade students from low to moderate socioeconomic statuses. Li found that 54% were bullied with traditional methods and a quarter of these students were subjected to cyberbullying. Of the victims, 34% reported the abuse to adults, and of all of the students sampled, 70% believed that adults who were aware of the incidents did not intervene to cease the cyberbullying. (Li, 2007).

Furthermore, victims have typical features of anxiety, insecurity, low self-esteem, poor social skills, few friends, and may be physically weaker than peers (Banks, 1997). According to a survey conducted by researchers at the National Institutes of Health (Wang, Iannotti, & Nasel, 2009), the highest depression scores were reported in bully victims. Bully-victims are more likely to feel depression than other groups. As a result of the depression, the victims could possibly lose interest in academic performance and withdraw from classroom activities, thus showing a decline in academic achievement. Previous research studies concluded that cyberbullying lowers the academic and the economic value of post-secondary education that has long been known as the promising pathway out of poverty (National Crime Prevention Council, 2013). In the economy of the 21st century, the college degree is the best way to get and keep a job. The U.S. Bureau of Labor Statistics (2013) had reported that unemployment rates decrease and wages increase as higher educational attainment occurs. "As of October 2009, the aggregate jobless rate for people with a high school degree or less was 12.2 percent, compared with 6.6 percent for those with some college or higher educational degree. Similarly, average yearly earnings jump each additional level of educational attainment" (Zhao, Liu, & Wolanin, 2012, p. 1). Fisher (2009) had reported that "in 2008, someone with an associate degree earned an average of $7,500 more than an individual with no schooling beyond high school" (as quoted by Zhao, Liu, & Wolanin, 2012, p. 1). While the post-secondary education leverages an opportunity to bring up students' economic status, a number of promising students, unfortunately, are unable to persist in the post-secondary educational environment. Cyberbullying causes interference with students continuing learning in higher education. Report of cyberbullying (Minor, Smith, & Brashen, 2013) announced cyberbullying caused a fear of not getting further learning opportunities and actually decreasing the rate of student retention.

Based on cyberbullying incidences and studies, educational researchers have recently devoted a great deal of attention to answering the question of how to protect students from cyberbullying in post-secondary education. Students have also expressed a need for academic intervention. For instance, similarities in college student responses in university cyberbullying case studies occurred between the student survey responses reported by Smith and Yoon (2012) and the focus group research by Baldasare et al. (2012). Overall college students thought that the university did not have to be involved in cyberbully events - that students should be able to handle it on their own. However, with further questioning and as certain cyberbullying scenarios became more extreme, university responsibility was advised by students, specifically policy creation. In the Baldasare et al. (2012), "nearly every focus group called for an update of the university policies to explicitly address cyberbullying" and "a zero-tolerance policy should be in place for any kind of online misbehavior taking place in an online learning environment" (p. 146).

CYBERBULLYING PERPETRATORS

In addition to understanding victims of cyberbullying, it is significant to investigate bullies in order to develop appropriate preventions and to apply relevant proactive protections for both victims and perpetrators. Who engages in cyberbullying behavior? Because cyberbullying is considered as an example of illegal behavior or activity occurring in the virtual and unreal world, cyber-bullies in college environments are considered as individuals who want to possess power or entertainment over victims (Doane et al., 2014). Therefore, cyberbullying perpetrators may have received some type of encouraging feedback when they instigated cyberbullying behavior (Görzig & Frumkin, 2013; O'Brien & Moules, 2013). In addition, because of anonymous environments of cyber settings, it is difficult to identify and locate perpetrators of cyberbullying and they may take advantage of anonymity (Barlett et al., 2016). For example, researchers found that cyber-bullies created their own false email accounts or web-based pages not using their real names bot others' names to insult, defame, and humiliate victims (Kokkinos et al., 2014; Renati, Berrone & Zanetti, 2012). Cyberbullying perpetrators benefit from technology. Burton and colleagues (2013) reported that online technology made cyberbullying more advanced and easier for cyber-bullies because more developed networks and more advanced electronic devices would be abused to harm other online users (Kyobe et al., 2016; Schenk et al., 2013). Cyber-bullies who are equipped technologically advanced devices and skills may have better and easier access to diverse online resources to harm victims emotionally and psychologically while they are not identified or caught. Therefore, online perpetrators are smart enough to utilize advanced technologies that were originally created with positive purpose in harmful and distorted ways. Thus, it may be inferred that the more cyber spaces are equipped with advanced technologies, the more perpetrators will harm others. Ironically, there have been patterns found among cyber-bully perpetrators and those patterns are related to their psychological characteristics. For example, according to Goodboy and Martin (2015) and Pieschl and colleagues (2013), cyberbullies are more likely to have maladaptive coping skills compared to those who never bullied others. Goodboy and Martin (2015) indicated that perpetrators' behaviors are originated from their external and internal energy: they internally believe that they have been wronged by others and feeling jealous would also cause those internal forces. Therefore, they harm others as an act of revenge. For external energy, researchers (Pieschl et al., 2013) attributed anonymous environments and encouragement from other peers as the major eternal forces of bullies' cyberbullying behaviors. However, according to Horner, Asher, and Fireman's study (2015), it is surprising that perpetrators are suicidal as much as cyberbully victims and bullies can be victims and vice versa. For additional psychological characteristics of cyber-bullies, Goodboy and Martin (2015) found that cyberbullying perpetrators are more likely to be morally disengaged compared to those who have not bullied. Individuals who bully others in cyber spaces are lacking the morality to feel guilty or bad about their harmful behaviors and consequences of those behaviors. In addition, by using a large-scale examination, Ryan and colleague (2011) found that cyber-bullies reported higher levels of distress psychological issue (e.g., depression, alcohol consumption) compared to their counterparts, and these problems eventually led bullies to commit additional destructive behaviors. This is another cycle of negative cause and effect, but morality and anonymous environments associated in cyberbullying because anonymity may cause immorality. Given the fact that cyberbullying perpetrators may be the ultimate victims after all, specialized treatment and interventions are necessary for cyber-bullies in this context. We will discuss more about psychological treatment and interventions in other solutions. Although researchers have attempted to confirm a profile of cyberbullying perpetrators (e.g., Slonje, Smith, & Frisén, 2013; Tokunaga, 2010), most studies explored students in K-12 settings. Therefore, with the need of established profile of college students who engage with cyberbullying behaviors, we investigated common personal profiles and tendency of cyber-bullies in postsecondary education such as gender, age, personality traits, and psychological issues. For gender differences in cyberbullying behaviors, Calvete and colleagues (2010) and Vandebosch and Van Cleemput (2009) found that male students are more likely to engage in cyberbullying behaviors compared to their female counterparts while Rivers and Noret (2010) and Sourander and colleagues (2010) reported higher rate of cyberbullying among female students than their male peers. It appears that existing literature on gender differences in cyberbullying behaviors is not consistent which will lead to the suggestions for future research. Studies investigated on the relationship between age and cyberbullying behaviors have somewhat inconsistent findings: some studies indicated that cyberbullying behaviors decrease as students become older (Raskauskas & Stoltz, 2007; Williams & Guerra, 2007) while Vandebosch and Van Cleemput (2009) found a positive correlation between age and cyberbullies. Given the fact that college students are more likely to engage with more online activities because they live apart from their families, they take more online courses, they meet their friends and colleagues in cyber spaces due to assignments and group projects compared to adolescents, it is assumed that college students may engage with more cyberbully behaviors. Therefore, it is important to explore an accurate rate of the behaviors among young adults. For psychological traits associated with cyberbullying, Carpenter (2012) indicated that narcissistic personality is associated with antisocial behaviors revealed on Facebook activities among students, and Gibb and Devereux (2014) addressed a possible association between narcissism and cyberbullying behaviors arguing that narcissistic individuals may feel socially less vulnerable. In addition to narcissism, there would be more psychological trait related to cyberbullying behaviors among college students. Thus, more systematic analysis on association between psychological trait and cyberbullies is necessary to understand this population.

CYBERBULLYING POLICIES AND SOLUTIONS

Developing a safe environment in post-secondary institutions to protect students from cyberbullying has become an increasingly emergent concern. The first legislation related to the prevention of cyberbullying was introduced in April 2009. As of February 2012, all but two of the 50 states in the United States have enacted anti-bully legislation, and 16 states have either anti-bullying policies, laws pending, or comments about the need for or status of their policies or laws (Hinduja & Patchin, 2012). The Megan Meier Cyberbullying Prevention Act is a federal act currently pending legislation (Hinduja & Patchin, 2012). The act states, "Whoever transmits in interstate or foreign commerce any communication, with the intent to coerce, intimidate, harass, or cause substantial emotional distress to a person, using electronic means to support severe, repeated, and hostile behavior, shall be fined under this title or imprisoned not more than two years, or both" (p. 14). As of September 2011, only eight state laws include cyberbullying. Currently, there is no federal law that defines cyberbullying (Hinduja & Patchin, 2012). Since cyberbullying is a relatively new area of research, little is known about the concept and policies of cyberbullying in post-secondary education. Few policies exist to prevent or reprimand the behavior (Brown et al., 2006).

U.S. law has not sufficiently covered this new form of abuse specifically because of freedom of speech issues, and because of this, cyberbullying policies themselves are problematic for educational institutions (O'Neil, 2008). However, because of extreme cases of life endangerment and death there are a few states that are employing laws as well as schools developing policies to deal with cyberbullying (O'Neil, 2008). Lane (2011) had argued that it is the school's responsibility and assured that cyberbullying policy and practices can be implemented successfully. In 2011, the U.S. Department of Education had released a comprehensive review of state anti-bullying laws as well as policies encompassing the discussion of school district policy development. The report noted that at the time, 36 states had language of anti-cyberbullying in laws or policies. Thirteen states extended a school's jurisdiction over cyberbully cases to both on- and off-campus and/or through the school's technological infrastructure if the behavior created a hostile campus environment. Cyberbullying and related behaviors are addressed in single or multiple laws. In some cases, cyberbullying appears in the criminal code of a state that may apply to juveniles. (U.S. Department of Education, 2011).

The U.S. Department of Education reviewed state laws and identified 11 key components common among many of those laws provided examples of the key components (U.S. Department of education, 2010). The 11 key components may be useful to those who are creating or improving anti-bullying laws or policies in their states. The 11 key components are:

1. Purpose statement;
2. Statement of scope;
3. Specification of prohibited conduct;
4. Enumeration of specific characteristics;
5. Development and implementation of LEA policies;
6. Components of LEA policies;
7. Review of local policies;
8. Communication plan;
9. Training and preventive education;
10. Transparency and monitoring;
11. Statement of rights to other legal recourse.

Policy discussion and creation on cyberbullying have generally centered on K-12 schools. However, since this form of abuse also affects colleges and universities, policy should be extended to higher education. Existing policy can also provide useful principles and provisions for higher educational institutions to use for addressing possible cyberbullying or other bullying behaviors on their campuses. Finally, as the incidence of cyberbullying may grow in the K-12 sector, colleges and universities should consider how this trend might ultimately affect their institutional climate. Post-secondary institutions could investigate the steps that need to be taken to ensure negative impacts to student learning and well-being are minimized.

OTHER SOLUTIONS

Given the fact that "it takes a village to raise a child," it takes every individual's efforts to develop safe environments for both cyber-bullies and victims in postsecondary education settings. First, it is important to understand the phenomenon of cyberbullying among college students because both cyber-bullies and cyberbullying victims are more likely to be at higher risk of psychological problems and their dropout rates are higher compared to their counterparts (Baldasare et al., 2012). Since the psychological problems will lead to other issues in academic performance (e.g., missing classes, not submitting assignments, not participating in discussions due to fear of being attacked), it is important to understand cyberbullying.

Second, as it is anticipated that more universities are moving their campuses into the online learning environments, awareness on severe cyberbullying within this digital college campus environments should be widely informed to all individuals in higher education institutions. Although cyberbullying is the phenomenon among students, administrators, faculty, advisors, leaders, and policy makers in college should be well aware of the realistic circumstances to understand the phenomenon and be alert.

Third, mental health professionals, faculty, and student affairs who work with students on campus need to know their assigned students and advisees well and periodically explore their up-to-date experiences on cyberbullying. Timely and appropriate investigations are necessary to prevent and protect cyberbullying and mental health professionals, faculty, and student affairs professionals are those who work closely with students who can access their needs and honest experiences. For this proactive protections, advanced educational sessions such as cyberbullying prevention workshops for mental health professionals, faculty, and student affairs professionals on campus are needed.

Fourth, mental health professionals, faculty, and staffs on campus need to know that the approach to and interpretation of cyberbullying behaviors should be differentiated according to students' psychological and cultural background. As we previously discussed, cyber-bullies are more likely to be distressed and associated psychological issues compared to their counterparts, therefore understanding their psychological background should be considered when working with them. In addition, the reason why considering cultural background is important is because culture play important roles to understand and interpret cyberbullying behaviors. For example, in collectivistic culture, deep engagement with their friends' lives and experiences can be a token of appreciation or friendship while some students may feel humiliated when their friends want to know their detailed daily lives. Some bullies may commit negative behaviors not knowing it is insulting or humiliating. Thus, understanding and interpreting cyberbullying behaviors should be considered with diverse perspectives.

Fifth, professors and instructors need to address the possible cyberbullying issues upfront before they begin the new classes, so that students are fully aware of the importance of safe online learning environments. Given the fact that online academic courses are another base for cyberbullying behaviors among college students, proactive preventions related online courses are necessary to prevent before it happens. Considering college students are easily exposed to learning environments and they are intellectually capable to comprehend and implement, it would be effective for instructors to educate their students during the initial stage of their online courses.

Lastly, creating and running campus wide anti cyberbully campaign or cyberbully prevention program would be helpful for students' awareness. Since campus wide events or psycho-educational workshops are effective for college students, age appropriate and situation appropriate campus wide programs to target students' awareness on cyberbully will be recommended.

CONCLUSION

This paper has sought to provide a review of the many facets of research on cyberbullying affecting post-secondary education. Research studies and statistics relay that cyberbullying is a problem for students of many backgrounds and ages, including disadvantaged students in higher education. Young adults utilize many technologies that can be used as weapons, from laptops to cell phones to specific social networking Internet sites. It is likely technologies will continue to change where students will acquire and use them to communicate with each other. Post-secondary education is likely to adopt these communication devices and applications for teaching and learning as well.

As technology will only become more ingrained in education, the negative effects of cyberbullying have to be acknowledged. It interferes with the promising future of students in post-secondary education, especially disadvantaged students, such as minority students or those in lower socio-economic groups. Cyberbullying creates a barrier to post-secondary students of lower socio-eco backgrounds? While a few research studies conducted have identified that cyberbullying is clearly occurring in higher education, it has had little to say definitively about how the problem might be remedied. Many students on campus of higher institutions are experiencing cyberbullying by their peers and instructors but there are few research studies to protect them from the cyberbullying attacks. Fortunately, the U.S. Department of Education (2011) has taken cyberbullying seriously by reviewing state anti-bullying laws and model policies.

What post-secondary education can do to help in delivering high quality, as well as safe, instruction is the core of our evolving learning environment. Many studies recommend policy adoption, which has been a focal point for secondary schools in the last decade. This article recommends it is necessary to research more about cyberbullying policy-making in higher education as well as its effects on students, especially in disadvantaged socio-economic circumstances.

REFERENCES

Akbulut, Y., Sahin, Y. L., & Eristi, B. (2010). Cyberbullying victimization among Turkish online social utility members. *Journal of Educational Technology & Society, 13*(4), 192–201.

Anderson, T., & Sturm, B. (2007). Cyberbullying from playground to computer. Young Adult Library Services, 24-27.

Ang, R. P., & Goh, D. H. (2010). Cyberbullying among adolescents: The role of affective and cognitive empathy, and gender. *Child Psychiatry and Human Development, 41*(4), 387–397. doi:10.100710578-010-0176-3 PMID:20238160

Baldasare, A., Bauman, S., Goldman, L., & Robie, A. (2012). Cyberbullying? Voices of college students. In C. Wankel (Ed.), *Cutting-edge technologies in higher education* (pp. 127–157). Emerald Group Publishing Limited.

Banks, R. (1997). Bullying in schools.

Barlett, C. P., Gentile, D. A., & Chew, C. (2016). Predicting cyberbullying from anonymity. *Psychology of Popular Media Culture, 5*(2), 171–180. doi:10.1037/ppm0000055

Bauchner, H. (2011, April 20). Benefits and risks of social media use in children and adolescents. *Journal Watch Pediatrics & Adolescent Medicine.*

Beale, A. V., & Hall, K. R. (2007). Cyberbullying: What school administrators (and parents) can do. *The Clearing House: A Journal of Educational Strategies, Issues and Ideas, 81*(1), 8–12. doi:10.3200/TCHS.81.1.8-12

Belsey, B. (2006). Bullying.org: A learning journey. *Bulletin – Newfoundland and Labrador Teachers Association, 49*(4), 20-21. Retrieved from http://www.nlta.nl.ca/files/documents/bulletins/bultn_jan_feb06.pdf

Brown, K., Jackson, M., & Cassidy, W. (2006). Cyberbullying: Developing policy to direct responses that are equitable and effective in addressing this special form of bullying. *Canadian Journal of Educational Administration and Policy, 57*, 8–11. Retrieved from http://www.umanitoba.ca/publications/cjeap/articles/brown_jackson_cassidy.html

Bryman, A. (1989). *Research methods and organization studies*. London, UK: Unwin Hyman.

Calvete, E., Orue, I., Estévez, A., Villardón, L., & Padilla, P. (2010). Cyberbullying in adolescents: Modalities and aggressors' profile. *Computers in Human Behavior, 26*(5), 1128–1135. doi:10.1016/j.chb.2010.03.017

Campbell, M. (2005). Cyberbullying: An older problem in a new guise? *Australian Journal of Guidance & Counselling, 15*(1), 68–76. doi:10.1375/ajgc.15.1.68

Clemans, K. H., Graber, J. A., Lyndon, S. T., & Sontag, L. M. (2011). Traditional and cyber aggressors and victims: A comparison of psychosocial characteristics. *Journal of Youth and Adolescence, 40*(4), 392–404. doi:10.100710964-010-9575-9 PMID:20680425

Conn, K. (2011). Cyberbullying and other student technology misuses in k-12 American schools: The Legal Landmines. *Widener Law Review, 89*(1).

Doane, A. N., Pearson, M. R., & Kelley, M. L. (2014). Predictors of cyberbullying perpetration among college students: An application of the theory of reasoned action. *Computers in Human Behavior, 36*, 154–162. doi:10.1016/j.chb.2014.03.051

Englander, E., Mills, E., & McCoy, M. (2009). Cyberbullying and information exposure: User-generated content in post-secondary education. *International Journal of Contemporary Sociology, 46*(2), 213–230. Retrieved from http://webhost.bridgew.edu/marc/user-generated%20data%20englander %20mills%20mccoy.pdf

Englander, E. K. (2007). Cyberbullying: The New Frontier. *Proceedings of the Twenty-Third Annual Pediatric Rehabilitation Conference*. Franciscan Hospital for Children and Boston University School of Medicine, Burlington, MA.

Firat, M., & Ayran, G. (2016). Cyberbullying among college students. *Turk Silahli Kuvvetleri Koruyucu Hekimlik Bulteni*, *15*(4), 322. doi:10.5455/pmb.1-1450776947

Francisco, S. M., Veiga Simão, A. M., Ferreira, P. C., & Martins, M. J. D. (2015). Cyberbullying: The hidden side of college students. *Computers in Human Behavior*, *43*, 167–182. doi:10.1016/j.chb.2014.10.045

Gibb, Z., & Devereus, P. (2014). Who does that anyway? Predictors and personality correlates of cyberbullying in college. *Computers in Human Behavior*, *38*, 8–16. doi:10.1016/j.chb.2014.05.009

Goodboy, A. K., & Martin, M. M. (2015). The personality profile of a cyberbully: Examining the dark triad. *Computers in Human Behavior*, *49*, 1–4. doi:10.1016/j.chb.2015.02.052

Görzig, A., & Frumkin, L. (2013). Cyberbullying experiences on-the-go: When social media can become distressing. *Cyberpsychology*, *7*(1), 4. doi:10.5817/CP2013-1-4

Hinduja, S., & Patchin, J. (2011, February). High-tech cruelty. *Educational Leadership*, *68*(5), 48–52.

Hinduja, S., & Patchin, J. (2012). State cyberbullying laws: A brief review of state cyberbullying laws and policies. Retrieved from http://www.cyberbullying.us/Bullying_and_Cyberbullying_Laws.pdf

Holladay, J. (2011). Cyberbullying. *Education Digest: Essential Readings Condensed for Quick Review*, *76*(5), 4–9.

Horner, S., Asher, Y., & Fireman, G. D. (2015). The impact and response to electronic bullying and traditional bullying among adolescents. *Computers in Human Behavior*, *49*, 288–295. doi:10.1016/j.chb.2015.03.007

Jones, C. G. (2011). Computer hackers on the cul-de-sac: Myspace suicide indictment under the Computer Fraud and Abuse Act sets dangerous precedent. *Widener Law Review*, *17*(1), 261–287.

Juvonen, J., & Gross, S. (2008). Extending the School Grounds? Bullying Experiences in Cyberspace. *The Journal of School Health*, *78*(9), 496–505. doi:10.1111/j.1746-1561.2008.00335.x PMID:18786042

Kokkinos, C. M., Antoniadou, N., & Markos, A. (2014). Cyber-bullying: An investigation of the psychological profile of university student participants. *Journal of Applied Developmental Psychology*, *35*(3), 204–214. doi:10.1016/j.appdev.2014.04.001

Kyobe, M. E., Oosterwyk, G. W., & Kabiawu, O. O. (2016). The nature of mobile bullying in the Western Cape high schools of South Africa. *African Journal of Information Systems*, 8(2), 45–69.

Lane, D. K. (2011). Taking the lead on cyberbullying: Why schools can and should protect students online. *Iowa Law Review*, 96(5), 1791.

Lenhart, A., Madden, M., Smith, A., Purcell, K., Zickuhr, K., & Rainie, L. (2011, November 9). Teens, kindness and cruelty on social network sites. *Pew Internet & American Life Project*. Retrieved from http://pewinternet.org/Reports/2011/Teens-and-social-media/Summary.aspx?view=all

Levy, P. (2011). Confronting cyberbullying: Experts say that schools need to stop worrying about external internet predators and take on the threat within: cyberbullying. *The Journal Technological Horizons In Education*, 38(5), 25.

Li, Q. (2007). New bottle but old wine: A research of cyberbullying in schools. *Computers in Human Behavior*, 23(4), 1–15. doi:10.1016/j.chb.2005.10.005

Li, Q. (2008). A cross-cultural comparison of adolescents' experience related to cyberbullying. *Educational Research*, 50(3), 223–234. doi:10.1080/00131880802309333

Luscombe, N. (2011). The dark side of social networking. *WWLP-TV*. Retrieved from http://www.wwlp.com/dpp/mass_appeal/family/the-dark-side-of-social-networking

Minor, M. A., Smith, G. S., & Brashen, H. (2013). Cyberbullying in Higher Education. *Journal of Educational Research and Practice*, 2(1), 15–29. Retrieved from http://scholarworks.waldenu.edu/cgi/viewcontent.cgi?article=1043&context=jerap

Nakamoto, J., & Schwartz, D. (2009). Is peer victimization associated with academic achievement? A meta-analytic review. *Social Development*, 19(2), 221–242. doi:10.1111/j.1467-9507.2009.00539.x

National Crime Prevention Council. (2013). What is Cyberbullying? Retrieved from http://www.ncpc.org/topics/cyberbullying/what-is-cyberbullying

National Institutes of Health. (2010). *Depression high among youth victims of school cyber bullying, NIH researchers report*. Retrieved from http://www.nih.gov/news/health/sep2010/nichd-21.htm

National Center for Vocational Education (NCVER). (2000). *Australian Vocational education and Training Statistics 2000: Students with a Disability in Vocational Education and Training*.

Noonan, B. J. (2011). Crafting legislation to prevent cyberbullying: The use of education, reporting, and threshold requirements. *Contemporary Health Law & Policy, Spring,* 330.

O'Brien, N., & Moules, T. (2013). Not sticks and stones but tweets and texts: Findings from a national cyberbullying project. *Pastoral Care in Education, 31*(1), 53–65. doi:10.1080/02643944.2012.747553

O'Neil, R. M. (2008). It's not easy to stand up to cyberbullies, but we must. *The Chronicle of Higher Education, 54*(44), A23.

Pieschl, S., Porsch, T., Kahl, T., & Klockenbusch, R. (2013). Relevant dimensions of cyberbullying—Results from two experimental studies. *Journal of Applied Developmental Psychology, 34*(5), 241–252. doi:10.1016/j.appdev.2013.04.002

Price, M., & Dalgleish, J. (2010). Cyberbullying: Experiences, impacts and coping strategies as described by Australian young people. *Youth Studies Australia, 29,* 51–59.

Raskauskas, J., & Stoltz, A. D. (2007). Involvement in traditional and electronic bullying among adolescents. *Developmental Psychology, 43*(3), 564–575. doi:10.1037/0012-1649.43.3.564 PMID:17484571

Renati, R., Berrone, C., & Zanetti, M. A. (2012). Morally disengaged and unempathic: Do cyberbullies fit these definitions? An exploratory study. *Cyberpsychology, Behavior, and Social Networking, 15*(8), 391–398. doi:10.1089/cyber.2012.0046 PMID:22823490

Rivers, I., & Noret, N. (2010). 'I h 8 u': Findings from a five-year study of text and email bullying. *British Educational Research Journal, 36*(4), 643–671. doi:10.1080/01411920903071918

Robson, C. (2002). *Real world research: A resource for social scientists and practitioner-researchers* (2nd ed.). Malden, MA: Blackwell.

Ryan, T., Kariuki, M., & Yilmaz, H. (2011). A comparative analysis of cyberbullying perceptions of preservice educators: Canada and Turkey. *The Turkish Online Journal of Educational Technology, 10*(3), 1–12.

Samarawickrema, G., & Stacey, E. (2007). Adopting Web-based learning and teaching: A case study in higher education. *Distance Education, 28*(3), 313–333. Retrieved from http://www.mrgibbs.com/tu/research/articles/Samarawickerema-adopting_WBE.pdf doi:10.1080/01587910701611344

Schenk, A. M., Fremouw, W. J., & Kelan, C. M. (2013). Characteristics of college cyberbullies. *Computers in Human Behavior*, *29*(6), 2320–2327. doi:10.1016/j. chb.2013.05.013

Schwartz, J. (2010, October 2). Bullying, suicide, punishment. The New York Times. Retrieved from http://www.612essentials.com/wp-content/uploads/2010/10/ Bullying-Suicide-Punishment-NYTimes.com_.pdf

Sellers, M., Wray, G., Meeker, N., & Moulton, S. (2009). Cyberbullying in higher education. In T. Bastiaens, & ... (Eds.), *Proceedings of World Conference on E-Learning in Corporate, Government, Healthcare, and Higher Education* (pp. 2298-2303). Chesapeake, VA: AACE.

Shanahan, S. J., & Kelly, J. G. (2012). How to Protect Your Students From Cyberbullying, Retrieved from http://chronicle.com/article/How-to-Protect-Your-Students/131306/

Shariff, S. (2005). Cyberdilemmas in the new millennium. *McGill Journal of Education*, *40*(3), 467–487. Retrieved from http://www.eric.ed.gov/ERICWebPortal/ sea rch/detailmini.jsp?_nfpb=true&_&ERICExtSearch_SearchValue_0=EJ73707 8&ERICExtSearch_SearchType_0=no&accno=EJ737078

Slonge, R., Smith, P., & Frisen, A. (2013). The nature of cyberbullying, and strategies for prevention. *Computers in Human Behavior*, *29*(1), 16–32.

Smith, J., & Yoon, J. (2013). Cyberbullying Presence, Extent, and Forms in a Midwestern Post-secondary Institution. *Information Systems Education Journal*, *11*(4).

Smith, P. K., Mahdavi, J., Carvalho, M., Fisher, S., Russell, S., & Tippett, N. (2008). Cyberbullying: Its nature and impact in secondary school pupils. *Journal of Child Psychology and Psychiatry, and Allied Disciplines*, *49*(4), 376–385. doi:10.1111/ j.1469-7610.2007.01846.x PMID:18363945

Solomon, G., & Schrum, L. (2010). *Web 2.0: How-To for Educators*. US: International Society for Technology in Education.

Sourander, A., Klomek, A. B., Ikonen, M., Lindroos, J., Luntamo, T., Koskelainen, M., & ... . (2010). Psychosocial risk factors associated with cyberbullying among adolescents: A population based study. *Archives of General Psychiatry*, *67*(7), 720–728. doi:10.1001/archgenpsychiatry.2010.79 PMID:20603453

Tokunaga, R. S. (2010). Following you home from school: A critical review and synthesis of research on cyberbullying victimization. *Computers in Human Behavior*, *26*(3), 277–287. doi:10.1016/j.chb.2009.11.014

U.S. Bureau of Labor Statistics. (2013). The Employment Situation. Retrieved March 27th 2013 from http://www.bls.gov/news.release/pdf/empsit.pdf

U.S. Department of Education. (2011). Analysis of State Bullying Laws and Policies. Retrieved from http://www2.ed.gov/rschstat/eval/bullying/state-bullying-laws/state-bullying-laws.pdf.

Valentino-DeVries, J. (2010, Sept.). Cyberbullying goes to college. *Wall Street Journal*. Retrieved from http://blogs.wsj.com/digits/2010/09/30/the-rutgers-students-suicide-cyberbullying-goes-to-college/

Vandebosch, H., & Van Cleemput, K. (2009). Cyberbullying among youngsters: Profiles of bullies and victims. *New Media & Society*, *11*(8), 1349–1371. doi:10.1177/1461444809341263

Walker, C.M., Rajan Sockman, B., & Koehn, S. (2011). An exploratory study of cyberbullying with undergraduate university students. *TechTrends: For Leaders in Education & Training, 55*(2), 31.

Wang, J., Iannotti, R. J., & Nansel, T. R. (2009). School bullying among adolescents in the United States: Physical, verbal, relational, and cyber. *The Journal of Adolescent Health*, *45*(4), 368–375.

Willard, N. (2007). Cyberbullying and cyberthreats: Responding to the challenge of online social aggression, threats, and distress. Research Press. Retrieved from http://www.ctap4.org/cybersafety/Documentaton.htm

Williams, K. R., & Guerra, N. G. (2007). Prevalence and predictors of internet bullying. *The Journal of Adolescent Health*, *41*(6 Suppl. 1), S14–S2. doi:10.1016/j.jadohealth.2007.08.018 PMID:18047941

Woods, R. H. (2001). Order in the virtual classroom. *Journal of Information, Law and Technology, 3*, 1-47. Retrieved from http://www.buscalegis.ccj.ufsc.br/revistas/index.php/buscalegis/article/viewFile/19359/18923

Wright, V. H., Burnham, J. J., Inman, C. T., & Ogorchock, H. N. (2009). Cyberbullying: Using virtual scenarios to educate and raise awareness. *Journal of Computing in Teacher Education*, *26*(1), 35–42.

Ybarra, M. L., Diener-West, M., & Leaf, P. J. (2007). Examining the overlap in internet harassment and school bullying: Implications for school intervention. *The Journal of Adolescent Health*, *41*(6), S42–S5. doi:10.1016/j.jadohealth.2007.09.004 PMID:18047944

Zhao, H., Liu, S., & Wolanin, N. (2012, June). College enrollment, persistence, and degree attainment for high school graduates in Montgomery County Public Schools, Maryland. Retrieved from http://montgomeryschoolsmd.org/departments/ sharedaccountability/reports/2012/College%20Enrollment%20Persistence%20 and%20Degree%20Attainment%20final.pdf

This research was previously published in International Journal of Cyber Behavior, Psychology and Learning (IJCBPL), 9(1); edited by Lijia Lin, pages 1-15, copyright year 2019 by IGI Publishing (an imprint of IGI Global).

Chapter 9
Legislative Response to Cyber Aggression:
Federal and State-Local Policy Reform

Ramona S. McNeal
University of Northern Iowa, USA

Susan M. Kunkle
Kent State University, USA

Mary Schmeida
Kent State University, USA

ABSTRACT

This chapter presents the federal and state-local legislative response to cyber aggression: stalking, harassment, and bullying. Along with other federal efforts, the federal Violence Against Women Act and its reauthorizations is identified as a cornerstone law in protecting the public on stalking and harassment. State-local laws have advanced in scope; yet, there are laggard states not yet entirely on board in passing legislation aligned with the advancement of technology used in cyber aggression. All three branches of government to some extent have had a voice in today's cyber policy. Judicial court cases have shaped policy decisions and several key cases are presented.

DOI: 10.4018/978-1-7998-1684-3.ch009

INTRODUCTION

Cyber aggression takes on varying forms including stalking, harassment, bullying, and nonconsensual pornography. See Table 1 of Chapter 1. These are behaviors restricted by laws and court rulings. Federal and state regulatory and administrative legislation fighting these dysfunctional behaviors have been incremental in the making. On the federal level, the 1994 Violence against Women Act (Public Law 103-322) is a cornerstone law to supporting stalking victims such as women and children. It authorized grants to states and tribal government to fight the aggression on the domestic level. With cyberbullying, there is no chief federal law that governs over the behavior. Instead, the federal government has devolved authority to states and school districts, and judicial decisions have had an impact on school discipline policy. In the fight against cyber aggression, states know the protective needs of their local best, but not all are on board. While the majority has some type of law protecting residents from "physical" aggression crimes, not all have updated to include the "cyber" of aggression. This chapter discusses government action or inaction on enacting regulatory and administrative cyber aggression laws on stalking, harassment, bullying, and nonconsensual pornography.

BACKGROUND

With nearly half (49%) of the world online (Pew Research Center, 2017) more people are susceptible to cyber aggression as criminals use technology to cyber stalk, harass, and bully. This is not surprising since obtaining electronics for criminal intent is easy. Most anyone can purchase a computer, multifunctional cell phone device and supporting software; and access to the World Wide Web is becoming less costly and free in some places. The traditional "physical" stalking, harassment, and bullying behaviors now have a digital counterpart. The U.S. Department of Health and Human Services (2015) reports cyber aggression as an "emergent concern," and not limited to "sending threatening texts, posting or distributing defamatory or harassing messages, and uploading or distributing hateful or demeaning images or videos intended to harm another" (USDHHS, 2015). Concerned about cybercrime, some Americans are taking counter measures to confront the unfriendly digital climate. A 2013 Pew Internet & American Life Project survey found as many as 55% of respondents reported avoiding online observation by people, employers, government, organizations, and other; while 86% of adult Internet users have taken measures to promote anonymity, privacy, and security online. To avoid surveillance, online safety behaviors range from masking personal information, clearing search histories, to using a public computer instead of personal home computer (Pew Internet & American Life Project, 2013).

The definition of stalking varies from state to state. Generally, it is "a course of conduct directed at a specific person that causes actual fear or would cause a reasonable person to feel fear" (U.S. Department of Justice Office on Violence against Women [USDOJOVW], 2017, p. 6). The cyber counterpart is the use of the Internet, email or other electronic communications to stalk, and generally refers to a pattern of threatening or malicious behaviors. It may be considered a most dangerous type of Internet harassment. The sanctions range from misdemeanors to felonies (National Conference of State Legislatures [NCSL], 2013a). This crime is under federal, state, District of Columbia and U.S. territories law (USDOJ, 2012). Cyber-harassment differs from cyberstalking since it may not involve a credible threat, and usually pertains to threatening or harassing email messages, instant messages, or to blog entries or websites dedicated solely to tormenting an individual (NCSL, 2013a), reference Table 1 of Chapter 1 on definitions. Not all states are keeping up with provisions that cover advanced technology methods being used by perpetrators for cybercrimes. Although federal laws (Violence against Women Act of 2005 & 2013) extended protective regulation to cover both interstate and intrastate cyberstalking, many states have not caught up with the newer forms of technology, such as Global Positioning Systems surveillance and videotaping. Some state laws use "broader language" to cover the many types of evolving stalking methods (physical and electronic) used by perpetrators, whereas others have separate laws (USDOJOVW, 2017; NCSL, 2013a). Some states approach cyber-harassment by including language addressing electronic communications in general harassment statutes, while others have created stand-alone cyber-harassment laws (NCSL, 2013a). Chapter 5 brings an empirical insight on why some states have taken the basic steps of updating existing stalking and harassment laws to now include electronic communication technology, and others not.

With cyberbullying, much like physical bullying, girls are more likely to be victims than boys. Popular methods are Internet instant messaging, chat rooms, e-mails and posted website messages (NCSL, 2011). There are no federal laws "directly addressing" bullying per se, as the responsibility has been devolved to the local government for policy making. Defining cyberbullying has not been clear cut for the states. While some states differentiate bullying from harassment, others say the two cannot be differentiated. The cyberbullying language in some state laws is the same for cyber-harassment. "In some cases, bullying overlaps with discriminatory harassment when it is based on race, national origin, color, sex, age, disability, or religion" (Antibullying Institute, 2017, p. 1).

As described in Chapter 1, cyber revenge pornography is a form of aggression facing minors and adults. Some refer to the behavior as sexual cyber-harassment, involuntary or non-consensual pornography, whereas doxing refers to the posting of personal information about another in an act of revenge. Cyber pornography involves "the dissemination or posting sexually explicit media without the consent of the individual in the media, particularly where the intent is to shame, humiliate, and frighten the person or otherwise cause them harm" (Lonardo, Martland & White, 2016, p. 80). A shorter definition by the State of Arkansas's Act 304 is the "unlawful distribution of sexual images or recording." Both the federal government and states are assuming a strict stance on this problem. All states have passed some type of legislation governing child pornography (Cyberbullying Research Center, 2015c).

GOVERNMENT RESPONSE TO CYBER AGGRESSION

In effort to protect the public from cyber aggression, federal laws have been passed and several are in response to some violent crisis event and/ or vulnerable group most in need of law. The federal government has made a commitment to assist the states on domestic crime with funding. Cyberstalking and harassments policies are largely aimed to protect females; cyberbullying is primarily geared to protect children and youth. Updating federal anti-discrimination and harassment laws to protect the lesbian, gay, bisexual, and transgender population has progressed.

The federal and state-local response to cyber aggression is primarily regulatory and administrative law. Lowi (1972) classifies public policy as falling into four major categories: distributive, re-distributive, regulatory, and constituent policy. Policy concerning the criminalization of cyberstalking, harassment and bullying activities can be conceptualized as regulatory and administrative policy. Specifically, these protective-type regulatory policies are designed to protect society by prohibiting harmful conditions (Ripley and Franklin, 1980, pp. 20, 24), and considered "only one of several ways governments seek to control society and individual conduct" (Lowi, 1972, p. 299). The political relationships in policymaking of regulatory policy are largely Congressional committees and sub-committees, the full House and Senate, executive agencies, and trade associations (Ripley and Franklin, 1980, p. 22). On the other hand, administrative reform policy (McNeal, Tolbert, Mossberger & Dotterweich, 2003), unlike regulatory policy does not involve the direct and coercive use of government power over citizens (Lowi, 1979). Administrative policy tells us "how" policy/ programs are to be carried out, and are technical rather than value-laden and non-salient with the public. Major players tend to be administrative officials even though state legislators play a role through budget processes or legislative oversight and professional networks (McNeal et al., 2003). In all, protecting against cyber aggression requires not only federal but state-local regulatory and administrative laws.

Violence Against Women Act as a Federal Cornerstone Law

Current federal laws fighting cyberstalking and cyber-harassment are largely built on early crime laws aimed at public safety. Initially, Congress enacted regulations protecting the public from violence such as (physical) stalking and harassment. The "cyber" counterpart was added to law by subsequent provisions. Prior to the 1970s, women were invisible victims of violent crimes, such as battering, harassment, stalking and policy centered on family domestic violence. For example, considered a domestic family issue, in 1984 the Family Violence Prevention and Services Act (Public Law 98-457) was passed assisting states to prevent family violence and to provide shelters and services to those victimized (Congressional Research Service, 2014). Modern day cyberstalking laws protecting women are rooted in these older concepts, and as family violence took on a modern-day social view, the laws were modernized. It was in the 1990s that society began to view stalking as a criminal conduct as falling within the jurisdiction of the federal and state criminal justice systems. Considered a legislative milestone in dealing with gender based violence against women, the 1994 Violence against Women Act often referred to as VAWA was enacted by Congress as Title IV of the Violent Crime Control and Law Enforcement Act of 1994 (Public Law 103-322). The 1994 VAWA gave state, local, and tribal law enforcement jurisdictions grant opportunities for the investigation and prosecution of violent crimes against women---domestic violence, sexual assault, dating violence, stalking, and other (USDOJ, 2016). "VAWA articulates the Congress's commitment to effective strategies for preventing and responding to domestic and sexual violence, holding offenders accountable, and ensuring safety, autonomy, and justice for victims" (USDOJOVW, 2015b, p. ix).

Much like the Civil Rights Act of 1964 (Public Law 88-352) with all its amendments improving the gesture of the law over time, the VAWA has expanded in scope now giving many a biased/ vulnerable group their law enforcement attention by way of federally funded programs on anti-stalking and harassment. The VAWA was reauthorized in 2000 and 2005 with broad bipartisan support, and again in 2013 with "some adversity" (Congressional Research Service, 2015). In both 2000 and 2005 the scope of protection and services for victims were expanded. Specifically, the Victims of Trafficking and Violence Protection Act of 2000 (Public Law 106-386) reauthorized the 1994 VAWA and its grant monies for policy implementation, in particular to support law enforcement actions that encouraged arrest policies. In 2000, other VAWA monies went to states for their domestic violence and sexual assault coalitions; and to Indian tribal governments to cover rural domestic violence and child abuse. The law improved the access to protection of battered immigrant women. In 2005, Congress reauthorized appropriations for VAWA through the Violence against Women and Department of Justice Reauthorization Act (Public Law 109-162) that modernized the goals of VAWA. Title I of P.L. 109-162 enhances judicial and law enforcement tools to fight violence against women. Title II improves services for victims of domestic violence, sexual assault, and stalking. Title V strengthens the healthcare system's response to aggressive crime. Among funding appropriations was a new program developed for cultural and linguistic services for victims because of today's changing cultural landscape; monies went to servicing children and women age 50 and over who are victim vulnerable; and higher education campus needs. Prioritized for monies was the underserved and rural American. The VAWA 2005 now gives the Attorney General power to authorize grants to Indian tribal governments and those organizations aimed at improving the capacity of Indian Tribal Government service to native women (Public Law 109-162, 2005) as these women have been victims to a high incidence of aggression. Since stalking methods have become more advanced through new technology (Internet, global positioning systems, etc.), the 2005 Act introduced "interstate cyberstalking" (USDOJOVW, 2017, p. 7). More recently in 2013, Congress reauthorized the VAWA through the Violence against Women Reauthorization Act of 2013 (Public Law 113-4), which expanded the definition of stalking to now include "intrastate cyberstalking" crimes. 2013 also reauthorized many of the existing grant programs for states and tribal governments from FY2014 through FY2018. The 2013 law further improved upon 2005 service access for many vulnerable groups historically discriminated (Public Law 113-4, 2013). In all, the federal government has passed many a law, but does not act alone in prohibiting cyberstalking and harassment. It has committed to provide national monetary aide through grants to lower levels of government, and makes federal agency assistance possible (falls under the executive branch of U.S. government) e.g. the U.S. Department of Justice and U.S. Department of Education.

Grant Funding to Fight Cyber Aggression

In the U.S., all 3 levels of government may be involved in putting a single piece of legislation into effect (Dye, 2008). The U.S. has created federal agencies to apply the principles of legislation, monitor policy implementation and evaluate its effectiveness; federal agencies largely collaborate with state-local agency bureaucrats in policy implementation and money is involved. In the case of the Violence against Women Act, a vertical implementation structure is used involving federal, state and local institutions and a host of policy actors. In 1995, the VAWA charged the Department of Justice to administratively create its Office on Violence against Women (OVW) to oversee VAWA grants, as grants are the primary method in funding the VAWA policy programs. Policy implementation is made difficult without funding. The OVW awarded greater than $6 billion in grants and cooperatives to state-local and tribal governments, non-profits and universities (Congressional Research Service,

2015, p. 4). The U.S. Department of Justice Office on Violence against Women and the National Center for Victims of Crime partnered in year 2000 to create a one-stop resource center to effectively interface with stalking in the U.S. This Stalking Resource Center provides government, practitioners, and victims with tools to improve the response of the criminal justice system, enhance victim safety, hold offenders accountable, give training on multiple related topics, etc. (Stalking Resource Center, 2017). The National Center for Victims of Crime has provided advocacy for victims of crime across the U.S. since 1985.

The grant programs are an important policy implementation tool for VAWA giving victims protection and concurrent services to fight aggression. Since 1994 through 2016, VAWA provisions were added authorizing multiple types of grants (formula and discretionary) to state governments, enforcement agencies, coalitions, including the actual victims of crime. Reported in 2016, the VAWA Office on Violence against Women administered 15 discretionary grants and 4 formula grant programs giving monies to institutions on domestic and sexual violence (p. vii). These grants cover many vulnerable women groups, including "culturally specific" underserved groups as with the Culturally Specific Services Program (CSSP). The 2013 VAWA reauthorization made "culturally specific" to mean racial and ethnic minority groups. The CSSP is a community program aiding racial/ ethnic minorities, and its subsequent 2014 expansion added victims of deaf or hard of hearing, underserved religious/ ethnic groups, and aiding the LGBT (lesbian, gay, bisexual, and transgender) populations (USDOJOVW, 2016, p. 130). As campus aggression has increased, VAWA grants also apply to higher education institutions. The Grants to Reduce Violent Crimes against Women on Campus Program aims at improving campus security, and the prevention and prosecution of aggression. The Department of Justice reports that 92 campus grants were awarded to 31 states for 2012-2015 (USDOJOVW, December 2016, p. 3-4).

A grant program awarded in large number is the Services, Training, Officers, Prosecutors Violence against Women Formula Grant Program [STOP] (USDOJ, 2015). The STOP grant formula is based on population and awarded to states and territories. The DOJ reports $269,532,798 awarded to states and territories during 2011 and 2012, with sub awards of $255,203,456 distributed to victim service agencies and organizations, coalitions, law enforcement, prosecutor offices, courts and other sub grantees (USDOJOVW, 2015b, p. x). Sub grantees receiving STOP funding have used the monies in various ways. The Commonwealth of Virginia, for example, has enhanced its Domestic Violence Intervention Project, educating its STOP stakeholders (including law enforcement and prosecutors) on the new technologies being used by stalkers. In Pennsylvania, the Helping All Victims in Need Project trains law enforcement "how" to build felony stalking charges and work with other municipalities. Ohio's Stalking Investigator initiative funds investigator liaison with multiple jurisdictions, to conduct surveillance on suspects, and funds the expertise to compile profiles of suspects to develop a big picture of the case (USDOJOVW, 2015b, p. 63-64). The total number of STOP sub grantee awards distributed across the states in 2011 totaled 3,338 led by Michigan at 370, followed by Ohio at 255, New York at 130, Minnesota 121, Maryland 119, Texas 116, and Utah at 101 awards (USDOJOVW, 2015b, p. 118). The U.S. Department of Justice (2015) reports domestic violence against American Indian and Alaskan Native women on reservations is high at "10 times the national average" (p. 3). In response to need, the 2013 VAWA broadened the responsibility of states distributing STOP funding to include tribal governments as potential recipients of monies. In addition, the Grants to Encourage Arrest Policies and Enforcement of Protection Orders program is also available, encouraging state-local government and the tribal government and its courts to take domestic violence / stalking as a "serious" crime encouraging arrest policies and policy enforcement (Congressional Research Service, 2015, p. 18-21).

Aside from the VAWA, the federal government has made other monetary commitment to help the states fight domestic crime with funding for prevention, prosecution, safety and housing, etc. The federal Omnibus Crime Control and Safe Streets Act of 1968 (Public Law 90-351) devolved much responsibility for citizen protection to the state-local governments. Here, Congress pledged to provide them with national monetary assistance through grants to prevent, detect and apprehend criminals, including the crime against women. This 1968 public law also prohibited the invasion of privacy done through wiretapping and electronic surveillance by criminals, thus laying a foundation for future laws prohibiting perpetrator surveillance as done in cyberstalking and cyber-harassment. In 1994, the Violent Crime Control and Law Enforcement Act (Public Law 103-322) authorized monies for transitional housing for female victims of domestic violence, sexual assault and stalking. In 2009, the American Recovery and Reinvestment Act (Public Law 111-5) authorized grant monies for state and local law enforcement activities connected to the Violence against Women Prevention and Prosecution Programs including monies for the victim housing assistance grants, previously authorized by the 1994 law.

Some may not consider the 1994 Violence against Women Act as the only cornerstone federal law on cyberstalking. Alongside the VAWA and its modernizing reauthorizations, 3 federal codes are considered in fighting cyberstalking---18 USC § 2261A, 18 U.S. Code § 875, and U.S. Code 47 § 223. The U.S. Code Title 18, Domestic Violence and Stalking §2261A added the use of "any interactive computer service or electronic communication service or electronic communication system of interstate commerce" to existing federal laws governing the physical stalking activities, and expanded the scope of stalking crimes to include the "intent" and "effects" of stalking on victims (18 USC § 2261A, 2012; University of North Carolina at Chapel Hill [UNC], 2017a; UNC, 2017b). The 18 U.S. Code § 875 (2012) added the cyberstalking penalties, and the U.S. Code 47 § 223 (2012) outlined the prohibited acts of obscene or harassing telephone calls (wire or radio telecommunications) for interstate or foreign communications and for the District of Columbia; covered the legal enforcement of stalking laws; and covered the defense to prosecution (UNC, 2017a; UNC, 2017b).

State-Local Cyberstalking Laws

States have picked up where federal government has left off in adopting cyberstalking laws to protect and punish. State laws are non-uniform. They vary in the modernization of old offline stalking laws to cyberstalking laws. In Chapter 5, we analyze over time why some states modify existing stalking or harassment legislation to include electronic communication and why others are laggard using regression and controlling for political constraints, interest group strength, state wealth, and state need or demand for updated laws. While some states are laggard others are leaders in passing cyberstalking laws. California is considered a leader having enacted a broad scope of administrative and regulatory laws protecting Californians on cyberstalking. This may be expected as California had the highest number count of victim complaints on Internet crime at 39,547 as submitted to the Federal Bureau of Investigation's Internet Crime Complaint Center for 2016 (FBI, 2017, p 19), see Table 1 *Victim Complaints about Internet Crime to FBI, 2016.* Historically, California was the first state to codify stalking as a crime in 1990, largely a result of homicide cases involving women victimized by stalking. In 1992 and 1993, an additional 45 states followed to enact laws criminalizing stalking (National Institute of Justice, 1996, pp. A1-A11). Today, California has both criminal and civil laws governing cyberstalking and cyber-harassment. They have expanded the scope of harassment, which can be a single "intentionally harassing contact" of threat or can be "obscene" language. Among California laws, personal information cannot be electronically disseminated to harass or cause emotional distress; the posting of pictures on the Internet of victims or revenge porn is illegal without permission; penalty is more severe with recidivism or minor age victims (Privacy Rights Clearinghouse, 2016). Theoretically, states learn about "good" policy ideas and "poor" ones from each other, and California has been observed by many for being a leader and innovative across different policy domains. Laggard states can save policy money by learning from the mistakes and practices of California before adopting their own laws.

Are these state laws adequate to protect victims? According to Goodno (2007), "state statutes that might be used to prosecute cyberstalking do not have clear and equal standards" and are inadequate to deal with the distinct issues of cyberstalking (p. 140, 156). The U.S. Department of Justice (2012) reports that among the differences, states vary relative to the level of fear and distress necessary for the stalking behavior

Table 1. Victim complaints about Internet crime to FBI, 2016

States With Highest # of Complaints	Count	States With Lowest # of Complaints	Count
California	39, 547	North Dakota	350
Texas	21,441	South Dakota	376
Florida	21,068	Wyoming	432
New York	16,426	Vermont	440
Illinois	9,177	Rhode Island	663
Maryland	8,361	Delaware	703
Pennsylvania	8,265	Montana	744
Virginia	8,068	Maine	770
Ohio	7,052	Nebraska	1,028
Washington	6,874	Hawaii	1,055

Note: The numbers in Table 1 are not a rank ordering since they do not consider the multiple variables involved with each crime case; they are based on the total number of victim complaints in each state, and territory including D.C.; count is aggregate for all Internet crimes but do include harassment/ threats of violence, social media, crimes against children. Source: Federal Bureau of Investigation Internet Crime Complaint Center. (2017), 2016 Internet Crime Report, p. 19.

to be elevated to the level of criminal and perpetrator intent. "Actual fear" typically requires testimony by the victim relative to lifestyle changes because of stalking. While some laws require actual fear by the victim, other laws have a "reasonable person standard" where the perpetrator behavior would cause a reasonable person to experience fear (USDOJ, 2012, p. 3). In their evaluation of cyberstalking laws across the states, Goodno (2007) recommends effective cyberstalking statutes to "criminalize conduct that either puts a 'reasonable person' in fear of bodily harm or causes severe emotional distress" and statutes need to directly target the situations where the cyber-stalker gets innocent third parties to do the harassing and stalking for them (p 133, 156). Goodno reports, using the reasonable person standard provides the "most successful way to prosecute cyberstalking" because it does not require physical proximity as with offline stalking; it addresses many of the issues resulting from a credible threat requirement; it does not require an unequivocal threat being sent to the victim; does not require the victim to prove that the cyber-stalker had the ability to follow through on the threat. Goodno (2007) considers the reasonable person standard as the appropriate standard to be used in cyberstalking laws (p. 139-140).

Aside from a variation on level of fear and distress, crime can vary according to general or specific intent. Most crimes require "general intent" meaning that the accused did what the law prohibits. Whereas, "specific intent" crimes typically require that the accused did what the law prohibits and intended to accomplish the precise act the law prohibits (Black's Law Dictionary, 1990, p. 810). States also vary on the level of severity of the crime committed. According to the Stalking Resource Center (2015), "less than 1/3 of states classify stalking as a felony upon first offense. More than 1/2 of states classify stalking as a felony upon second or subsequent offense or when the crime involves aggravating factors" such as victim age under 16 years and victimization more than once (p 1).

Cyber Pornography Laws

Revenge pornography is a form of harassment/bullying. Cyber pornography is governed by a collection of laws that regulate perpetrator use of electronic means to transmit sensitive images of child porn. In 1967, the U.S. Congress called obscenity and pornography a "national concern" asking for a coordination of all levels of government on the matter, and created an advisory Commission on Obscenity and Pornography. Made up of multidisciplinary specialists, they researched the causal relationship of pornography to antisocial behavior to give "advisable action" to Congress (Public Law 90-100, 1967) and established a scientific understanding on this type of aggression. It was later that advanced technology use in pornography, such as the computer had made the government decision making agenda. Responding to the visual possibilities that could be created using the Internet at that time, the Child Protection Act of 1984 (Public Law 98-292) updated an older law, the Protection of Children against Sexual Exploitation Act of 1977 (Public Law 95-225) modernizing the language of pornographic sensitive images that previously meant "obscene visual or print medium" to the newer language of "visual depiction" of pornographic material. The 1984 Child Protection Act also strengthened the criminal and civil forfeiture of the property used in the pornography crime, and reinforced the customs laws on judicial forfeiture of property. Another law advancing the regulations against cyber revenge pornography is the 1988 Child Protection and Obscenity Enforcement Act of 1988 (Public Law 100-690). This 1988 law made it illegal to use a computer to transport, receive or possess "with intent to distribute" visual depiction of minors either interstate or in foreign commerce. Later, the 1998 Protection of Children from Sexual Predators Act, Title II, expanded the "jurisdictional base for prosecution of production of child pornography" to include the use of the computer in receiving and handling of materials for a visual depiction of a child (Public Law 105-314, 1998). In 1996, the Child Pornography Prevention Act (H.R. 4123, 1995-1996) closed loopholes from previous laws and again updated the capabilities of advanced technology on pornography. Since newer technology had already evolved with capability to create and further modify images of children making them "virtually indistinguishable" from real images, the 1996 law also broadened the definition of a "visual depiction." Some defendants claim the newer definition violated their First Amendment rights and challenged it in court.

In addition to the collection of federal laws that govern over child pornography, the states are passing their own sexting laws. As defined in Chapter 1, sexting is the sending of a naked or partially naked picture of oneself to another person using an advanced technology medium typically done through text messaging. In 2013, about 20 states had some type of law covering sexting by minors, 26 states had laws on cyber revenge pornography, and 18 states had no law. Penalty laws vary. For example, in Utah, the first offense for minors who are involved in sexting is considered a misdemeanor, but considered a felony for all other offenses. In Rhode Island, the minor disseminating a sexually sensitive image of self to others is committing a "status offense" and sent to family court (Cyberbullying Research Center, 2015c). Adults, however, can receive a stricter penalty when it comes to cyber pornography as seen in Illinois state law. Illinois violators get court determined forfeiture of property (such as computer or even profits) and forfeiture of any "contractual right of any kind affording a source of influence over any enterprise" that is related to child pornography, aggravated child pornography, or "non-consensual dissemination of private sexual images" (State of Illinois, 2015).

Florida is a leader, having passed a range of sexual cyber-harassment and revenge pornography laws with implementation beginning in 2015. This may be expected (analyzed in Chapter 5), as Florida followed California and Texas at a count of 21,068 in the number of Internet crime victim complaints submitted to the FBI for 2016 (FBI, 2017), see Table 1. Florida defines "image" of a sexually explicit image to include but not limited to any photograph, picture, motion picture, film, video, or representation. Their penalties vary and include misdemeanor of the first degree and felony of the third degree for the person who has one prior conviction and commits a second or subsequent offense (Florida Legislature, 2015). In cases of multiple images transmitted within 24 hours it is considered a "single" offense. Florida penalty allows for counseling or some other "informal" type of sanction, and persons can seek civil remedies. Their law addresses both the sending and receiving of sexting for those under age 18 years. Minors receiving images without request and not having distributed the image(s) and having reported the incident to authority are not considered to have committed a sexting offense (Cyberbullying Research Center, 2015c). Florida authorizes law enforcement to arrest without warrant anyone that he or she has probable cause to believe has committed sexual cyber-harassment; authorizes a search warrant issued in "specified" instances; specifies the circumstances of offense, and more (Florida Legislature, 2015). Chapter 5 empirically explores why some states have a higher legal penalty for committing a crime of revenge porn while others do not.

Cyberbullying Laws

Although the federal government has been active in passing cyberstalking laws to protect women, it has devolved responsibility on cyberbullying and accompanying child harassment onto the states and its school districts. There is no cornerstone federal law for cyberbullying as seen with cyberstalking. The federal government has however governed over schools receiving federal funds by requiring them to assume a serious anti-bullying agenda. Recently, the 2017 Congress the Tyler Clementi Higher Education Anti-Harassment Act of 2017, not yet law, was introduced as House bill 2151 and as Senate bill 954 aimed at the higher education setting. This bill targets harassment in higher education that is associated with a student's (actual or perceived) race, color, national origin, sex, sexual orientation, gender identification, disability, or religion. It defines electronic communication used in cyber harassment broadly so as to reflect newer cyber methods: "any transfer of signs, signals, writing, images, sounds, or data of any nature transmitted in whole or in part by a wire, radio, electromagnetic, photo electronic, or photo optical system" (House of Representatives 2151, June 2017). As discussed in Chapter 2, based on its legislative history, the Tyler Clementi Higher Education Anti-Harassment Act of 2017 is not expected to become law. Currently in Congressional committee, the Safe Schools Improvement Act of 2017 targets student bullying and harassment (House of Representatives 1957, 2017). It would amend the Elementary and Secondary Education Act of 1965, which is aimed "to strengthen and improve educational quality and educational opportunities in the Nation's elementary and secondary schools" (Public Law 89-10, p. 27). As a federal incentive to get local level government to move on anti-bullying and harassment of youth, the Safe Schools Improvement Act of 2017 would require those districts receiving federal monies to adopt codes regulating school bullying and harassment of students (Human Rights Campaign, 2017; H.R. 1957). Schools receiving federal funding are expected to resolve bullying and harassment complaints, cyber and otherwise. Several federal agencies are available to aid them; the U.S. Department of Education Office for Civil Rights and the U.S. Department of Justice Civil Rights Division are available to assist (Antibullying Institute, 2017, p. 1).

Basically, cyberbullying of youth is considered a local policy matter best resolved by the locale more in tune with the regional needs. To keep up with digital advances used by bullies, some states have been innovative through adopting laws in response to their devolved authority, whereas other states remain laggard. States are experimenting with legal strategies. Many a state cyberbullying law overlaps with its harassment laws. Since perpetrator harassment can spill over into cyberstalking, some states reflect this by covering many of the types of cyber aggression in a single law, while others are more specific to differences in crime. For example, Minnesota and

Nebraska's statutes on stalking and harassment can also be applied to prosecution of cyberbullying. Kentucky considers cyberbullying between students as part of its concept of cyber-harassment, punishable as a class B felony. New Mexico defines electronic bullying to include but not limited to "hazing, harassment, intimidation or menacing acts of a student which may, but need not be based on the student's race, color, sex, ethnicity, national origin, religion, disability, age or sexual orientation" (NCSL, July 2010; January 2013b).

As with cyberstalking, cyberbullying laws passed by states are largely regulatory and administrative. In addition to enacting anti-bullying regulations governing the entire state, states are also passing administrative laws devolving much authority to the local school districts to implement the state law, to design procedures on enforcement, and to create their own local policies tailored to their specific needs. New Hampshire for example devolves authority to the school board of every school district, while in Idaho power is also given to school officials to penalize cyber-harassment. Oregon empowers community stakeholders in effort to push a local "participatory" policymaking idea with "parents, school employees, volunteers and community representatives" to model their laws (NCSL, January 2013b). Vermont promotes student participation in advisory adding a secondary student to their Advisory Council on Harassment, Hazing, and Bullying (NCSL, January 2013). Some states have codified federal standards into statute, such as federal case laws allowing "schools to discipline students for off-campus behavior that results in a substantial disruption of the learning environment at school" (Cyberbullying Research Center, 2016, p. 1). Florida's 2008 Jeffery Johnston Stand Up for All Students Act requires that if school networks are being used by students, then Internet bullying means "on or off" the school zone. In addition to school zone, California extends the scope of cyberbullying laws to include school personnel (NCSL, 2013b). In all, the state government and local school districts (government units) have assumed an intergovernmental policy relationship with their anti-cyberbullying campaign.

Theoretically, policies tend to remain stable for extended periods of time until new information or events take place drawing attention to a problem and elevating it onto political agenda (Baumgartner & Jones, 1993; Cobb & Elder, 1971). This is consistent with the finding that legislative action on school bullying occurred after a focusing event such as the 1999 Columbine (Colorado, USA) school shootings in 1999. As a result of this 1999 crisis event, Georgia was a pioneer in adopting anti-bullying laws, including a law requiring its schools to implement "character education programs" that specifically addressed bullying prevention. Forty-six states followed Georgia from 1999-2000 enacting more than 120 separate bills either introducing or amending bullying statutes in their education or criminal codes. The four states that were laggard in following Georgia's lead were Hawaii, Michigan, Montana, and South Dakota who did not pass these laws (U.S. Dept. of Education, 2011). Except for Michigan (historically an early adopter of policy across many different policy domains), Hawaii, Montana and South Dakota may have a lesser need to adopt Internet crime laws (see Table 1). Just as Georgia pioneered in anti-bullying laws, Utah in 2001 became the first to include language for cyberbullying. More legislative action on the "cyber" of bullying did not happen until 2007 (Cyberbullying Research Center, 2015a) and state momentum picked up around 2010 where 21 new bills were passed, and 8 bills were signed into law through April 30, 2011 (U.S. Dept. of Education, 2011). In contrast to Utah being an early adopter, Montana has been laggard in passing cyberbullying laws. In 2015, Montana became the last state to adopt policy and practically speaking, it was strictly symbolic. The law provided a definition of bullying but did not mandate any actions to be taken. Montana is not a state with a high need for cyber policy given that its Internet crime rate is amongst the lowest reported to the FBI. In contrast to the majority of states, the FBI (2017) shows Montana having low reported Internet crime, based on a count of 744 victim complaints in 2016 (see Table 1). This suggests an association between the occurrence of Internet crime and the need for law; empirically explored in Chapter 5.

Today, according to the Cyberbullying Research Center (2017), 49 states require schools to have a policy governing bullying, 16 states have laws that include off-campus behaviors, and 44 states have criminal sanctions for cyberbullying or electronic harassment (2017). Those 6 states lacking criminal sanctions are Maine, Minnesota, Nebraska, New Hampshire, New Mexico, and Wyoming (Cyberbullying Research Center, 2017). Except for Minnesota, the 5 others had a lower number of reported Internet crime for 2016, which may or may not be a reason for not passing criminal sanctions, see Table 1 (FBI, 2017). The fight against bullying is not limited to state government. As a leader, the capital of the U.S., District of Columbia, adopted the Youth Bullying Prevention Act of 2012, which is an administrative law framing "how" bullying prevention efforts may be modeled by stakeholders citywide. It uses "a public health framework with three levels of prevention practices and strategies." The first level of prevention practices and strategies is on the persons in need of prevention action; the second is on persons at risk and the places of risk for this victimization; and third is the strategic responses to the incidents (Urban Institute Justice Policy Center, 2013, p. 3).

State bullying laws can also be shaped by judicial decisions on school discipline or the lack of discipline to bullying and harassment. In *Zeno v. Pine Plains Central School District* (2012) the school failed to adequately protect a student from harassment. The plaintiff, a high school student, received a final award of $1 million in damages because his school failed to protect him from harassment (on and off school property) for nearly 3-and-a-half years. The student was subjected to "verbal racial attacks" and physical attacks. Although the school disciplined students for the bullying and suspended one student for 45 days, the school district had not taken "definitive action" ensuring that the aggression had stopped. Zeno brought action "contending that the District was deliberately indifferent to his harassment." A jury found the District liable in violating Title VI of the Civil Rights Act of 1964. Schools are required to respond in the short-term with discipline and in the long-term with a plan to manage the issue (U.S. Court of Appeals, 2012; McNeal, Kunkle, & Bryan, 2016). The Civil Rights Act of 1964 is a federal law to prevent bias toward race, color, religion, sex, or national origin (Public Law 88-352, 1964).

Some stakeholders argue that school district bullying policies restrict student speech of what can and cannot be posted on the Internet, as some accused of violating school policy claim their schools have violated their First Amendment on freedom of speech. "Overall, U.S. courts are oriented toward supporting First Amendment rights of free expression of students. Certain expressions, however, are not protected and allow intervention and discipline" (p. 3). These expressions include the disruption of the school learning environment by bullying/ harassment; impeding the educational process and school discipline; the obstruction of civil rights of other students; the use of school computers to harass others (Cyberbullying Research Center, 2015b). As state laws on bullying are adopted, courts are playing a role defining what schools are legally permitted to do to protect students, with some legal constraints presenting a barrier to state adoption of cyberbullying laws. Recent language in federal bills, such as the Safe Schools Improvement Act of 2017, have a specific provision reinforcing that the bill does not alter legal standards or federal laws protecting the freedom of speech or expression (House of Representatives 1957, 2017).

Judicial decisions have influenced subsequent court decisions related to cyberbullying. For example, in case law *Tinker v. Des Moines Independent Community School District*, a precedent court decision was used to regulate cyberbullying (U.S. Supreme Court, 1969). In Tinker, the Court ruled that the school violated the First Amendment rights of those students who wore black armbands to school as a symbolic protest to the Vietnam War. The Court ruled that a student's right to free speech was not absolute, but to restrict student speech or actions school officials must show that student actions violated the rights of other students or constitute a "substantial disruption" to the school's ability to maintain order. Courts have extended the substantial disruption standard of the Tinker decision to cyberbullying. Since cyberbullying differs from other types of bullying in that it can occur 24/ 7 and can reach a bigger audience than traditional offline bullying, federal courts have been extending the Tinker standard to include actions that have taken place off school grounds. For example, in *Doninger v. Niehoff,* a student posted on their public blog that a school event was cancelled and urged school peers to harass the school administrator. The Second Circuit Court agreed on the school's discipline to bar the student from participating in student government, deciding that the student's blog constituted a substantial disruption (U.S. Court of Appeals, 2008). In all, court cases have played a role in shaping cyberbullying policy for federal, state and school districts. All three branches of government are involved on bullying issues by passing and shaping legislation, and having a check and balance on each other.

Government Initiatives Protecting the LGBT Population

Crimes toward lesbian, gay, bisexual, and transgender (LGBT) persons occur every hour in the U.S. (Human Rights Campaign, 2017b). According to the 2015 Gay, Lesbian & Straight Education Network's National School Climate Survey, 20% of LGBT students reported bias due to gender expression (House Concurrent Resolution 49, 2017). Congress declares violence motivated by actual or perceived gender, gender identity, or sexual orientation a serious issue (Public Law 111-84, 2009). In response, federal laws have been passed. Landmark is the Civil Rights Act of 1964 (Public Law 88-352) signed into law by former President Lyndon Johnson. This Act aims to enforce constitutional rights to vote, "confer jurisdiction upon the district courts of the United States to provide injunctive relief against discrimination," to prevent discrimination in public accommodations and institutions and in government funded programs toward race, color, religion, sex, or national origin (Public Law 88-352, 1964). Although there is some contention among citizens on the meaning of the Act's use of the word "sex" as some claim it has meaning beyond one's biological sex, the 1964 Act is considered a foundation for subsequent laws and court cases.

Responsibility to prohibit aggression (hate) crimes toward the LGBT persons is largely being placed on institutions receiving federal monies. Those institutions, such as schools receiving government funding are required to comply with government anti-LGBTQ aggression initiatives. According to the government website Stopbullying.gov, "when students are harassed based on their actual or perceived sexual orientation, they may also be subjected to forms of sex discrimination recognized under Title IX" (2014). Title IX of the Education Amendments of 1972 is a federal administrative law on educational institutions receiving federal dollars to prohibit sex discrimination. It applies to primary, secondary, colleges, universities and educational training programs in the U.S. (USDOJ, August 2015). Newer laws follow the 1972 idea on anti-harassment and anti-discrimination of LGBT persons. For example, the federal Don't Block LGBTQ Act of 2016, was introduced in the House to prohibit primary and secondary education schools or libraries receiving "discount rates" for Internet from blocking Internet access to lesbian, gay, bisexual, transgender, or queer (H.R. 6254, 2015-2016). The 2017 Safe Schools Improvement Act, in committee, is a bipartisan bill requiring school districts receiving federal dollars to adopt codes against bullying and harassment and against bias of race, color, national origin, sex, sexual orientation, gender identity, disability, and religion (H.R. 1957, 2017-2018). In addition to schools who receive monies, are the recipients of the VAWA grants. The VAWA of 2013 with its LGBT provision is aimed at "discrimination for LGBT people appearing within a federal funding statute." The VAWA Culturally Specific Services Program gives LGBT victims protection and services (USDOJOVW, 2016, p. 54).

Laws protecting the LGBT population from bias are not limited to cyberspace, school settings, and those institutions receiving federal monies. According to the National Conference of State Legislators, many states have passed laws similar to the federal civil rights acts protecting vulnerable populations from bias in employment and public accommodation. California for example includes sex, gender identity, gender expression, sexual orientation in their law against both public and private employment discrimination. To this list Colorado adds victims of stalking, domestic violence and sexual assault (NCSL, 2017). More than 200 U.S. cities and counties have passed policy banning gender identity discrimination. Transgender persons as public employees may be protected through ordinances, charter provisions and like (American Civil Liberties Union, 2017).

CONCLUSION

All three branches of U.S. government to some extent have had a voice in today's cyber policies. Overall, federal policy fighting cyber aggression has been incremental with the "cyber" added later to older family domestic violence laws protecting women and children against physical aggression. The federal government, all 50 states, the District of Columbia, and U.S. territories have adopted some type of policy addressing stalking crime (USDOJOVW, 2017). However, fast paced digital advances used by criminals and a slow legislative process creates a "lag" in the making of modern cyber laws. Not all states have picked up where the federal government has left off in passing strict protective regulations and accompanying administrative policy. While some states are passing specific laws differentiating cyber aggression from its physical offline form, other states are laggard by either passing a few law(s) having broad language to cover the evolving methods of cyber aggression, or relying on existing cyber laws to cover multiple types of digital aggression. In all, state laws are not uniform and vary in extent of protective coverage and perpetrator penalty.

Cyberbullying tends to be an issue for younger aged Americans although older adults can also face this type of aggression. The federal governing authority over cyberbullying has largely been devolved to the states and school districts, but the feds still have a hand in the matter requiring those schools receiving federal school funding to take aggression seriously. Responsibility to prohibit aggression (hate) crimes toward the LGBT population is also largely being placed on institutions receiving federal monies. Several 2017 federal bills have been introduced to protect the LGBT person(s). The magnitude of state actions reflecting the evolving political and policy environment relative to bullying in schools suggests that legislators are repeatedly refining legislative expectations for schools in response to emerging problems such as cyber bullying (U.S. Dept. of Education, 2011). U.S. Courts have played a role in shaping state bullying policy. In the next chapter, community anti-bullying programs are discussed.

REFERENCES

American Civil Liberties Union. (2017). *Know your rights: transgender and the law*. Retrieved June 15, 2017, from https://www.aclu.org/know-your-rights/transgender-people-and-law

Antibullying Institute. (2017). *Bullying facts and the challenge to be met*. Retrieved June 23, 2017, from http://antibullyinginstitute.org/facts#.WS8Tdfn1DIU

Baumgartner, F. R., & Jones, B. D. (1993). *Agendas and instability in American politics*. Chicago: The University of Chicago Press.

Black, H. (1990). *Black's law dictionary* (6th ed.). St. Paul, MN: West Group.

Cobb, R., & Elder, C. (1971). The politics of agenda setting. *The Journal of Politics*, *33*(4), 892–915. doi:10.2307/2128415

Congressional Research Service. (2014). *The violence against women act: overview, legislation, and federal funding*. Retrieved June 23, 2017, from https://www.crs.gov

Congressional Research Service. (2015). *The violence against women act: overview, legislation, and federal funding*. Retrieved June 23, 2017, from https://www.crs.gov

Cyberbullying Research Center. (2015a). *State cyberbullying laws: A brief review of state cyberbullying laws and policies*. Retrieved June 5, 2017, from https:// from www.cyberbullying.org

Cyberbullying Research Center. (2015b). *Cyberbullying legislation and case law implications for school policy and practice*. Retrieved June 5, 2017, from https:// www.cyberbullying.org

Cyberbullying Research Center. (2015c). *State sexting laws*. Retrieved June 5, 2017, from https://www.cyberbullying.org

Cyberbullying Research Center. (2016). *State cyberbullying laws. a brief review of state cyberbullying laws and policies*. Retrieved June 5, 2017, from https://www.cyberbullying.org

Cyberbullying Research Center. (2017). *Bullying laws across America.* Retrieved June 5, 2017, from https://www.laws.cyberbullying.org

Dye, T. R. (2008). Understanding public policy (12th ed.). Upper Saddle River, NJ: Pearson Prentice Hall.

Federal Bureau of Investigation Internet Crime Complaint Center. (2017). *2016 Internet Crime Report.* Retrieved December 29, 2017, from http://www.ic3.gov/media/annualreports.aspx

Goodno, N. H. (2007, Winter). Cyberstalking, a new crime: Evaluating the effectiveness of current state and federal Laws. *Missouri Law Review, 72*(1), 125–197.

House Concurrent Resolution 49. (2017). *Supporting the goals and ideals of GLSEN's 2017 Day of Silence in bringing attention to anti-lesbian, gay, bisexual, transgender, and queer name-calling, bullying, and harassment faced by individuals in schools. 115th Congress, 1st Session.* Retrieved July 10, 2017, from https://www.govtrack.us/congress/bills/115/hconres49

House of Representatives 1957. (2017-2018). *Safe Schools Improvement Act of 2017.*

House of Representatives 2151. (June 2017). *Tyler Clementi Higher Education Anti-Harassment Act of 2017.*

House of Representatives 4123. (1995-1996). *Child Pornography Prevention Act of 1996. 104th Congress.*

House of Representatives 6254. (2015-2016). *Don't Block LGBTQ Act of 2016.*

Human Rights Campaign. (2017). *Federal legislation.* Retrieved June 23, 2017, from http://www.hrc.org/resources/federal-legislation

Human Rights Campaign. (2017b). *Hate crimes law 2017.* Retrieved June 23, 2017, from http://www.hrc.org/resources/hate-crimes-law

Legislature, F. (2015). *Senate Bill 538.* Retrieved December 26, 2017, from https://www.flsenate.gov/Session/Bill/2015/0538/BillText/er/PDF

Lonardo, T., Martland, T., & White, D. (2016). A legal examination of revenge pornography and cyber-harassment. *Journal of Digital Forensics, Security and Law., 11*(3), 79–105.

Lowi, T. (1972). Four systems of policy, politics and choice. *Public Administration Review, 33*(4), 298–310. doi:10.2307/974990

McNeal, R., Kunkle, S., & Dotterweich-Bryan, L. (2016). State-Level Cyberbullying Policy: Variations in Containing a Digital Problem. In G. Crews (Ed.), *Critical Examinations of School Violence and Disturbance in K-12 Education* (pp. 62–82). Hershey, PA: Information Science Reference. IGI Global. doi:10.4018/978-1-4666-9935-9.ch005

McNeal, R., & Schmeida, M. (2015). Digital Paranoia: Unfriendly Social Media Climate Affecting Social Networking Activities. In J. P. Sahlin (Ed.), *Social Media and the Transformation of Interaction in Society* (pp. 210–227). Hershey, PA: Information Science Reference. IGI Global. doi:10.4018/978-1-4666-8556-7.ch011

McNeal, R., Tolbert, C., Mossberger, K., & Dotterweich, L. J. (2003). Innovating in digital government in the American states. *Social Science Quarterly*, *84*(1), 52–70. doi:10.1111/1540-6237.00140

National Conference of State Legislators. (2013b). *State bullying legislation since 2008*. Retrieved June 5, 2017, from http://www.ncsl.org/research/education/bullying-legislation-since-2008.aspx

National Conference of State Legislators. (2017). *State laws on employment-related discrimination*. Retrieved June 5, 2017, from http://www.ncsl.org/research/labor-and-employment/discrimination-employment.aspx

National Conference of State Legislatures. (2010). *Cyberbullying and the states*. Retrieved June 5, 2017, from http://www.ncsl.org/research/civil-and-criminal-justice/cyberbullying-and-the-states.aspx

National Conference of State Legislatures. (2011). *Overview: School bullying*. Retrieved June 5, 2017, from http://www.ncsl.org/research/education/school-bullying-overview.aspx

National Conference of State Legislatures. (2013a). *Cyberstalking and cyber harassment laws*. Retrieved June 5, 2017, from http://www.ncsl.org/research/telecommunications-and-information-technology/cyberstalking-and-cyberharassment-laws.aspx

National Institute of Justice. (1996). *Domestic violence, stalking, and antistalking legislation – an annual report to congress under the violence against women act* (NCJ 160943). Retrieved June 1, 2017, from https://www.ncjrs.gov/pdffiles/stlkbook.pdf

Pew Internet & American Life Project. (2013). *Anonymity, privacy, and security online*. Retrieved July 10, 2017, from http://pewinternet.org/Reports/2013/Anonymity-online.aspx

Pew Research Center. (2015). *Mobile messaging and social media 2015*. Retrieved July 10, 2017, from http://www.pewinternet.org/2015/08/19/mobile-messaging-and-social-media-2015/

Pew Research Center. (2017). *The Internet of things connectivity binge: what are the implications?* Retrieved July 10, 2017, from http://www.pewinternet.org/2017/06/06/the-internet-of-things-connectivity-binge-what-are-the-implications/

Privacy Rights Clearinghouse. (2016). *Online harassment & cyberstalking*. Retrieved June 5, 2017, from https://www.privacyrights.org

Public Law 103-322. (1994). *Violent Crime Control and Law Enforcement Act of 1994.*

Public Law 105-314. (1998). Protection of Children from Sexual Predators Act of 1998.

Public Law 106-386. (2000). *Trafficking and Violence Protection Act of 2000.*

Public Law 109-162. (2005). *Violence against Women and Department of Justice Reauthorization Act.*

Public Law 111-5. (2009). *American Recovery and Reinvestment Act of 2009.*

Public Law 111-84. (2009). *Matthew Shepard and James Byrd, Jr. Hate Crimes Prevention Act.*

Public Law 113-4. (2013). *Violence against Women Reauthorization Act of 2013.*

Public Law 88-352. (1964). *Civil Rights Act of 1964.*

Public Law 89-10. (1965). *Elementary and Secondary Education Act of 1965.*

Public Law 90-100. (1967). *Act Creating the Commission on Obscenity and Pornography.*

Public Law 90-351. (1968). *Omnibus Crime Control and Safe Streets Act of 1968.*

Public Law 95-225. (1978). *Protection of Children against Sexual Exploitation Act.*

Public Law 98-292. (1984). *Child Protection Act of 1984.*

Public Law 98-457. (1984). *Family Violence Prevention and Services Act.*

Ripley, R. B., & Franklin, G. A. (1980). *Congress, the bureaucracy, and public policy*. Homewood, IL: The Dorsey Press.

Stalking Resource Center. (2015). *Stalking fact sheet*. Retrieved June 23, 2017, from https:// www.victimsofcrime.org/src

Stalking Resource Center. (2017). *Stalking resource center services*. Retrieved June 23, 2017, from https://victimsofcrime.org/our-programs/stalking-resource-center/about-us

State of Illinois Public Act 098-1138. (2015). *An Act Concerning Criminal Law.*

Stopbullying.gov. (2014). *Federal laws*. Retrieved June 15, 2017, from https://www.stopbullying.gov/laws/federal/index.html

U. S. Department of Health & Human Services. (2015). *What is cyberbullying?* Retrieved January 5, 2015, from http://www.stopbullying.gov/

U. S. Department of Justice Office on Violence Against Women. (2016a). *The 2016 biennial report to congress on the effectiveness of the grant programs under the violence against women act*. Retrieved June 15, 2017, from http://www.ovw.usdoj.gov

University of North Carolina at Chapel Hill. (2017a). *Cyberstalking federal criminal statutes*. Retrieved June 5, 2017, from http://cyberstalking.web.unc.edu/federal-criminal-statutes/

University of North Carolina at Chapel Hill. (2017b). *Cyberstalking policy reform*. Retrieved June 5, 2017, from http://cyberstalking.web.unc.edu/policy-reform/

Urban Institute Justice Policy Center. (2013). *Citywide model bullying prevention policy*. Retrieved July 5, 2017, from https://www.urban.org

U.S. Court of Appeals, Second Circuit. (2008). *Doninger v. Niehoff*. 527 F.3d 41.

U.S. Court of Appeals, Second Circuit. (2012). *Zeno v. Pine Plains Central School District*. 702 F.3d 655.

U.S. Department of Education, Office of Planning, Evaluation and Policy Development, Policy and Program Studies Service. (2011). *Analysis of state bullying laws and policies*. Retrieved June 23, 2017, from http://www.ed.gov/about/offices/list/opepd/ppss/index.html

U.S. Department of Justice. (2015). *Overview of title IX of the education amendments of 1972, 20 U.S.C. A§ 1681 ET. SEQ*. Retrieved June 5, 2017, from https://www.justice.gov/crt/overview-title-ix-education-amendments-1972-20-usc-1681-et-seq

U.S. Department of Justice Office of Justice Programs. (2012). *Stalking victims in the United States – revised - Bureau of Justice statistics special report* (NCJ 224527). Retrieved June 23, 2017, from http://www.bjs.gov/content/pub/pdf/svus_rev.pdf

U.S. Department of Justice Office on Violence Against Women. (2015a). *2014 tribal consultation report*. Retrieved June 5, 2017, from http://www.ovw.usdoj.gov

U.S. Department of Justice Office on Violence Against Women. (2015b). *STOP program 2014 report part A*. Retrieved June, 15, 2017, from http://www.ovw.usdoj.gov

U.S. Department of Justice Office on Violence Against Women. (2016b). *Report to congress on the 2013-2015 activities of grantees receiving federal funds under the grants to reduce violent crimes against women on campus program*. Retrieved June 15, 2017, from http://www.ovw.usdoj.gov

U.S. Department of Justice Office on Violence Against Women. (2017). *2014 report to congress grant funds used to address stalking*. Retrieved June 15, 2017, from http://www.ovw.usdoj.gov

U.S. Supreme Court. (1969). *Tinker v. Des Moines Independent Community School District*. 393 U.S. 503.

47. USC § 223. (2012). *Obscene or Harassing Telephone Calls in the District of Columbia or in Interstate or Foreign Communications*.

18. USCS § 2261A. (2012). *Stalking*.

18. USCS § 875. (2012). *Interstate Communications*.

This research was previously published in Cyber Harassment and Policy Reform in the Digital Age edited by Ramona S. McNeal, Susan M. Kunkle, and Mary Schmeida, pages 52-78, copyright year 2018 by Information Science Reference (an imprint of IGI Global).

Chapter 10
Troll Farm:
Anonymity as a Weapon for Online Character Assassination

Leslie J. Reynard
Washburn University, USA

ABSTRACT

Anonymity can create cowards. Perceptions of mistreatment can create an urge for revenge. And online social media platforms create opportunities to exact vengeance. This chapter provides an overview of online character assassination as it has evolved within a profusion of social media sites offering forums for uncensored airing of opinions. When opinions constitute political speech, they can be life-threatening. When opinions are commercial speech rating character and competence of professionals, digital defamation can threaten livelihood. In commercial arenas, victims often feel helpless to protect their reputations; however, some legal remedies may be available. This essay investigates the nature of abusive communication online, the role anonymity plays in digital attacks, and psychological characteristics associated with trolls and cyber-bullies. Case studies of individuals' efforts to defend themselves from online character assassination illustrate concepts discussed and strategies being used for online reputational self-defense.

INTRODUCTION

In a virtual marketplace of ideas, where uploaded information has a global, eternal audience and is under little to no administrative control as to its truth value or ethical weight, ideas can become weapons. Character assassination using online postings to websites – and the emotional, psychological, social, and economic turmoil the

DOI: 10.4018/978-1-7998-1684-3.ch010

inevitably results from such attacks – is a burgeoning problem worldwide. Chetty and Alathur offer a focused overview both of the "dark side" of advances in Internet Technologies (Its), especially social media evolving alongside their benefits to humanity. Their study focuses primarily on delineating the relationships among hate speech, terrorism, and cyberterrorism Within their definitions and descriptions, online character assassination would be a form of extremism they place beneath the umbrella of extremist hate crime or hate speech (Chetty and Alathur, 2018). In this chapter, this form of hate speech or hate crime is explored in relation to ways that anonymity facilitates this form of violence, whether it be rhetorical or physical.

Virtual speech acts transmitted via the internet generally may allocated into one of two categories based upon intent and material purpose: political speech acts or commercial speech acts. Online communication of both categories carried out using social media sites can also be either categorized either as productive and prosocial or destructive and abusive, based upon both intent and outcomes. Figure 1 depicts this fourfold framework of virtual communication dimensions, providing sub-types of online speech acts within each dimension.

Character assassination is earmarked by its personal nature, its viciousness and its deliberate lack of truth. Such speech acts maliciously deployed as weapons to destroy an individual's reputation can fall into either the pollical and commercial dimensions of online speech acts. It may be apparent in the diagram that all four dimensions and varieties of online message types that comprise them may encourage message-creators to be either braver or more malignant if their communications are posted online under the protection of anonymity. In the case of character assassination, anonymity within the commercial speech dimension is likely to result in permanent, irreversible damage to one's good name. However, in the realm of political communication, anonymity can operate either to the public good or result in the actual assassination of its human target. While this chapter has as its primary focus the commission of character assassination through social media using an example of a professor who was targeted by a disgruntled student, an example of a politically motivated online cyberterrorism campaign powered by anonymity that resulted in the murder of a journalist is presented.

Technical, psychological, and legal throughputs that contribute to the expanding scope and escalating complexity of abusive communication online include:

- The proliferation of social media platforms that provide staging areas for online attacks on character.
- The phenomenon that has become known as the Streisand Effect (where raising the issue of damaging online communications actually worsens the impact by drawing attention to it) as well as audience-generated hurdles to reputational self-defense such as comment sections of news sites.

Figure 1. Categories of social media speech acts

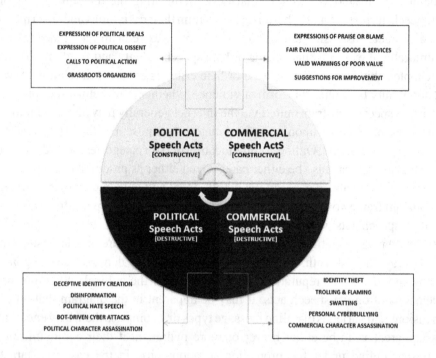

- In the United States, competing laws that protect rights to privacy on the one hand and rights to speak one's mind on the other have produced a double bind. It is difficult to defend simultaneously both sets of contradictory protections offered by the Bill of Rights when one undermines the other. This is particularly true with respect to online commercial speech that constitutes defamation. In this balancing act, safeguards to freedom of speech and association guaranteed by the First Amendment are pitted against Fourth Amendment guarantee that one's right to privacy is sacrosanct (Chemerinsky, 2017).
- The critical role that anonymity plays in facilitating the free expression of dissent while at the same time enabling the abusive dissemination of false or threatening messages is a key concern. Balancing safeguards to individuals' free expression while at the same time protecting rights to privacy and safety is a stumbling-block to developing workable protocols and legislation of digital speech, especially on social media sites.

In order to successfully balance Constitutional protections for American citizens and possibly to provide a model for worldwide application (since there are no national boundaries in cyberspace, and the problem is global), the issue of online character assassination could best be addressed at the national level and a protocol developed that can work on a state-by-state basis as well as in application to international issues. This chapter will provide historical foundation as to social media development, psychological and economic insight as to its use as a weapon, and balanced discussion of issues related to online character assassination.

Chapter Objectives

Abusive, defamatory, and threatening online content is increasingly problematic worldwide; legislative and organizational control mechanisms have not been developed that adequately contain or manage malignant content. Thus, information relating to legal definitions and legal actions is provided, from the perspective of a communication studies scholar with a focused interest defamation rhetoric and its role in conflict management and in First Amendment issues related to online journalism, but who is not a lawyer. More detailed information regarding specific causes of action and advice as to pursuit of legal claims should be directed to a licensed attorney who specializes in those specific areas of representation. Ultimately, having a clear understanding of the threat that digital incivility poses to online communities, what constitutes actionable defamation, and ways to mitigate the wave of incivility and virtual violence that increasingly hallmarks online communication can offer a foundational line of defense against it.

Chapter Objectives

Embedded within a primary framework that examines the agonic engagement of virtuous anonymity and the malignant anonymity which emboldens online character assassination are four micro-level objectives.

The first objective of this chapter is to understand ways that the ability to "speak" anonymously in online venues can be both a blessing and a curse for human societies. Toward this end, the chapter describes the evolution of Web 2.0 social media sites in tandem with an increasingly virulent communication environment that fosters cyberbullying, trolling, and other forms of abusive communication (Gerrie, 2017; Obar & Wildman, 2015; Valentine, 2017). While political speech is a more fragile virtual arena, commercial speech as it affects professionals and public figures is a primary focus of this chapter. The role of anonymity and character traits associated with cyberbullying, trolling, and online defamation are primary objects of consideration. The case of US-based Saudi journalist Jamal Khashoggi is offered example of an online character assassination campaign which ended as an actual assassination.

A second, related, objective is to address the problem of protecting oneself from virtual character assassination, often complicated by the anonymity accorded to virtual attackers and laws that protect that anonymity (Obar & Wildman, 2015; Santana, 2014). The conflicting ideals of the First Amendment, which protects free speech, and the Fourth Amendment, which protects privacy, must be considered insofar as they affect legal remedies for victims of cyber-attacks on their character. Attacks on reputation are especially heinous when the professional status and livelihood of the victims is at stake.

Thus, a third objective of this chapter is to focus on interactive social media sites as arenas for digital hate speech and understand the growing "culture of hate" perpetrated by cyberbullies, trolls, and other cyberhaters.

A final objective is to provide a broad foundational understanding of what constitutes actionable defamation as a civil cause of action, with possible legal and extra-legal strategies for online reputation management. The case Dr. Sally Vogl-Bauer is an example of a reputational attack launched against an American college professor by a former student. This cautionary tale illustrates that defending against an anonymous online campaign is often a futile effort and that efforts to maintain or restore one's good name can, ironically, intensify the spotlight on the victim of defamation.

BACKGROUND

The Anonymity Conundrum

Similar to other crowd phenomena, such as the bystander effect (where people in a group are less likely to come to the aid of another person than if they were alone), groupthink (where the sense of group membership can obscure errors in judgment and lapses in critical thinking leading to bad outcomes), and the spiral of silence (where individuals measure the appropriateness of their own feelings against their perception of the feelings of the majority), troll behavior emerges from a combination of psychological and situational factors. This disquieting new form of mob mentality has come to be known as the *online disinhibition effect*. Factors contributing to the emergence of a virtual mob include lack of effective regulation and control, a sense that consequences are not likely, asynchronous communication among the parties, leanness of the medium (which means nonverbal and visual cues that usually accompany meaningful communication are absent), a solipsistic mindset wherein one perceives themselves as the only "real" creature that exists, generational differences, and most importantly, anonymity (Dawson, 2017; Santana, 2014; Stein, 2015; Suler; 2004; Twenge & Campbell, 2008). Disinhibition can be benign or even beneficial, in facilitating the free expression of ideas and also in instances where anonymous strangers share experiences online in a mutually supportive manner with all parties benefitting (Bouchard, 2016). More often, anonymity in online communications is toxic, as occurs in trolling and cyberbullying. Where *benign disinhibition* tends to be curative and productive, *toxic disinhibition* is dangerous and destructive – often deliberately so.

People abiding in this category are app to explore places on the internet that they would never visit in the real world... toxic disinhibition may be simply a blind catharsis, a fruitless repetition of compulsion, and an acting out of unsavory needs without any personal growth at all. (Santana, 2014, p. 22, quoting Suler, 2004)

A number of studies specifically focusing on anonymity in computer mediated communication (CMC) find support for the hypothesis that anonymity is a key ingredient in online aggression, impoliteness, incivility, trolling and cyberbullying (Bartlett, 2015; Santana, 2014; Zimmerman & Ybarra, 2016).

On the Internet, Nobody Knows You're a Dog

Peter Steiner's cartoon of a key-boarding dog talking to another dog about his online activities was published in the New Yorker magazine, the deep and ominous meaning of that statement was not as readily acknowledged as it would be today. The sardonic humor of an ambitious canine pretending to be a human in order to network with others on the internet, 25 years later, has taken on more ominous connotations.

Whether anonymity is being used "properly" depends upon the situation, the communicator, and the subject matter of the communicator. In cases of political speech, the ability to remain anonymous often can be a matter of life or death; in case of commercial speech relating to assessments of professional competence, anonymity can be a weapon of character assassination. Anonymity is the basis for progressive tendencies because

[E]very country has a limit on which political opinions are allowed, and there are always people who want to express forbidden opinions, like racial agitation in most democratic countries... The border between illegal and legal but offensive use is not very sharp and varies depending on the law in each country. (Palme & Berglund, 2012, p. 3, 4)

This grey area between legality and illegality of certain speech acts constitutes the primary field of considerations of digital defamation and conflicting notions of management and control of online speech. Permissibility of certain forms of speech is further complicated in the United States and similar democracies where culturally imposed "political correctness" mandates constrain the free expression of opinions. Laws often simultaneously protect and prohibit anonymity. These laws are not consistent either in application in specific countries and even less so if a focus is on international consensus-building relative to rights to speech *vs.* rights to anonymity *vs.* rights to privacy.

In the US, the First and Fourth Amendments exemplify protection of free speech that is not congruent with protection of the right to privacy. French law requires that Internet speech be presented with the true identity of the communicator. In Sweden, Internet service providers (ISPs) are accountable for content disseminated on their sites, while in the United States, Section 230 of the Communications Decency Act provides qualified immunity to ISPs. According to some European studies, there is a propensity to legislative and judicial bias against anonymity. "For example, U.S. Supreme Justice Scalia said, 'The very purpose of anonymity is to facilitate wrong by eliminating accountability'" (Palme & Berglund, 2012, quoting Froomkin, 1995).

Digital Speech Offenses

While the boundless virtual terrain of cyberspace offers incredible opportunities to advance humanity, it also expands the playing field for nefarious human behavior. An entirely new realm of criminal acts and forms of civil torts has come into being through the agency of Internet platforms. Cybercrimes and cybertorts are domestic and international issues of growing concern to legislators, legal practitioners and scholars.

The category of cybercrime encompasses online behaviors that would make an individual liable for criminal prosecution if they were committed in the material world. These include cyberterrorism, identity theft, cyberstalking, election manipulation, denial of service attacks, and inciting to violence. Other online behaviors may not be crimes but are actionable in courts of law – cybertorts - are those that "use the internet or computers to commit a negligent or intentional civil wrong against others" (Penn State Research Wiki, n.d.). Online defamation is a cyber tort.

The potential exists for the Internet to enable perpetrators to launch attacks from the cybersphere to damage or destroy power grids, computer networks, or other networked resources that drive 21st century human life. Malicious code embedded by remote network access can disrupt communication and information management systems and wreak havoc for individuals and for international organizations. As the Penn State researchers put it:

These threats are all around us and are now ever-present because our current society tends to be connected constantly. This interconnectivity often allows these cyber threats to go undetected.

Quoting Deloitte's 2010 cyber security watch survey, the Penn State researchers further note that

Hackers are the greatest cyber threat, over insiders, criminal organizations and foreign entities "... because on a global and national scale the typical approaches to cybersecurity are not nearly keeping pace."

Opinion manipulation by online influencers is entering public awareness, especially in light of an alleged Russian *troll farm* which attempted to manipulate the 2016 US Presidential election via other social media. especially Facebook. But this is not solely an American problem. Writing in 2015 for presentation at an International Conference on computational language learning held in Beijing China, a group of scholars addressed the problem of online opinion manipulation trolls as manifested in Eastern Europe, Asia, and the Middle East. The ready availability of online forums provides "the opportunity for corporations, governments and others to distribute rumors, misinformation, speculation and he's other dishonest practices to manipulate user opinion" (Mihaylov, Georgiev & Nakov. 2015).

Those authors noted that Europeans had become aware of online opinion manipulation during the Ukraine crisis. In order to determine ways to distinguish internet trolls from well-meaning civilian commentators, they performed statistical analyses of the largest internet community forum linked to the Bulgarian newspaper, *Dnevnik*. Although it appears to have been a well-constructed experiment, the authors ultimately characterized it as "much of a witch hunt" (Mihaylov, Georgiev & Nakov, 2015, p. 313), suggesting that the data needs to be rechecked manually in the future rather than relying solely computer-generated results. In the end, the authors determined that there is currently no reliable way to recognize our Define who and what and online troll is. "We solve this issue pragmatically: we assume that a user who is called a troll by several people is likely to be one (p.310).

Although this chapter focuses primarily on defamatory online communication perpetrated against individuals in their professional capacities, which is considered to be commercial commentary, trolls who engage in online political commentary have become far more dangerous. While such operations pose a threat to life and democratic political processes, issues of anonymity, technological and governmental management of social media platforms, and protections for individuals similarly challenge the management of sites that facilitate commercial speech.

Anonymity and Character Assassination Online

Science fiction devotees are familiar with the concept of cloaking – as in *cloaking devices* that permit the Starship *Enterprise* to navigate uncharted interstellar territories in the fictional futures of the *Star Trek* chronicles. The cloak of invisibility also is a common theme of folktales, fairy stories, and myths across many cultures through many eras. The magical power of invisibility can facilitate heroic actions or villainous travesties. In much the same way, the cloak of anonymity in communication situations in the present time empowers persons to feel safe in sharing opinions that may otherwise be kept secret – bravely in some cases, nefariously in others. In certain venues, identity is protected by legal standards (as in information shared with attorneys, law enforcement, or medical practitioners) and in other cases identity is protected by religious conventions (as in confessions to a priest). In these instances, anonymity masks the individual's identity for a public good, in order to encourage sharing of information that might otherwise remain hidden.

It would be difficult to overstate the importance of anonymity to political speech worldwide. In the pre-revolutionary period in America, anonymity might be lauded as a critical strategy enabling independence from Great Britain. Sedition laws forced pamphleteers agitating for the establishment of an independent country had to operate behind a mask of anonymity in order to survive the publication of their ideas. Similarly, founding fathers James Madison, Alexander Hamilton and John Jay, authoring the Federalist Papers as *Publius*, found it necessary to publish using pseudonyms.

In the present time, safeguarding one's life in some cases and one's economic well-being in other instances mandates obscuring one's identity to disseminate ideas that contradict the values and practices of established authorities and power elites. In other cases, however, norms of civility (which have often morphed into extremes of political correctness conventions) come into play where anonymous hate speech or speech characterized as hate speech comes into play. In most instances, the free exchange of ideas has been the life force of a wave of democracies established worldwide in the past 30 year. Often, this has been contingent upon one's ability to communicate anonymously. Bloggers and citizen journalists have been the driving force in political activism taking place in online forums; many of these commentators have been targeted for literal assassination because of their inflammatory ideas when unmasked by enemies to their ideals. Social media have served conflicting roles in the advance of democratic urges globally and in their suppression.

Anonymity, Trolls, Bots, and the Death of Jamal Khashoggi

An October 20th, 2018, *New York Times* article provided and in an in-depth analysis of the operations of a Saudi Troll Army and a suspected Twitter Insider who helped engineer the kidnapping and murder of Jamal Khashoggi, a Saudi living in the United States and working as a columnist for *The Washington Post*.

In many parts of the world, exposition of political and religious ideas is subsumed as one and the same, as theocratic power structures control all aspects of life in those countries. Penalties for sedition are strict and severe; even more grievous are penalties imposed for blasphemy in countries whose rule of law is based in religious tenets. Much has been written in the past decade or so about the gruesome executions of Bangladeshi bloggers – assumed to be unofficially state-sanctioned – whose expressed democratic ideals in their blogs that constituted blasphemy. Within cultures where Islamic Sharia law is the fundamental basis of all forms of life practices and activities, political speech is often deemed blasphemous. Saudi Arabia holds to a strict interpretation of Sharia law and, in conjunction with authoritative political rule, constraints on dissent are rigid.

Many Saudis had hoped that Twitter would democratize discourse by giving everyday Citizens Voice, but Saudi Arabia has instead become an illustration of how authoritarian governments can manipulate social media to silence or drown out critical voices while spreading their own version of reality. (Benner, et al., 2018)

The tragic fate of Jamal Khashoggi, the Saudi journalist advocating for democratic policies - especially free speech - in his native country while a legal resident of Virginia writing for *The Washington Post*, exemplifies the dangers of openly publishing unsanctioned, subversive political ideas. His murder inside the Saudi Embassy in Turkey in October 2018 is being seen as the culmination of a Web-based conspiracy originating at the highest levels of the Saudi government The crime is still under investigation as of the writing of this chapter, but it is becoming clear that a highly organized Internet-based operation of online trolls, humans not bots, was at the center of the conspiracy.

The *New York Times* reports that anti-dissident activities of an army of "Twitter trolls" based in Riyadh projected a disquieting foreshadowing of what was to become a political assassination. According to sources that include friends of Khashoggi, other dissident Saudi ex-pats, Middle East scholars, and cyber-tech experts, a concerted effort to silence him and other critics of Saudi Crown Prince Mohammed bin Salman weaponized social media, especially Twitter. It was reported that Khashoggi had been the victim of a campaign of psychological cyber warfare in the months preceding his death. His friend Maggie Mitchell Salem reported that each morning Khashoggi would check his cell phone and find himself the target of a plethora of venomous Twitter attacks. Salem states that "he would wake up to the equivalent of sustained gunfire online" (Benner, Mazzetti, Hubbard & Isaac, 2018).

Avoiding mistaking correlation with causation, it still should be noted that Saudi Arabia had the largest one-year increase in social media usage in 2018, up 31% since January, 2017 (Kemp, 2018; We Are Social, 2018). Twitter is the most popular social media platform not only for interpersonal communication but also per news in the Kingdom of Saudi Arabia in the aftermath of the Arab Spring uprisings of 2010.

In the Khashoggi case, conflicting forces of democratic ideals and state-supported constraints of personal freedoms were heavily involved in internet-based communication, and those communications had opposing objectives. It might seem that government control of technological infrastructures and of internet functionalities that give authorities the ability to unmask those acting anonymously on the Internet would have a chilling effect on anti-authoritarian speech. However, according to Mark Owen Jones, an expert on the Persian Gulf and the Arabian peninsula,

In the Gulf, the stakes are so high for those who engage in dissent that the benefits of using social media are outweighed by the negatives, and in Saudi Arabia in particular. (quoted in Benner, et al., 2018)

The Khashoggi tragedy humanizes the anonymity conundrum and magnifies the dilemma of operationalizing dueling freedoms – the right to privacy coexisting with the right to speak - that faces those who must resolve that dialectic as it concerns online interactions. Further discussion of this point is undertaken in the Conclusions section dealing with future directions in research and legislation. Political commentary is crucial to the furtherance of democratic processes worldwide, and political speech often depends upon the speaker's right to anonymity. This goes to the crux of the issues presented in this chapter.

Commercial speech and the right to be protected from defamatory commentary, while offering a lower level of threat to life, remains a threat to global enterprises and personal well-being. While character assassination is clearly less grave than literal assassination, overcoming challenges to control, legislation and adjudication of communication abuses could establish the groundwork for preventing bloodshed that is the extreme consequence of free speech. Digital defamation and character assassination stems from the same heinous urges of people who want to hurt others physically and use social media to facilitate those objectives.

Social Media and Online Character Assassination: The State of the Art

A category of civil actions called "privacy torts" have evolved, extending classical definitions of torts of defamation, libel, and slander. Civil torts now include invasion of privacy, rights to control one's likeness, "false light" claims, and claims of "intrusion upon seclusion" (Mitrano, 2010). The emergence of these more recent communication-based causes of action are, to a great extent, the result of increasingly sophisticated communication technology.

Electronic media offers not only increasingly detailed surveillance of individuals but also establishes a network of web-based forums for commentary on individuals' activities that is global, permanent, and irrevocable (Neher & Sandin, 2017). Because of the Internet... " we not only have speech, we have endurance for all time, international scope and the potential for reverberation of that invasion or libelous statement to do real damage to people in terms of lost employment, emotional and reputational harm." (Mitrano, 2012)

The proliferation of social media sites, especially sites which review professionals such as doctors, attorneys, professors, and others whose reputations are based upon credibility and competence, have resulted in an increasing number of lawsuits for cyber-defamation (Bhimji, 2018; Boyle, 2017; Brooks, 2014; Browning, 2008; Davis, 2000; Ernst, 2018; Flaherty, 2014; Forde, 2008; Greenfield, 2014; Hur & Sequeira, 2018; Jackson, 2018; Licea, 2018; Rolfe & Douglas, 2018; Spencer, 2011; Stewart, 2016; Woodward, 2009).

Efforts are being made at state and federal levels to develop legal frameworks to manage key issues such as what liability should an internet service provider have for statements posted by their users, when should anonymity be relinquished and by what standard, and how might conflicts between mandates of the 1st and 4th amendments in cases of defamation be resolved (Balica, 2017; Cheung & Schultz, 2017; Gerrie, 2017; Nilsson, 2017; Siler, 2016; Young & Laidlaw, 2017).

As we move through the early 21st century, the core definitions of social constructs such as truth, news, and communication are being reconstructed as cultural concepts impacted by the norms and practices of those within a variety of information communities. The norms, values, and practices of professional journalists have been supplanted by the important activities of bloggers, online commentators, and other types of citizen journalists. Commentary abounds. And within this abundance of commentary, arises an abundance of potentially defamatory statements.

Although reputational crises in the virtual environment have become a global phenomenon, this chapter focuses primarily on its manifestation in the United States and Canada. Americans are guaranteed freedoms set forth in the Bill of Rights to the Constitution. Two of these, the First and the Fourth Amendments, are in dialectical opposition when considering matters of abusive communication, specifically defamatory speech acts which put the author of the communication in jeopardy of legal liability for publishing those ideas. In cases of defamation, specifically online defamation, these areas of Americans rights are on a collision course (Chemerinsky, 2017; Hopkins, 2017; Nilsson, 2017).

Actionable Online Character Assassination

Defamation, libel and slander are categories of speech which may be the basis of lawsuits in state courts, filed by persons about whom statements are made which can be shown to have caused harm to that person's reputation. To prevail in a lawsuit based upon defamation, libel or slander, the plaintiff generally must prove that the derogatory statement was false and was presented as a statement of fact and not as an opinion. Unless the statement was so abhorrent on its face that it falls into categories of *per se* defamation (set out on a state-by-state basis), the false statement also must be shown to have caused actual harm to the person's or organization's reputation. The person bringing suit usually must also show that the harmful statement of fact was made recklessly and without due diligence as to its truth or falsity. If the person who is alleging defamation, libel or slander is a public figure, then *malice* must also be proven. Malice is based upon the intentionality underlying the publication (Bhimji, 2018; Solmecke, 2013; Valentine, 2017).

Generally, *libel* is a form of defamation published as a written communication, while *slander* is a spoken or audible message. Both libel and slander can and do occur with increasing frequency on websites (Gerrie, 2017; Valentine, 2017). An individual may be slandered on a website, discussion board, blog, or review if the statement made is part of a video or podcast or audio file (Bhimji, 2018; Valentine, 2017).

Expansion of Social Media Proliferates Abusive Communication

Virtual defamation is an increasingly important area of legal practice, both in the United States and globally. Web 2.0, also known as the Participatory and Social Web, began evolving early in the 2000s due in part to changes in the way that web pages are designed and disseminated. This version of the World Wide Web provides a more dynamic and Interactive and interconnected internet, is more user-friendly, provides a high degree of user-generated content, and allows for greater collaboration and vitality of shared information. Moving away from earlier .html versions of websites that were essentially online bulletin boards and messaging sites spurred development of a multitude of social media sites, the most commonly used being Facebook and Twitter as of this writing. (Obar & Wildman, 2015) the number and types of social media platforms worldwide continues to expand rapidly.

Essentially, and most importantly for the purposes of this chapter, the shift to Web 2.0 can be characterized as a shift from user as consumer to user as participant." (Obar & Wildman, 2015. p.6) The critical element of Web 2.0 functionality is the continual input of content, which is "continuously modified by all users in a participatory and collaborative fashion." (Kaplan & Haenlein, 2010, p. 61) Control and regulation of the vast and interconnected network of virtual information providers and the virtual structures that facilitate communication in this network is incredibly challenging, and increasingly so as the Web expands (Balica, 2017; Brenner, 2006; Ober & Wildman, 2015; Young & Laidlaw, 2017).

The nature of virtual communication and digital communication technologies create unique challenges in terms of policy development and controls over Web content, including abusive communication generally and defamatory communication specifically. Whereas communication mediums that pre-existed the Internet and virtual communication platforms was relatively slow-moving in terms of novel developments and use-practices, tended to weed out newcomers to the benefit of established providers, and could be managed and controlled by essentially similar sets of rules and regulations.

In the case of virtual / digital communication technologies, the rate of change is so rapid and varied, that regulatory agencies do not have the luxury of time to gather information, ruminate on alternatives and potential outcomes of legislative protocols, "make adjustments while developing rules that applied, with some variation, to all providers of a given type of communication service" (Obar & Wildman, 2010, p. 15-16). Obar & Wildman note further that a second critical difference between old and new communication functionalities lies in the ways that users interact in online venues. Although there is great potential for benefit from these "new forms of socialization" generated online, there is just as much danger of harm:

[S]ocial media can facilitate injurious forms of social interaction, such as sexting, online stalking, and cyber-bullying that by any standards should be suppressed. How to craft laws and regulations that suppress what is harmful while preserving still the functionalities that facilitate positive forms of interaction is a challenge ... (Ober & Wildman, 2015, p. 16)

Thus, extreme and rapid changes in communication technology, types of user interaction (especially within a social climate of pervasive incivility such as we see in the past several years), the potential for abuse that the cloak of anonymity in virtual domains provides, and the permanence of Internet-generated messages greatly complicates the establishment of control over malignant communication in virtual environments.

Another consideration that bears reflection, in terms of the challenges and pitfalls of social media communication relates to notions of ethical communication and loss of control over one's "sent" messages. Ethics scholar William W. Neher cautions that

Unlike face-to-face communication, we do not always know if the intended person (and only that person) has received the message or how the message was interpreted ... The more people who have access to a message, the less any one person might control it. With the world as audience, there is little or no confidentiality or safety in sending it... The point is that digital communication can [and should] be considered public communication. (Neher & Sandin, 2017, p. 282)

Applying this thinking to the subject of social media defamation, a further point that should be considered is the ability of receivers to use screen-shots and other re-sending strategies to share the original sender's message. Thus, where actionable defamation is concerned, a claim of unintentional sharing of libelous or slanderous material may not offer protection from a lawsuit.

Social media sites are expected to continue their exponential growth and to become increasingly important globally due to the heavy involvement in these by Millennial users, who have "transformed every domain from entertainment to retail" (Bhangadia, 2017). Social media are, more and more, not only a marketplace for goods also of ideas. They are big business. The commercial importance and complexity of social media sites in both the virtual world and the real world further contribute to control challenges.

The following are striking statistics about social media use as of mid-October 2018 presented in the global social media research summary developed and maintained by We Are Social, a London UK-based firm. (We Are Social monitors and continually updates information on global social media use and global marketing strategies which tap into online capabilities.)

- Globally, internet users numbered 4.2 billion, an increase of 7% over 2017 figures
- Of these, 3.4 billion were social media users, an increase of 10% over those counted in September, 2017
- Two-thirds of the population of planet Earth used mobile phones, with 60% of these being Internet-connected smart phones
- Worldwide, there are 5.1 billion mobile phone users
- Between July and September of 2018, 68 million people went online for the first time; this is an increase of 1.5% in only 3 months
- 320 million people became first time users of social media between September, 2017, and October, 2018

Whereas only 7% of Americans interacted using social media a decade ago, that percentage has now increased to 65%. Facebook is by far the most heavily used of the social media sites with over 2 billion active users globally (Kemp, 2018; Smith & Anderson, 2018).

Marketing researchers and media scholars applying demographic information, including generational categories, are able to track popularity of specific social media sites and usage trends connected to these. The current generational classification schemed, building upon US Census figures and the Pew Center's fine-tuning of the time-frames for each, is:

- Silent generation: 1928 to 1945
- Baby Boomers: 1946 to 1964
- Generation X: 1965 to 1980
- Millennials: 1981 to 1996
- Post-millennials (as yet without a nickname): 1997 to present

Important to this discussion of online communication behaviors, these categories are defined in great part by the dominant "new" technological innovations impacting the period in which they became cognizant of the world around them. For example, television became a major force an American life during the Baby Boomer generation. Generation X saw computers generally, and personal computer specifically, have a massive impact upon daily life. While Millennials can still recall landlines and rotary phones, that generation also witnessed the development and implementation of the Internet and social media. It should also be noted that the Millennial generation further can be defined by their memories as impressionable children of the attacks on the World Trade Center on September 11, 2001 and personal experience of the economic downturn of the 2008 recession (Duggan, 2014; Smith & Anderson, 2018; We Are Social, 2018)

Although all age categories are well-represented, users within the Millennial category are seen to be the heaviest participants on social media (Bhangadia, 2017; Chaffey, 2018; Duggan, 2014; Twenge & Campbell, 2008). This point becomes relevant in the discussion which follows of psychological traits attributed to cyberbullies, including Internet trolls.

Researchers also have attempted to develop a framework whereby social media may be categorized and defined by type. This endeavor – which is more complicated than it would appear at first glance – is a necessary stage in developing legislation or protocols by which defamation in the virtual realm may be identified, litigated, and controlled. There is scholarly consensus that six major types exist. These are summarized and discussed in Kaplan and Heinlein's 2010 paper setting out the challenges and opportunities of social media. The six categories they define are blogs, social networking sites such as Facebook, virtual social worlds such as Second Life, collaborative projects such as Wikipedia, content communities like YouTube, and virtual game worlds like World of Warcraft.

Kaplan and Haenlein apply relevant public communication theories and media studies theories to develop their typology table, including Erving Goffman's early work on face and self-presentation, media richness theories as described by Daft & Langel in 1986, and social presence theory, discussed by Short, Williams and Christy in 1976. They classify social media according to high medium or low levels of social presence / *media richness* on one axis and high or low according to *self-presentation* / *self-disclosure* on the second axis.

The Kaplan & Haenlein paper was published in 2010, just ahead of the rapid proliferation of online commentary and rating sites individuals can access today to publish what are essentially opinion-based reviews of experiences they've had with a variety of organizations and individuals. Messages are often published anonymously on these sites; anonymity somewhat confounds the usefulness of the typology described above. This is especially true relative to the dimensions of self-presentation and self-disclosure. The author is deliberately withholding disclosure and presentation of "self" when posting anonymously or with a pseudonym. It may be that an additional category is needed in order to apply relevant communication and media theories to the effects and ramifications of such rating sites. This is especially so when posts under consideration concern professionals and become subject matter in a defamation suit.

The overarching aim of this chapter is to describe, to understand and to manage malevolent communicators who use online technologies to disparage or otherwise injure individuals and organizations. The following discussion presents issues related to anonymity, characteristics of digital character assassinations, including cyber bullies and trolls, and strategies for managing and mitigating the challenges that abusive communicators impose on others.

"A Culture of Hate": Anonymity, (In)incivility and Trolls

The cover story of the October 18, 2016, issue of *Time Magazine* was entitled "Why We're Losing the Internet to the Culture of Hate." Aside from the familiar red *TIME* title, the only image on the white background of that cover is a flame-haired, pointy-eared little troll with a demonic smirk, busily typing on a laptop. The thesis of the *Time* special issue is that "trolls are ruining the internet." And the way they're doing it is to pervert a technology that is well oriented toward sharing ideas, values, wisdom, hopes, by turning it into a dark and eerie cyber-forest where bad, dangerous things are lurking.

Human beings indulging in variety of misbehaviors online have come to be known as *trolls*. The word may summon the image of a fisherman trailing a line while moving along the water or of a mean and smelly little creature who lurks under a bridge to frighten and extort tolls from travelers, depending upon one's cultural experiences. Both definitions properly capture the essence of the activity characterized as *trolling* in Internet venues. Trolls feed on attention, especially negative reactions, and exact psychological tolls upon their targets. Trolls are often *phishing* for data or entry into others' online accounts; the term *catfishing*, an extreme form of anonymity and identity theft morphed together, lures someone online into believing that they are forging a real relationship with someone who does not actually exist. Other specialized troll behaviors include *doxxing* (where personal financial and other sensitive data is released to the public), *flaming* (pulling others into heated and in civil discussions over usually trivial points of view), and *swatting* (summoning emergency or law enforcement personnel to someone's actual home – all just for the *lulz* (laughs). In the latter case, swatting has led to the deaths of innocent people clue when they resist law enforcement personnel who show up at their doors. Another form of vile troll behavior that is occurring with increasing frequency is an extreme form of cyberbullying known as RIP-trolling. This occurs when bereaved families are subjected to heartless taunts and insults of their deceased loved one. In similar behavior, cyberbullies and trolls attempt to shame their targets into such self-loathing and despair that they become suicidal.

Although liberals and progressives engage in trolling to some extent, "trolling has become the tool of the alt-right" (Stein, 2016). Digital troll voices tend to be racist, sexist, misogynistic, anti-Semitic, anti-immigrant, and generally anti" anything that the majority value and find praiseworthy. This is because, at its core, troll behavior can be seen to have its genesis in fearful self-loathing and envy. However, attempting to categorize persons likely to be trolls on the basis of age, gender, political likes, dislikes, and other demographic and psychographic data would be to misunderstand that persona. People who troll are not readily identifiable by distinguishing characteristics such as an intimidating scowl, a curled lip, or a nasty laugh triggered by other people's pain.

Jessica Moreno, formerly Reddit's (an online news aggregator feed with user-generated content) head of community, points to the actions of users within one Reddit online community called *fatpeoplehate* as instrumental in her decision to leave her job there. She and her husband, also a former Reddit employee, eventually had to move away from their home and conceal their new location when Reddit trolls became angry at her efforts to decommission the *fatpeoplehate* site. Administrative responsibilities and privileges of her Reddit position gave her access to the real personal identification of anonymous posters, so she was able to know who the people behind the anonymous hate posts were. She noted that the troll personality isn't what one might think it is at first glance.

The idea of the basement dweller drinking Mountain Dew and eating Doritos isn't accurate... they would be a doctor, a lawyer, and inspirational speaker, a kindergarten teacher. They've been normal person. It's more complex than just being good or bad. (Stein, 2016)

Psychographic Characteristics of Cyberhaters

In virtual communication communities, abusive communication has become so widespread that, according to one researcher, 80% of young participants see it as "commonplace" (Stein, 2016). A 2014 study of the online environment by the Pew Research Center determined that a large majority of people who are active online have experienced hurtful communications to some extent. The age group of their respondents is linked to the venue in which the hurtful communication was encountered. Where internet users age 50 and older who had been hurt by a communication reported that the most recent incident happened in an email account, a large number of young adults age 18 to 29 (especially males) reported the most recent abusive communication they had experienced happened in online gaming. Analyzing responses by gender, 79% of women reporting named social networking sites as the location where they most often experienced abusive communication, compared to 59% of men reporting this. Overall, 66% of those who experienced abusive communication online stated that the harassment occurred on a social networking site or app.

In the same Pew Research Center study, 68% of respondents thought that the online environment "was more enabling of social support, with 31% disagreeing." At the same time, 92% of respondents felt that the online environment allowed people to be more critical of others, with only 7% disagreeing. The study also elicited number of first-person reactions to being targeted by anonymous online cruelty:

Cowards hiding beyond a keyboard and the anonymity of the internet provides were verbally abusive.

A disagreement in a chat ...people are ten feet tall and bulletproof behind a screen.

People who disagree acting out in ways that would never be acceptable when dealing with someone in person.

A 2016 survey of 1,000 Americans indicated that about one-quarter had been victims of online harassment in some form or knew someone who had been. Twenty percent of the victims were concerned about repercussions to themselves professionally; 20% reported being fearful about going into public; and 29% actually feared for their lives and well-being. "Experts believe that it's going to get worse" (Chastain, 2018).

Digital Haters: Who Does That?

A number of researchers have attempted to delineate the difference between a *cyberbully* and a *troll* (Bishop, 2014; Buckels, Trapnell & Paulhus, 2014; Shahan & Hara, 2010; Zezulka & Seigfried-Spellar, 2016). Again, there is consensus that anonymity has a stimulating effect on aggressive online communication, making attack communication more likely when anonymity is added to a constellation of personality traits.

A workable definition of online trolling is "the practice of behaving in a deceptive, destructive, or disruptive manner in a social setting on the Internet with no apparent instrumental purpose (Buckels, Trapnell & Paulhus, 2014). The pointlessness of the troll activity is one dividing line between trolling and cyberbullying. One of the first systematic studies examining the behaviors of Internet trolls focused on differentiating trolls from hackers operating in *Wikipedia*. That 2010 study characterized both behaviors as forms of virtual vandalism. Common features shared by trolls and hackers included their hidden identity as they undertake deceptive online behavior, the intentionality of their destructive acts, and the repetitive nature of the behaviors (Shachaf & Hara, 2010, pp. 363-365). A subsequent study tracked the changing characterizations of online trolling behaviors to develop a typology and construct a matrix of trolling types. Generally, the meaning of *trolling* has expanded from simply meaning dialogic flaming on a discussion board and otherwise provoking heated exchanges for shared enjoyment to meaning all forms of online abuse perpetrated purely for the troll's amusement. Broadly defined, the more recent definition encompasses

... a group of people looking for a new villain to attack in order to escape their own insecurities. And there are the counter culture groups who enjoy identifying as trolls as they know it is seen as deviant by others, making their subversive and transgressive humor that much more enjoyable. (Bishop, 2014, p.13)

The same study also charts trolling behaviors in terms of grades "... namely, playtime, tactical, strategic and domination, with the first the least severe, and the last most severe" Bishop, 2014, p.19).

The type of abusive communication this chapter focuses on most closely, defamatory trolling on internet rating sites, best fits the third category, also called "strategic cyberbullying." These trolls are described as going out of their way "to cause problems, but without a sustained and plan long-term campaign." Such messages are typically posted on websites that "are open to a wide audience, where many can see the message posted and then move on" (ibid., p. 20.)

The Dark Triad of personality - that is characteristics of narcissism, Machiavellianism, and psychopathy, often more narrowly framed as sadism - is a psychological link from children who bully in the real world to people who grow up to be trolls online (Buckels, Trapnell & Paulus, 2014). Other characteristics statistically significant in studies of abusive online behaviors include aggression, deception, and disruption. Generally, the pointlessness of the behaviors is underscored by the obscurity of the transgressor's intent and the cloak of anonymity (ibid., p. 98). Researchers have found that "cyberbullying is often perpetrated by heavy internet users, and disagreeable persons use mobile technologies more than others" (ibid., p. 97). Citing previous research, the authors stated that

...those with antisocial personality disorder use Facebook more frequently than others, indicating that dark personalities leave large digital footprints. After all, trolling culture embraces a concept virtually synonymous with sadistic pleasure: in troll-speak, "lulz" ... Internet trolls displayed high levels of the Dark Tetrad traits and a BFI profile consistent with those traits. It was sadism, however, that had the most robust associations with trolling of any of the personality measures ... [Associations were] so strong that it might be said that online trolls are prototypical everyday sadists ... both trolls and sadists feel satisfaction at the distress of others. Sadists just want to have fun and the internet is their playground! (ibid, p. 98, p. 100-101)

Several quantitative analyses of generational differences among Americans have delineated four categories of individuals whose major life experiences (and technological advances that defined their youth and young adulthood). Insights as to generational aspects of a propensity toward incivility and abusive communication support those findings insofar as younger Internet users are concerned.

Twenge and Campbell's 2008 longitudinal study covered an 80-year time frame in an analysis of hundreds of psychological profiles of college students throughout that time, a sample of more than 1.4 million people. The four categories broken out of this meta-analysis were:

- Veterans (a/k/the Silent Generation) 1922 to 1945
- Baby Boomers 1946 to 1964
- Generation X 1965 to 1980
- Millennials 1980 to 2000

These time frames correspond generally to those established by the US Census Bureau and the Pew Center for research. Findings identified a set of specific traits statistically significant for Millennials which differentiate that demographic in terms of communication style, interpersonal interactions, personal and professional objectives, and psychological profile. These include:

- A decreased need for social approval
- A simultaneous increase in both self-esteem and narcissism
- An expectation of continual praise and a resistance to criticism
- An external locus of control (placing agency and accountability for outcomes outside oneself)
- Higher levels of anxiety and depression
- Increased assertiveness (in Millennial females)

Further, this research specifically associates the Dark Triad of personality traits with the Millennial generation, especially as these are manifested in the workplace and, one might assume, other similarly public spheres (Trapnell & Paulus, 2014; Twenge & Campbell, S.M., 2008; Twenge, Miller & Campbell, W.K., 2014).

Identifying and attempting to understand the personality characteristics of cyberbullies and internet trolls is increasingly the focus of scholarly research. The objective ultimately is to mitigate the effects of these people on internet discourse specifically and on norms of civility generally. A 2016 study of cyberharassment analyzed self-reports of those who engaged in cyberbullying, trolling, neither behavior, or both behaviors. Generally speaking, few factors differentiate cyberbullies from internet trolls; cyberbullies tended to be less extroverted and score higher on neuroticism than those who engaged only in trolling behaviors. The study suggests that an individual who is likely to engage in cyberbullying is probably just as likely to engage in trolling. Shared characteristics included low internal moral values, low conscientiousness, and especially, low self-esteem (Zezulka & Seigfried-Spellar, 2016). Turning attention to such online rating sites as RateMyProfessor.com, these psychological traits provide some illumination of the motives of defamatory trolling.

Interactive Online Sites as Arenas for Digital Hate Speech

When online news media began allowing for reader comments at the end of news stories, that provided an entry into all forms of emotional abuse in what could be called the Forum of Mean-Spirited Opinions. Originally, the commentary areas were anonymous. In response to the increasing incivility on the site, however, newspapers began requiring identification or requiring that users log into a Facebook or similar account prior to being able to post. That had some effect on increasing civility on the newspaper sites (Santana, 2015). However, many online opinion sites which publish reviews of such professionals such as doctors, dentists, and college professors continue to allow comments to remain anonymous. These sites have sometimes become rhetorical battlegrounds where allegations of defamation are being brought with increasing frequency and some increase in their success.

Character assassination is not constrained by national boundaries. A variety of cyber-tort issues are being raised around the globe over negative ratings and false narratives posted by individuals that are alleged by their targets to be nothing more than libel, slander, defamation, invasion of privacy, or otherwise actionable.

A 2014 report notes of 23% increase in defamation cases filed in the UK in the previous year. "The growth in the number of reported defamation cases is partly due to a sharp rise in claims brought over defamatory material publish through social media and websites" (Greenslade, 2014). Because these posts are anonymous, making it difficult to uncover the truth or falsity of the posted information, it is also difficult to determine who the person is behind the mask of anonymity who is making the statement or to understand why they are doing so. Thus, successful prosecution of digital defamation is extremely difficult.

Twenge and Campbell discuss the concept of a "psychological contract" that exists in organizational relationships, whereby the authoritative and subordinate parties negotiate beliefs and understandings of the terms of their shared objectives. This negotiation is not necessarily deliberate or even consciously undertaken in real life but, instead, exists in the minds of the parties – often in very different forms. This can lead to both functional and emotional repercussions when it becomes evident that no real agreement underpins the shared tasks and goals. Incongruence between the expectations of the employer and the employee can lead to perceptions that one or more obligations of the employer or unfulfilled. Since the subordinate likely does not have a sense of operational power, that can lead to blows struck behind the mask of an anonymous rating site.

Narrowing consideration now to ways that powerless individuals may feel safe in expressing dislike or disapproval of experiences they've shared with certain professionals, such as doctors, dentists, and college professors, the notion of what might be considered a broken promise (from the point of view of the subordinate) can manifest in feelings of anger and hurt that might cause the individual to turn to an anonymous forum in order to strike back at the perceived transgressor. This form of aggressive or abusive online communication that is potentially actionable in courts of law could be called *defamation trolling* to differentiate it from other forms of online incivility and allow for a clearer and closer investigation of that behavior with an eye toward understanding, controlling, and mitigating its ill effects.

Professor rating sites such as RateMyProfessor.com offer a lens through which the type of abusive communication that occurs on rating sites can be analyzed. Taking a logical leap but without attempting to quantify it, assume for purposes of this reflection that because the majority of college students fall between the ages of 18 and 25, the majority of individuals posting content to RateMyProfessors are likely to be members of the Millennial generation. This may enhance understanding whether and how the personality traits connected with the Millennial generation manifest themselves in teacher ratings. When content alleged to be libelous or injurious to the target's professional reputation is posted on such sites, this is not necessarily done so deliberately or consciously, but may be deflecting difficult emotions into online statements that could meet the standards for actionable defamation.

The Case of Sally Vogl-Bauer

Case number 2013-001140 filed in the Walworth County Wisconsin Circuit Court on December 11, 2013, attracted a great deal of attention because it involved a professor's defamation action against a former student, a more novel occurrence then than currently.

Dr. Sally Vogl-Bauer, a tenured professor of Communication at the University of Wisconsin at Whitewater, had been made the target of a campaign of extreme online vitriol by Anthony Llewellyn, a graduate student she'd taught. In her court filing, Dr. Vogl-Bauer stated that the student's false and defamatory online statements had caused her "substantial economic, reputational and emotional injuries," and she requested actual and punitive damages as well as the legal costs of the suit. According to the student, however, Dr. Vogl-Bauer treated him abusively and unfairly to such an extent that she caused him to drop out of graduate school in 2013. Llewellyn accused Vogl-Bauer of calling him a "horrible student," "screaming and lashing out at him," accusing him of plagiarism, mocking him for a learning disability, and causing him to be dismissed from the University (Brooks, 2014; Flaherty, 2014; Greenfield, 2014).

Included among a large repertoire of retaliatory communications, were reviews of her teaching Llewellyn posted on a rating site called TeacherComplaints.com, similar narratives on several blog sites, a YouTube video entitled *Sally Vogl-Bauers' Garbage*, letters of complaint about Vogl-Bauer to her department at the University, to the Eastern Communication Association (a professional group to which she belonged), the Better Business Bureau, and the Federal Trade Commission. Additionally, a number of online communications similar to those that clearly were authored by Llewellyn carried similar content, although posted under other names.

Vogl-Bauer's attorney, Timothy Edwards, speaking on her behalf, made it clear that there was no argument that a student has a right to express unhappiness with a teacher's instructional methods and assessment approaches. In this case though, according to Edwards, the student went too far in making statements that went far beyond permissible statements of opinion into the realm where they were not only false but also defamatory. The objective of the Vogl-Bauer lawsuit was to draw a line between what is protected speech and what is defamation.

The case raises questions about the line between rating and defaming one's professor, and of what, if any, ethical and legal obligations students have in publicly assessing professors' performance. ... When you make false statements of fact repeatedly about another person with the intent of harming them, that's over the line. If you truthfully say, in my experience, this isn't a good teacher, I didn't have a good experience, she was late and that's your opinion, that's fair. (quoted in Greenfield, 2014)

Prior to filing the lawsuit, Vogl-Bauer and her attorney repeatedly requested the student to remove the defamatory postings and video, but Llewellyn refused to do so. Llewellyn states, "I don't feel I've went [sic] too far with my videos and comments because everything posted basically communicates exactly how Sally Vogl-Bauer treated me" (Brooks, 2014).

The apparently endless communication attack by Llewellyn finally forced Vogl-Bauer to resort to the courts in order to protect her professional reputation. Her attorney states a strong claim as to the permanent effects of a virtual attack on character:

Persistent defamation of one's peers and within a small professional Community can be devastating to the career of a well-respected professional such as Ms. Vogel Bauer. Students have a right to express their opinion, but when you go so far beyond that, into a concerted effort to attack somebody's reputation because things didn't go your way, that's much different. (ibid)

Ultimately, the case was settled without a trial. The widespread reports of the conflict, both in publications catering to higher education and in mainstream media, attracted quite a bit of attention and a polarized audience of commentators. Some of those commenting online made references to similar lawsuits where physicians and dentists have filed similar defamation actions against anonymous posters claiming to be disgruntled patients. As public awareness of these conflicts chains out into the online community, the attention the legal actions and controversies that arise around them attracts a great deal of attention. Individuals who are already embarrassed by content they found to be defamatory that they went on record with a lawsuit then get to experience the Streisand Effect firsthand. This is the phenomenon that occurs when an attempt to obscure or remove negative information on the internet actually attracts far more attention than it would have had the efforts to erase it had not been launched.

The Vogl-Bauer case also illustrates the complexity and ubiquity of containment challenges inherent in managing online commentary within the larger issue of controlling online content while, at the same time, fostering a climate of free speech and inquiry. There are various forms of privilege and qualified privilege that enable a person to post statements without fear of reprisal. But statements also are made that place the individual making them at risk for liability for defamation. While statements of opinion are permitted, making false statements – even those presented under the guise of opinion – are prohibited, especially when these cause harm.

REPUTATIONAL SELF-DEFENSE: IMPLICATIONS AND RECOMMENDATIONS

As discussed above, abusive communication published on Internet sites is not an American phenomenon. It is not a North American phenomenon, nor is it an issue facing only developed, Westernized countries. It is a global issue. Legislative and policy-making bodies encounter daunting challenges in attempting to address this increasingly salient issue. Even defining the terms – social media, defamation, bullying *versus* trolling, and other concepts similarly associated with online communication – is very difficult. Agreement on a policy-making vocabulary is unlikely to become less complex in the future, due to the rapid proliferation of technological advances and new behaviors that accompany each new Internal functionality.

Chetty and Alathur's "Hate Speech Review in the Context of Online Social Networks" (2018) aims at categorizing online forms of terrorism and extremism, providing as well a compendium of their research of international legal frameworks that illustrate a fairly substantial corpus of shared human values encoded into "accepted declarations and conventions supporting fundamental rights to every human being (p. 111). Tables illustrating their findings summarize articles from five international bodies promulgating pro-social norms for free speech as well as efforts to control and restrict hate speech. They find "that the view of all the treaties are almost the same with some added restrictions on hate speech by the [International Convention on the Elimination of all forms of Racial Discrimination]" (pp. 111-114). This research in combination with applications of US state and federal attempts to elucidate, define, and control actionable online speech acts may provide a solid starting-point for workable international conventions.

The issue of anonymity is a critical one to consider in devising an e-form of control over abusive internet communication and determining what, if any, forms of speech must be prohibited. There are compelling and prosocial reasons for an anonymity to be permitted, both in real world mediums and even more so, in the virtual world. While in some ways anonymity protects virtual character assassins, it also protects those who desire to freely share ideas and values related to democratic principles, allowing them to escape political assassination. While online defamation poses a risk to some professionals' livelihood and anonymity enables that risk, the lack of anonymity for certain online commentators seeking to further humanistic ideals is a threat to life itself. Identifying perpetrators, human and bot, linking behaviors to situational triggers. Identifying, predicting, and controlling these communications is greatly enhanced by developments in machine learning and artificial intelligence classifiers that translate Twitter and similar social media data into meaningful categories distinguishing between hate speech, especially those responses "with a focus on race, ethnicity, or religion" (Burnap and Williams, 2015, p. 223).

Ideally, legal, judicial, and policy-building best practices for managing online communication will be developed to an extent where an international framework can be developed that will permit for a set of standards that might tap into whatever core human values, if such can be determined, will offer guiding principles for adaptation and adoption within local and national communities. Artificial intelligence classifiers may be quite useful in sorting bots from humans and "used to forecast the likely spread of cyber hate in a sample of Twitter data" (*ibid*).

Individual actions at the institutional and individual levels could foster workable communication practices and establish educational objectives oriented toward ameliorating the growing and dense cloud of incivility overhanging today's communication networks, both on the internet and in the material world. Young students might learn in school to consider a variety of ethical approaches, both to daily life and to generic communication situations. Understanding the boundaries between free speech and prohibited speech, especially when publishing ideas on the Internet and especially through social media, is a good first step in training people to communicate ethically and honorably. Appealing to self-interest in teaching that the truth is an absolute defense in most cases where defamation is alleged, people might prefer to tell the truth simply to avoid consequences of defaming.

CONCLUSION

Anonymity is critical to democratic discourse and often empowers an individual's ability to exercise free speech, so it is protected by law in many venues including the United States. In balancing the right to privacy with the right to express one's opinion, a double bind arises. It is important to understand the intention underlying the public statement. Is it a heartfelt opinion based on an actual experience? Is it cyberbullying of a perceived enemy? Is it narcissistic externalization of a toxic lack of self-esteem? Or is it mean-spirited troll behavior sadistically acted out simply for the lulz?

The quandary arises when one must conclude that some form of unmasking the communicator is necessary to carry forward any legal action for defamation in most venues. Some preliminary speculation and assumptions about categories of persons most likely to be posting material alleged to be defamatory may be helpful, thus the focus on definition of terms.

It is important to recognize that online trolling behavior and norms of incivility are on the ascendant, mirroring the numerous chasms of cultural hostility developing within increasingly polarized factions. Hating is contagious, and haters can be found at every level of human enterprise. Anyone can be a troll; celebrities can be and are trolls, spreading toxicity even more potently than everyday people, because their fame and wealth add to their authority. The negative halo of their fame endows their words with a powerful virulence that causes abusive, malignant communications to metastasize and cultivate virtually any arena for commentary into a troll farm.

At the same time, the Internet empowers individuals as commentators and publishers to an extent never before experienced. Individuals have as much power to spread goodwill and amity via the Internet as they do to troll and cyber-hate. Message boards and commentary sites attached to media allow individuals to model effective engagement in online communications and to contribute to civility in the public cybersphere. Thus, education as to the rights and responsibilities that attach to free speech is critical as is the modeling of ethical communication practices by individuals working in virtual conversations, either as active participants or passive observers with the ability to post commentary. In this way, virtual realms can be cultivated to move beyond a farm that grows cyberbullies and trolls.

REFERENCES

Balica, R. (2017). The Criminalization of Online Hate Speech: It's Complicated. *Contemporary Readings in Law and Social Justice*, 9(2), 184–190. doi:10.22381/CRLSJ92201710

Banerjee, S. (2018). Analysis of user-generated comments posted during live matches of the Cricket World Cup 2015. *Online Information Review*, 42(7), 1180–1194. doi:10.1108/OIR-01-2017-0015

Barlett, C. P. (2015). Anonymously hurting others online: The effect of anonymity on cyberbullying frequency. *Psychology of Popular Media Culture, 4*(2), 70–79. doi:10.1037/a0034335

Bartlett, C. P., Gentile, D. A., & Chew, C. (2016). Predicting cyberbullying from anonymity. *Psychology of Popular Media Culture, 5*(2), 171–180. doi:10.1037/ppm0000055

Benner, K., Mazzetti, M., Hubbard, B., & Isaac, M. (2018, Oct. 20). Saudis' image makers: A troll army and a Twitter insider. *The New York Times*. Retrieved from https://www.nytimes.com/2018/10/20/us/politics/saudi-image-campaign-twitter.html

Bhangadia, M. (2017, Nov. 8). How the dynamics of social media platforms are changing [Blog post]. *Entrepreneur*. Retrieved from https://www.entrepreneur.com/article/304360

Bhimji, S. S., & Gossman, W. G. (2018). *Defamation*. StatPearls Publishing. Retrieved from: https://www.ncbi.nlm.nih.gov/books/NBK531472/

Bishop, J. (2014). Representation of 'trolls' in mass media communication: A review of media-texts and moral panics relating to 'internal trolling.'. *International Journal of Web Based Communities, 10*(1), 7–24. doi:10.1504/IJWBC.2014.058384

Bouchard, K. L. (2016). Anonymity as a double-edge sword: Reflecting on the implications of online qualitative research in studying sensitive topics. *Qualitative Report, 21*(1), 59–67. Retrieved from https://nsuworks.nova.edu/tqr/vol21/iss1/5

Brenner, S. W. (2006). Should online defamation be criminalized? *Miss. LJ, 76*, 705. Retrieved from https://www.researchgate.net/publication/228199163

Brooks, K. (2014, May 30). Professor sues former student for YouTube video, claims defamation. *The College Fix*. Retrieved from https://diverseeducation.com/article/11101/

Browning, L. (2008, May 1). Law professor accuses students of defamation. *New York Times*. Retrieved from https://www.nytimes.com/2008/05/01/us/01legal.html

Buckels, E. E., Trapnell, P. D., & Paulhus, D. L. (2014). Trolls just want to have fun. *Personality and Individual Differences, 67*, 97–102. doi:10.1016/j.paid.2014.01.016

Bunge, N. (2018, Nov. 28). Students rating teachers doesn't just hurt teachers. It hurts students. *The Chronicle of Higher Education*. Retrieved from https://www.chronicle.com/article/Students-Evaluating-Teachers/245169

Burnap, P., & Williams, M. L. (2015). Cyber hate speech on Twitter: An application of machine classification and statistical modeling for policy and decision-making. *Policy and Internet, 7*(2), 223–242. doi:10.1002/poi3.85

Cavna, M. (2013, July 31). 'Nobody knows you're a dog': As iconic Internet cartoon turns 20, creator Peter Steiner knows the joke rings as relevant as ever. *The Washington Post*. Retrieved from https://www.washingtonpost.com/blogs/comic-riffs/post/nobody-knows-youre-a-dog-as-iconic-internet-cartoon-turns-20-creator-peter-steiner-knows-the-joke-rings-as-relevant-as-ever/

Chaffey, D. (2018). Global social media research summary 2018. *Smart Insights*. Retrieved from https://www.smartinsights.com/social-media-marketing/social-media-strategy/new-global-social-media-research/

Chastain, R. (2018, Jan. 16). The complete guide to understanding and dealing with online trolls [Blog post]. Retrieved from https://betterhumans.coach.me/the-complete-guide-to-understanding-and-dealing-with-online-trolls-4a606ae25c2c

Chemerinsky, E. (2017). Fake News and Weaponized Defamation and the First Amendment. *Sw. L. Rev., 47*, 291.

Chetty, N., & Alathur, S. (2018). Hate speech review in the context of online social networks. *Aggression and Violent Behavior, 40*, 108–118. doi:10.1016/j.avb.2018.05.003

Cheung, A. S., & Schulz, W. (2017). Reputation protection on online rating sites. *Stanford Technology Law Review, 21*(310). doi:10.2139srn.3037399

Cyber Crimes and Torts. (n.d.) In *Penn State University Wikispaces*. Retrieved from https://wikispaces.psu.edu/display/IST432TEAM4/Cyber+Crimes+and+Torts

Davis, J. (2000, March 13). Libel-by-linking: Case could be landmark in Cyberspace. *Editor & Publisher*. Retrieved from http://www.editorandpublisher.com/news/libel-by-linking/

Dawson, J. (2018, March 30). Who is that? The study of anonymity and behavior. *Association for Psychological Science*. Retrieved from https://www.psychologicalscience.org/observer/who-is-that-the-study-of-anonymity-and-behavior

Duggan, M. (2014). Part 2: The online environment. *The Pew Research Center, Internet & Technology*. Retrieved from http://www.pewinternet.org/2014/10/22/part-2-the-online-environment/

Ernst, D. (2018, June 21). Jordan B. Peterson hits university with $1.5M defamation lawsuit. *The Washington Times*. Retrieved from https://www.washingtontimes.com/news/2018/jun/21/jordan-b-peterson-hits-wilfrid-laurier-university-/

Flaherty, C. (2014, May 23). Rating or defaming: Professor sues student over his online reviews of her course. *Inside Higher Ed*. Retrieved from https://www.insidehighered.com/news/2014/05/23/professor-sues-student-over-his-online-reviews-her-course

Forde, D. (2008, May 1). Professor sues students for character defamation. *Diverse Issues in Higher Education*. Retrieved from https://diverseeducation.com/article/11101/

Froomkin, A. M. (1995). Anonymity and its enemies. *Journal of Online Law*. Retrieved from http://edu/law/publications/jo//95_96/frooomkin

Gerrie, W. (2017). Say what you want: how unfettered freedom of speech on the internet creates no recourse for those victimized. *Catholic University Journal of Law and Technology*. Retrieved from https://scholarship.law.edu/jlt/vol26/iss1/4

Greenfield, S. H. (2014, May 24). Sensitive Sally smacks special snowflake student silly [Blog post]. *Simple Justice*. Retrieved from https://blog.simplejustice.us/?s=vogl-bauer

Hopkins, W. (2017). Defamation, actual malice and online republication: Lessons learned from Eramo v. Rolling Stone, et al. *Appalachian JL, 17*, 127.

Hur, E., & Sequeira, K. (2018). Professor files for defamation in lawsuit. *University of Southern California Daily Trojan*. Retrieved from https://dailytrojan.com/2018/11/11/professor-files-for-defamation-in-lawsuit/

Jackson, S. (2018, Jan. 29). 'Deplorable' NYU professor sues university, colleagues for defamation. *Washington Square News*. Retrieved from https://nyunews.com/2018/01/28/01-28-news-rectenwald/

Kaplan, A. M., & Haenlein, M. (2010). Users of the world, unite! The challenges and opportunities of social media. *Business Horizons, 53*, 59-68. Retrieved from http://www.elsevier.com/locate/bushor.doi:10.1016/j.bushor.2009.09.003

Legal Information Institute. (n.d.). *47 U.S. Code § 230 - Protection for private blocking and screening of offensive material*. Retrieved from https://www.law.cornell.edu/uscode/text/47/230

Licea, M. (2018, Jan. 13). 'Deplorable' NYU professor sues colleagues for defamation. *New York Post*.

Mihaylov, T., Georgiev, G., & Nakov, P. (2015). Finding opinion manipulation trolls in news community forums. In *Proceedings of the Nineteenth Conference on Computational Natural Language Learning* (pp. 310-314). Academic Press.

Mitrano, T. (2012, Nov. 30). Invasion of privacy, defamation, libel: Type 4 privacy law [Blog post]. *Inside Higher Ed.* Retrieved from http://insidehighered.com/blogs/law-policy-and-it

Neher, W. W., & Sandin, P. J. (2017). Ethics and online communication. In *Communication Ethics* (2nd ed.; pp. 279–301). New York: Routledge.

Nilsson, A. (2017). *Personality rights, defamation and the internet: Considerations of private international law* (Thesis). Retrieved from http://lup.lub.lu.se/student-papers/record/8909002

Obar, J. A., & Wildman, S. S. (2015). *Social media defamation and the governance challenge: An introduction to the special issue* (Working Paper, prepared for the Governance of Social Media special issue of Telecommunications Policy). Retrieved from http://ssm.com/abstract=2633190

Palme, J. (2012). Anonymity on the Internet [Blog post]. Retrieved from https://people.dsv.su.se/~jpalme/society/anonymity.html

Rolph, D., & Douglas, M. (2018). Rebel Wilson's pitch perfect defamation victory. *Entertainment Law Review, 37.* Retrieved from: https://ssrn.com/abstract=3148794

Santana, A. D. (2014). Virtuous or vitriolic: The effect of anonymity on civility in online newspaper reader comment boards. *Journalism Practice, 8*(1), 18–33. doi: 10.1080/17512786.2013.813194

Shachaf, P. & Hara, N. (2010). Beyond vandalism: Wikipedia trolls. *Journal of Information Science, 36*(30), 357-370.

Short, J., Williams, E., & Christie, B. (1976). *The social psychology of telecommunications*. Hoboken, NJ: John Wiley & Sons, Ltd.

Siler, E. B. (2016). Yelping the way to a national statutory standard for unmasking Internet anonymity. *Wake Forest Law Review, 51*(189).

Smith, A., & Anderson, M. (2018). Social media use in 2018. *Pew Research Center, Internet & Technology*. Retrieved from http://www.pewinternet.org/2018/03/01/social-media-use-in-2018/

Solmecke, C. (2013, Nov. 6). Defamation on Facebook and its legal consequences [Blog post]. *Wilde Beuger Solmecke Rechtsanwalte*. Retrieved from https://www.wbs-law.de/eng/defamation-eng/defamation-on-facebook-and-its-legal-consequences-47984/

Spencer, G. (2011, Aug. 12). Widener Law School faces objections. *Delaware County Daily Times*. Retrieved from https://www.delcotimes.com/news/spencer-widener-law-school-faces-objections/article_fa7767be-23a7-5344-a703-d8cf98754c03.html

Stein, J. (2016). How trolls are ruining the Internet. *Time Magazine*, 18.

Stewart, R. (2016, May 12). Facebook defamation case sets new standard for social media commentary [Blog post]. *Ontario Trial Lawyers Association Blog*. Retrieved from http://otlablog.com/facebook-defamation-case-sets-new-standard-for-social-media-commentary/

Suler, J. (2004). The online disinhibition effect. *Cyberpsychology & Behavior, 7*(3), 321–326. doi:10.1089/1094931041291295 PMID:15257832

Twenge, J. M., & Campbell, S. M. (2008). Generational differences in psychological traits and their impact on the workplace. *Journal of Managerial Psychology, 23*(8), 862–877. doi:10.1108/02683940810904367

Twenge, J. M., Miller, J. D., & Campbell, W. K. (2014). The narcissism epidemic: Commentary on modernity and narcissistic personality disorder. *Personality Disorders, 5*(2), 227–229. doi:10.1037/per0000008 PMID:24796568

Valentine, S. (2017). Defamation in the Internet age: The law and social media. *McCague Borlack, LLC*. Retrieved from http://mccagueborlack.com/emails/articles/defamation-social-media.html

Verhofstadt, G. (2018, Dec. 2). Mark Zuckerberg has lost control of Facebook. *Project Syndicate*. Retrieved from https://www.project-syndicate.org/commentary/mark-zuckerberg-has-lost-control-of-facebook-by-guy-verhofstadt-2018

We Are Social. (2018). *The state of the Internet in Q4 2018*. Retrieved from https://wearesocial.com/us/

Zezulka, L. A., & Seigfried-Spellar, K. C. (2016). Differentiating cyberbullies and Internet trolls by personality characteristics and self-esteem. *Journal of Digital Forensics, Security and Law, 11*(3), 5.

Zimmerman, A. G., & Ybarra, G. J. (2016). Online aggression: The influences of anonymity and social modeling. *Psychology of Popular Media Culture, 5*(2), 181–193. doi:10.1037/ppm0000038

ADDITIONAL READING

David, J. (2016). How to Protect (Or Destroy) Your Reputation Online: The Essential Guide to Avoid Digital Damage, Lock Down Your Brand, and Defend Your Business. Wayne, NJ: Career Press.

Dietrich, G. (2014). *Spin Sucks: Communication and Reputation Management in the Digital Age*. Que Publishing.

Gerrie, W. (2017). *Say what you want: How unfettered freedom of speech on the internet creates no recourse for those victimized*. Catholic University Journal of Law and Technology.

Lanier, J. (2018). *Ten Arguments for Deleting Your Social Media Accounts Right Now*. Henry Holt & Co.

MacKenzie, J. (2015). *Psychopath Free: Recovering from Emotionally Abusive Relationships With Narcissists*. Berkeley, CA: Sociopaths, and Other Toxic People

McNamara, L. (2008). Reputation. Oxford, UK: Oxford University Press.

Neher, W. W., & Sandin, P. J. (2017). *Communication Ethics* (2nd ed.). New York: Routledge.

Patchen, J. W., & Hinduja, S. (2013). Words Wound: Delete Cyberbullying and Make Kindness Go Viral. Golden Valley, MN: Free Spirit Publishing.

Siler, E. B. (2016). Yelping the way to a national statutory standard for unmasking Internet anonymity. *Wake Forest Law Review, 51*(189).

Twenge, J. M., & Campbell, W. K. (2010). *The Narcissism Epidemic: Living in the Age of Entitlement*. New York: Atria Books.

KEY TERMS AND DEFINITIONS

Abusive Communication: In this context, an online message that is false, derogatory or demeaning, uncivil, bigoted, or logically likely to cause hurt or harm to the target/subject of that communication.

Anonymity: As used in this chapter, the condition wherein an online commentator's actual identity is not made available. In addition to pure anonymity, where no identifying information is provided, this also would include situations where the commentator uses a pseudonym or an avatar for self-representation.

Communications Decency Act of 1996, Section 230: Federal law that creates freedom from liability for content of online forums which publish information, either visual or spoken by third parties, which may be defamatory. Internet service providers (ISPs) have used this act to absolve themselves from responsibility for online defamation. It also makes it difficult to identify, prosecute or sue for anonymous communications posted online.

Cyber-Bullying: A form of malevolent online abusive communication which intentionally demeans or otherwise targets the victim. Among younger internet users, this would include what they often term as creating *drama* or *pranking* or *punking*, the creation of memes or other disparaging, hurtful depictions of a victim.

Dark Triad of Personality Traits: Psychological attributes that produce a cluster of personality disorders that includes narcissism, Machiavellianism, or psychopathology (each of which manifests along a spectrum of behaviors for that trait). Psychopathy is sometimes discussed more narrowly as *sadism*. When an individual has these personality traits at the more extreme end of the spectra and the traits act together in the thought patterns and behaviors of that person, it often indicates an aggressive person with high regard for self and low regard for others which causes them to victimize other people. The Dark Triad is seen as statistically relevant in cyber-bullying and online troll behaviors.

Defamation *per Quod*: An allegation that a defamatory statement was made which falls outside the categories of obviously defamatory statements that produce defamation *per se*. In these cases, evidence that the individual suffered damage because of the statement must be presented to support and prove the charge.

Defamation *per Se*: Most states in the US have determined communication types that are so damaging to individuals' and organizations' reputations that the statements are false doesn't have to be proven. It is enough simply to prove that they have been published in order to prevail on a suit for defamation. Types of statements that can result in defamation *per se* vary by state. They include claiming someone suffers from a "loathsome" disease (which has come to include allegations of mental illness), engages in "abnormal" sexual behaviors, engages in criminal activity of various kinds, or making statements that are so extreme that the allegation itself is likely to injure one's reputation in their trade, business or profession.

Lulz: Internet slang term that evolved as the plural form of LOL (*laughing out loud*), when acronyms were used to depict a non-verbal affective dimension of communication prior to emoticon innovations. *Just for lulz*, meaning "for laughs," often in a mean-spirited vein as part of trolling behavior.

Machiavellianism: A personality characteristic that is one of the Dark Triad marked by an end-justifies-the-means attitude and a high willingness to manipulate people and situations to achieve one's ends.

Malice, Related to Defamation: Knowingly and deliberately communicating false or harmful information or doing so without investigating and with "reckless disregard" for the truth. In many venues, public figures must demonstrate malice as part of their burden of proof when bringing a defamation action.

Narcissism: A personality trait manifesting as extreme self-centeredness, desire for approving attention and praise, belief in one's "specialness," lack of empathy, a tendency to exploit others, resistance to criticism, and a sense of entitlement. One of the Dark Triad personality traits linked to cyber-bullying and trolling.

Psychopathy: Sometimes called "anti-social personality disorder" or "sociopathy," manifests as absence of remorse for bad behaviors, lack of empathy or compassion for others, often superficial charm, failure to learn from mistakes, displays disregard for the rights or feelings of others. One of the Dark Trial traits (also characterized as sadism) linked to cyber-bullying and trolling.

Streisand Effect: The phenomenon that occurs when one attempts to censor online information backfires by actually attracting more attention to the information once the attempt to remove it from view is made known. The name comes from an invasion of privacy situation that arose when Barbra Streisand's mansion was photographed by a professional who was charting the Malibu coastline; the pictures were published the photographers web-site. Prior to Streisand's lawsuit, the pictures were viewed only a few times. After the lawsuit, however, the photos received over 1,000,000 views. Relevance here is that lawsuits filed against rating sites such as Yelp or RateMyProfessor for defamatory content will often draw an extraordinary level of attention to the contested posting.

This research was previously published in Handbook of Research on Deception, Fake News, and Misinformation Online edited by Innocent E. Chiluwa and Sergei A. Samoilenko, pages 392-419, copyright year 2019 by Information Science Reference (an imprint of IGI Global).

Chapter 11
Digital Privacy Across Borders:
Canadian and American Perspectives

Lorayne P. Robertson
University of Ontario Institute of Technology, Canada

Heather Leatham
University of Ontario Institute of Technology, Canada

James Robertson
University of Ontario Institute of Technology, Canada

Bill Muirhead
University of Ontario Institute of Technology, Canada

ABSTRACT

This chapter examines digital privacy and key terminology associated with the protection of online personal information across two countries and through an education lens. The authors raise awareness of the identified risks for students as their online presence grows. The authors highlight some of the potential consequences of a lack of awareness of the risks associated with sharing information online. They outline the obligations of multiple parties (from the vendor to the end user) when students use online apps, including the teachers and parents who want to protect students' digital privacy. Employing policy analysis and a comparative approach, they examine federal, national, and local legislation, as well as curriculum responses to this issue in the USA and Canada. When the authors compare federal policy responses from these two countries, they find that they differ in instructive ways. The chapter concludes with a focus on risk abatement, including solutions and recommendations.

DOI: 10.4018/978-1-7998-1684-3.ch011

INTRODUCTION

Privacy is important to many people who want to guard their personal information closely, but the ease of access to online tools that require a user's personal information makes it increasingly difficult to be a private person in the 21st century. Most people would say that they want the right to protect their privacy, meaning that they want to have the right to control whether or not other people have access to information about their lives. Personal privacy, where people can feel certain that they are not being observed or disturbed by other people, is no longer *a given* in the digital age. Wherever there are people, there may be video surveillance recording their activities, a global positioning system (GPS) capturing their locations, and devices tracking their conversations through email and phones (Goodman, 2015). Many new device applications carry with them digital aspects that erode both solitude and privacy. Some examples include vehicles and devices that have GPS trackers, wearable technology that tracks fitness data and activities, and the Internet of Things (IoT), including home appliances, which track and exchange personal data regarding the lives we live. While people are on mobile devices constantly communicating with each other, online services are tracking user activities and may be co-mingling data for purposes of behavioural advertising (Stoddart, 2011). Most technology users know they need to offer some information in order to communicate, but they may not understand how the vendors could be compromising their privacy. In other words, there are "costs" to being connected, and one of them is privacy.

This chapter focuses specifically on the right to privacy and the protection of privacy for children and adolescents. When it comes to youth, the protection of personal information assumes a higher importance because there are greater risks to their safety and security and they cannot give informed consent because of their age (Berson & Berson, 2006). The authors review current information regarding the sharing of students' personal information online and find that both individuals and organizations may be unknowingly complicit in providing third party access to student information. Conversely, both individuals and organizations can take steps to increase student privacy. The authors identify new tools as well as the awareness needed to make informed judgments regarding how to participate safely in an interconnected, online world. This chapter also examines policy responses designed to control access to the personal information of vulnerable populations, comparing some of the American policy responses with those originating in Canada. The chapter concludes with some recommendations for risk abatement for both individuals and organizations interested in protecting students' digital privacy.

BACKGROUND

In earlier times, teachers and parents cautioned children not to share personal information with a stranger or any person they had just met (usually in person and in real time). There was an expectation that information (about children's lives and their activities) was disclosed only to those with close ties to them, such as their families or caregivers, and only in supervised settings. Names, addresses, and pictures that might identify a child, known as personally identifiable information or PII, were captured on paper files in the school office or the doctor's office and often there were no mechanisms to connect these discrete paper files from one organization to the next. Use of technology in that era was also simpler; there were expectations that children used technology only under adult supervision, for example using a telephone that was centrally located in the home. In other words, personal information about students was more protected, both through adult supervision and a lack of access.

The safeguarding of privacy was also simpler in previous times such as when privacy and security were managed by curtains in houses and locks on doors and fences. In the present era, however, it is becoming much more difficult to protect personal information because the lock it to maintain security metaphor has been challenged in multiple overt and subtle ways. The likelihood of losing control of access to anyone's PII on the internet has expanded exponentially, and this has significantly increased the level of potential risk to children and adolescents (Berson & Berson, 2006; O'Keeffe & Clarke-Pearson, 2011). In addition, the North American expectation of privacy has changed in significant ways; people have become more accustomed to others knowing about their day-to-day activities. Some of the reasons for this can be linked to new technologies, new behaviours, and consumerism.

While it is a given that people in general are sharing more about themselves online, these new online activities have implications for children's digital privacy. Steinberg (2016) points out that these new personal and social habits shape children's online identities "long before these young people open their first email" (p.839). She explains that sharenting, which is a term that describes how parents share the details about the lives of their children online, has had little attention in legal analysis, and the rights of children and parents may be at odds. Well-intentioned parents may be posting without thinking about how these postings might affect their children later in life due to the reach and longevity of the Internet (Steinberg, 2016). Studies in the US indicate that parents manage Facebook privacy settings by restricting postings of their children's images and birthdays to their friends setting, but the average number of reported friends is 150 people, which means that parents are sharing information to relatively large groups even if their Facebook privacy setting is not public (Minkus, Liu & Ross, 2015). According to Steinberg, however, while parents guard children's privacy by controlling the publication of children's images by outside organizations, parents' decisions around posting online are also a source of potential harm that has not been addressed. Children have no option to control the initiation of a digital footprint that may not be erasable (Steinberg, 2016).

Privacy is about access and control over who has access to someone else's personal information. Gülsoy (2015) describes digital privacy as "the right to privacy of users of digital media" (p.338). There is, however, much more to the definition of digital privacy when you unpack the *privacy* aspect. For example, there is *an* expectation of privacy unless a person has granted access to their information to another person or organization. Individuals want the right to decide if they will provide or withhold consent for access to this information and they may want to limit that access. For this reason, if a person or an organization is collecting information about people, they need to say how they plan to use the information (purpose) and how long they will keep the information (Stoddart, 2011). While it may have been easier to control access to information in pre-digital times, this does not tell the full story or explain the complexities associated with digital privacy in the present era. There are trade-offs, or paradoxes, apparent in the information-sharing systems of the digital era. Most of these trade-offs have to do with convenience. While it is considered good practice to take steps to control access to digital information using controls such as passwords, another common practice is for people to allow access to their personal information when they agree to the terms of use for free online applications. So there are very real contradictions between a user's expressed desire to protect their personal information and their online practices.

Other reality shifts have created new privacy imperatives. The protection of students' private information in North America is a concern because students spend more of their personal time on social media and digital apps at a time when schools and classrooms are also moving toward online applications. A recent Canadian study finds that there has been a major shift in online activity for adolescents in the past decade, and online access among those surveyed was virtually universal at 99% (Steeves, 2014). These two categories of activity blur the lines between personal and educational spaces. Recent advances in cloud-based storage, internet connectivity, and the widespread availability of new applications for educational purposes complicate solutions for the protection of students' private information. A recent news article from British Columbia, Canada highlights some of the issues that can emerge. According to Telford (2017), parents were asked to give permission for their pre-teens to use the Google Education App while in school, knowing that the information collected would include PII such as the student's name, the school name, and the grade level of the student. The parents were informed that the information would be stored in servers outside of Canada and would be subject to US law enforcement, including the USA PATRIOT Act (U.S. Congress, 2001). One parent expressed concerns about the use of online technology for students in schools and discussed how there were no alternatives for parents other than giving permission or declining to give permission for their son or daughter to participate in essential and valuable classroom activities (Telford, 2017). The reality is that adolescents in North America are online constantly, in and out of school, whether they're accessing the internet from their phones for socializing purposes or searching for information online (O'Keeffe & Clarke-Pearson, 2011; Steeves, 2014). Welcome to the complexity of online learning in education!

CONTEXT

Canadians and Americans are engaged on the Internet, and are possibly some of the most engaged globally (Canadian Internet Registration Authority (CIRA), 2017) with an internet penetration rate that varies at around 88% (internetlivestats.com). The mobile phone is the digital tool of choice for instant messaging (86%), gaming (80%), and social media (69%) which are the favoured online activities of younger Canadians (CIRA, 2017). Similarly, in the US, the number of pre-teens and teens online has experienced a dramatic increase, with one recent poll reporting that American students log into social media on average more than 10 times a day (O'Keeffe & Clarke-Pearson, 2011). This increase in time spent online has implications for digital privacy and the protection of students' PII. According to the annual report of the Privacy Commissioner to Canada's parliament, the majority of Canadians feel that they are losing control of their personal information due to their online activity (Office of the Privacy Commissioner (OPC), 2017a). Therefore, whether students' online participation occurs during school hours or outside of school hours, there are risks to their privacy (O'Keeffe & Clarke-Pearson, 2011; Leatham & Robertson, 2017) in addition to the risks posed due to the archival nature of information posted on social media and in the data storage settings of any apps being used.

The lack of policies for the protection of students' digital privacy is an example of an innovation-policy gap, which has been defined by Davis (2014), in international terms, as the point at which the speed of progress of technology creates a gap between the innovators and policymakers. He finds that there is a critical need to build collaborative spaces in order to discuss questions of data ethics and protocols. However, digital privacy is bound to the architecture of its associated technology. In that sense, a policy might be outdated as soon as a new technology emerges. Another complication is due to the disappearance of borders; people who are online can cross multiple borders, leading to jurisdictional questions, and this makes policy solutions more challenging (Davis, 2014). Another gap that has been identified in the search for solutions is the discrepancy between some parents' online technical skills and knowledge when compared to the online knowledge and skills of their children (O'Keeffe & Clarke-Pearson, 2011).

To summarize the context, the changing digital habits of North Americans, including youth, require new approaches to digital supervision (Berson & Berson, 2006; Madden et al., 2013; O'Keeffe & Clarke-Pearson, 2011; Palfrey, Gasser & Boyd, 2010; Steeves, 2014). The protection of students' PII has implications for schools and school district policies and practices (Leatham & Robertson, 2017). In Canada, the official position is that the solutions to digital privacy issues need to combine both legislation (e.g., national and provincial) as well as education for the end users (OPC, 2017a). Legislative policies and education provided by parents or delivered through the curriculum should work together in their approaches, although this intention may not always succeed. For example, creating firewalls and filters at the school district level to prevent access to new educational apps could be counterproductive if the goal is to build empowered, critical, and digitally-literate 21st century learners (and not deter the early technology innovators). Due to two factors: the advent of educational apps, and the increased student online presence out-of-school, it is likely that policy updates at many levels will be required. This includes national policies to control how vendors can use personal information; provincial and state legislation to direct school and vendor operations in different regions; and local school district policies such as acceptable use policies (for example, contracts for students who bring their own devices (BYOD) to school) that parents and students need to sign to indicate awareness of school rules. In addition, students, teachers, and parents will need to become more aware of the responsibilities, affordances, and risks associated with digital participation. They will need both the tools and the awareness to make informed judgements about participation in an interconnected, online world.

Digital Privacy

Canada's former privacy commissioner, Jennifer Stoddart, has been credited with saying that, "Privacy begins with the individual" (Berkow, 2011). Little has been written, however, about how individuals learn that they have a *right to privacy* and the steps they can take to protect it. Research is not definitive regarding who has the major responsibility for teaching internet safety and supervising online participation for children at vulnerable ages. MediaSmarts, a Canadian non-profit organization dedicated to media literacy education, surveyed more than 5,000 Canadian students in grades 4 through 11, finding that many of the students (41%) report that they learn about privacy settings from their parents, while a smaller percentage (15%) report that they learn about privacy settings from their teachers. In the MediaSmarts report, students state that their teachers are more likely to help them search for information online and deal with cyberbullying than teach them about digital privacy (Steeves, 2014). This is reflected in the results of a recent study from Ontario, Canada finding that teachers lack general knowledge about policies on the protection of student privacy (Leatham, 2017). In the US context, one American Academy of Pediatrics report on the impact of social media prescribes the roles of doctors, parents, and youth in the protection of PII but not the schools (O'Keeffe & Clarke-Pearson, 2011). These findings highlight the importance of educating everyone, not only the end users (the students), but also educating parents, caregivers, and teachers about the protection of student information and privacy, until students can make independent and informed decisions about their own privacy protection.

This issue of "who is responsible" for supervising access to data used to be simpler. When PII was filed in different physical locations that were not connected to each other, the rules governing its collection and how long the information could be retained were addressed at the level of the organizations that collected the data. There are several changes which transpired with the advent of the internet: a) data are interconnected, searchable, and more easily accessible; b) with the more interactive nature of the web beginning with Web 2.0, children and adolescents are actively (and possibly unknowingly) contributing to the collections of online information; and c) the students' level of awareness of digital privacy and risks is currently unknown. If the premise is that people have a right to privacy unless they have waived that right, then until students are old enough to give informed consent, their rights should be protected. Solutions to this issue, however, are not that easily determined.

Due to their constant online presence, young people are unknowingly increasing their own risks. O'Keeffe and Clarke-Pearson (2011) report that adolescents essentially pose risks to themselves and to each other when they overshare information online or post incorrect information about themselves and others. Given that they lack awareness of privacy issues, they will post inappropriate material online about themselves and each other without understanding that what they have posted cannot be taken down. This has implications for their future job prospects, and future academic careers. Their lack of awareness may also make them a target for fraud, identity theft, or other serious criminal offences (O'Keeffe & Clarke-Pearson, 2011).

This leads to the question of 'consent'. Most users have seen at least one terms of use agreement - the kind that you click through in order to get to an online app. This issue of consent needs to be addressed presently for adults and youth alike because of the lack of transparency and the level of complication in these vendor consent agreements (OPC, 2017a). There are other factors complicating the matter: the seeming anonymity of the internet somehow encourages the public documentation of many aspects of children's lives by their parents and caregivers on sites such as Facebook and creates a "desensitization to the loss of control over their personal information" (Berson & Berson, 2006, p.137). A present reality is that future employers will be able to scan through decades of an applicant's life by researching them online. The information found is generally based on what the applicant's parents have contributed while documenting many personal aspects of their lives online, followed by the applicant's own postings throughout their life. This open sharing needs to be balanced by a consideration that, where information is so readily available, it can be used for ulterior motives and commercial purposes (Goodman, 2015).

According to Stoddart (2011), approximately half of Canadians are aware that their online activities are being tracked. Once Canadians are made aware of these practices, they find them to be intrusive (Stoddart, 2011). But, not every user is aware of the tracking of their information. Larger forces are at play to capture big data in surreptitious ways. The subsequent sale of their browsing histories to third parties is a practice known as *behaviour tracking*. According to Goodman, online apps that appear to be free are making a profit from selling the information that they collect (2015). Many people do not realize that the collection of personal information and the sale of that information to third parties - when users are unaware of this tracking - is a large criminal industry that affects one in five US and EU citizens through identity theft and the stealing of billions of dollars through medical and tax fraud (Goodman, 2015). Illegally collected personal information is a valuable asset to criminals committing fraud. A recent Equifax digital breach of security has identified the vulnerability of everyone's digital footprint (Federal Trade Commission, 2017). The breach made available the personal information of millions of people globally. Scott (2013) finds that *online behavioural advertising* is a concern across borders, leaving the question open regarding which country will write the rules in an era when personal data crosses the globe in seconds. According to the Electronic Privacy Information Center (EPIC) in the US, companies who profile or track individuals to target them through advertising, using a practice called *list brokerage*, have developed criteria to cross-reference information to classify individuals into fifteen main categories (such as families who live in the country, working town people, etc.) and then subcategories. The list brokers link to individual identities through data such as date of birth, health information, telephone number, utilities usage, and memberships. They aggregate information also from online and offline purchases, loyalty cards, financial and property records, phone records, credit records, magazine subscriptions, and public records. This profiling of customers is called *personalization*. EPIC reports that these lists or profiles are quite affordable to advertisers with some companies charging sixty-five dollars for a thousand names (EPIC, n.d.).

Indications are that young people do care about privacy and want to protect their information as reported by Steeves (2014) in Canada at MediaSmarts, and Palfrey et al. (2010) at Harvard Law School. Also in the US, Berson and Berson (2006) report that young people do not realize that their online contributions collectively create a digital dossier about themselves that consists of their preferences and their information. Added to that, children and adolescents often serve unwittingly as information brokers to provide data about their friends. Even adults do not realize that these digital dossiers are public domain documents that can be provided or sold to third parties without necessarily alerting the end users (Berson & Berson, 2006).

Another important consideration is that data disclosed online are "often persistent, searchable, and hard to delete" a concept which has been called digital permanence (Palfrey et al. 2010, p. 11). When teens and pre-teens are learning self-regulation and decision-making, they are susceptible to peer pressure and advertising. As online users, they create a digital footprint on each site they visit, which is an online record of web activity including their personal information and preferences. This digital footprint can put children and adolescents at risk because it connects elements of the information that identify them or their PII. Youth users also need to understand that, even though they're managing their privacy settings on Facebook, they have no control over how their friends manage their privacy settings; the implications of this can affect their life chances when something is shared inadvertently or without their permission (Marwick & Boyd, 2014).

The extent to which North American youth are aware of the strategies used to gain information from them online and also their level of awareness that their online digital wanderings are being tracked and sold is not known. According to a Pew Internet survey (Madden et al., 2013) American teens are increasingly more likely to share information online and they are increasingly sharing information that identifies themselves. The median teen user of Facebook has 300 friends and 79 followers on Twitter. The Facebook profiles most often have private settings (60%) or partially private (friends of friends), while most teens have public Twitter accounts. Almost all (91%) post photos of themselves and 92% post their real name to the profile that they use the most often. Most of them (82%) post their birth date, and 71% post their school name and the city or town where they live. Some teens even enable the inclusion of their location information as they are posting (Madden et al., 2013). What is surprising and perhaps concerning is that, in Canadian studies, almost one in three students in Grades 4-6 (10-12 years old) have a Facebook account, despite the age 13 requirement set by Facebook for participation (Steeves, 2014).

Early research findings indicate that educational interventions can help. A recent study in Singapore finds that students are generally unaware of their privacy risks, but those who are aware disclose less PII on Facebook (Liu, Ang & Lwin, 2013). However in North America, there is a dearth of information on student awareness of issues of digital privacy, and a lack of research on targeted interventions to empower students to protect their PII. Based on the recent calls to protect digital privacy and students' PII, significant and compelling research questions emerge, including: What legislation exists in the US and Canada to guide the protection of privacy in general and specifically, the privacy of students as they venture out into digital territory? What policies, guidelines, and best practices exist in either country to guide the work of schools, parents, and teachers? What are the essential online safety skills that students and teachers need to acquire before they take a digital leap into places unknown, and how can they acquire these digital safety skills? What, if anything, can be learned by comparing the Canadian and American approaches to digital privacy? These are some of the topics addressed in the next section.

Risk Abatement Legislation

In this section, the authors compare the different legislative and policy approaches that have been taken in the US and in Canada with respect to the protection of students' digital privacy. Policy analysis is an important research tool because it helps to frame studies about policy in instructive ways and allows for the identification of gaps. Fowler (2004) states that policy analysis (including monitoring and evaluation) is essential to the improvement of public education-related policy. Additionally, Ball (1994) argues that it is essential to consider not only the official texts of policies but also to examine the discourse of those who are creating and influencing policy. The authors examine some American and Canadian policy texts, which do not necessarily represent a definitive list, but an illustrative list, in order to compare the approaches taken in both countries.

The US has laws that relate to the sharing of student PII in education. The *Children's Online Privacy Protection Act, 1998* (COPPA) (Federal Trade Commission (FTC), 1998) designates the age of 13 as the minimum age to have an online profile (O'Keeffe & Clarke-Pearson, 2011). While COPPA initially was seen to deter predatory online practices targeting young internet users, more recent research indicates that many underage users report that they are using social media sites. This has stirred debate regarding the efficacy of the age restriction policies (Boyd, Hargittai, Schultz & Palfrey, 2011). To the best of the authors' knowledge, there is no parallel national Canadian legislation designed specifically to protect children and adolescents with respect to online privacy using age restrictions.

Another US example is the *Children's Internet Protection Act* (CIPA) (2000) which was created to prevent children from seeing harmful or obscene content over the internet. As of July 2012, American schools who receive CIPA funding are required to educate minors about what is appropriate online behaviour and responses to cyberbullying, which includes information about interactions in social networking sites and in chat rooms (California Department of Education, 2017). The Department of Education (US) Office of Educational Technology, from which CIPA is administered, provides information on how to protect student privacy by offering both requirements and best practices (Privacy Technical Assistance Center (PTAC), 2014).

A third US example is the *Family Educational Rights and Privacy Act* (FERPA, 1974) which falls under the US Department of Education's control and addresses students' educational records. It was written pre-internet and includes the protection of parents' information as well as students' information. FERPA regulates the disclosure of student information for the purposes of large scale testing to improve instruction. The metadata from these tests can be used if the PII is stripped (PTAC, 2014). Also, on the US Department of Education website, information about the protection of student privacy is provided for specific users such as parents or educators on a site entitled, *Protecting Student Privacy* (US Department of Education, 2016). Added to the legislation regarding students' PII, California was one of the first state legislatures to address the issue of list brokerage. It passed a bill that allows persons in California to ask businesses where they have sold their personal information for direct marketing purposes (EPIC, n.d.).

In Canada, policies have been directed more broadly at, for example, industries and municipalities. The primary legislation protecting individuals' privacy rights online is not a single policy, but different pieces of umbrella legislation. The *Personal Information Protection and Electronic Documents Act* (PIPEDA) (2016) establishes privacy law for private-sector organizations in Canada. Significantly, PIPEDA promotes eight key principles for fair information practices in Canada. According to the Centre for International Governance Innovation (CIGI, 2013), these are:

- **Notice:** Users should be informed when information is collected, for what purpose, how long it will be used, and how it will be shared.
- **Choice:** Users should have a choice about whether or not they share their information.
- **Access:** Users should be able to check and confirm their information on request.
- **Security:** The users' information should be protected from unauthorized access.
- **Scope:** Only the required information can be collected.
- **Purpose:** The purpose for collecting the information should be disclosed.
- **Limitations:** There should be a time limit on how long the information will be held.
- **Accountability:** Organizations should ensure that their privacy policies are followed.

Education in Canada is under the purview of the individual provinces and territories as is the protection of privacy information. In Ontario, the *Freedom of Information and Protection of Privacy Act* (FIPPA) has been in effect since 1988 and was revised to include hospitals in 2012, but it does not govern schools. Schools fall under the *Municipal Freedom of Information and Protection of Privacy Act* (MFIPPA) (1991) which applies to every municipality in Ontario, including district school boards. It provides the right of access to records and to a person's own information. It also requires municipalities to protect personal information by specifying how information may be collected, used, retained, and disposed. MFIPPA has not been updated in the digital realm.

The Canadian Privacy Commissioner has repeatedly stated that Canadian privacy laws are falling behind and need to catch up to U.S. and EU legislation (Stoddart, 2011). In a national report (OPC, 2017a), the privacy commissioner finds that, without improving how privacy is protected online, Canadians could have insufficient trust to enable the digital economy to grow. This could compromise the ability of Canadians to benefit from innovations. The solutions, in the view of the OPC, fall into two categories: 1) an increase in the accountability of organizations through *policy compliance*, and 2) a focus on educating the end users of technology. Some of these recommendations include:

- That organizations should be held accountable for more transparency in their privacy practices through legislation;
- That there should be a shift in focus toward educating the individual user;
- That guidelines on how to de-identify personal information in order to become more privacy-protective should be provided to end users;
- That children should be taught about privacy at a young age; and
- That privacy should be incorporated into the school curriculum (OPC, 2017a).

This national report on privacy raises attention about the need to consider multiple types of risk abatement for children, adolescents, and teachers who pursue online learning (OPC, 2017a). One of the means of risk abatement is through curriculum or curriculum policies. Another key means of addressing privacy issues is through broad educational approaches such as digital citizenship. These approaches are reviewed, in general terms, in the next section.

EDUCATION AND EMPOWERMENT

Canadian Curriculum Approaches

In Canada, there have been calls recently for more targeted digital citizenship approaches. One submission to Digital Canada 150 calls for privacy education to be introduced into the secondary school curriculum in all provinces (Warfield, 2010) but this may be too late to address digital privacy in light of data showing that students are online and creating digital footprints at much earlier grades. While it might be assumed that digital citizenship and the protection of PII is a significant issue for all schools to address, a review of the approaches to digital citizenship across Canada reveals a broken curriculum policy context of approaches.

According to Hoechsmann and DeWaard (2015), approaches to teaching digital citizenship in Canada vary. The BC curriculum has a framework for digital literacy that is used also by the Yukon. Alberta has a framework for student learning which includes the ethically-responsible use of technology. Saskatchewan uses the term digital fluency, not citizenship. Manitoba has a model for Information and Communications Technology (ICT) across the curriculum that includes ethical and responsible use. Quebec students are supposed to use ICT with critical judgement. The Maritime Provinces discuss technological literacy. The Northwest Territories and Nunavut promote the ethical use of ICT with a technology in education framework that does not mention digital citizenship (Hoechsmann & DeWaard, 2015).

Outside of the curriculum, in 2012, the Alberta government published a *Digital Citizenship Policy Development Guide* for schools and administrators to help them understand digital citizenship and facilitate the development of local, school authority-based policies (Government of Alberta, 2012). In 2017, the Alberta Privacy Commissioner, in conjunction with the Alberta Teachers' Association, hosted two seminars that included the topic of digital privacy in the classroom. Elsewhere, in New Brunswick, they started piloting a grade 11 program with CyberNB and Blue Spurs where students use a kit from Blue Spurs which contains eight lessons (including the Internet of Things (IoT) and cyber security) (Burgos, 2017).

The largest Canadian province, Ontario, has a scattered approach across curriculum policies where one curriculum mentions cyberbullying and another defines digital privacy but overall the curriculum policies are silent on digital citizenship. Instead, what is promoted within Ontario are digital citizenship modules on the Ontario Software Acquisition Program Advisory Committee (OSAPAC, 2015) website for both elementary and secondary schools. Its *School Leader Learning Series* helps school administrators engage in discussions about the role of digital learning in the classroom. The Ontario Privacy Commissioner (2011) has published three specific guides for education: for Grades 5, 10, and 11/12 entitled *What Students need to Know* on the topic of privacy and the internet (OPC, 2011).

The federal Office of the Privacy Commissioner for Canada provides web links that can be used by teachers of specific grades (without ties to any specific curriculum), which their office promotes as resources for privacy education. These link to the individual provincial privacy commissioners' sites, which may or may not be education-specific. The most well-known national digital citizenship resource is from MediaSmarts, which has guides for teachers, parents, and school resource officers to help students navigate the online world safely. Their digital literacy framework is called *Use, Understand and Create* (MediaSmarts, 2016). In 2017, the Canadian Civil Liberties Association (CCLA) created a privacy booklet, called the *Peer Privacy Protectors Guidebook*, in conjunction with a national student advisory panel, which made the topic of privacy understandable to teenagers. For example, they reworded the Instagram privacy policy to make it comprehensible (CCLA, 2017).

American Curriculum Approaches

The American approach to digital citizenship in curriculum is equally multi-faceted. Gardner (2013) is not alone in calling for a national curriculum on digital citizenship. A recent survey of 500 educational professionals across multiple jurisdictions in the US estimated that approximately half of the teachers and administrators in their districts were aware of, and teaching about digital citizenship, but that some teachers have yet to accept technology which is holding back the development of digital citizenship curriculum (Hollandsworth, Dowdy & Donovan, 2011). Because many schools have not fully embraced technology, approaches range from no supervision of students' online participation, to very strict firewalls and not allowing students to use their mobile devices in school. Instead, the approach needs to be a combination of policy supports and strategies to engage communities in supporting students and empowering students to make good choices about digital citizenship. Hollandsworth et al., advocate that everyone needs to be on board to bring digital citizenship standards into the US curriculum policies. They recommend more teacher awareness of online affordances and risks, and a concerted effort to provide a coherent digital citizenship curriculum, starting in the early years. They raise the concern that, without a national set of standards for digital citizenship, private providers of curriculum may attempt to meet the gap in curriculum policies (Hollandsworth et al., 2011).

Also within the US, companies such as Common Sense Education have created their own digital citizenship curriculum. This stand-alone curriculum is mapped to the American English Language Arts Common Core Standards, American Association of School Librarians (AASL), and the International Society for Technology in Education (ISTE) standards (Common Sense Education, 2017). In 2017, Google joined the digital citizenship advocacy in creating a game-based learning platform called *Be Internet Awesome* to complement their teacher curriculum. Educators complete a five-unit interactive program in order to be able to download a Digital Citizenship and Safety curriculum to use in classrooms (Hadid, 2017).

According to Davis and James (2013), multiple educational curricula were developed in the US to promote responsible, safe, and ethical online behaviours. Examples include commercial products such as the i-SAFE's Internet Safety and public programs such as Web Wise Kids (http://www.webwisekids.org/). They also report that, in some jurisdictions, the use of these types of curriculum supports are mandated as components of educational programs. In order to qualify for educational technology funds from the federal government, schools must take steps to educate children about appropriate online behaviour (Davis & James, 2013). According to Willard (2012) the *Protecting Children in the 21st Century Act* added a provision to CIPA that schools should educate minors about how to interact with others on social media. The concern with some of the commercially-available programs, however, was that they might promote fear without providing age-appropriate information (Willard, 2012).

California, a state which appears at the forefront of digital citizenship and student online protection, participated in a Digital Citizenship Week per the recommendation of the California Education Technology Blueprint (2014-2017) entitled: *Empowering Learning* (California Department of Education, 2017). The second recommendation states that the Department of Education needs to "ensure student safety by outlining policies and best practices to prevent cyberbullying and protect student data" (p.12). They promote the use of the aforementioned curriculum as a means of satisfying CIPA as well as the Blueprint recommendations.

In general, the American approach appears to be multi-pronged on many fronts. This is supported by Hollandsworth et al. (2011) who argue that digital citizenship will need to be taught through multiple means and through multiple years of schooling in order to tackle the challenges and reap the rewards of online learning.

SUMMARY AND RECOMMENDATIONS

While a review of approaches across every state and province is outside the purview of this chapter, there are some conclusions that can be drawn from this broad policy analysis. In both Canada and the US, there is overarching legislation aimed at protecting students' digital privacy. The legislation in the US is more targeted and has recently been updated to reflect the protection of youth's digital privacy. In Canada, the federal legislation that regulates industries (PIPEDA) has recently been updated but there is no similar national initiative for schools. Additionally, the federal privacy commissioner provides support for educating children and adolescents with respect to good privacy practices (OPC, 2017b). With respect to curriculum development, while individual state or provincial educational departments do make mention of digital citizenship, there appears to be a lack of a cohesive, coherent, and common national strategy for teaching students about the benefits and consequences of online participation. The reason for this may be the recent emergence of international guidelines for educators and students. These guidelines focus on overarching principles, and the guidelines themselves are designed to cross borders.

Personal Data Protection: Some Guidelines for Schools

In 2016, an international conference for the Privacy and Data Protection Commissioners created a set of guidelines for students in schools, the *Personal Data Protection Competency Framework for School Students*. They did not present this as a policy but as a competency framework intended to help educators teach about digital privacy (International Working Group on Digital Education (IWG), 2016). They created this framework with the understanding that the focus is to teach students to be "responsible, ethical and civic minded" in the digital age (IWG, p.3). The framework is legislation agnostic in the sense that it is designed to work with the laws for data protection in each country. The framework has nine guiding principles and each is described with its own list of knowledge and skills. The goal is to create a common base of knowledge and skills on digital privacy in education and disseminate this information in order to protect personal privacy and personal information in education.

The first principle is personal data. Students should understand that personal data is any data that identifies an individual. Students should learn how to discern which information is particularly sensitive, something which can vary from country to country. They also need to know how their online presence can be traced back using technical data and metadata. The second principle is the understanding that privacy is a human right that should be protected, and how their actions can affect their own privacy and the privacy of others. The third principle is an understanding of the digital environment's technical aspects and how digital space is structured. This includes an understanding of the risks associated with the digital space and what is meant by digital security. Students should also learn how to ensure the security of their digital environment. The fourth principle is to learn about the key players in the digital environment, and how systems are used for commercial purposes to offer free services to establish personal user profiles. Student users need to know what data are collected and stored while online. The fifth principle is the understanding that there are some key rules which are important for data protection, such as people's rights to be informed about who is collecting their personal information, for what purpose, and how long data will be stored. End users also need to know how to work with data protection authorities (IWG, 2016).

The sixth principle is one that deals with many of the issues that have been raised in this chapter. Under this principle, students should be taught that it is necessary to control the use of personal information. Students should learn how to investigate the nature of the space where they are sharing information and monitor the content and information about them that exists online. Also, students should be taught to participate online in ways that respect other people, including not sharing others' information without their consent. The seventh principle is about encouraging students to seek the consent of parents to access online services and to monitor the information about them located online. The eighth principle focuses on students' rights to use technology to protect and secure their data. Examples include managing their settings and refusing geolocation, for example. The final (ninth) principle is one of digital citizenship which includes learning to assess the reliability and credibility of information, and identifying inappropriate or illegal content (IWG, 2016).

This international framework addresses both issues of education and empowerment for youth. It takes into consideration research that youth do care about their privacy (e.g., Palfrey et al., 2010) and that they need to work together with concerned adults such as their parents and teachers to build their skills in a digital era. In a similar vein, privacy regulators have also established a Global Privacy Enforcement Network (GPEN) comprised of 60 privacy regulators in 39 jurisdictions. They, too, have identified that participation in school on certain types of software, digital learning resources and teaching platforms that are internet-based may be putting students at risk. They caution that educators should minimize the identifiability of students who are participating online, be aware of the terms of service, and seek parental permission (GPEN, 2017).

Cyber Hygiene: Some General Guidelines for Parents

The problems with accidentally or intentionally sharing PII, media, and information online have been reviewed earlier in this chapter. Because PII can be shared accidentally or intentionally, there are some key messages and strategies that should be communicated to the students, parents, and the teachers to help protect students' PII and help them to be safer online.

Parents are key. They have the most opportunity to protect, influence, and educate children. They are also role models, so it is important for them to model the same type of online behaviour and decision-making they want from their children. Parents need to be aware of their own digital footprints, including the level to which their digital footprints can affect their children's digital footprints. Parents can help by being more aware of how much of their child's information they are sharing on their own social media accounts and by setting boundaries to minimize risks for their children (Steinberg, 2016). To do this, they need to configure their privacy settings to ensure that strangers cannot see their children's pictures. They need to advise their friends and family not to repost any images on their own (and possibly less secure) social media profiles. Parents should avoid posting or tagging images using their child's name, birthday, and year of birth, or any other elements of PII.

Parents can discern the level to which their online presence or that of their children is publicly available if they search for themselves or their children from a computer outside the home, or ask a friend or family member to investigate their online presence.

There are paid services that will do this as well; many of those services will also offer to assist with deleting online data and PII. Software filtering is another option that allows parents to filter software by inclusion, by exclusion, or by content analysis. Websites can be filtered as well for which lists are allowed and which are restricted. These technical controls can be implemented but should not be used in isolation. Education, dialogue, and awareness, combined with these technical tools, are more likely to be effective (Palfrey et al., 2010). It is important for parents to tell children that the controls are for their safety and not because they are not trusted.

More parent education and dialogue should occur around family, child, and parent social media accounts and by helping to increase parental understandings surrounding the age restrictions designed to protect children. There is still debate over the appropriate age to possess social media accounts and share online. Given the role that parents have as child protectors, much more discussion and awareness needs to happen so that parents manage online access for these vulnerable populations. The answer is not always to restrict access, however, as there are other possibilities.

One alternative to restriction is activism. The Government of Canada encourages parents to talk with their children about the risks of being online, sharing PII, and being critical of the information found online (Government of Canada, 2017). Perhaps even more importantly, children and adolescents need to be aware about privacy and the Internet. Parents should discuss the importance and function of privacy settings, location services, password sharing, online predators, online scams, liking, and friending. It is important for parents to talk with young people about being critical consumers of their media. In general, education is better than blocking access, so that children are able to understand the issues, risk, and the importance of protecting their privacy. Parents can support this process by keeping the dialogue open with their children and encouraging them to ask questions and report content they have seen that might be offensive or hurtful.

One of the dialogues that can be opened between parents and children is to encourage them to come to adults with questions or for permission to download an app. When children show parents an app that they would like to use, parents and children can then read the privacy agreement together. This will help everyone understand how the app will be using their personal information or sharing it with outside parties. It is important for parents to check for statements in the privacy policy that discuss sharing data with outside parties when they close the account or delete the app. Parents (or any end users) should look for any information about whether or not their data can be sold and whether the new owner of the information has to comply with the privacy agreement. Also, parents should be aware that there are privacy settings for both the app and for the mobile device itself. Most smartphones allow the user to modify the privileges of the apps on their phone. End users need to confirm and check these privacy and app privilege settings regularly.

FINAL THOUGHTS

The intent of this chapter was not to provide a definitive or exhaustive list of the issues of digital privacy or the ways that digital privacy for students can be protected. The intent of the chapter was to raise awareness of the issues of digital privacy and review some of the helpful policies and practices that can help to protect students' privacy. The review of policies from different jurisdictions reveals a multiplicity of approaches to inform new policy development. More awareness surrounding how children and adolescents may be at risk and how the adults in their lives can become better informed about practices to protect them when they are online is needed. An example of one of these protective practices includes careful attention to the terms of use agreements associated with online applications. In general, there are multiple ways to minimize the identifiability of students and the collection of their PII in online applications in schools, such as the creation of pseudonyms through teacher-managed lists. Parents need to be able to provide informed consent that includes an awareness of the risks and rewards associated with online participation in learning. What has emerged from many sources is the need to provide timely advice to students based on their internet usage, to empower them to take control of access to their information, and to teach them how to protect their own information and the information of others.

REFERENCES

Ball, S. (1994). What is Policy? Text, trajectories and toolboxes. In S. Ball (Ed.), *Education Reform* (pp. 14–27). Buckingham, UK: Open University Press.

Berkow, J. (2011). Canadians careless with private data, privacy watchdog warns. *Financial Post*. Retrieved from http://business.financialpost.com/technology/canadians-not-cautious-enough-with-digital-communications-privacy-commissioner-says

Berson, I. R., & Berson, M. J. (2006). Children and their digital dossiers: Lessons in privacy rights in the digital age. *The International Journal of Social Education*, *21*(1), 135–147.

Boyd, d., Hargittai, E., Schultz, J., & Palfrey, J. (2011). Why parents help their children lie to Facebook about age: Unintended consequences of the 'Children's Online Privacy Protection Act'. *First Monday, 16*(11). Retrieved from http://journals.uic.edu/ojs/index.php/fm/article/view/3850/3075

Burgos, M. (2017). 'Cutting-edge technology' to be implemented in school curriculums. *Canadian Broadcasting Corporation*. Retrieved from http://www.cbc.ca/news/canada/new-brunswick/cybersecurity-blue-kit-1.4201962

California Department of Education, Educational Technology Initiative. (2014). *Empowering learning. A blueprint for California Education technology 2014–2017.* Retrieved from https://www.cde.ca.gov/eo/in/documents/yr14bp0418.pdf

California Department of Education. (2017). *Digital citizenship week.* Retrieved from https://www.cde.ca.gov/ls/et/dc/dcwk2017.asp

Canadian Civil Liberties Association (CCLA). (2017). *Peer privacy protectors guidebook.* Retrieved from https://ccla.org/peer-privacy-protectors-guidebook/

Canadian Internet Registration Authority (CIRA). (2017). Retrieved from https://cira.ca/factbook/domain-industry-data-and-canadian-Internet-trends/internet-use-canada

Centre for International Governance (CIGI). (2013). *Big data, big responsibilities: Recommendations to the Office of the Privacy Commissioner on Canadian privacy rights in a digital age.* Retrieved from https://www.cigionline.org/publications/big-data-big-responsibilities-recommendations-office-privacy-commissioner-canadian

Common Sense Education. (2017). *Digital citizenship.* Retrieved from https://www.commonsense.org/education/digital-citizenship

Davis, K. (2014). Bridging the innovation-policy gap. *SAIS Review (Paul H. Nitze School of Advanced International Studies), 34*(1), 87–92.

Davis, K., & James, C. (2013). Tweens' conceptions of privacy online: Implications for educators. *Learning, Media and Technology, 38*(1), 4–25. doi:10.1080/17439 884.2012.658404

Electronic Profiling Information Center (EPIC). (n.d.). Retrieved from https://epic.org/privacy/profiling/

Federal Communications Commission. (2000). *Children's Internet Protection Act.* Retrieved from https://www.fcc.gov/consumers/guides/childrens-internet-protection-act

Federal Trade Commission. (1998). *Children's Online Privacy Protection Rule (COPPA).* Retrieved from https://www.ftc.gov/enforcement/rules/rulemaking-regulatory-reform-proceedings/childrens-online-privacy-protection-rule

Federal Trade Commission. (2015). *Complying with COPPA: Frequently asked questions*. Retrieved from https://www.ftc.gov/tips-advice/business-center/guidance/complying-coppa-frequently-asked-questions

Federal Trade Commission. (2017). *The Equifax data breach: What to do*. Retrieved from https://www.consumer.ftc.gov/blog/2017/09/equifax-data-breach-what-do

FERPA. (1974). *Family Educational Rights and Privacy Act of 1974, Pub. L. 93-380, title V,Sec 513, Aug. 21, 1974,88 Stat. 571*. Retrieved from https://www2.ed.gov/policy/gen/guid/fpco/ferpa/index.html

Fowler, F. (2004). *Policy Studies for Educational Leaders: An Introduction*. Pearson.

Freedom of Information and Protection of Privacy Act (FIPPA). (1990). Retrieved from https://www.ontario.ca/laws/statute/90f31

Gardner, J. (2013). *Why America's kids need a national Digital Citizenship curriculum*. Venture Beat. Retrieved from https://venturebeat.com/2013/12/08/why-americas-kids-need-a-national-digital-citizenship-curriculum/

Global Privacy Enforcement Network (GPEN). (2017). *GPEN Sweep 2017: User controls over personal information*. Retrieved from https://www.privacyenforcement.net/sites/default/files/2017%20GPEN%20Sweep%20-%20International%20Report.pdf

Goodman, M. (2015). *Future crimes: Everything is connected, everyone is vulnerable and what we can do about it*. Anchor.

Government of Alberta. (2012). *Digital Citizenship Policy Development Guide*. Retrieved from https://open.alberta.ca/publications/9781460103517

Government of Canada. (2017). *Children online: Keeping your child safe online*. Retrieved from https://www.getcybersafe.gc.ca/cnt/prtct-yrslf/prtctn-fml/chld-sf-en.aspx

Gülsoy, T. Y. (2015). Advertising ethics in the social media age. In *Handbook of Research on Effective Advertising Strategies in the Social Media Age* (pp. 321–338). Hershey, PA: IGI Global. doi:10.4018/978-1-4666-8125-5.ch018

Hadid, G. (2017). Bringing digital citizenship into the school curriculum [Blog]. Retrieved from https://www.blog.google/topics/education/bringing-digital-citizenship-school-curriculum/

Hoechsmann, M., & DeWaard, H. (2015). *Mapping digital literacy policy and practice in the Canadian education landscape: MediaSmarts.* Retrieved from http://mediasmarts.ca/teacher-resources/digital-literacy-framework/mapping-digital-literacy-policy-practice-canadian-education-landscape

Hollandsworth, R., Dowdy, L., & Donovan, J. (2011). Digital citizenship in K-12: It takes a village. *TechTrends, 55*(4), 37–47. doi:10.100711528-011-0510-z

International Working Group on Digital Education (IWG). (2016). *Personal data protection competency framework for school students.* International Conference of Privacy and Data Protection Commissioners. Retrieved from https://icdppc.org/wp-content/uploads/2015/02/International-Competency-Framework-for-school-students-on-data-protection-and-privacy.pdf

Internetlivestats.com. (n.d.). Retrieved from http://www.internetlivestats.com/internet-users/canada/

Leatham, H. (2017). *Digital privacy in the classroom: An analysis of the intent and realization of Ontario policy in context* (Master's thesis). Retrieved from https://ir.library.dc-uoit.ca/xmlui/handle/10155/816

Leatham, H., & Robertson, L. (2017). Student digital privacy in classrooms: Teachers in the cross-currents of technology imperatives. *International Journal for Digital Society, 8*(3). Retrieved from http://infonomics-society.org/ijds/

Liu, C., Ang, R. P., & Lwin, M. O. (2013). Cognitive, personality, and social factors associated with adolescents' online personal information disclosure. *Journal of Adolescence, 36*(4), 629–638. doi:10.1016/j.adolescence.2013.03.016 PMID:23849657

Madden, M., Lenhart, A., Cortesi, S., Gasser, U., Duggan, M., Smith, A., & Beaton, M. (2013). Teens, social media, and privacy. *Pew Research Center, 21,* 2-86. Retrieved from http://www.pewinternet.org/2013/05/21/teens-social-media-and-privacy/

Marwick, A. E., & Boyd, D. (2014). Networked privacy: How teenagers negotiate context in social media. *New Media & Society, 16*(7), 1051–1067. doi:10.1177/1461444814543995

MediaSmarts. (2016). *Use, Understand & create: A digital literacy framework for Canadian schools.* Retrieved from http://mediasmarts.ca/sites/mediasmarts/files/pdfs/digital-literacy-framework.pdf

Minkus, T., Liu, K., & Ross, K. W. (May, 2015). Children seen but not heard: When parents compromise children's online privacy. In *Proceedings of the 24th International Conference on World Wide Web* (pp. 776-786). International World Wide Web Conferences Steering Committee. 10.1145/2736277.2741124

Municipal Freedom of Information and Protection of Privacy Act (MFIPPA). (1991). Retrieved from https://www.ontario.ca/laws/statute/90m56

O'Keeffe, G. S., & Clarke-Pearson, K. (2011). The impact of social media on children, adolescents, and families. *Pediatrics, 127*(4), 800–804. doi:10.1542/peds.2011-0054 PMID:21444588

Office of the Privacy Commissioner of Canada. (2017b). *External educational resources and information*. Retrieved from https://www.priv.gc.ca/en/about-the-opc/what-we-do/awareness-campaigns-and-events/privacy-education-for-kids/fs-fi/yth_res/

Office of the Privacy Commissioner of Canada (OPC). (2017a). *Real fears, real solutions: A plan for restoring confidence in Canada's privacy regime. 2016-17 Annual Report to Parliament on the Personal Information Protection and Electronic Documents Act and the Privacy Act*. Retrieved from https://www.priv.gc.ca/media/4586/opc-ar-2016-2017_eng-final.pdf

Ontario Privacy Commissioner (OPC). (2011). *What students need to know*. Retrieved from https://www.ipc.on.ca/wp-content/uploads/Resources/up-flyer_w.pdf

Ontario Software Acquisition Program Advisory Committee. (2015). *Digital citizenship*. Retrieved from https://www.osapac.ca/dc/

Ontario Software Acquisition Program Advisory Committee (OSAPAC). (2017). *School leader learning series*. Retrieved from https://www.osapac.ca/school-leader-learning-series/

Palfrey, J. G., Gasser, U., & boyd, d. (2010). *Response to FCC notice of inquiry 09-94: Empowering parents and protecting children in an evolving media landscape*. Retrieved from https://papers.ssrn.com/sol3/papers.cfm?abstract_id=1559208

Personal Information Protection and Electronic Documents Act (PIPEDA). (2016). Retrieved from https://www.priv.gc.ca/en/privacy-topics/privacy-laws-in-canada/the-personal-information-protection-and-electronic-documents-act-pipeda/

Scott, E. M. (2013). Protecting consumer data while allowing the web to develop self-sustaining architecture: Is a trans-Atlantic browser-based opt-in for behavioral tracking the right solution. *Pac. McGeorge Global Bus. & Dev. LJ, 26*, 285.

Steeves, V. (2014). *Young Canadians in a wired world. Phase III: Life online*. Ottawa, Canada: MediaSmarts. Retrieved from http://mediasmarts.ca/sites/mediasmarts/files/pdfs/publication-report/full/YCWWIII_Life_Online_FullReport.pdf

Steinberg, S. B. (2016). Sharenting: Children's Privacy in the Age of Social Media. *Emory Law Journal, 66,* 839.

Stoddart, J. (2011). Privacy in the era of social networking: Legal obligations of social media sites. *Saskatchewan Law Review, 74,* 263.

Telford, H. (2017). Parents ask schools to sign away children's privacy rights. *Vancouver Sun.* Retrieved from http://vancouversun.com/opinion/op-ed/opinion-public-schools-ask-parents-to-sign-away-childrens-privacy-rights

U.S. Congress. (2001). *(USA PATRIOT ACT) United and Strengthening America by Providing Appropriate Tools Required to Intercept and Obstruct Terrorism Act of 2001. Pub. L. No. 107-56,115 Stats. 272 (2001).* Retrieved from https://www.congress.gov/bill/107th-congress/house-bill/03162

U.S. Department of Education, Privacy Technical Assistance Center. (2014). *Protecting Student Privacy while using online educational services: Model terms of service.* Retrieved from https://tech.ed.gov/wp-content/uploads/2014/09/Student-Privacy-and-Online-Educational-Services-February-2014.pdf

U.S. Department of Education, Privacy Technical Assistance Center. (2016). *Protecting Student Privacy while using online educational services: Model terms of service.* Retrieved from https://studentprivacy.ed.gov/

U.S. Department of Education, Office of Educational Technology. (2017). *Learning.* Washington, DC: United States Government. Retrieved from https://tech.ed.gov/netp/learning/

Warfield, A. (2010). *A pragmatic approach to encouraging ICT innovation in Canada.* Consultation paper. Retrieved from https://www.ic.gc.ca/eic/site/028.nsf/eng/00466.html

Willard, M. (2012). Protecting children in the 21st century. *District Administration, 34*(3), 86–87.

This research was previously published in Emerging Trends in Cyber Ethics and Education edited by Ashley Blackburn, Irene Linlin Chen, and Rebecca Pfeffer, pages 234-258, copyright year 2019 by Information Science Reference (an imprint of IGI Global).

Section 3
Technological Solutions

Chapter 12
Technological Help to Prevent and Reduce Cyberbullying

Gilberto Marzano
Rezekne Academy of Technologies, Latvia

ABSTRACT

This chapter intends to present the most common technological solutions that can be implemented to prevent and reduce cyberbullying. Three main questions will be addressed: How can children stay safe online? What can the information technology (IT) industry do to combat cyberbullying? How effective is automatic cyberbullying detection? The chapter will illustrate the progress that has been made to reduce cyberbullying through technological means and discuss the notion of industry self-regulation. Indeed, the IT industry has a responsibility to respect societal obligations towards users, especially when users are children. While many companies in the industry are working responsibly on solutions for the safer use of technology, some global internet service providers are involved in the illicit use of users' personal data. As a consequence, problems of online safety cannot be solved locally, but through concerted actions undertaken at an international level.

INTRODUCTION

Home is no longer a private space. It is penetrated by social networks, rooms for online chatting, and virtual spaces for shopping, entertainment, and socialization.

Children and youngsters perceive the internet, smartphones, and related technologies as essential tools for their social life. Until a few years ago, many parents had difficulties in using the new technologies themselves, and didn't understand the risk hidden in them. In fact, plenty of parents candidly admit that it was their children who taught them how to use the internet.

DOI: 10.4018/978-1-7998-1684-3.ch012

Today, the situation is completely different. Parents know how to manage digital technologies, and are able to protect their children by activating parental control tools.

In this regard, applications have been implemented to fight cyberbullying by using blocking and filtering options on a computer. Parents can prevent access to dangerous websites using commercial as well as open source and freeware programs that provide functions of parental control. Most of these functions enable parents to check the internet activities of their children, prevent their access to certain websites, and limit the time they spend online. However, whilst such preventive measures are useful, they are not infallible since parental controls can be bypassed. In the same vein, a child can use a computer or a smartphone where no filters are configured. Moreover, the proliferation of mobile technologies offers ever more new opportunities for accessing the internet.

Trying to avoid the problem of cyberbullying by preventing children from using the internet altogether is, however, not the answer. In fact, it has been observed that banning a child's access to the internet is not only impossible but can, paradoxically, actually damage their educational and social development (Coyne & Gountsidou, 2013).

Taking the drastic step of completely banning children from using the internet and smartphones, may not, in any case, solve the actual cyberbullying itself, as the following case illustrates.

To avoid acts of online bullying, the parents of a young girl, whom we will refer to as E., prevented her from surfing on the internet in their absence, and only allowed her to use an old mobile phone that was not equipped with multimedia functions and an internet connection. When E. was thirteen, however, she became a victim of cyberbullying. How could this happen? Some of her classmates showed her that there were messages on Facebook denigrating and ridiculing her. These messages were posted by other classmates who, in front of her, behaved in a kind and friendly manner. The consequence was that E. was doubly upset: she could not understand why her friends were denigrating her and, at the same time, she was unable to respond. Indeed, she could not connect to the internet herself and, consequently, was reliant on friends to see the hurtful messages concerning her. This created serious stress problems for E., and eventually her parents were forced to move her to a different school.

In this light, it is remarkable that, in 2010, a law was approved in France that banned the use of smartphones during any teaching activity (Shaban, 2018; Smith, 2018). Going further, in fact, the French parliament have recently (July 30, 2018) banned smartphones along with other kinds of internet-connected devices such as tablets from schools entirely. This prohibition has been imposed on schoolchildren between 3 and 15 years of age. French secondary schools are left to decide whether to adopt the phone ban for their students.

In the regard, Shariff observed a few years ago that:

The 'weapons' being used in attempts to control cyber-bullying consist of lobbying by teachers' unions, parents and school administrators who want their governments to implement laws and policies that censor social communication tools such as Facebook and YouTube from being accessed at schools. Some call for bans on cellular and mobile phones that have photographic and text-messaging capabilities. Others want to restrict computer use while children are at school; impose school board monitored firewalls; and enforce zero-tolerance policies that include suspensions and, in some cases expulsion (Education Act, R.S.O., 1990), as deterrents to bullying. (Shariff, 2008, p. 3)

Many psychologists share the conviction that cyberbullying is essentially a relational and personality problem. Accordingly, in order to prevent it, they suggest intervening in the relational behavior and attitudes of young people (Goodboy & Martin, 2015; Kowalski, Giumetti, Schroeder, & Lattanner, 2014; van Geel, Goemans, Toprak, & Vedder, 2017).

Nevertheless, the positive contribution that technological interventions has in reducing cyberbullying and mitigating its effects should not be left unevaluated. Strategies of cyberbullying prevention should focus either on the study of aspects of socialization, or on researching solutions for the automatic detection of cyberbullying.

Applications for the automatic detection of cyberbullying are still at an experimental stage, but advances being made in relation to cybersecurity, for example algorithms developed for detecting invalid information (Kumar, Jiang, Jung, Luo, & Leskovec, 2018), could be applied to cyberbullying.

All this said, of course, any technical remedy remains useless without an adequate educational endeavor on the part of children, parents, and teachers.

In this chapter, the contribution of technology to the prevention and reduction of cyberbullying will be discussed, and the issue of the IT industry's societal obligations will be explored.

Stay Safe Online

In 2007, the UK government commissioned a review on the risks that children face from the internet and video games. It was aimed at protecting children from these risks, enabling them to play video games and surf the internet in a safe and informed way. The review was known as the *Byron Review*, after its author Dr. Tanya Byron, a clinical psychologist specialized in child and adolescent mental health.

The results of the Byron Review were published on April 27, 2008 in a report entitled *Safer Children in a Digital world*. In the report, the author argued for the involvement of the IT industry in restricting access to harmful and dangerous content online:

[...] industry should ensure that computers sold for use in the home in the UK should have Kite marked parental control software which takes parents through clear prompts and explanations to help set it up and that ISPs offer and advertise this prominently when users set up their connection.

[...] search providers should agree to make it obvious to users what level of search is on (e.g. safe or moderate) and give users the option to 'lock it' on and that every search engine have a clear link to child safety information and safe search settings on the front page of their website – this is particularly important as most parents are comfortable using search functions. (Byron, 2008)

Byron was persuaded that the safety of children on the internet should involve representatives from the industry, third sectors, child sectors, parents, and government institutions. Moreover, in her opinion, firms should have to implement a voluntary code of practice defining the minimum standards to which the industry must subscribe. An independent monitoring system, based on self-assessment, should also be created. The Byron strategy is synthetized in the following points of the report's executive summary:

- In relation to the internet, we need a shared culture of responsibility with families, industry, government, and others in the public and third sectors all playing their part to reduce the availability of potentially harmful material, restrict access to it by children, and increase children's resilience.
- I propose that we seek to achieve gains in these three areas by having a national strategy for child internet safety which involves better self-regulation and better provision of information and education for children and families" (Byron, 2008).

At the time that Byron was conducting her study, the IT industry was just starting to concern itself with users' safety, however, remarkable progress has been made in the decade since then.

In 2008, in concomitance with the Byron Review, the European Commission created ESNTF (the European Social Networking Task Force) involving a broad group of stakeholders, such as social networks providers, scientists, and organizations dealing with child care. The ESNTF worked to develop guidelines for minimizing online potential harm to children and young people. The result was the *Seven Safer Social Networking Principles* (ESNTF, 2009):

Principle 1: Raise awareness of safety education messages and acceptable use policies among users, parents, teachers, and carers in a prominent, clear and age-appropriate manner.

Principle 2: Work towards ensuring that services are age-appropriate for the intended audience.

Principle 3: Empower users through tools and technology.

Principle 4: Provide easy-to-use mechanisms to report conduct or content that violates the terms of service.

Principle 5: Respond to notifications of illegal content or conduct.

Principle 6: Enable and encourage users to employ a safe approach to personal information and privacy.

Principle 7: Assess the means for reviewing illegal or prohibited content/conduct.

In 2010, The *Child Exploitation and Online Protection* command (CEOP) of the UK National Crime Agency introduced the *Click CEOP*, a safety or panic button, to provide children, young people, parents, and professionals with trusted online safety advice, help, and support. It also included access to an online mechanism for reporting known or suspected child sexual exploitation or child sexual abuse directly to CEOP (Figure 1).

Facebook agreed on the suggestion of allowing users to report offensive content but disliked the graphic of the CEOP button, since they believed it would intimidate and confuse people. Facebook preferred a different "report button" to provide users with the option to report to CEOP as well as to other moderators (Barnet, 2010).

At the end of the 2010s, many software providers such as Google and Microsoft started to focus on developing tips and advice for staying safe on the Web.

Figure 1. The CEOP safety button

In 2010, Google launched the Google Family Safety Center intended to help children to safely use the internet and handle cyberbullies (Google, 2010).

The introduction to *Get off to a safe start* has remained the same:

There are so many fascinating things to do and explore online, but there are also times when the Internet can be a little bit scary. Just like in the offline world, it's important to keep yourself safe and secure. Whether you're a new Internet user or an old hand, it's good to stay updated on the best practices when it comes to sharing your data online and browsing safely.

The list of advice for staying more secure on the web cover the following areas:

- Secure your passwords
- Sign in and out
- Manage multiple accounts
- Check your Gmail settings
- Use secure networks
- Lock your screen or device
- Keep your device clean
- Online shopping safety
- Is Google Calling or is it a Scam?

One of first of the big software providers to engage in online safety was Microsoft, starting to develop programs to protect children on the internet at an early time. In fact, in the middle of the 2000s, together with other partners, Microsoft created the *Web Watchers*, a program to support online safety.

The *Web Watchers* was launched in 2005. It was an internet security and safety program aimed at providing teachers in the U.S. with age-appropriate and curriculum-valid lessons to help students better understand the opportunities and risks of the internet (Microsoft, 2005).

Nowadays, Microsoft offers many free applications for parental control which allow them to manage their children's computer activity: which websites were visited, the programs used, and the length of time spent on the computer. In particular, Microsoft parental controls provide:

- Web restrictions. It is possible to restrict the websites that children can visit, make sure children only visit age-appropriate websites, prevent or allow file downloads, and set up filters to block or allow particular content.

- Time limits. It is possible to set time limits to control when children are allowed to log on to the computer. Time limits prevent children from logging on during the specified hours and, if they are already logged on, they will be automatically logged off.
- Games. It is possible to control access to games, choose an age rating level, choose the types of content you want to block, and decide whether you want to allow or block unrated or specific games.
- Allow or block specific programs. This function prevents children from running specific programs.

However, in the last few years, an increasing number of software solutions have been developed in order to supervise the online activity of children. These are necessary as parents cannot control what kids are doing online alone, since kids are continuously connected and use a wide range of devices to communicate.

Usually, parental control software runs both on computers and mobile devices, and allows parents to block unwanted web content, limit screen time, restrict the use of risky applications, and more. Most products available on the market support Windows and Android and many of them are also compatible with mac OS and iOS.

Content filtering functions allow access to be blocked to websites that match particular categories such as hate, violence, and porn. However, these functions work with secure (HTTPS) sites and a smart teen could bypass the filter by using a secure anonymizing proxy website or an anonymizing browser. Nevertheless, many products can now keep a detailed log of the web activity of the user, and can help parents to control the online activity of their kids to some degree.

Recent advances in products provide functions to track the viewing history of kids on YouTube and video streaming channels, check their location, or even remotely lock down a device to force them to stop them using it entirely, perhaps while they are at school.

Geofencing is a new feature. Geofencing is a location-based service which uses GPS, RFID, Wi-Fi, or cellular data to trigger a pre-programmed action when a mobile device or RFID tag enters or exits a virtual boundary set up around a geographical location, which could be a museum, monument, park, or specific building (Wong, Sang, & Peng, 2017). Depending on the application, a geofence service could prompt mobile push notifications, trigger text messages or alerts, or even disable certain technology.

Geofencing applications are currently being experimented in many sectors, such as marketing, audience engagement, and security. Specific solutions have also been implemented for online child safety (Day, Wise, Sigler & Roarke, 2016).

Table 1 shows the main functions of parental control products.

Table 1. The main functions of parental control products

Function	Type
Time scheduler	Basic
Content filtering	Basic
Filter HTTPS sites	Basic
Access scheduling	Basic
Social Network monitoring	Basic
Remote management	Recommended
Geofencing	Advanced
Location tracking	Advanced

Source: author's own elaboration

In this regard, the *Australian Government's Cybersafety Help B*utton initiative introduced in 2010 also merits a mention. It was designed in order to provide internet users, particularly children and young people, with easy online access to cybersafety information and advice. Recently, the *eSafety Commission* substituted the button with a form for *cyberbullying complaints* contained in a set of extended cybersafety information and resources. Figure 2 shows a section of the form available for reporting cyberbullying episodes.

Recently, Topcu-Uzer and Tanrikulu have analyzed 16 apps specifically related to cyberbullying (2018). Most of these (11) aim to enhance cyberbullying prevention measures by providing practical information, whilst the others focus on intervention (4) or on both prevention and intervention (1).

Figure 2. A section of the form provided by the Australian government to report a cyberbullying event
Source: Office of the eSafety Commissioner, https://esafety.gov.au/complaints-and-reporting/cyberbullying-complaints/i-want-to-report-cyberbullying

Section 4 – What is happening?

Tell us as much as possible about the cyberbullying.

What has been happening? Have you told friends, family or anyone else? Do you have support? How are you feeling about the cyberbullying? Is there anything else we should know?	*Enter text here*
How long has this been going on for?	☐ Just today ☐ Up to one week ☐ Up to one month ☐ Longer than one month

What the IT Industry Can Do

Firms operating within the IT industry are involved with cyberbullying safety to varying degrees, since the IT industry encompasses a variety of subjects, from Internet Service Providers (ISPs), mobile phone producers, social networking site developers and providers, developers of computer games, providers of chat and messenger apps, and so on. Additionally, the same organization might provide users with a number of services that could require different types of safety actions.

Age control is a crucial aspect for the protection of children. The most popular instant messaging apps state in their policies that users must be a minimum of 13 years of age. In their community guidelines, social network providers declare that threats and violence, harassment and bullying, hate speech, and impersonation are banned.

Some apps provide a function to report cyberbullying incidents, for example SnapChat advises its users:

If you ever experience any harassment, bullying, or any other safety concern, you can always report it right to us! Every report we receive is reviewed by someone at Snapchat, usually within 24 hours.

Together we can make Snapchat a safer place and a stronger community.

To report a Story on Snapchat, just press and hold on the offending Snap until a button appears in the bottom-left corner. Tap it to report the Story and let us know what's going on. (Snapchat Support, 2018)

Social media companies such as Facebook, Twitter, Instagram, Snapchat, LinkedIn, Pinterest, Tumblr, Reddit, and YouTube all have policies against bullying and cyberbullying that are published in their websites, and often collect and present tips that could help their users. However, although these companies emphasize that their user's safety is paramount to them, it has been observed that

[...] specific criteria of effectiveness, evidence of effectiveness, or the details behind how the effectiveness of this effort is measured remain difficult to determine in the case of established and new companies alike. (Milosevic, 2018, p. 121)

Internet Service Providers also offer parental control and network-level filters.

Google with Gmail, and Microsoft with Outlook, have implemented filters to block messages containing harassing, offensive, and threatening content, and provide users with a service to report abuse. Microsoft users, for example, are advised as follows:

* Customers who wish to report **abuse** *about harassment, impersonation, child exploitation, child pornography etc., received* **from a outlook.com account** *should send their complaint to abuse@outlook.com with all the relevant information (abuse@hotmail, or abuse@outlook.com)*

* If you are being threatened please call your local law enforcement.

* If you wish to report abuse against a non-Microsoft account, please send the complaint to abuse@xxxxxx.com, where xxxxxx.com is the text that appears after the "@" symbol in the sender's e-mail address. For example, if the unwanted email came from someone@mymail.com then report the email message to abuse@mymail. com. You can also use the site http://abuse.net to identify the correct abuse reporting address. (Microsoft, 2018)

Chatroulette, a social chat website launched in 2009 that has been the source of many controversies over the years with problems of nudity, harassment, and stalking, provides users with clear rules and regulations for using their chat service, two of its restrictions being:

1. Deceptive behavior is a restriction here on **chatroulette**:
    ◦ Troubling others with vulgar, intimidating comments;
    ◦ Teasing other **chatroulette users** in concerns of their color, birth, race etc.;
    ◦ Degrading others' dignity through text, image, or video chat.
2. It is not allowed to behave disgracefully with other chat partners:
    ◦ Chatting and showing bare chest without a face;
    ◦ Maltreat your chat companion with sexual abuse;
    ◦ Asking to get involved in sex or intercourse virtually;
    ◦ Displaying the body parts that are not socially acceptable;
    ◦ Exhibiting the genital body organs;
    ◦ Touching, scratching, rubbing, or putting your hands on private parts;
    ◦ Directing camera angle lower than your chest;
    ◦ Doing any sexually or physically intimate activity.

Currently, the IT industry is both implementing technical features and empowering users in their efforts towards keeping kids safe online (Nocentini, Zambuto, & Menesini, 2015).

Table 2 synthetizes the main types of solutions currently being developed.

Table 2. Information and Communication engagement for keeping kids safe online

Implementing technical features	Empowering users
• Blocking messages • Providing filtering • Monitoring internet usage • Activating instant alerts • Setting time limits • Defining community guidance • Providing services for reporting abuse	• Providing education and guidance on safe internet use • Offering tips to stop cyberbullying

In the last few years, mobile operators have been multiplying their investments in staying safe online. In 2015, GSMA, an organization that represents the interests of mobile operators worldwide, established a partnership with Child Helpline International (CHI) aimed at helping young people deal with issues such as cyberbullying, sexual extortion, and online privacy. Mats Granryd, director general, reported that in 2018, GSMA started an initiative called Mobile Alliance Against Child Sexual Abuse Content with the involvement of more than 100 mobile operators from 65 different countries around the world. Under this initiative, members sign up to deliver on three objectives (Granryd, 2018):

- To notify law enforcement of abusive content and aim to have it removed at source.
- To support the implementation of a reporting-mechanism, such as a hotline, in all countries where they operate.
- To work towards restricting access, where allowed, to URLs or websites which feature child sexual abuse content, and to do this by using INTERPOL or other international organizations' lists of known sites.

Wide-ranging efforts are being made, both at a public and private level, to improve the performance of automatic detection of unbecoming, harmful, and threatening content. Indeed, the fight against terrorism has made automatic content detection a very important task for state security. Numerous algorithms are being experimented for military purposes (cyberwar) as well as for the detection of fake news (Shu, Sliva, Wang, Tang, & Liu, 2017). One can expect that within a relatively short time, this research will lead to commercial and low-cost apps that are useful for combatting cyberbullying.

Automatic Detection of Cyberbullying

On May 15 2018, Facebook published its first report detailing the activities it has instigated to enforce its community standards (Facebook, 2018). Media consider this report to be the company's response to the increased scrutiny it has been under following the Cambridge Analytica scandal and other revelations that have emerged relating to the US presidential election in 2016 (Magid, 2015).

The report covers the period from October 2017 to March 2018. However, Facebook said it could not estimate the prevalence of posts containing violating content. For example, the company stated that it is still developing measurement methods for detecting hate speech and, accordingly, is unable to provide reliable data for the reported period.

In fact, Figure 3 reveals that the Facebook algorithms flagged only 38% of identified hate speech posts over the period, meaning that 62% were only addressed because users had reported them.

It is clear, then, that the development of the Facebook platform for the automatic detection of problematic posts is a work in progress and still at an experimental stage, as one particular episode illustrates. In July 2018, the algorithm developed to remove advertisements with sexually oriented content (but which also routinely flag artistic or educational nudes) censored a series of promotions for the Belgian region of Flanders because they featured works by Flemish artists mostly known for their detailed depictions of lush, curvaceous women and cherubs (BBC News, 2018).

Figure 3. Facebook statistics on identification of hate speech posts
Source: Facebook, 2018

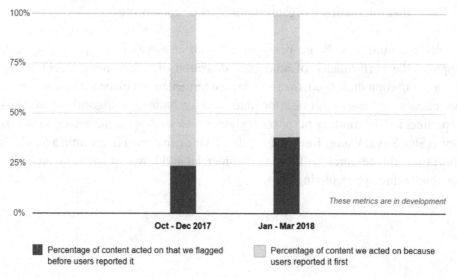

This said, the reliance on automatic monitoring of social networks and the automatic detection of dangerous and harmful content is, absolutely, an essential route, given the immense volume of posts that people make on a daily basis.

Furthermore, although parental control tools might block undesirable content, and many social networks make use of keyword lists to intercept harmful posts, these capabilities are not enough to combat cyberbullying. Often, cyberbullies send subtle and implicitly harassing messages in which no offensive word actually appears.

Intelligent applications are being experimented in the field of the content analysis of social networks that might be able to find a solution to this problem. Since the 1960s, automatic content analysis has been a scope of investigation for researchers interested in information retrieval and natural language processing. The difficulties related to natural language analysis emerged early on. At the end of the 1960s, Salton, one of the most eminent researchers in the field of information retrieval observed:

If the information items to be dealt with are written documents or books, the basic elements are words in the natural language, and the larger units are sentences, paragraphs, or chapters. Unhappily, although it is relatively easy to isolate the individual word in a text, an interpretation of the meaning of the words is much more difficult. Furthermore, there is no-well-defined set of rules by which the individual words in the language are combined into meaningful word groups or sentences. Specifically, the correct identification of the meaning of word groups depends at least in part on the proper recognition of syntactic and semantic ambiguities, on the correct interpretation of homographs, on the recognition of semantic equivalences, on the detection of words relations, and on general awareness of the background and environment of a given utterance. (Salton, 1969, pp. 152-153)

Despite these difficulties, however, important advances have been made in the field of automatic content analysis over the last decades, and the research is moving so fast these days that it is sometimes hard to keep up (Appavu, Rajaram, Muthupandian, Athiappan, & Kashmeera, 2009; Schwartz & Ungar, 2015; Willig & Rogers, 2017).

Currently, the most promising solutions to cyberbullying detection are based on hybrid (Dadvar, Trieschnigg, & de Jong, 2014) and supervised or semi-supervised machine learning approaches (Nahar, Al-Maskari, Li, & Pang, 2014). Supervised approaches involve the construction of a classifier based on labeled training data, whereas semi-supervised approaches rely on classifiers that are built from a training corpus containing a small set of labeled and a large set of un-labelled instances (Van Hee et al., 2018).

Building effective applications for automatic cyberbullying detection is, though, far from easy. For example, online conversations lack the signals of a face-to-face interaction such as intonation, facial expressions, and gestures, which makes them more ambiguous than real-life conversations (Duarte, Llanso, & Loup, 2018; Vandebosch & Van Cleemput, 2009). As such, the receiver may sometimes get the wrong impression that they are being offended or ridiculed when that was not the intent. In this regard, we can wonder how a machine can be expected to detect the sarcastic expression that frequently occurs in forums, blogs, and microposts if it is difficult for even a human to recognize it. Nevertheless, in 2013, the news spread that the French company Spotter had indeed managed to develop an analytics tool that was able to identify sarcastic comments posted online (BBC News, 2013). Nowadays, the researchers who are working on sarcasm detection follow different approaches (Maynard & Greenwood, 2014; Tsur, Davidov, & Rappoport, 2010).

Community Moderation

In her book regarding the cyberbullying policies of social media companies (2018), Tijana Milosevic analyzed the state of the art for how companies deal with cyberbullying. She is persuaded that social media companies play an important role in addressing cyberbullying, and the aim of her book was to analyze how these companies address cyber risks, what policies have been developed, and what the real remedies are. The author denounces that there is an overall lack of transparency within social media companies:

While the more established companies appear to succeed in projecting an image of decisive and effective handling of bullying, they nonetheless provide extremely limited information about their operational policies. A widespread use of non-disclosure agreements (NDAs) in the industry prevents much insight into concrete evidence for the effectiveness of anti-bullying enforcement mechanisms, in both the less established and more established companies alike. (Milosevic, 2018, p. 6)

The author observes that, nowadays, social media platforms have begun to introduce flagging or reporting options for users. In this way, part of the responsibility for moderation is transferred to users. Flagging is a mechanism for reporting offensive content to a social media platform that is present in many social media platforms, including Facebook, Twitter, Vine, Flickr, YouTube, Instagram, etc. By using flagging or reporting options, users can express their concerns and feedback regarding particular content.

Social media companies point to user flagging to legitimize their own content management decisions as a measurable expression of "community standards".

However, although flags have becoming a ubiquitous mechanism of social media governance, they cannot be assumed to be a means to directly represent community sentiments. In fact, the algorithms that are behind the processing of flags are not transparent and stable (Crawford & Gillespie, 2016). Furthermore, flagging could offer a legitimation to remove undesired content on behalf of the user community at large. Flags on social media could be used to legitimize the content management by social media companies under the pretense of upholding community decisions, since their algorithms would be the measure of the community expression.

Milosevic argues that a debate is necessary regarding the critical consequences of the privatization of the digital public sphere, and to address the challenges presented by cyber threats, especially by cyberbullying. Indeed, she urges that this debate should also encompass the risks related to community moderation by private entities which pursue commercial interests.

Facebook is currently testing a feature that allows users to "downvote" comments (Figure 4). The downvote function should allow users to signal that a comment is "inappropriate, uncivil, or misleading." Facebook has pointed out that this is not a "dislike" button per se, but is simply a measure for collecting responses and feedback for comments (Constine, 2018). But then again, who trusts Facebook these days?

Look for Signs of Cyberbullying

Adults, especially parents, should actively search for signs of cyberbullying in their children.

They need to integrate automatic parental controls with their own analysis of the behavior of their children, looking for anything that appears odd.

Figure 4. An example of a downvote
Source: Constine, 2018

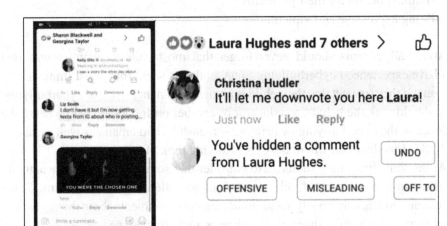

There are certain recognizable signs that may indicate the existence of problems of cyberbullying. Parents should be alert to these signs and explore whether any cyberbullying problem has arisen. Ignoring the following signs can lead to serious consequences:

- Unexplainable injuries, since teens may physically injure themselves by cutting, burning, or enacting other forms of self-harm as a way of coping with emotional pain;
- Depressive state, frequent headaches or stomachaches;
- Fake illnesses;
- Lost or destroyed personal items;
- Changes in eating behavior, such as skipping meals or eating too much;
- Difficulty in sleeping and frequent nightmares;
- Loss of interest in schoolwork;
- Not wanting to go to school;
- Avoidance of social situations;
- Decreased self-esteem.

However, parents should also be able to recognize signs that correspond to a cyberbully's behavior. These are:

- Having relationships with bullies;
- Getting involved in verbal or physical fights;
- Having unexplained extra money or new items such as pens, smartphones, watches, etc.;
- Blaming others for their problems;
- Being aggressive and violent.

Above all, parents should never forget that most children won't report that they have experienced cyberbullying to an adult. As such, they must immediately intervene if they suspect that their child is involved in an incidence of cyberbullying. They should seek the help of an educator or another professional, and preserve the evidence of the cyberbullying by printing screenshots and emails as well as saving the URL of the location where the cyberbullying took place.

At the same time, they should also consider that some adolescents are actually engaging in a new form of self-aggression, so-called digital self-harm. Some adolescents post, anonymously, mean and derogatory comments about themselves on social media. Teens bully themselves online as a way to manage feelings of sadness and self-hatred, and to gain attention from their friends (Patchin & Hinduja, 2017).

Table 3.

Acronym	Meaning
1174	Party meeting place –nude club
143, 459, ILU	I love you
182	I hate you
420	Marijuana
53X	Sex
8	Oral sex
9	Parent watching
99	Parent gone
Broken	Hungover from alcohol
CID	Acid (the drug)
GNOC	Get naked on camera
IPN	I am posting naked
LH6	Let's have sex
NIFOC	Naked in front of a computer
PRON	Porn
SUGARPIC	Suggestive or erotic photo

Finally, in seeking to protect their children, parents need to understand the language they use to communicate among themselves. Some of the more essential internet acronyms that parents need to know are shown in Table 3.

CONCLUSION

In his introduction to *In Real life*, Doctorow observes:

This is the golden age of organizing. If there's one thing the Internet's changed forever, it's the relative difficulty and cost of getting a bunch of people in the same place, working for the same goal. That's not always good (thugs, bullies, racists, and loonies never had it so good), but it is fundamentally game-changing. (Doctorow & Wang, 2014, p. viii)

A brief examination of the technological tools available for preventing and intervening in cases of cyberbullying confirms Doctorow's claims. Cyberbullying is a complex phenomenon since technology is disrupting the dynamics of socialization.

However, the same technology can also help to prevent and reduce cyberbullying by providing automatic filtering and monitoring programs. Nevertheless, relying only on technology is not sufficient to eradicate cyberbullying. Combatting cyberbullying requires an orchestrated action that includes, of course, technology, but also encompasses other forms of interventions such as regulatory statements by internet service providers and social network providers, and effective and continuous educational program for children, parents, and teachers. Moreover, although the efficacy of anti-cyberbullying measures introduced by technological tools have been proclaimed in many experimental studies (Garaigordobil & Martínez-Valderrey, 2015; Menesini & Salmivalli, 2017), these benefits have yet to be demonstrated on a large scale. To evaluate the effects of such tools, larger investigations are required, and appropriate standards and procedures for evaluation need to be defined.

In this regard, a study by the European Commission that benchmarked a number of parental control tools available on the market between 2012 and 2017 suggested that most parental control tools fail to sufficiently address the needs of the parents to protect children against online risk (Vulcano, Angeletti, Chancen, & Croll, 2017). The study found that some tools are good at filtering adult content, but they also over-block non-harmful content. In general, the tools are not able to block violence or self-harm:

The overall effectiveness of tools, in general, is low for both PC and mobile tools. Those with a high rate of over-blocking consequently have a low under-blocking rate and vice versa. [...] Content-filtering tools are less effective when dealing with user-generated content, which is difficult to categorize. In fact, tools present lower effectiveness with user-generated and Web 2.0 content. In all qualitative tests conducted on web 2.0, all the tools failed. (Vulcano, Angeletti, Chancen, & Croll, 2017, p. 32)

The study underlines that the effectiveness of parental controls, however, varies according to the particular social and specific familial context. It seems that highly educated parents are more successful in using available parental control tools, while children of lower educated classes are more exposed to unsafe internet use.

Finally, regarding the use of technological tools, there are other problematic elements that should be considered. In many aspects, internet technology appears to be market sensitive, and recent revelations about the selling of personal data has provided a timely warning about the risk that social networks can be used in a discriminatory and/or manipulative way, even invading the sphere of individual liberty, for example, by invoking community moderation or applying other non-transparent forms of e-democracy.

Paradoxically, policy makers should, at the same time, focus on the safe use of the tools that have been developed for the safe use of the internet by children and adolescents.

REFERENCES

Appavu, S., Rajaram, R., Muthupandian, M., Athiappan, G., & Kashmeera, K. S. (2009). Data mining based intelligent analysis of threatening e-mail. *Knowledge-Based Systems*, 22(5), 392–393. doi:10.1016/j.knosys.2009.02.002

Barnet, E. (2010). Facebook refuses to add safety buttons saying they 'confuse' and 'intimidate' users. *The Daily Telegraph*. Available at: https://www.telegraph.co.uk/technology/facebook/7585688/Facebook-refuses-to-add-safety-buttons-saying-they-confuse-and-intimidate-users.html

BBC News. (2018, July 24). *Facebook angers Flanders with Rubens ban*. Available at: https://www.bbc.co.uk/news/technology-44936601

BBC News. (2013, July 3). *Authorities use analytics tool that recognizes sarcasm*. Available at: https://www.bbc.co.uk/news/technology-23160583

Byron, T. (2008). *Safer children in a digital world: The report of the Byron Review: Be safe, be aware, have fun*. Available at: http://dera.ioe.ac.uk/7332/7/Final%20Report%20Bookmarked_Redacted.pdf

Constine, J. (2018). Facebook confirms test of a downvote button for flagging comments. *Techcrunch.com*. Available at: https://techcrunch.com/2018/02/08/facebook-downvote-button/

Coyne, L., & Gountsidou, V. (2013). The role of industry in reducing cyberbullying. In P. K. Smith & G. Steffgen (Eds.), *Cyberbullying through new media* (pp. 83–98). Psychology Press.

Crawford, K., & Gillespie, T. (2016). What is a flag for? Social media reporting tools and the vocabulary of complaint. *New Media & Society*, 18(3), 410–428. doi:10.1177/1461444814543163

Dadvar, M., Trieschnigg, D., & de Jong, F. (2014, May). Experts and machines against bullies: A hybrid approach to detect cyberbullies. In *Canadian Conference on Artificial Intelligence*, (pp. 275-281). Springer. 10.1007/978-3-319-06483-3_25

Davidov, D., Tsur, O., & Rappoport, A. (2010, August). Enhanced sentiment learning using twitter hashtags and smileys. In *Proceedings of the 23rd international conference on computational linguistics: posters*, (pp. 241-249). Academic Press.

Day, I. R. W., Wise, E., Sigler, S., & Roarke, J. P. (2016). *U.S. Patent No. 9,485,206*. Washington, DC: U.S. Patent and Trademark Office.

Doctorow, C., & Wang, J. (2014). *In real life*. Macmillan.

Duarte, N., Llanso, E., & Loup, A. (2018, January). Mixed Messages? The Limits of Automated Social Media Content Analysis. *FAT Conference*. Available at: https://cdt.org/files/2017/12/FAT-conference-draft-2018.pdf

ESNTF. (2009). *Safer Social Networking Principles for the EU*. Available at: https://www.sbs.ox.ac.uk/cybersecurity-capacity/system/files/European%20Commission%20-%20Safer%20Social%20Networking%20Principles.pdf

Facebook. (2018). *Community Standard Enforcement Preliminary Report*. Available at: https://transparency.facebook.com/community-standards-enforcement#hate-speech

Garaigordobil, M., & Martínez-Valderrey, V. (2015). The effectiveness of Cyberprogram 2.0 on conflict resolution strategies and self-esteem. *The Journal of Adolescent Health*, *57*(2), 229–234. doi:10.1016/j.jadohealth.2015.04.007 PMID:26206445

Goodboy, A. K., & Martin, M. M. (2015). The personality profile of a cyberbully: Examining the Dark Triad. *Computers in Human Behavior*, *49*, 1–4. doi:10.1016/j.chb.2015.02.052

Google. (2010). *Announcing our new Family Safety Center*. Available at: https://googleblog.blogspot.com/2010/09/announcing-our-new-family-safety-center.html

Granryd, M. (2018, March 28). Blocking child sexual abuse content is common sense. *NetClean*. Available at: https://www.netclean.com/2018/03/28/mats-granryd-gsma-blocking-child-sexual-abuse-content-is-common-sense/

Kowalski, R. M., Giumetti, G. W., Schroeder, A. N., & Lattanner, M. R. (2014). Bullying in the digital age: A critical review and meta-analysis of cyberbullying research among youth. *Psychological Bulletin*, *140*(4), 1073–1137. doi:10.1037/a0035618 PMID:24512111

Kumar, S., Jiang, M., Jung, T., Luo, R. J., & Leskovec, J. (2018, February). MIS2: Misinformation and Misbehavior Mining on the Web. *Proceedings of the Eleventh ACM International Conference on Web Search and Data*. Available at: https://www. researchgate.net/publication/322971747_MIS2_Misinformation_and_Misbehavior_Mining_on_the_Web

Magid, L. (2015, May 15). Facebook reports numbers on nudity, sex, violence, hate speech and other banned contents. *Forbes*. Available at: https://www.forbes.com/sites/larrymagid/2018/05/15/facebook-reports-numbers-on-nudity-sex-violence-hate-speech-and-other-banned-content/#55fb38772968

Maynard, D. G., & Greenwood, M. A. (2014, March). Who cares about sarcastic tweets? investigating the impact of sarcasm on sentiment analysis. In LREC 2014 Proceedings. ELRA.

Menesini, E., & Salmivalli, C. (2017). Bullying in schools: The state of knowledge and effective interventions. *Psychology Health and Medicine*, 22(sup1), 240–253. doi:10.1080/13548506.2017.1279740 PMID:28114811

Microsoft. (2018). *To report abuse*. Available at: https://answers.microsoft.com/en-us/outlook_com/forum/osecurity-oother/fraudulent-hotmail-account/713d7303-6054-47ac-9e20-4795d2f0bb18

Microsoft. (2005, March 23). *Web Watchers: Teaching Kids to Stay Safe Online*. Available at: https://news.microsoft.com/2005/03/23/web-watchers-teaching-kids-to-stay-safe-online/

Milosevic, T. (2018). *Protecting Children Online? Cyberbullying Policies of Social Media Companies*. The MIT Press. doi:10.7551/mitpress/11008.001.0001

Nahar, V., Al-Maskari, S., Li, X., & Pang, C. (2014, July). Semi-supervised learning for cyberbullying detection in social networks. *Australasian Database Conference*, 160-171. 10.1007/978-3-319-08608-8_14

Nocentini, A., Zambuto, V., & Menesini, E. (2015). Anti-bullying programs and Information and Communication Technologies (ICTs): A systematic review. *Aggression and Violent Behavior*, 23, 52–60. doi:10.1016/j.avb.2015.05.012

Patchin, J. W., & Hinduja, S. (2017). Digital self-harm among adolescents. *The Journal of Adolescent Health*, 61(6), 761–766. doi:10.1016/j.jadohealth.2017.06.012 PMID:28935385

Rowland, W. D. I., Wise, E., Sigler, S., & Roarke, J. P. (2016). *U.S. Patent No. 9,485,206*. Washington, DC: U.S. Patent and Trademark Office.

Salton, G. (1968). *Automatic information organization and retrieval*. McGraw-Hill.

Schwartz, H. A., & Ungar, L. H. (2015). Data-driven content analysis of social media: A systematic overview of automated methods. *The Annals of the American Academy of Political and Social Science, 659*(1), 78–94. doi:10.1177/0002716215569197

Shaban, H. (2018, July 31). France bans smartphones in schools. *The Washington Post*. Available at: https://www.washingtonpost.com/technology/2018/07/31/france-bans-smartphones-school/?noredirect=on&utm_term=.bdce77a99648

Shariff, S. (2008). *Cyber-bullying: Issues and solutions for the school, the classroom and the home*. Routledge. doi:10.4324/9780203928837

Shu, K., Sliva, A., Wang, S., Tang, J., & Liu, H. (2017). Fake news detection on social media: A data mining perspective. *ACM SIGKDD Explorations Newsletter, 19*(1), 22–36. doi:10.1145/3137597.3137600

Smith, R. (2018, July 31). France bans smartphones from schools. *CNN*. Available at: https://edition.cnn.com/2018/07/31/europe/france-smartphones-school-ban-intl/index.html

Snapchat Support. (2019). *Report Abuse on Snapchat*. Available at: https://support.snapchat.com/en-US/a/report-abuse-in-app

Topcu-Uzer, C., & Tanrikulu, I. (2018). Technological solution for cyberbullying. In M. Campbell & S. Bauman (Eds.), *Reducing cyberbullying in schools: international evidence-based best practices* (pp. 33–47). Academic Press. doi:10.1016/B978-0-12-811423-0.00003-1

van Geel, M., Goemans, A., Toprak, F., & Vedder, P. (2017). Which personality traits are related to traditional bullying and cyberbullying? A study with the Big Five, Dark Triad and sadism. *Personality and Individual Differences, 106*, 231–235. doi:10.1016/j.paid.2016.10.063

Van Hee, C., Jacobs, G., Emmery, C., Desmet, B., Lefever, E., Verhoeven, B., . . . Hoste, V. (2018). *Automatic Detection of Cyberbullying in Social Media Text*. Available at: https://arxiv.org/abs/1801.05617

Vandebosch, H., & Van Cleemput, K. (2009). Cyberbullying among youngsters: Profiles of bullies and victims. *New Media & Society, 11*(8), 1349–1371. doi:10.1177/1461444809341263

Vulcano, M. A., Angeletti, M. R., Chancen, S. D., & Croll, C. (2017). Benchmarking of parental control tools for the online protection of children. *European Union*. Available at: https://ec.europa.eu/digital-single-market/en/news/benchmarking-parental-control-tools-online-protection-children

Willig, C., & Rogers, W. S. (Eds.). (2017). *The SAGE handbook of qualitative research in psychology*. Sage. doi:10.4135/9781526405555

Wong, J., Sang, D., & Peng, C. S. (2017). An Android Geofencing App for Autonomous Remote Switch Control. World Academy of Science, Engineering and Technology. *International Journal of Computer and Information Engineering, 4*(3), 288–296.

KEY TERMS AND DEFINITIONS

Automatic Cyberbullying Detection: The implementation of methods to automatically analyze the content of messages to detect harming, harassing, and abusive sentences as well as insulting words.

Byron Review: A study commissioned in 2007 by the UK government and conducted by Tanya Byron on the risks children face from the internet and video games.

Information Retrieval: A sector of the computer sciences that focuses on implementing solutions for searching information in large collections of resources, both structured and unstructured, such as natural language texts, images, and videos.

Machine Learning: A field of artificial intelligence (AI) that aims to provide systems with the ability to automatically learn and improve from experience without being explicitly programmed.

Parental Control Tools: Various blocking capabilities serving mainly for controlling young users when they are online.

This research was previously published in Cyberbullying and the Critical Importance of Educational Resources for Prevention and Intervention edited by Gilberto Marzano and Joanna Lizut, pages 119-143, copyright year 2019 by Information Science Reference (an imprint of IGI Global).

Chapter 13
Empowering Technology Use to Promote Virtual Violence Prevention in Higher Education Context

Miftachul Huda
*Universiti Teknologi Malaysia,
Malaysia*

Budi Rismayadi
*Buana Perjuangan University,
Indonesia*

Aminudin Hehsan
*Universiti Teknologi Malaysia,
Malaysia*

Kamarul Azmi Jasmi
*Universiti Teknologi Malaysia,
Malaysia*

Singgih Basuki
*Sunan Kalijaga State Islamic
University, Indonesia*

Bushrah Basiron
*Universiti Teknologi Malaysia,
Malaysia*

Mohd Ismail Mustari
Universiti Teknologi Malaysia, Malaysia

ABSTRACT

This chapter aims to explore the pattern to use technology as an attempt to promote virtual violence prevention. A literature review from referred journals and books was conducted. The findings reveal that technology use, in particular an effort to solve the emerging issues of violence promotes the solution with an innovative approach designed in HE. With technology use in attempting violence prevention insights, an innovative way to strengthen technology use wisely with underlying the compassionate skills to promote the preventive action of violent forms is needed. Attempts to promote virtual violence prevention in higher education should be combined with empowering

DOI: 10.4018/978-1-7998-1684-3.ch013

technology use to focus comprehensively on encouraging diverse learners with personal and social awareness in digital interaction. This chapter is expected to contribute in dealing with exploring the systematic approach in nurturing the self-awareness and social concern in digital interaction to be potentially applied in HE.

INTRODUCTION

In the last decade, the recent feature of communication device has been developed in following the trends adopted across the world. Among them which can be viewed include smartphone application such as WhatsApp, telegram, Facebook and others. Generated with the featured generations of communication, the patterns of delivering information with sophisticated process and more convenient way have been shifted using the new technologies' enhancement. It can be seen in the attempt to enhance the demand for social presence, it is necessary to strengthen digital-mediated communication including WhatsApp, Facebook, telegram, and Instagram with more convenient way to enjoy connecting with other users in the variety of purposes. This particular view points out the design feature to enable individual personality to have the interpersonal relationship which is basically derived from face to face-based communication through the digital model (Huda et al., 2017a). Referring to live interaction tendency, adopting the new paradigm shift with virtual means will lead to the process mode into more efficiency. In terms of the initiative with a rapid development to facilitate the communication patterns, the systematic basis is usually engaged with computer-mediated communication (CMC) for instance (Thurlow, Lengel, & Tomic, 2004) or Instant Messaging (IM) where both will benefit to increase the particular approach to enable the communication basis into interpersonal relationships (Chung & Nam, 2007). As an attempt to utilise the technology tools simultaneously with such benefits like helping the students learning and innovative teaching (Anshari et al, 2017; Ahad & Anshari, 2017; Huda et al, 2017b).

However, since there have been challenging issues such as lack of humanity which comes from the lack of affection in the messages (Berson & Berson, 2005), the orientation basis in addressing the interaction strength refers to the extent that the systematic approach to be applied among the individuals with others should be taken into consideration by addressing the potential values to underlie the interaction basis. Although it has both chances and challenges, especially in the digital age based communication pattern, an entire improvement of technology innovation generated into the particular tools in both visual and audio contents should be simultaneously transmitted with the balance of ethical responsibility (Huda et al., 2017b). This is because the convenient service provided from the certain feature design in the smartphone device would potentially lead to the immoral behaviour such as the pattern risky activities, disclosing personal information where this refers to the problematic online practices (Berson & Berson, 2005). With regard to the impact of such worrying problematic issues, promoting the sense of the way to communicate with others is required necessarily to take concern into morality engaged in the virtual basis. It becomes entirely a pivotal role to deliver the sense of social presence to address the ethical responsibility in underlying the social presence in order to operate the instrument among the users. In the effort to performing the interaction mode basis from live interaction to virtual interaction, the initiative to deliver the information by enabling the medium of social affection within the sense of presence of face-to-face communication refers to the various types belonging to the invention of instant messaging software applications for instance. By proposing a model with the innovative way to empowering technology use to promote virtual violence prevention in higher education context, this chapter attempts to elucidate the stages employed amidst the users in empowering technology use through nurturing innovative approach. It attempts to deal with strengthening awareness of personal and social basis referring to the collaborative skills associated with empathy as the foundation in digital interaction to be framework model of violence actions prevention in the Higher education (HE) setting.

Towards Virtual Violence Prevention in Higher Education

Virtual violence has been an obviously serious issue spread along with social media platform. Among the emergence of the violence issue includes alive bullying and cyberbullying where both indicate the particular category in creating the tendency to lead to the aggressive behaviour which needs to consider with aggressive behaviour. Providing the solution with an innovative approach needs to confirm the way of generating information through social media platform (Wright, 2016). Moreover, the provoking dilemma during the last few decades needs to enhance such kind of thoroughly solving initiation by approaching the supervision extent in guiding the counselling service for instance using the smartphone application (Huda et al., 2017c). In this view, the mediation of providing the service on the feeling impact should be enlarged through the guidance approach in the sense that would lead to transmit the strategy initiation in transforming the entire system within the application. The strategical approach in underlying the way to be good in which the systems can manage the device well referring to the procedural stage needs to enhance the overall consistency in gathering the supervisors valuably with underperforming the continuous development. It addresses to always engage with compassionate feeling in the sense that give insights into such feeling mediated in underlining the curriculum program. The valuable insight may be concerned to play a key role in underpinning the brutal issue of violence. Starting from the leaders and stakeholders of HE, attempts to promote character performance in using the digital device would lead with an in depth trait to create the well conducive circumstance.

In line with addressing the potential insights transmitted into attitudes and beliefs towards the violence issues, the need to maintain the skill approached in consolidating the conflict in strengthening the norm of an appropriate behavioural response should be considered in order to contribute to make the environmental basis in the campus circumstance. In terms of creating the environment with minimising the risk set into achieving the stability with peace co-existence, the initiation of campus policy attempts to provide the platform to promote the violence prevention. In addition to the way which starts from the task and duty, the entire basis of organising the prevention has to be enforced with addressing community law and campus cultural form (Espelage et al., 2013). This attempt with influential basis in enforcing the cultural initiation norm has a point of view in contributing the socialization approach in outlining the prevention insights on the virtual violence. Towards the risk of violence attack in the campus life environment, the way of extending the socialization amongst all members should be associated entirely with making the circumstance typically on the feeling approach basis. This is because this initiative would point out the reason of attempting to maintain the wide range of factors leading to the violence. Such factors related to the human behavioural existence should be addressed in particular approach on the violent event leading to the behaviour circumstance. From the predisposing potential for violent issues, creating the situation to solve violence behaviour has to do with attempts to reduce the tendency in a multi-component initiative of the violence complexity. Referring to the particular risk elements of the violent events for instance, the typical dynamics of campus violence would lead to take into account designing an effort to settle and manage concisely into addressing the arrangement of identifying factors lead to the campus incidents issues (Drysdale, 2010). With this regard, the actual condition is needed to perpetrate adequately in addressing the violence issues along with the settings on the skills for negotiating conflict.

In line with negotiating the conflict initiation, this initiative should start from the basic setting of technology use, since it has been developed with its recent feature as a new medium to assist the human interaction. Moreover, the utilization of technology in every aspect has both chance and challenge respectively. The issue of violence in the virtual basis can be viewed from Social Network Site (SNS) basis in the way which should cater the interaction process among the users wisely in the well performed act. Applied in the violence prevention, the initiative of technology use should be considered in a particular way with addressing the moral integrity for instance compassionate feelings (Huda et al., 2017d). In the interaction process with such potential value in generating the moral engagement, this particular act will potentially lead to drive into the violence prevention insights. Moreover, an example with approaching the development of multimedia perspectives such as smart talk helps people to control emotions using interactive assessment likes animation and games (Moksin et al., 2018; Tang, 2014). In the view of giving solution with approaching such initiatives, violence prevention can be undertaken with a wide range of technology medium. Promoting the knowledge understanding among the users will enable to fully enlarge this initiative in the basis of solution insights.

Challenges of Violence Factor and Virtual Interaction Prevention

About the challenges of virtual violence emerged in the last decades, this worrying issues have been arisen among the youth in both school context (Conoley & Goldstein, 2004) and higher education (Drysdale, 2010). Such violence issues here indicate that the emergence of the behavioural crisis should be taken into serious consideration in solving the systematic programs. The numbers of this challenging issue vary from bullying (Cross et al., 2004) and cyberbullying (DeHue, Bolman, & Völlink, 2008). Moreover, the impact caused from this issue can be viewed into the bullying victimisation (Campbell, 2005). From these forms of examples, there can be indicator for the perpetration among the students, mainly in the higher education (HE) context. In terms of the fact for those involving violence, the most likely the experiential basis seems to be the school-aged students. About the ranging number of violent issues, the complex phenomenon is increasingly seen from both students' interaction and teachers' behavioural performance (Klewin, Tillmann & Weingart, 2003). In this view, both individual and groups have been a similar point of view arising the emergence of conflicts such as miscommunication. The potential risk leading to the issues with the matters on the human interaction refers to the lack of integrity due to coercive or manipulative language that aims to induce fear, guilt, shame, etc. Communication skills need to strengthen the way of looking at the violent modes including the conflict divert in the sense which needs a particular attention among the users (Huda et al., 2017e). This view should be confirmed through clarifying the needs associated with the extent of perceptions, feelings and requests in transforming the rules to give insights in preventing the violence issues. As a result, the violence issue in this view in forming the process of preventive action towards violent forms should be prepared with pointing out an innovative approach in the way to nourish the feeling of compassion together with self-empowerment skills.

In terms of performing the skills of feeling compassionate associated with nurturing the moral values integrated among those involved in the school, the need to point out the factors leading to the violence has to be determined in both individual characteristics and attributes of campus and community environments

(Langford, 2004). Among those involved into the multiple influence levels, individual background with social group including institution and community and also public policy can be organized referring to public factors. In this view, the framework of social ecological basis as this model might be enlarged to point out the model of safety basis to cater behavioural circumstance by which to determine the public concern shaped with the societal factors. In terms of strengthening the nature to solve these issues, it is necessary to take serious concern about factors set across the following examples possibly giving insights into influencing the type of violence mainly in HE context. One of them is factors from the personal behaviour involved in the school context including individual factors (Murphy & Van Brunt, 2016). This can be viewed among student and teacher where the awareness of violence issues should be transmitted among them. The following factor is about the inter-individual relationship where the environment has a role to influence the behavioural tendency to others. In this situation, the maturity of beliefs and attitudes about violence issues should be transmitted to response by addressing the norms of appropriate acts. As a result, the institutional regulation needs to consequently accommodate the campus policies with designing the procedures to give insights in preventing the violence existence. Through settings with the high-risk in contributing the solution to minimize the violence issues, creating the campus environment in a conducive way has to be strengthened appropriately. At this point of view, the community engagement becomes a pivotal element to enhance the high rates of awareness to possess mutual understanding about the violence impact.

In line with extending the enforcement of community involvement to tackle violence, creating public policy to maintain the impact of societal influences leading to the negative behavioural extent has to do with enhancing the campus life. This refers to influence potential value which can be managed with the cultural contributions. Through attempting such socialization using the social media for instance, the convergence of elements leading to the violence is required to stabilise the situation by which to make the circumstance well with maintaining the peaceful circumstance among the members (Kardefelt-Winther, 2014). In this view, attempts to predispose the potential element of creating violent behavioural acts in the sense that leads to the situation to some risk of violent events need to accommodate the mutual involvement into the societal level. It can be viewed through consolidating the complexity of violence to emphasise that such efforts might potentially minimise the extent of violence. Towards the initiatives designed with multicomponent in addressing the typical dynamics as an attempt to reduce the violence behaviour, the arrangements in creating the extent of personal behaviour play a significant role in solving any kind of incidents or assault which can give impact to the victim. At this point of view, such factors which can potentially contribute to the violence event should counteract in enhancing the circumstance of campus conditions where to be safety attainment can be achieved.

Featured Technology Improvement and Misbehavior Potential

The design of featured technology improved through such portable devices has a valuable benefit to assist the human life in terms of communication and interaction, business and other purposes. With more convenient in delivering any service, application device is developed to transmit the insightful contribution in underlying the interaction mode basis among the users. Through enhancing to attract the necessary merit in terms of the workplace coordination and organization consolidation, the useful essence especially in the way to support the complex work with the primary use of workplace among the people group needs to gather in discussing the topics designed to transmit the information (Schultze, 2010). It can be used to deliver the information through social media where the user can see from the screen from their mobile phone. With regard to the extent of communication among the users in both physical and virtual mode, the initiative in the workplace setting is seemingly to be more effective in an attempt to establish the sensitive essence within the work groups to enable in helping the workers interact with their peers (Ramirez & Broneck, 2009). In order to getting successful in fostering friendships by increasing communication and connectivity with co-workers, it is necessary to enhance the atmosphere where all the workers may have chance with the means to introduce levity and intimacy into the work place or in any other relation. It is necessary to elaborate the significant participation among others to lead to the organizational communications in the workplace setting with the effective and efficient basis in improving relationships among them.

However, apart from such benefits clearly mentioned above, the challenging issues derive from a wide range of causes varying from the lack of caring in the interaction basis. As a result, the additional impact will result in misbehaviour conduct in the sense that this potency might behave the tendency to the violence. In some cases, the violence issue was caused due to overlapping the activities between university and societal stage with a minimum control in maintaining the good morality (Huda et al., 2017e). In this view, both campus and community traits should construct the initiative in facilitating the circumstance in the sense that generates the violence factors to look at the main root of issues (Murphy & Van Brunt, 2016). The nature of violence in resulting the possibility to influence others needs to be clearly enhanced to provide the prevention insights in accommodating individual, social, institutional and community basis engagement.

Towards the improvement of featured technology, this chance may potentially lead to challenge in the sense that refers to the misbehaviour conduct which traits the potential violence. As a result, attempts to the prevention insights in this view should create the forum among those involved in the programs in order to lead to possess the responsibility awareness since they are together consolidating the response to influence towards the incidents of violence prevention. About the level of individual influence, this initiative refers to violence prevention through dealing or negotiating process among students, staff and lecturers meanwhile for group. It is a responsibility among the group norms with institutional rules to become the bystander response towards the violence incidents. In this view, stakeholder of policy making needs to assure the overall initiative including the rules to combat the violence issues in the way which can be undertaken regularly in evaluating the campus integrity initiation. At this point of view, the extent of communities is necessary to maintain the rules in evaluating the enforcement of community law initiated to violence prevention. With regard to the engagement into the social interactions intimated to take a serious concern of relationships, recent technology advancement and internet strength designed into the mobile application has an important influence on transmitting the communication (Huda et al., 2017f). It points out the extent of technologies leading to the major shift in human social interactions mode. Towards raising the experience of intimacy among interpersonal relationship, the inquiry in looking at the way of these technologies would give an impact into online intimacy and well-being. With this regard, the intimacy prepared in the virtual based-social interactions becomes an outstanding matter to maintain the integrity of experiential interaction basis in the sense that addresses the stages in shaping the online intimacy concern.

In addition, the potential impact caused from the online intimacy among the users in this regard becomes an experiential value to maintain the context of relationship between live interaction and virtual one. With online social interactions, the general sense of shedding the light on the extending level of interactions intimacy to influence the affection among the users should gather the social interactions in online basis with pointing out the components of intimacy in online. Exploring the potential contribution especially for social support with self-disclosure refers to the aims at guiding the directions of online intimacy to indirectly tackle the potential impact being the fundamental attainment of solving initiation . In terms of the access to information in building techno-spatial configurations, sometimes both privileges and discrimination configured by the spatial seclusion could be attributed to affect information-sharing patterns. It can be seen for instance the intimacy basis through practicing technology usage with pointing out the network intimacy coming from personal support among the members (Sugimoto-Matsuda & Braun, 2014). Apart from this, between disclosure and closeness under internet environment, the challenges may emerge with lending the intimacy, which perceived with the formal tool of computer-mediated communication. For instance, the disclosure of information that is usually kept private defines interactions and relationships as intimate, differentiating them from casual interactions and relationships (Contreras-Castillo, Pérez-Fragoso, & Favela, 2006). As a result, attempts to achieve the mutual sharing of information prepared with the emotions into the intimate romantic interactions are required to possess the awareness about the possible occurrence which may happen. Referring to the network intimacy which may emerge among friends and family members, the challenge may come from the interaction pattern within virtual conversations.

Trough supplying techniques which may be applied to the interpersonal sphere, this awareness will lead to increase the performance of individual basis together with self-censorship or even between users in close relationships. With offering the space of communication pattern more physical distance, the entire concern to the extent additionally users' technology devices with possessing more control enhancement on interpersonal communications is required to be aware of face-to-face based-interaction (Thurlow, Lengel & Tomic, 2004). For example, there is a blocking system tool for most smartphone devices in allowing the users to remove the others from their lists. This is very useful to avoid instant messaging from the ones set out to notify the effects of messenger on interpersonal relationship. With regard to the interpersonal relationship to engage with allowing users to remove other users by blocking system, attempts to set out some of the informants reported with referring to the real-time promoted the way to the communication stage from face to face to the digital touch screen. As popularly known into the interaction mode, it is worthwhile to possibly concern in allowing the people to virtually remain in contact anytime, and anywhere. As a result, effective and social intimacy to promote the steep advancement of frequent conversation actually encourages the desire in creating the atmosphere with focusing on casual environment to be more relaxed to engage into the digital communication (Almunawar et al., 2017). With this regard, interpersonal communication integrated into the face-to-face mode together with digital basis aims to enhance the influences on the relationships to get close among the members including friends, family and colleagues.

Empowering Technology Use to Promote Virtual Violence Prevention in Higher Education Context

Attempts to build the environment by which to empower technology use have been an insightful view to commit in trust and intimacy mainly in the digital world interaction. This initiative has to be enlarged in combatting the virtual violence insights as an attempt to preventive action within HE context. As a pivotal rule in embarking the raise of putting trust in the virtual communication basis, it is necessary to entirely engage the awareness attainment of violence impact amidst the campus life circumstance. This distinctive enhancement needs to convince the recognition with more open to receive an extent of reliability to transmit information clearly. In terms of transferring the set of recognisable values to enhance the basic tenet, this regard attempts to build trust basis in the sense which the reliability to possess the knowledge understanding of violence prevention should be undertaken more attractive with a reciprocal agreement in giving insights into credibility basis. As a result, the technology use with pointing out the influential basis to complete work with keeping credibility outlines the initial point of view as a result of knowing the other users. In the HE context, the students would have their colleagues to transfer information about the academic concern while misbehaviour conduct may be the major issue to solve in building virtual communication integrity (Guinalíu & Jordán, 2016). This includes manual setting of interaction to the digital-based communication with addressing the procedural stage to be easily employed amidst societal life at large. Beyond face to face mode of interaction, the important value in establishing the commitment of putting trust is surely needed to employ the construction ability in the virtual world. With a powerful essence in generating the consistent assumption easily to execute the credential way, formatting the rule of mechanical manner can entirely be engaged into the additional purpose to minimise violence issue. Through attempting the virtual interaction basis, the challenges of embarking violence from featured technology raise need to prepare the strategy with a particular approach in maintaining the awareness of caring based integrity enhancement (Galassi, 2017). With regard to enhancing the sense in attempting the interaction model like instant based communication message, providing this particular approach will eventually need to develop human connection freely and wisely. This significant essence attempts to enlarge assisting the goal-driven initiative by providing the way to help through technology-driven anonymity. To which attempts such initiations need to confirm the particular attention in terms of offering all-important personal touch which is critical in developing intimacy, the key ingredient role of trust has to be entirely involved in the basis of establishing relationships with best practice easily observing communication application amidst the users at large and the students in particular.

In line with protection assurance which the students may undertake to keep from violence issues both from bullying and cyberbullying, attempts to have an initiation to securing system can be set up in the sense which re-energizes the valuable discourse towards prevention insights. Through protecting violence issues, the style of technology use in this view needs to develop the systematic approach in benefiting the valuable contribution as an important attempt considered to determine the prevention enforcement (Huda et al., 2018a; Huda et al., 2018b; Huda, 2018). With this regard, the nature of particular feeling for instance compassionate based empathy becomes a pivotal value with a protective initiation to be integrated amongst the students. As a result, it is considered to give a direction with significant role to drive the communication skills. In this view, the strategies with committing the entire principles communication management to underlie verbal and physical interaction should enlarge transforming environmental basis with strengthening cultural approach amidst the HE context. Attempts to enlarge the integration of mindfulness amongst understanding, feeling and caring essence could enhance making situations to be more empathetic with each other in fostering the compassionate communication (Slonje & Smith, 2008). As a result of assisting the users to get engaged entirely with no particular blaming personal criticisms, promoting the solution to solve the violence issues through being committed to take care with compassionate empathy basis is potentially considered as the way to adopt the technology use with the concern to take aware of the violence issues. Following the way in the adoption of technology use in HE context, determining many factors to lead to violence has to be involved with being careful engagement to build the systematic approach in transmitting information into the users. Concerning generally oriented framework in reducing violence issues, achieving with systematic solution is necessary to point out strengthening the detailed descriptions about the major anti-bullying initiation programs. With regard to behaving awareness in the interaction, the program in presenting caring with compassion in underlying the digital human communication within societal community needs to strengthen the key role in transmitting the way to synergise entire basis of empathy combined with the sympathy enhancement. Through embarking the initiative to strengthen the consciousness in achieving the caring, the necessary act to put integrity with the compassionate skills is required to enlarge the approach in the sense which performs the empathy (Huda et al., 2017d). Enhancing the way to maintain the compassionate basis should give insights to combat violence as an integrated prevention. Towards the specific exploration about caring involvement connected specifically into the bully and cyberbully issue (DeHue, Bolman, & Völlink, 2008; Slonje & Smith, 2008), the initiation to accept the kind of experience would gather the conceptual framework with transmitting the difficult feelings by taking the kindness in recognising the compassion. With referring to the experiential enhancement in acknowledging the element of wisdom, performing self-actualisation more fully to cover the substance is an outstanding value to let the digital interaction committed to the compassionate enhancement.

In line with getting close through social interaction, strengthening the way of technology use should be wisely integrated with feelings compassion in the sense which refers to the empathy (Greeno et al., 2017). This initiative is potentially considered to enhance the consciousness in covering the caring insights together with recognizing the extent of kindness and understanding oneself with others. With a particular essence of caring transmitted into the self-awareness, attempts to enhance the learning process by fully understanding the emotion feeling need to embrace in responding the compassionate-based initiation. It aims to achieve the potential nature with expressing constructively into an additional involvement of feeling compassionate through working with the orientation to the engaged process systematically on online communications basis for instance Social Network Site (SNS). It could become a pivotal element to have a key role in resulting the empowerment of technology use as an attempt to promote virtual violence prevention in HE context.

Attempts to promote virtual violence prevention in particular with referring to give insights into designing an innovative solution approach should be enlarged in the combination basis designed in HE context. As a result, strengthening the strategy in the technology use with generating the application on keeping compassionate feeling needs to transmit into the preventive solution insights in predicting the appropriate way in the sense that maintain the convenient essence among the users. In this view, the role of school leader and stakeholders has a key consideration to transmit the core behaviour essence of bullying in which significant supervision as the medium in generating the potential value of compassionate basis needs to bring along with the mediation through pointing out the considerable guidelines (Cross et al., 2004). With this regard, the valuable insight to strengthen critical analysis with underlying to promote the innovative approach would enable individual development in empowering good moral behaviour as the consequent enhancement with a particular attention to feeling compassionate (Huda & Kartanegara, 2015). The initiated way in delivering the process could be significantly engaged into online communications designed into promoting virtual violence prevention in HE context. It is necessary to pay particular attention to make orientation in the technology use wisely with the commitment to enlarge using SNS as a result in empowering self-foundation with entire awareness of misbehaviour potential caused from the featured technology improvement.

Enhancing Interpersonal Interaction With Technology Use in the Digital Age

Enhancing the interpersonal communication with pointing out interpersonal interaction would lead to increase the extent of social relationships with more satisfaction in the virtual world. This can be achieved with attempting to induce the positive mediation in the effort to give insight into the recent relocation to use the communication channel through expressing thoughts together with sharing experience into other users (Espelage et al., 2013). As a result, taking care of the effect which may happen with addressing the mutual understanding would lead directly to increase the users' satisfaction among the individual basis within the interpersonal relationship. Towards the virtual interpersonal relationships in using the technology to engage with building the friendships seems likely to generate the social interaction configured into the quality with a positive effect on their interpersonal relationships in real life. As a result, sustaining the various social relationships among the users in acquainting the extent of relationships should do with tending other users in the way to stress an overall positive impact on personal wellbeing (Maseleno et al., 2017). In terms of strengthening the weak relationships among the users, the use of virtual interaction basis with an effective enhancement to communicate with others should be paid serious attention to enable them maintain the level of trust during the interaction and communication. Considering potential time and cognitive constraints in examining the impact of social network site use (SNS) on social relationships for instance should be considered in particular essence with an entire maintenance to gather long-distance relationship. Between self-identity and social-identity with interpersonal interaction to help the users achieve the ethical responsibility, the extent of intimacy basis inquiry is basically engaged to get access the information delivered across technology tool (Huda et al., 2017; Moksin et al., 2018). It refers to the particular attribution including external events such as interactions with paying serious attention on personal thoughts and feelings strengthened with the modern interpersonal relations and communication.

In line with engaging interaction under the meaningful extent, attempts to get intimated towards the social relationships refer to play a pivotal basis in underlying the key components through influencing general framework illustration. About the social factors leading to cyberbullying for instance, the recent and widespread integration of Internet and mobile communication technologies into daily lives is changing the principal modalities through which we keep in touch with others. With this regard, such critical light of these changes needs to maintain the way of getting interpersonal communication experience in the context of online social engagement could give insights in influencing the outcomes style of digital human. Amidst the digital age where to signify the multiple levels to influence the good feedback including health and wellbeing, social network characteristics size in maintaining social-structural conditions should give an entire governance to always keep on encountering such upstream effects of cultural and socioeconomic factors leading to the violence. With this regard, density and reciprocity become an initial consequence with addressing downstream effects into interpersonal behaviour in the sense that could gather psychosocial mechanisms involving intimate interactions. In terms of getting social interaction to effect ultimately in transmitting behavioural, psychological and physiological pathways, the capacity in directing social connectivity linked more directly to particular outcomes in terms of the social contexts can be considered at multiple levels into the effects of combining the exposition of internet connection. Towards the explosion in enabling social networking with online applications, facilitating the interactions within interpersonal disinhibition to consolidate intimate self-disclosure can potentially enhance the raise of one's social capital in the sense that increased connectivity (Huda et al., 2017g). Through online social networking basis, it needs to necessarily view the mode of meaningful social connections to look at describing the condition of certain aspects of internet-mediated interactions. As a result, increased online disinhibition has to do with increasing self-disclosure-based favour online intimacy. Attempts to promote increased satisfaction in online interpersonal interactions can facilitate meaningful and intimate social interactions in the way that points out highlighting the potential of this medium for cultivating such feeling involving empathy and compassion through high-quality social engagement online.

With regard to outlining the impact of social online communication in digital basis, the entire consideration to be involved with pointing out the extent of online interactions has to bring along with the online resources quality. In terms of the relation to the outcomes in making advanced into the psychological behaviour, attempts to energize the benefits with draw-backs of this social interaction medium need to confirm the sense that synergise technology and human psychology (Loke, 2016). At this point of view, the systematic exploration of online communication to give insights into the digital human interaction within the specific relationship on shedding light on the aim of enhancing interpersonal interaction should point out reintegrating the entire consideration in identifying the potential value in starting points of the extent of knowledge understanding (Huda et al., 2017h). Through this emerging field to identify the stage of understanding the way of digital communication to give a positive feedback in influencing the digital human interaction, the systematic approach to begin with determining the characteristic elements in the digital communication has an entire direction to guide with a fundamental online social interaction. As a result of identifying the stage of multimodal components with online social interactions, attempts to build online social interactions refer to address self-disclosure and social support in the sense that could determine to shed light on the potential contribution of online interaction.

Supporting Technology Use With Engaging Emotional Feeling

The effort to determine the social support in transmitting the technology use wisely to engage into emotional essence has a role to direct with a simultaneous integrity in generating particular attention of perceived support availability. Especially in determining the particular attention to enlarge social engagement, an important mediator with many aspects in covering emotional feeling associated with transmitting instrumental design of informational support would become a point of view attributed to facilitate the social emotional aspects (Huda et al., 2017a). As a result, this initiative referring to the social support in benefitting the digital interactions may help individuals obtain the capability with confidence to use any kind of technology with being consistently careful. It is necessary to address certain aspects of promoting to facilitate self-disclosure interactions with an influential basis of interpersonal communication in the digital age. As an important ability to cope with emotional issues, self-disclosure in enhancing SNS should refer to recognise the significant element to deliver online relationships with an overview in mediating positive feedback concerning online support communities (Huda et al., 2016a). The starting point of instruments developed in assessing meaningful companionship through online relationships requires operationalization to enhance the development of appropriate assessment measured with the actual experience of the different online environments features.

In line with addressing an important accessibility in performing the individual ability to communicate with others, attempts to perceive in expressing different online interactions should begin with ranging from shared communication in the context of live basis to obtain the settings to shared experiences mainly in the digital age. In particular, the way to take advantage of social networks in virtual worlds attempts to focus on online social experience to be more involved with multiple media to gain a clear understanding about digital online communication (Kardefelt-Winther, 2014). As an attempt to develop measures in establishing online interaction models, the extension with an important form to convey the direction in incorporating interpersonal relationship could be undertaken with a better understanding of recognising the necessary involvement into the social interaction (Huda et al., 2017i; Huda et al., 2017j). In this view, the incorporation of accomplishing the existing measurement tools would be modified with addressing the physiological responses in online social experiences. In order to shed light on potential physiological mechanisms, the assessments model would also be important to contribute to health and well-being in determining the way of online experiences (Kross et al., 2013). As a result, examining social interactions in online contexts needs to enhance the practical applicability through which the way of technology use might become an important element to generate psychological practice in the digital era. With being involved into the nature of human social interactions in the digital age, addressing this critical inquiry of violence issues has to be updated to continue the commitment integrity along with continuing to evolve better understanding of the immediate and long-terms effects caused by violence event into the psychological effect.

In addition to the basis of environments with continuously accessible wireless technologies, it is necessary to recognise some of the worrying issues including the tendency growing temptations into misuse behaviour such as cheating, plagiarism, and bullying through the digital technology devices. Through getting early preparatory experiences, the initiation of using computers and mobile phones provide the conjunction with engaging the practicing responses to problematic situations (Almunawar et al., 2017; Huda et al., 2017j). It is worthwhile to be aware of risky situations in order to develop appropriate techniques way adequately though simplistic cautions and authoritative rules (Maseleno et al., 2018). Prepared with the media-saturated culture for instance, the potential value in approaching safety awareness should be enlarged into the basis of comprehensive process with a broader part of safety program. Attempts to understand the particular situation through putting the responsibility awareness are required to prepare the intervention of risk emanated across such efforts with the collaborative basis including understanding the rules with the knowledge to solve wisely (Huda et al., 2016b), and also the knowledge understanding towards the global phenomena committed to the ethical values in the context of advancement and the perfection of the individual and the society at large (Huda et al., 2016c). In the effort to avoid violent situations, engaging the ability in showing the social awareness with personal integrity needs to work together in improving the prosocial decision making demonstrated through interpreting the instruction in interpreting conflict issues by improving their behavioural cues associated with resolution skills. Moreover, the additional initiative by focusing on harm avoidance is entirely engaged into the sensation-seeking behaviours basis in the way which can be obtained through prosocial response (Huda et al., 2017h). In terms of minimizing the clues that would typically lead to the cyberbullying and any other violence issue in cyberspace, it is necessary to enhance the achievement of diminishing the effectiveness of the cognitive component of empathy. This may point out the beneficial inclination through the prevention programs prepared in designing repercussions to safeguard the communication skills basis in the digital age (Schultze, 2010). It is a pivotal view to behave the social responsibility with the ethical values to embed into the behavioral principle (Huda et al., 2016d). It is also an essential component of transmitting the sensitivity of the way of online communications referring to the impact among others in preventing harmful online communication. To be designed in raising the extent of effective internet awareness, the entire initiation may be achieved through the digital literacy together with necessitating the internet safety to accommodate the personal and social replication within the computer interface. Towards the amplification of awareness in frightening in cyberspace, the extent of ability to engage in training with undesirable effort is necessary to expand the making of sense into obtaining the experiential communication basis with more expansive ways of thinking about the sensory data in cyberspace.

Strengthening Responsibility With Social Awareness in Digital Era

As an effort to have responsibility with engaging social awareness, strengthening interaction quality in digital era has to be managed into outlining preventive insights in interfering the initiation associated with prosocial skills integrity. In this view, accessibility into the real-world behaviour through digital device may lead to the opportunity in assisting the human life needs in terms of communication and interaction with others (Sugimoto-Matsuda & Braun, 2014). In attempting to have knowledge understanding both chances and challenges of the violence phenomena popularly among the users, the initiative to broaden the opportunity with more attractive enhancement should engage with pointing out the prevention insight towards abusive behaviours and violent potentials. With this regard, considering the way to make online communication along with transmitting information into others is entirely the initiated accessibility in delivering service into actual purpose. Since the more active users in social media, the more potential to lead to get involved into such violence including bully, threaten and harass and consequently will impact to exploit victims (Wright, 2016). This challenging issue may need to get solved through strengthening responsibility awareness in suggesting the users in having the online activity to avoid the access of potential offenders with being more expansive pool of victims. The consequence is inextricably linked to the strictly pointing out behavioural repercussions with addressing revealed emotional implications where the internet gave the impact apart from the benefiting the imitation through intellectual activity.

Frequently with making such activities through online basis, the contrary act will always happen into the actual purpose, being dramatically increased to point out the social life impact. In this view, transmitting virtual connection to the information delivery may need to have the securing system in order to protect the anonymity status of questionable web page. It is valuable insights into prevention initiation, since this becomes a worrying risky potency to prevent the way in social media use with online communication trough an exposure to the violence potential. With this regard, the risky potency of anonymity should be considered in particular approach to have the relationships in both virtual interaction and live basis. Through pointing out the balance between the two, an exposure of professional and ethical integrity should be an inherent online communication part leading to the violence prevention. In this view, the exploitation coming from increasing the risk for identity deception has to attempt transforming the fluid identity in an online basis to personalise the users with being aware of positive and negative impact. This will result in determining the experiential basis to expand the learning enhancement in the digital age. In terms of the online basis interaction associated with the tendency to diminish self-regulation, self-construction with extending the experiment in engaging the behavioural substance refers to the tendency potentials with an affective feedback to commit to share disclosures to enhance the prevention insights towards aggressive interaction. With this regard, harmful impact inflicted from misbehaviour conduct needs to concern about reducing the cyberspace disregard with the pervasive enlightenment of contributing the initiative negotiated as an anticipated task. In determining the responsibility awareness with an appropriate guideline, getting engaged to keep in working together with directing into a good condition should be enlarged into the digital technology users. Through guiding with a particular supervision, the exertion of technology adoption with process and management skills should be taken appropriately and wisely into consideration in the sense that can point out the adaptive teaching competencies in digital era (Huda et al., 2016a). In particular to supporting the application guideline in big data approach for instance, the extent of responsibility engagement with the multichannel of sources of knowledge aims to extract the new insights of value involved into assessing the insights of adaptive teaching competencies (Huda et al., 2017h). As a result, it is necessary to maintain the way which can lead to the balance orientation into the circumstance in digital era.

In conjunction with connecting the digital communication integrally made a connection into the global understanding of the chance and challenges of SNS, the responsibility engagement can be enhanced through pointing out such moral expertise qualities including mutual safety, comfortability, and privacy concern. Such these should be provided in the way to make a positive feedback from internet literacy with requiring continuum of skills in terms of message delivery from any kind of online device. Attempts to construct the responses towards interpreting perspectives in the way to respond into the others might address the influential basis through combining actions with understanding the nuances of opinions shared especially misperceiving communications in a digital environment. With achieving the competency in the technology basis, learning enhancement can be commenced in the way to see the particular approach through filtering environmental concern set out in order to maximise the knowledge understanding about the violence issue coming from the internet communication impact. As a result, creating the online environment made to carefully engage in enabling the optimal structure should start with building the responsibility based communication skills. With embarking the competency basis on digital technology communication, attempts to rote the basic rules in transmitting the social interaction together with the personal behavioural enhancement need to behave an active engagement in the context of refining the capable skill trait in order to combat the violence potentials.

CONCLUSION

This chapter explored the initiation of technology use with transmitting the responsibility awareness and also interpersonal interaction. With technology use in attempting violence prevention insights, any form in the issue of violence is needed an innovative way to strengthen technology use wisely with underlying the compassionate skills to promote the preventive action of violent forms. Referring to the framework model, attempts to promote virtual violence prevention in higher education context should be combined with empowering technology use to focus comprehensively on encouraging diverse learners with personal and social awareness including empathy, collaborative skills, and conflict literacy as the main foundation in digital interaction. Specifically, this chapter is expected to contribute in dealing with exploring the systematic approach in nurturing the self-awareness and social concern in digital interaction to be potentially applied in HE. This initiative is supposed to enhance in giving awareness of the impact on anti-social behaviour. Elucidating this innovative approach in nurturing compassionate based empathy performances becomes a wide exchange to propose framework model in the effort to prevent violence actions. Among the main strategic strengths for guiding the user's online interaction is empowering technology use to promote virtual violence prevention in higher education context. It refers to enhance interpersonal interaction with technology use in digital age in the way which is supporting technology use with engaging emotional feeling aspect. Followed into strengthening the responsibility with social awareness in digital world towards the potential nature, an additional involvement of enhancing interpersonal interaction with technology use in digital age has to be oriented to the process which could be engaged systematically into online communications. As a result to empowering technology use to promote virtual violence prevention in HE context, engaging emotional feeling responsibility with social awareness entails to point out promoting the solution with an innovative approach designed in HE to generate the preventive solution with predicting the appropriate strategy to be recommended amongst the school leader and stakeholders.

REFERENCES

Ahad, A. D., & Anshari, M. (2017). Smartphone Habits Among Youth: Uses and Gratification Theory. *International Journal of Cyber Behavior, Psychology and Learning*, 7(1), 65–75. doi:10.4018/IJCBPL.2017010105

Almunawar, M. N., Anshari, M., Susanto, H., & Chen, C. K. (2017). How People Choose and Use Their Smartphones. *Management Strategies and Technology Fluidity in the Asian Business Sector*, 235.

Anshari, M., Almunawar, M. N., Shahrill, M., Wicaksono, D. K., & Huda, M. (2017). Smartphones usage in the classrooms: Learning aid or interference? *Education and Information Technologies*, 1–17.

Berson, I. R. (2003). Grooming cybervictims: The psychosocial effects of online exploitation for youth. *Journal of School Violence*, 2(1), 5–18. doi:10.1300/J202v02n01_02

Berson, I. R., & Berson, M. J. (2005). Challenging online behaviors of youth: Findings from a comparative analysis of young people in the United States and New Zealand. *Social Science Computer Review*, 23(1), 29–38. doi:10.1177/0894439304271532

Bosworth, K., Espelage, D., & DuBay, T. (1998). A computer-based violence prevention intervention for young adolescents: Pilot study. *Adolescence, 33*(132), 785. PMID:9886006

Campbell, M. A. (2005). Cyber Bullying: An Old Problem in a New Guise? *Australian Journal of Guidance & Counselling, 15*(01), 68–76. doi:10.1375/ajgc.15.1.68

Conoley, J. C., & Goldstein, A. P. (Eds.). (2004). *School violence intervention: A practical handbook.* Guilford Press.

Contreras-Castillo, J., Pérez-Fragoso, C., & Favela, J. (2006). Assessing the use of instant messaging in online learning environments. *Interactive Learning Environments, 14*(3), 205–218. doi:10.1080/10494820600853876

Cross, D., Pintabona, Y., Hall, M., Hamilton, G., & Erceg, E. (2004). Validated guidelines for school-based bullying prevention and management. *International Journal of Mental Health Promotion, 6*(3), 34–42. doi:10.1080/14623730.2004.9721937

DeHue, F., Bolman, C., & Völlink, T. (2008). Cyberbullying: Youngsters' experiences and parental perception. *Cyberpsychology & Behavior, 11*(2), 217–223. doi:10.1089/cpb.2007.0008 PMID:18422417

Drysdale, D. A. (2010). *Campus attacks: Targeted violence affecting institutions of higher education.* DIANE Publishing.

Espelage, D., Anderman, E. M., Brown, V. E., Jones, A., Lane, K. L., McMahon, S. D., ... Reynolds, C. R. (2013). Understanding and preventing violence directed against teachers: Recommendations for a national research, practice, and policy agenda. *The American Psychologist, 68*(2), 75–87. doi:10.1037/a0031307 PMID:23294044

Galassi, J. (2017). *Strengths-based school counseling: Promoting student development and achievement.* Routledge.

Greeno, E. J., Ting, L., Pecukonis, E., Hodorowicz, M., & Wade, K. (2017). The role of empathy in training social work students in motivational interviewing. *Social Work Education, 36*(7), 794–808. doi:10.1080/02615479.2017.1346071

Guinalíu, M., & Jordán, P. (2016). Building trust in the leader of virtual work teams. *Spanish Journal of Marketing-ESIC, 20*(1), 58–70. doi:10.1016/j.reimke.2016.01.003

Haber, M. G., Cohen, J. L., Lucas, T., & Baltes, B. B. (2007). The relationship between self-reported received and perceived social support: A meta-analytic review. *American Journal of Community Psychology, 39*(1-2), 133–144. doi:10.100710464-007-9100-9 PMID:17308966

Hawkins, J. D., Smith, B. H., Hill, K. G., Kosterman, R., Catalano, R. F., & Abbott, R. D. (2003). Understanding and preventing crime and violence. In *Taking stock of delinquency* (pp. 255–312). Springer US. doi:10.1007/0-306-47945-1_8

Huda, M. (2018). (accepted for publication). Empowering Application Strategy in the Technology Adoption: Insights from Professional and Ethical Engagement. *Journal of Science and Technology Policy Management.*

Huda, M., Anshari, M., Almunawar, M. N., Shahrill, M., Tan, A., Jaidin, J. H., ... Masri, M. (2016a). Innovative Teaching in Higher Education: The Big Data Approach. *The Turkish Online Journal of Educational Technology, 15*(Special issue), 1210–1216.

Huda, M., Haron, Z., Ripin, M. N., Hehsan, A., & Yaacob, A. B. C. (2017g). Exploring Innovative Learning Environment (ILE): Big Data Era. *International Journal of Applied Engineering Research, 12*(17), 6678–6685.

Huda, M., Jasmi, K. A., Alas, Y., Qodriah, S. L., Dacholfany, M. I., & Jamsari, E. A. (2017j). Empowering Civic Responsibility: Insights From Service Learning. In S. Burton (Ed.), *Engaged Scholarship and Civic Responsibility in Higher Education* (pp. 144–165). Hershey, PA: IGI Global; doi:10.4018/978-1-5225-3649-9.ch007

Huda, M., Jasmi, K. A., Basiran, B., Mustari, M. I. B., & Sabani, A. N. (2017h). Traditional Wisdom on Sustainable Learning: An Insightful View From Al-Zarnuji's Ta 'lim al-Muta 'allim. *SAGE Open, 7*(1), 1–8. doi:10.1177/2158244017697160

Huda, M., Jasmi, K. A., Embong, W. H., Safar, J., Mohamad, A. M., Mohamed, A. K., ... Rahman, S. K. (2017d). Nurturing Compassion-Based Empathy: Innovative Approach in Higher Education. In M. Badea & M. Suditu (Eds.), *Violence Prevention and Safety Promotion in Higher Education Settings* (pp. 154–173). Hershey, PA: IGI Global. doi:10.4018/978-1-5225-2960-6.ch009

Huda, M., Jasmi, K. A., Mohamed, A. K., Wan Embong, W. H., & Safar, J. (2016d). Philosophical Investigation of Al-Zarnuji's Ta'lim al-Muta'allim: Strengthening Ethical Engagement into Teaching and Learning. *Social Science, 11*(22), 5516–5551.

Huda, M., Jasmi, K. A., Mustari, M. I., Basiron, B., Mohamed, A. K., Embong, W., ... Safar, J. (2017c). Innovative E-Therapy Service in Higher Education: Mobile Application Design. *International Journal of Interactive Mobile Technologies, 11*(4), 83–94. doi:10.3991/ijim.v11i4.6734

Huda, M., Jasmi, K. A., Shahrill, M., Hehsan, A., Mustari, M. I., Basiron, B., & Gassama, S. K. (2017a). Empowering Children with Adaptive Technology Skills: Careful Engagement in the Digital Information Age. *International Electronic Journal of Elementary Education, 9*(3), 693–708.

Huda, M., & Kartanegara, M. (2015). Islamic Spiritual Character Values of al-Zarnūjī's Ta 'līm al-Muta 'allim. Mediterranean Journal of Social Sciences, 6(4S2), 229-235.

Huda, M., Maseleno, A., Jasmi, K. A., Mustari, I., & Basiron, B. (2017e). Strengthening Interaction from Direct to Virtual Basis: Insights from Ethical and Professional Empowerment. *International Journal of Applied Engineering Research*, 12(17), 6901–6909.

Huda, M., Maseleno, A., Muhamad, N. H. N., Jasmi, K. A., Ahmad, A., Mustari, M. I., & Basiron, B. (2018b). Big Data Emerging Technology: Insights into Innovative Environment for Online Learning Resources. *International Journal of Emerging Technologies in Learning*, 13(1), 23–36.

Huda, M., & Sabani, N. (2018). Empowering Muslim Children's Spirituality in Malay Archipelago: Integration between National Philosophical Foundations and Tawakkul (Trust in God). *International Journal of Children's Spirituality*, 1–14.

Huda, M., Sabani, N., Shahrill, M., Jasmi, K. A., Basiron, B., & Mustari, M. I. (2017i). Empowering Learning Culture as Student Identity Construction in Higher Education. In A. Shahriar & G. Syed (Eds.), *Student Culture and Identity in Higher Education* (pp. 160–179). Hershey, PA: IGI Global. doi:10.4018/978-1-5225-2551-6.ch010

Huda, M., Shahrill, M., Maseleno, A., Jasmi, K. A., Mustari, I., & Basiron, B. (2017f). Exploring Adaptive Teaching Competencies in Big Data Era. *International Journal of Emerging Technologies in Learning*, 12(3), 68–83. doi:10.3991/ijet.v12i03.6434

Huda, M., & Siregar, M., Rahman, S.K.A., Mat Teh, K.S., Said, H., Jamsari, E.A., … Ninsiana, W. (2017b). From Live Interaction to Virtual Interaction: An Exposure on the Moral Engagement in the Digital Era. *Journal of Theoretical and Applied Information Technology*, 95(19), 4964–4972.

Huda, M., Teh, K. S. M., Nor, N. H. M., & Nor, M. B. M. (2018a). Transmitting Leadership Based Civic Responsibility: Insights from Service Learning. *International Journal of Ethics and Systems*, 34(1), 20–31.

Huda, M., Yusuf, J. B., Jasmi, K. A., & Nasir, G. A. (2016b). Understanding Comprehensive Learning Requirements in the Light of al-Zarnūjī's Ta'līm al-Muta'allim. *SAGE Open*, 6(4), 1–14. doi:10.1177/2158244016670197

Huda, M., Yusuf, J. B., Jasmi, K. A., & Zakaria, G. N. (2016c). Al-Zarnūjī's Concept of Knowledge ('ilm). *SAGE Open*, 6(3), 1–13. doi:10.1177/2158244016666885

Kardefelt-Winther, D. (2014). A conceptual and methodological critique of internet addiction research: Towards a model of compensatory internet use. *Computers in Human Behavior*, *31*, 351–354. doi:10.1016/j.chb.2013.10.059

Keith, S., & Martin, M. E. (2005). Cyber-bullying: Creating a culture of respect in a cyber world. *Reclaiming Children and Youth*, *13*(4), 224.

Klewin, G., Tillmann, K. J., & Weingart, G. (2003). Violence in school. In *International handbook of violence research* (pp. 863–884). Springer Netherlands. doi:10.1007/978-0-306-48039-3_43

Kross, E., Verduyn, P., Demiralp, E., Park, J., Lee, D. S., Lin, N., ... Ybarra, O. (2013). Facebook use predicts declines in subjective well-being in young adults. *PLoS One*, *8*(8), e69841. doi:10.1371/journal.pone.0069841 PMID:23967061

Langford, L. (2004). *Preventing violence and promoting safety in higher education settings: Overview of a comprehensive approach.* Higher Education Center for Alcohol and Other Drug Abuse and Violence Prevention.

Lewis, C., & Fabos, B. (2005). Instant messaging, literacies, and social identities. *Reading Research Quarterly*, *40*(4), 470–501. doi:10.1598/RRQ.40.4.5

Loke, S. W. (2016). Technology Trends: Working Life with 'Smart Things'. In Communicating, Networking, Interacting (pp. 13-20). Springer International Publishing.

Maseleno, A., Pardimin, Huda, M., Ramlan, Hehsan, A., Yusof, Y.M., Haron, Z., Ripin, M.N., Nor, N.H.M., and Junaidi, J. (2018). Mathematical Theory of Evidence to Subject Expertise Diagnostic. *ICIC Express Letters*, *12*(4), 369. doi:10.24507/icicel.12.04.369

Maseleno, A., Huda, M., Siregar, M., Ahmad, R., Hehsan, A., Haron, Z., ... Jasmi, K. A. (2017). Combining the Previous Measure of Evidence to Educational Entrance Examination. *Journal of Artificial Intelligence*, *10*(3), 85–90. doi:10.3923/jai.2017.85.90

Miller, D. (1999). *Principles of social justice.* Academic Press.

Moksin, A. I., Shahrill, M., Anshari, M., Huda, M., & Tengah, K. A. (2018). The Learning of Integration in Calculus Using the Autograph Technology. *Advanced Science Letters*, *24*(1), 550–552.

Murphy, A. L., & Van Brunt, B. (2016). *Uprooting Sexual Violence in Higher Education: A Guide for Practitioners and Faculty.* Taylor & Francis.

Othman, R., Shahrill, M., Mundia, L., Tan, A., & Huda, M. (2016). Investigating the Relationship Between the Student's Ability and Learning Preferences: Evidence from Year 7 Mathematics Students. *The New Educational Review, 44*(2), 125–138.

Plaga, J. A., Kosnik, W., Lacson, F., Thomas, J., & Whitmore, M. (2016, September). Recent Trends in Human Systems Integration. *Proceedings of the Human Factors and Ergonomics Society Annual Meeting, 60*(1), 494–498. doi:10.1177/1541931213601112

Pollet, T. V., Roberts, S. G., & Dunbar, R. I. (2011). Use of social network sites and instant messaging does not lead to increased offline social network size, or to emotionally closer relationships with offline network members. *Cyberpsychology, Behavior, and Social Networking, 14*(4), 253–258. doi:10.1089/cyber.2010.0161 PMID:21067280

Ramirez, A. Jr, & Broneck, K. (2009). IM me': Instant messaging as relational maintenance and everyday communication. *Journal of Social and Personal Relationships, 26*(2-3), 291–314. doi:10.1177/0265407509106719

Schultze, U. (2010). Embodiment and presence in virtual worlds: A review. *Journal of Information Technology, 25*(4), 434–449. doi:10.1057/jit.2010.25

Slonje, R., & Smith, P. K. (2008). Cyberbullying: Another main type of bullying? *Scandinavian Journal of Psychology, 49*(2), 147–154. doi:10.1111/j.1467-9450.2007.00611.x PMID:18352984

Stevens, G., Seedat, S., & van Niekerk, A. (2004). Understanding and preventing violence. *Self, Community & Psychology*, 13-19.

Sugimoto-Matsuda, J. J., & Braun, K. L. (2014). The role of collaboration in facilitating policy change in youth violence prevention: A review of the literature. *Prevention Science, 15*(2), 194–204. doi:10.100711121-013-0369-7 PMID:23430580

Tang, J. (2014). Graphics, Animation, and Games. In *Beginning Google Glass Development* (pp. 249–295). Apress.

Thurlow, C., Lengel, L., & Tomic, A. (2004). Computer mediated communication. *Sage (Atlanta, Ga.)*.

Valkenburg, P. M., & Peter, J. (2013). The differential susceptibility to media effects model. *Journal of Communication, 63*(2), 221–243. doi:10.1111/jcom.12024

Wright, M. F. (2016). Cyber Victimization on College Campuses Longitudinal Associations With Suicidal Ideation, Depression, and Anxiety. *Criminal Justice Review, 41*(2), 190–203. doi:10.1177/0734016816634785

KEY TERMS AND DEFINITIONS

Digital Age: The period of the introduction of the personal computer with subsequent technology in providing the ability to transfer information freely and quickly in human history characterized by the shift from traditional industry. Expanded to include online and social media, the industrial revolution is brought through industrialization into an economy based on information computerization.

Higher Education: A public or non-profit educational institution beyond high school specifically providing by colleges and graduate schools and professional schools. Institution authorized by law to provide a program of education beyond. It is also stated as tertiary education which is in the third stage, third level, and post-secondary education taken to include undergraduate and postgraduate education.

Responsibility With Social Awareness: An entire improvement of technology innovation generated into the particular tools in both visual and audio contents should be simultaneously transmitted with the balance of ethical responsibility. It can usually be identified through the characteristics of intimacy in online social interactions, its multimodal components, and its caveats.

Technology Use: The adoption of reliability with possessing the knowledge to individualize instruction into the collection of techniques, skills, methods, and processes used in the production of goods or services through accomplishing the objectives. For instance, within the computer networks called integrated learning systems, teachers can prescribe individual learning paths for students, where this is called scientific investigation.

Virtual Interaction: An effective enhancement to communicate with others through social network site (SNS) use on social relationships. The consideration in particular essence with an entire maintenance to gather long-distance relationship should be involved with an effective attainment to communicate with others to enable them to maintain the level of trust during the interaction and communication.

Virtual Violence: The kind of behavioral quality which is ethically problematic with aggression leading to the extreme where it refers to violence physically experienced coming from entertainment involving television, video, film, music, computer. In this regard, technology must be utilized for violence prevention and solution.

This research was previously published in Intimacy and Developing Personal Relationships in the Virtual World edited by Rejani Thudalikunnil Gopalan, pages 272-291, copyright year 2019 by Information Science Reference (an imprint of IGI Global).

Chapter 14
Brute Force Search Method for Cyberbullying Detection

Michal E. Ptaszynski
Kitami Institute of Technology, Japan

Fumito Masui
Kitami Institute of Technology, Japan

ABSTRACT

In this chapter, the authors present a method for automatic detection of malicious internet contents, based on a combinatorial approach resembling brute force search algorithms, with application to language classification. The method automatically extracts sophisticated patterns from sentences and applies them in classification. The experiments performed on actual cyberbullying data showed advantage of this method to previous methods, including the one described in Chapter 4. Pros and cons of this method when compared to previous ones are also discussed in this chapter.

INTRODUCTION

Brute-force search algorithms, also known as exhaustive search algorithms, are a general group of algorithms applying combinatorial approach to problem solving. In particular, such algorithms firstly generate all possible answers to a problem, and then test the answer for its success. Combinatorial algorithms are especially useful in tasks where it is difficult to estimate a probable answer to narrow the scope of search. Therefore they have been traditionally used in password breaking and data decryption (Narayanan & Shmatikov, 2005; Paar, Pelzl & Preneel, 2010).

DOI: 10.4018/978-1-7998-1684-3.ch014

However, due to their minimal requirements when it comes to initial knowledge base, combinatorial algorithms have been also useful in Natural Language Processing, for example, in dependency parsing (Covington, 2001), stemming (Mishra & Prakash, 2012), or specific and novel tasks, such as extraction and analysis of emoticons (Ptaszynski et al., 2010).

However, brute-force approach often faces the problem of exponential and rapid growth of function values during combinatorial manipulations. This phenomenon is known as combinatorial explosion (Krippendorff, 1986). Since this phenomenon often results in very long processing time, combinatorial approaches have been often disregarded. We assumed however, that combinatorial explosion can be handled on modern hardware to the extent needed in our research. Moreover, optimizing the combinatorial approach algorithm specifically to problem requirements should shorten the processing time making it advantageous in the task of processing harmful language.

The method proposed in this chapter is original in following regards. As was pointed out by previous research (Ptaszynski et al., 2010), language used in cyberbullying messages is often deceptive and messy, and it is difficult to grasp a simple set of features to detect it. Therefore, to create a flexible model of cyberbullying, we applied a novel automatic feature extraction procedure. In research on machine learning, or applying any kind of machine learning to solve real world problems, one can use one of two approaches to feature extraction, namely, either automatic feature extraction (later called bottom-up approach) or select some custom predefined features (later called top-down approach, e.g., hand-crafting a lexicon of characteristic terms, etc.). The latter, although sometimes providing satisfying results, requires deep knowledge of the problem beforehand, meaning that the researchers need to figure out valid features themselves, which is inefficient.

In grand majority of NLP research, also in cyberbullying detection, applying the bottom-up approach, the features extracted automatically are typically based on separate words (as in e.g., bag-of-words) (Ptaszynski et al., 2010). Although instead of simple words one can use in text classification parts-of-speech or concepts (Sahlgren & Cöster, 2004), the sophistication of extracted pattern still does not exceed one token. A smaller number of research applies ngrams (usually unigrams to tetragrams of words or letters) (Damashek, 1995; Ponte & Croft, 1998; Siu & Ostendorf, 2000).

Recently, researchers have started to apply slightly more generalized version of ngrams, namely, skip-grams (Guthrie et al., 2006), which allow one controlled "skip", or a gap of a controlled distance. This however is still far from the definition of a pattern proposed here, namely, allowing any number of "skips" with a flexible dynamic distance, which in mathematical terms refers to "ordered combinations without repetitions." This kind of pattern extraction has not been widely applied till

Figure 1. A graphical summary of the whole method

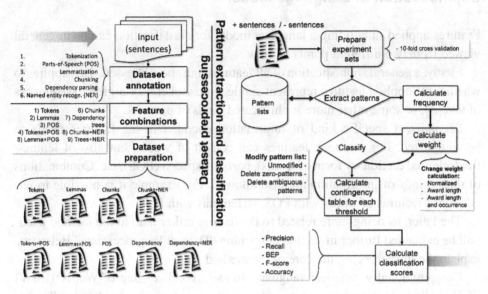

now due to the computational cost it requires to train. The method proposed here takes advantage of the recent computing technologies allowing multiple cores and large amounts of memory to overcome this problem and compute such patterns in a sufficient time. We assumed this method of feature extraction will provide features of the sophistication level previously unused in cyberbullying detection research.

Outline of the chapter is as follows. Firstly, we describe the proposed method and the ways we decided to preprocess the applied dataset in this research. We explain the evaluation settings, and thoroughly analyze the results. Finally, we discuss the pros and cons of the method proposed in this chapter.

SENTENCE PATTERN EXTORTION METHOD DESCRIPTION

In this section we explain all parts of the proposed method, step by step. At first we describe general types of features we apply in this research and explain our feature extraction method. Next, we describe all ways of weight calculation for the applied features. Then, we present the applied classifier. Finally we describe the threshold optimization as a method to optimize the classifier performance. A graphical summary of the whole method was represented in Figure 1.

Sophistication of Language Model

Features applied in building a language model for classification can be in general viewed from two different points of view.

Firstly, a general sophistication of all features must be addressed. This applies to whether the applied features represent single words/tokens, or n-grams (sequences of tokens), or some other more sophisticated kinds of patterns.

Secondly, a specific kind of information encoded in the features needs to be recognized. For example, features can consist of words, but also of lemmas (undeclensed dictionary form of words), parts-of-speech (POS), etc. Combinations of those kinds of information are also allowed. For example it is possible to use combined features of words with POS, or lemmas with POS.

The latter, as being more related to the dataset rather than to the method itself, will be explained further in section describing "Dataset Preprocessing." Below we explain the former, being the core of the method.

Computationally simplest language model is called Bag-of-Words (BoW) (Zellig, 1954). It considers a piece of text or document as an unordered collection of words. BoW thus disregards grammar and word order. Although recently there has been proposed a generalization of BoW model using semantic concepts instead of words (Bag-of-Concepts) (Cambria & Hussain, 2012), the general rule remains the same, disregarding the order of elements within input, and longer strings of elements (e.g., phrases).

An approach in which word order is retained is broadly called the n-gram approach. In terms of probabilistic theory its basis was firstly formulated by Markov (1971). The n-gram approach perceives a given input (e.g., sentence) as a set of n-long ordered sub-sequences of words. This allows matching the words while retaining the sentence word order. However, the n-gram approach when applied to language, still allows only for simple sequence matching, while disregarding more sophisticated sentence structure.

An example of such sophisticated pattern, can be explained as follows. A following sentence (in Japanese) *Kyō wa nante kimochi ii hi nanda !* (What a pleasant day it is today!) contains a common and widely studied language pattern *nante * nanda !* (asterisk "*" used as a marker of disjointed elements). Similar cases can be easily found in other languages, for instance, in English. An exclamative sentence "Oh, she is so pretty, isn't she?", contains a pattern "Oh * is so * isn't *?" which is a typical example of a *wh*-exclamative sentence pattern (Beijer, 2002; Sasai, 2006; Potts & Schwarz, 2008). The existence of such patterns in language is common and well recognized in linguistics. However, it is not possible to discover them using n-gram approach.

An example of a language model aimed to go beyond BoW and n-grams is the skip-gram model (sometimes also called skipped n-gram or distanced n-gram). It assumes that some words within an n-gram could be not adjacent, but skipped over. In theory this should allow extraction of most of frequent language patterns from a corpus. However, there are some major drawbacks in research studying skip-gram modeling. These include for example, assuming that a skip can appear only in one place (Huang et al., 1992). The above-mentioned English sentence example clearly indicates that frequent and easily recognizable language patterns can consist of elements appearing sometimes on the beginning of a sentence, another time in the middle, or at the end. Multiple gaps between them are also common, which cannot be covered by the skip-gram language model. Moreover, the number of skipped elements is recorded for each gap. For example, a 2-skip-3-gram can only allow 2 skips (omitting two words) between the elements, which means that the model considers as different patterns two cases in which the first gap has 2 skips, and second has 5 skips. Since the model assumes full control of the skip-length, the 2-skip-3-gram and 5-skip-3-gram consisting of the same elements (words) are represented as different entities and can never refer to the same pattern in a corpus. This assumption is unrealistic, since one can easily imagine that the same pattern, appearing in two sentences of different length, will be separated by gaps of different sizes. To illustrate this problem in Table 1 we compared which of the above-mentioned language models is capable of discovering particular patterns present in the two sentences below. The last column on the right represents capability of the language model based on the idea of language combinatorics (LC), applied in this research.

1. John went to school today.
2. John went to this awful place many people tend to generously call school today.

The language modeling method discussed in this chapter is capable of dealing with any of the sophisticated patterns. This is due to the fact that we define sentence pattern as *any ordered non-repeated frequently occurring combination of sentence elements*. This definition allows extraction of all possible frequent meaningful linguistic patterns from unrestricted text. Moreover, by a "frequent pattern" we consider a combination which occurs in a corpus at least twice. This differs from the traditional approach to building BoW language models, where one usually uses all extracted words, even if their occurrence is equal to 1. This is due to the fact that single words usually do not reach high occurrence rates, and most of them are rare. Therefore not using all of them, or using only those with occurrence = 2 or higher, could significantly decrease the Recall rate in classification process (not many features would be found). With sophisticated patterns the situation is different. They are extracted in enormous numbers and using all of them would make the

Table 1. Comparison of capabilities of different language models to capture certain patterns from a hypothetical corpus consisting of two sentences, (1) and (2) (○ = capable, × = incapable)

pattern	model			
	BoW	**n-gram**	**skip-gram**	**LC**
John	○	○	○	○
John went	×	○	○	○
John * to	×	×	○	○
John * school	×	×	×	○
John * to * today	×	×	×	○

classification process inefficient. By using the above cut-off rate, we conform to the general definition of "a pattern" (as something that appears repeatedly, or "at least twice"), get rid of the least useful patterns, and retain those which in fact appear most often.

Feature Extraction With Language Combinatorics

To extract the patterns of cyberbullying messages we first applied the idea of Language Combinatorics (Ptaszynski et al., 2011). This idea assumes that linguistic entities, such as sentences can be perceived as bundles of ordered non-repeated combinations of elements (words, punctuation marks, etc.). Furthermore, the most frequent combinations appearing in many different sentences can be defined as sentence patterns. The idea was applied in SPEC or Sentence Pattern Extraction arChitecture – a custom feature extraction and classification system, which we also applied in the experiment.

We assumed that for the task of cyberbullying detection, where actual harmful meaning is often hidden and indirect, applying such sophisticated patterns with disjointed elements should provide better results than the usual bag-of-words or n-gram approach. As long as patterns are defined as ordered combinations of sentence elements, they could be automatically extracted by generating all ordered combinations of sentence elements, verifying their occurrences within a corpus, and filtering out those the combinations which appear only once.

From the fact that the method first extracts all possible patterns from a sentence with brute force inspired algorithm, we decided to call the method *pattern extortion*, to distinguish it from typical *pattern extraction* methods based on n-grams or single tokens.

Formally, in this method, firstly, ordered non-repeated combinations are generated from all elements of all input sentences in a training set. In every n-element sentence there is k-number of combination clusters, such as that $1 \leq k \leq n$, where k represents all k-element combinations being a subset of n. The number of combinations generated for one k-element cluster of combinations is equal to binomial coefficient, represented in equation 1. In this procedure the system creates all combinations for all values of k from the range of $\{1, ..., n\}$. Therefore the number of all combinations is equal to the sum of combinations from all k-element clusters of combinations, like in equation 2.

$$\binom{n}{k} = \frac{n!}{k!(n-k)!} \tag{1}$$

$$\sum_{k=1}^{n}\binom{n}{k} = \frac{n!}{1!(n-1)!} + \frac{n!}{2!(n-2)!} + ... + \frac{n!}{n!(n-n)!} = 2^n - 1 \tag{2}$$

Next, all non-subsequent elements are separated with an asterisk ("*"). All patterns generated this way are used to extract frequent patterns appearing in a given corpus. For comparison, we also applied more traditional n-gram model.

Weight Calculation

After combinatorial patterns are extracted, their occurrences O are calculated, separately for the positive (here, meaning "harmful") side O_{pos} and the negative side (here meaning "non-harmful") side O_{neg}. The occurrences of each pattern j are further used to calculate normalized pattern weight w_j according to equation 3.

$$w_j = \left| \frac{O_{pos}}{O_{pos} + O_{neg}} - 0.5 \right| *2 \tag{3}$$

The weight can be later modified in several ways. Two features are important in weight calculation. A pattern is the more representative for a corpus when, firstly, the longer the pattern is (length k), and the more often it appears in the corpus (occurrence O). Thus the weight can be modified by

- Awarding length (later: LA), by multiplying normalized weight w_j by pattern length k_j, which provides a weight with awarded length W_{LA}, like in equation 4, or
- Awarding length and occurrence (later: LOA), by multiplying normalized weight w_j by pattern length k_j and overall pattern occurrence ($O_{pos} + O_{neg}$), which provides a weight with awarded length and occurrence w_{LOA}, like in equation 5.

$$w_{LA} = w_j * k_j \qquad (4)$$

$$w_{LOA} = w_j * k_j * (O_{pos} + O_{neg}) \qquad (5)$$

The list of frequent patterns generated in the process of pattern generation and extraction can be also further modified. When two collections of sentences of opposite features (such as "positive vs. negative" or "harmful vs. non-harmful") are compared, a generated list of patterns will contain patterns that appear uniquely in only one of the sides (e.g. uniquely positive patterns and uniquely negative patterns) or in both (ambiguous patterns). Therefore the pattern list can be further modified by

- Erasing all ambiguous patterns[1] (later: AMB),
- Erasing only ambiguous patterns which appear in the same number on both sides (later zero patterns, or 0P).

Moreover, a list of patterns will contain both the sophisticated patterns (with disjointed elements) as well as more common n-grams. Therefore the experiments on the proposed method were performed with both

- Patterns (PAT), and
- N-grams (NGR) only.

Classification

The proposed classifier is a function defined as a sum of weights of patterns found in the input sentence, like in equation 6.

$$\text{score} = \sum w_j, \left(1 \geq w_j \geq -1\right) \qquad (6)$$

It produces a harmfulness score for each analyzed sentence. The score alone does not yet specify whether a sentence should be considered harmful or not, however, a good guess is that the higher above zero is the score the more harmful patterns it contains, or, to put it in more straightforward terms, the more it resembles a style of writing usually found in cyberbullying. On the other hand, the lower below zero the score, the more it resembles non-harmful way of writing. However, an intuitive rule of thumb, with zero as a universal threshold does not apply to pattern-based method, since even a one word difference in a sentence can produce much larger number of patterns on one of the sides (harmful or non-harmful), and thus cause an imbalance in the data. Therefore we also performed a threshold optimization to specify which threshold should be used for the applied data.

Threshold Optimization and Heuristic Rules

If the initial collection of sentences was biased toward one of the sides (e.g., more sentences of one kind, or the sentences were longer, etc.), there will be significantly more patterns of a certain kind. Thus to avoid bias in the results, instead of applying a static rule of thumb, threshold was optimized automatically.

All above settings were automatically verified in the process of evaluation, based on 10-fold cross validation, to choose the best model. The metrics used in evaluation were standard Precision (P), Recall (R), balanced F-score (F) and Accuracy (A). These scores were calculated for every threshold and compared to choose the optimal model.

Finally, to deal with the combinatorial explosion mentioned on the beginning of this chapter we applied two heuristic rules. In the preliminary experiments (Ptaszynski et al., 2011), we found out that the most valuable (frequently appearing) patterns in language are up to six element long, thus we limited the scope of pattern extraction to $k \leq 6$. Therefore, the procedure of pattern generation will (1) generate up to six elements patterns, or (2) terminate at the point where no frequent patterns were found.

EVALUATION EXPERIMENT

Dataset Preprocessing and Feature Selection

The proposed method takes as an input sentences separated into elements (words, tokens, etc.). In original transcription of Japanese language (the language of applied dataset) spaces, like in English are not used. Therefore we needed to preprocess the dataset and make the sentences separable into elements. We did this in several ways to check how the preprocessing would influence the results. We used MeCab[2], a morphological analyzer for Japanese and CaboCha[3], a Japanese dependency structure analyzer, to preprocess the sentences from the dataset in the following ways.

- **Tokenization:** All words, punctuation marks, etc. are separated by spaces (later: TOK).
- **Lemmatization:** Like the above but the words are represented in their generic (dictionary) forms, or "lemmas" (later: LEM).
- **Parts of Speech:** Words are replaced with their representative parts of speech (later: POS).
- **Tokens With POS:** Both words and POS information is included in one element (later: TOK+POS).
- **Lemmas With POS:** Like the above but with lemmas instead of words (later: LEM+POS).
- **Chunks:** Larger sub-parts of sentences divided in grammatical clusters, such as noun phrase, verb phrase, predicates, etc., but without dependency relations (later: CHUNK).
- **Dependency Structure:** Same as above, but with information regarding in what relation a chunk is with previous one, the following one, and other chunks (later: DEP).
- **Chunks With Named Entities:** Chunks with added information on what named entities (private name of a person, organization, numericals, etc.) appear in the sentence. The information is provided by the dependency structure analyzer (later: CHUNK+NER).
- **Dependency Structure With Named Entities:** Both dependency relations and named entities are provided (later: DEP+NER).

Feature extraction from sentences is done automatically, according to procedure explained in section "Feature Extraction with Language Combinatorics." Next, language model is generated automatically using the extracted features. In this context, the dataset preprocessing methods represented above can be understood as feature selection preset for the experiment.

Five examples of preprocessing are represented in Table 2. Theoretically, the more generalized a sentence is, the less unique and frequent patterns it will produce, but the produced patterns will be more frequent. This can be explained by comparing tokenized sentence with its POS representation. For example, in the sentence from Table 2 we can see that a simple phrase *kimochi_ii hi* ("pleasant day") is be represented by a POS pattern as ADJ N. We can easily assume that there will be more ADJ N patterns than *kimochi_ii hi*, because many word combinations can be represented by this POS pattern. On the other hand, there are more words in the dictionary than POS labels. Therefore POS patterns will come in less variety but with higher occurrence frequency. By comparing the result of the classification using different preprocessing methods we can find out whether it is better to represent sentences as more generalized or as more specific.

Experiment Setup

The preprocessed original dataset provides nine separate training and test sets for the experiment (tokenized, POS-tagged, tokens with POS, lemmatized, lemmas with POS, chunks, dependency relations, chunks with named entities, dependency with named entities). The experiment was performed nine times, one time for each kind of preprocessing to choose the best option. For each version of the dataset a 10-fold cross validation was performed and the results were calculated using standard Precision, Recall, balanced F-score and Accuracy for each threshold within the whole threshold span. In one experiment 14 different versions of the proposed classifier are compared with 10-fold cross validation condition. Versions of the classifier represent combinations of weight calculation and pattern list modification explained in section "Weight Calculation," and are in order: PAT, PAT-0P, PAT-AMB, PAT-LA, PAT-LA-0P, PAT-LA-AMB, PAT-LOA, NGR, NGR-0P, NGR-AMB, NGR-LA, NGR-LA-0P, NGR-LA-AMB, NGR-LOA. Since the experiment was performed for nine different versions of preprocessing, we obtained overall number of 1260 experiment runs (9 datasets * 14 classifier versions in 10-fold cross-validation). There were several evaluation criteria. Firstly, we looked at which version of the algorithm achieved highest balanced F-score, and highest Accuracy within the threshold span. This is referred to as threshold optimization. However, theoretically, an algorithm could achieve its best score for one certain threshold, while for others it could perform poorly. Therefore we also looked at break-even points (BEP) of Precision and Recall. This shows which version of the algorithm is more balanced. Finally, we checked the statistical significance of the results. We used paired t-test because the classification results could represent only one of two classes (harmful or non-harmful). To choose the best version of the algorithm we compared separately the results achieved by each group of modifications, eg., "different pattern weight calculations", "pattern list modifications" and "patterns vs n-grams". We also compared the performance to previous methods, which we consider a baseline. This refers primarily to SO-PMI-IR based methods (Matsuba et al., 2011; Nitta et al., 2013; Ptaszynski et al., 2016), including the method described in previous chapter, which were based on the same data.

Table 2. Three examples of preprocessing of a sentence in Japanese; N = noun, PP = postpositional particle, ADV = adverb, ADJ = adjective, AUX = auxiliary verb, SYM = symbol, 1D, 2D, ... = depth of dependency relation, *0, *1, *2, ... = phrase number.

Sentence: 今日はなんて気持ちいい日なんだ!
Transcription in alphabet: *Kyōwanantekimochiiihinanda!*
Glosses: Today TOP what pleasant day COP EXCL
Translation: What a pleasant day it is today!

Preprocessing examples

–**Tokenization:** *Kyō wa nante kimochiii hi nanda !*
–**POS:** N PP ADV ADJ N AUX SYM
–**Tokens+POS:** *Kyō* [N] *wa*[PP] *nante*[ADV] *kimochi_ii*[ADJ] *hi*[N] *nanda*[AUX] *!*[SYM]
–**Chunks:** *Kyō wa nante kimochi_ii hi_nanda!*
–**Dependency relations:** *0 3D *Kyō wa* *1 2D *nante* *2 3D *kimochi_ii* *3 -1D *hi nanda!*

RESULTS AND DISCUSSION

We analyzed the results in a number of ways to obtain as objective perspective as possible.

Firstly, we analyzed the results for each feature set separately, to find out which weight calculation method and which pattern list modification achieved highest results for each set. We looked at the highest F-score and Accuracy. We also checked break-even point of Precision and Recall (BEP) for each version of the classifier. We also calculated statistical significance between all results within each feature set.

Secondly, we compared the results among all feature sets to find out whether there exists a stable pattern in results, e.g., if patterns were always better than n-grams, or if it is more effective to use all patterns, or only the unique ones, etc.

Following, we analyzed, whether the method works better on more generalized of more specific feature sets.

Finally, we calculated statistical significance between the best results of each feature set.

Lastly, we compared the best and the worst results of the proposed method to previous methods.

Results Separately for Each Feature Set

Tokenized Set

At first, we looked at the dataset preprocessed with the simplest method, namely, tokenization.

Highest achieved Precision was 0.861 and was obtained by both patterns and n-grams when zero-patterns were deleted from pattern lists. Second best Precision was achieved by pattern list containing all patterns/n-grams (0.858). However, when all ambiguous patterns were deleted, the highest achieved Precision suddenly dropped to 0.820. Awarding length usually caused drop in Precision. The results for best Precision were represented in Table 3.

The highest achieved F-score was 0.778 and was obtained by patterns when zero-patterns were deleted from pattern lists. Second best F-score was achieved by pattern list containing all patterns/n-grams (0.724). Deleting all ambiguous patterns caused drop in F-score to 0.690. Awarding length also caused drop in F-score. The results for best F-score were represented in Table 4.

The highest achieved Accuracy was 0.776 and was obtained by patterns when all ambiguous patterns were deleted from pattern lists. This stands in contradiction to the above results for best Fscore, however, second best Accuracy was achieved by pattern list containing all patterns/n-grams (0.766). Awarding length, similarly to above results, caused drop in Accuracy. The results for best Accuracy were represented in Table 5.

When it comes to statistical significance, differences between most results were statistically significant, meaning, they could not be considered as a matter of chance. Pairs which tended to be not statistically significant included those which differed only in one kind of characteristics, e.g., PAT-0P and NGR-0P, which were also two best scores for highest Precision and highest F-score (former). Results of T-test for F-scores and Accuracies among all system results for tokenized dataset were represented in Table 6.

Lemmatized Set

The second simplest way of data preprocessing, after tokenization, was lemmatization. In this process all declensed and conjugated words are simplified to their dictionary forms. Therefore, lemmatization provides less specific, thus less numerous, but more frequently appearing features. This makes lemmatization more generalized than tokenization.

The highest achieved Precision for lemmatized dataset was higher than for tokens, and reached 0.902 when patterns were used with length awarded weighting and zero-patterns deleted. Differently to tokenized dataset, where different weighting and pattern list modifications caused negative influence, for lemmas the influence was in most cases positive, especially when it comes to awarding length in weight calculation.

The highest achieved F-score for lemmatized dataset was also higher then for tokenized set, and reached 0.79 for n-grams. Highest scores of pattern-based

Table 3. Comparison of best Precision within the threshold span for each version of the classifier for tokenized dataset. Best classifier version within each preprocessing kind - highlighted in bold type font

	Highest Precision within threshold			
	Pr	Re	F1	Acc
PAT-ALL	0.858	0.242	0.377	0.610
PAT-0P	**0.861**	**0.249**	**0.387**	**0.614**
PAT-AMB	0.820	0.491	0.614	0.699
PAT-LA-0P	0.838	0.150	0.255	0.571
PAT-LA	0.839	0.143	0.244	0.568
PAT-LA-AMB	0.755	0.562	0.644	0.697
NGR-ALL	0.859	0.243	0.378	0.611
NGR-0P	**0.861**	**0.249**	**0.387**	**0.614**
NGR-AMB	0.820	0.491	0.614	0.699
NGR-LA	0.840	0.144	0.245	0.568
NGR-LA-0P	0.838	0.150	0.254	0.570
NGR-LA-AMB	0.754	0.563	0.645	0.697

Table 4. Comparison of best F-score within the threshold span for each version of the classifier for tokenized dataset. Best classifier version within each preprocessing kind - highlighted in bold type font. In case of identical results for F-score, the best score was optimized for Accuracy.

	Highest F-score within threshold			
	Pr	Re	F1	Acc
PAT-ALL	0.724	0.842	0.778	0.766
PAT-0P	**0.724**	**0.842**	**0.778**	**0.766**
PAT-AMB	0.690	0.889	0.777	0.751
PAT-LA-0P	0.697	0.796	0.743	0.73
PAT-LA	0.656	0.856	0.742	0.709
PAT-LA-AMB	0.666	0.826	0.738	0.712
NGR-ALL	0.723	0.842	0.778	0.766
NGR-0P	0.724	0.841	0.778	0.765
NGR-AMB	0.690	0.889	0.777	0.751
NGR-LA	0.654	0.855	0.741	0.708
NGR-LA-0P	0.696	0.796	0.743	0.730
NGR-LA-AMB	0.666	0.826	0.737	0.711

Table 5. Comparison of best Accuracy within the threshold span for each version of the classifier for tokenized dataset. Best classifier version within each preprocessing kind - highlighted in bold type font. In case of identical results for Accuracy, the best score was optimized for F-score.

	Highest Accuracy within threshold			
	Pr	Re	F1	Acc
PAT-ALL	0.724	0.842	0.778	0.766
PAT-0P	**0.785**	**0.718**	**0.750**	**0.766**
PAT-AMB	0.778	0.760	0.769	0.776
PAT-LA-0P	0.736	0.713	0.724	0.734
PAT-LA	0.740	0.708	0.723	0.735
PAT-LA-AMB	0.715	0.703	0.709	0.718
NGR-ALL	0.723	0.842	0.778	0.766
NGR-0P	0.784	0.718	0.749	0.766
NGR-AMB	0.777	0.759	0.768	0.776
NGR-LA	0.740	0.708	0.723	0.735
NGR-LA-0P	0.737	0.713	0.725	0.735
NGR-LA-AMB	0.714	0.702	0.708	0.717

Table 6. Results of t-test (p-values) for F-scores and Accuracies among all system results for tokenized dataset.

F-score	PAT--ALL	PAT--AMB	PAT--LA	PAT-LA--AMB	PAT--LA-0P	NGR--ALL	NGR--AMB	NGR--LA	NGR-LA--AMB	NGR--LA-0P	NGR--0P	PAT--0P
PAT-ALL		.000***	.002**	.002**	.002**	.920	.000***	.002**	.002**	.002**	.005**	.004**
PAT-AMB			.000***	.128	.000***	.000***	.068	.000***	.130	.000***	.000***	.000***
PAT-LA				.004**	.001***	.002**	.000***	.429	.004**	.001***	.003**	.003**
PAT-LA-AMB					.004**	.002**	.128	.004**	.023*	.004**	.002**	.002**
PAT-LA-0P						.002**	.000***	.001***	.004**	.147	.002**	.002**
NGR-ALL							.000***	.002**	.002**	.002**	.005**	.005**
NGR-AMB								.000***	.130	.000***	.000***	.000***
NGR-LA									.004**	.001***	.003**	.003**
NGR-LA-AMB										.004**	.002**	.002**
NGR-LA-0P											.002**	.002**
NGR-0P												.853
PAT-0P												

Accuracy												
PAT-ALL		.000***	.006**	.000***	.005**	.998	.000***	.006**	.000***	.005**	.001***	.001***
PAT-AMB			.000***	.272	.000***	.000***	.110	.000***	.265	.000***	.000***	.000***
PAT-LA				.000***	.000***	.006**	.000***	.697	.000***	.000***	.008**	.008**
PAT-LA-AMB					.000***	.000***	.268	.000***	.004**	.000***	.000***	.000***
PAT-LA-0P						.005**	.000***	.000***	.000***	.225	.006**	.006**
NGR-ALL							.000***	.006**	.000***	.004**	.001***	.001***
NGR-AMB								.000***	.261	.000***	.000***	.000***
NGR-LA									.000***	.000***	.009**	.009**
NGR-LA-AMB										.000***	.000***	.000***
NGR-LA-0P											.006**	.006**
NGR-0P												.802
PAT-0P												

$*p \leq 0.05, **p \leq 0.01, ***p \leq 0.001$

classifier ranged lower in general. Similarly to tokenized dataset, awarding length caused drop in highest achieved F-score. Also, deleting either zero-patterns or all ambiguous patterns/n-grams caused occasional drop in scores, indicating that such patterns usually contribute positively to classification with lemmas. The results for best F-score were represented in Table 8.

Results for the highest Accuracy within threshold confirm the above results for F-score. The highest result was achieved by n-grams, and reached 0.79. Here also pattern list and weighting modifications decreased the results in general. The results for best Accuracy were represented in Table 9.

The differences among all versions of the classifier were in most cases statistically significant, usually on 0.1% level. Similarly to tokenized dataset, the results, when not significant usually had only one difference, e.g., PAT-0P and NGR-0P, or NGR-AMB and NGR-LA-AMB. Unfortunately, version of the classifier which achieved the highest top scores, namely, NGR-ALL (using all ngrams in classification), did not reach statistical significance with pattern-based classifiers, which decreases the reliability of n-gram-based scores. The results of T-test (p-values) for F-scores and Accuracies among all system results for lemmatized dataset were represented in Table 10.

Table 7. Comparison of best Precision within the threshold span for each version of the classifier for lemmatized dataset. Best classifier version within each preprocessing kind - highlighted in bold type font.

	Highest Precision within threshold			
	Pr	Re	F1	Acc
PAT-ALL	0.871	0.276	0.419	0.627
PAT-0P	0.871	0.276	0.419	0.627
PAT-AMB	0.872	0.207	0.334	0.598
PAT-LA-0P	**0.902**	**0.208**	**0.338**	**0.602**
PAT-LA	0.872	0.293	0.438	0.633
PAT-LA-AMB	0.886	0.236	0.372	0.612
NGR-ALL	0.887	0.307	0.457	0.642
NGR-0P	0.886	0.329	0.48	0.651
NGR-AMB	0.810	0.597	0.687	0.735
NGR-LA	0.894	0.25	0.391	0.619
NGR-LA-0P	0.896	0.187	0.31	0.592
NGR-LA-AMB	0.807	0.609	0.694	0.738

Table 8. Comparison of best F-score within the threshold span for each version of the classifier for lemmatized dataset. Best classifier version within each preprocessing kind - highlighted in bold type font.

Highest F-score within threshold				
	Pr	Re	F1	Acc
PAT-ALL	0.715	0.82	0.764	0.753
PAT-0P	0.715	0.82	0.764	0.753
PAT-AMB	0.717	0.818	0.764	0.753
PAT-LA-0P	0.701	0.797	0.746	0.734
PAT-LA	0.714	0.811	0.76	0.749
PAT-LA-AMB	0.707	0.789	0.746	0.737
NGR-ALL	**0.713**	**0.885**	**0.79**	**0.77**
NGR-0P	0.713	0.885	0.79	0.769
NGR-AMB	0.713	0.864	0.781	0.763
NGR-LA	0.722	0.851	0.781	0.767
NGR-LA-0P	0.722	0.851	0.781	0.766
NGR-LA-AMB	0.724	0.818	0.768	0.758

Table 9. Comparison of best Accuracy within the threshold span for each version of the classifier for lemmatized dataset. Best classifier version within each preprocessing kind - highlighted in bold type font.

Highest Accuracy within threshold				
	Pr	Re	F1	Acc
PAT-ALL	0.765	0.724	0.744	0.756
PAT-0P	0.765	0.724	0.744	0.756
PAT-AMB	0.765	0.724	0.744	0.756
PAT-LA-0P	0.748	0.718	0.732	0.744
PAT-LA	0.763	0.717	0.740	0.753
PAT-LA-AMB	0.749	0.717	0.733	0.745
NGR-ALL	**0.787**	**0.781**	**0.784**	**0.790**
NGR-0P	0.785	0.783	0.784	0.789
NGR-AMB	0.759	0.786	0.772	0.773
NGR-LA	0.770	0.762	0.766	0.773
NGR-LA-0P	0.769	0.766	0.768	0.773
NGR-LA-AMB	0.755	0.771	0.763	0.766

Table 10. Results of t-test (p-values) for F-scores and Accuracies among all system results for lemmatized dataset.

F-score	PAT-ALL	PAT-AMB	PAT-LA	PAT-LA-AMB	PAT-LA-OP	NGR-ALL	NGR-AMB	NGR-LA	NGR-LA-AMB	NGR-LA-OP	NGR-OP	PAT-OP
PAT-ALL		.002**	.000***	.000***	.000***	.422	.001**	.001***	.001***	.001***	.222	.000***
PAT-AMB			.005**	.000***	.000***	.741	.001**	.001***	.001***	.001***	.421	.002**
PAT-LA				.000***	.000***	.803	.001**	.001**	.001***	.001**	.842	.000***
PAT-LA-AMB					.001***	.002**	.014*	.014*	.003**	.024*	.002**	.000***
PAT-LA-0P						.002**	.009**	.034*	.002**	.065	.003**	.000***
NGR-ALL							.002**	.001**	.001**	.001**	.005**	.422
NGR-AMB								.004**	.002**	.005**	.002**	.001**
NGR-LA									.002**	.001***	.001**	.001***
NGR-LA-AMB										.003**	.001**	.001***
NGR-LA-0P											.001**	.001***
NGR-0P												.222
PAT-0P												

Accuracy	PAT-ALL	PAT-AMB	PAT-LA	PAT-LA-AMB	PAT-LA-OP	NGR-ALL	NGR-AMB	NGR-LA	NGR-LA-AMB	NGR-LA-OP	NGR-OP	PAT-OP
PAT-ALL		.000***	.000***	.000***	.000***	.310	.002**	.004**	.000***	.002**	.443	.000***
PAT-AMB			.003**	.000***	.000***	.202	.003**	.009**	.000***	.004**	.296	.000***
PAT-LA				.000***	.000***	.087	.007**	.045*	.000***	.020*	.135	.000***
PAT-LA-AMB					.000***	.000***	.165	.001***	.421	.001***	.000***	.000***
PAT-LA-0P						.000***	.283	.001**	.224	.002**	.000***	.000***
NGR-ALL							.000***	.000***	.000***	.000***	.000***	.310
NGR-AMB								.008**	.000***	.013*	.000***	.002**
NGR-LA									.000***	.000***	.000***	.004**
NGR-LA-AMB										.000***	.000***	.000***
NGR-LA-0P											.000***	.002**
NGR-0P												.443
PAT-0P												

$*p \leq 0.05, **p \leq 0.01, ***p \leq 0.001$

POS-Tagged Set

Comparing to previous datasets, POS-tagging provides the most generalized way of preprocessing. A small number of features is extracted, however their occurrences are very high.

When it comes to comparison of the highest achieved scores, the highest Precision reached 0.934 (although for Recall = 0.031), however, all other compared measures were in general much lower than for tokenized, and lemmatized datasets, and reached at best 0.677 and 0.612, for F-score and Accuracy, respectively. This dataset also had the highest number of cases where differences between classifier versions were not statistically significant. There was also no consistency to which version of the classifier performs best for this dataset.

This could suggest that the classifier performs poorly for highly generalized datasets, or in practice, for low number of features, even if their occurrences are numerous.

Results for highest Precision, F-score and Accuracy were represented in Tables 11, 12 and 13. Results for T-test were represented in Table 14.

Table 11. Comparison of best Precision within the threshold span for each version of the classifier for POS-tagged dataset. Best classifier version within each preprocessing kind - highlighted in bold type font.

	Highest Precision within threshold			
	Pr	Re	F1	Acc
PAT-ALL	0.776	0.048	0.091	0.518
PAT-0P	0.776	0.048	0.091	0.518
PAT-AMB	0.796	0.019	0.037	0.507
PAT-LA-0P	0.761	0.114	0.198	0.539
PAT-LA	0.776	0.048	0.091	0.518
PAT-LA-AMB	0.758	0.119	0.205	0.540
NGR-ALL	0.917	0.022	0.042	0.510
NGR-0P	0.917	0.021	0.041	0.510
NGR-AMB	0.652	0.196	0.302	0.546
NGR-LA	**0.934**	**0.031**	**0.060**	**0.514**
NGR-LA-0P	0.910	0.032	0.062	0.514
NGR-LA-AMB	0.656	0.308	0.419	0.574

Table 12. Comparison of best F-score within the threshold span for each version of the classifier for POS-tagged dataset. Best classifier version within each preprocessing kind - highlighted in bold type font.

	Highest F-score within threshold			
	Pr	Re	F1	Acc
PAT-ALL	0.526	0.950	0.677	0.547
PAT-0P	0.526	0.950	0.677	0.547
PAT-AMB	**0.528**	**0.946**	**0.677**	**0.550**
PAT-LA-0P	0.524	0.952	0.676	0.543
PAT-LA	0.526	0.950	0.677	0.547
PAT-LA-AMB	0.526	0.949	0.677	0.547
NGR-ALL	0.518	0.959	0.672	0.533
NGR-0P	0.520	0.954	0.673	0.537
NGR-AMB	0.500	1.000	0.666	0.500
NGR-LA	0.528	0.935	0.675	0.551
NGR-LA-0P	0.530	0.930	0.675	0.552
NGR-LA-AMB	0.565	0.764	0.650	0.588

Table 13. Comparison of best Accuracy within the threshold span for each version of the classifier for POS-tagged dataset. Best classifier version within each preprocessing kind - highlighted in bold type font.

	Highest Accuracy within threshold			
	Pr	Re	F1	Acc
PAT-ALL	0.577	0.779	0.663	0.604
PAT-0P	0.577	0.779	0.663	0.604
PAT-AMB	0.578	0.776	0.663	0.605
PAT-LA-0P	0.639	0.461	0.536	0.600
PAT-LA	0.577	0.779	0.663	0.604
PAT-LA-AMB	0.640	0.463	0.537	0.600
NGR-ALL	**0.635**	**0.528**	**0.576**	**0.612**
NGR-0P	0.635	0.527	0.576	0.612
NGR-AMB	0.545	0.774	0.640	0.564
NGR-LA	0.624	0.539	0.578	0.607
NGR-LA-0P	0.626	0.540	0.580	0.609
NGR-LA-AMB	0.587	0.650	0.617	0.596

Table 14. Results of t-test (p-values) for F-scores and Accuracies among all system results for POS-tagged dataset.

F-score	PAT-ALL	PAT-AMB	PAT-LA	PAT-LA-AMB	PAT-LA-0P	NGR-ALL	NGR-AMB	NGR-LA	NGR-LA-AMB	NGR-LA-0P	NGR-0P	PAT-0P
PAT-ALL		.146	.000***	.009**	.009**	.086	.001***	.002**	.001**	.002**	.090	.000***
PAT-AMB			.146	.009**	.009**	.088	.001***	.002**	.001**	.002**	.093	.146
PAT-LA				.009**	.009**	.086	.001***	.002**	.001**	.002**	.090	.000***
PAT-LA-AMB					.076	.014*	.004**	.000***	.002**	.000***	.014*	.009**
PAT-LA-0P						.014*	.004**	.000***	.002**	.000***	.014*	.009**
NGR-ALL							.001**	.003**	.002**	.003**	.576	.086
NGR-AMB								.082	.005**	.092	.001**	.001***
NGR-LA									.014*	.007**	.003**	.002**
NGR-LA-AMB										.015*	.002**	.001**
NGR-LA-0P											.003**	.002**
NGR-0P												.090
PAT-0P												

Accuracy	PAT-ALL	PAT-AMB	PAT-LA	PAT-LA-AMB	PAT-LA-0P	NGR-ALL	NGR-AMB	NGR-LA	NGR-LA-AMB	NGR-LA-0P	NGR-0P	PAT-0P
PAT-ALL		.065	.000***	.000***	.000***	.501	.000***	.000***	.000***	.000***	.474	.000***
PAT-AMB			.065	.000***	.000***	.656	.000***	.000***	.000***	.000***	.629	.065
PAT-LA				.000***	.000***	.501	.000***	.000***	.000***	.000***	.474	.000***
PAT-LA-AMB					.152	.000***	.043*	.628	.000***	.845	.000***	.000***
PAT-LA-0P						.000***	.052	.729	.000***	.965	.000***	.000***
NGR-ALL							.000***	.000***	.000***	.000***	.854	.501
NGR-AMB								.055	.000***	.040*	.000***	.000***
NGR-LA									.001***	.002**	.000***	.000***
NGR-LA-AMB										.001***	.000***	.000***
NGR-LA-0P											.000***	.000***
NGR-0P												.474
PAT-0P												

$*p \leq 0.05, **p \leq 0.01, ***p \leq 0.001$

Tokenized Set With POS

Dataset containing both tokens and POS information provides a feature set more specific than the original tokenized dataset.

Precision score was better for this dataset and reached 0.89 when either all patterns or all n-grams were used. Further modifications only decreased the results, although for second best Precision, corresponding F-score and Accuracy were much higher. The results for best Precision were represented in Table 15.

For F-score as well as for Accuracy, the highest results were obtained when zero-patterns were deleted from pattern list, and reached 0.796 and 0.784, respectively. Using all patterns, as well as deleting all ambiguous patterns caused decrease in results. Other modifications also did not cause any improvement.

Unfortunately, many of T-test results indicated lack of statistical significance. For the two best classifier versions (PAT-0P, NGR-0P) the differences were usually significant only for cases with no weight modifications. The results of T-test (p-values) for F-scores and Accuracies among all system results for tokenized dataset with POS information were represented in Table 18.

Table 15. Comparison of best Precision within the threshold span for each version of the classifier for dataset containing tokens with POS information. Best classifier version within each preprocessing kind - highlighted in bold type font.

	Highest Precision within threshold			
	Pr	Re	F1	Acc
PAT-ALL	**0.890**	**0.336**	**0.487**	**0.647**
PAT-0P	0.885	0.342	0.494	0.649
PAT-AMB	0.873	0.417	0.565	0.678
PAT-LA-0P	0.868	0.121	0.212	0.551
PAT-LA	0.868	0.092	0.167	0.539
PAT-LA-AMB	0.837	0.434	0.572	0.675
NGR-ALL	**0.890**	**0.336**	**0.487**	**0.647**
NGR-0P	0.886	0.344	0.496	0.650
NGR-AMB	0.873	0.417	0.565	0.678
NGR-LA	0.868	0.092	0.167	0.539
NGR-LA-0P	0.868	0.121	0.212	0.551
NGR-LA-AMB	0.837	0.434	0.572	0.675

Table 16. Comparison of best F-score within the threshold span for each version of the classifier for dataset containing tokens with POS information. Best classifier version within each preprocessing kind - highlighted in bold type font.

	Highest F-score within threshold			
	Pr	Re	F1	Acc
PAT-ALL	0.754	0.840	0.795	0.783
PAT-0P	**0.756**	**0.839**	**0.796**	**0.784**
PAT-AMB	0.717	0.844	0.775	0.755
PAT-LA-0P	0.706	0.767	0.735	0.724
PAT-LA	0.700	0.775	0.736	0.722
PAT-LA-AMB	0.709	0.728	0.719	0.715
NGR-ALL	0.754	0.840	0.795	0.783
NGR-0P	**0.756**	**0.839**	**0.796**	**0.784**
NGR-AMB	0.717	0.844	0.775	0.755
NGR-LA	0.700	0.775	0.736	0.721
NGR-LA-0P	0.706	0.768	0.736	0.724
NGR-LA-AMB	0.709	0.728	0.719	0.715

Table 17. Comparison of best Accuracy within the threshold span for each version of the classifier for dataset containing tokens with POS information. Best classifier version within each preprocessing kind - highlighted in bold type font.

	Highest Accuracy within threshold			
	Pr	Re	F1	Acc
PAT-ALL	0.809	0.743	0.775	0.784
PAT-0P	**0.756**	**0.839**	**0.796**	**0.784**
PAT-AMB	0.741	0.809	0.774	0.763
PAT-LA-0P	0.736	0.708	0.722	0.727
PAT-LA	0.731	0.715	0.723	0.726
PAT-LA-AMB	0.718	0.710	0.714	0.715
NGR-ALL	0.809	0.744	0.775	0.784
NGR-0P	**0.756**	**0.839**	**0.796**	**0.784**
NGR-AMB	0.741	0.809	0.774	0.763
NGR-LA	0.731	0.715	0.723	0.726
NGR-LA-0P	0.735	0.707	0.721	0.726
NGR-LA-AMB	0.717	0.710	0.714	0.715

Table 18. Results of t-test (p-values) for F-scores and Accuracies among all system results for tokenized dataset with POS information.

F-score	PAT-ALL	PAT-AMB	PAT-LA	PAT-LA-AMB	PAT-LA-0P	NGR-ALL	NGR-AMB	NGR-LA	NGR-LA-AMB	NGR-LA-0P	NGR-0P	PAT-0P
PAT-ALL		.000***	.906	.128	.815	.583	.000***	.905	.128	.825	.001***	.001***
PAT-AMB			.000***	.005**	.000***	.530	.000***	.005**	.000***	.000***	.000***	.000***
PAT-LA				.031*	.005**	.905	.000***	.783	.031*	.018*	.956	.964
PAT-LA-AMB					.034*	.128	.005**	.031*	.315	.033*	.146	.145
PAT-LA-0P						.814	.000***	.005**	.034*	.218	.949	.941
NGR-ALL							.000***	.904	.128	.824	.001***	.001***
NGR-AMB								.000***	.005**	.000***	.000***	.000***
NGR-LA									.031*	.016*	.957	.965
NGR-LA-AMB										.033*	.146	.145
NGR-LA-0P											.958	.950
NGR-0P												.101
PAT-0P												

Accuracy	PAT-ALL	PAT-AMB	PAT-LA	PAT-LA-AMB	PAT-LA-0P	NGR-ALL	NGR-AMB	NGR-LA	NGR-LA-AMB	NGR-LA-0P	NGR-0P	PAT-0P
PAT-ALL		.000***	.074	.010*	.064	.577	.000***	.074	.010*	.066	.001**	.001**
PAT-AMB			.000***	.486	.000***	.000***	1.000	.000***	.487	.000***	.000***	.000***
PAT-LA				.005**	.001***	.074	.000***	.834	.005**	.002**	.093	.091
PAT-LA-AMB					.006**	.010*	.486	.005**	.575	.006**	.013*	.013*
PAT-LA-0P						.064	.000***	.001***	.006**	.048*	.081	.080
NGR-ALL							.000***	.074	.010*	.065	.002**	.002**
NGR-AMB								.000***	.487	.000***	.000***	.000***
NGR-LA									.005**	.002**	.093	.092
NGR-LA-AMB										.006**	.013*	.013*
NGR-LA-0P											.082	.081
NGR-0P												.208
PAT-0P												

$*p \leq 0.05, **p \leq 0.01, ***p \leq 0.001$

Lemmatized Set With POS

The dataset preprocessed to contain both lemmas and POS information (LEM+POS) is theoretically more generalized then TOK+POS, but more specific then tokenized only (TOK) or lemmatized only (LEM). The results for previous ways of preprocessing (TOK, LEM, POS) indicated, that lemmas alone, although being more generalized than tokens, were more effective. On the other hand, parts-of-speech, although providing even higher level of generalization, scored much lower. By combining lemmas with POS and comparing the results to TOK+POS we can evaluate, whether POS, although causing negative influence alone, could contribute positively to overall results, when they are combined with other features. From the results on TOK+POS we could hypothesize that there might be some improvement.

Best achieved Precision reached 0.956 and was the highest of all previous results for any dataset. This score was achieved by pattern-based dataset with all ambiguous patterns removed. However, both unmodified pattern- or n-gram-based classifier also achieved very high scores, 0.954 and 0.948, respectively. The results for best Precision were represented in Table 19.

Results for both best achieved F-score and Accuracy indicated similar tendencies, with n-gram-based unmodified classifier achieving F1=0.803 and A=0.808. These results confirm positive influence of lemmas comparing to simple tokens and further support contribution of POS information, but only when it is used with other features as well. The results for best F-score and Accuracy were represented in Tables 20 and 21, respectively.

T-test results for both F-score and Accuracy were in most cases either extremely statistically significant (p≤0.001) or very statistically significant (p≤0.01). The results of T-test for F-scores and Accuracies among all system results for lemmatized dataset with POS information were represented in Table 22.

Chunk-Separated Set

While tokenization and lemmatization divide sentence by words or morphemes, sentence parsing splits a sentence by unified meaningful chunks, thus usually consisting of more than one word. The simplest way of parsing is shallow parsing, or chunking, in which chunks are simply separated by spaces with no additional information provided on relations between the chunks.

Table 19. Comparison of best Precision within the threshold span for each version of the classifier for dataset containing lemmas with POS information. Best classifier version within each preprocessing kind - highlighted in bold type font.

Highest Precision within threshold			
	Pr	Re	F1	Acc
PAT-ALL	0.954	0.114	0.204	0.565
PAT-0P	0.954	0.114	0.204	0.565
PAT-AMB	**0.956**	**0.119**	**0.212**	**0.567**
PAT-LA-0P	0.929	0.200	0.330	0.602
PAT-LA	0.954	0.114	0.204	0.565
PAT-LA-AMB	0.929	0.209	0.341	0.606
NGR-ALL	0.948	0.233	0.374	0.619
NGR-0P	0.948	0.119	0.212	0.567
NGR-AMB	0.932	0.205	0.336	0.604
NGR-LA	0.922	0.197	0.325	0.600
NGR-LA-0P	0.923	0.167	0.283	0.587
NGR-LA-AMB	0.892	0.266	0.409	0.626

Table 20. Comparison of best F-score within the threshold span for each version of the classifier for dataset containing lemmas with POS information. Best classifier version within each preprocessing kind - highlighted in bold type font.

	Highest F-score within threshold			
	Pr	**Re**	**F1**	**Acc**
PAT-ALL	0.752	0.817	0.783	0.779
PAT-0P	0.752	0.817	0.783	0.779
PAT-AMB	0.759	0.813	0.785	0.782
PAT-LA-0P	0.725	0.809	0.765	0.756
PAT-LA	0.752	0.817	0.783	0.779
PAT-LA-AMB	0.732	0.805	0.766	0.760
NGR-ALL	**0.807**	**0.798**	**0.803**	**0.808**
NGR-0P	0.808	0.795	0.802	0.808
NGR-AMB	0.754	0.809	0.781	0.778
NGR-LA	0.733	0.794	0.763	0.756
NGR-LA-0P	0.720	0.825	0.769	0.757
NGR-LA-AMB	0.729	0.800	0.763	0.757

Table 21. Comparison of best Accuracy within the threshold span for each version of the classifier for dataset containing lemmas with POS information. Best classifier version within each preprocessing kind - highlighted in bold type font.

	Highest Accuracy within threshold			
	Pr	**Re**	**F1**	**Acc**
PAT-ALL	0.817	0.737	0.775	0.791
PAT-0P	0.817	0.737	0.775	0.791
PAT-AMB	0.818	0.733	0.773	0.790
PAT-LA-0P	0.757	0.765	0.761	0.765
PAT-LA	0.817	0.737	0.775	0.791
PAT-LA-AMB	0.762	0.759	0.761	0.766
NGR-ALL	**0.807**	**0.798**	**0.803**	**0.808**
NGR-0P	0.808	0.795	0.802	0.808
NGR-AMB	0.788	0.764	0.776	0.784
NGR-LA	0.783	0.738	0.760	0.770
NGR-LA-0P	0.776	0.760	0.768	0.775
NGR-LA-AMB	0.729	0.800	0.763	0.757

Table 22. Results of t-test for F-scores and Accuracies among all system results for lemmatized dataset with POS information.

F-score	PAT-ALL	PAT-AMB	PAT-LA	PAT-LA-AMB	PAT-LA-OP	NGR-ALL	NGR-AMB	NGR-LA	NGR-LA-AMB	NGR-LA-OP	NGR-OP	PAT-OP
PAT-ALL		.000***	.000***	.001***	.001***	.034*	.000***	.001***	.000***	.001***	.048*	.000***
PAT-AMB			.000***	.001***	.001***	.024*	.000***	.001**	.001***	.002**	.032*	.000***
PAT-LA				.001***	.001***	.034*	.000***	.001***	.000***	.001***	.048*	.000***
PAT-LA-AMB					.002**	.001***	.282	.001***	.000***	.001***	.001**	.001***
PAT-LA-OP						.001***	.340	.001***	.000***	.001***	.001**	.001***
NGR-ALL							.001***	.001**	.001***	.002**	.001**	.034*
NGR-AMB								.058	.038*	.002**	.001***	.000***
NGR-LA									.000***	.001***	.002**	.001***
NGR-LA-AMB										.000***	.001***	.000***
NGR-LA-OP											.003**	.001***
NGR-OP												.048*
PAT-OP												
Accuracy												
PAT-ALL		.002**	.000***	.000***	.000***	.018*	.000***	.000***	.000***	.001**	.027*	.000***
PAT-AMB			.002**	.000***	.000***	.012*	.000***	.001***	.000***	.002**	.016*	.002**
PAT-LA				.000***	.000***	.018*	.000***	.000***	.000***	.001*	.027*	.000***
PAT-LA-AMB					.000***	.000***	.098	.000***	.000***	.000***	.000***	.000***
PAT-LA-OP						.000***	.128	.000***	.000***	.000***	.000***	.000***
NGR-ALL							.000***	.000***	.000***	.001**	.003**	.018*
NGR-AMB								.010*	.019*	.000***	.000***	.000***
NGR-LA									.000***	.000***	.000***	.000***
NGR-LA-AMB										.000***	.000***	.000***
NGR-LA-OP											.001**	.001**
NGR-OP												.027*
PAT-OP												

$*p \leq 0.05, **p \leq 0.01, ***p \leq 0.001$

Chunking provides more generalized preprocessing than tokenization or lemmatization, but is less generalized then POS.

Highest achieved Precision was 0.875, which is higher than for tokens alone, but lower than for lemmas or POS. The results for best Precision were represented in Table 23.

Results for F-score and Accuracy were much lower than for all other sets, with F1=0.658 and A=0.640 (Tables 24 and 25, respectively). Similarly, the differences between the classifier versions were rarely statistically significant (Table 26).

Dependency Parsed Set

Dependency parsing of a sentence, or deep parsing, refers to splitting a sentence into chunks with their syntactic interrelations. It is more specific than chunking, however, unless really large dataset is in use, it often provides lower results than simple tokenization, due to small number of extracted frequent features to build a reliable language model.

Table 23. Comparison of best Precision within the threshold span for each version of the classifier for chunk-separated dataset. Best classifier version within each preprocessing kind - highlighted in bold type font.

	Highest Precision within threshold			
	Pr	Re	F1	Acc
PAT-ALL	0.852	0.109	0.194	0.548
PAT-0P	0.845	0.112	0.198	0.548
PAT-AMB	0.849	0.087	0.158	0.534
PAT-LA-0P	0.845	0.115	0.202	0.549
PAT-LA	0.851	0.110	0.195	0.548
PAT-LA-AMB	0.850	0.088	0.160	0.535
NGR-ALL	0.848	0.110	0.195	0.547
NGR-0P	0.873	0.071	0.131	0.532
NGR-AMB	0.808	0.107	0.188	0.541
NGR-LA	0.856	0.111	0.197	0.549
NGR-LA-0P	**0.875**	**0.072**	**0.133**	**0.533**
NGR-LA-AMB	0.819	0.106	0.188	0.541

Table 24. Comparison of best F-score within the threshold span for each version of the classifier for chunk-separated dataset. Best classifier version within each preprocessing kind - highlighted in bold type font.

	Highest F-score within threshold			
	Pr	Re	F1	Acc
PAT-ALL	0.490	1.000	0.658	0.490
PAT-0P	0.490	1.000	0.658	0.490
PAT-AMB	0.490	1.000	0.658	0.490
PAT-LA-0P	**0.490**	**1.000**	**0.658**	**0.490**
PAT-LA	0.490	1.000	0.658	0.490
PAT-LA-AMB	0.490	0.999	0.658	0.490
NGR-ALL	0.490	1.000	0.658	0.490
NGR-0P	0.490	1.000	0.658	0.490
NGR-AMB	0.490	1.000	0.658	0.490
NGR-LA	**0.490**	**1.000**	**0.658**	**0.490**
NGR-LA-0P	**0.490**	**1.000**	**0.658**	**0.490**
NGR-LA-AMB	0.490	0.999	0.658	0.490

Table 25. Comparison of best Accuracy within the threshold span for each version of the classifier for chunk-separated dataset. Best classifier version within each preprocessing kind - highlighted in bold type font.

	Highest Accuracy within threshold			
	Pr	Re	F1	Acc
PAT-ALL	0.656	0.587	0.620	0.638
PAT-0P	0.656	0.587	0.620	0.638
PAT-AMB	0.644	0.604	0.624	0.631
PAT-LA-0P	**0.658**	**0.589**	**0.622**	**0.640**
PAT-LA	0.655	0.587	0.619	0.638
PAT-LA-AMB	0.645	0.605	0.625	0.631
NGR-ALL	0.655	0.586	0.619	0.638
NGR-0P	0.657	0.586	0.620	0.639
NGR-AMB	0.606	0.635	0.620	0.613
NGR-LA	0.656	0.589	0.621	0.639
NGR-LA-0P	0.657	0.587	0.620	0.639
NGR-LA-AMB	0.606	0.637	0.621	0.613

Table 26. Results of t-test for F-scores and Accuracies among all system results for chunk-separated dataset.

F-score	PAT-ALL	PAT-AMB	PAT-LA	PAT-LA-AMB	PAT-LA-0P	NGR-ALL	NGR-AMB	NGR-LA	NGR-LA-AMB	NGR-LA-0P	NGR-0P	PAT-0P
PAT-ALL		.006**	.084	.005**	.002**	.187	.030*	.035*	.015*	.005**	.109	.002**
PAT-AMB			.007**	.045*	.015*	.005**	.215	.008**	.048*	.014*	.007**	.009**
PAT-LA				.005**	.002**	.003**	.034*	.083	.017*	.008**	.227	.012*
PAT-LA-AMB					.010**	.004**	.413	.006**	.079	.009**	.006**	.007**
PAT-LA-0P						.001***	.056	.002**	.026*	.255	.048*	.007**
NGR-ALL							.026*	.000***	.013*	.003**	.051	.002**
NGR-AMB								.036*	.044*	.055	.031*	.042*
NGR-LA									.018*	.011*	.372	.071
NGR-LA-AMB										.025*	.017*	.021*
NGR-LA-0P											.009***	.025*
NGR-0P												.940
PAT-0P												

Accuracy	PAT-ALL	PAT-AMB	PAT-LA	PAT-LA-AMB	PAT-LA-0P	NGR-ALL	NGR-AMB	NGR-LA	NGR-LA-AMB	NGR-LA-0P	NGR-0P	PAT-0P
PAT-ALL		.098	.342	.057	.000***	.000***	.126	.004**	.102	.000***	.002**	.000***
PAT-AMB			.113	.044*	.857	.026*	.151	.229	.111	.349	.986	.459
PAT-LA				.066	.000***	.000***	.132	.025*	.107	.000***	.003**	.000***
PAT-LA-AMB					.582	.015*	.199	.134	.147	.645	.696	.290
PAT-LA-0P						.000***	.277	.001***	.232	.012*	.641	.011*
NGR-ALL							.084	.000***	.067	.000***	.000***	.000***
NGR-AMB								.165	.117	.392	.276	.210
NGR-LA									.135	.001***	.017*	.063
NGR-LA-AMB										.331	.231	.173
NGR-LA-0P											.005**	.001***
NGR-0P												.058
PAT-0P												

$*p \leq 0.05, **p \leq 0.01, ***p \leq 0.001$

Results of our experiment confirmed this. While the highest Precision reached 0.868, best Fscore and Accuracy were the worst of all datasets, and reached F=0.658 and A=0.58, meaning that cyberbullying classification with the use of dependency parsing is close to random coin flipping. T-test results were also almost never statistically significant.

Results for highest Precision, F-score and Accuracy were represented in Tables 27, 28 and 29, respectively. Results for T-test were represented in Table 30.

Chunk-Separated Set With Named Entities

Named entities, such as private names of people, companies, dates, numericals, etc., provide additional level of generalization for analyzed sentence. We applied named entity recognition (NER) to shallow and deep parsing to find out how such additional generalization would influence the results.

The results were in general lower than for chunks alone, but higher than for dependency parsing.

Results for highest Precision, F-score and Accuracy were represented in Tables 31, 32 and 33, respectively. Results for T-test were represented in Table 34.

Table 27. Comparison of best Precision within the threshold span for each version of the classifier with dependency parsed dataset. Best classifier version within each preprocessing kind - highlighted in bold type font.

	Highest Precision within threshold			
	Pr	Re	F1	Acc
PAT-ALL	0.865	0.070	0.130	0.537
PAT-0P	0.865	0.070	0.130	0.537
PAT-AMB	0.860	0.069	0.129	0.537
PAT-LA-0P	0.866	0.071	0.131	0.537
PAT-LA	**0.868**	**0.071**	**0.131**	**0.537**
PAT-LA-AMB	0.860	0.069	0.129	0.537
NGR-ALL	0.865	0.071	0.130	0.537
NGR-0P	0.850	0.070	0.129	0.537
NGR-AMB	0.860	0.069	0.129	0.537
NGR-LA	0.865	0.070	0.130	0.537
NGR-LA-0P	0.862	0.069	0.129	0.537
NGR-LA-AMB	0.856	0.069	0.128	0.537

Table 28. Comparison of best F-score within the threshold span for each version of the classifier with dependency parsed dataset. Best classifier version within each preprocessing kind - highlighted in bold type font.

	Highest F-score within threshold			
	Pr	Re	F1	Acc
PAT-ALL	0.490	1.000	0.658	0.490
PAT-0P	0.490	1.000	0.658	0.490
PAT-AMB	0.490	1.000	0.658	0.490
PAT-LA-0P	**0.491**	**1.000**	**0.658**	**0.491**
PAT-LA	**0.491**	**1.000**	**0.658**	**0.491**
PAT-LA-AMB	**0.491**	**1.000**	**0.658**	**0.491**
NGR-ALL	0.490	1.000	0.658	0.490
NGR-0P	0.490	1.000	0.658	0.490
NGR-AMB	0.490	1.000	0.658	0.490
NGR-LA	**0.491**	**1.000**	**0.658**	**0.491**
NGR-LA-0P	**0.491**	**1.000**	**0.658**	**0.491**
NGR-LA-AMB	**0.491**	**1.000**	**0.658**	**0.491**

Table 29. Comparison of best Accuracy within the threshold span for each version of the classifier with dependency parsed dataset. Best classifier version within each preprocessing kind - highlighted in bold type font.

	Highest Accuracy within threshold			
	Pr	Re	F1	Acc
PAT-ALL	0.671	0.336	0.448	0.580
PAT-0P	0.671	0.336	0.448	0.580
PAT-AMB	0.659	0.340	0.448	0.574
PAT-LA-0P	**0.671**	**0.336**	**0.448**	**0.580**
PAT-LA	0.670	0.335	0.447	0.579
PAT-LA-AMB	0.659	0.340	0.449	0.574
NGR-ALL	0.671	0.336	0.448	0.580
NGR-0P	0.672	0.335	0.447	0.580
NGR-AMB	0.659	0.340	0.449	0.574
NGR-LA	0.671	0.336	0.448	0.580
NGR-LA-0P	0.672	0.335	0.448	0.580
NGR-LA-AMB	0.659	0.340	0.449	0.574

Table 30. Results of t-test for F-scores and Accuracies among all system results for dependency parsed dataset.

F-score	PAT-ALL	PAT-AMB	PAT-LA	PAT-LA-AMB	PAT-LA-0P	NGR-ALL	NGR-AMB	NGR-LA	NGR-LA-AMB	NGR-LA-0P	NGR-0P	PAT-0P
PAT-ALL		.176	.576	.238	.969	.000***	.184	.211	.180	.010**	.000***	.023*
PAT-AMB			.136	.057	.160	.108	.177	.154	.492	.240	.242	.219
PAT-LA				.186	.291	.186	.143	.862	.139	.016*	.025*	.062
PAT-LA-AMB					.218	.152	.221	.209	.000***	.318	.321	.294
PAT-LA-0P						.014*	.168	.462	.163	.011*	.019*	.045*
NGR-ALL							.113	.020*	.113	.000***	.000***	.000***
NGR-AMB								.161	.253	.253	.255	.231
NGR-LA									.157	.000***	.000***	.010*
NGR-LA-AMB										.240	.244	.222
NGR-LA-0P											.814	.533
NGR-0P												.354
PAT-0P												
Accuracy												
PAT-ALL		.600	.998	.516	.007**	.000***	.529	.149	.568	.036*	.136	.029*
PAT-AMB			.598	.000***	.818	.653	.003**	.631	.187	.790	.714	.673
PAT-LA				.514	.023*	.190	.528	.351	.566	.081	.260	.230
PAT-LA-AMB					.713	.566	.704	.543	.000***	.685	.615	.581
PAT-LA-0P						.048*	.728	.010*	.780	.403	.018*	.005**
NGR-ALL							.580	.591	.620	.142	.405	.475
NGR-AMB								.557	.165	.700	.629	.594
NGR-LA									.598	.058	.270	.235
NGR-LA-AMB										.751	.677	.638
NGR-LA-0P											.015*	.053
NGR-0P												.360
PAT-0P												

$*p \leq 0.05, **p \leq 0.01, ***p \leq 0.001$

Table 31. Comparison of best Precision within the threshold span for each version of the classifier for chunks with NER. Best classifier version within each preprocessing kind - highlighted in bold type font.

	Highest Precision within threshold			
	Pr	Re	F1	Acc
PAT-ALL	0.637	0.165	0.262	0.546
PAT-0P	0.637	0.167	0.265	0.546
PAT-AMB	0.644	0.199	0.304	0.551
PAT-LA-0P	0.540	0.783	0.639	0.545
PAT-LA	0.592	0.698	0.641	0.543
PAT-LA-AMB	0.546	0.761	0.635	0.542
NGR-ALL	**0.768**	**0.242**	**0.368**	**0.586**
NGR-0P	0.749	0.251	0.376	0.585
NGR-AMB	0.724	0.186	0.297	0.558
NGR-LA	0.736	0.252	0.375	0.582
NGR-LA-0P	0.730	0.270	0.395	0.585
NGR-LA-AMB	0.644	0.209	0.315	0.552

Table 32. Comparison of best F-score within the threshold span for each version of the classifier for chunks with NER. Best classifier version within each preprocessing kind - highlighted in bold type font.

Highest F-score within threshold				
	Pr	Re	F1	Acc
PAT-ALL	0.551	0.902	0.684	0.575
PAT-0P	0.552	0.903	0.685	0.577
PAT-AMB	0.541	0.913	0.680	0.565
PAT-LA-0P	0.508	0.964	0.666	0.511
PAT-LA	0.507	0.984	0.669	0.515
PAT-LA-AMB	0.508	0.967	0.666	0.513
NGR-ALL	**0.563**	**0.879**	**0.686**	**0.603**
NGR-0P	0.560	0.864	0.680	0.599
NGR-AMB	0.554	0.851	0.671	0.587
NGR-LA	0.579	0.820	0.678	0.616
NGR-LA-0P	0.546	0.904	0.681	0.583
NGR-LA-AMB	0.523	0.906	0.664	0.548

Table 33. Comparison of best Accuracy within the threshold span for each version of the classifier for chunks with NER. Best classifier version within each preprocessing kind - highlighted in bold type font.

Highest Accuracy within threshold				
	Pr	Re	F1	Acc
PAT-ALL	0.596	0.668	0.630	0.602
PAT-0P	0.598	0.670	0.632	0.603
PAT-AMB	0.593	0.708	0.645	0.602
PAT-LA-0P	0.540	0.783	0.639	0.545
PAT-LA	0.592	0.698	0.641	0.543
PAT-LA-AMB	0.546	0.761	0.635	0.542
NGR-ALL	**0.659**	**0.647**	**0.653**	**0.655**
NGR-0P	0.655	0.646	0.650	0.651
NGR-AMB	0.622	0.568	0.594	0.613
NGR-LA	0.625	0.596	0.610	0.623
NGR-LA-0P	0.626	0.605	0.616	0.625
NGR-LA-AMB	0.588	0.663	0.624	0.603

Table 34. Results of t-test for F-scores and Accuracies among all system results for dataset separated by chunks with NER.

F-score	PAT-ALL	PAT-AMB	PAT-LA	PAT-LA-AMB	PAT-LA-0P	NGR-ALL	NGR-AMB	NGR-LA	NGR-LA-AMB	NGR-LA-0P	NGR-0P	PAT-0P
PAT-ALL		.006**	.021*	.021*	.021*	.017*	.051	.153	.127	.599	.017*	.016*
PAT-AMB			.026*	.026*	.025*	.010*	.018*	.020*	.339	.073	.010**	.008**
PAT-LA				.047*	.088	.004**	.003**	.009**	.009**	.012*	.004**	.021*
PAT-LA-AMB					.088	.004**	.003**	.010**	.010**	.013*	.004**	.022*
PAT-LA-0P						.004**	.003**	.010**	.009**	.012*	.004**	.021*
NGR-ALL							.027*	.008**	.005**	.005**	.046*	.015*
NGR-AMB								.026*	.002**	.008**	.027*	.041*
NGR-LA									.013*	.000***	.007**	.099
NGR-LA-AMB										.030*	.004**	.142
NGR-LA-0P											.004**	.438
NGR-0P												.015*
PAT-0P												

Accuracy	PAT-ALL	PAT-AMB	PAT-LA	PAT-LA-AMB	PAT-LA-0P	NGR-ALL	NGR-AMB	NGR-LA	NGR-LA-AMB	NGR-LA-0P	NGR-0P	PAT-0P
PAT-ALL		.911	.029*	.026*	.031*	.031*	.010**	.002**	.000***	.000***	.028*	.046*
PAT-AMB			.023*	.021*	.025*	.033*	.011*	.003**	.000***	.000***	.031*	.559
PAT-LA				.028*	.063	.003**	.000***	.002**	.000***	.001***	.003**	.028*
PAT-LA-AMB					.214	.003**	.001***	.003**	.000***	.001***	.003**	.025*
PAT-LA-0P						.004**	.001***	.003**	.000***	.001***	.003**	.030*
NGR-ALL							.462	.334	.392	.863	.374	.034*
NGR-AMB								.520	.456	.659	.497	.012*
NGR-LA									.866	.000***	.345	.002**
NGR-LA-AMB										.089	.403	.000***
NGR-LA-0P											.921	.000***
NGR-0P												.031*
PAT-0P												

$*p \leq 0.05, **p \leq 0.01, ***p \leq 0.001$

Dependency Parsed Set With Named Entities

When it comes to dependency parsing supported with named entity recognition, the results were in general lower than for chunks with NER, but higher than for dependency parsing. The differences between the results were also more often statistically significant.

This suggests, that named entities, even for not very big datasets, contribute positively to dependency parsing-based classification, although the contribution is not strong enough to make the classification much better than random guessing.

Results for highest Precision, F-score and Accuracy were represented in Tables 35, 36 and 37, respectively. Results for T-test were represented in Table 38.

Table 35. Comparison of best Precision within the threshold span for each version of the classifier for dependency parsed set with NER. Best classifier version within each preprocessing kind - highlighted in bold type font.

Highest Precision within threshold				
	Pr	Re	F1	Acc
PAT-ALL	0.529	0.160	0.246	0.513
PAT-0P	0.547	0.167	0.256	0.516
PAT-AMB	0.611	0.185	0.284	0.531
PAT-LA-0P	0.513	0.805	0.627	0.529
PAT-LA	0.513	0.805	0.627	0.528
PAT-LA-AMB	0.518	0.507	0.513	0.527
NGR-ALL	0.699	0.100	0.174	0.521
NGR-0P	0.688	0.101	0.176	0.520
NGR-AMB	0.619	0.216	0.320	0.536
NGR-LA	**0.718**	**0.010**	**0.020**	**0.513**
NGR-LA-0P	0.708	0.010	0.019	0.513
NGR-LA-AMB	0.647	0.196	0.301	0.536

Table 36. Comparison of best F-score within the threshold span for each version of the classifier for dependency parsed set with NER. Best classifier version within each preprocessing kind - highlighted in bold type font.

Highest F-score within threshold				
	Pr	Re	F1	Acc
PAT-ALL	0.500	0.983	0.662	0.509
PAT-0P	0.499	0.980	0.661	0.508
PAT-AMB	0.490	1.000	0.658	0.490
PAT-LA-0P	0.499	0.982	0.662	0.509
PAT-LA	0.499	0.982	0.662	0.509
PAT-LA-AMB	0.490	0.999	0.657	0.490
NGR-ALL	0.500	0.981	0.662	0.509
NGR-0P	**0.500**	**0.982**	**0.663**	**0.510**
NGR-AMB	0.490	1.000	0.658	0.490
NGR-LA	0.500	0.981	0.662	0.509
NGR-LA-0P	0.500	0.981	0.662	0.509
NGR-LA-AMB	0.490	0.999	0.657	0.490

Table 37. Comparison of best Accuracy within the threshold span for each version of the classifier for dependency parsed set with NER. Best classifier version within each preprocessing kind - highlighted in bold type font.

	Highest Accuracy within threshold			
	Pr	**Re**	**F1**	**Acc**
PAT-ALL	0.519	0.766	0.618	0.534
PAT-0P	0.519	0.769	0.620	0.535
PAT-AMB	0.611	0.185	0.284	0.531
PAT-LA-0P	0.513	0.805	0.627	0.529
PAT-LA	0.513	0.805	0.627	0.528
PAT-LA-AMB	0.518	0.507	0.513	0.527
NGR-ALL	0.547	0.615	0.579	0.556
NGR-0P	**0.551**	**0.617**	**0.582**	**0.559**
NGR-AMB	0.533	0.512	0.522	0.540
NGR-LA	0.548	0.614	0.579	0.557
NGR-LA-0P	0.549	0.616	0.581	0.558
NGR-LA-AMB	0.536	0.516	0.526	0.543

Table 38. Results of t-test for F-scores and Accuracies among all system results for dependency parsed dataset with NER.

F-score	PAT-ALL	PAT-AMB	PAT-LA	PAT-LA-AMB	PAT-LA-0P	NGR-ALL	NGR-AMB	NGR-LA	NGR-LA-AMB	NGR-LA-0P	NGR-0P	PAT-0P
PAT-ALL		.444	.063	.515	.063	.015*	.056	.021*	.079	.023*	.019*	.019*
PAT-AMB			.000***	.017*	.000***	.672	.005**	.735	.007**	.786	.718	.378
PAT-LA				.008**	.246	.019*	.000***	.018*	.000***	.020*	.021*	.072
PAT-LA-AMB					.007**	.216	.004**	.224	.004**	.239	.230	.557
PAT-LA-0P						.019*	.000***	.018*	.000***	.020*	.021*	.072
NGR-ALL							.353	.093	.458	.014*	.000***	.015*
NGR-AMB								.277	.002**	.251	.323	.048*
NGR-LA									.373	.005**	.506	.019*
NGR-LA-AMB										.340	.422	.067
NGR-LA-0P											.098	.022*
NGR-0P												.018*
PAT-0P												

Accuracy	PAT-ALL	PAT-AMB	PAT-LA	PAT-LA-AMB	PAT-LA-0P	NGR-ALL	NGR-AMB	NGR-LA	NGR-LA-AMB	NGR-LA-0P	NGR-0P	PAT-0P
PAT-ALL		.045*	.010*	.381	.009**	.001**	.000***	.001***	.000***	.001***	.001***	.065
PAT-AMB			.003**	.042*	.002**	.883	.000***	.955	.000***	.979	.979	.079
PAT-LA				.036*	.356	.001***	.000***	.001***	.000***	.001***	.001***	.008**
PAT-LA-AMB					.034*	.584	.000***	.533	.000***	.495	.496	.484
PAT-LA-0P						.001***	.000***	.001***	.000***	.001***	.001***	.007**
NGR-ALL							.017*	.079	.006**	.004**	.005**	.001***
NGR-AMB								.023*	.002**	.035*	.037*	.000***
NGR-LA									.008**	.019*	.307	.001***
NGR-LA-AMB										.014*	.015*	.000***
NGR-LA-0P											.999	.001***
NGR-0P												.001***
PAT-0P												

$*p \leq 0.05, **p \leq 0.01, ***p \leq 0.001$

Table 39. Break-even points for all feature sets and all classifier versions

	TOK	LEM	POS	TOK +POS	LEM +POS	CHUNK	DEP	CHUNK +NER	DEP +NER
PAT	0.761	0.751	0.613	0.785	0.781	**0.633**	0.566	0.603	0.510
PAT-0P	0.763	0.751	0.613	**0.786**	0.781	0.632	0.551	0.605	0.512
PAT-AMB	**0.770**	0.751	0.613	0.764	0.782	0.629	**0.591**	0.603	0.514
PAT-LA	0.729	0.748	0.613	0.726	0.781	0.632	0.568	--	0.505
PAT-LA-0P	0.729	0.737	0.596	0.726	0.760	**0.633**	0.549	--	0.505
PAT-LA-AMB	0.711	0.737	0.594	0.715	0.761	0.629	**0.591**	--	0.516
NGR	0.761	**0.784**	**0.614**	0.785	**0.802**	0.632	0.566	**0.655**	0.547
NGR-0P	0.762	**0.784**	0.613	**0.786**	**0.802**	0.632	0.551	0.652	**0.548**
NGR-AMB	**0.770**	0.767	0.570	0.764	0.777	0.612	**0.591**	0.610	0.526
NGR-LA	0.729	0.767	0.605	0.726	0.762	**0.633**	0.551	0.619	0.546
NGR-LA-0P	0.729	0.768	0.607	0.726	0.769	0.631	0.559	0.622	**0.548**
NGR-LA-AMB	0.711	0.762	0.596	0.715	0.750	0.613	0.589	0.589	0.529

Break-Even Point Analysis

Except detailed analysis for each dataset, we also looked at the results from a wider perspective.

One of the popular methods of evaluation in text classification studies has been estimation of a break-even point, or BEP. It is a cross point of Precision and Recall, where both those scores (and F-score in result) are in equality, meaning that the classifier is the most balanced. The higher the BEP, the more balanced the classifier can be considered.

We calculated BEP for all versions of the proposed classifier. The results were represented in Table 39. Since versions with weight modified by awarding both pattern length and occurrence rarely obtained BEP within threshold range, we excluded them from further analysis.

In the analysis we looked at four things, namely, 1) which classifier version got the highest BEP, 2) which classifier version usually got the highest BEP for different dataset preprocessing, 3) which preprocessing usually provided highest BEP, and 4) what was the highest achieved BEP, and by which dataset/classifier combination.

When it comes to classifier version most often achieving top scores, although often pattern-based and n-gram-based classifiers achieved similar, or even the same BEP scores, n-grams more often achieved the highest score. Moreover, the highest score of all was also achieved by n-gram-based classifier, and reached P=R=F1=0.802.

When it comes to dataset preprocessing method that usually scored highest, it was the lemmatized dataset combined with part-of-speech information. The highest score of all, mentioned above was also achieved by this feature set.

Also, clustering the dataset preprocessing methods into more generalized (POS, CHUNK, DEP, CHUNK+NER, DEP+NER, with BEP scores below 70%) and more specific (TOK, LEM, TOK+POS, LEM+POS, with BEP scores above 70%), provides a meaningful insight. The classifier usually performs better on more specific feature sets. In other words, the method provides better results when it can extract large number of features, even if their occurrence is not very high.

Although tokens with POS were the most numerous, the fact that lemmas with POS achieved the highest result needs to be addressed. Lemmatizing a sentence means that declensed and conjugated forms of words are unified. This makes it not only easier to extract frequent patterns, but is also advantageous in classification, since a pattern consisting of dictionary word forms applied to also lemmatized test data has much broader coverage. This provides the optimal setting for a classifier to use multiple specific features on the one hand, but on the other hand also be generalized to the extent allowing it to capture a broad range of cases.

Comparison Between Feature Sets

Apart from analyzing BEPs, we also compared the highest achieved F-scores for each dataset. These two evaluation measures rarely go together, since it would be difficult to have the highest F-score in the place of BEP. However, we can see which of the best achieved F-scores is closest to BEP. We can also follow the tendencies in

Figure 2. Best F-scores for each dataset preprocessing, ordered from left to right, with corresponding Precision, Recall and Accuracy. Classifier version that achieved the score - in brackets.

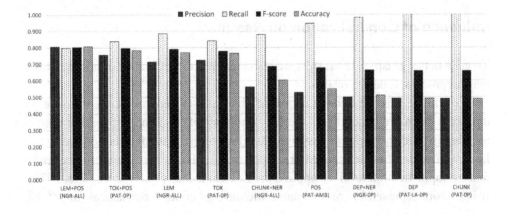

results and check if they correlate between the two evaluation measures. The results were represented in Figure 2. We ordered the datasets by their highest F-score from left to right.

The best score was achieved by lemmatization with POS information. The results was F1=0.803 with P=0.807, R=0.798, and A=0.808. This confirms the winning setting for BEP, with nearly identical F-score (0.802).

Interestingly, while the winning settings showed high consistency between Precision and Recall, close to BEP, for other dataset preprocessing settings, the lower was the F-score, the wider was also the gap between Precision and Recall. This is meaningful not only for the fact that the F-score, and therefore the general performance, of such a dataset is lower, but also provides further insight into the influence of generalization on results. Here, similarly to BEPs, the results can be clustered into two groups: with a small gap between P and R, and with a wide gap. This grouping is the same as for BEP analysis.

When it comes to the question whether it is more useful to use pattern- of n-gram-based classifier, although the very best score was achieved by n-grams, both settings appeared as the highest interchangeably. For example, second best was pattern-based classifier using pattern list with zero-patterns deleted, which achieved F1=0.796, P=0.756, R=0.839, and A=0.784. Third best was n-gram based classifier, fourth - again - patterns, etc. This suggests that we need to perform more experiments, most desirably on a wider threshold span to answer this question.

The most optimal classifier settings were the unmodified one, or the one with zero-patterns deleted. This suggests, that, although ambiguous patterns appear both in cyberbullying as well as in normal messages, it is more effective to use then in classification. This is an interesting insight, since, in previous research it has been often considered that only words/patterns that are specifically characteristic to cyberbullying should be used. For example, Fujii et al. (2010) refereed to them as "gray words/patterns" in comparison to "black words/patterns" appearing only in harmful messages and opted for disregarding gray words as noise.

Influence of Generalization on Results

To get a better grasp on the results we also analyzed the influence of how a dataset was preprocessed on the results.

To achieve this we needed a quantifiable dataset generalization measure. A dataset is the more generalized, the fewer number of frequently appearing unique features is used in its preprocessing. Therefore to estimate dataset generalization level we decided to calculate feature sophistication level. As the exact measure of feature sophistication level we applied the Lexical Density (LD) score (Ure, 1971). It is a score representing an estimated measure of content per lexical units for a

Table 40. Analysis of influence of dataset generalization on results

Dataset Preprocessing	No. of unique unigrams	No. of all unigrams	Feature Density	Highest achieved F-score	Highest unmodified F-score	BEP
DEP	12802	13957	0.917	0.658	0.658	0.591
DEP+NER	12160	13956	0.871	0.663	0.662	0.548
CHUNK	11389	13960	0.816	0.658	0.658	0.633
CHUNK+NER	10657	13872	0.768	0.686	0.684	0.655
TOK+POS	6565	34874	0.188	0.796	0.795	0.786
TOK	6464	36234	0.178	0.778	0.778	0.770
LEM+POS	6227	36426	0.171	0.803	0.783	0.802
LEM	6103	36412	0.168	0.790	0.764	0.784
POS	13	26650	0.000	0.677	0.677	0.614

(Left axis: Feature sophistication — high → low)

	unique 1ngr with			FD with		
	F1	F1-unmod.	BEP	F1	F1-unmod.	BEP
Pearson Correlation Coefficient (p-value)	-0.450 (p=0.224)	-0.453 (p=0.221)	-0.431 (p=0.247)	-0.735 (p=0.0242)	-0.736 (p=0.024)	-0.706 (p=0.0336)
with statistical significance (p-value)		F1 & BEP 0.9681 (p=0.00002)			F1-unmod. & BEP 0.9595 (p=0.00004)	

given corpus, and is calculated as the number of all unique words from the corpus divided by the number of all words in the corpus. However, since in our research we use a variety of different features, not only words (tokens), and the LD can vary depending on which features or feature combinations were used, we will further call this measure Feature-based Lexical Density, or shortly, Feature Density (FD).

After calculating FD for all used datasets we calculated Pearson's correlation coefficient (ρ- value) to see if there is any correlation between dataset generalization (FD) and the results. Pearson's coefficient can achieve scores from 1.0 (meaning there is a perfect positive correlation), through 0.0 (no correlation) to -1.0 (perfect negative correlation).

As the results we used the highest achieved F-scores. However, since the highest overall F-scores were sometimes achieved by different versions of the classifier (all patterns, or zero-patterns deleted; with length awarded, or not, etc.), we also used an unmodified version of the classifier (PAT-ALL). As an equivalent set of results we also used BEPs. Finally, we verified whether the correlations were statistically significant.

The first intuition about the correlation of dataset generalization with the results was that the less unique features are used in its preprocessing the lower the results would be. However, there was no correlation between unique unigrams of datasets and the overall results.

On the other hand, Feature Density score revealed an interesting correlation. There was a somewhat strong negative correlation (around -0.7) between the results and FD. This means that the results are better when the feature density is low. The correlation was not ideal due to the fact that the preprocessing method resulting in the lowest FD (POS-tagged dataset) achieved some of the lowest results. Interestingly, preprocessing methods resulting in very high FD (dependency parsing, etc.) also achieved similarly low results. This could suggest that there could be an even better way of preprocessing.

For the given datasets the scores are growing along with decreasing FD, until the lowest FD is reached, which also obtained low results. Therefore in the future we plan to use the FD measure to find a preprocessing method with optimal Feature Density, resulting in even better results.

The analysis of influence of dataset generalization on results is represented in Table 40.

Statistical Significance of Results

As a final step in analysis of results of the proposed method, we analyzed statistical significance of the highest achieved F-scores for each dataset preprocessing. As a measure of significance we used Student's paired T-test, since the results represented either one of two sides (cyberbullying/harmful or non-harmful), and we compared all pairs of optimized methods (that achieved the highest F-scores for the certain dataset). Results of T-test for best F-scores for each dataset was represented in Table 41. We were most interested in how the best method (LEM+POS/NGR-ALL) compared to other methods, especially the worst ones. The worst methods (based on chunking, dependency parsing and only POS), always differed significantly with better methods (based on tokens, lemmas and those combined with POS). Usually the difference was very significant ($p \leq 0.01$), or even extremely significant ($p \leq 0.001$). There were some cases, where the difference did not reach significance (eg., CHUNK/PAT-0P vs. LEM+POS/NGR-ALL), which indicates we need to perform further experiments on wider threshold span to obtain more result samples for comparison.

Table 41. Results of T-test for best F-scores for each dataset

	TOK+POS (PAT-0P)	LEM (NGR-ALL)	TOK (PAT-0P)	CHUNK+NER (NGR-ALL)	POS (PAT-AMB)	DEP+NER (NGR-0P)	DEP (PAT-LA-0P)	CHUNK (PAT-0P)
LEM+POS (NGR-ALL)	0.0005 ***	0.0284 *	0.0353 *	0.3062	0.0028 **	0.0878	0.0001 ***	0.1416
TOK+POS (PAT-0P)		0.7225	0.091	0.0035 **	0.0004 ***	0.4689	0.0001 ***	0.0001 ***
LEM (NGR-ALL)			0.0214 *	0.0102 *	0.0031 *	0.5168	0.0001 ***	0.0018 **
TOK (PAT-0P)				0.0576	0.0027 **	0.2423	0.0001 ***	0.0018 **
CHUNK+NER (NGR-ALL)					0.003 **	0.0329 *	0.0001 ***	0.0004 ***
POS (PAT-AMB)						0.002 **	0.0213 *	0.0091 **
DEP+NER (NGR-0P)							0.0001 ***	0.0013 **
DEP (PAT-LA-0P)								0.0001 ***

$*p \leq 0.05, **p \leq 0.01, ***p \leq 0.001$

Comparison With Previous Methods

After specifying optimal settings for the proposed method, we compared it to previous methods. In the comparison we used the methods proposed in Matsuba et al., (2011) and Nitta et al. (2013) and their most recent improvement in Ptaszynski et al. (2016), all of which were explained and presented together in previous Chapter. Moreover, since these methods extract cyberbullying relevance values from the Web (in particular Yahoo! API), apart from comparison to the reported results we also repeated their experiment to find out how the performance of the Web-based method changed during the years. The details on the re-evaluation experiment were explained in previous Chapter. Finally, to make the comparison more fair, we compared both best and worst results of the method proposed here. As the evaluation metrics we used the same one used in the previous research, namely, area under the curve (AUC) on the graph showing Precision and Recall together. The results were represented in Figure 3.

The highest overall results when it comes to AUC were obtained by the best settings of the proposed method (based on all n-grams and normalized feature weight). Although the method starts low, it quickly reaches over 95% of Precision and keeps this score even around 60% of Recall. Moreover, even when the method loses Precision, the loss is not sudden or steep, but decreases slowly, keeping a high Precision around 70% even when Recall reaches 90%. This method also outperformed all of the previous methods.

Figure 3. Comparison between the proposed method (best and worst performance) and previous methods.

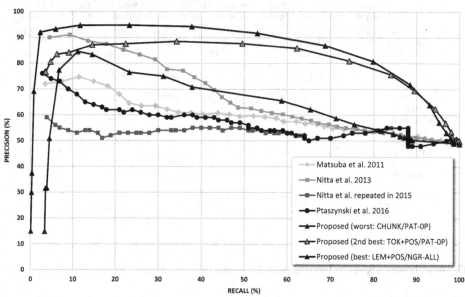

The second-best method (tokens with POS, all patterns, no weight modification) starts from a high 77% and also retains the Precision between 80% and 90% for most of the threshold. Although the highest originally reported Precision score (Nitta et al., 2013) was better than this second-best, the performance of that previous method quickly decreased due to quick drop in Precision for higher thresholds. What is important, even the worst method proposed here (based on separation by chunks with zero-patterns deleted) was still better then all other previous research except the original ones reported in 2013.

Finally, while the numerical results were in favor of the proposed approach, we also wanted to know to what extent the patterns automatically recognized by the proposed method cover the manually selected seed words in the previous research (Matsuba et al., 2010, 2011; Nitta et al., 2013). The comparison of the extracted patterns with seed word list applied in previous research revealed that all seed words applied in previous methods appeared in the list of patterns automatically extracted by the proposed method. This can be interpreted as follows. Firstly, the official governmental definition of cyberbullying (Ministry of Education, Culture, Sports, Science and Technology, 2008) and the intuition of researchers, on which previous approaches were mostly based, were generally correct. Secondly, using the automatically extracted patterns it could be possible to improve previous approaches in the future.

CONCLUSION AND FUTURE WORK

In this chapter we proposed a novel method for automatic detection of Internet forum entries that contain cyberbullying (CB). The proposed method applies a combinatorial algorithm, resembling brute force search algorithms, in automatic extraction of sophisticated sentence patterns, and used those patterns in text classification of CB entries. We tested the method on actual CB data obtained from Human Rights Center. We performed experiments on nine different feature sets. The settings that came out as optimal consisted of word lemmas with part-of-speech information. The results showed the proposed method outperformed all previous methods. Moreover, even the worst version of the proposed method achieved higher scores than previous methods. Apart from achieving much better performance, the proposed method was also more efficient as it requires minimal human effort.

For the near future we consider the following paths of further development of this particular method. To improve the detection method itself, we plan to apply different ways of dataset preprocessing to find out whether the performance can be further improved and to what extent. We have found out that too few highly generalized features (such as parts-of-speech alone), resulting in low Feature Density (FD), as well as too much of over-specific features (sentence chunks with dependency relations), resulting in very high Feature Density, cause similarly low performance. On the other hand, feature set that is to some extent generalized but also plentiful (lemmas with POS) resulting in not-too-high and not-too-low FD, achieves the highest scores. We will pursue this path to find out optimal FD for the applied dataset, and for the proposed method in general.

REFERENCES

Cambria, E., & Hussain, A. (2012). *Sentic Computing: Techniques, Tools, and Applications*. Dordrecht, The Netherlands: Springer. doi:10.1007/978-94-007-5070-8

Covington, M. A. (2001). A fundamental algorithm for dependency parsing. *Proceedings of the 39th annual ACM southeast conference*, 95-102.

Damashek, M. (1995). Gauging similarity with n-grams: Language-independent categorization of text. *Science, 267*(5199), 843–848. doi:10.1126cience.267.5199.843 PMID:17813910

Fabian Beijer, F. (2002). *The syntax and pragmatics of exclamations and other expressive/ emotional utterances*. Working Papers in Linguistics 2, The Dept. of English in Lund.

Fujii, Y., Ando, S., & Ito, T. (2010). Yūgai jōhō firutaringu no tame no 2-tangokan no kyori oyobi kyōki jōhō ni yoru bunshō bunrui shuhō no teian [Developing a method based on 2-word co-occurence information for filtering harmful information] (in Japanese). *Proceedings of The 24th Annual Conference of The Japanese Society for Artificial Intelligence (JSAI2010)*, 1-4.

Guthrie, D., Allison, B., Liu, W., Guthrie, L., & Wilks, Y. (2006). A closer look at skipgram modelling. *Proceedings of the 5th international Conference on Language Resources and Evaluation (LREC-2006)*, 1-4.

Huang, X., Alleva, F., Hon, H.-W., Hwang, M.-Y., & Rosenfeld, R. (1992). The SPHINX-II Speech Recognition System: An Overview, Computer. *Speech and Language, 7*(2), 137–148. doi:10.1006/csla.1993.1007

Klaus Krippendorff, K. (1986). Combinatorial Explosion. In *Web Dictionary of Cybernetics and Systems*. Principia Cybernetica Web.

Markov, A. A. (1971). Extension of the limit theorems of probability theory to a sum of variables connected in a chain. John Wiley and Sons.

Matsuba, T., Masui, F., Kawai, A., & Isu, N. (2010). Gakkō hikōshiki saito ni okeru yūgai jōhō kenshutsu [Detection of harmful information on informal school websites] (in Japanese). *Proc. of The 16th Annual Meeting of The Association for Natural Language Processing (NLP2010)*.

Matsuba, T., Masui, F., Kawai, A., & Isu, N. (2011). Gakkō hi-kōshiki saito ni okeru yūgai jōhō kenshutsu wo mokuteki to shita kyokusei hantei moderu ni kansuru kenkyū [A study on the polarity classification model for the purpose of detecting harmful information on informal school sites] (in Japanese). *Proceedings of The Seventeenth Annual Meeting of The Association for Natural Language Processing (NLP2011)*, 388-391.

Ministry of Education, Culture, Sports, Science, and Technology (MEXT). (2008). *'Netto-jō no ijime' ni kansuru taiō manyuaru jirei shū (gakkō, kyōin muke)* ["Bullying on the Net" Manual for handling and collection of cases (for schools and teachers)] (in Japanese). MEXT.

Mishra, U., & Prakash, C. (2012). MAULIK: An effective stemmer for Hindi language. *International Journal on Computer Science and Engineering, 4*(5), 711.

Narayanan, A., & Shmatikov, V. (2005, November). Fast dictionary attacks on passwords using time-space tradeoff. In *Proceedings of the 12th ACM conference on Computer and communications security* (pp. 364-372). ACM. 10.1145/1102120.1102168

Nitta, T., Masui, F., Ptaszynski, M., Kimura, Y., Rzepka, R., & Araki, K. (2013). Detecting Cyberbullying Entries on Informal School Websites Based on Category Relevance Maximization. *Proceedings of the 6th International Joint Conference on Natural Language Processing (IJCNLP 2013)*, 579-586.

Paar, C., Pelzl, J., & Preneel, B. (2010). *Understanding Cryptography: A Textbook for Students and Practitioners*. Springer. doi:10.1007/978-3-642-04101-3

Ponte, J. M., & Croft, W. B. (1998). *A Language Modeling Approach to Information Retrieval*. Research and Development in Information Retrieval. doi:10.1145/290941.291008

Potts, C. & Schwarz, F. (2008). *Exclamatives and heightened emotion: Extracting pragmatic generalizations from large corpora*. Ms., UMass Amherst.

Ptaszynski, M., Dybala, P., Matsuba, T., Masui, F., Rzepka, R., Araki, K., & Momouchi, Y. (2010). In the Service of Online Order: Tackling Cyber-Bullying with Machine Learning and Affect Analysis. *International Journal of Computational Linguistics Research*, *1*(3), 135–154.

Ptaszynski, M., Maciejewski, J., Dybala, P., Rzepka, R., & Araki, K. (2010). CAO: A fully automatic emoticon analysis system based on theory of kinesics. *IEEE Transactions on Affective Computing*, *1*(1), 46–59. doi:10.1109/T-AFFC.2010.3

Ptaszynski, M., Masui, F., Nitta, T., Hatakeyama, S., Kimura, Y., Rzepka, R., & Araki, K. (2016). Sustainable cyberbullying detection with category-maximized relevance of harmful phrases and double-filtered automatic optimization. *International Journal of Child-Computer Interaction*, *8*, 15–30. doi:10.1016/j.ijcci.2016.07.002

Ptaszynski, M., Rzepka, R., Araki, K., & Momouchi, Y. (2011). Language combinatorics: A sentence pattern extraction architecture based on combinatorial explosion. *International Journal of Computational Linguistics*, *2*(1), 24–36.

Sahlgren, M., & Cöster, R. (2004, August). Using bag-of-concepts to improve the performance of support vector machines in text categorization. In *Proceedings of the 20th international conference on Computational Linguistics* (p. 487). Association for Computational Linguistics. 10.3115/1220355.1220425

Sasai, K. (2006). The Structure of Modern Japanese Exclamatory Sentences: On the Structure of the Nanto-Type Sentence. *Studies in the Japanese Language*, *2*(1), 16–31.

Siu, M., & Ostendorf, M. (2000). Variable n-grams and extensions for conversational speech language modeling. *IEEE Transactions on Speech and Audio Processing*, *8*(1), 63–75. doi:10.1109/89.817454

Ure, J. (1971). Lexical density and register differentiation. In G. Perren & J. L. M. Trim (Eds.), *Applications of Linguistics* (pp. 443–452). London: Cambridge University Press.

Zellig, H. (1954). Distributional Structure. *Word*, *10*(2/3), 146–162.

ENDNOTES

[1]   By ambiguous patterns we refer to those patterns which appear on both the harmful side as well as in the non-harmful side. If a pattern appears on both sides it is ambiguous whether it is harmful or non-harmful, and its normalized weight is in the range from 0.99(9) to -0.99(9). Moreover, if an ambiguous pattern appears on both sides in the same occurrence, then its weight is equal 0, thus zero-patterns.

[2]   http://taku910.github.io/mecab/

[3]   https://taku910.github.io/cabocha/

This research was previously published in Automatic Cyberbullying Detection edited by Michal E. Ptaszynski and Fumito Masui, pages 85-132, copyright year 2019 by Information Science Reference (an imprint of IGI Global).

Chapter 15
Entropy Based Identification of Fake Profiles in Social Network:
An Application of Cyberbullying

Geetika Sarna
Netaji Subhas Institute of Technology, India

M.P.S. Bhatia
Netaji Subhas Institute of Technology, India

ABSTRACT

Cyberbullying is a felonious act carried out against the victim by sending harassing/ embarrassing/ abusing information online. Normally offenders create fake profiles in order to hide their identity for unscrupulous activities. Assuming a fake identity is very harmful as the real picture of the offender is not visible, and also it can become difficult to entrap them. Sometimes, some trustworthy friends can also take advantage of the fake identity in order to harm the victim. Culprits can reveal victim's personal information like financial details, personal history, family, etc., and along with it, he can harass, threaten or blackmail the victim using fake profiles and permeates that information on the social network. So, it is necessary to resolve this issue. In this article, the authors used the concept of entropy and cross entropy to identify fake profiles as entropy works on the degree of uncertainty. Also, this article shows the comparison of proposed method with the existing classifiers.

DOI: 10.4018/978-1-7998-1684-3.ch015

INTRODUCTION

Cyberbullying is the online fight against the victim in order to show the power by unfair means. Offender sends unacceptable material in the form of text, images, videos and audios as well. They normally take the help of online social networks for doing such types of illegal activities as the information diffuses very fast and reach to large number of audience on social network which may harm the fame of victim. This may put the victim into depression or he may commit suicide. Normally the offender creates fake identity for executing such types of unlawful activities in order to save himself by hiding the identity. The mischievous behaviour on social media is normally created by the fake profiles with different alias in order to hide the identity. So, it needs to be identified and controlled so that no one could harm by this in the context of reputation, fame and also life.

The study showed that the chances of cyberbullying were approximately seven times higher between current or former friends and dating partners than between young people who had neither been friends nor dated each other. "A common concern regarding cyberbullying is that strangers can attack someone, but here we see evidence that there are significant risks associated with close connections," said Diane Felmlee, Professor at Pennsylvania State University, in the US. "Competition for status and esteem can be one reason behind peer cyberbullying," Felmlee added. In addition, lesbian, gay, bisexual, transgender, and queer (LGBTQ) youth were four times as likely as their heterosexual peers to be victimised on a cyber platform. Friends, or former friends, are particularly likely to find themselves in situations in which they are struggling for the same school, club, ranks and or sport positions and social connections (Cyberbullying more common among friends, dating partners, 2016).

According to the Centers for Disease Control and Prevention (CDC), suicide is the third leading cause of death which estimates up to approximately 4,400 deaths every year out of which at least 100 suicide attempts are committed among young people. More than 14 percent of high school students have considered suicide and nearly 7 percent have attempted it (Bullying Statistics. Anti-bullying Help, Facts and more, 2016).

Nobullying.com is an online forum aimed at educating, advising, counselling and all importantly, helping to stop bullying, in particular, cyber bullying. You can read so many real stories regarding cyberbullying on this site. We would like to discuss few of them which will clear the purpose of this paper. Ryan Patrick Halligan was a 13-year-old student in Vermont, USA. Ryan Halligan was bullied by his classmates in school as well as cyber bullied online and committed suicide at the innocent age of 13. There were no criminal charges filed following Ryan's death because there was no criminal law at that time (Nobullying, 2015). Megan, Missouri woman struggled with attention deficit disorder and depression because of her over weight. A person named Josh Evans created a fake account to convince Megan to talk. After spending time with her online for few days, he started ignoring her by sending cruel messages and finally she committed suicide (Nobullying, 2016). There are lot more cases of cyberbullying come in front of our eyes daily with the loss of life of someone.

Existing methods used machine learning classifiers for classification of fake profiles. In this paper, we identified the fake profiles using entropy and cross entropy. Machine Learning classifies the data based on the features extracted and on the other hand, entropy works on the concept of uncertainty or impurity of information gathered from the features for classification. Here, single feature is being used so entropy is analysed as the best method than the other classifiers. We used clustering with Jaro-Winkler distance for making the set of similar names extracted from Twitter and Levenshtein Distance for comparing the words extracted from the messages with bad word dictionary. All the three techniques are discussed below in brief.

Entropy

Entropy is a measure of the amount of uncertainty or impurity associated with a set of probabilities. Entropy is given by:

$$H(P) = -\sum p(x_i) \log_2 p(x_i) \tag{1}$$

Jaro-Winkler Distance

Jaro-Winkler distance is used for comparing the strings. As this algorithm compares the prefix of the strings also, therefore, the main use of this algorithm is in the area where we need the comparison of names. Jaro-Distance d_j is given by:

$$d_j = \begin{cases} 0 & if \quad m = 0 \\ \dfrac{1}{3}\left(\dfrac{m}{|s_1|} + \dfrac{m}{|s_2|} + \dfrac{m-t}{m} \right) & otherwise \end{cases} \tag{2}$$

where:

m = number of matching characters
t = half the number of transpositions
s_1 and s_2 be the two strings.

Jaro-winkler Distance d_w is given by:

$$d_w = \begin{cases} d_j & if \ d_j < b_t \\ d_j + \left(lp\left(1 - d_j\right)\right) & otherwise \end{cases} \tag{3}$$

where:

l = length of the common prefix at the start of the string
p = constant scaling factor with standard value =.1

Levenshtein Distance

Levenshtein distance is named after Vladimir Levenshtein, who invented this distance in 1965. In information theory, the Levenshtein distance is a string metric used for measuring the difference between two strings. Basically, the Levenshtein distance between two strings is the minimum number of single-character updations (i.e. insertions, deletions or substitutions) required to alter one word into the other. Levenshtein Distance $lev_{s,t}(|s|,|t|)$ is given by:

$$lev_{s,t}(i,j) = \begin{cases} \max(i,j) & if \min(i,j) = 0 \\ \min \begin{cases} lev_{s,t}(i-1,j)+1 \\ lev_{s,t}(i,j-1)+1 \\ lev_{s,t}(i-1,j-1)+1_{(s_i \neq t_j)} \end{cases} & otherwise \end{cases} \tag{4}$$

where s,t are two strings.

In section 2, we give the related work and proposed method is discussed in section 3. Results are given in section 4 and at last but not least, the conclusion and future work is given in section 5.

THE RELATED WORK

Galán-García et al. (2014), detected fake profiles on twitter by comparing the content generated by both the troll profiles as well as real user profiles. Fire et al. (2014), detected fake users using the dataset of Facebook. Tang et al. (2012), detected fake profiles using features like Age, Gender, College Degree, Avatar photo, Personal information in the profile, Authentic pictures, advertisements, Profile Completeness, Number Of friends, length of membership, gender of Majority of mutual friends, comments on their posts on Facebook using one of the machine learning classifier named decision tree classifiers. Perez et al. (2013) detected suspicious profiles from those users who normally access social networks through smartphones on the basis of activity of profile and visibility of profile. Conti et al. (2012), identified fake profiles from Facebook on the basis of pattern found in the online social network structure. Liu et al. (2008), predicted trust between users in online communities using the dataset of Epinion by employing two factors: user factor and interaction factor. Sarkar et. al. (2015) find trust between two entities in real application using fuzzy Logic and Ant colony Model. Singh M. Et Al(2014), classify the malicious, non-malicious user and celebrity on Twitter using user characteristics. Coa q. et. Al (2012), developed tool SybilRank to identify the fake user by giving them the rank based on the social graph properties. Rizi et.al. (2014), detected the clone identities based on the profile similarity and relationship strength. Egele et al. (2013), developed tool called COMPA which detected anomalous accounts based on the sudden change in behaviour of user. They also considered the change is malicious or legitimate. Xiao C. et.al (2015), classified the group of fake accounts created by single user and the legitimate user using user characteristics like name, email, company. Meligi A. et al. (2015), proposed a framework based on social graph which is used to extract the trusted instances from the graph based on the communication between the users. Ahmed F. et al. (2013) distinguished the normal and spam profiles based on the statistical features. They applied proposed model on facebook as well as Twitter also. Sarna et al. (2017) find the credibility of user based on the category of bullying to which he belongs. Sarna et al. (2016) used machine learning techniques to distinguish between the severity of bullying in messages in social media.

Konstantinidis (2005), computed the Levenshtein distance of the Regular Language. Yujian et. al (2007), proposed a Generalized Levenshtein Distance (GLD) to fine the distance between two strings with the complexity of O(|X|.|Y|), where X and Y are two strings. Su et al. (2008), proposed a hybrid plagiarism method using Levenshtein Distance and Smith Waterman algorithm.

THE PROPOSED METHOD

The key objective of this paper is to use the proposed method efficiently in order to improve the classification of fake social profiles. Identification of fake profiles is very important as some unexpected users can do the crime online by assuming the fake identity. Offenders create fake identity so that no one can see the real identity or picture and recognize them. Also the victims can easily entrapped by them and trust them in short time. Framework for proposed method is given below in Figure 1.

Proposed method consists of following modules.

Figure 1. Proposed framework for identification of fake profiles

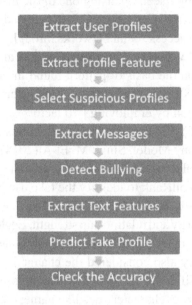

Extract User Profiles

Initially we extracted the user profiles from the Twitter and make the clusters of similar names based on similarity index calculated by Jaro-Winkler Distance. The implementation is done in Python. This step is necessary because miscreants create the fake profile using the name of celebrities, politicians, writers, authors, other famous personalities and also friends to develop the trust in victim. Here, for making the clusters, we consider two features: length of common prefix of two words and number of matching characters on the basis of which similarity index is calculated between two words using Jaro-Winkler Distance. Algorithm for creating the clusters of similar words is called CSW (Clusters of Similar Words).

Steps for the Algorithm of CSW

len: length (len) of common prefix
m: the number of matching characters(m)
j: Jaro-Winkler distance
    1.   Take first word as seed.
    2.   Take second word as new item.
    3.   Compare seed and new item and find the smallest one.
    4.   Find the length (len) of common prefix at the start of the word and the number of matching characters(m).

5.   Two cases arise:

if(len $\geq$ 1) //case 1

$$\left(m > \frac{1}{2}(\text{length of the smallest word})\right) \text{ then find the Jaro-Winkler (j)}$$

else //case 2

if (half the length of the first string exists in the second string or half the length of
     the second string exists in the first string),

set len=1,

find the Jaro-Winkler distance(j)

Here, in case 1, we have taken len $\geq$1 because we want first few characters of both the words should be same and m > half the length of the smallest word because we want a large number of matching characters in order to get similar words. In case 2, we have set len=1 for showing the presence of half of the prefix of the one string in the second string.

6.   If j $\geq$ 0.8, then put both the words in one cluster else use the word as a seed and create the separate cluster. Here, we have taken 0.8 for the similarity of two words in order to get the most similar strings. For Example: Parveen, Parveen123 and Parv1. If the maximum part of the word matches only then those words will be considered.

Example

Example 1: Parveen and Parvleen1

Length of common prefix=4 which is greater than 1 and matching characters=7 which is more than the half of the smallest string. So, the string can be considered. Jaro-Winkler Distance(j)=.955.So, both the strings should be in the same cluster.

Example 2: Parveen and Parveet123geet

Length of common prefix =6 which is greater than 1 and matching characters=6 which is more than the half of the smallest string. So, the string can be considered. Jaro-Winkler Distance(j)=.90. So, both the strings should be in the same cluster.

Example 3: Reena and Teena

Length of common prefix =0 which is not greater than 1 and also half part of one string is not present in the other such as *Ree* is not in *Teena* or *Tee* is not in *Reena*. So, these strings are not considered in the same cluster.

Example 4: BillGates and RealBillGates
Here, half of string BillGates=BillG which exist in the second string. Jaro-Winkler Distance(j) = .84. So, both the strings should be in the same cluster.

7. Select the most accurate seed from the existing clusters by finding the RMSE (Root Mean Square Error) after addition of the new item. The item which is having low RMSE value in the cluster will become the new seed for the cluster. RMSE is calculated as:

$$RMSE = \sqrt{\frac{\sum_{i=1}^{n}(x-x_i)^2}{n}}$$

where x is the predicted jaro distance value which is always one because the similarity index of two same string is always one as we expect the most similar strings and x_i is the observed Jaro Distance between two strings.

8. Repeat steps 2-7 for the all the new items to form clusters of similar names.
9. Assess only those clusters whose degree is more than one. This step is called cluster pruning.
   Def: Degree of the cluster is the number of items present in the cluster.
   Def: Cluster Pruning: Cluster pruning is to cut down those clusters which are unwanted. It is helpful in reducing the number of clusters.
10. Check the accuracy of clusters: Accuracy of cluster is tested by swapping the seed with the seed of some other cluster and find the RMSE. If RMSE decreases, it means cluster is not accurate and needs re-clustering.

Above algorithm generates the clusters of the similar name when applied on the set of screen names extracted from Twitter:

- **Extract Profile Features:** Consider one cluster of user name from the group of clusters formed in the previous module and extract the features of the user profile. The first feature is the number of friends the user follows and second is the status of profile whether the profile is verified or not. The number of friends of the verified account will become the threshold which is used for detecting the suspicious profile. Activity and visibility of profile are two main factors for vigorous connectivity of users in social media. Activity of user means how much the user actively send messages to other users and visibility means to what extent user profile is visible to others mean how much the user get response from others. Hence, we have considered friend feature;

- **Select Suspicious Profiles:** Next Step is to select the suspicious profiles after comparing all the unverified profiles with the verified profile based on the number of friends:

$$fd_u^{vo} = fd_u^v - fd_u^o \qquad (5)$$

where, fd_u^v is the number of friends of verified user v, fd_u^o is the number of friends of other unverified user and fd_u^{vo} is the difference of number of friend between user v and user o.

If $fd_u^{vo} > 0$, indicates user v prefer to create friends and user o create network just for some limited purpose. Normally a reliable user has approximately 100 to 350 friends on social network.

If $fd_u^{vo} \geq$ +(half of number of friends of user v)or $fd_u^{vo} \leq$ -(half of number of friends of user v), the user v can be considered as the suspicious user:

- **Extract Messages:** In this step, we extracted the messages of suspicious profiles using the code written in Python;
- **Detect Bullying:** In this step, we detected bullying in messages by comparing the keywords in the messages with the bad word Dictionary. Our bad word dictionary contains 768 keywords which are the negative personality adjectives like ugly, dirty etc. and bad words like bitch, fuck etc. So the keywords of the messages are basically the adjectives which we choose with the help of Stanford Post tagger. Comparison between keywords of messages and bad word dictionary is done using Levenshtein Distance. Normally, the last few characters of the word are different based on the verb and comparison degrees. For example: Ugly to Uglier, worse to worst. So, the maximum difference between two words is 3. If the Levenshtein Distance is less than equal to 3, then the word matches with the dictionary else not.

Example

Consider two strings: cheat and cheater:

// Cheat is present in the bad word dictionary and decision need to be taken about cheater //word
Smallest string = cheat
Here matching percentage of smallest string with other string =100%
Levenshtein Distance between two strings =2

Here Levenshtein Distance is less than equal to three, so, cheater will also be considered as bad word:

- **Extract Text Features:** In this step, we extracted the number of profane words from each message. Profane words are those which are matching with the bad word dictionary. A number of profane words will be the feature for detecting the fake profiles in the case of cyberbullying. More the number of profane words in the messages, more the chance of being it a fake profile. This module consider profane words for detecting bullying messages because without profane words, it would become difficult to get more accurate results and challenging to distinguish between bullying and non-bulling messages and. Bad or profane words are the basis of cyberbullying;
- **Predict Fake Profiles:** In this module, we have found the entropy of the profile based on the profane words. Messages with profane words are declared as bullying messages and the remaining messages are declared as non-Bullying messages.

For example: Entropy for profile is calculated as:

$$H(P) = -P_B \log_2(P_B) - P_{NB} \log_2(P_{NB}) \tag{6}$$

where $-P_B \log_2(P_B)$ be the entropy of Bullying messages and $-P_{NB} \log_2(P_{NB})$ be the entropy of Non-Bullying Messages. The category which is having less value of entropy indicates less uncertainty of that category means if the entropy of bullying messages is less than the non-bullying messages then we can say that the uncertainty or impurity of bullyingness in messages of profile is less which results in pure bullying profile. If the degree of the entropy of bullying messages is less than 50% of the entropy of profile means the profile is suspicious.

- **Check the accuracy:** In this module, we compared the suspicious profile and undoubted profile. We examined the cross-entropy of the suspicious profile and the profile which is unsuspicious and verified. If cross-entropy approaches zero, it means the profile is not fake else the profile is fake. The cross-entropy is calculated by the formula:

$$H(P, m1) = -\sum p(x_i) \log_2(m1(x_i)) \tag{7}$$

where P is the undoubted profile and m1 be the profile to be predicted.

RESULTS

The initial step is to gather profiles with similar names. We got 9000 profiles from Twitter by considering the followers and following relations and apply CSW algorithm on the screen name to form clusters. Then we extracted the profile features named number of friends and the status of the profile. Then compare the number of friends of verified user with the other entire users. Figure 2 shows only two clusters.

The similarity index between users according to CSW algorithm and RMSE value is given in Table 1. The user name in the oval in Table 1 is the seed. The RMSE value of the seed is very less as compared to the other users. So, for new words, the seed will be same till the RMSE value of seed is less.

It is analysed from Table 2 that the accuracy of CSW algorithm is much better than Jaro_Winkler Distance. The results are shown in Table 3 which exhibits that the case of @billgates_s, @BillGatesAdvice and @BRBillGates are extremely different from the verified account. So, we can consider these cases as suspicious profiles. Next step is to extract the messages of the suspicious profiles and find the number of profane words of each message by comparing it with the bad word dictionary using the Levenshtein Distance. We got a negligible number of bad words in suspicious profiles, so the entropy of the bullying messages is negligible which indicates the suspicious profiles against user Bill Gates are not fake profiles and not involved in cyberbullying. The details of those users whose screen name is similar to the Britney

Figure 2. Cluster of similar name using CSW algorithm

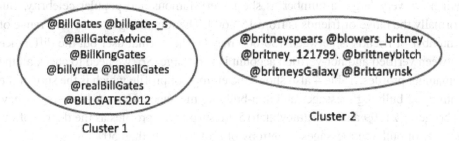

@BillGates @billgates_s
@BillGatesAdvice
@BillKingGates
@billyraze @BRBillGates
@realBillGates
@BILLGATES2012

Cluster 1

@britneyspears @blowers_britney
@britney_121799. @brittneybitch
@britneysGalaxy @Brittanynsk

Cluster 2

Table 1. Matrix for similarity index by CSW algorithm and RMSE between user for Cluster 1

Screen Name	@BillGates	@billgates_s	@BillGatesAdvice	@BillKingGates	@billyraze	@BRBillGates	@realBillGates	@BILLGATES2012	RMSE
@BillGates	1	.98	.97	.93	.86	.94	.84	.97	.2364
@billgates_s	.98	1	.98	.90	.84	.89	.78	.98	.3119
@BillGatesAdvice	.97	.98	1	.85	.81	.82	.75	.97	.3946
@BillKingGates	.93	.90	.85	1	.82	.85	.78	.87	.3970
@billyraze	.86	.84	.81	.82	1	.75	.66	.82	.5694
@BRBillGates	.94	.89	.82	.85	.75	1	.81	.85	.4378
@realBillGates	.84	.78	.75	.78	.66	.81	1	.74	.6358
@BILLGATES2012	.97	.98	.97	.87	.82	.85	.74	1	.3763

Table 2. Comparison between words using Jaro_winkler and CSW method

	Jaro_winkler	CSW
Total Number Of Keywords Compared with Dictionary	1000	1000
Total Error	202	97
Error Rate	20.2%	9.7%
Accuracy Rate	79.8%	90.3%

Table 3. Details of users with screen name similar to Bill Gates

S.No.	Screen Name	Number of Friends	Status	Difference
1	@BillGates	169	Verified	0
2	@billgates_s	7566	Not Verified	-7397
3	@BillGatesAdvice	6487	Not Verified	-6318
4	@BillKingGates	0	Not Verified	169
5	@billyraze	302	Not Verified	-133
6	@BRBillGates	1890	Not Verified	-1721
7	@realBillGates	81	Not Verified	88
8	@ BILLGATES2012	216	Not Verified	-47

are shown in Table 4. The @britneyspears has the verified account with 396K friends which are very large in number as she is very famous and popular celebrity. But normally the range of friends is from 150-600. The remaining users whose range of a number of friends is between 150-600 may be the normal user but the difference between verified and not-verified account is very large. So, we need to check all the remaining profiles. Table 4 also shows the entropy of profile which is the sum of the entropy of bullying messages and non-bullying messages. Here, @blowers_britney, @britney_121799 and @brittneybitch15 are suspicious profiles as the degree of the entropy of bullying messages in entropy of profile is less than 50%.

Results of cross entropy between user @britneyspears and other users with screen name similar to Britney is given in Table 5. The result shows that the cross entropy of user @britneybitch05 is very near to the entropy of user @britneyspears which indicates the user is not suspicious. But the user @blowers_britney, @ britney_121799 and @britneybitch15 are very much fake and suspicious as there is very large difference between the cross entropy and entropy of user @britneyspears. Here cross entropy is used as the metric to check the accuracy of the result obtained using entropy.

Table 4. Details of Users with screen name similar to Britney

S. No.	Screen Name	Number of Friends	Status	Entropy of Bullying Messages	Entropy of Non-Bullying Messages	Entropy of Profile	Suspicious
1	@britneyspears	396K	Verified	0.181	0.054	0.235	No
2	@blowers_ britney	251	Not Verified	0.196	0.407	0.602	yes
3	@ britney_121799	511	Not Verified	0.427	0.530	0.958	yes
4	@ brittneybitch88	573	Not Verified	0.530	0.436	0.966	no
5	@ brittneybitch15	513	Not Verified	0.500	0.500	1.000	yes
6	@_ brittneybitch_	169	Not Verified	0.482	0.282	0.764	no
7	@ brittneybitch21	214	Not Verified	0.531	0.411	0.942	no
8	@ britneysGalaxy	939	Not Verified	0.314	0.125	0.439	no
9	@ brittneybitch05	219	Not Verified	0.487	0.289	0.776	no

Table 5. Cross entropy between user @britneyspears and other users with screen name similar to Britney

S. No.	Unsuspicious Profile	Profiles to be Predicted	Cross Entropy of Bullying Messages	Cross Entropy of Non-Bullying Messages	Cross Entropy
1	@britneyspears	@blowers_britney	0.009	2.659	2.668
2	@britneyspears	@britney_121799	0.026	1.345	1.371
3	@britneyspears	@brittneybitch88	0.052	0.689	0.741
4	@britneyspears	@brittneybitch15	0.038	0.962	1.000
5	@britneyspears	@_brittneybitch_	0.083	0.349	0.432
6	@britneyspears	@brittneybitch21	0.057	0.617	0.674
7	@britneyspears	@britneysGalaxy	0.133	0.132	1.330
8	@britneyspears	@brittneybitch05	0.082	0.360	0.442

Table 6. Comparison of various classifiers with the proposed method

Classifiers	Accuracy
SVM	76%
Decision Tree	66%
AdaBoost	71%
Proposed Method	79%

The comparison of various classifiers with the proposed method is given in Table 6. The table shows that the accuracy of the proposed method is more than the other classifiers. Reason behind this is the proposed method works on the entropy and tells that how much the profile is uncertain or bullying on the basis of single feature i.e. profane words. This value of uncertainty more accurately helps to identify the suspicious profiles. Also, cross-entropy helps to compare the two profiles on the basis of their entropy. But other methods need more features to give more accurate results. Here, the cross entropy has also been used to do the cross-validation which is very easy and can work well with large datasets.

DISCUSSION

The proposed method discussed in section 4 has been implemented for the detection of fake profiles responsible for cyberbullying. Administrator can detect the suspects using this simple approach which require only profane words. Then he can use method proposed by Sarna et al. (2017) to find the credibility of user based on the category of bullying to which he belongs. Credibility of user will give the idea to the victim in the context of further communication or also in accepting the friend request from him. This may prevent the victim from entrapping in the conspiracy of culprit, hence, saves victims life from cyberbullies.

CONCLUSION AND FUTURE WORK

The purpose of this experiment it to restrict the fake profiles in order to make the social network a more reliable source of information sharing. In this paper, we proposed clustering algorithm for similar words (CSW) which we used for making the clusters of similar names. The main limitation of CSW is it creates large number of clusters. So, we also employed cluster pruning to reduce the number of clusters and make the algorithm efficient. This paper shows how entropy is helpful in detecting the fake profiles and cross entropy is helpful in finding the accuracy. As users assume a fake identity in various areas like terrorism, extremist etc., the proposed method is helpful in detecting the fake profiles in those areas also. But the only difference is the keywords. Keywords used are domain dependent. This experiment is based only on cyberbullying, so we used profane words as the feature to detect fake profiles. Similarly, in the case of terrorism, keywords related to that area will be used like ISIS, Taliban etc. The different dictionary will be used in different domains. But the method of identification of fake profiles is same. In all the cases, entropy and cross entropy can be used to get best results. Also, the cross-entropy can be further use for the classification and the prediction of the category profiles.

In this paper, we used two set of features: profile feature that includes a number of friends and status of profile and text feature including profane words. In future, we wish to use more features to get better results. As large amount of information is available or posted on social network, consequently, we get a large number of new keywords. We will also try to handle new emerging keywords and make out our dictionary up to date in future work.

REFERENCES

Ahmad, F., & Abulaish, M. (2013). A Generic Statistical Approach for Spam Detection in Online Social Networks. *Computer Communications, 36*(10-11), 1120–1129.

Bullying Statistics. (2016). Anti-bullying Help, Facts and more. Retrieved from http://www.bullyingstatistics.org/content/bullying-and-suicide.html

Cao, Q., Sirivianos, M., Yang, X., & Pregueiro, T. (2012). Aiding the Detection of Fake Accounts in Large Scale Social Online Services. In *Proceedings of the 9th USENIX conference on Networked Systems Design and Implementation*. ACM.

Conti, M., Poovendran, R., & Secchiero, M. (2012). FakeBook: Detecting Fake Profiles in Online Social Networks. *Paper presented in IEEE International Conference on Advances in Social Networks Analysis and Mining (ASONAM)*, Istanbul.

Cyberbullying more common among friends, dating partners (2016, August 23). The National Youth Violence Prevention Resource Center.

Egele, M., Stringhini, G., Kruegel, C., & Vigna, G. (2013). COMPA: Detecting Compromised Accounts on Social Networks. In NDSS symposium.

Fire, M., Kagan, D., Elyashar, A., & Elovici, Y. (2014). Friend and Foe? Fake profile identification in online social networks. *Journal Of Social Network Analysis and Mining, 4*(1), 1–23.

Galán-García, P., Puerta, J. G., Gómez, C. L., Santos, I., & Bringas, P. G. (2014). Supervised Machine Learning for the Detection of Troll Profiles in Twitter Social Network: Application to a Real Case of Cyberbullying. *Paper presented at Advances in Intelligent Systems and Computing* (pp. 419-428). Springer.

Konstantinidi, S. (2005). Computing the Levenshtein Distance of a Regular Language. In *Proceedings of IEEE ISOC ITW2005 on Coding and Complexity* (pp. 113-116).

Liu, H., Lim, E., Lauw, H., Le, M., Sun, A., Srivastava, J., & Kim, Y. (2008). Predicting Trusts among Users of Online Communities – an Epinions Case Study. In *Proceedings of the 9th ACM conference on Electronic commerce*, Chicago, IL (pp. 310-319).

Meligy, A., Ibrahim, H., & Torky, M. (2015). A framework for detecting cloning attacks in OSN based on a novel social graph topology. *International Journal of Intelligent Systems and Applications*, *7*(3), 13–20.

Perez, C., Lemercier, M., & Birregah, B. (2013). A dynamic approach to detecting the suspicious profiles on social platforms. *Paper presented in IEEE International Conference on Communications*, Budapest. 10.1109/ICCW.2013.6649223

Rizi, F., Khayyambashi, M., & Yousefi, M. (2014). A new approach for finding cloned profiles in online social networks. *International Journal of Network Security*, *6*.

Ryan Patrick Halligan. (2015, December 22). Nobullying.com. Retrieved from https://nobullying.com

Sarkar, M., Banerjee, S., & Hassanein, A. E. (2015). Evaluating the degree of trust under context sensitive relational database hierarchy using hybrid intelligent approach. *International Journal of Rough Sets and Data Analysis*, *2*(1), 1–21. doi:10.4018/ijrsda.2015010101

Sarna, G., & Bhatia, M. P. S. (2016). An approach to distinguish between the severity of bullying in messages in social media. *International Journal of Rough Sets and Data Analysis*, *3*(4), 1–20. doi:10.4018/IJRSDA.2016100101

Sarna, G., & Bhatia, M. P. S. (2017). *Content based approach to find the credibility of users in social networks: an application of cyberbullying. International Journal Of Machine Learning and Cybernetics*, *8*(2), 677-689.

Singh, M., Bansal, D., & Sofat, S. (2014). Detecting malicious users in Twitter using classifiers. In *Proceedings of the 7th International Conference on security of Information and Networks* (p. 247).

Su, Z., Ahn, B., Eom, K., Kang, M., Kim, J., & Kim, M. (2008). Plagiarism Detection Using the Levenshtein Distance and Smith-Waterman Algorithm. *Paper presented in 3rd International IEEE Conference on Innovative Computing Information and Control (ICICIC'08)*, China. 10.1109/ICICIC.2008.422

Tang, R., Lu, L., Zhuang, Y., & Fong, S. (2012). Not Every Friend on Social Network Can be Trusted: An Online Trust Indexing algorithm. *Paper presented at IEEE/WIC/ACM International conference on Web Intelligence and Intelligent Agent Technology (WI-IAT)*, China. 10.1109/WI-IAT.2012.84

The Megan Meier Story. (2016, September 18). Nobullying.com. Retrieved from https://nobullying.com

Xiao, C., Freeman, D., & Hwa, T. (2015). Detecting Clusters of Fake Accounts in Online Social Networks. In *Proceedings of the 8th ACM workshop on Artificial Intelligence and Security* (pp. 91-101). ACM. 10.1145/2808769.2808779

Yujian, L., & Bo, L. (2007). A normalized Levenshtein distance metric. *IEEE Transactions on Pattern Analysis and Machine Intelligence, 29*(6), 1091–1095.

This research was previously published in International Journal of Virtual Communities and Social Networking (IJVCSN), 9(4); edited by Subhasish Dasgupta and Rohit Rampal, pages 18-30, copyright year 2017 by IGI Publishing (an imprint of IGI Global).

Related Readings

To continue IGI Global's long-standing tradition of advancing innovation through emerging research, please find below a compiled list of recommended IGI Global book chapters and journal articles in the areas of cyber bullying, cyber aggression, and technology tools. These related readings will provide additional information and guidance to further enrich your knowledge and assist you with your own research.

Adomi, E. E., Eriki, J. A., Tiemo, P. A., & Akpojotor, L. O. (2016). Incidents of Cyberbullying Among Library and Information Science (LIS) Students at Delta State University, Abraka, Nigeria. *International Journal of Digital Literacy and Digital Competence*, 7(4), 52–63. doi:10.4018/IJDLDC.2016100104

Ahad, A. D., & Anshari, M. (2017). Smartphone Habits Among Youth: Uses and Gratification Theory. *International Journal of Cyber Behavior, Psychology and Learning*, 7(1), 65–75. doi:10.4018/IJCBPL.2017010105

Akmam, J., & Huq, N. (2016). Living Parallel-ly in Real and Virtual: Internet as an Extension of Self. In A. Novak & I. El-Burki (Eds.), *Defining Identity and the Changing Scope of Culture in the Digital Age* (pp. 230–239). Hershey, PA: IGI Global. doi:10.4018/978-1-5225-0212-8.ch014

Alim, S. (2016). Cyberbullying in the World of Teenagers and Social Media: A Literature Review. *International Journal of Cyber Behavior, Psychology and Learning*, 6(2), 68–95. doi:10.4018/IJCBPL.2016040105

Alim, S. (2017). Twitter Profiles of Organisations Fighting Against Cyberbullying and Bullying: An Exploration of Tweet Content, Influence and Reachability. *International Journal of Cyber Behavior, Psychology and Learning*, 7(3), 37–56. doi:10.4018/IJCBPL.2017070104

Andoh-Quainoo, L. (2020). Examining the Psychosocial Dimensions of Young People's Emergent Social Media Behavior. In M. Desjarlais (Ed.), *The Psychology and Dynamics Behind Social Media Interactions* (pp. 368–389). Hershey, PA: IGI Global. doi:10.4018/978-1-5225-9412-3.ch015

Andriakaina, E. (2016). Public History and National Identity: The 1821 Revolution as Metaphor for the "Greek Crisis". In A. Novak & I. El-Burki (Eds.), *Defining Identity and the Changing Scope of Culture in the Digital Age* (pp. 56–79). Hershey, PA: IGI Global. doi:10.4018/978-1-5225-0212-8.ch005

Arslan, G. (2018). Psychological Maltreatment and Internet Addiction: Is Psychological Maltreatment a Risk Factor? In B. Bozoglan (Ed.), *Psychological, Social, and Cultural Aspects of Internet Addiction* (pp. 90–108). Hershey, PA: IGI Global. doi:10.4018/978-1-5225-3477-8.ch005

Ayscue, L. M. (2016). Perception of Communication in Virtual Learning Environments: What's in It for Them? In B. Baggio (Ed.), *Analyzing Digital Discourse and Human Behavior in Modern Virtual Environments* (pp. 25–39). Hershey, PA: IGI Global. doi:10.4018/978-1-4666-9899-4.ch002

Baggio, B. G. (2016). Why We Would Rather Text than Talk: Personality, Identity, and Anonymity in Modern Virtual Environments. In B. Baggio (Ed.), *Analyzing Digital Discourse and Human Behavior in Modern Virtual Environments* (pp. 110–125). Hershey, PA: IGI Global. doi:10.4018/978-1-4666-9899-4.ch006

Bagwell, T. C., & Jackson, S. L. (2016). The Mode of Information – Due Process of Law and Student Loans: Bills of Attainder Enter the Digital Age. In R. Cropf & T. Bagwell (Eds.), *Ethical Issues and Citizen Rights in the Era of Digital Government Surveillance* (pp. 16–34). Hershey, PA: IGI Global. doi:10.4018/978-1-4666-9905-2.ch002

Balakina, J., & Frolova, N. (2020). Education via Social Net Sites: Challenges and Perspectives. In M. Desjarlais (Ed.), *The Psychology and Dynamics Behind Social Media Interactions* (pp. 343–367). Hershey, PA: IGI Global. doi:10.4018/978-1-5225-9412-3.ch014

Benvenuti, M., Błachnio, A., Przepiorka, A. M., Daskalova, V. M., & Mazzoni, E. (2020). Factors Related to Phone Snubbing Behavior in Emerging Adults: The Phubbing Phenomenon. In M. Desjarlais (Ed.), *The Psychology and Dynamics Behind Social Media Interactions* (pp. 164–187). Hershey, PA: IGI Global. doi:10.4018/978-1-5225-9412-3.ch007

Betts, L. R. (2018). The Nature of Cyber Bullying Behaviours. In M. Khosrow-Pour, D.B.A. (Ed.), Encyclopedia of Information Science and Technology, Fourth Edition (pp. 4245-4254). Hershey, PA: IGI Global. doi:10.4018/978-1-5225-2255-3.ch368

Bisen, S. S., & Deshpande, Y. (2018). The Impact of the Internet in Twenty-First Century Addictions: An Overview. In B. Bozoglan (Ed.), *Psychological, Social, and Cultural Aspects of Internet Addiction* (pp. 1–19). Hershey, PA: IGI Global. doi:10.4018/978-1-5225-3477-8.ch001

Bishop, J. (2018). Evaluating the Risk of Digital Addiction in Blended Learning Environments: Considering ICT Intensity, Learning Style, and Architecture. In B. Bozoglan (Ed.), *Psychological, Social, and Cultural Aspects of Internet Addiction* (pp. 169–185). Hershey, PA: IGI Global. doi:10.4018/978-1-5225-3477-8.ch009

Boursier, V., & Manna, V. (2018). Problematic Linkages in Adolescents: Italian Adaptation of a Measure for Internet-Related Problems. In B. Bozoglan (Ed.), *Psychological, Social, and Cultural Aspects of Internet Addiction* (pp. 253–282). Hershey, PA: IGI Global. doi:10.4018/978-1-5225-3477-8.ch014

Boylu, A. A., & Günay, G. (2018). Loneliness and Internet Addiction Among University Students. In B. Bozoglan (Ed.), *Psychological, Social, and Cultural Aspects of Internet Addiction* (pp. 109–125). Hershey, PA: IGI Global. doi:10.4018/978-1-5225-3477-8.ch006

Bozoglan, B. (2018). The Role of Family Factors in Internet Addiction Among Children and Adolescents: An Overview. In B. Bozoglan (Ed.), *Psychological, Social, and Cultural Aspects of Internet Addiction* (pp. 146–168). Hershey, PA: IGI Global. doi:10.4018/978-1-5225-3477-8.ch008

Brkljačić, T., Majetić, F., & Wertag, A. (2018). I'm Always Online: Well-Being and Main Sources of Life Dis/Satisfaction of Heavy Internet Users. In B. Bozoglan (Ed.), *Psychological, Social, and Cultural Aspects of Internet Addiction* (pp. 72–89). Hershey, PA: IGI Global. doi:10.4018/978-1-5225-3477-8.ch004

Cameron, C. A., & Mascarenas, A. (2020). Digital Social Media in Adolescents' Negotiating Real Virtual Romantic Relationships. In M. Desjarlais (Ed.), *The Psychology and Dynamics Behind Social Media Interactions* (pp. 83–106). Hershey, PA: IGI Global. doi:10.4018/978-1-5225-9412-3.ch004

Campbell, M. A., Whiteford, C., Duncanson, K., Spears, B., Butler, D., & Slee, P. T. (2017). Cyberbullying Bystanders: Gender, Grade, and Actions among Primary and Secondary School Students in Australia. *International Journal of Technoethics*, *8*(1), 44–55. doi:10.4018/IJT.2017010104

Casaregola, V. (2016). Who "Screens" Security?: Cultures of Surveillance in Film. In R. Cropf & T. Bagwell (Eds.), *Ethical Issues and Citizen Rights in the Era of Digital Government Surveillance* (pp. 57–76). Hershey, PA: IGI Global. doi:10.4018/978-1-4666-9905-2.ch004

Chamakiotis, P., & Panteli, N. (2016). The World is your Office: Being Creative in a Global Virtual Organization. In B. Baggio (Ed.), *Analyzing Digital Discourse and Human Behavior in Modern Virtual Environments* (pp. 87–108). Hershey, PA: IGI Global. doi:10.4018/978-1-4666-9899-4.ch005

Chen, B., & Luppicini, R. (2017). The New Era of Bullying: A Phenomenological Study of University Students' Past Experience with Cyberbullying. *International Journal of Cyber Behavior, Psychology and Learning*, 7(2), 72–90. doi:10.4018/IJCBPL.2017040106

Chen, I. L., & Shen, L. (2016). The Cyberethics, Cybersafety, and Cybersecurity at Schools. *International Journal of Cyber Ethics in Education*, 4(1), 1–15. doi:10.4018/IJCEE.2016010101

Cline, B. J. (2016). The Electric Soul: Faith, Spirituality, and Ontology in a Digital Age. In A. Novak & I. El-Burki (Eds.), *Defining Identity and the Changing Scope of Culture in the Digital Age* (pp. 251–270). Hershey, PA: IGI Global. doi:10.4018/978-1-5225-0212-8.ch016

Comas-Forgas, R., Sureda-Negre, J., & Calvo-Sastre, A. (2017). Characteristics of Cyberbullying Among Native and Immigrant Secondary Education Students. *International Journal of Cyber Behavior, Psychology and Learning*, 7(1), 1–17. doi:10.4018/IJCBPL.2017010101

Costa, C., Sousa, C., Rogado, J., & Henriques, S. (2017). Playing Digital Security: Youth Voices on their Digital Rights. *International Journal of Game-Based Learning*, 7(3), 11–25. doi:10.4018/IJGBL.2017070102

Demirtepe-Saygili, D. (2020). Stress, Coping, and Social Media Use. In M. Desjarlais (Ed.), *The Psychology and Dynamics Behind Social Media Interactions* (pp. 241–267). Hershey, PA: IGI Global. doi:10.4018/978-1-5225-9412-3.ch010

Desjarlais, M. (2020). Online Self-Disclosure: Opportunities for Enriching Existing Friendships. In M. Desjarlais (Ed.), *The Psychology and Dynamics Behind Social Media Interactions* (pp. 1–27). Hershey, PA: IGI Global. doi:10.4018/978-1-5225-9412-3.ch001

Desjarlais, M. (2020). The Effects of Virtual Likes on Self-Esteem: A Discussion of Receiving and Viewing Likes on Social Media. In M. Desjarlais (Ed.), *The Psychology and Dynamics Behind Social Media Interactions* (pp. 289–312). Hershey, PA: IGI Global. doi:10.4018/978-1-5225-9412-3.ch012

Eckert, S., & Steiner, L. (2016). Feminist Uses of Social Media: Facebook, Twitter, Tumblr, Pinterest, and Instagram. In A. Novak & I. El-Burki (Eds.), *Defining Identity and the Changing Scope of Culture in the Digital Age* (pp. 210–229). Hershey, PA: IGI Global. doi:10.4018/978-1-5225-0212-8.ch013

Edwards, S. B. III. (2016). The Right to Privacy Is Dying: Technology Is Killing It and We Are Letting It Happen. In R. Cropf & T. Bagwell (Eds.), *Ethical Issues and Citizen Rights in the Era of Digital Government Surveillance* (pp. 103–126). Hershey, PA: IGI Global. doi:10.4018/978-1-4666-9905-2.ch006

El-Burki, I. J., & Reynolds, R. R. (2016). It's No Secret Justin Wants to Be Black: Comedy Central's Justin Bieber Roast and Neoliberalism. In A. Novak & I. El-Burki (Eds.), *Defining Identity and the Changing Scope of Culture in the Digital Age* (pp. 15–28). Hershey, PA: IGI Global. doi:10.4018/978-1-5225-0212-8.ch002

Endong, F. P. (2018). Selfie-Objectification as a Facet of the Social Media Craze Among Youths in Nigeria: A Socio-Cultural Discourse. In B. Bozoglan (Ed.), *Psychological, Social, and Cultural Aspects of Internet Addiction* (pp. 236–252). Hershey, PA: IGI Global. doi:10.4018/978-1-5225-3477-8.ch013

Englander, E. K., & McCoy, M. (2017). Pressured Sexting and Revenge Porn in a Sample of Massachusetts Adolescents. *International Journal of Technoethics*, 8(2), 16–25. doi:10.4018/IJT.2017070102

Farmer, L. S. (2016). Using Virtual Environments to Transform Collective Intelligence. In B. Baggio (Ed.), *Analyzing Digital Discourse and Human Behavior in Modern Virtual Environments* (pp. 149–163). Hershey, PA: IGI Global. doi:10.4018/978-1-4666-9899-4.ch008

Firdhous, M. F. (2016). Cyber Espionage: How Safe Are We? In R. Cropf & T. Bagwell (Eds.), *Ethical Issues and Citizen Rights in the Era of Digital Government Surveillance* (pp. 176–207). Hershey, PA: IGI Global. doi:10.4018/978-1-4666-9905-2.ch010

Fiske, R. R. (2016). The Borders of Corruption: Living in the State of Exception. In R. Cropf & T. Bagwell (Eds.), *Ethical Issues and Citizen Rights in the Era of Digital Government Surveillance* (pp. 1–15). Hershey, PA: IGI Global. doi:10.4018/978-1-4666-9905-2.ch001

Force, C. M. (2016). How Middle School Principals of Small Rural Schools Address Cyberbullying. *International Journal of Cyber Behavior, Psychology and Learning*, 6(1), 27–41. doi:10.4018/IJCBPL.2016010102

Gao, M., Zhao, X., & McJunkin, M. (2016). Adolescents' Experiences of Cyberbullying: Gender, Age and Reasons for Not Reporting to Adults. *International Journal of Cyber Behavior, Psychology and Learning*, 6(4), 13–27. doi:10.4018/IJCBPL.2016100102

Gur, S., Blanchard, A. L., & Walker, L. S. (2016). Impacts on Society: Informational and Socio-Emotional Support in Virtual Communities and Online Groups. In B. Baggio (Ed.), *Analyzing Digital Discourse and Human Behavior in Modern Virtual Environments* (pp. 181–195). Hershey, PA: IGI Global. doi:10.4018/978-1-4666-9899-4.ch010

Hacker, K. L., Acquah-Baidoo, B., & Epperson, A. (2016). Reconciling the Needs for National Security and Citizen Privacy in an Age of Surveillance. In R. Cropf & T. Bagwell (Eds.), *Ethical Issues and Citizen Rights in the Era of Digital Government Surveillance* (pp. 78–102). Hershey, PA: IGI Global. doi:10.4018/978-1-4666-9905-2.ch005

Hartzel, K. S., & Gerde, V. W. (2016). Using Duality Theory to Reframe E-Government Challenges. In R. Cropf & T. Bagwell (Eds.), *Ethical Issues and Citizen Rights in the Era of Digital Government Surveillance* (pp. 35–56). Hershey, PA: IGI Global. doi:10.4018/978-1-4666-9905-2.ch003

Ho, H. K. (2016). Embodying Difference on YouTube: Asian American Identity Work in "Shit Asian Dads Say". In A. Novak & I. El-Burki (Eds.), *Defining Identity and the Changing Scope of Culture in the Digital Age* (pp. 1–14). Hershey, PA: IGI Global. doi:10.4018/978-1-5225-0212-8.ch001

Hollenbaugh, E. E., Ferris, A. L., & Casey, D. J. (2020). How Do Social Media Impact Interpersonal Communication Competence?: A Uses and Gratifications Approach. In M. Desjarlais (Ed.), *The Psychology and Dynamics Behind Social Media Interactions* (pp. 137–163). Hershey, PA: IGI Global. doi:10.4018/978-1-5225-9412-3.ch006

Hussain, Z., & Pontes, H. M. (2018). Personality, Internet Addiction, and Other Technological Addictions: A Psychological Examination of Personality Traits and Technological Addictions. In B. Bozoglan (Ed.), *Psychological, Social, and Cultural Aspects of Internet Addiction* (pp. 45–71). Hershey, PA: IGI Global. doi:10.4018/978-1-5225-3477-8.ch003

Ingle, S., & Kuprevich, C. L. (2016). Workforce Development in Behavioral Healthcare and the Increased Use of Technology: Is It Working or Not? Are We Asking the Right Questions? In B. Baggio (Ed.), *Analyzing Digital Discourse and Human Behavior in Modern Virtual Environments* (pp. 40–59). Hershey, PA: IGI Global. doi:10.4018/978-1-4666-9899-4.ch003

Joseph, J. J. (2020). Facebook, Social Comparison, and Subjective Well-Being: An Examination of the Interaction Between Active and Passive Facebook Use on Subjective Well-Being. In M. Desjarlais (Ed.), *The Psychology and Dynamics Behind Social Media Interactions* (pp. 268–288). Hershey, PA: IGI Global. doi:10.4018/978-1-5225-9412-3.ch011

Joseph, J. J., & Florea, D. (2020). Clinical Topics in Social Media: The Role of Self-Disclosing on Social Media for Friendship and Identity in Specialized Populations. In M. Desjarlais (Ed.), *The Psychology and Dynamics Behind Social Media Interactions* (pp. 28–56). Hershey, PA: IGI Global. doi:10.4018/978-1-5225-9412-3.ch002

Kang, Y., & Yang, K. C. (2016). Analyzing Multi-Modal Digital Discourses during MMORPG Gameplay through an Experiential Rhetorical Approach. In B. Baggio (Ed.), *Analyzing Digital Discourse and Human Behavior in Modern Virtual Environments* (pp. 220–243). Hershey, PA: IGI Global. doi:10.4018/978-1-4666-9899-4.ch012

Kato, S., Kato, Y., & Usuki, K. (2020). Associations Between Dependency on LINE Text Messaging and Occurrence of Negative Emotions in LINE Group Chats. In M. Desjarlais (Ed.), *The Psychology and Dynamics Behind Social Media Interactions* (pp. 188–209). Hershey, PA: IGI Global. doi:10.4018/978-1-5225-9412-3.ch008

Kidd, D., & Turner, A. J. (2016). The #GamerGate Files: Misogyny in the Media. In A. Novak & I. El-Burki (Eds.), *Defining Identity and the Changing Scope of Culture in the Digital Age* (pp. 117–139). Hershey, PA: IGI Global. doi:10.4018/978-1-5225-0212-8.ch008

Knibbs, C., Goss, S., & Anthony, K. (2017). Counsellors' Phenomenological Experiences of Working with Children or Young People who have been Cyberbullied: Using Thematic Analysis of Semi Structured Interviews. *International Journal of Technoethics*, 8(1), 68–86. doi:10.4018/IJT.2017010106

Kowalsky, M. (2016). Analysis of Initial Involvement of Librarians in the Online Virtual World of Second Life. In B. Baggio (Ed.), *Analyzing Digital Discourse and Human Behavior in Modern Virtual Environments* (pp. 126–148). Hershey, PA: IGI Global. doi:10.4018/978-1-4666-9899-4.ch007

Lai, F. T., & Kwan, J. L. (2018). Socioeconomic Determinants of Internet Addiction in Adolescents: A Scoping Review. In B. Bozoglan (Ed.), *Psychological, Social, and Cultural Aspects of Internet Addiction* (pp. 127–145). Hershey, PA: IGI Global. doi:10.4018/978-1-5225-3477-8.ch007

Ling, K. C., Ling, C. P., Zhimin, W., Hung, K. K., & Leong, L. H. (2017). The Impacts of Reactive Aggression and Friendship Quality on Cyberbullying Behaviour: An Advancement of Cyclic Process Model. *International Journal of Cyber Behavior, Psychology and Learning*, 7(2), 49–71. doi:10.4018/IJCBPL.2017040105

Loutzenhiser, K. (2016). Public Administrators, School Safety, and Forms of Surveillance: Ethics and Social Justice in the Surveillance of Students' Disabilities. In R. Cropf & T. Bagwell (Eds.), *Ethical Issues and Citizen Rights in the Era of Digital Government Surveillance* (pp. 232–248). Hershey, PA: IGI Global. doi:10.4018/978-1-4666-9905-2.ch012

Macur, M., & Pontes, H. M. (2018). Individual Differences and the Development of Internet Addiction: A Nationally Representative Study. In B. Bozoglan (Ed.), *Psychological, Social, and Cultural Aspects of Internet Addiction* (pp. 221–235). Hershey, PA: IGI Global. doi:10.4018/978-1-5225-3477-8.ch012

Martins, M. J., Simão, A. M., Freire, I., Caetano, A. P., & Matos, A. (2016). Cyber-Victimization and Cyber-Aggression among Portuguese Adolescents: The Relation to Family Support and Family Rules. *International Journal of Cyber Behavior, Psychology and Learning*, 6(3), 65–78. doi:10.4018/IJCBPL.2016070105

Masrom, M. (2016). E-Government, E-Surveillance, and Ethical Issues from Malaysian Perspective. In R. Cropf & T. Bagwell (Eds.), *Ethical Issues and Citizen Rights in the Era of Digital Government Surveillance* (pp. 249–263). Hershey, PA: IGI Global. doi:10.4018/978-1-4666-9905-2.ch013

McLaughlin, B., Hull, S., Namkoong, K., Shah, D., & Gustafson, D. H. (2016). We All Scream for Ice Cream: Positive Identity Negotiation in the Face of Cancer. In A. Novak & I. El-Burki (Eds.), *Defining Identity and the Changing Scope of Culture in the Digital Age* (pp. 81–98). Hershey, PA: IGI Global. doi:10.4018/978-1-5225-0212-8.ch006

McNeal, R. S., Schmeida, M., & Holmes, J. (2016). The E-Government Surveillance in the United States: Public Opinion on Government Wiretapping Powers. In R. Cropf & T. Bagwell (Eds.), *Ethical Issues and Citizen Rights in the Era of Digital Government Surveillance* (pp. 208–230). Hershey, PA: IGI Global. doi:10.4018/978-1-4666-9905-2.ch011

Metin-Orta, I. (2020). Online Social Networking and Romantic Relationships. In M. Desjarlais (Ed.), *The Psychology and Dynamics Behind Social Media Interactions* (pp. 57–82). Hershey, PA: IGI Global. doi:10.4018/978-1-5225-9412-3.ch003

Millman, C. M., Winder, B., & Griffiths, M. D. (2017). UK-Based Police Officers' Perceptions of, and Role in Investigating, Cyber-Harassment as a Crime. *International Journal of Technoethics*, 8(1), 87–102. doi:10.4018/IJT.2017010107

Mou, N. Z., & Islam, M. S. (2016). Re-Routing the Masculinity Myths in Bangladeshi Fashion Adverts: Identifying a New Wave among the Youths. In A. Novak & I. El-Burki (Eds.), *Defining Identity and the Changing Scope of Culture in the Digital Age* (pp. 170–191). Hershey, PA: IGI Global. doi:10.4018/978-1-5225-0212-8.ch011

Myers, Z. R., Swearer, S. M., Martin, M. J., & Palacios, R. (2017). Cyberbullying and Traditional Bullying: The Experiences of Poly-Victimization Among Diverse Youth. *International Journal of Technoethics*, 8(2), 42–60. doi:10.4018/IJT.2017070104

Nene, M. J., & Gupta, P. (2018). CyberPsycho Effect: A Critical Study on the Impact of Internet Addiction. In B. Bozoglan (Ed.), *Psychological, Social, and Cultural Aspects of Internet Addiction* (pp. 186–198). Hershey, PA: IGI Global. doi:10.4018/978-1-5225-3477-8.ch010

Niedt, G. (2016). Social Media Affordances and the Capital of Queer Self-Expression: Facebook, Ello, and the Nymwars. In A. Novak & I. El-Burki (Eds.), *Defining Identity and the Changing Scope of Culture in the Digital Age* (pp. 99–116). Hershey, PA: IGI Global. doi:10.4018/978-1-5225-0212-8.ch007

Novak, A. N., & Richmond, J. C. (2016). The Phrase Has Been Hijacked: Studying Generational Communication on Feminism through Social Media. In A. Novak & I. El-Burki (Eds.), *Defining Identity and the Changing Scope of Culture in the Digital Age* (pp. 156–169). Hershey, PA: IGI Global. doi:10.4018/978-1-5225-0212-8.ch010

Novoselova, V. (2016). Digitizing Consumer Activism: A Thematic Analysis of Jezebel.com. In A. Novak & I. El-Burki (Eds.), *Defining Identity and the Changing Scope of Culture in the Digital Age* (pp. 140–154). Hershey, PA: IGI Global. doi:10.4018/978-1-5225-0212-8.ch009

Oluwole, J. O., & Green, P. C. III. (2016). *Censorship and Student Communication in Online and Offline Settings* (pp. 1–622). Hershey, PA: IGI Global. doi:10.4018/978-1-4666-9519-1

Oravec, J. A. (2018). Cyber Bullying. In M. Khosrow-Pour, D.B.A. (Ed.), Encyclopedia of Information Science and Technology, Fourth Edition (pp. 1695-1703). Hershey, PA: IGI Global. doi:10.4018/978-1-5225-2255-3.ch148

Pina, A., Holland, J., & James, M. (2017). The Malevolent Side of Revenge Porn Proclivity: Dark Personality Traits and Sexist Ideology. *International Journal of Technoethics*, 8(1), 30–43. doi:10.4018/IJT.2017010103

Rive, P. B. (2016). Virtual Design Teams in Virtual Worlds: A Theoretical Framework using Second Life. In B. Baggio (Ed.), *Analyzing Digital Discourse and Human Behavior in Modern Virtual Environments* (pp. 60–86). Hershey, PA: IGI Global. doi:10.4018/978-1-4666-9899-4.ch004

Robson, G., & Olavarria, C. M. (2016). Big Collusion: Corporations, Consumers, and the Digital Surveillance State. In R. Cropf & T. Bagwell (Eds.), *Ethical Issues and Citizen Rights in the Era of Digital Government Surveillance* (pp. 127–144). Hershey, PA: IGI Global. doi:10.4018/978-1-4666-9905-2.ch007

Rodríguez-de-Dios, I., & Igartua, J. (2016). Skills of Digital Literacy to Address the Risks of Interactive Communication. *Journal of Information Technology Research*, 9(1), 54–64. doi:10.4018/JITR.2016010104

Rosette, O. N., Kazemeyni, F., Aghili, S., Butakov, S., & Ruhl, R. (2016). Achieving Balance between Corporate Dataveillance and Employee Privacy Concerns. In R. Cropf & T. Bagwell (Eds.), *Ethical Issues and Citizen Rights in the Era of Digital Government Surveillance* (pp. 163–175). Hershey, PA: IGI Global. doi:10.4018/978-1-4666-9905-2.ch009

Rosewarne, L. (2017). "Nothing Crueler than High School Students": The Cyberbully in Film and Television. *International Journal of Technoethics*, 8(1), 1–17. doi:10.4018/IJT.2017010101

Rowe, N. C. (2016). Privacy Concerns with Digital Forensics. In R. Cropf & T. Bagwell (Eds.), *Ethical Issues and Citizen Rights in the Era of Digital Government Surveillance* (pp. 145–162). Hershey, PA: IGI Global. doi:10.4018/978-1-4666-9905-2.ch008

Samli, R. (2018). A Review of Internet Addiction on the Basis of Different Countries (2007–2017). In B. Bozoglan (Ed.), *Psychological, Social, and Cultural Aspects of Internet Addiction* (pp. 200–220). Hershey, PA: IGI Global. doi:10.4018/978-1-5225-3477-8.ch011

Sarna, G., & Bhatia, M. (2016). An Approach to Distinguish Between the Severity of Bullying in Messages in Social Media. *International Journal of Rough Sets and Data Analysis*, 3(4), 1–20. doi:10.4018/IJRSDA.2016100101

Shang, G. N. (2016). The Self of the Camera: Popular Practices of Photography and Self-Presentation in the New Social Media. In A. Novak & I. El-Burki (Eds.), *Defining Identity and the Changing Scope of Culture in the Digital Age* (pp. 240–250). Hershey, PA: IGI Global. doi:10.4018/978-1-5225-0212-8.ch015

Shen, L. (2018). Treatment of Internet Addiction. In B. Bozoglan (Ed.), *Psychological, Social, and Cultural Aspects of Internet Addiction* (pp. 284–309). Hershey, PA: IGI Global. doi:10.4018/978-1-5225-3477-8.ch015

Smyth, S. J., Curran, K., & Mc Kelvey, N. (2018). Internet Addiction: A Modern Societal Problem. In B. Bozoglan (Ed.), *Psychological, Social, and Cultural Aspects of Internet Addiction* (pp. 20–43). Hershey, PA: IGI Global. doi:10.4018/978-1-5225-3477-8.ch002

Sterner, G., & Felmlee, D. (2017). The Social Networks of Cyberbullying on Twitter. *International Journal of Technoethics*, 8(2), 1–15. doi:10.4018/IJT.2017070101

Stodt, B., Wegmann, E., & Brand, M. (2016). Predicting Dysfunctional Internet Use: The Role of Age, Conscientiousness, and Internet Literacy in Internet Addiction and Cyberbullying. *International Journal of Cyber Behavior, Psychology and Learning*, 6(4), 28–43. doi:10.4018/IJCBPL.2016100103

Sweeny, J. (2017). Gendered Violence and Victim-Blaming: The Law's Troubling Response to Cyber-Harassment and Revenge Pornography. *International Journal of Technoethics*, 8(1), 18–29. doi:10.4018/IJT.2017010102

Switzer, J. S., & Switzer, R. V. (2016). Virtual Teams: Profiles of Successful Leaders. In B. Baggio (Ed.), *Analyzing Digital Discourse and Human Behavior in Modern Virtual Environments* (pp. 1–24). Hershey, PA: IGI Global. doi:10.4018/978-1-4666-9899-4.ch001

Tai, Z., & Liu, X. (2016). Virtual Ties, Perceptible Reciprocity, and Real-Life Gratifications in Online Community Networks: A Study of QQ User Groups in China. In B. Baggio (Ed.), *Analyzing Digital Discourse and Human Behavior in Modern Virtual Environments* (pp. 164–180). Hershey, PA: IGI Global. doi:10.4018/978-1-4666-9899-4.ch009

Tellería, A. S. (2016). Liquid Communication in Mobile Devices: Affordances and Risks. In B. Baggio (Ed.), *Analyzing Digital Discourse and Human Behavior in Modern Virtual Environments* (pp. 196–219). Hershey, PA: IGI Global. doi:10.4018/978-1-4666-9899-4.ch011

Triberti, S., Sebri, V., Savioni, L., Gorini, A., & Pravettoni, G. (2020). Avatars for Clinical Assessment: Digital Renditions of the Self as Innovative Tools for Assessment in Mental Health Treatment. In M. Desjarlais (Ed.), *The Psychology and Dynamics Behind Social Media Interactions* (pp. 313–341). Hershey, PA: IGI Global. doi:10.4018/978-1-5225-9412-3.ch013

Walker, J. A., & Jeske, D. (2016). Understanding Bystanders' Willingness to Intervene in Traditional and Cyberbullying Scenarios. *International Journal of Cyber Behavior, Psychology and Learning*, 6(2), 22–38. doi:10.4018/IJCBPL.2016040102

Wang, W., Cheung, B. C., Leung, Z. C., Chan, K., & See-To, E. W. (2017). A Social Media Mining and Analysis Approach for Supporting Cyber Youth Work. *International Journal of Knowledge and Systems Science*, 8(2), 1–16. doi:10.4018/IJKSS.2017040101

Wigfall, J. (2016). Nothing Random about Taste: Toni Morrison and the Algorithmic Canon. In A. Novak & I. El-Burki (Eds.), *Defining Identity and the Changing Scope of Culture in the Digital Age* (pp. 43–55). Hershey, PA: IGI Global. doi:10.4018/978-1-5225-0212-8.ch004

Wright, M. F. (2016). The Roles of Age, Gender, and Ethnicity in Cyberbullying. In A. Novak & I. El-Burki (Eds.), *Defining Identity and the Changing Scope of Culture in the Digital Age* (pp. 192–208). Hershey, PA: IGI Global. doi:10.4018/978-1-5225-0212-8.ch012

Wright, M. F. (2020). Cyberbullying: Negative Interaction Through Social Media. In M. Desjarlais (Ed.), *The Psychology and Dynamics Behind Social Media Interactions* (pp. 107–135). Hershey, PA: IGI Global. doi:10.4018/978-1-5225-9412-3.ch005

Yau, J. C., Sun, B. T., & Moreno, J. D. (2020). Addicting Content, Blue Light, and Curtailed Sleep: The ABCs of Social Media Use and Sleep. In M. Desjarlais (Ed.), *The Psychology and Dynamics Behind Social Media Interactions* (pp. 211–240). Hershey, PA: IGI Global. doi:10.4018/978-1-5225-9412-3.ch009

Yu, S. (2016). Using Mixed Methods to Understand the Positive Correlation between Fear of Cyberbullying and Online Interaction. *International Journal of Virtual Communities and Social Networking*, 8(3), 29–36. doi:10.4018/IJVCSN.2016070103

Zhang, Y. (2016). The Personalized and Personal "Mass" Media – From "We-Broadcast" to "We-Chat": Reflection on the Case of Bi Fujian Incident. In A. Novak & I. El-Burki (Eds.), *Defining Identity and the Changing Scope of Culture in the Digital Age* (pp. 29–42). Hershey, PA: IGI Global. doi:10.4018/978-1-5225-0212-8.ch003

Index

Ensure Quality Research is Introduced to the Academic Community

Become an IGI Global Reviewer for Authored Book Projects

Premier Reference Source

Emerging GIS Applications for Emergency and Disaster Management

Premier Reference Source

Managerial Strategies and Green Solutions for Project Sustainability

Premier Reference Source

Comparative Approaches to Using R and Python for Statistical Data Analysis

Premier Reference Source

Solutions for High-Touch Communications in a High-Tech World

The overall success of an authored book project is dependent on quality and timely reviews.

In this competitive age of scholarly publishing, constructive and timely feedback significantly expedites the turnaround time of manuscripts from submission to acceptance, allowing the publication and discovery of forward-thinking research at a much more expeditious rate. Several IGI Global authored book projects are currently seeking highly-qualified experts in the field to fill vacancies on their respective editorial review boards:

Applications and Inquiries may be sent to:
development@igi-global.com

Applicants must have a doctorate (or an equivalent degree) as well as publishing and reviewing experience. Reviewers are asked to complete the open-ended evaluation questions with as much detail as possible in a timely, collegial, and constructive manner. All reviewers' tenures run for one-year terms on the editorial review boards and are expected to complete at least three reviews per term. Upon successful completion of this term, reviewers can be considered for an additional term.

If you have a colleague that may be interested in this opportunity, we encourage you to share this information with them.